Strategic Supply Chain Alignment

To Lea

for all her love and support over the years.

Strategic Supply Chain Alignment

Best practice in supply chain management

Editor John Gattorna

Assistant Editors

Theresa Jones
Alister Danks
Yamini Dhillon
Lucinda Holdforth

Gower

Published by
Gower Publishing Limited
Gower House
Croft Road
Aldershot
Hampshire GU11 3HR
England

Gower
Old Post Road
Brookfield
Vermont 05025
USA

British Library Cataloguing in Publication Data
Strategic supply chain alignment
    1.Business logistics 2.Strategic planning
    I.Gattorna, John
    658.7

    ISBN 0-566-07825-2

Library of Congress Cataloging-in-Publication Data
Strategic supply chain alignment / edited by John Gattorna.
        p.   ca.
    Includes index.
    ISBN 0-566-07825-2 (hardback)
    1. Business logistics. 2. Delivery of goods--Management.
I. Gattorna, John.
HD38.5.S87 1998
658.7--dc21   98-16752
                                   CIP

Typeset by SetPoint, Middlesex and printed in Great Britain by MPG Books Ltd, Bodmin, Cornwall

Contents

Acknowledgements

This project had a long gestation. It all started when Gower Publishing asked me to follow up the fourth edition of the very successful *Handbook of Logistics and Distribution Management* (1990) with a fifth edition. That was in late 1995 and I was just in the transition from my own consulting business to Andersen Consulting. So things were delayed for a year while I tried to fathom how this huge, successful, very sophisticated organization worked; in this regard I am grateful for the patience shown by Chris Simpson, Julia Scott and Solveig Servian at Gower Publishing.

By early 1997 I was ready for the task, and I could already see the possibilities of having the vast resources and talent of Andersen Consulting behind me to generate a book unlike any other hitherto available on the subject of supply chain management, featuring new authors and predominantly unpublished material. The opportunity was too good to miss, and so I gathered an outstanding team of people around me as we designed, refined and built the content that you are about to see. For their tireless work, often in conjunction with demanding consulting work going on at the same time, special thanks to Theresa Jones, Alister Danks, Yamini Dhillon and Lucinda Holdforth; their dedication and tenacity have been outstanding. Thanks also to Carmel McCauley of Future Perfect Communications who assisted us with the final editing process.

Of course, a project of this scale in a firm like Andersen Consulting requires strong support and sponsorship from the top, and in this regard I want to acknowledge Greg Owens (global managing partner of the supply chain management practice) who unreservedly put his not insignificant influence behind the project, together with Dave Anderson (European managing partner of the supply chain practice) and Peter Fuchs (global managing partner of the strategic services practice). To the three of you, my sincere appreciation for the faith you had in the project.

You cannot produce a book like this without the contribution of a large number of very talented individuals. There are 67 authors involved in the 38 chapters which comprise this book, and every one is outstanding in their field. Six of the chapters have been written by my colleagues in academia and industry, to whom I owe a very special vote of thanks. It is relationships like this that enable us to incorporate the latest supply chain management research into our consulting work to deliver value to our clients.

The numerous contributors from Andersen Consulting also deserve special thanks because I know that your contributions were developed on top of an already killer workload. Based on my observations of how my Andersen Consulting colleagues responded so positively to the invitation to be part of this book, it is no mystery why Andersen Consulting has been so successful over the last nine years; I have never seen such a gathering of talented people in a single organization, anywhere!

I would also like to acknowledge the invaluable assistance given to me by Elizabeth Kim, Paul Littman and Howard Leibman during the writing of my two chapters in this book (including one with Cathy Walt).

Of course, irrespective of how good the final product is, all the effort amounts to nothing if the marketplace remains blissfully unaware of its availability. I'm sure such a fate will not befall this book because of all the support and creative ideas that Jim Wejman, Fiona Gibson, Karen Morgan, Daphne Katz and Karen Livius have provided throughout. We are fortunate to have such an outstanding marketing team on the job.

Finally, to Julia Scott, publisher at Gower Publishing, whose patience and accommodating manner during the last year or so have made her a delight to work with, our special thanks.

John L. Gattorna
Sydney, June 1998

Foreword

Let there be no doubt about the vital relevance of supply chain management to firms today.

Supply chain management is no longer a matter for the operational and functional areas of the firm—today it is a strategic issue demanding top-level management attention. Indeed, the quality of a firm's supply chain performance can mean the difference between business prosperity and failure.

Those companies which have moved themselves to the forefront of supply chain management have reaped clear rewards in terms of performance and shareholder returns. Benetton (quick response), Wal-Mart (very low supply chain costs), Microsoft (virtual manufacturing and logistics), Whirlpool (direct consumer delivery), Motorola (mass customization) and Peapod (home shopping) are examples of high-performing companies drawing on—and creating—the world's best supply chain management practices.

Today most supply chain innovation is confined to product manufacturing and retail firms. The next wave of change will embrace the service industries (such as banking, insurance, healthcare and entertainment), which will be forced to follow the lead of product companies in providing supply chain excellence to a more demanding generation of consumers. Smart service firms will seize the prize that awaits them through creative supply chain management.

Perhaps the biggest breakthrough in prospect lies in achieving truly integrated decision support systems that link all the parties along a particular supply chain. A comprehensive supply chain information system will make visible to managers all the opportunities to improve performance along the length and breadth of the network, ensuring that all parties improve their decision making and their capacity to contribute to, and benefit from, the optimum supply chain.

Strategic in outlook, challenging in terms of content and ideas and accessible to the general reader, this book offers an invaluable opportunity to the business executive looking to capture the latest thinking on supply chain management. This collection of contemporary readings, many of them hitherto unpublished material, reflects the best thinking of the world's leading supply chain practitioners and experts.

Together with all the contributors to this book, I wish you good reading and express the sincere hope that the 'value added' to your business as a result of dipping into a few chapters of particular interest will inspire you to do more and go further in search of superior corporate performance.

Gregory J. Owens, Managing Partner
Global Supply Chain Management Practice
Andersen Consulting
Atlanta, June 1998

Introduction

The drive towards strategic alignment in the supply chain

The 1990s have seen a dramatic change in the way that we do business. Rapid advances in technology and increasing regulatory freedom have changed the rules of competition. Companies are now competing globally and traditional barriers between industries are breaking down. To cope with these changes and achieve superior performance, business leaders are moving towards new business paradigms that allow their companies to work more closely with their traditional and new business partners to adapt to the rapidly changing marketplace. This improved integration is the very essence of supply chain management. Supply chain leaders are reconsidering the linkages, not only between functions within their own company, but with other organizations up and down the supply chain.

As part of this transformation, we have seen successive generations of operating paradigms deliver new lessons in performance. The pursuit of functional excellence developed into a focus on business process excellence, with firms breaking down their functional silos and reorganizing around 'core' logistics-related processes.

More recently we have seen the emergence of network excellence in the form of efficient consumer response and other integrating mechanisms that link raw material providers, manufacturers, distributors and retailers along a seamless supply chain. These approaches emphasize shared resources and information, eliminating duplication, enabling rapid information flows and, ultimately, delivering smooth product flows. In the near future lies the prospect of virtual supply chains in which most functions are entirely 'outsourced'.

With so much emphasis on the technological and process elements of supply chain management, it is no surprise that one simple, vital element has received so little attention: human behaviour. The fact is that people and their behaviour both generate and amplify the pulses that reverberate through the supply chain—at the consumer level, inside the firm or between firms. An understanding of human behaviour and its implications for supply chain design and management forms the missing ingredient in contemporary thinking about supply chain strategy. Master this and we have all the ingredients for creating an 'unfair competitive advantage' with your supply chain. It is exactly this insight which is the driving inspiration for this book.

The traditional view of logistics was very narrowly defined. It focused on the physical movement of goods and (more recently) information, from suppliers to customers and their consumers. This led to a pre-occupation with internal functions and processes within the firm in the name of increased efficiency, which has seen the introduction of useful techniques such as materials requirement planning, distribution requirements planning, and just-in-time manufacturing.

This narrow definition of logistics takes no account of different customer types and the different demands they place on the business. Nor does it facilitate the full organizational response required to meet these demands effectively. The reality is that materials and finished products only move through the supply chain because of consumer behaviour at the end of the pipeline or the behaviour of certain parties inside a particular channel. There is no magic in that insight, and yet many firms and indeed whole channels have long operated without recognizing this essential connection.

It is our contention that a new framework is required that integrates the formulation of logistics strategy with the human factors that both create the demand outside the firm and form the core capability inside the firm to deliver the prescribed strategy to the marketplace. We argue the need for a Strategic Alignment Model that brings together the external market's dynamics, the firm's strategic response(s) and the firm's internal capability to execute this desired alignment, through the appropriate subcultures and leadership style(s) built into the organization.

Customers (and consumers) place different demands on an organization. We have only to look at our weekly and monthly sales patterns for confirmation of this. What is not so readily obvious is that these demand patterns are driven by different human behaviours internal and external to the firm. For example, firms in the channel distort the flow of product via promotional campaigns, credit terms, customer incentives, internal policies and product characteristics (e.g. freshness). Patterns of behaviour at the consumer level vary significantly. Some behaviours are motivated by cyclical needs and seasonal effects and fashions, while the buying behaviours related to other product types are stable and predictable, based on maintenance or hygiene patterns such as repeat purchases of toothpaste or consumer durables.

These different customer (and consumer) behaviours drive different flows of product through an organization or series of channels. And these different flows require tailored logistics responses through some form of 'multiple alignment' capability. For example, an identical can of Coca-Cola will move along dramatically different pathways to fulfil demand in its three main channels: supermarkets, vending machines and corner stores. So the logistics infrastructure has to respond to the differ-

The Strategic Alignment Model in brief

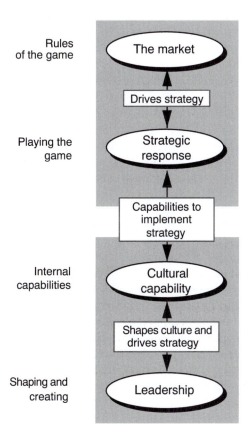

Rules
of the game — The market

Drives strategy

Playing the
game — Strategic
response

Capabilities to
implement
strategy

Internal
capabilities — Cultural
capability

Shapes culture and
drives strategy

Shaping and
creating — Leadership

ent types of customer and consumer behaviour represented by each of these channels, including recognizing that the volume passing through each channel may well vary over time.

The Strategic Alignment Model seeks to improve the alignment between markets, strategy, culture and leadership, on the premise that the better the alignment, the better the bottom-line performance. IBM's fall and rise constitute a good example of effective realignment. The problem in the past has been that different metrics have been used to measure performance at each of the four levels. Market researchers and corporate strategists use entirely different language to describe the marketplace. Equally, strategists rarely communicate with change management specialists interested in behaviour at the individual or team level.

The model, by its very nature, needs to be dynamic in order to respond to changes at each level. Just as humans change their behaviour in different situations or environments, so do companies and markets.

When the New Zealand dairy industry was deregulated in 1995 the previously monopolistic NZ Dairy Group awoke to a market in transition. Rather than selling 95 per cent of its produce to one customer, the Dairy Board, the company now had to compete in an open market. In order to adapt, it had to formulate a new strategy that matched the new market conditions. However, while it was relatively easy in principle to design a new strategy, developing the capability to deliver or execute it was more complex. The culture that had developed during the monopolistic period had to change radically to realign with the new competitive intensity in the market and the desired strategic response. To achieve this, the company needed a different leadership style. A new CEO was appointed who understood the current marketplace and was able to set a fresh vision for the future that aligned with current customer requirements.

The Strategic Alignment Model emphasizes the interaction between the formulation of strategy and its execution. Formulating effective strategies requires an operational response to be developed that is consistent with the understanding of the market, its customer segments and the behaviour of each of these segments. But the intended strategy, which resides in the minds and plans of senior management, will be very different to the strategic outcome if there is a misalignment between the intention and the capabilities of the firm.

It is this crucial interface between cultural capability and strategy that has been the missing link in understanding how to shape and successfully deliver winning strategies to the competitive marketplace. We now know that a common culture and single, all-purpose response to the market will not be sufficient. Instead, what is required is multiple alignments between customer segments and internal organization structures, with the appropriate array of strategies acting as the bridge.

How the model operates

To put the model into action, the range of buying behaviours and competitive situations for a given product category must first be determined. This involves identifying the different market segments, the key customer values, the marketplace dynamics and the causes of varying demand patterns. Then the corresponding range of appropriate strategic responses is formulated to meet the logistics requirements of each market segment.

Different channels require different sets of skills to manage them effectively. So to ensure that the organization can execute its strategies it must have internalized the appropriate cultural capability, usually manifested in the diverse skill cultures necessary to meet customer requirements. Finally the leadership team must have a broad capacity to understand, shape and drive the agreed logistics strategy into the marketplace.

The Strategic Alignment Model

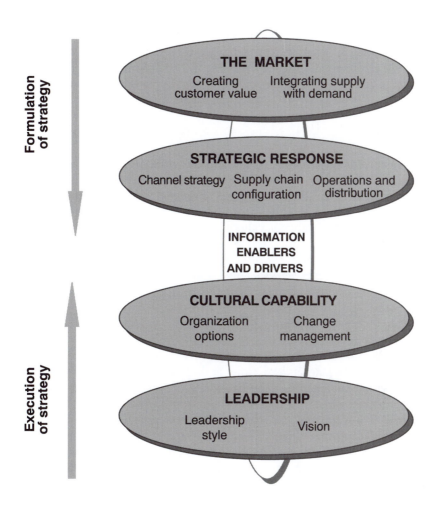

If conditions change in the marketplace, a ripple effect runs through the entire model. Strategies must be reformulated and the organizational capability redefined. The only problem is that, in large organizations, it is relatively easy to write a new strategy in response to a changing market, but achieving rapid change in the underlying cultures is exceedingly difficult and takes a significant amount of time—hence the flight to outsourcing in recent years, on the premise that it is easier to engage an external organization for a particular task than to find or invent the capability within the existing organization.

The Strategic Alignment Model has another element that flows beneath each of the four levels and ties the whole framework together: logistics information drivers and enablers. Superb information is critical to ensure that a firm obtains, synthesizes and shares the market data necessary to implement responsive strategies along the entire supply chain.

We have organized the chapters in this book around the core concepts in the Strategic Alignment Model. The authors, however, contribute as individual experts, and each chapter can be read independently for its insights and perspectives on contemporary supply chain challenges.

Part I—The market

The market is the structure, conditions and forces for change in a given industry, all of which shape a finite range of customer buying behaviours (or segments). Consideration is given to the methods that can be used to segment the marketplace effectively and the strategies that companies can adopt to create greater value for the customer. Best practice methods of integrating supply and demand are highlighted which enable companies, and indeed entire supply chains, to capture, analyse and respond effectively to market signals and align themselves accordingly.

Part II—Strategic response

Strategic response is the way a company responds to the main segments identified in the marketplace, either at the end-consumer level or at some level within the channel. The consideration of strategic response has three distinct aspects. Analysis of channel strategy focuses on the ways in which a company can develop different channels, including the emerging consumer direct channel, to create value in the network. Supply chain configuration focuses on the management of relationships and networks that are vital to a company's capacity to achieve supply chain excellence. Operationalizing the strategy involves consideration of best practice in the core manufacturing and distribution functions.

Part III—Cultural capability

Culture is the set of shared understandings within a company: the 'glue' holding together the diverse values and beliefs, the assumptions about reality, and the visible patterns of behaviour that an organization manifests in the marketplace. Techniques are explored to help business leaders understand the strengths and weaknesses of their organizational culture and lift and shape cultural capability to ensure that internal strengths are capable of driving towards and meeting strategic objectives.

Part IV—Leadership

Leadership is a core supply chain issue. When success depends on understanding and bringing together the many complex and disparate elements in the marketplace, in the firm itself and in the key partnerships along the supply chain, then assumptions about leadership styles and models need to be challenged. Part 4 explores the latest thinking about leadership and applies it in the supply chain context.

Part V—Information enablers and drivers

Information systems enable existing strategies to be implemented and drive new strategies to be created, while information flows provide the linkages that enable the supply chain to operate effectively. The authors focus on some of the hottest issues and opportunities in using information technology and information to drive and enable supply chain success.

Part VI—Special interest

Here the aim is to demonstrate the application of supply chain principles across various industries and geographies. The principles are the same, but the outcomes are different.

Conclusion

This collection of articles seeks to assist business managers and supply chain specialists alike to gain new insights into the parameters that they must manage for superior supply chain performance, and the dynamic interaction between these parameters.

Most of the material presented in this book is new and previously unpublished. It reflects next-generation thinking about management of the supply chain for success. And while there will be many differing perspectives on the issues, some key themes emerge. Most powerful of all is the message of alignment—a message about the sophisticated integration of all the attributes so that the supply chain operates as a single, integrated, cost-effective system.

Supply chain performance is going to be a key indicator of overall corporate success into the twenty-first century. Now is the time to become part of that success story.

New approaches to strategy
Dynamic alignment of strategy and execution

Peter Fuchs, Andrew Young and Alida Zweidler-McKay

Over the past two decades both strategic positioning and excellent execution have emerged as drivers of sustainable success. But the pace of change and the growth of strategic alternatives have forced companies to think again about how to formulate strategy and create competitive advantage. Companies are learning that the key to success lies in the alignment between strategic positioning and execution.

Strategy formulation processes are changing to enable companies to create and sustain alignment in their organizations. Companies are using more sophisticated planning tools and adopting a more dynamic and iterative approach to strategy. And they are experimenting more with the details of strategy, rather than merely implementing formal long-range plans. But companies need the internal capacity to follow this path—structure, culture and systems must all support a flexible organization that is geared to change.

Introduction

Today's competitive environment is more demanding than ever. Two factors in particular are affecting the way in which companies can conduct business successfully.

First, companies across a broad range of industries are facing rapid change and growing uncertainty. Under these conditions, they find it increasingly difficult to establish a sustainable competitive advantage. Company planners have less time to develop and implement strategies.

Secondly, in the context of this uncertainty, strategic experts have expressed a variety of opinions about the drivers of success. Companies must sort through a wide array of complex and often conflicting advice in developing their strategies.

The increasing complexity and pace of change inevitably have a dramatic impact on how successful companies operate. Achieving a competitive edge demands a fresh approach to both strategy formulation and execution.

An emerging view

In the face of this complexity, companies are finding that focusing in isolation either on aspects of strategic positioning or execution capabilities does not lead to a sustainable competitive edge. A more dynamic and iterative view of strategy is emerging.

Traditionalists have described strategy as a process of analysing the competitive environment and determining a unique strategic position within it. But the potential for companies to maintain competitive advantage through unique positioning has been eroded by the explosion in the availability of competitive information. Unique positioning alone is no longer sustainable.

Many successful companies have already realized that the ability to execute well has become a key part of competitive strategy. Excellence in execution at least partially protects companies from the ravages of rapid change and copycat strategies. Winning companies like Wal-Mart, British Airways and McDonald's have shown that simple, widely known strategies can be eminently successful if the execution of the strategy is a step above the competition. But execution excellence without the right strategic positioning is not enough. Eventually, the advantages won through improvements such as total quality management, outsourcing, reengineering and benchmarking are eliminated as competitors catch up (Porter, 1996).

In isolation, neither unique strategic positioning nor execution excellence is sufficient to create sustained competitive advantage. The emerging view of strategy is that success depends on developing and aligning a unique combination of positioning and execution capabilities. Successful strategy is about building a system of mutually complementary elements.

The paper chase: Wausau Paper Mills

Wausau Paper Mills manufactures printing, writing and speciality paper products and sells them throughout the US and in international markets. In the US paper and forest products industry, Wausau is only a small player in terms of sales, assets or production capacity. It does not rank in the top 30 in any of these categories. However, when it comes to financial performance, Wausau sets the industry standard. Over the period 1986–96, it multiplied shareholder value more than ten times and outperformed the industry average by more than a staggering 700 per cent. Financial analysts predict that Wausau will continue to do well.

Many other players in the industry would appear to hold some competitive advantages over Wausau, in particular the economies of scale that many thought were requirements for profitability in the industry. And in a commodity business like paper, a unique product position is very easily copied. So what

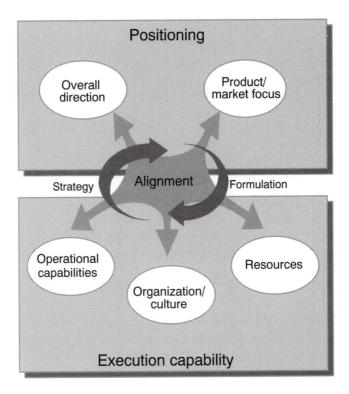

Figure 1.1   An emerging view of strategy

sets Wausau apart in this highly competitive business?

Wausau's success is not a result of positioning alone. It has developed a combination of strategy and execution capabilities that is unique and difficult to imitate.

Wausau's strategic position

Wausau is a lean and flexible niche player. The company has successfully focused on creating or occupying niche markets, typically gaining a significant market share in a segment (for example, it has a 40 per cent market share in pressure-sensitive labels) and realizing operating margins well above average. If one of the segments in which Wausau operates becomes crowded, it quietly exits and goes on to find another speciality product. In the early 1980s, for example, Wausau provided 3M with the lightweight yellow paper the latter used for its hugely successful 'Post-It Notes'. When other paper companies entered this market three years later and 3M asked Wausau to cut its prices, the company declined and left the business.

Wausau enters and leaves markets more often than competitors, but this is part of a definite strategy. Overall, it concentrates its efforts on just a few product segments. This niche strategy seems to be paying off.

The second component of Wausau's positioning is its focus on lean operations. Although it has significantly increased its production capacity over the last few years, it has no ambition to become self-sufficient or to integrate vertically. This sets it apart from many of its competitors and proves to be an excellent position in a highly cyclical industry suffering from production over-capacity.

Wausau's execution capabilities

Wausau is the industry leader in identifying and exploiting new business opportunities, demonstrating both flexibility and creativity in its willingness to move to new product lines as they become more profitable.

Wausau acquired Rhinelander Paper, a struggling producer of interior liners for cereal boxes and pet foods. Seeing a market opportunity, it turned the company into an early producer of microwaveable popcorn bags. As others entered that market, Wausau again repositioned Rhinelander, this time producing pressure-sensitive labels with great success.

Wausau has also demonstrated strong skills in commercializing new products. For example, in experimenting with coloured paper, it developed 'Astrobrights', a superior speciality paper that fades less quickly than rival products. Wausau's product became so popular that customers would ask for it by name—a remarkable achievement in an environment that usually does not emphasize brand names.

Over time, Wausau has developed some of the best distribution capabilities in the industry to meet customers' needs for timely delivery. Today, approximately 75 per cent of all items are shipped within 24 hours, a service level much higher than that found at most other paper companies. Ongoing distribution initiatives indicate that the company is not resting on its laurels and intends to distance itself even further from its competition.

Wausau is also skilled at developing and maintaining strategic relationships, with both customers and suppliers. Learning that a major customer was suffering from rising pulp prices, Wausau developed a paper that uses less pulp. In order to reduce its own energy costs, it entered an agreement with a nearby electric utility to build a high-efficiency power plant next to one of its mills.

Alignment at work at Wausau

Wausau's success is built on the tight alignment between its positioning and execution capabilities. To support its position as a niche player that rapidly enters, exploits and exits markets, it must identify market opportunities and adapt to changing buyer values. Strong customer relationships help Wausau identify unique customer needs. Its abilities to develop and commercialize new products further support this positioning. The company's strong distribution capabilities support these customer relationships and allow it to expand geographically. Its skills in developing strategic relationships allow it to maintain lean, flexible operations without the inertia created by upstream or downstream integration.

Each of these examples illustrates the important connections between Wausau's positioning and capabilities. Wausau leads its industry because specific components of its positioning and execution capabilities mutually reinforce each other.

The new strategy process

We now begin to see some implications for the process of formulating strategies. The traditional process begins with industry and competitor analysis, moves on to developing and testing hypotheses and making recommendations, and ends with implementation. In the modern uncertain environment, that process is far too linear. To maintain alignment between the various parts of the organization, a dynamic and iterative approach is now required. Companies must constantly prepare for, anticipate and adapt to changing market conditions. Speed and flexibility are key requirements.

Dynamic and iterative process

In the changing environment, companies cannot afford to plan according to a single view of the future. Instead, successful companies are open-minded. They are able to develop multiple strategic options and they frequently experiment with new ideas. They are able to modify their course midstream, in response to feedback from the market and changing conditions.

The dynamic and iterative strategy process that is now required differs significantly from the traditional, formal planning procedure. In place of a discrete annual or biannual strategy process, planning has become a continuous management responsibility. The dynamic nature of strategy formulation is indicated by the pair of curved arrows on the strategy framework in Figure 1.2.

Sophisticated and creative tools

The proliferation of information means that companies can know more about their performance than ever before. Advanced technologies are now available to help them sort through and understand this information. By investing in these technologies, companies can take some of the

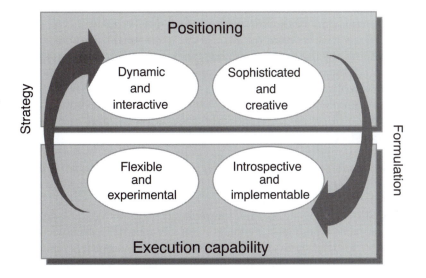

Figure 1.2   The new strategy process

guesswork out of planning, to make better-informed, fact-based decisions.

Companies are also using more creative tools to facilitate the development of multiple strategic options. Instead of trying to base strategy formulation purely on best-guess predictions, they are learning to develop more robust planning processes that help them prepare for a range of futures.

In the early 1970s, Shell Oil Company pioneered 'scenario planning', a technique that involves developing strategic responses to a number of potential future scenarios. By encouraging its managers to consider a range of hypothetical situations, Shell was uniquely prepared for the OPEC oil embargo of 1973–4. By the 1980s it had moved from being the weakest of seven petrochemical giants to becoming the strongest of the oil companies (Miller, 1992).

Modern analysis and planning tools allow companies to prepare for, anticipate and respond to changes in their competitive environment. When change occurs, these companies are able to adapt their planning much more quickly than are their competitors.

An introspective view

The paired arrows on the strategy framework have a second meaning. Strategy is not a one-way process; it is no longer sufficient to plan according to the environment and then build appropriate capabilities. Successful companies are skilled at introspection and coldly assess their own strengths and weaknesses in developing their strategies.

A position that is based on the market environment, without attention to the company's unique abilities, may be easily imitated. But the sum total of the organization—its people, technology, processes, culture and the way it has developed its own capabilities—is hard to copy. No two companies are alike. A strategy that utilizes the company's unique combination of resources, capabilities and culture has a greater chance of sustained differentiation in the marketplace.

A natural implication of formulating a strategy based in part on the company's strengths is that this strategy will be implementable. A company will experience fewer barriers to implementing a strategy based on its unique abilities than will the competition.

Hartford Steam Boiler is a multinational property and casualty insurance company whose positioning is built on specific skills. It insures equipment for target customers in industries such as utilities, paper manufacturing, oil refining and food processing. Over the years it has developed a sophisticated knowledge base and an extensive corps of engineers with expertise in inspecting and insuring manufacturing equipment. Building on this expertise, the company has also developed an inspection services unit to help clients prevent losses. By leveraging its existing capabilities, it has been able to expand its position to provide a broader range of services to its customers. The expansion of Hartford Steam Boiler's services makes it difficult to imitate (Heskett, Sasser and Hart, 1990).

Improving home improvement: Home Depot

Home Depot's strategic position

In 1978, Home Depot revolutionized the home improvement market by creating a unique strategic positioning. Its large, low-cost, no-frills warehouse concept provided consumers with a deeper and broader merchandise assortment than the traditional, small, high-priced hardware store. Home Depot's unique combination of one-stop shopping, competitive prices and highly knowledgeable, service-oriented personnel enabled it rapidly to overtake its competitors to become the world's largest and most profitable home improvement retailer.

Home Depot's execution capabilities

Home Depot's superior execution has been the key differentiating factor compared to others who have moved to copy its positioning. In particular, Home Depot has built its skills in attracting, retaining and motivating high-performance employees, sharing knowledge and best practices across the organization, encouraging innovation, leveraging technology, managing inventories and controlling costs.

Home Depot's execution capabilities fit well with its positioning. No-frills, warehouse-style stores, sophisticated inventory management and replenishment systems, and direct purchasing support its low-cost and broad assortment positioning. It has invested in state-of-the-art technology systems to increase its efficiency and effectiveness, including computerized point-of-sale systems, barcode scanning, electronic data interchange with vendors, rapid replenishment and a satellite communications network connecting stores and headquarters. It hires employees with appropriate skills—often trade professionals—to provide customers with expert advice and to train other employees. The hiring criteria also include measures to select people with a customer-friendly demeanour, while a sophisticated labour-scheduling system and separate phone centre (for handling telephone requests) ensure that these employees will be available in the stores to serve customers.

Home Depot's responsive positioning

Home Depot has shown the willingness and ability to make adjustments to its strategy. It invests in experiments to keep pace with changes in customer values and tests new market opportunities. A decentralized management structure allows store managers the flexibility to experiment with local market variations. To sustain its aggressive growth rates, Home Depot has expanded its initial positioning to adapt to changing business environments and market opportunities. For example, it has successfully reached out to the professional segment by expanding commercial credit programmes, offering on-site delivery services and updating its lines of professional products. Technology has also supported its strategy-formulation process. In 1991 the company replaced aging in-store systems with a relational database management system to enhance its ability to track performance.

Home Depot's day-to-day flexibility

Flexibility is good, particularly in a world of ever more demanding customers. However, too much of a good thing can be bad and can cause confusion and inefficiency. Home Depot demonstrates well how to maintain a high degree of flexibility in day-to-day operations throughout the organization while at the same time providing employees with a clear sense of an overall direction. Company policies are not treated as sacrosanct. Employees see them as guidelines and are given the freedom to overstep them if that will achieve the company's objectives more effectively. A sense of personal responsibility, training, incentive systems and a widely used corporate communication network are instrumental in balancing consistency and flexibility.

In support of strategy: the flexible organization

Companies must continuously adapt to maintain the alignment between the changing environment, their strategic position and their capabilities. Strategies must constantly be updated to reflect new information. New skills must be developed. The process of planning has changed too—planners must learn to cope with uncertainty in new ways. With change as the dominant paradigm, companies are finding that flexibility is a crucial capability.

In order to remain flexible, organizations need to believe that change does not demand a crisis. The change dynamic should be viewed as an opportunity and not a threat; a chance to do something better, not a personal risk.

3M is well known as a flexible organization. The company developed a core culture and ideology that encouraged originality, experimentation and a willingness to try new ideas. This 'can do' attitude and an internally flexible organization that allow ideas to come up from the 'shop floor' are key to the company's success (Collins and Porras, 1994).

Most companies have difficulty achieving 3M's level of change readiness. As human beings, we expect to be 'in control'. We are wary of change and that fear can fossilize into inertia. We become comfortable in our own situations and, unless there is a real threat or crisis, will find ways to maintain the status quo. Research shows that, for most organizations, only an externally driven threat triggers action for change; an internal threat more frequently reinforces the inertia. However, in today's rapidly changing world, companies that are only able to change during times of crisis will be unable to keep up.

Building a flexible organization requires the development of a culture, structure and performance measures. Critical elements of this organization include a clearly articulated company direction, open channels of communication both from the top down and the bottom up and suitable performance measures. When the company's overall direction is clear, and performance measures and expectations are appropriately aligned, employees can be given the flexibility to make more decisions on their own—leading to faster decision making and the ability to respond quickly to market dynamics.

A company that has successfully developed a flexible organization is Compaq. Founded in 1982 to manufacture and sell portable IBM-compatible personal computers, the company has developed into an $18 billion organization that is a major player in today's PC market. Compaq's success is based on a lean and flexible organization, a culture that supports sales excellence and performance measures that focus on bottom-line results. When Compaq started to enter the PC business, rather than establishing its own salesforce it granted exclusive rights to dealers and suppliers. This proved to be very effective and allowed it to build an international dealer network within a few years. To achieve its vision of becoming a 'top enterprise computing company', Compaq has found a new way of leveraging partnerships to enter new businesses. Its partnership with Microsoft provided the base from which to enter the emerging PC server market by combining its unique hardware and software strengths. Compaq encourages its management to be 'in the middle of things' and measures executives' contribution to growth and the bottom line very carefully. While Compaq has had some notable difficulties making their complex supply chain run smoothly, it is doing well what many others have failed to do: designing a structure and culture to address the realities of fast-changing markets.

Conclusion

Strategic positioning and excellence in execution are, in isolation, insufficient to generate sustainable advantage. Creating and sustaining tight alignment between the parts of the organization is now the key to success. To facilitate alignment, modern strategy-formulation processes are more dynamic and iterative. Companies are learning to deal with the uncertain future by being open-minded about strategy, by experimenting and by adapting to new information more quickly. In support of the emerging model of strategy, the ability to change is becoming a key distinctive capability. Companies that can generate and sustain a dynamic, integrated approach to strategy and its execution will emerge as winners in a tough marketplace.

References

Collins, J.C. and Porras, J.I. (1994) *Built to Last: Successful Habits of Visionary Companies*, HarperCollins, New York.

Heskett, J.L., Sasser, W.E. and Hart, C.W.L. (1990) *Service Breakthroughs: Changing the Rules of the Game*, Free Press, New York.

Miller, D. (1992) 'The Icarus paradox: how exceptional companies bring about their own downfall', *Business Horizons*, 35 (1), Jan/Feb, 24–35.

Porter, M.E. (1996) 'What is strategy?', *Harvard Business Review*, 74 (6), Nov/Dec, 61–78.

Strategic supply chain management
Creating shareholder value by aligning supply chain strategy with business strategy

Robert Evans and Alister Danks

Management of the supply chain has evolved over the last two decades from an emphasis on integrating logistics and lowering costs to providing better products and services to customers, quickly and cheaply. Now, with the advent of the twenty-first century, the challenge is to take supply chain management to a more strategic level within the firm. This chapter describes how to formulate and establish a supply chain strategy and, most importantly, how to align the strategy with the organization's overall business strategy. By elevating supply chain management to the heart of decision making in the boardroom, and uniting corporate and supply chain goals, companies can boost profitability and growth and substantially increase their shareholder value.

Introduction

The role of supply chain management within an organization has changed considerably over the last three decades.

In the 1970s supply chain management, then known primarily as 'distribution', was focused on the integration of warehousing and transportation within the firm. In addition, the high, double-digit interest rates that existed in most countries during the decade encouraged firms to pay particular attention to their use of capital. Supply chain managers focused heavily on reducing inventories. At this point, the focus was principally on how the firm could make internal changes that would reduce inventories and distribution costs. Even efforts to reduce plant and supplier lead times, and consequently safety stocks, can be considered as being internally focused, since lead times were considered primarily as 'inputs' to the forecasting and procurement processes.

In the 1980s the focus of supply chain management shifted to the reengineering of supply chain cost structures. Attention was directed to integrating the firm's supply chain processes in a manner that would

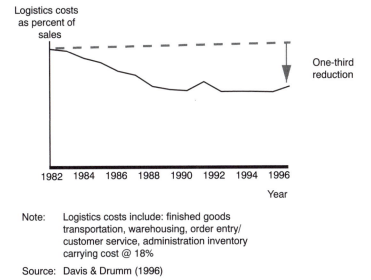

Note: Logistics costs include: finished goods
        transportation, warehousing, order entry/
        customer service, administration inventory
        carrying cost @ 18%

Source: Davis & Drumm (1996)

Figure 2.1   North American logistics costs: 1982–96

lower supply chain operating costs and reduce supply chain assets. These efforts were not without considerable rewards. According to Herbert W. Davis & Co., North American supply chain costs, including finished goods transportation, warehousing, order entry, customer service, administration and inventory carrying costs, declined by nearly one-third between 1982 and 1990, as shown in Figure 2.1.

As the 1980s came to a close, the focus of supply chain management shifted from reducing costs to improving customer service. The benefits of improving the performance of the supply chain included revenue growth and higher profitability through greater market share and price premiums *vis-à-vis* the firm's competitors. Given this new area of focus, it is not surprising that the progress in reducing supply chain operating costs and supply chain assets, so prevalent during the 1980s, slowed considerably. Since 1990, reported supply chain costs in North America have been largely unchanged (see Figure 2.1). While it could be argued that any realized supply chain cost 'savings' were reinvested in higher levels of service during this period, thus accounting for the lack of reported progress in reducing costs, it is hard to find any quantitative evidence that customer service increased substantially during this period.

The interest in improving customer service intensified during the early 1990s. Growth, long considered the responsibility of product development, sales and marketing in many firms, emerged as an objective of the supply chain organization as well.

The continuing need to reduce supply chain costs and supply chain assets, the increased importance of customer service and the emerging focus on growth resulted in many firms considering yet another implication of their supply chain operations channel structure and effectiveness. While some companies are adding new channels or eliminating existing ones, the more innovative players are entering into new arrangements with channel participants, aiming to broaden their customer base, reduce costs and deepen their customer relationships.

Now with a new decade (and a new century) looming, another wave of change is sweeping over supply chain operations in most firms: the evolution of strategic supply chain management. The emerging view is that supply chain management can both drive and enable the business strategy of many firms, rather than only forming part of a firm's operational strategy, as has been the traditional view. This chapter puts forward a framework for developing a supply chain strategy, but also describes how to align the strategy with business strategy. Without this critical alignment, supply chain strategy will be isolated from the firm's broader vision and ultimately hampered in its effectiveness. Successful alignment will enable value enhancement throughout the firm.

Value creation through strategic supply chain management

The power of aligning supply chain strategy with a company's business strategy can be seen in the success of three major US companies. Wal-Mart, Coca-Cola and Dell Computer have easily outperformed their competitors in terms of shareholder value growth; over the eight years from 1988–96, Wal-Mart's growth exceeded its industry average by nearly 250 per cent, Coca-Cola's by nearly 500 per cent and Dell Computer's by over 3000 per cent (according to the Stern Stewart EVA™ 1000 Database). These three companies have all demonstrated the strategic power of the supply chain.

Wal-Mart has built its growth and financial success in the US around the supply chain. Its store expansion process involves first constructing a distribution centre in a targeted area and then building stores whose minimal inventories are replenished daily by the distribution centre. Combined with its other supply chain competencies in procurement, use of point-of-sale retail data and 'flow-through' distribution, Wal-Mart maintains a significant cost-of-goods-sold advantage that underpins its dominant 'everyday low price' marketing strategy.

While the Coca-Cola Company is traditionally viewed as a brand-driven company, the impact of the supply chain on its success cannot be overstated. Coke has invested billions over the last several years to acquire many of its largest independent bottlers, giving it a substantial distribution advantage over its arch rival Pepsi-Cola. It has been noted that while Pepsi frequently wins the advertising war, Coke wins the supply chain war, particularly in fast-growing markets outside the US where Coke gets more than 70 per cent of its profits.

Dell Computer has fundamentally reshaped the manufacturing and retailing of computers in the US through its approach to the supply chain. Dell's 'retail direct' strategy involves processing orders directly from customers (many via its Website), building computers to the customer's order and delivering them within five days. To support this logistical approach, Dell requires its suppliers to maintain inventories within approximately 15 minutes of its manufacturing plants. Since it has only 14 days of work-in-process and finished goods inventory, Dell sells computers that are about 60 days 'newer' than its competitors whose supply chains are configured more traditionally. In an industry where component prices fall 15 per cent to 25 per cent a year, this translates into about a 6 per cent cost-of-goods-sold advantage. Dell's much larger competitors (including IBM, Apple and Hewlett-Packard) are all scrambling to match its cost and customer service advantage.

In all cases, companies that have unleashed the strategic power of the supply chain have done so in order to increase shareholder value. Value theory holds that to increase the value of a company, cash earnings must be increased in excess of the company's full cost of capital in a sustainable fashion. As shown in Figure 2.2, the supply chain can directly affect both profitability and invested capital. Improved customer service and

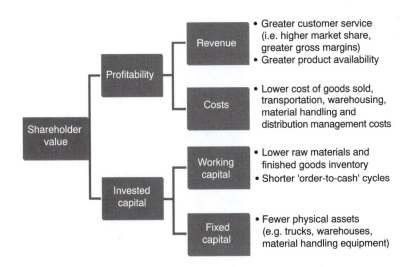

Figure 2.2   Impact of supply chain management on cash earnings

Table 2.1
Impact of logistics on profitability and growth

Profitability measure	Logistics driver(s) (Performance *vis-à-vis* competitors)	Percent of total variance explained (R^2)
Impact on profitability		
• Return on sales	• Low-cost distribution	7%
• Return on assets	• Responsiveness to market • Low-cost distribution	12%
• Return on investment	• Responsiveness to market • Delivery reliability	12%
Impact on growth		
• Sales growth	• Delivery speed • Responsiveness to market	16%
• ROS growth	• Responsiveness to market • Delivery reliability	12%
• ROI growth	• Responsiveness to market • Delivery reliability	16%

Source: Morash, Droge and Vickery (1996)

product availability drive revenue growth, while efficient logistic operations can dramatically reduce operating costs. Leaner operations and shortened lead times reduce inventory and working capital requirements, while network optimization and outsourcing can decrease the need for physical assets and thus the amount of fixed capital invested.

Substantial evidence is emerging of the impact of the supply chain on the profitability of the firm. In their 1996 study of the highly competitive US furniture industry, Morash, Drose and Vickery identified and quantified the impact of the supply chain on profitability and growth. The researchers surveyed 65 chief executives of furniture manufacturers and measured their financial performance and their degree to which they had implemented eight major strategic supply chain capabilities: pre-sale customer service; post-sale customer service; delivery speed; delivery reliability; responsiveness to target markets; widespread distribution coverage; selective distribution coverage; and low total cost distribution.

Analysis of the survey results identified that four key supply chain capabilities were significantly related to financial performance. 'Delivery speed, reliability, responsiveness to target markets and low cost total distribution represent the true order-winners for sustained competitive advantage,' the study found.

Table 2.1 shows that supply chain drivers account for up to 16 per cent of the variability in the firm's profitability, and up to 28 per cent of the variability in its growth. The results also show that firms must develop and implement a range of strategic supply chain capabilities to satisfy multiple performance objectives. While responsiveness to market and delivery reliability are most important for return investment measures, low-cost distribution was found to be the main driver of return on sales.

To realize shareholder value fully, firms must begin to formulate strategies that capture the full profit potential inherent in the supply chain. This requires a systematic, structured framework within which alternative supply chain strategies can be identified and evaluated.

Four dimensions of the strategic supply chain

The framework for formulating a supply chain strategy consists of four key dimensions: sourcing strategy, demand flow strategy, customer service strategy and supply chain integration strategy, as illustrated in Figure 2.3. By focusing on these four dimensions and developing the answers to ten key questions, managers will be in a position to formulate effective supply chain strategies that meet the needs of the market and integrate with supply chain partners to deliver improved shareholder value. In turn, the strategy developed needs to be assessed and aligned with the overall business strategy of the firm, as shown later in Figure 2.8.

Strategic supply chain begins with the customer (as used here, 'customer' refers to the 'end-user customer' to differentiate this final user of the product and/or service from intermediate supply chain entities). Customer service strategy deals with how the firm responds to the needs and expectations of its customers in a manner that maximizes profitability.

How the firm 'senses and responds' to its customers is a primary determinant of its overall success. Demand flow strategy defines the linkage between the firm's customers and the sources of the products and services that the firm provides to the marketplace.

Sourcing strategy determines where and how products and services are produced and has a significant impact on the firm's product and service cost structure and associated risks.

Finally, supply chain integration establishes the degree of integration of a firm's information, finances, operations and decision making with those of the participants in the company's supply chain, including

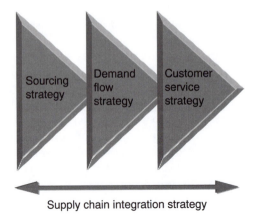

Figure 2.3   Four dimensions of strategic supply chain management

retailers, wholesalers, dealers, distributors, manufacturers, suppliers and supply chain services providers.

The four dimensions are summarized below. However, each element is discussed in greater detail in the relevant chapters of the book.

Customer service strategy

Formulating a customer service strategy involves addressing three steps: customer service segmentation, cost-to-serve analysis and revenue management (see Figure 2.4).

Customer service segmentation

Customer service strategy begins by identifying the unique segments of the firm's customer base. A variety of techniques and approaches can be used to identify service needs and expectations, including surveys, focus groups, demographic analysis and analysis of large-scale customer information databases. The outputs of this process are customer service needs and expectations for each relevant customer/product/ geographic segment.

Cost-to-serve

Next, an analysis of the firm's current customer service delivery cost structure must be developed and the costs of meeting the newly identified service levels by customer segment determined. Those firms that have implemented activity-based costing (ABC) accounting systems will typically find this a relatively straightforward task. Without ABC capability, this analysis must be conducted on a project basis.

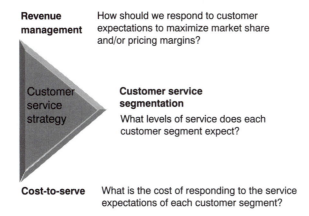

Revenue management   How should we respond to customer expectations to maximize market share and/or pricing margins?

Customer service strategy

Customer service segmentation
What levels of service does each customer segment expect?

Cost-to-serve   What is the cost of responding to the service expectations of each customer segment?

Figure 2.4   Three elements of customer service strategy

Revenue management

Finally, the determination of the appropriate response to the identified needs and expectations of each customer segment must be completed. Few firms carry out this analysis, resulting in a situation where customer service needs and expectations are known, but the response which maximizes the firm's profitability and growth is undetermined.

This is the critical element in the formulation of the firm's customer service strategy but, unfortunately, it is frequently underdeveloped. Consider the impact of failing to understand fully this dimension of the supply chain strategy. Suppose a firm accurately determines the service needs and expectations of each relevant customer segment. Furthermore, assume that all of the costs required to achieve this level of service are fully known. Finally, assume that the firm acts to achieve the desired level of customer service. A fundamental question nevertheless remains: how will customers respond to the new level of service?

This behavioural outcome is frequently unknown. Will customers reward the firm with greater market share, higher price premiums *vis-à-vis* competitors or both—and to what degree? At a very simple level, consider the dramatic differences of two alternative behavioural responses, one that focuses on market share and one that focuses on price premiums. Should the former occur, the firm will need to provide additional production capacity to meet the higher demand. In the second case, no additional capacity is required, but product prices should be adjusted immediately.

Revenue management is the process of determining the market share and price premium impact of the behavioural responses of customers to alternative levels of customer service. These behavioural responses include purchase, repurchase (typically referred to as 'loyalty') and

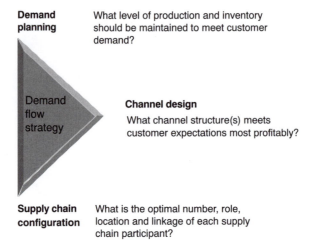

Demand planning
What level of production and inventory should be maintained to meet customer demand?

Demand flow strategy

Channel design
What channel structure(s) meets customer expectations most profitably?

Supply chain configuration
What is the optimal number, role, location and linkage of each supply chain participant?

Figure 2.5   Three elements of demand flow strategy

recommendations (which influence the behaviour of other customers). Analytical techniques include factor analysis, regression analysis, dynamic conjoint analysis and other multivariate statistical techniques.

Demand flow strategy

There are three elements to formulating a firm's demand flow strategy—channel design, demand planning and supply chain configuration (see Figure 2.5).

Channel design

A variety of alternative structures exist through which the firm's products and services reach the end-user customer. While most firms have sold their products and services through retailers, wholesalers, dealers and distributors, advances in information and communications technology such as the Internet and World Wide Web have fostered the development of an increasing number of 'direct' channels whereby firms sell directly to their end-user customers.

The choice of channel structures is of critical importance since this can directly influence both the level of customer service provided and the associated distribution costs.

Demand planning

Determining the level of production and inventory required to meet end-user customer demand is a critical function at most firms. (The more traditionally named activities of forecasting, distribution resource planning (DRP), manufacturing resource planning (MRP) and inventory control are collectively referred to here as demand planning.) This 'sense and respond' process is critical to meeting end-user customer demand successfully while minimizing costs and assets both within the firm and across its supply chain.

A large number of new software tools are available that provide the firm with increased levels of demand planning support, including Manugistics, I2, Red Pepper and others. Many of these software tools will support demand planning not only within the firm, but across its supply chain partners as well.

Supply chain configuration

Determining the optimal number, location and role of each supply chain participant is a critical element of the firm's overall supply chain strategy. The definition of the distribution network commits financial capital in the form of facilities, equipment and other assets, and establishes certain limits on the overall operating cost effectiveness of the firm and its supply chain partners.

Sourcing strategy

Formulating a Sourcing Strategy requires consideration of the make or buy decision, capacity management and manufacturing management, as shown in Figure 2.6.

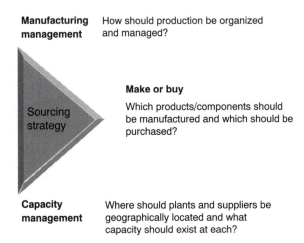

Manufacturing management How should production be organized and managed?

Sourcing strategy

Make or buy
Which products/components should be manufactured and which should be purchased?

Capacity management Where should plants and suppliers be geographically located and what capacity should exist at each?

Figure 2.6   Three elements of sourcing strategy

Make or buy

The decision as to whether to manufacture or purchase a product and/or service (as well as their subcomponent elements) affects both the firm's product/service cost structure and its exposure to risks such as labour cost changes, labour disputes, exchange rate volatility, transportation interruptions, political restrictions and changes in taxation

Capacity management

The firm must determine where its plants and suppliers will be located geographically and the level of capacity that will exist at each. While the supply chain configuration element discussed in the earlier section is related, capacity management is focused at the detailed plant/supplier location and capacity decisions that are subject to risks including labour cost changes, labour disputes, exchange rate volatility, transportation interruptions, political restrictions and changes in taxation.

Manufacturing management

Traditional approaches to production planning and control systems, seeking to maximize efficiency and utilization, are no longer adequate in a customer-centred world. Firms wanting to compete successfully need to look to new concepts, processes and technologies to help them adapt to this new era and to ensure that their production processes optimize the balance between customer satisfaction and efficiency.

The way in which a firm establishes its sourcing strategy must reflect risk-adjusted trade-offs. This is especially true in the automotive industry where just-in-time (JIT) manufacturing requires reliable and consistent supplies. When a fire swept through the Aisin Seiki Co. plant in Japan, Toyota was left without a supply of brake cylinders and proportioning valves. The fire on Saturday shut down production of 16 200 vehicles by Tuesday, costing the firm an estimated $200 million in profits. While at first glance this may be viewed as an ineffective sourcing strategy, Toyota officials stated that they believed the long-term benefits of JIT arrangements far exceeded the $200 million cost. Thus, Toyota's sourcing strategy adequately reflected both the economic benefits and associated business risks of where products were produced, who produced those products and how production was managed.

Supply chain integration strategy

Linkages among the participants in the firm's supply chain are a key dimension of the firm's overall supply chain strategy. The answers to three questions form the foundation of a supply chain integration strategy.

To what degree should the firm integrate across its supply chain?

In recent years, many firms have thought about and discussed integration with their supply chain partners as if the concept were universally applicable. This, however, is likely not to be the case. Consequently, the first issue which must be addressed is the degree to which the firm should integrate across its supply chain with its supply chain partners. These supply chain partners are probably also considering the same question.

The answer is determined by the shareholder value creation opportunities which may exist from pursuing a supply chain integration strategy. This shareholder value may be created directly by improving the customer service and/or cost performance of the supply chain, or it may be created indirectly by positioning the firm and its (selected) supply chain partners in such a way as to 'lock out' competing firms from achieving similar gains.

Different industries and different firms within each industry are likely to develop different supply chain integration strategies based on the customer segments to be served, the products and services offered and the geographic locations involved.

The impact of developing an appropriate supply chain integration strategy can be significant. A recent study by Andersen Consulting sought to identify the Economic Value Added™ (EVA™) impact of supply chain integration in the personal computer (PC) industry. This study of more than 150 companies in the global PC supply chain identified several significant areas of supply chain integration where the EVA™ impact on the participants was compelling. For example, the study showed that inter-enterprise postponement of manufacturing (that is, moving final assembly of PCs from the manufacturer/assembler to the distributor/retailer) created significantly lower inventory and increased the EVA™ for both the manufacturer/assembler and the distributor/retailer, as shown in Figure 2.7. (EVA™ is a registered trademark of Stern Stewart & Co.)

While this suggests that significant EVA™ creation opportunities may be developed through a supply chain integration strategy, it is also clear that not all participants benefit to the same degree. Only by evaluating the EVA™ impact of every supply chain integration option on each participant in the firm's supply chain can this initial question be answered.

What types of supply chain integration are required?

Fundamentally, supply chain integration has four forms—information, decision, financial and operational.

Information integration enables firms across the supply chain to share useful information. For example, it is widely known that Wal-Mart and Proctor & Gamble (P&G) share information regarding the retail sales of

Annual inventory turns

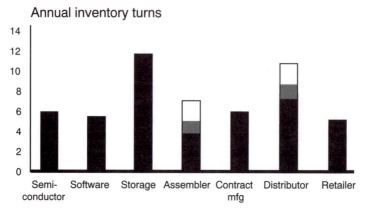

- Turns improve from
  - 5.1 up to 7.3 turns per year for assembler (up to 45%)
  - 7.5 up to 10.7 turns per year for distributor (up to 45%)

EVA™ as percent of revenues

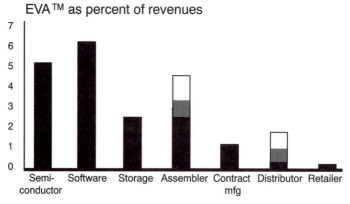

- EVA™ as percent of revenue improves
  - from 2.7 up to 4.7% for assembler
  - from 0.4 up to 1.6% for distributor
- Total value grows by $80 to $245
  - $20 to $85m from capital efficiencies
  - $60 to $160m from enhanced revenues

Figure 2.7   EVA™ creation through supply chain integration: the global personal computer industry

P&G products at Wal-Mart stores. This information enables P&G to do a better job of managing its production of these products and provides Wal-Mart with greater 'in store' availability.

Decision integration supports the planning and control functions of management across multiple firms within the supply chain. For example, General Motors' subsidiary Saturn manages the inventories of service parts at its independently owned dealers. Saturn determines which parts to stock at each dealer, determines when the dealer should reorder from Saturn and how much should be ordered. By sharing decision making, both Saturn and its dealers achieve higher levels of parts availability for their end-user customers, lower overall inventory levels and inventory obsolescence, and reduced transportation and parts handling costs.

Financial integration changes the terms and conditions of payment across the supply chain. For example, a manufacturer may accept payment at the time its products are sold *by* a retailer rather than demand payment at the time the goods are sold *to* the retailer. This type of integration changes the ownership of inventory, and hence capital costs, and can reduce the costs of managing accounts payable and accounts receivable.

Operational integration encompasses the sharing of physical and human assets between participants within a supply chain. For example, a manufacturer may provide floor space within its plant to one or more of its suppliers for the purpose of producing components for the assembly line. Beyond the savings in the fixed costs of plant and equipment, such arrangements enable both parties to respond more quickly to production changes and to reduce overall cycle times and costs.

Should supply chain integration be pursued 'physically' or 'virtually'?

The concept of 'linkages' among participants in a supply chain is not new. Earlier in the twentieth century the concept was frequently referred to as 'vertical integration'. Firms such as Ford Motor Company often controlled all of the elements of the supply chain from the mining of ore, to the production of steel, to the assembly of automobiles, to the sale to the end-user customer. These vertically integrated firms encompassed all four forms of supply chain integration: information, decision, financial and operational.

In the 1990s, these linkages have taken on a different form, whereby multiple, independently owned firms have built 'virtual' supply chain linkages. These virtual linkages, often enabled by advances in information technology, are seen as a way to realize the benefits of supply chain integration while avoiding the perceived negative impacts of vertical integration. Virtual integration has allowed a small group of Swedish entrepreneurs to establish GANT men's clothing as a global brand, now available in 23 countries. High-quality and top-fashion garments are designed, produced, distributed and sold through a tightly controlled network, with minimal investment in physical assets. Production is outsourced and most sales outlets are under franchising agreements. GANT Stores has used IT to develop and leverage the company's network organization with efficient transfer of sales and inventory information, coordination of design and production activities and clear communication of advertising and promotion activities.

Nevertheless, some companies are pursuing supply chain integration in 'physical' terms. For example, AutoNation USA, a 'mega-retailer' of automotive products and services in the US which began business in 1994, is rapidly acquiring auto dealerships, building its own used vehicle retail 'superstores' and vehicle reconditioning centres and acquiring commercial rental car companies (to secure a source of used vehicles) and other companies in the automotive supply chain. This has prompted companies such as General Motors and Ford Motor Company to pursue a 'physical' supply chain integration strategy whereby they are acquiring previously independently owned dealers in selected geographic areas.

Consequently, the firm must choose between 'physical' and 'virtual' supply chain integration as part of its overall supply chain strategy.

Aligning supply chain strategy with business strategy

Supply chain strategy does not exist in isolation within the firm. As discussed in the previous chapter, the alignment between the firm's business strategy and its execution is a critical factor in the firm's success. Here we examine the alignment between the firm's overall strategy and its supply chain activities in particular (see Figure 2.8).

Wal-Mart's devotion to building customer loyalty through everyday low pricing and ready availability of goods has contributed to the firm's rapid rise over the last decade. However, to achieve this inventory replenishment had to become a centrepiece of its competitive strategy. This strategic vision was realized through adopting largely invisible supply chain concepts such as cross docking or 'flow-through' distribution. The fact that an operational detail such as cross-docking became a vital link in Wal-Mart's business strategy demonstrates that effective business strategy requires the achievement of a dynamic balance between the functional details and the broader competitive position. Supply chain management by nature plays an integral role in achieving that balance because it spans the key corporate functions as well as the links with a firm's suppliers and customers.

Business strategy in its simplest form addresses three fundamental questions that define how a firm will compete:

■ What products/services should the firm sell?
■ What customer segments should the firm serve?
■ In what geographic markets should the firm operate?

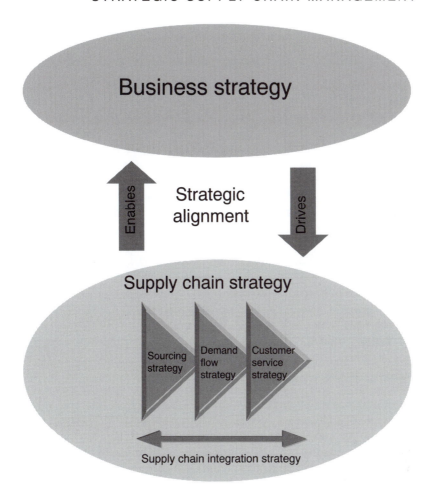

Figure 2.8   Achieving alignment of supply chain strategy and business strategy

The answers to these questions depend, in part, on the supply chain strategy the firm seeks to implement. Similarly, the answers to these business strategy questions will determine the context within which the firm's supply chain strategy is developed. The question of alignment then becomes critical.

It is of little value to introduce the new 'customer service leadership' brand advertising, for example, if the customer service performance reality is not consistent with that image. Ultimately, the degree of integration that exists between the firm's business strategy and its supply chain strategy is determined by the level of resources applied to each. An evaluation of the commitment of resources to implementing the supply chain strategy should be undertaken to assure that the development of key supply chain capabilities is aligned with the development of key capabilities in other areas of the firm.

Aligning supply chain strategy and execution

In practice, the execution of many supply chain strategies is complicated by the number of entities that are involved in the supply chain. By definition, a supply chain extends across more than one division or department of a single company; it affects several areas of responsibility within a company and often crosses company borders.

Effectively aligning supply chain strategy and execution requires alignment between groups, whether within a single company or across companies. These entities must:

- pursue the same goal; and
- act at the right speed.

Pursue the same goal

There must be alignment between each firm's supply chain strategy and those of its supply chain partners, both internal and external. Unfortunately, many firms have little knowledge or understanding of the intent of their external partners' supply chain strategies.

Perhaps the best way to determine common goals is to involve all supply chain participants, both internal and external to the firm, in formulating the supply chain strategy. To make this participation productive, a shared view must exist of the impact of the supply chain strategy on end-user customers and the shareholders of the various supply chain partners. This typically requires a greater understanding of the customer service and financial performance of the supply chain than readily exists. Substantial effort is required to develop this shared view of the 'outcomes' that are desirable to all supply chain participants.

Act at the right speed

The speed of change is critical. The firm must be aware that, to the extent it is pursuing a supply chain strategy that involves supply chain integration, the rate at which its supply chain partners are able to change is a key consideration. Creativity in developing the 'financial integration' aspects of the firm's supply chain integration strategy is critical since its supply chain partners are unlikely to have the same degree of available resources to pursue implementation, nor will the shareholder value benefits be realized by all supply chain participants at a level proportional to their implementation investment.

What should the pace of change be? The firm must change at a rate that is equal to or greater than the rate of change of its competitors (depending on whether competitive parity or a competitive disadvantage exists). This is particularly challenging since many of the firm's supply chain partners are also members of its competitors' supply chain. The old adage to 'be first and be right' has probably never been more appropriate.

Alignment in action—Caterpillar Inc.   CASE STUDY

Aligning supply chain strategy with business strategy

The widely recognized success of Caterpillar Inc.'s global service parts business illustrates the power of strategic alignment between the firm's business strategy and its supply chain strategy.

Caterpillar manufactures and sells products that require a high degree of post-sale parts and service support. Industry surveys typically show that the level of this support is often customers' first or second most important consideration when buying new equipment. Caterpillar's logistics expertise in its global service parts business, as typified by its 'parts delivery in 48 hours, or the parts are free' guarantee, not only generates profitable parts sales, but also contributes directly to the firm's equipment market share and price premium position.

Aligning supply chain strategy and execution

For many years, Caterpillar's participation in the agricultural equipment industry was minimal, despite the fact that the firm's 1925 origins were firmly rooted in the agricultural industry of southern California. Again, the logistics of its parts and service business played a significant role. Like construction equipment owners, farmers require a high degree of post-sale parts and service support. But Caterpillar's service parts logistics strategy was built around fewer than 250 dealers worldwide. Other agricultural equipment manufacturers, who often had thousands of dealers, had a logistics network that was able to deliver superior post-sale parts and service support to the North American farmer. While Caterpillar certainly had the engineering and manufacturing expertise to manufacture competitive agricultural equipment products, its post-sale support logistics capabilities at that time were not responsive to customer service requirements. The timing wasn't right.

During the 1980s and early 1990s, however, the confluence of changes such as the deregulation of transportation in the North American logistics industry and rapid increases in logistics information technology created a new opportunity for Caterpillar. Now able to align the performance of its post-sale parts and service logistics strategy with its business strategy in the agricultural industry, it found itself in a much stronger competitive position. Suddenly its business strategy and post-sale logistics strategy could proceed at the same speed.

While many companies struggle to align their business strategy and logistics strategy 'internally', Caterpillar's pursuit of 'same goal' alignment even extends 'externally' across its service parts supply chain. Not only do specific parts availability goals exist for its dealers and suppliers, but Caterpillar's parts availability tracking system reports on why any particular customer's parts order cannot be filled. The power of aligning the logistics strategy goals of each member of the supply chain with Caterpillar's overall business strategy and leveraging their combined actions is considerable.

Conclusion

This chapter has described a framework for establishing a supply chain strategy and for ensuring that this strategy is aligned with the firm's overall business strategy. As the supply chain has evolved from a cost focus to a customer focus and, now and in the decade ahead, to a strategic focus, the need to think strategically about it has never been greater.

Ultimately, the success of any supply chain strategy is only as great as the firm's ability to execute it. Throughout this book readers will find a comprehensive guide not only to understanding the market and formulating the appropriate strategic response, but also to the ingredients necessary for the successful execution of that strategy. A winning supply chain strategy, combined with operational excellence, can ensure success for the firm, its shareholders and its customers.

References

Davis, Herbert W. and Drumm, William (1996) 'Logistics costs and customer service levels', Council of Logistics Management Annual Conference.

Ericsson, Dag (1995) 'Virtual integration: information technology the enabler in globalization', Unisource, Stockholm.

Kent, John L. Jr. and Flint, Daniel J. (1997) 'Perspectives on the evolution of supply chain thought', *Journal of Business Logistics*, 18 (2), 15–29.

Morash, Edward A., Droge, Cornelia L.M. and Vickery, Shawnee K. (1996) 'Strategic supply chain capabilities for competitive advantage and firm

success', *Journal of Business Logistics*, 17 (1), 1–22.
Stern Stewart EVA™ 1000 Database provided courtesy of Stern Stewart & Co.
Note that EVA™ is a registered trademark of Stern Stewart & Co.

Part I
The Market

Overview

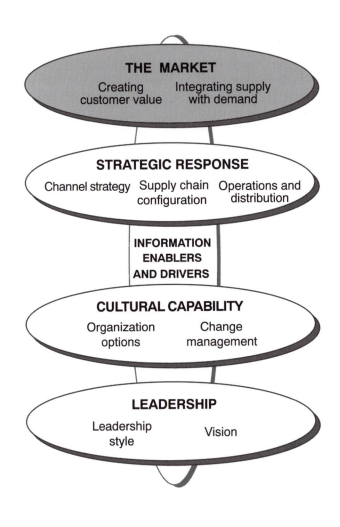

Leaders in supply chain management know that management of the supply chain represents only half of the business equation. While much attention has been paid to finding new and better ways to reduce inventory and increase stockturns, little attention is being paid to understanding, creating and managing demand more effectively. The reality is that superb supply and demand chain management is the contemporary challenge confronting supply chain practitioners, and will be the basis for competitive success or failure for many businesses.

A condition of superb supply and demand management is an intimate relationship with customers. The most effective—indeed the only—way to develop a close customer relationship is by understanding customer buying behaviours and designing and sustaining a supply chain tailored to deliver value to each customer segment. Customer segments may typically include the cost-conscious buyers, the time-sensitive payers and those with specialized requirements, among others. Sometimes circumstances move customers from one segment to another—in an emergency, for example, swift response may become critical to the normally cost-conscious customer. Or a young single customer marries and starts a family, moving into a new segment.

Companies looking to succeed need to understand their customers and consumers, their present needs, their stage of life and their consumption values. Different industries and firms will usually service one segment more than the others. But even for niche businesses some form of customer segmentation will almost certainly be necessary to ensure long-term survival. In Chapters 3, 4 and 5 the contributors analyse different strategies for segmenting customers and the ways in which the supply chain can address their needs, across everything from the needs of different categories of beer customers, right through to understanding the segment-of-one and implementation of mass customization.

A key part of understanding and retaining customers is to draw them into the company's orbit, through integrating the supply and demand chain. This means moving the supply chain from supplying customers indiscriminately according to forecast demand, to supplying customers with precision according to their actual demand and their stated requirements. That way the company lines up its supply chain to match and mirror the demand requirements of its customers—and is capable of moving with customers as their needs change. Chapters 6 through 13 analyse ways in which companies do this, including everything from time compression techniques, to the possibilities of efficient consumer response, to smoothing demand volatility. The tools and techniques discussed in these chapters are all directed to managing an intimate relationship with customers through the supply chain, and they offer the latest thinking and experience of leading companies and practitioners.

Aligned logistics operations
Tailoring logistics to the needs of customers
Liane Torres and John Miller

In the drive for reduced supply chain costs and improved efficiency, many companies have adopted a 'one-size-fits-all' mentality when it comes to providing logistics services. But customers come in all shapes and sizes and have vastly divergent logistics needs. Companies need to understand the differences in customer requirements and align their logistics operations to customer segments based on these differences. This chapter outlines how companies can achieve alignment in a cost-effective way, using a three-step approach. Alignment offers benefits that go far beyond cost efficiency: it promises greater market share and competitive power.

Introduction

Logistics has traditionally been viewed as a narrow function: the activities involved in storing and delivering products. These activities are seen to tie up large capital investment, but are not particularly difficult to accomplish. The traditional focus has been to achieve the required throughput (pallets or boxes delivered) with the minimum amount of cost.

This mindset leads naturally to a strategy, whether developed deliberately or by default, of simplifying logistics operations as much as possible by providing a single, standard level of service to all customers. Some organizations even actively discourage, or ignore, special customer requirements as these are seen to detract from logistics' goal of maximum efficiencies.

More often that not, this standard level of service is developed from a purely internal perspective, that is, with very little or no customer involvement. The service standards are set because it is convenient for the organization's logistics operations, not for its customers.

Many manufacturing organizations approach logistics in this way. A large Australian beverage manufacturer, for instance, provided a 'one-size-fits-all' delivery service. This meant exactly the same service to all its customers, who ranged from large grocery chains and large hospitality establishments to small independent restaurants and corner stores. While the purchase volumes, delivery size, timing and ordering drivers varied greatly within their customer base, every customer received the same level of service, at the same flat rate per box.

Service standardization in the pursuit of efficiency in the supply chain is admirable. However, the mindset that values only efficiency needs to be challenged. The supply chain has other, equally important goals in addition to cost efficiency.

The new mindset

The prevalent logistics mindset must move from one of complexity reduction and cost efficiencies, to one of revenue and margin enhancement, to the extent of providing for occasional 'profitable inefficiencies'.

The provision of logistics services represents a great, untapped area for providing increased value added to the purchase transaction. When customers purchase, they buy more than the product. They also buy the bundle of services around the product provided by the supplier. This bundle includes components such as pricing flexibility, promotions/ deals/discounts, credit and payment terms, merchandising support, after-sales support and delivery or logistics service. Because the logistics service is manifested in every transaction with the customer, it has the most significant impact on customers' internal operations.

Customers' requirements for logistics services, however, vary by customer or product. The 'one-size-fits-all' approach to logistics service often consists of an 'average' service level that tends to over-service some customers while under-servicing others.

This can also apply to ordering situations. At a large pharmaceutical company, all orders were processed as emergencies, although 85 per cent were replenishments, as the company thought all its customers needed the short delivery turnaround. As the company was over-servicing its market, the costs were too high. This is best illustrated by the standard cost–service level trade-off curve (Figure 3.1). Selecting one 'average' service level implies opportunities for improved service, at a higher cost-to-serve, for some customers, while reducing the service and therefore generating cost savings for others. The supplier's challenge then is to identify and capitalize on these opportunities. The supplier may choose to increase service to some customers, and in that way enhance its revenue opportunities, or to minimize service to other customers, which will not only better match the customers' needs but reduce costs for both the manufacturer and the customer.

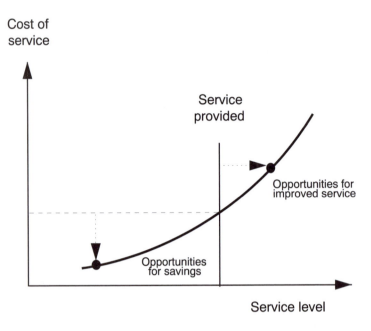

Figure 3.1   The cost of service versus service level trade-off

Increasing service: enhancing revenue and keeping customers

Enhanced revenue is one typical result of providing an 'above-average' level of service to selected customers. For example, a few customers—large retailers and mass merchandisers come to mind—are more sophisticated and demanding in the logistics support services they require, compared to other organizations. Some of these services include support for electronic data interchange (EDI) and efficient consumer response (ECR), joint forecasting and planning programmes, display-ready pallets, rainbow pallets, direct-to-store deliveries, customer case labelling and shelf-ready preparation, to name a few. 'Preferred supplier' status and the potential for increased selling space or time are some examples of carrots dangled by customers to induce suppliers to provide a specialized logistics service.

For example, a large Australian retailer has guaranteed to its 'preferred suppliers'—that is, those that accept EDI purchase orders, provide EDI advance shipping notices (ASNs) and supply merchandise in a shelf-ready state (already price-ticketed, barcoded and on hangers)—a 24-hour turnaround through the retailers' distribution centres and on to the selling floor. The retailer prioritizes the processing and movement of these suppliers' products through their internal distribution network by setting up a 'fast-track' channel in their distribution centres. This results in an increased selling cycle for these 'preferred suppliers' at the expense of those who are not ready or willing to tailor their logistics services.

For certain industries, especially those that deal with large retailers, suppliers have no choice but to tailor logistics services. Some retailers will simply not deal with suppliers who cannot provide these services. The retailer described above has put a programme in place to stop dealing with suppliers who cannot provide the level of service required within 24 months; and does not accept new suppliers who cannot provide the same level of service.

Today's manufacturers need to support a more complex distribution channel mix. Most manufacturers will tend to sell through a multitude of mechanisms including distributors, selling direct to large customers, and through a variety of retail formats, from corner stores to mass merchants, warehouses and convenience stores, for which the logistics requirements will vary significantly.

In addition, revenue-enhancement opportunities also exist through charging premiums for higher levels of logistics service. For example, a large chemical manufacturer in the USA offered a vendor-managed inventory programme using telemetry technology, where remote electronic monitoring was used to track the volume of material at its customers' sites. The manufacturer was able to save on delivery costs and also charge customers a premium for the service, as the requirement for customers' stocktake and ordering activities was removed. Another benefit to the manufacturer was that the information relating to actual customer use for the product allowed it to manage and plan internal production schedules more effectively, reduce finished goods inventory, cut raw material costs and reduce the number of emergency line changeovers.

Minimizing service: matching needs and reducing costs

At the same time, providing a 'below-average' logistics service to selected customers offers an excellent way for organizations to improve the return on assets and funds employed in their logistics activity. For example, a large office equipment manufacturer used a next-day delivery service for all spare parts to service agents on the assumption that these were urgently required for emergency customer repairs. After analysing the true nature of requirements, the manufacturer realized that some parts requirements were not urgent at all, but were used to top up the agents' inventories. A system for slower and lower-cost 'standard' deliveries was established.

In addition, an increased understanding of customer profitability through better information systems and costing tools such as activity-based costing allows organizations to realize the true cost-to-serve for their customers. This new insight has driven organizations either to modify service levels or develop specific cost-reduction programmes, based on the contribution a customer makes to the bottom line.

At a large US paper products manufacturer, some strategically important, powerful customers were found to be costing the company more than they should in sales support. A large mass-merchant customer was a problem account as it changed orders at the last minute, causing expensive shipments (from out-of-service sources) and expensive line changeovers. For this mass merchant, a specific programme of cross-functional selling was used to identify cost-reduction programmes that would benefit both organizations. Compared to another large mass merchant, the difference in margin was several percentage points.

The provision of logistics services aligned to the unique requirements of the customer provides many potential benefits to an organization, including competitive advantage, revenue enhancement, margin enhancement and cost reduction. It does, however, represent a significant shift from the traditional 'one-size-fits-all' logistics approach.

While cost efficiency will always be a target, logisticians must include the objective of a customized logistics service to their brief. The new logistics challenge, then, is to provide tailored logistics services cost effectively to customers.

In working with several organizations in different industries, a three-step approach has been developed for tailoring services cost effectively, as summarized in Figure 3.2 and described in detail below.

Segment customers from a logistics perspective

Building the capability to provide tailored services above and beyond the standard levels traditionally offered by suppliers carries the risk of a cost blowout for logistics. Providing these 'extra' services on an unplanned or *ad hoc* basis could result in additional cost-to-serve for certain customers that cannot be recovered from the margins associated with them. For example, a large consumer products goods manufacturer found itself investing in several different EDI delivery support and invoicing systems in an effort to support the varying standards required by its main customers. The key to building cost-effective tailored logistics services is to segment customers to find the right balance between the 'one-size-fits-all' and the 'segment-of-one' approaches (Figure 3.3).

Segment customers from a logistics perspective

- Identify logistics service requirements across the entire customer base
- Understand the logistical and economic drivers for the requirement of services
- Create a logical grouping for those customers with similar requirements
- Identify opportunities to deliver service to customer groups throughout the entire supply chain

Design levels of service for each segment

- Identify opportunities to differentiate based on service bundles
- Determine customers' strategic attractiveness
- Develop specific service strategies that address the strategic attractiveness
- Build a business case for new service offerings, considering cost-to-serve
- Test service offerings with customers

Reconfigure logistics operations

- Align logistics strategy with strategies of other customer-facing activities, e.g. sales, merchandising, marketing, customer service
- Determine the impact of the new service strategies on the distribution network configuration and operations
- Determine the impact of service strategies on existing third-party contracts

Figure 3.2   Approach for tailoring services cost effectively

Finding this balance requires the development of a reasonable number of groups, or segments, of customers that are similar enough to have common logistics needs. This enables the organization to build economies of scale into the provision of tailored services. In determining the appropriate segmentation, companies can borrow from the approaches used in the sales and marketing disciplines. Sales and marketing have traditionally invested significant amounts of time and effort in segmenting the customer and consumer base, designing a suite of tailored or account-specific products and non-logistics offerings, such as merchandising support and promotions. These efforts have typically resulted in increased revenues by tailoring products to major consumer segments.

One-size-fits-all

Standard logistics service
provided to all customers

- Cost-reduction focus
- Simplification of logistics
  activity through
  standardization
- Low cost-to-serve

Segment-of-one

Logistics service
customized for every customer

- Customer service
  focus
- Provide customized
  service for each
  customer
- High cost-to-serve

Logistically distinct
segmentation

Customers segmented
according to logistics
requirements

- Segments significantly
  different
- Segments large enough to
  build critical mass in service
  provision

Figure 3.3   The segmentation balance

A similar approach to segmentation is proposed from a logistics perspective. This involves focusing on specific logistics needs or logistically
different product characteristics.

Bases for logistics segmentation

The 'science' of segmenting customers from a logistics perspective does
not differ significantly from traditional sales and marketing segmentation. Primary market research segmentation tools such as cluster and
factor analysis apply in defining these segments; the main difference lies
in the factors used in defining the segments. These will, of necessity, be
highly logistics specific and range from strategic to operational levels of

Table 3.1
Logistics segmentation factors

Example factors	Specifics
Buying relationship	
• Demand forecasting	Limited, extensive, joint forecasts/schedules
• Price determination	Basic, volume, agreed returns on investment
Ordering and billing	
• Order entry mechanism	Phone, facsimile,EDI
• Billing mechanism	Invoice, COD, EFT, EDI
• Order confirmation	Immediate, 2 days
• Order tracking	Visibility, barcoding
Delivery and support services	
• Use of time slots	None, strict
• Driver unloading role	None, expected
• Order receiving	ASN, automated receiving support
• Delivery requirements	Special pallets, special barcodes
Ordering complexity	
• Variability of demand	Low, medium, high
• Regularity of orders	High, medium, low
• Order predictability (size and product mix)	High, medium, low
• Order frequency	Weekly, monthly
• Average order sizes	Boxes, pallets, truck loads
Delivery complexity	
• Drop-off points	Central, single, multiple
• Site accessibility	Low, medium, high
• Emergency deliveries	None, expected
• Requirement for reverse logistics	None, expected

detail, as shown in Table 3.1. These factors are roughly broken down into two distinct types: customers' logistics needs, including order types, and product characteristics.

Examples of customer-unique logistics needs that drive segmentation can be found in Table 3.1. For example, the large Australian beverage company mentioned earlier used a combination of ordering characteristics, physical handling and customer sophistication as the main factors in defining the segments around which it built a new logistics infrastructure.

Companies will also need to distinguish between the significantly different demand patterns in their customer orders, such as between regular replenishment and emergency orders. For example, a large telecommunications provider found that its internal customers had different demand requirements for the same products. Requirements ranged from emergency orders to planned build requirements to scheduled maintenance. To meet these varying needs successfully, the provider configured its demand planning and inventory management processes and storage support infrastructure for each different demand type.

Product characteristics, to the extent that these define significant differences in logistics operations, can also be used as a segmentation driver and as bases around which unique capabilities are built. Product differences are usually driven by unique handling characteristics. For example, a large processed foods manufacturer identified different flow characteristics requirements of different products through its own distribution network and established two distinct channels, 'flow-through' and 'flexibility', to support specific products.

Defining customer groups and their requirements may be accomplished in a variety of ways. Approaches range from sophisticated market research, using detailed customer surveys, focus groups and quantitative analytical tools, to using internal focus groups and interviews conducted with sales and logistics personnel. The most appropriate approach for a particular organization depends on the trade-off between the time and cost of the exercise and the requirement for stringent statistical validity of the results. Experience shows that statistical validity is typically not a high priority for logistics segmentation, as there are often only a few major logistics segments that can be easily tested internally and externally before tailored services are designed.

In defining customers' logistics requirements, organizations should also focus on understanding their own performance versus their competitors'. This will provide great insight into the priority of each service factor and how well these service requirements are being met. Where a high-priority service is not being met by the market, there is an opportunity to differentiate. If a service requirement is being met by most of the competition, then it must play catch-up. In addition, a focus on non-priority service requirements can be avoided. A large Australian process industry manufacturer realized in the process of logistics segmentation that none of the major players in the industry was sufficiently meeting its customers' most basic logistics requirements. As a result, it first focused on getting its product delivered on time and in full to all customers before offering specialized logistics services.

Logistics segmentation versus sales segmentation

Ideally, customers should be segmented according to their overall requirements and services offered accordingly. However, the most likely situation is that a sales segmentation will already exist. It is possible for a sales-developed segmentation to differ from a logistics-developed one. The previously mentioned beverage manufacturer found that its logistics segmentation varied slightly from its sales segmentation and that both segmentation approaches were valid. It required internal alignment between sales and logistics personnel in offering a consistent selling message to the market.

Design levels of service for each segment

When customer segments have been defined, the next step will be to design specific service offerings for each of the segments. As the segmentation itself is driven by service requirements, this step should be relatively straightforward. However, as in any instance when service offerings are being defined, the key for any organization is not to go bankrupt in the process. The overall process for developing new services is an iterative one, as shown in Figure 3.4.

The first step is to develop a full understanding of the organization's current capabilities and define a 'first cut' of the segment-specific services. In addition to the customer requirements, the strategic attractiveness of a customer relationship also dictates whether or not a service

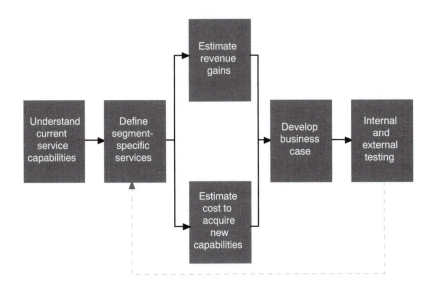

Figure 3.4   Process for developing new services

- Leverageable relationship
- Potential for sales growth
- Potential to partner
- Importance of customer

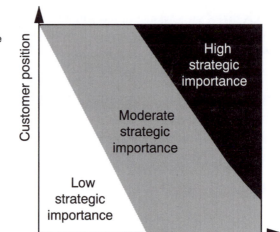

Figure 3.5   The strategic importance of a customer relationship

should be offered. A framework used in determining the strategic importance of a customer to an organization is presented in Figure 3.5. The strategic importance of the relationship, which depends on the combination of both the relationship potential of a customer and the customer's importance in the market. For example, in the case of most large retail chains, especially in Australia where the trade is highly concentrated, customers have large volumes with limited potential for partnering. Manufacturers have almost no control over whether and how much logistics services are to be provided to retailers. In other cases the customers' future market potential, such as current business size and forecast growth, may dictate whether additional services are warranted.

In most cases, organizations will find that additional services are required, new capabilities must be built and new pricing mechanisms must be developed. Organizations have to put together the business case for providing new services, including both the costs associated with the provision of these services, driven by the gap between current and required capabilities, and the likelihood of recovery of these costs through either higher prices or increased sales volume. As mentioned earlier, the increased use of information systems and availability of customer profitability information, and the use of tools such as activity-based costing, will greatly assist in this step.

Any new service offering will need to be tested both internally, with sales and marketing personnel, and externally, with customers. Internal testing is required to ensure alignment between sales offerings, such as pricing and credit terms, and logistics offerings. For example, at the beverage manufacturer, one of the service changes that logistics wanted to implement was to eliminate fixed delivery charges and move to a variable delivery charge based on the size of the delivery. This, however, was in potential conflict with sales pricing policies then in place. Joint sales and logistics offerings had to be developed to retain consistency and avoid marketplace confusion.

External testing is also required to ensure that additional services add value to customers, and that customers are willing either to pay a premium for the service or to support increased sales volume. These tests could be done through customer focus groups, one-on-one interviews or customer surveys. Changes to services coming out of these tests typically mean a review of the business case, as both revenue and cost estimates could be altered significantly.

Reconfigure logistics operations

The next challenge is to 'operationalize' the new offerings, not just in the day-to-day warehousing and transport operations, but also in other customer-facing activities and customer service-supporting assets and systems.

The main impacts on the organization can be divided into three components: on processes employed, on the assets and technology used, and on the people involved, which includes both employees and any third-party logistics providers.

Process implications

The challenge in defining new processes is to ensure the new services are provided in a cost-effective and efficient manner. For example, the provision of extended services to retailers, through barcoding, presenting merchandise in a shelf-ready state or constructing special pallets, will require additional processing steps within the production or distribution facility. Or, in another example, changes in the flow of product by creating distinct 'cross-dock' or flow-through pathways through the distribution centre may be required for specific products or customers. The challenge is to identify the most cost-effective area in which to perform the additional activities without causing too much disruption to the overall product flow. The following questions can help bring to the surface the issues associated with process changes:

■ What new activities need to be performed by the manufacturer? Where is the best place to perform these activities (for example, at point of manufacture, after packaging or after picking)?

■ What are the expected volumes of product and numbers of customers that will be affected by the change? What is the best way of implementing the new processes without disrupting the flow of 'other' products?

■ How are individual processes affected: receiving, put-away, storage, picking, despatch, transport planning, scheduling and routing?

■ What changes to forecasting, production planning, inventory management and distribution management processes and policies need to be introduced?

■ What changes to sales and marketing processes and policies need to be introduced?

Assets and technology implications

The appropriate level of assets used and the right enabling technology must be identified. The additional services that most sophisticated customers demand tend to be technology related, such as EDI orders and ASNs, and pallet and product barcoding. In addition, most of the new activities that need to be introduced in the factory or warehouse will have to be supported by advanced systems, for example systems to support cross-docking operations, advanced transport scheduling and routing. Changes to asset use and configuration may also be required, as mentioned in the earlier example of setting up distinct product-flow pathways through the distribution centre or in instances where specialized vehicles may be designed for specific customers, as is the case in the soft drink industry in Australia. The following questions can assist in teasing out the issues associated with asset and technology changes:

■ What changes to asset configuration are required, for example reconfigured warehouses and assets, numbers of facilities, new and specialized material handling and delivery equipment?

■ What changes to sales, order management and customer service systems are required to support the new processes?

■ What changes or upgrades to production planning, supply chain planning, warehouse and transport management systems are required to support the new service offerings?

People implications

It is crucial to identify and address organizational issues to ensure effective implementation of the new services. In all instances, changes to work flows and the introduction of new systems will necessitate training and work changes. Agreements with third-party logistics contractors, with which most organizations are involved, will more often than not also be required. An understanding of the impact of work changes on contracts associated with labour unions and third-party contractors will need to be developed. The people-change issues can be brought to the surface by the following questions:

- Who will be performing the new or changed processes? What is the impact of these changes on current workplace agreements?
- What training is required to support the performance of these new processes?
- What key supply chain roles need to be redefined?
- What changes to the logistics and sales organization are required to support the new processes?
- What changes to existing third-party logistics arrangements must be made to support the new processes?
- What new third-party arrangements must be made to support the new processes?
- What are the implications for other areas of the organization, for example customer service, after-sales support?

Aligned logistics operations in action

The organization is a large US-based paper products manufacturer that supplies paper products to retailers throughout the country. The challenge was to use logistics as a tool to gain a competitive advantage, increase potential sales volume, and decrease overall costs.

From interviews with a large number of customers of varying size, geographic coverage and channel, the project team identified that all customers viewed order accuracy, fill rate and on-time delivery as very important. In contrast, the varying importance of other service requirements indicated a potential opportunity for the organization to differentiate itself. The team plotted the relative importance of these service factors on Figure 3.6.

The team learned that while the organization was performing well on the basic requirements, all paper suppliers are doing well in these areas, so these requirements present no opportunity for differentiation. For the other services providing an opportunity to set apart the organization's offerings (in the upper left-hand corner), the team heard that they did not consistently deliver many of these. An opportunity in the lower left corner would have been developed

Importance
to customers

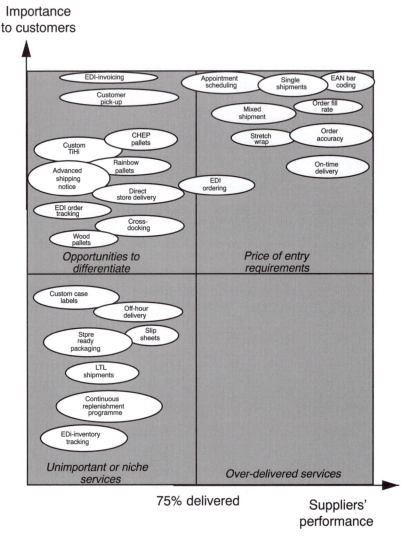

75% delivered

Suppliers'
performance

Figure 3.6 Customer ratings of logistics service offerings

if an important customer considered it important, and if the economics
supported it.

Four distinct customer segments emerged when the degree of importance
placed on logistics by the customer was combined with their relative level of
logistics sophistication. The team called these Traditional, Followers, Internal
Focus and Partners (see Figure 3.7).

The strategic attractiveness of each customer was evaluated in two dimensions: 'customer potential' and 'company potential'. The cost-to-serve for a
customer, including the logistics and non-logistics costs of delivering a finished
product, was also determined.

Followers

- Open to most basic information linkages
- Relies on vendor to offer new services, rather than driving the relationship
- Not consistently measuring vendor performance
- Beginning to seek change in performance on logistics
- Focusing on standardization rather than flexibility
- Order cycle 6-8 days
- Inventory turns 25-35

Partners

- Integrated logistics with category management
- Pushing utilization of sophisticated information linkages
- Interested in programmes to optimize supply chain to drive out system costs
- Requires highest performance on basic, as well as sophisticated performance requirements
- Desire to select delivery and packaging services on an order specific basis
- Order cycle 3 days or less
- Inventory turns 50 or greater

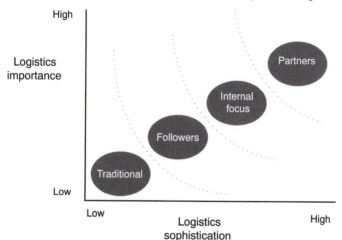

Traditional

- Traditional buying organization
- Not expecting increased services
- Little focus on information
- Order cycle greater than 7 days
- Inventory turns 20 or less

Internal focus

- Some category management implemented, not integrated with logistics
- Less developed information linkages
- More focused on managing internal logistics issues and network
- Somewhat demanding on basic and sophisticated performance requirements
- Like flexibility of choosing logistics services
- Order cycle 4 days or less
- Inventory turns 35 to 50

Figure 3.7   Segmentation of customers

The combination of cost-to-serve and strategic attractiveness factors guided the team in setting their new logistics service strategies (Figure 3.8).

Followers

Selectively grow volume with low-cost customers who compete successfully via:
- Providing supply chain leadership through a standard service offering that maximizes efficiency
- Implementing a pricing strategy that penalizes exceptions. Use cost savings and shift of volume from higher-cost customers to fund increased investments with partners and internal focus

Partners

Invest to drive volume via:
- Developing partnering relationships utilizing cross-functional account teams
- Agreeing on value-added service offerings which mutually reduce costs focused on information-enabled offerings

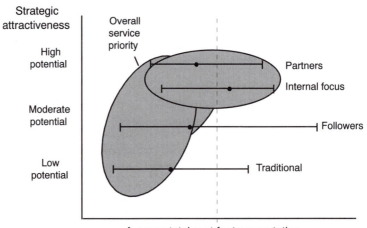

Traditional

Selectively offer standard services with set pricing to low-cost customers near mills. Provide significantly longer lead times with reduced fill rate and on-time delivery performance. Shift volume from higher-cost customers to fund increased investment with partners and internal focus

Internal focus

Selectively invest to drive volume via:
- Providing value-added services that:
  - Customers are willing to pay for
  - Reduce cost, and/or,
  - Lead directly to share and volume growth
- Educating customers on cost of inefficient service practices to bring about change and lead to partnering relationship

Figure 3.8   New logistics service strategies

Conclusion

Aligning logistics operations with customer segments is a departure from the traditional manufacturing approach of providing a 'one-size-fits-all' level of logistics service for all customers. External factors such as growing variability in the services customers require, as well as internal factors including a desire to improve return on assets and funds employed on logistics activities, are compelling organizations to provide a range of logistics services tailored to distinct customer and product segments.

By following the approach outlined here for developing these tailored services, organizations will be able to develop proactively logistic operations that are aligned to customers' requirements, both today and in the future. The benefits associated with alignment go well beyond the efficiencies on which logisticians have traditionally focused. These include:

- higher market penetration, with service offerings geared towards selling more to existing customers and attracting new customers;
- greater customer loyalty—if a company reliably provides the services customers require, and develops partnerships where required, customers have no reason to switch providers;
- product availability—with lower inventory, through understanding customer needs and focusing on service, demand planning programmes are aligned with requirements; and
- profit growth through increased sales volumes resulting from better aligned service offerings and an improved understanding of cost-to-profit relationships of new service offerings.

CHAPTER

4

Customer support logistics
The key to customer satisfaction
Robert Evans and Doug Castek

The priority given in recent years to the customer as the chief driver of business activity has put the performance of customer support organizations firmly in the spotlight. If companies are to succeed in capturing the hearts of their many customer segments, they must look not only at the products they sell, but also at the level of support provided before and after the sale. Achieving seamless customer support means ensuring that logistics considerations are given primacy in the customer support structure. This chapter outlines four models for customer support logistics and describes the forces of change that will affect future success. Paying proper attention to the role of logistics in customer support can ensure that the right part, the right tools and the right information arrive at the right time. By doing this, companies will deliver customer satisfaction and motivate purchasing loyalty in the future.

Introduction

Customer support can be defined as a series of primarily after-sale activities that are aimed at reinforcing total customer satisfaction and building ongoing customer loyalty. Its focus is to provide value to the customer by delivering time-sensitive, user-friendly and value-adding information and services that maximize product availability and productivity, as well as minimize customer expenditures of energy, time and cost. Customer support logistics refers to the role of logistics in improving the performance of customer service operations. The term 'customer' in this sense refers to the person who actually uses the product or service, rather than a customer within the supply chain.

Customer service knows few industry boundaries: customer support operations exist in any company that manufactures or uses products in conducting its business. For example, car makers, computer manufacturers and electronics, equipment and consumer durables manufacturers must provide customer support to their end-user customers. Service providers such as telecommunications companies, utilities and transportation operators must perform or acquire customer support services for the physical assets, such as facilities and equipment, used in their businesses. Similarly, manufacturers must also offer customer services for the physical assets used in making their products.

In addition, numerous companies treat customer support as an independent business, separate from any products which they may manufacture or use in the conduct of their business, and, in effect, compete with the customer support organizations provided by product manufacturers. As examples consider automotive parts and service companies and computer service providers.

Customer support is often understood to be an 'after-market' activity, but increasingly these operations are involved 'before' the sale occurs. Product manufacturers, for instance, are increasingly bundling customer support services with the product so that customers buy not only the product but the ongoing parts and service. Customer support organizations may also be involved in the design and engineering of products to ensure that service can be performed effectively later. Highlighting a firm's customer support performance can also be part of product marketing.

Customer service consists of three principal components, as illustrated in Figure 4.1:

- service parts management, including managing the inventory, sourcing, transportation and distribution centre design required to provide service parts;
- service management, involving the technology, equipment, scheduling, information and design involved in servicing and repairs; and

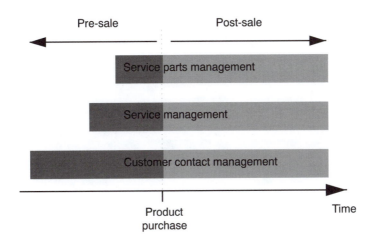

Figure 4.1   The three components of customer support

■ customer contact management: encompassing parts and service marketing, problem resolution, service staff recruitment and training, and customer research.

Importance of customer support

Companies are increasingly discovering that there are three primary benefits of providing effective customer support.

First, satisfied customers behave in a manner that can benefit the firm in the longer term. These customers can increase the firm's product, service parts and service market share and help the company achieve a price premium over competitors. Purchasing loyalty showed by contented buyers will reduce the sales and marketing costs associated with creating new customers. Further, the recommendations of satisfied customers can positively affect the purchasing behaviour of other customers.

A second benefit of customer support is the profits that can be generated by customer support activities. In some industries, service parts, service and, in some instances, customer contact revenues and profits can be considerable. In the automotive industry, for example, customer support provides a disproportionate level of manufacturers' and dealers' profits, as shown in Table 4.1.

Finally, customer support activities used to support the assets used in their businesses can substantially improve both operational effectiveness and efficiency and financial performance. For example, the availability (often referred to as 'uptake') of the assets that comprise the network of a telecommunications services provider is a significant determinant of the overall level of end-user customer satisfaction as well as the profitability of the firm. Similarly, a manufacturer whose plant is inoperable

Table 4.1
Customer support profits in the automotive industry

	Proportion of sales	Proportion of profits
Service parts (manufacturer)	10%	25%
Service parts/ service management (dealer)	25%	75%

Source: Andersen Consulting industry analysis

due to the failure of a key piece of equipment incurs substantial costs related to the lost production.

Customer support service trade-off model

Apart from considering the benefits of customer support, companies must also take account of the cost of providing differing levels of service to customers. The effective customer support organization of the future will develop strategies that will enhance the overall profitability of not only the internal service organization but the parent as well. To meet these challenges, many will attempt to balance the cost-to-serve against the quality of the service rendered. Figure 4.2 is an example of how many service organizations continually balance cost versus quality.

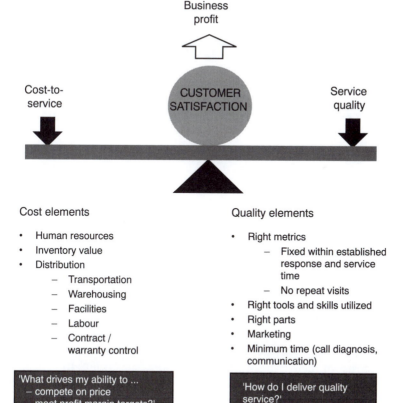

Figure 4.2   Customer support service trade-off

Table 4.2
Key customer support logistics activities

Key customer support logistics area	Primary logistics challenge
Service parts inventory management	Maximizing parts availability with minimum inventory and costs
Service parts warehousing	Maximizing order fulfilment effectiveness while minimizing costs
Service parts transportation	Providing rapid parts delivery while minimizing costs
Service parts order processing and fulfilment	Maximizing order entry and processing while minimizing costs
Service parts sourcing	Finding and developing low-cost/high-quality sources of supply
Service parts procurement	Ensuring timely delivery of high-quality parts at minimum costs
Service technician capacity planning	Maintaining the appropriate number of technicians to support demand
Service technician scheduling	Ensuring service technician capacity is effectively utilized
Service technician dispatch	Managing deployment of service technicians on an hour-to-hour basis
End-user service requirements determination	Accurately identifying customer satisfaction needs and expectations
End-user customer service management	Managing appropriate response to customer service issues

Models for customer support logistics

Logistics plays a central role in the delivery of customer support and as such is a critical determinant of a firm's level of customer support performance. Ultimately, customer support is about delivering the right parts, service technicians, tools and information to the right location, at the right time, at the lowest possible cost. The extent of logistics activities in key customer support functions is shown in Table 4.2.

Logistics-based activities can account for more than 90 per cent of the total costs of delivering customer support, according to Andersen Consulting industry analysis. It is thus critical to develop a strategic approach to logistics that will deliver logistics activities according to the needs of the customer and the requirements of the organization. Four customer support logistics models exist, listed below. These vary according to the diverse competitive and supply chain environments faced by companies operating in different industries; each presents its own supply chain challenges.

Dealer channel model

The dealer channel model is perhaps the most common customer support logistics model. This model is characterized by manufacturers who sell the products they produce through a number of dealers, typically independently owned. While it is the responsibility of the dealers to provide customer support to end-user customers, the manufacturer often plays a significant role in supporting dealers in this effort.

Companies in the automotive, agricultural equipment, construction equipment, industrial equipment and transportation equipment industries tend to provide customer support to their end-user customers through the dealer channel model.

Saturn

General Motors' wholly owned subsidiary Saturn designs, manufactures and markets automobiles in the US market through independently owned dealers. When GM created Saturn, one of its primary business objectives was to provide a high, luxury-car level of after-sale customer support, even though the Saturn product line is priced in the $13 000 to $20 000 range. Traditionally, manufacturers utilizing the dealer channel model took responsibility for managing their own parts inventories and relied on their dealers to manage parts inventories owned and held by the dealers.

Saturn took a different approach. The company and its dealers are linked by a sophisticated information system that enables Saturn to 'see' the part inventory availability and sales data of each of its dealers. It uses this information to create replenishment orders to restock dealer inventories of service parts. This new approach ensures that all service parts supply chain planning decisions are driven by customer demand, thereby reducing inventory throughout the supply chain and improving parts availability to customers. Saturn dealer parts availability, as experienced by customers, is consistently in the 90 to 95 per cent range versus typical dealer inventory availability levels of 70 to 80 per cent. This exceptionally high level of parts availability is not achieved by maintaining excessive inventories. Typical Saturn dealer parts inventory 'turnover' (i.e. parts sales divided by inventory) is six to seven turns per year, compared to an industry norm of two to four turns per year.

This innovative supply chain relationship has redefined the channel dealer model and has prompted both Saturn's competitors and other firms outside the automotive industry who utilize the dealer channel model to pursue similar operating strategies.

Field service model

The field service model is also frequently encountered and is character-ized by a manufacturer that sells its products directly to end-users. The manufacturer also typically provides customer support to end-user cus-tomers through its own field service organization or through a third-party organization under a contractual arrangement.

Companies in the computer, consumer electronics, office equipment, aerospace, medical equipment and consumer durables industries typi-cally employ the field service model to provide support to customers.

Depicted in Figure 4.3 is the typical network of a medical diagnostics equipment manufacturer, distributor and customer support provider.

From a logistics perspective, there are several challenges that stress the ability to provide high levels of service in the field service model eco-nomically. These key challenges include:

- inventory deployment, moving inventory between many stocking locations, including central and regional warehouses and local stock-ing locations;
- parts planning and field engineer coordination;
- parts usage reporting;
- split inventory responsibility, including central and remaining net-work and the field engineer's needs;
- use of premium transportation for high-value and low-usage parts, including air freight such as sonic air and parts depots;
- lifecycle planning, including new products, growth and maturity (in-use) products, post-production products and obsolete products;
- part characteristics, such as part value disparity, the small number of parts 'driving' a large proportion of the usage and many low usage parts; and
- reverse flow, such as part return policies and repair of defective parts.

Traditionally, to be effective, the field service model deployed by many companies requires significant levels of inventory. A 1992 survey by Andersen Consulting for computer and office equipment industries indi-cated that the average months of supply of inventory was 13.8. Additionally, a study from the Association of Field Service Management International and Coopers & Lybrand in 1993 showed that 4.6 months of inventory for high-technology companies (such as computer, medical equipment and office equipment manufacturers) was a best demonstrat-ed practice and that inventory carrying costs represented about 50 per cent of total logistics costs.

Through study and correlation of data completed by these authors, it appears that service parts inventory turns are driven by one key factor. Design consistency across product offerings appears to affect a service

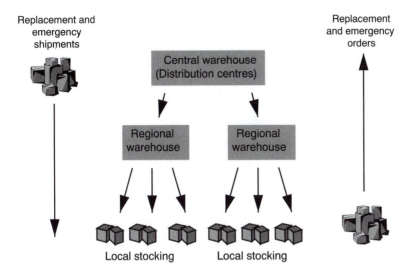

Replacement and emergency shipments

Replacement and emergency orders

Central warehouse (Distribution centres)

Regional warehouse

Regional warehouse

Local stocking

Local stocking

Stocking point decision hierarchy

Central warehouse
- Replenishes regional warehouses
- Handles emergency stockout orders as a last resort
- Stocks all parts

Regional warehouses
- Possibly multiple
- Replenish local stocking locations
- Stock majority of parts
- Handle emergency stockout orders from local stocking locations

Local stocking locations
- Stock high-usage parts
- Variety of locations
  - branch offices
  - customer sites
  - field engineer's vehicle/home

Figure 4.3   Field service model network

organization's ability to drive inventory turn ratios higher. Those that utilize common designs and parts across products tend to have lower inventory investment.

It is therefore imperative to integrate these concepts when designing new equipment.

Network asset model

The network asset model is characterized by a service provider or manufacturing firm that has a substantial 'network' of assets, typically plants

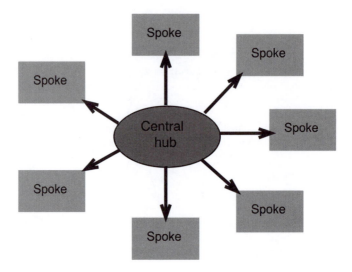

Stocking point decision hierarchy

Central hub
- Replenishes regional warehouses 'minor' material safety
- Holds 'networks' safety stock
- Stocks all parts
- Sends job kits to spokes based on weekly demand on orders

Spoke locations
- Spokes carry minor material and bulk items (poles, transformers, etc)
- Kits from hub are staged on the dock for future delivery or directly on to trucks
- Large jobs (e.g. capital) are shipped directly to spoke or at point of use in field
- Spoke locations hold emergency and storm material

Figure 4.4   Networking asset model (electric utility example)

and equipment, which must be effectively maintained to support the ongoing business of the firm. Customer support is provided in four ways. The firm may:

- employ its own staff to provide customer support;
- contract with a third party to provide customer support;
- engage the suppliers of its assets to provide customer support for their products; and
- utilize a combination of all three methods.

The network asset model is often referred to as operations and maintenance, or O&M. Virtually every manufacturing and service provider, such as telecommunications, utilities and transportation firms, employs the network asset model to support its operations.

Depicted in Figure 4.4 is a storeroom network of an electricity utility that supports maintenance, emergency, repair and customer hook-ups.

To enable this type of network structure to operate effectively, it is imperative that the asset manager sets priorities with regard to the work required in order profitably to support and maintain the future infrastructure, while continuing to complete customer-driven demands. Integrated Resource Planning (IRP) is an integrated methodology that

Doing the right thing the right way ...

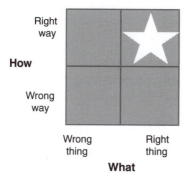

... requires adopting an integrated approach

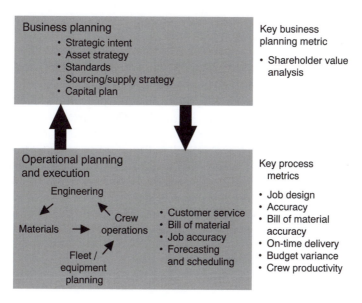

Figure 4.5   Integrated resource planning (IRP) methodology

Table 4.3
Results of 'hub and spoke' and IRP
implementation at a US electricity utility

Action	Results against baseline
Hub and spoke	
• Inventory carrying costs	15% reduction
• Transportation costs	1% increase
• Warehouse labour	10% reduction
IRP methodology	
• Line crew productivity	8% increase

Andersen Consulting has developed to support organizations utilizing the network asset model. The premise of IRP is to integrate business/infrastructure planning with operational planning execution. Figure 4.5 outlines the methodology.

From a logistics perspective, several challenges stress the ability to provide high levels of service economically in the network asset model. These key logistics challenges include:

■ inventory deployment, such as central stocking (safety stock consolidation), local stocking, line crew trucks and spoke inventory locations;
■ system and infrastructure planning, such as new technology, standards and obsolete in-service infrastructure;
■ part characteristics, including part value disparity, a small number of parts 'driving' usage and many low-value parts.

A southern-based US electrical utility recently reconfigured its storeroom network to the 'hub and spoke' design and implemented an IRP methodology in its wires business. Implementation resulted in the improvements shown in Table 4.3. These types of improvements reaped millions in annual savings and positioned the organization for pending deregulation.

Retail model

The retail model is typically employed by companies that are competitors to the customer support organizations of product manufacturers.

Firms using the retail model do not manufacture or sell the products for which they provide customer support. The retail model is characterized by firms that maintain a network of owned or independent retailers who are in the business of providing customer support services for other companies' products.

Retail automotive service parts chains, automotive lubrication chains, automotive service chains, agricultural and construction equipment service parts distributors and computer retailers who offer repair services are firms utilizing the retail model to deliver customer support.

Repco Auto Parts and Auto Service, Australia

CASE STUDY

Repco is an Australian automotive parts retailing and service chain that models itself closely on AutoZone in the US. Repco operates 280 branches covering most suburbs and towns in Australia with a distribution network that provides daily replenishment to all but the most remote branches. The business is a mixture of pure retailing, trade sales (supply of parts to car repairers) and actual servicing of vehicles. Some of the newer sales branches have been set up as superstores with extensive product displays, careful attention to facings, large specials bins and a layout designed to appeal to the non-technical shopper. Behind the scenes, delivery vans make frequent runs from each branch to local service businesses who order parts by telephone, fax or computer. The Repco service sites compete with other local vehicle service operators and are rarely co-located with sales branches.

Repco aggressively competes with vehicle dealers to supply common replacement parts, particularly for vehicles that are out of warranty. Using its high brand awareness in Australia, it markets a wide range of Repco-branded products including filters, oils, brake parts, clutch parts and even hand tools. Only a few strongly branded products such as sparkplugs avoid sharing shelf space with a Repco equivalent. Such strong control of its product assortment gives Repco a great deal of freedom to pick the most profitable product mix and store format for each location.

Backing up Repco's branch network is a 'sell one, replace one' replenishment system that efficiently ensures same-day or overnight delivery of a core range of parts. Rare parts and specialized tools can be supplied from a national slow-mover distribution centre within a day or two. This distribution approach promises scale economies, lower inventories and lower costs than a typical dealer channel model spare parts network.

The important characteristic of the retail model is that companies such as Repco do not have to consider the impact of their customer support activities on future product sales. That is the manufacturer's and dealer's problem.

Retail model companies are free to optimize their own business without having to service every possible customer need or obscure parts requirement.

Customer support model variations

A combination of customer support models may exist within an individual firm. An automotive manufacturer, for example, may employ the dealer channel model to support the products it sells while simultaneously utilizing the retail model (with its dealers as the 'retailers') to provide customer support to the end-user customers of other automotive manufacturers.

The importance of key logistics areas differs depending on the customer support model employed, illustrated in Table 4.4.

Forces of change

Five forces of change will affect the planning and delivery of customer support in the decade ahead.

- changing customer expectations regarding customer support;
- changing channels of customer support delivery;
- product proliferation;
- use of technology;
- globalization.

Force 1. Changing customer expectations

Customers' actions speak louder than their words. Evidence from recent studies (cited in the *Harvard Business Review*, 1995) shows that products such as personal computers and cars only maintain buyer loyalty by achieving the very highest levels of customer satisfaction—anything less than 100 per cent is not good enough. New business measures such as lifetime customer value are becoming of paramount importance. Pressure is coming on customer support organizations to put in place practices and measures that focus on meeting heightened customer expectations.

At the prestige end of the car industry, companies like BMW and Lexus have been setting high standards for personalized service to their customers. In most countries they offer breakdown service, owners' clubs, loan vehicles and free service pick-up and delivery. Some of these offerings are being copied by lower-priced new entrants such as Daewoo, a phenomenon that is helping raise customer expectations across the industry.

Table 4.4
Importance of key logistics areas in each customer support model

Key logistics area	Dealer channel model	Field service model	Field asset model	Retail model
Service parts inventory management	Critical	Critical	Critical	Critical
Service parts warehousing	High	High	High	High
Service parts transportation	High	High	Moderate	Moderate
Service parts order processing and fulfilment	High	High	Moderate	High
Service parts sourcing	High	High	High	Critical
Service parts procurement	High	High	High	High
Service technician capacity planning	Moderate	Critical	High	Moderate
Service technician dispatch	Moderate	Critical	Critical	Moderate
End-user customer service	Low	Critical	Moderate	Low
Requirement determination	Critical	Critical	High	High
End-user customer service management	Critical	Critical	High	High

Importance indicators:

Critical	Greatest importance to competitive success; logistics operational excellence is required
High	Significant importance to competitive success; high level of logistics performance required
Moderate	Of little importance to competitive success; logistics operational parity required
Low	Not a competitive discriminator; logistics operational sufficiency required

At the same time as expanding high-profile customer services, companies have to keep improving basics such as parts availability. Too few companies today can accurately measure and manage their parts order fill rate. Yet one of the keys to satisfying customers is providing a range of service options, allowing the customer to make informed choices such as faster delivery at a higher cost, and then ensuring that the customer's choice is delivered in full, on time, as agreed. The customer support organizations that will prosper in future will be customer driven, responsive and consistent in meeting their promises, even for basics such as delivery of parts on time.

Force 2. Changing channels of delivery

A power shift to retailers is under way in many automotive markets, especially in the US where it has already occurred in consumer electronics and office equipment. Category killers and superstores have been the clear winners in consumer and office products, but the scale and complexity of the automotive industry are driving a different sort of solution where multiple channels are likely to coexist.

Examples of emerging channels that threaten to take profitable volume away from the existing dealer channel include automotive parts chains entering the service business, used-car superstores providing extended warranties with on-site service, and 'supplier direct' initiatives where parts makers sell direct to the retailer, circumventing the vehicle manufacturer and dealers. Given the importance of customer support to dealer profits and brand loyalty in the automotive and industrial products industries, decisions to oppose or embrace these emerging channels will affect manufacturers' competitive positions for some time to come.

Force 3. Product proliferation

Product development times are being quickly reduced, creating not only more products but those that exist as 'current' products for shorter and shorter periods. These tighter cycle times complicate customer support considerably by adding complexity, especially in the form of more part numbers, more parts and service publications and more specialized service equipment.

Proliferation is also apparent in the variety of materials used and manufacturing techniques adopted as designers struggle to reconcile conflicting objectives—on the one hand low emissions, low energy impact and low cost; on the other hand marketing requirements for more space, performance, gadgets and features. The result can be products that require completely new service techniques, skills and tools. Consider the impact of electronic engine management systems on car servicing over the last decade and, for a select few dealers, the requirements for specialized training to repair the aluminium body of the new Audi A8.

Table 4.5
A new basis of competition

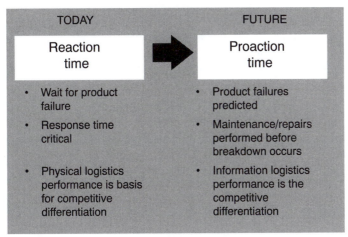

TODAY	FUTURE
Reaction time	**Proaction time**
• Wait for product failure	• Product failures predicted
• Response time critical	• Maintenance/repairs performed before breakdown occurs
• Physical logistics performance is basis for competitive differentiation	• Information logistics performance is the competitive differentiation

Force 4. Use of technology

While exploiting the marketing opportunities provided by the product proliferation trend, manufacturers have developed a number of technology-based initiatives to manage the negative impacts on customer support. Leading companies are taking specific action to reduce part number proliferation. Product information is often distributed electronically, avoiding the cost of updating paper-based manuals. Products are becoming increasingly 'serviceless' (for example, most cars now use sparkplugs which last 100 000 kilometres). The most complex industrial products, such as aircraft, cars and heavy trucks, are getting 'smarter', using self-diagnosis, evaluation and reporting systems built in to either the product or the servicing equipment.

The most advanced service technologies allow aircraft such as the Boeing 777 to transmit real-time analysis to a service centre, which schedules service and parts requirements for the next maintenance stop, greatly reducing unplanned stops and aircraft downtime. As the trend towards 'smarter' products develops we can expect to move customer support slowly from competing on the basis of 'reaction time' to 'proaction time', as highlighted in Table 4.5.

Force 5. Globalization

Increasingly companies are finding that they must source and deliver customer support information, parts and service on a global basis. As products are increasingly being designed for and sold in all major markets, so customer support is most economically provided in a consistent manner worldwide. Many companies are responding to the global challenge by enrolling the help of third-party specialists. Pioneering examples include Land Rover's use of Caterpillar Logistics Services to handle its service parts inventory and distribution around the world. Other prominent users of third parties to provide global service parts distribution are Case Corporation and Perkins Engines.

Conclusion

Business leaders wishing to put the needs of the customer at the centre of their activities must look closely at the role of logistics in delivering satisfactory customer support. Key customer services such as supplying parts, quickly and at minimum cost, rely primarily on high-level logistics expertise. This chapter has described how four models of customer support logistics can provide different structures for ensuring superior and timely customer service. Particular logistics functions possess different levels of importance in each model; all play a role in the long-term prosperity of the business. In the future, higher levels of customer expectations along with new technologies, multiple channels for delivery and product proliferation will pose even greater challenges for customer support organizations. Clever management of customer needs through carefully planned logistics structures will help deliver the ever-elusive business goal of customer satisfaction.

Postponement for mass customization
Satisfying customer demands for tailor-made products

Hau Lee

In today's competitive market, it is easy for companies to lose control of global supply chain efficiency as product varieties proliferate and product lifecycles get shorter and shorter. The symptoms of lost control are increasing costs in inventory, logistics and manufacturing, while customer service actually deteriorates. Yet the pressure to satisfy the diverse needs of the marketplace continues to mount. Now the proliferation of product variety has pushed companies to find ways to mass customize their products in a cost-effective manner. How can this be achieved? Companies such as Hewlett-Packard, among others, are using a powerful design concept, known as design for postponement, to address the mass customization challenge. This concept calls for a reconfiguration of the product and process designs to counteract the complexity and uncertainty factors that paralyse supply chains. This powerful concept, when implemented, has led to dramatic value creation for companies, as mass customization allows them to penetrate new markets and increase market share for current customer segments; improve customer satisfaction by offering more personalized products and increased product availability; and significantly lower inventory investment.

Introduction

The ability to offer and deliver a highly customized product quickly and efficiently to a customer has become a competitive differentiator in many industries. The growing global market, with its multiple local options, rapidly changing technologies resulting in overlapping product lifecycles, the expanding tastes and needs of diverse customers and the trend of channel distributors towards customized channel brands, drives companies to offer proliferating product options. Faced with such product variety and increasing pressure for customer service, the challenge of effective delivery becomes an issue of corporate survival. It has been suggested that time and mass customization are two of the most important areas in which companies can develop a competitive edge in the 1990s.

Mass customization allows companies to penetrate new markets and capture customers whose special or personal needs could not be met by standard products. Yet mass customization by brute force is both excessively costly and inefficient. Customers would only be disappointed if the time or cost of customizing the products went beyond their expectation, and certainly this could be a nightmare for companies who could not fulfil their promise for mass customization. Hence, mass customization, while an important goal for many companies, is not easily achievable without inordinate cost and asset inefficiencies in a supply chain.

Building an agile workforce and organizational structure is a necessary ingredient for mass customization. Other methods help, such as reducing cycle times and improving manufacturing responsiveness. For example, the use of electronic data interchange and computer-aided ordering can reduce the times incurred to transmit and process customer orders, and the use of air transport can cut down transportation lead times. Techniques such as investing in flexible manufacturing systems not only allow for faster cycle times but also improve responsiveness to the variable product mix found in a given factory. Finally, the latest developments in electronic commerce help strengthen communication links and can enhance decision-making capabilities for firms operating in the supply chain.

While they are noteworthy and definitely steps in the right direction, neither logistics improvements, better information flow, shorter cycle times nor flexible factories will allow a company to compete effectively in the future. Product and process design offer much greater potential. Indeed, it is generally recognized that 80 per cent of the manufacturing cost of a product is determined by the design of the product. The opportunity lies in the integration of product design and the supply chain. Some visionary companies have experimented with product design and supply chain restructuring as a means to achieve mass customization effectively. The idea is to design products and realign the manufacturing and distribution activities in a supply chain, so that the customization steps that lead to product variety occur at the most efficient point of a supply chain and at the lowest total supply chain cost.

The underlying principle for designing products and processes so that supply chain efficiency can be optimized is 'postponement'. Postponement is about delaying the timing of the crucial processes in which the end products assume their specific functionalities, features, identities or 'personalities'. Such customization processes would take place after some key information about the customers' specific needs or requirements is revealed. Hence, postponement can be viewed as an information strategy. The delay of the customization steps is only valuable if the information about the customers' needs can be captured quickly and accurately. Design for postponement refers to the design of

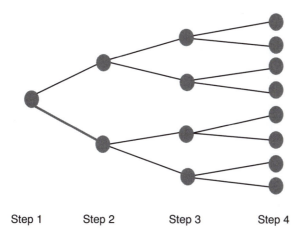

Step 1   Step 2   Step 3   Step 4

Figure 5.1   Product structure

the products or the processes so that postponement is possible.

Consider the way product variety is created. It usually follows a product structure that is often tree-like in nature. The product thus starts as a common single engine. As it moves along the manufacturing process (or a supply chain) more features are added and it assumes more and more of the identity of the end product. Figure 5.1 depicts an example of the product structure or hierarchy.

Three basic concepts form the fundamentals of design for postponement: pull postponement, logistics postponement and form postponement. These concepts, properly implemented, can add tremendous value to companies.

Pull postponement

Consider Figure 5.1, which describes how a common product engine can become multiple end products while going through various steps or processes of a supply chain. Companies operating under a build-to-stock environment complete all the processes and have finished goods inventory stocked for customers. As the manufacturing of the product is completed prior to the placement of customer orders, the build plan is totally based on forecast. At the other extreme, a company waits for the customer order to come in so that, armed with the information on the full specificity of the order, the whole supply chain process can be activated to build and deliver the product. No incorrect product is produced, but this is at the expense of excessive waiting time by the customer for the product. Most companies operate somewhere in between the pure build-to-stock and build-to-order system. Some of the early steps in the supply chain are run based on forecast and the semi-finished products are stocked. The remaining customization steps are only completed on receipt of the customer order. The point from which the process switches from a build-to-forecast (push) mode to the build-to-order (pull) mode is often called the push–pull boundary, or a decoupling point.

Pull postponement refers to making the decoupling point *earlier* in the process. Fewer process steps will be performed under forecast resulting in fewer stocks of semi-finished products being held. More steps are performed on learning about the exact specification of the customer order. In that way, more process steps are postponed until after the order is revealed.

There are some basic elements required in order for pull postponement to be successful:

■ The process steps must be sequenced so that the less differentiating steps (steps that result in less fan-out in the product structure) are performed prior to the decoupling point. With fewer fan-outs, forecasts are easier and more accurate. Accurate forecast is a key success driver in order that the build-to-forecast processes can be carried out effectively.
■ The process steps after the decoupling point can be performed flexibly and fast. This is important if customers are to receive a good response time. Under high time pressure, it is also important that these steps can be performed precisely and at a quality standard.
■ Accurate order capture is the key success driver for the build-to-order process. The system must be in place to record the customer's exact order (configuration and specification) and transmit it to start the fulfilment process.

 # National Bicycle

In 1986, National Bicycle, a Japanese bicycle company, was faced with strong competition from other Japanese, Korean and Taiwanese bicycle manufacturers. The population of Japan was not growing and bicycles were becoming more and more durable, so that the demand for bicycles was declining rapidly, threatening the company's existence. National Bicycle had been successful in improving the cost efficiency of bicycle manufacturing, but there was only so much it could achieve with cost reduction when demand was limited. Instead, the company embarked on an ambitious strategy—it wanted to grow the market by providing personalized bicycles for customers. Customers could choose from a variety of options such as colour patterns, frames, pedal types, handlebar widths, toe clips, calligraphies and so on. In fact, the number of options exceeded 11 million! This was truly a mass customization strategy. National Bicycle estimated that it could tap into the market of customers whose body

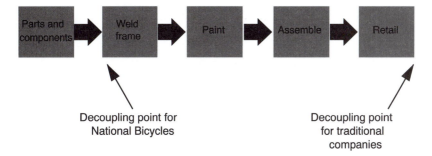

Figure 5.2   **Pull postponement at National Bicycles**

sizes or preferences were such that they could not find the right bicycles from stock at stores, and that personalized bicycles could make the standard sports bicycle into a fashion product and increase the customers' appetite for new products on a periodic basis.

How could National Bicycle pursue this mass customization strategy without going bankrupt through astronomical costs? The trick was pull postponement. The company carefully redesigned the supply chain process with a different decoupling point to traditional bicycle companies. Figure 5.2 describes the steps involved in a typical bicycle supply chain. Traditional bicycle companies had their decoupling point at the end of the supply chain process, so that bicycles were built to stock and stored by retailers. Some bicycles had their decoupling points right before final assembly, but National Bicycle aggressively moved the decoupling point to before frame welding and painting. This enabled it to have tremendous flexibility to respond to the multitudes of options requested by customers.

In order to make this pull postponement strategy work, National Bicycles had to conduct some significant reengineering:

■ The components and subassemblies had to be standardized so that there were not too many product fan-outs prior to the decoupling point, while retaining enough combinations to create the necessary variety in the end products.
■ The steps after the decoupling point were designed in such a way that they could be performed quickly and accurately. National Bicycle picked some of its best workers to perform these tasks. In addition, investment in barcoding every bicycle with appropriate computer-controlled machines enabled these tasks to be done accurately.
■ National Bicycle created a 'fitting machine' that was installed at the retailer. Together with samples of components, these fitting machines were used to obtain the exact specification desired by the customer. The key was to make sure that customers' orders were captured accurately. The orders were faxed back to the factory.

The result was tremendous. While the Japanese bicycle market continued to decline in subsequent years, National Bicycle was the lone shining star, having doubled its sales in the same period. Pull postponement had enabled National Bicycle to create a new market for mass customization.

As a major apparel manufacturer, Benetton used to manufacture its product by first dyeing yarns into various colours and then knitting the coloured yarns into finished products (different styles and sizes). Mismatch of inventory of finished garments with different colours resulted in costly end-of-season markdowns. Chairman Luciano Benetton was credited with the innovative reengineering of the supply chain by reversing the dyeing and knitting stages. Bleached yarns are now knitted into the various styles and sizes and then dyed into the different coloured end products when the season's fashion preferences become more established. For this change, the yarns have to be treated in a strong chemical solution to increase their receptiveness to dye. Such a change was considered to be a significant breakthrough in improving Benetton's operational performance. Inventory reduction, better customer service, increasing sales and fewer writedowns have been reported.

The Benetton example illustrates how pull postponement can work. Rather than having the decoupling point at the finished sweater level, the reversal of the dyeing and knitting operations was accompanied by shifting the decoupling point to just after the knitting operation, but before the dyeing operation. In this way, the dyeing step—customization—was performed in build-to-order mode.

Logistics postponement

The second postponement strategy calls for the redesign of the tasks or modules involved in a supply chain process (see Figure 5.1) so that some of the customization steps can be performed downstream closer to the customers. For example, instead of having all the tasks performed at a central factory far away from customers, design changes might be made so that some of the downstream steps are performed at distribution centres, often geographically located closer to the main customer markets. Indeed, some steps may be performed at the retail or distribution channel, which is even closer to the customer. Finally, product design changes might make it possible for the final configuration of the product to be carried out by the customers themselves. We call this strategy logistics postponement, since postponement is enabled by relocating the customization steps.

In order for logistics postponement to be successful, companies must take steps to ensure that any customization performed downstream will not lead to quality degradation; that the downstream sites have the capability to perform the task without excessive cost and time, and potentially to procure the necessary components or modules for the customization; and that the engineering team is able and willing to design products and processes so that the customization steps can be deferred to the downstream sites effectively.

As an example, consider Hewlett-Packard's (HP) Deskjet printers which have to be localized for global markets—such as power supply voltages, power cords and plugs, and language options for keyboards and manuals. In the past, printers were manufactured and localized at the factory and then shipped to distribution centres in California, Singapore and Germany. Except for the California destination, shipments by sea were customary, with a transit time of about one month.

The variety of localized versions of the product, coupled with increasing pressure for product availability, had resulted in millions of dollars of inventory tied up at the distribution centres, which often led to excruciatingly expensive write-offs near the end of the product lifecycle. Shipping by air would certainly reduce the lead time from the factory to the distribution centres, but this approach would reduce profits considerably. Instead, HP redesigned the product so that only one generic printer was manufactured at the factory and shipped to the distribution centres. Specifically, this required the printer to be redesigned so that the power supply module would be the last component incorporated. This module could then be added at the distribution centres (along with the appropriate plug and language-specific manual). Safety stocks of the generic printers could now be significantly reduced while distribution centres sourced and stocked those elements needed to 'localize' the product. Due to the 'risk pooling' of safety stock, the general investment in inventory could be greatly reduced. This strategy is illustrated in Figure 5.3.

A stunning pay-off resulted from localizing printers in the distribution centres. The generic printer was more compact than the previously pre-localized versions from the factory. It was found that these sleeker models could be bulk shipped so that many more units could be loaded on each pallet. Consequently, freight cost was cut by about a half and the new design shaved millions of dollars off the unit transportation costs.

Similarly, Philips has modularized the design of its electronic devices so that the 'bundling' of accessories can be carried out at the distribution centres instead of at the factory, a concept identical to that for the HP Deskjet printer.

Certainly, logistics and pull postponement could be used as a combined strategy. Take the example of colour matching paints at your local hardware store. The production of paints in different colours formerly took place at a factory as a single process. Individual stores had to stockpile different paints, but the customer always seemed to ask for paint that was slightly different to those stocked. The development of low-cost

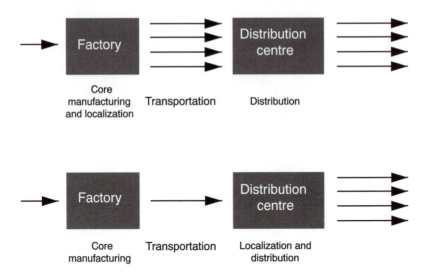

Figure 5.3   Deskjet printer supply chain before and after postponement

chromatography has made it possible to modularize the paint production process. Generic paint (tint base) is made at the factory, as are the multiple colour pigments. Hardware and paint stores stock the generic paint and the colour pigments, which they combine to match a customer's colour sample on demand. This innovation provides the customer with a virtually unlimited number of consistent colour choices. This is an example of a combination of logistics and pull postponement: the customization step to differentiate the product into many coloured paints was postponed from the factory to the retail stores, while the decoupling point was shifted from the finished goods level to prior to the mixing step.

The personal computer industry is also moving aggressively towards the use of logistics and pull postponement to improve its order fulfilment process. First, the decoupling point is moved from the finished goods level to just prior to final assembly and testing. Secondly, the assembly and testing phase is moved from the factory to distribution centres. This is the strategy being pursued by more and more companies, including computer manufacturers such as Compaq, IBM and HP.

Form postponement

A third postponement strategy calls for a fundamental change of the product structure, using designs that standardize some of the compo-

Before standardization

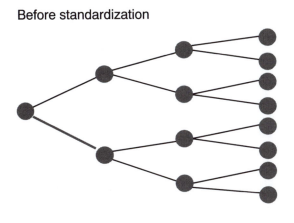

After standardization

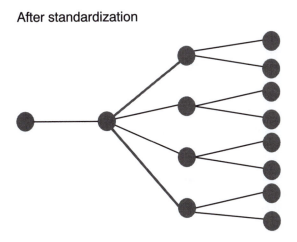

Figure 5.4   Form postponement through standardization

nents or process steps. Consider Figure 5.1 again. If some early steps can be standardized so that the outputs of these steps are undifferentiated, then effectively the point of product differentiation is delayed. Figure 5.4 illustrates how standardization leads to postponement. We call this form postponement because postponement is achieved through the change in the form of the product structure.

When HP was developing its new network printer a few years ago, it utilized a combination of logistics and form postponement as a means to meet the product variety challenge. The network printer is a high-end laser printer that has networking capabilities and special functionalities. It had many configurable options and features, such as memory, stapling ability, firmware, system software, fax modems, paper handling, linkage to print server, scanner and printer stand. The network printer division at HP outsourced the procurement and assembly of the product's main engine to a Japanese partner. After being integrated into the printed circuitboard made by HP, the key engine, including the power supply and fuser unit, would be shipped to HP's distribution centres by sea.

Recognizing that the many thousands of configurable options for the product would be a nightmare for forecasting and production planning, special efforts were spent in the design of the products so that most of the customization, such as the installation of paper input units, cabinet stands, fax modems, paper output units, stapler upgrade package, memory and print server linkage, could be carried out at the distribution centres. This meant that all the options could be installed as accessories at the distribution centres. In addition, the localization of the product through the inclusion of driver software disks, manuals, power cords and front panels (with the correct mix of languages) is also done at the distribution centres, following a logistics postponement strategy.

Consider a key engine manufactured by a Japanese assembly partner based on two different power and fuser units—110V for North America and 220V for Europe. In the past, the long lead time in the manufacture of the key engine and the difficulty in forecasting demands in North America and Europe would have resulted in high inventory on one continent while stockouts occurred on the other. But if the engine is redesigned using a universal power supply and fuser, the product does not need to be differentiated until it is loaded at the port to be shipped to its final destination. A side benefit of a universal power supply in this case is the ease of transshipping the products from one continent to another, whenever significant imbalances of demand and supply existed. When production of the key engine begins in Japan, all that is needed is the aggregate quantity worldwide, instead of having to forecast the mix of 110V and 220V engines if a dedicated power supply was used. This is an example of form postponement, as the standardization of the power supply and fuser unit changed the form of the product structure. Figure 5.5 illustrates this concept.

The circuit breaker division at General Electric is another example of using both form and logistics postponement to create value. With increasing product variety, the circuit breaker division had not been profitable for some time. Eventually, the product was redesigned. The number of parts was reduced from 600 000 to just 300 in a standardized unit (form postponement) and the final product was configured at distribution (logistics postponement).

In addition to standardizing the modules or subassemblies, processes can also be standardized to enable form postponement. In disk drive manufacturing, a key time-consuming stage is the testing and burn-in of the disk drive. A major manufacturer that produces different types of

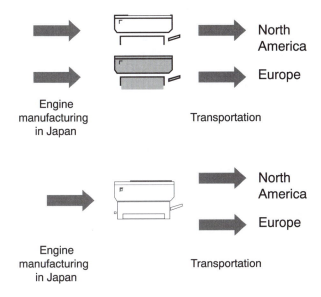

**Figure 5.5   Network printer supply chain before and after
form postponement**

disk drives for computer manufacturers such as AT&T, Next Computer
and HP has found that because its customers often revise their orders,
matching supply with demand has been difficult. One problem results
from the need to insert a PCB (printed circuitboard) during the testing
of disk drives. Each type of disk drive requires a distinct PCB. Hence,
the insertion of the PCB immediately defines the personality of the end
product. An engineer studied the testing and burn-in process and discovered that the whole process can be decomposed into two subprocesses, the first consisting of standard tests that are common to all
end products, and the second consisting of customized tests and burn-in
that are specific to each individual end product. Once this possibility for
decomposition was identified, the engineer designed a special PCB which
the company called the 'coupon board' and which allows the standard
common tests to be performed when the board is inserted. Once the
coupon board has fulfilled its mission, it can be removed and the actual
PCB inserted so that the remaining customized tests and burn-in can be
carried out. In this way, the company successfully postponed the point of
product differentiation, through the decomposition of the testing process
and the division of tasks between the standard subprocess and the customized subprocess.

Postponement enablers

To successfully use postponement, there are at least four enablers or building blocks. These are not 100 per cent necessary, but they certainly help make postponement easier.

First, products or processes should be modular in structure. Product modularity, defined here as the ability to build and test the product in modules rather than as a complete unit, requires the module interface to be redesigned so that they can easily be assembled and tested as a total unit. Such modularity provides several benefits:

- It separates the composition of the end products into parts and/or subassemblies that are common and those that are not. This separation allows for the use of common parts and subassemblies in an earlier stage of the production process, effectively enabling standardization of this stage.
- It allows production of the modules to be carried out independently. In fact, production of the modules can be done in parallel, thereby saving significant production cycle time.
- It also enables modules or subassemblies that differentiate the product to be built separate from the main factory.
- There tend to be more possible decoupling points in the supply chain process for a modular product.

Process modularity does for operational processes what product modularity does for products. Without process modularity, the complete process must be done as one, often leading to long cycle times and inflexibility in meeting the demands of multiple end products. Redesigning a process into subprocesses can potentially enable postponement for the following reasons:

- A subprocess can be postponed to a location closer to the customers, such as logistics postponement.
- The subprocess steps can be resequenced to create new decoupling point opportunities, such as the reversal of dyeing and knitting in the Benetton case.
- Some of the subprocesses can be standardized, enabling form postponement.

Since postponement is often made possible through the design of products and processes, a key enabler is that the company's design engineers should be aware of the importance of supply chain management, so that they are keenly pursuing design for postponement opportunities. Most design engineers tend to focus on measures such as product functionality, product performance or narrowly defined material costs. Supply chain performance is often not a consideration in the product development and design cycles. It is only recently that design engineers have begun to recognize the importance of design for manufacturability. This, of course, is still too narrowly focused, as the costs and performance outside the factory are not captured. Supply chain performance requires the consideration of inventory, logistics, transportation efficiencies, customs and duties, customer responsiveness and flexibility. It is only through understanding the full implications of design on supply chain performance that we can see more designers making product or process designs that support postponement.

Postponement is a strategy that often involves multiple functions or organizations in collaboration. For example, form postponement may require a supplier to design a standard component. Logistics postponement may require distribution centres or the channel partner to take over some customization steps that used to be carried out by manufacturing. Research and development functions have to be involved. In some cases, pull postponement requires marketing to reposition the product in the marketplace.

Finally, postponement may not be free. As can be seen from the above examples, postponement may result in higher per unit manufacturing cost. The universal power supply and fuser module for the HP network printer was more costly to make than a dedicated power supply and fuser; the standardization of the parts in GE's circuit breaker resulted in an increase in material costs because more copper is used; customization by the channel partners instead of at the factory can be more costly through the loss in economies of scale and added training and overhead; and knitting the garment before dyeing may be more time consuming and costly because of the added chemical treatment step. To determine what degree of postponement is best for the company, and to justify why it is so, requires the ability to quantify the costs and benefits of postponement. Analytical models are often powerful as a means to help motivate or justify postponement.

Conclusion

As it is increasingly recognized that most of the costs of products and services can only be influenced by their design, we see greater potential in the use of design for postponement principles. The movement towards mass customization is inevitable, given current competitive forces and technological advancements. Trying to implement mass customization by brute force is not the solution. Design for postponement offers the greatest leverage.

The quality movement has taught several important lessons. First, with design for quality taking over control of quality as a mainstream approach for quality improvement, the use of design for mass customization is only natural. But such an approach results in an increasing need for multifunctional teams to work together and communicate with one another effectively. Many of the examples described in this chapter happened because of the collaborative efforts of manufacturing, engineering, distribution and, in some cases, marketing. Cross-functional integration is vital. In addition, in some of the examples the design principles were implemented with the involvement of suppliers or channel partners. In a similar way, collaborative efforts among multiple companies in a supply chain are also a necessary ingredient for successful design for supply chain projects.

Finally, analysis of the total costs and benefits of alternative designs is crucial. Such analysis is required not only to determine the best designs that give optimal supply chain efficiency, but also to facilitate functional and inter-company collaboration to make the designs possible. Only with careful planning and subsequent cooperation will mass customization work most effectively.

Contrary to popular belief, mass customization does not have to be excessively costly. By avoiding the errors associated with 'brute force' mass customization and by carefully applying the set of design principles outlined in this chapter, companies can realize true competitive advantage. The results, in the form of improved profit margins and more satisfied customers, will speak for themselves.

References

Child, P., Diederichs, R., Sanders, F.-H. and Wisniowski, S. (1991) 'The management of complexity', *Sloan Management Review*, 33 (1), 73–9.

Dapiran, P. (1992) 'Benetton—global logistics in action', *Asian Pacific International Journal of Business Logistics*, 5, 7–11; and Harvard Business School (1986) 'Benetton (A) and (B)', Harvard Teaching Case 9-685-014.

Feitzinger, E. and Lee, H.L. (1997) 'Mass customization at Hewlett-Packard: the power of postponement', *Harvard Business Review*, 75 (1), 116–21.

Fisher, M., Jain, A. and MacDuffie, J.P. (1993) 'Strategies for product variety: lessons from the auto industry', working paper, The Wharton School, University of Pennsylvania.

Lee, H.L. and Billington, C. (1994) 'Designing products and processes for postponement', in Dasu, S. and Eastman, C. (eds) *Management of Design: Engineering and Management Perspectives*, Kluwer Academic Publishers, Boston.

Lee, H.L. and Sasser, M. (1995) 'Product universality and design for supply chain management', *International Journal of Production Planning and Control*, Special issue on supply chain management, 6 (3), 270–77.

Lee, H.L., Feitzinger, E. and Billington, C. (1997) 'Getting ahead of your competition through design for mass customization," *Target*, 13 (2), 8–17.

Pine, B.J., Victor, B. and Boynton, A.C. (1993) 'Making mass customization work', *Harvard Business Review*, 71 (5), Sept/Oct, 108–19.

Stalk, G. and Hout, T.M. (1990) *Competing Against Time: How Time-Based Competition is Reshaping Global Markets*, Free Press, New York.

Zarley, C. (1995) 'Manufacturers race to install full build-to-order capabilities', *Reseller News*, March 6; and 'IBM allows channel to perform final assembly on PCs', *Reseller News*, May 29.

6

The supply–demand nexus
From integration to synchronization
Jeff Beech

Companies wanting to achieve state-of-the-market supply chain management can no longer afford to focus on supply-side efficiencies. They need to use their business strategy to drive them towards integration of their demand and supply regimes to build a platform for achieving competitive advantage. But even internal supply and demand integration is only part of the journey. Ultimately enterprises will need to achieve an objective understanding of the supply and demand processes along the chain and manage those processes cooperatively, to eliminate waste and to create greater value for all the partners.

Introduction

Contemporary supply chain management has been heavily focused on improvements in supply-side processes, with attention devoted to hot agenda items such as how to move inventory more efficiently. But companies that want to manage their supply chain superbly can only achieve this goal if they recognise the fundamental nexus between supply and demand—and its implications for strategy and its implementation. All too often, however, as companies sift through their supply-side opportunities, they ignore the demand factor.

There is an interdependent relationship between supply and demand: companies need to understand customer demand so that they can manage it, create future demand and, of course, meet the level of desired customer satisfaction. Demand defines the supply-chain target, while supply-side capabilities support, shape and sustain demand.

Companies trying to achieve state-of-the-market in supply chain management therefore need to look beyond the supply chain to a new operating model of supply and demand chain management.

They can achieve this by:

■ applying a holistic strategy framework; and
■ moving beyond integration to synchronization.

The strategic imperative of the demand–supply nexus

Faced with eroding profits companies have two solutions: cut costs or attract more business. And even though they may never be able to cut their costs sufficiently to close the gap, many companies choose to concentrate on efficiency measures because they are the easiest to understand, articulate and implement.

But no matter how hard it is to determine how to build more value for customers, if companies want to reach the next stage of competitive advantage in supply chain management, they need to think beyond simple efficiency issues and towards value creation opportunities. They need to articulate their value proposition to the customer and drive a comprehensive supply and demand chain strategy from that critical insight. Only when companies have determined the nature of the benefit they propose to provide to the customer can they set about defining the strategy to realize that benefit.

Useful initiatives such as efficient consumer response, with its long list of best practices, will only be bewildering to companies that have not first developed their own strategy and a clear definition of their basic value proposition. Quite simply, they won't know where to start. Not every best practice is necessarily going to support and drive company strategy—so companies need a clear idea about where they are heading if they want to select the right initiatives to take them there.

When we consider how tangentially the marketing and operations arms of a business will typically interact, it becomes obvious that putting together the supply–demand nexus can only occur in the context of an overall perspective. The wide gulf between the supply and demand sides of a business can only be breached by a comprehensive umbrella strategy.

Integrated supply and demand chain strategy

All of us have heard outstanding success stories when a new product or service offering is developed and delivered effectively and efficiently to its target market. These examples make it clear that it is possible to integrate supply with demand.

The challenge is to develop a strategy that is achievable and sustainable beyond a few specialized instances. This challenge can only be met by developing a holistic strategic framework that leverages the generation and understanding of demand effectiveness with supply efficiency. Such a framework provides a strategic anchor to prevent the supply and

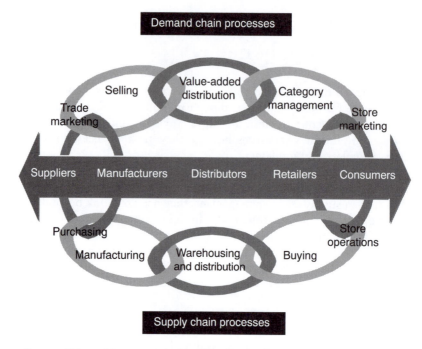

Source: This model was conceived by Steve Sotzing, further developed in a
publication created by Jeff Beech for the food industry titled 'Supply Meets
Demand', and established in a paper at Andersen Consulting by Steve Sotzing
and Bill Copacino.

Figure 6.1   The supply and demand chains

demand components of a business from drifting away from each other.

The basis of the holistic strategy framework is the integrated supply
and demand chain model, shown in Figure 6.1. The model is designed
around two key principles. First, organizations must bring a multi-enterprise view to their supply chains. They need to be capable of working
cooperatively with other organizations in the chain rather than seeking
to outdo them. Secondly, they must recognize the distinct supply and
demand processes that must be integrated in order to gain the greatest
value.

The holistic strategy framework therefore involves three key
elements:

- the core processes of the supply and demand chains, viewed from a
  broad cross-enterprise vantage point rather than as discrete
  functions;
- the integrating processes that create the links between the supply and
  demand chains; and
- the supporting infrastructure that makes such integration possible.

Core processes of supply and demand chains

Many organizations operate by managing each business process as an isolated, discrete function. Different departments operate in 'functional silos', often unaware how their activities affect each other's performance, while each is measured and rewarded separately for differing and, indeed, sometimes opposing goals. The same scenario is played out in a larger sense across the whole supply chain, with trading partners operating in strategic isolation: duplicating activities, creating independent business activities, forming business systems that have difficulty interacting with each in an efficient manner, and viewing each other as competitors for, rather than partners in, creating profit. This typically results in misalignment of activities, as departments or trading partners each pursue their own agendas, as well as duplication of efforts and assets.

To gain the maximum benefit, organizations need to identify the core processes across the demand and supply chain, as well as exploring the impact of each of these processes on the different functions and organizations across the various chains.

The core processes of the demand chain include product development, trade marketing, selling, value-added distribution, category management and store marketing. These must be managed in concert with supply chain processes which include the purchasing of raw materials, manufacturing, warehousing and distribution, purchasing of finished goods and store operations.

Each of the core processes in the demand chain consists of numerous subprocesses, creating ample opportunity for organizations to improve efficiency and effectiveness. The integration of these processes is the key concept. By considering each of the processes as they flow from one end of the supply chain to the other, different functional departments within a single company, or even companies at different points along the way, can synchronize their activities to maximize efficiency and returns.

In order to understand the demand-side processes, organizations must focus on coordinated improvements in two spheres of activity: the movement of information and the movement of services and physical materials. The first involves communicating demand from the point of purchase, back up through the levels of the supply chain. The second involves shortening the time it takes to produce and deliver product from the point at which demand is communicated until it reaches the end user. Attempts to improve these processes can affect every component of the supply chain, from how manufacturers operate their production lines and source raw materials, to the logistics systems used to distribute finished goods, to the ways retailers put product on the shelf or deliver them to their customers' homes, as well as the information flows required to manage the processes and subprocesses in between.

On the physical side, one way in which companies are speeding up the movement of goods is through such systems as flow-through distribution and cross-docking to eliminate warehousing wherever possible, in order to keep products moving. Warehouses themselves can add value if they are transformed from storage depots into flow-through distribution centres, where product is mixed and matched to create combined orders to customer specifications, without going into storage. Continuous replenishment is another way to align supply more closely with demand, by shipping more frequent orders that can be tied more closely to daily fluctuations in demand.

Like so many aspects of improved supply chain efficiency, these logistical approaches depend on quicker, more accurate communication on demand to higher levels in the supply chain so that supply processes can be shaped to meet customer needs. Better communication of demand can mean improving the visibility of known demand, actual purchases or orders to all levels of the supply chain simultaneously so that suppliers upstream have better information to work with. It can also mean more effective systems for forecasting demand.

It should be noted that the core processes of distribution provide a link in both supply and demand chains. As a supply chain link, distribution focuses on efficiency: efficient handling, product flow, transportation and delivery. As a demand chain link, distribution focuses on meeting all demand and service requirements and maximizing flexibility. Creating value-added distribution approaches such as cross-docking, mixed pallets and advance shipment notifications, as well as more advanced capabilities in postponement and product transformation, help achieve both goals. The integrating processes that synchronize the supply and demand chain include planning and servicing.

By analysing and controlling processes more efficiently end to end, companies have already begun to integrate their supply more closely with demand, dramatically reduce inventory investment, achieve better return on assets and deliver better value to customers. They have thus been able to enhance profitability while achieving significant competitive advantage in the marketplace.

In the ideal replenishment scenario, the consumer's purchase of an item at the store checkout automatically triggers a series of activities, from raw goods suppliers to retailers, necessary to replace that item on the shelf. While this is impossible in the real world for the vast majority of products, trading partners can use the techniques of supply chain management to bring their processes together as close to the paradigm as possible.

For example in the grocery industry, this translates to the sharing of point-of-sale (POS) data, collected by retailers at the checkout with trading partners further up the supply chain who are responsible for the production and movement of goods. It can also mean the development of better decision-support tools that can take actual historical movement generated by POS data and separate normal replenishment volume from lift factors associated with promotional activities or other events, and use this data to forecast future demand more accurately. Another way to improve forecast accuracy is to remove factors that contribute to uncertainty, which in the grocery industry has been the heavy use of push-oriented trade promotions. One example is off-invoice allowances, which reward distributors for buying rather than selling products.

Integrating processes

Planning processes

In order to achieve planning process integration (see Figure 6.2), organizations must focus on the development of channel strategies; planning of manufacturing, inventory, distribution and transportation; demand planning and forecasting; and marketing and promotional planning. While planning activities usually occur within a company, the information concerning timing and quantity must be shared across company boundaries. If each trading partner in the chain develops its own plans in isolation, there is no way to integrate the supply and demand chain processes that they share.

Service processes

Service processes include such functions as credit, order management, load planning, billing and collection, dispute resolution, promotion management and coordination of special and promotional shipments. These must be geared to coordinating the flow of resources smoothly between trading partners. The infrastructure needed to support this integrated management model includes information technology as well as finance, human resources and other administrative activities.

Supporting infrastructure

While information technology is needed to handle routine transactions in an efficient manner, it will also play an ever more critical role in facilitating the rapid sharing of planning, production and purchasing information; and capturing and analysing production, distribution and sales data at new levels of detail and complexity. Information technology provides the integrating tools that make it possible to convert data into meaningful pictures of business processes, markets and consumers that are needed to feed company strategies, in order to develop competitive advantage.

On the administrative side, such elements as flow path economics, which helps companies understand the real drivers of cost, and new

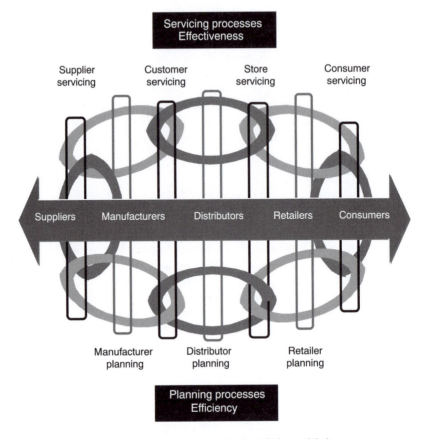

Beyond the core processes of the supply and demand chains and their constituent subprocesses stand the integrating processes of planning and servicing. These elements cut across the supply and demand chains and link participants across the business systems.

Figure 6.2   Integrating processes in the supply and demand chains

performance and measurement standards that align functions in accordance with total process goals are critical to achieving integration.

The integrated supply and demand chain model, though challenging, will eventually become widespread. It provides the holistic strategic framework from which businesses can develop strategies that leverage both demand effectiveness and supply efficiency (see Figure 6.3).

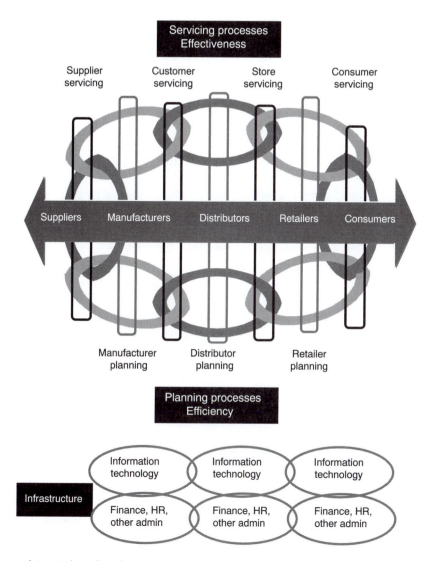

Integrated supply and demand chain management requires the support of a
two-part infrastructure consisting of information technology and finance,
human resources and other administration.

**Figure 6.3   Enabling integrated supply and demand chain
management**

Moving beyond integration to synchronization

Most industries are still doing much more of what would be termed integrated logistics, rather than actual supply and demand chain management. They are integrating their internal logistics processes; taking sales information, for example, and using it to replenish stock from their own warehouses, but not taking the extra step of linking directly to vendors. It is the linking between enterprises that can lead to the ultimate goal of moving beyond supply chain efficiency to integrating supply with demand (see Figure 6.4). The performance outcome is synchronization.

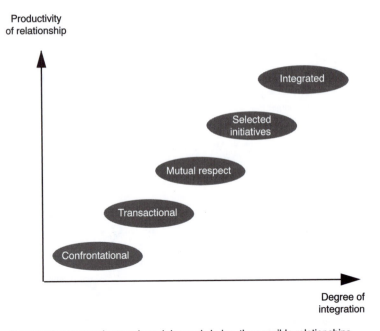

In partnering across the supply and demand chains, the possible relationships range from the confrontational relationship that was once the norm, when the 'salesperson' called on the 'buyer' to get today's order, to the truly integrated long-term relationship. Between the extremes are relationships that vary in focus: the transactional relationship concentrates on supply-side links, especially logistics and order management; the relationship of mutual respect zeroes in on areas of mutual interest; the relationship based on selected initiatives looks for specific 'win–win' opportunities, often tested in limited-scale pilot programmes. As integration increases, so does the likelihood of benefits to both partners.

Figure 6.4   Spectrum of alliances in the supply and demand chains

Not all companies or functions within a company will evolve towards a synchronized supply and demand chain at the same rate. Most businesses will need to be able to work with a portfolio of business systems that follow different models. There are four distinct models, each of which creates a different performance environment.

The first is the pipeline model, which is defined as functionally oriented and structured. It is driven by critical mass and the search for efficiency in an environment where bigger is generally considered better: the biggest distribution network, the biggest manufacturing network... In the traditional pipeline system, information flow is basically one way and is used to control transactions.

The second is the supply chain model, which shifts the emphasis to flexibility and velocity. In this model, companies achieve these goals through captured assets, their own manufacturing, their own distribution, their own transportation. Measures of success put more weight on factors like effectiveness and balance capacity, rather than straight efficiency which is the measure of success of the pipeline. Under the supply chain model, information technology becomes more necessary for effective operation, and companies start to look for ways to link the information inputs and outputs of their isolated system.

Third is the integrated demand chain model, where the emphasis shifts from effectiveness to customer service, providing customized services to certain customers. This moves into the realm of distributed assets. Rather than owning assets, companies look to outsource functions to achieve a high level of flexibility in providing services. There is a shift in focus to communication and linkages between the various outsourced functions and distributed assets. With the integrated demand chain and its distributed assets, information and technology assume greater importance as the key enablers of linkages that keep all the different assets aligned and operating in sync.

The fourth possibility, which is just beginning to emerge, is the network model. In this instance enterprises are made up of networks of logical assets, which comprise the virtual corporation. The model delivers 'absolute precision' by synchronizing numerous virtual entities or assets to work together to a common goal. Finally, in the network model, information technology becomes more than an enabler; it is in fact the key strategic asset.

The incentive for moving towards full supply–demand integration comes in terms of new market value-creation opportunities that affect the value proposition and the value-recovery capability from which each enterprise can benefit by working together differently.

Today it is impossible for a company to operate in isolation and achieve its full potential. The model described above takes a process view of what is going on in the chain—selling, distributing, processing/converting, sourcing, supplying and so on—without regard to who

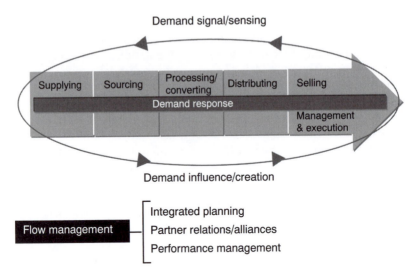

Demand signal/sensing

Demand influence/creation

Interdependence: The ultimate goal is to move beyond supply chain efficiency and to focus on integrating supply with demand. The performance outcome is synchronization.

Figure 6.5   Synchronizing the supply and demand chains

in the chain owns or performs the process. This process approach creates an intensified demand response capability that extends beyond and across enterprises. The capability is driven by demand in two ways. First, it is dependent on sharing demand signal and sensing information. Secondly, it recognizes that each enterprise is involved in demand influence and creation through outside activities including advertising, promotion and so on, and that these activities need to be factored in. In order to develop this demand-response capability, there is a requirement for enterprises to work together (see Figure 6.5).

The greatest opportunities for achieving cost reductions and attracting new business typically involve multi-enterprise interdependencies, such as continuous replenishment programmes, instead of companies trying to do their own internal supply chain management.

Conclusion

In the future companies will no longer compete as individual entities, rather they will compete as networks or chains of trading partners. Companies that recognize this are starting to identify potential partners and develop the kinds of organizational and technological capabilities that facilitate seamless flows of goods and information between their organizations.

As companies look beyond their borders and form alliances with trading partners designed to enhance the total net outcome of their joint supply chain efforts, many are taking a new look at the roles they play in various processes and who should perform which value-adding activities and when.

When companies act in isolation, pursuing competitive advantage on an individual basis, it may make some sense to seek to control and own internally as much as possible of each process and its related assets. When they join together to work in an integrated fashion towards a common end, however, each can concentrate on developing its own core competencies and seek out partners to supply complementary abilities.

An example of this would be vendor-managed inventory (VMI) programmes, where vendors may have better decision-support systems and more knowledge and control over the logistical processes involved, to enable them to make better decisions on how to replenish customers' warehouses with the input of necessary movement information from retail partners.

The benefit will come from supply chain partners looking at their core competencies and those of trading partners and using tools such as flow path management to determine where the most cost-efficient and effective points are for such activities to take place. Rational decisions can be made in partnership on how best to structure processes that cut across company boundaries.

This means understanding the fundamental workings of trading partners' business processes and developing unified systems and processes that span organizations. It also means sharing information on how activities within each organization drive costs so that the processes that eliminate cost on one side can be reengineered for more overall efficiency.

In addition, it means sharing information on demand, as well as strategies on how to capitalize on that demand, both up and down the supply chain between trading partners. This approach is about extending the enterprise into customers' organizations. This extension needs to be a win–win situation in which all players, manufacturers, wholesalers, brokers, retailers and third-party external service providers feel they have an equal investment in each other's success.

References

Beech, Jeff (1996) 'Supply meets demand', supplement to *US Distribution Journal*, Jan 15.

Efficient consumer response
From harmful competition to winning collaboration in the grocery industry
David Sharpe and Richard Hill

Efficient consumer response (ECR) has transformed the once adversarial relationship between manufacturers and retailers in the grocery industry. By emphasizing cooperation rather than competition and through focusing on consumer needs and satisfaction, ECR provides a framework for achieving the twin goals of the grocery industry: top-line sales growth with cost reduction or cost containment. ECR has provided tangible benefits, allowing companies to compete with new market entrants and retain market share. The next step for ECR will be to move to even deeper levels of mutually beneficial cooperation to stimulate and inspire consumer demand.

Introduction

Throughout the 1960s and 1970s competition in the grocery industry was mainly between branded consumer goods manufacturers. The brand, the product, outlet distribution and heavy advertising and promotion were the weapons in this war. But by the 1980s and 1990s the balance of power had shifted to the retailers. The focus of competition moved to central distribution, own-label products, supply chain efficiency and electronic point-of-sale scanning. Competition was now between the manufacturer and the retailer. Both sides fought for control of the supply chain and battled for their share of shelf space with own-label and branded merchandise. Costs were shuttled between organizations, resulting in higher costs overall and reduced margins for weaker players in the value chain.

With the competition focused on price and gross margins, consumer interests were marginalized. Consumers wanted quality, freshness, service and choice at a reasonable cost. Instead of choice and service, they were offered complexity through non-essential variety. Instead of quality, they were encouraged by aggressive and widespread promotional activity to switch stores searching for the latest bargains. Consumers did not get what they wanted; instead they got higher prices, confusion and dissatisfaction.

The situation was summed up in a 1995 report for the US Food Marketing Institute:

> Today's supply chain consists of a series of individual companies, each pushing (or selling) product to the next player in the supply chain. Each transaction adds substantial costs: selling expense, buying expense, purchase ordering, order processing, order assembly, shipping, receiving, checking, put away, invoicing, paying, deducting, reconciling and more. Further, receivables average several weeks for each transaction. Very little, if any of these costs add value to the ultimate product or service the consumer receives.

At the same time new entrants were changing the market. Limited-range, deep discounters and efficient mass merchandisers were selling comparable product at significantly lower prices. The total market was shrinking, with real spending on groceries remaining static or declining. Eating out and take-away food consumption increased dramatically to nearly 50 per cent of consumers' 'share of stomach', resulting in loss of business to the traditional supermarket outlet. Consumers had become increasingly sophisticated, demanding better value at lower prices.

For supermarkets, these changes brought to a halt an extended period of uninterrupted profitable growth. Volume growth slowed, or even reversed. Margins were squeezed as prices were reduced to compete with discount formats. Supermarkets had already pushed their suppliers so hard that there was little room for further benefits. They knew that 65 to 75 per cent of their revenue was sunk in the cost of goods. Unless they could reduce this cost they could not compete. A way had to be found to help suppliers reduce their own costs and subsequently recoup some of that benefit in lower purchase prices.

Consumer goods manufacturers were also in a difficult situation. Supermarket concentration, with its associated increase in buying power, had progressively reduced net margins from about 10 to 7 per cent. As eating out increased and supermarket food sales remained static, manufacturers tried to improve their share through a wider variety of packs, colours and flavours. While this marginally increased sales, it disproportionately increased costs through greater supply chain complexity. In an attempt to boost volumes, spending on promotion grew massively. In fact, manufacturer spending on trade and consumer promotions increased from 8 to 17 per cent of total sales between 1978 and 1994 (Andersen Consulting analysis). This huge increase in promotional activity often increased costs along the supply chain from raw materials suppliers right through to sales operations. The peaks and troughs in demand forced suppliers and production operations into expensive overtime, only to be under capacity in following periods. Promotional sales were difficult to predict, causing either excess inventory that later had to be cleared at a discount, or product shortages and lost sales.

The whole industry was caught in a deadly embrace. Historic ways of trading had created a high-cost environment that was preventing a response to increased competition. The old ways of growing the business had created more cost than the incremental profit they generated. A new strategic response was required—one that recognized that the old business model had run its course. The industry had to change and the means to achieve that change was ECR, which had originated in the US in 1993 and had been adopted by retailers and consumer goods manufacturers on every continent by 1996.

The evolution of ECR

The objective of ECR, as defined by the First Official ECR Europe Conference of 1996, is 'to fulfil consumer wishes better, faster and at less cost'. This objective translates into two key initiatives: first, reductions in inventory and logistics waste, thereby permitting price reduction or higher margins or both; and second, strengthening brand propositions that are compatible between manufacturer and retailer in order to meet consumer needs, thereby stimulating category growth and increasing revenue.

The power of ECR lies in cooperation and the sharing of information and expertise between trading partners towards a common goal of increased consumer satisfaction. ECR is a tool for integrating previously separate aspects of the supply chain to deliver increased value to the consumer. ECR takes a process view, defining four core processes that span all supply chain players, as shown in Figure 7.1.

The roots of ECR can be traced back to the just-in-time, quick response, total quality and partnership approaches that transformed the automotive, electronics and textile industries.

In ECR these ideas were allied with two unique aspects of the grocery business: category management and the rich source of consumer data available from electronic point-of-sale scanning. Category management moved the focus away from brands and products to a holistic view of the total category, or consumer, offer. More importantly, by focusing the category on the consumer and applying insight into what the consumer valued, range rationalization and reduced complexity could be achieved without loss of sales. In some cases a simplified range, which was better presented, actually increased total sales. Electronic point-of-sale (EPOS) data provided accurate information about what was selling where, and could be used to drive the replenishment process and shared with trading partners to help them better manage their supply chain processes. Analysis of the shopping basket revealed which products were purchased together to allow better targeting of promotions and range decisions.

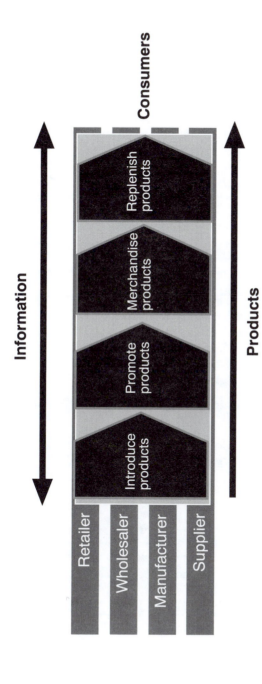

Figure 7.1   Consumer ECR takes a process view of the supply chain

Making ECR work

ECR is structured around 14 'improvement concepts', as outlined by ECR Europe in *The Official European ECR Scorecard* (see Figure 7.2). These cover areas that have long been recognized as ripe for improvement but difficult to address because of their cross-functional nature. They can be summarized as:

- *demand management*, which covers those activities focused on improving the product offering to consumers;
- *supply management*, which covers several initiatives designed to improve the flow of product through the supply chain; and
- *enabling technologies,* which are activities that act as enablers for the other ECR improvement concepts, many of which are related to electronic commerce.

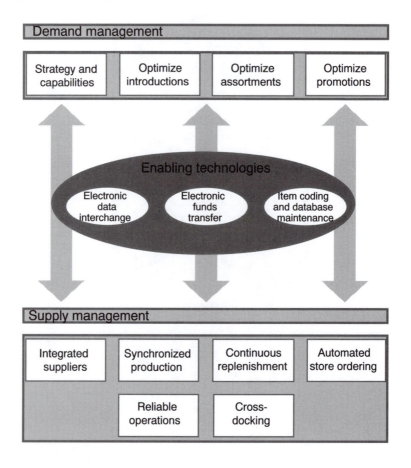

Figure 7.2   ECR improvement concepts

Integrated implementation

ECR improvement concepts are not easy to achieve. They deliver most benefit when implemented as an integrated whole, rather than a set of individual best practices. They need to be considered from the perspective of their impact on all trading partners, not just one link in the total supply chain.

While ECR is an industry movement, responsibility for its implementation lies with individual companies. Two trading partners working towards a mutually beneficial objective can rapidly achieve significant benefits. Undoubtedly the greatest barriers to ECR implementation centre around organization and attitudes.

Attitude change—historical trading relations

ECR requires fundamental changes in attitudes. Instead of regarding trading partners as potential competition, companies need actively to establish cooperative relationships with selected trading partners. Rather than manufacturers developing products and selling them to, and through, retailers, manufacturers and retailers must jointly identify and target products needed to support an enhanced consumer offer. Instead of information being closely guarded and only shared when absolutely necessary, ECR encourages the sharing of information so that all players in the supply chain have a consistent and up-to-date view of real demand.

In particular, it requires a change in the dominant historical mindset in which, for the last 20 years, success has been defined by dominance and negotiating muscle. ECR requires initiatives to be mutually beneficial. However, unless early agreement is reached on the basis of benefit sharing, old dominant behaviour patterns mean that the strongest will take all. Not all ECR activities result in gain for both parties. Unless ways are found to link costs and benefits across different initiatives, then the full scope of the improvement is not accessible. Historically, information represented power and sales data was not generally available unless purchased from retailers. Open sharing of data represents a significant cultural change that organizations need to embrace for ECR to become a reality.

For retailers, this change in attitude means a change from a gross-margin mentality and efforts to push costs to manufacturers, to a search for the lowest-cost, total supply chain solution. For manufacturers, this means moving away from a push mentality and competing on share of shelf space, to establishing a strong strategic position in the category which contributes to overall category growth. For both, it means gaining a better understanding of the consumer at the point of purchase and using sales to pull replenishment.

The spirit of ECR has been captured by Birds Eye Wall's, a Unilever frozen food company in the United Kingdom. It defines ECR as 'the process which facilitates the true working together to achieve ultimate consumer satisfaction, maximising business efficiency for mutual benefit'.

Overcoming functional silos

The majority of manufacturers and retailers achieved success in the past through excellence in separate supply chain activities. However, these individual operations could not manage cross-functionally and as a result became functional silos. A single point of contact usually operated between buyer and seller, with all communication and activity focused through these individuals. Over time, this raised the power of the buying or commercial function to preeminence, with success being measured and rewarded at the level of gross margin or sales.

ECR, in contrast, views consumer satisfaction, category sales and lowest total cost and hence net margin as the most appropriate measures of performance. In addition, it requires an organizational structure that interfaces at every level and function as part of a trading relationship, giving more open communication with activities coordinated by category managers and account managers. ECR is a strategic cross-functional initiative, which, to be successful, requires sustained sponsorship at the chief executive officer level. Without this sponsorship, there remains a risk that historical functional attitudes will override the difficult trade-off decisions that will need to be made.

In addition to new organizational structures, ECR calls for people with a different, broader set of skills than previously. Sales personnel cannot become account managers, nor buyers become category managers, without a good understanding of the consumer, logistics, finance and category management. ECR therefore requires retraining and reskilling of the organization's traditional front line. In the short term this often means increased headcount, which in the longer term is more than offset by reductions elsewhere. But combined with new skills there needs to be a new attitude: one based on cooperation, factual analysis and negotiation, and a passion for consumer satisfaction.

ECR is often seen as merely a collection of best practices—and just about every organization can genuinely claim to be implementing many of its improvement concepts already. More of a problem is a perception of the idea as another business fad, a 'buzzword' that is not relevant to day-to-day business. The truth is, of course, that it does not matter what ECR is called so long as the practices and principles are accepted and applied. Many organizations facing this barrier have chosen to align ECR ideas with an existing business initiative, thereby achieving ownership and acceptance, and preventing confusion by introducing potentially conflicting terminology.

The benefits of ECR

Several studies have been conducted to investigate the impact of the adoption of ECR. These studies have clearly demonstrated the significant benefits that flow from a complete industry-wide adoption of its principles. Cost savings are estimated to be between 5.5 and 6.3 per cent of costs, depending on market and corporate maturity. Sales increases are predicted, but not quantified, and would be likely to vary because of differing levels of latent demand by product category. Most importantly, the imperatives, objectives and actions of ECR are shown to be a good strategic fit with some key business issues. While it does not necessarily provide all the answers, it does provide a new framework in which to tackle strategic questions of cost, service profitability and growth.

The benefits of ECR vary from country to country, and also between distribution channels. In the US, Europe and Australia, industry-level studies have been conducted to assess its impact. The results are summarized in Table 7.1.

These studies show that the potential for cost reduction varies from 5.5 to 6.3 per cent of total costs. Europe, with its more developed retail supply chains, has already achieved a greater proportion of the potential benefit than its US counterparts. The overall similarity in these numbers reflects the fact that in western economies, the cost structures of consumer goods supply chains are remarkably similar. The picture on inventory reductions is, however, very different by market, as seen in Table 7.2.

The two key drivers for inventory reduction in the consumer supply chain area are smoother flow of product from manufacturer to retail

Table 7.1
Estimated ECR cost reductions

	Grocery market total costs (US$bn)	ECR reduction potential (% of total costs)	ECR reduction potential (US$bn)
Europe	491	5.5%	26.9
Australia	18	6.2%	1.1
US	307	6.3%	19.3

Table 7.2

Estimated ECR inventory reductions

	Grocery market average inventory (days)	ECR reduction potential (%)	ECR reduction potential (days)
Europe	43	42%	18
Australia	50	28%	14
US	104	41%	43

shelf and better alignment of production quantities to retail sales.

In Europe, and especially in the UK and the Netherlands, much of the potential for improved inventory management had been achieved before these ideas were formalized into the concept of ECR. Daily deliveries to stores from central distribution centres eliminated the need for most of the backroom stock in stores. High levels of electronic point-of-sale data capture, combined with automated store-level, sales-based ordering, ensured accurate ordering that further reduced in-store inventories. Increased supplier delivery frequencies and reduced order sizes kept distribution centre stock to a minimum. In total, a typical supermarket chain would have a total of 10 to 15 days of inventory, with the balance of the 43 days being with manufacturers and their suppliers.

By contrast, many of these initiatives were less advanced in the US. This is reflected in the starting position of 104 days and the greater reduction potential of 43 days, as shown in Table 7.2. It should also be noted that the inventory position in Europe was driven by retailer actions and by forcing changes on their suppliers to create a smoother flow of product. However, the potential inventory reductions through closer synchronization of production to retail sales had not been achieved anywhere in the world, and remained the greatest untapped source of future inventory reduction. These factors explain the differing starting points and improvement potential of the two geographies. However, these average regional figures still mask some very significant differences in local country industry structures. For example, the fragmentation of the Italian grocery industry, according to Nielsen Europa (1993), contrasts markedly with the concentration of the UK and the Netherlands, as shown in Table 7.3.

With such a different market structure, with different economics and dynamics, the response to ECR has been very different.

Table 7.3
Percentage of market for top three retail chains

Italy	11
UK	40
Netherlands	60

In Italy, the uptake of ECR thinking happened much earlier than in the UK, as the Italian market felt a greater competitive threat from new market entrants (especially deep discounters) than did the dominant UK grocery industry. The response in Italy has focused on industry-level initiatives, on the achievement of critical mass within the industry and on logistics-related cost reduction. In effect this meant that a relatively inefficient supply chain moved quickly to become more efficient. The main method was through the establishment of common standards that could be used to drive economies of scale through transport consolidation. This contrasts with the UK where inventory and cost reduction had already been achieved, driven by retailer dominance, and therefore the main thrust of ECR was focused on category management and revenue-enhancement opportunities.

Critical mass

Initial studies assume an industry-wide adoption of ECR principles. This means that part of the benefit comes from organizations adopting operating practices based on common industry standards. Only one study by ECR Italia (Toja, 1996) has addressed the impact of critical mass on the achievement of benefits, as summarized in Table 7.4.

In markets with high retailer concentration, the achievement of industry standards has been hampered by investments in differing physical equipment by major competitors, perpetuating multiple standards and higher

Table 7.4
Benefit from reengineering the supply chain
in Italy

One-to-one actions	5.2%
Critical mass	2.7%
Total	7.9%

than necessary costs. The above data suggests that one-third of benefits are associated with achieving a critical level of industry participation, and this final third of benefit can only begin to be taken when at least 50 per cent of traded volume or transactions are operating under the new processes.

Of course, all of these industry-level figures are, of necessity, averages and a simplification of the complex reality of the trading relationships between manufacturers and retailers in the grocery supply chain. Nevertheless, they illustrate the potential prize, and more importantly serve as a reminder of the benefit of end-to-end integration of the supply chain.

Moving to demand-side improvements

The evolution of ECR in different markets provides insight into how it can best be applied in different market circumstances. Early work in the concept focused on supply-side initiatives—cost reduction, reliability and service improvement. Essentially the objective of this work was to remove the negative aspects of supply-side performance that prevented progress on demand-generation activities. In markets, or in organizations, where supply-side performance was already at an acceptable level it was then possible to tackle the more difficult, but ultimately more rewarding, area of demand stimulation. Furthermore, this change brings with it a move away from industry-wide programmes to specific initiatives between individual retailers and manufacturers, tailored to deliver specific business objectives. These are shown in Figure 7.3.

None of the initial industry-wide studies satisfactorily deal with this important issue of ECR's contribution to increasing sales. The main reason is that there is little available data. The methods of leveraging strategic category captaincy relationships between manufacturers and retailers is a jealously guarded source of competitive advantage. Furthermore, the results that are available do not produce the banner headlines of the industry-level figures. Some product categories, such as detergents, have little prospects for sales growth as there is low untapped latent demand. The challenge in this type of category is cost minimization and profit maximization. On the other hand, impulse-driven categories such as snack foods, beverages and biscuits have repeatedly shown that collaborative category management can result in 10 to 20 per cent growth in total sales, as significant latent demand can be stimulated by better assortment and visual merchandising.

Implementation

ECR cannot be implemented at a market level. Industry bodies can provide standards, arrange education and raise awareness, but implementation of the

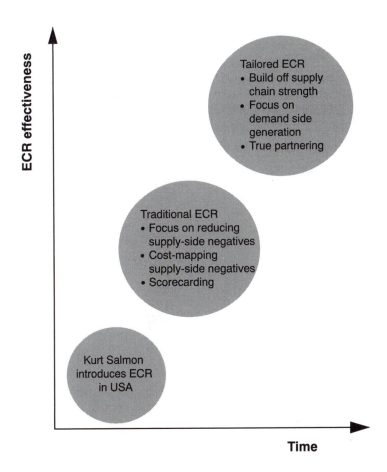

ECR effectiveness

Tailored ECR
• Build off supply chain strength
• Focus on demand side generation
• True partnering

Traditional ECR
• Focus on reducing supply-side negatives
• Cost-mapping supply-side negatives
• Scorecarding

Kurt Salmon introduces ECR in USA

Time

Figure 7.3 The evolution of ECR

concepts relies on individual company-to-company initiatives. Thus the first steps are pilots and trials of new ways of working, of trading with customers or suppliers. If the pilots are successful with one trading partner or category, then they can be expanded to others. In this way, critical mass is eventually achieved both for organizations and markets. However, critical mass is not a prerequisite for achieving significant benefits, as Figure 7.4 illustrates.

This concerns a consumer goods manufacturer whose products generated a strong cashflow, but low margins, for its retail customers. Its products, and its competitors' products in the category, were often heavily promoted, resulting in significant swings in traded volume. The company wished to take advantage of the increased interest in joint working with retailers to establish projects that would result in win–win situations, and in the long term strengthen its position in the category.

The overall approach is illustrated in Figure 7.5. The first step was to establish a common understanding internally of the company's existing capabilities

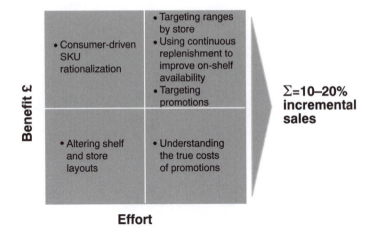

Figure 7.4   Case study benefits

through maturity profiling and benchmarking, using industry standard tools, and to identify potential projects. The next step was to flesh out each project in more detail and to discuss these both internally and with customers. From this, a short list of two projects was identified, for which a rigorous business case was developed ensuring an adequate return on the investment. The key issue for both projects was the amount of resource the manufacturer would need to commit to the project for it to be successful. Once the projects had been signed off, they were launched with a joint retailer and manufacturer workshop, to ensure alignment of objectives and commitment to a common goal. A key feature of this was a demonstration of commitment from the boards of both the retailer and the manufacturer.

The projects identified several initiatives that could be used to drive up both sales and profit contribution. The first 'quick win' was achieved by adjusting shelf layouts to create a display that was more visually appealing and easier to shop. Next, an analysis of sales by stocktaking unit (SKU) in the retailer, in comparison with national sales, showed an imbalance in certain key sub-categories. By reducing the number of SKUs, and at the same time changing the mix to match consumers' needs better, a further increase in sales was achieved. Importantly, this also resulted in a larger profit margin, as the new SKU mix was more heavily weighted to higher-margin, premium products. Through a progressive series of actions, which moved from the easy and generic (overall layout) to the more difficult and specific (targeted ranges by store), the partnership succeeded in achieving increases of up to 20 per cent in top-line sales, and up to a 7 per cent increase in profit contribution for the category as a whole.

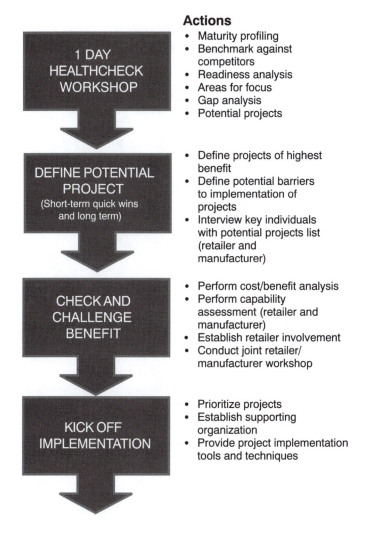

Actions
- Maturity profiling
- Benchmark against competitors
- Readiness analysis
- Areas for focus
- Gap analysis
- Potential projects

- Define projects of highest benefit
- Define potential barriers to implementation of projects
- Interview key individuals with potential projects list (retailer and manufacturer)

- Perform cost/benefit analysis
- Perform capability assessment (retailer and manufacturer)
- Establish retailer involvement
- Conduct joint retailer/ manufacturer workshop

- Prioritize projects
- Establish supporting organization
- Provide project implementation tools and techniques

1 DAY HEALTHCHECK WORKSHOP

DEFINE POTENTIAL PROJECT
(Short-term quick wins and long term)

CHECK AND CHALLENGE BENEFIT

KICK OFF IMPLEMENTATION

Figure 7.5   ECR implementation approach

The future of ECR

One of the underlying principles of ECR is that more can be accomplished by organizations working together rather than independently. Research conducted in 1996/7 by Andersen Consulting for ECR Europe found that most ECR-related initiatives had centred around working together to reduce costs. As the concept expands to include demand-side initiatives, working together will need to encompass innovation, to grow

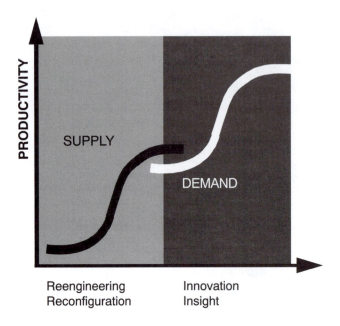

Figure 7.6   The focus of working together will change

the business and to stimulate consumer demand. This shift from a cost-reduction to an innovation focus can be depicted as moving from the world of reengineering and reconfiguration of existing processes, to the world of innovation and insight as the key drivers to improve consumer loyalty and further stimulate demand. The key enabler of this change will be a deeper understanding of consumer preferences and behaviour gained from analysing a variety of data sources, but especially the detailed sales transactions linked to loyalty card information.

The research shows that while the traditional ECR areas of assortment, promotions and product introductions were considered as high-benefit areas, other areas, such as consumer and brand loyalty, meal solutions and development of alternative channels, also ranked highly on many companies' lists. Companies were also asked to indicate the areas in which they were most comfortable working together with their trading partners. This defined their 'comfort zone' which, as can be seen from Figure 7.7, does not necessarily match the benefit rankings.

Traditional ECR areas such as promotions, range and space were well within the comfort zone. The high-benefit areas of loyalty and alternative channels, which tend to be of individual benefit to either the manufacturer or the retailer, were outside the comfort zone and as a consequence were unlikely to be the subject of joint projects.

BENEFIT

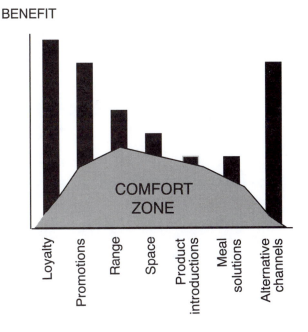

Figure 7.7   The 'working together' comfort zone

New layers of business—extending the scope of consumer fulfilment

ECR is about responding to consumers' needs—so understanding what consumers want is vital. Consumer research conducted at Andersen Consulting's SMART STORE in Europe and the US showed that consumers want:

■ convenience—they do not want to spend any more time than necessary to complete their shopping;
■ ideas and solutions—they do not only shop to replenish goods, they also seek ideas, solutions, recommendations and advice;
■ information—more than ever they require nutritional, chemical content, origin and other product-specific information;
■ value—they always want value for money;
■ entertainment—if they are going to spend several hours per week in stores, they want to be stimulated, interested and entertained; and
■ control—most importantly, consumers want to decide how, when and where they shop.

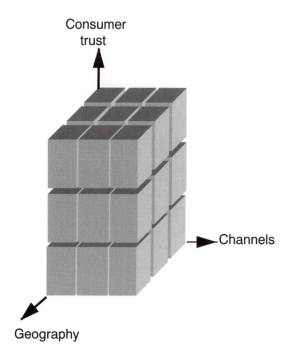

Figure 7.8   New layers of business

How should this insight into consumer values affect the future of ECR? Historically, companies have survived by profitable growth achieved by either expanding through selling products through new channels, or taking existing products into new geographic markets. Many markets are now saturated and traditional expansion will not automatically lead to profitable growth. ECR provides a vehicle for fulfilling consumers' wishes better, faster and at less cost; that is, maintaining or improving profitability by improving operational efficiency. As the research has shown, working together on ECR projects has been between retailers and manufacturers, primarily focused on efficiency improvement and structured along traditional ECR lines. These relationships will continue, but the next step will be to use the trust that has been built up with consumers, through reliable brands, consistent service and value delivery to add new layers of business (Figure 7.8).

In the future, working together will not be restricted to manufacturers and retailers cooperating to drive cost out of the industry, but will also include other companies who want to extend relationships with consumers. More and more companies will be joining forces not only to facilitate and satisfy consumers with additional levels of convenience and service, but also to stimulate and inspire demand for their own products and services. Examples include retailers forming alliances with the following types of businesses:

- petrol companies;
- banks and financial services;
- medical services;
- postal services; and
- dry-cleaning services.

Conclusion

ECR provides a framework for addressing the two key issues facing the grocery industry: combining top-line sales growth with cost reduction or containment. As part of their overall business strategy, it has allowed companies to compete with new market entrants and retain market share. However, where the main focus of ECR remains on working together to reduce costs rather than focusing on satisfying the needs of the consumer, its full potential will never be realized.

When the concept is fully developed and implemented, companies will move from measuring performance in terms of market and category share, to measuring performance in terms of overall share of consumer spending. Similarly, retailers and manufacturers will move from a product focus to a consumer focus. Overall consumer profitability will become a much more important measure than is product profitability. Companies will have to be highly efficient to remain in business. However, efficiency alone will not be a sustainable source of differentiation or competitive advantage. Innovation, based on a deep understanding of consumer needs, will become the leading source of differentiation and competitive advantage in the future. ECR will evolve from being about who can best 'facilitate and satisfy' consumer demand to who can best 'stimulate and inspire' that demand.

References

ECR Europe (1996) *Proceedings of 1st Official ECR Europe Conference*, ECR Europe.
ECR Europe (1997) *The Official European ECR Scorecard*, ECR Europe.
Hill, R. (1997) *Demand-side Priorities and Vision, Proceedings of 2nd Official ECR Conference*, Andersen Consulting/ECR Europe.
Morehouse, J. and Bowersox, D. (1995) *Supply Chain Management: Logistics for the Future*, US Food Marketing Institute.
Pearce, A.M. (1996) *Efficient Consumer Response*, Birds Eye Wall's Ltd.

Performance Measurement Operating Committee (1994) *Performance Measurement: Applying Value Chain Analysis to the Grocery Industry*, US Joint Industry Project on Efficient Consumer Response.

Toja, E. (1996) *ECR in Europe, Common Issues, Shared Solutions—Future Opportunities*, Institute of Grocery Distribution, UK.

Components of demand planning

Putting together the details for success

Todd Smith, Jay Mabe and Jeff Beech

With the growing recognition that competitive success will depend on supply chain performance in meeting consumer needs, companies are increasingly focused on achieving excellence in their demand-planning process. It has become increasingly important to understand the consumer's demand behaviour and to match this with the timely supply of goods. There is no magic pill that companies can take to achieve this goal. This chapter sets out the seven key actions for success which, put together during the establishment of a demand planning strategy, will ensure that a company can compete effectively.

Introduction

Consumers are becoming accustomed to getting the products they want, when they want them and in the manner they want. Even those products that were once restricted by geographic coverage or higher pricing are now becoming widely available. As the market expands, traditional shopping channels are also changing. Consumers can buy goods via the Internet, consumer direct channels and home shopping television networks.

For organizations this shift in consumer expectations has two main implications. First, it is much harder to understand and predict consumer behaviour; and secondly, organizations must manage the availability of their product lines effectively if they are to succeed in meeting customer requirements.

One way to achieve this goal is to get closer to consumers and tailor internal company processes to meet their needs. Once companies align their internal processes, further opportunities for improvement lie in integrating this information across all partners: contractors, co-packers and suppliers. Integration throughout the supply chain results in more assured decision making, shorter, consolidated supply chains, reduced inventory levels and more responsive customer service (this has been discussed in detail in Chapter 6). But a critical first step for companies is to ensure that their own houses are in good order.

The benefits of doing this are significant. Research has shown that modest improvements in forecast accuracy will have dramatic effects on lowering overall supply chain costs. Best practice measures show forecast error rates at a stock-keeping unit (SKU) level at 25 per cent. However, most companies currently operate with error rates of 40 to 50 per cent, and thus have a big opportunity to achieve significant gains by relatively small improvements to their demand-planning processes and organizations.

So, how are companies coming to grips with the demanding 'new' consumer and integrating their supply chain? Many have recognized the need to refocus their efforts on establishing a more strategic and robust demand-planning process. Today's companies have realized that they must address seven key components: organization; business alignment; practices; process; integration; performance measures; and technology. Failing to address any one of these components is likely to result in mediocrity.

Demand-planning organization

Getting the organization right is a critical first step in establishing excellence in demand planning. This essentially involves business alignment—ensuring that all the strategies employed in demand planning are in sync with, and supportive of, the overall business strategy. Each of the six components must begin by asking the question: what is necessary to support the business strategy? This can best be achieved if the individuals involved in demand planning are part of a distinct unit, rather than spread across different parts of the organization. When demand forecasting is only a small part of an individual's many responsibilities, he or she rarely spends time working to improve the accuracy of projections.

Demand planning requires a commitment to three guiding principles. First is focus. Best-practice companies achieve focus with a distinct supply- and demand-planning organization with people 100 per cent dedicated to demand planning within it. Second is ownership. The organization must foster ownership of demand forecasts across the company and an attitude shift from 'my number' to 'our number'. Third is balance. To be effective, demand-planning organizations must have the authority to balance supply and demand in accordance with strategic objectives.

Corporate structure

Companies have traditionally aligned the demand-planning organization based on two requirements. The first is accountability. Given the impact that poor forecasting can have on business performance, it is no wonder that demand planning is often required to report to operations or to be divided along performance-reporting lines. The second is communication. Some companies have decided that communication is the most important organizing principle and have aligned demand planning closely with the sources of input to forecasting, typically placing it in marketing. An issue with this model is that the analytical skills required in supply and demand planning are more frequently found in operations instead of marketing.

Best-practice companies are now beginning to consider a third option, namely maximizing the value delivered by combined supply and demand planning. This has driven a trend towards giving planning global scope and responsibilities.

Hybrid structures can also be effective. One communications company had been developing product forecasts and supply plans by sales region. It reorganized to create a 'centralized' planning organization, but left planners in their existing, regional locations. Each planner became solely responsible for planning one or more product lines company-wide, but was also responsible for collecting insights from local sales and marketing managers on all products to pass to other planners. This approach allowed the company to reap simultaneously the scale benefits of a centralized organization and the communications benefits of a decentralized organization.

Organization structure

Within a combined supply- and demand-planning organization two models dominate: the functional specialist and the product planner. In the functional specialist model, each individual is 100 per cent dedicated to a single activity, such as demand forecasting, inventory planning or production planning. In the product planner model, a single individual is responsible for all planning activities for one or more product lines. Each model has its pros and cons. The product planner model maximizes communication across functions, excels at some aspects of balancing supply and demand and typically yields the highest job satisfaction. However, it does not address contention for scarce supply resources. The functional specialist model maximizes focus and the scope of supply decisions at the expense of communication and accountability. The circumstances of each company will rightly dictate the model and hybrid models can also be found (for instance, demand forecasting and inventory planning follow a product planner model with a functional specialist in production planning).

Skill sets

Individual demand planners require a specific set of skills to be successful. At the core of this skill set are analytical abilities, coupled with the ability to use statistical analysis tools. Planners without these skills are typically unable to execute statistical forecasting effectively. Computer skills are required to apply statistical approaches using the latest demand-planning technology. If any sort of consensus process is being employed, then communication, negotiation and facilitation skills are also critical. These skills are largely outside the ability of an organization to develop and should form the basis for hiring new staff. Other abilities that need to be developed over time include expertise in the application of forecasting techniques and product knowledge.

Business alignment

Differentiation in the way market needs are addressed must be incorporated into all business processes—and not into marketing approaches alone. To this end, many companies are beginning to tailor their approach to demand planning by segmenting the way they treat both their customers and products when establishing demand parameters.

Organizational structures are beginning to appear that specifically tailor customer service, joint forecasting and product-delivery mechanisms to key customers. For example, one company has aligned its customer-service and demand-planning organizations into three distinct groups, focusing on key customers (60 per cent of its business), middle-market customers (25 per cent of its business) and low-end customers. All processes and performance measures are aligned with these groups and the business is reported and conducted along these lines. The company has improved overall customer service by 15 per cent, while lowering inventories by 15 per cent and overall logistics costs by 20 per cent. More and more companies are aligning their businesses to meet their specific customer needs. Some of these companies are doing this before customers demand this service, while others are being dragged along by their customers' demands.

Practices

Our experience indicates that there are several demand-planning best practices that apply broadly across products, channels and industries. These practices should act as the foundation of any demand-planning process design. They are:

- integrated forecasting, planning and execution;
- a cross-functional forecasting process;
- top-down, bottom-up and adjustment capabilities;
- pull-based demand signals;
- statistical techniques; and
- performance monitoring and tracking.

Integrated forecasting, planning and execution

In many companies, second-guessing of forecasts or the existence of multiple forecasts across distribution and manufacturing is common. While almost everyone will acknowledge that forecasts are often wrong, few managers take potential forecast errors into account when making inventory, distribution and production plans. Best-practice companies, by contrast, take an integrated approach to planning. To begin with, the entire enterprise runs on a single forecast, developed in a process designed to discourage or eliminate second-guessing. Distribution and production are driven by actual customer demand, to the extent that it is known, and by the single forecast if it is not. Finally, both distribution and production plans explicitly allow for some level of forecast error (based on measurements of past performance) with buffers of inventory and capacity. Companies that have adopted this best practice benefit through lower inventories, higher product availability and reduced expediting costs through more accurate, synchronized plans.

Cross-functional forecasting

A cross-functional forecasting process is the key to developing a single demand forecast that can be agreed by the whole organization. Typically, demand plans are either prepared in isolation by individual functions (sales, marketing, operations, finance) or decreed by some central forecasting group. In the first case, the individual plans are often at odds with each other and with corporate goals. In the second, individual functions often have great latitude to interpret the forecast as to mix and timing. This, combined with a poor understanding of underlying assumptions, often yields a set of plans with significant disagreements. Discrepancies between plans then lead to high inventories and lost sales opportunities. The situation is made worse by a lack of clear accountability for forecast accuracy and an inability to reconcile functional plans to each other due to differences in unit of measures (such as revenue for sales, units for manufacturing), level of detail and/or timing.

The best practice is to prepare a single forecast with input from all functional groups. Demand forecasting is 'owned' by a group in one function (usually marketing or operations) which generates a baseline, statistical forecast and handles forecast administration and performance monitoring. This group also acts as a focal point for the collection and incorporation of 'market intelligence' on factors that might cause demand to differ from the statistical baseline. Differences between functional plans and expectations and the baseline are reconciled during a consensus meeting and adjustments incorporated as required. Addressing issues and building a mutual understanding of forecasting assumptions during the consensus meeting is the primary vehicle for eliminating second-guessing later on.

An important issue that often comes up in the context of developing a consensus plan is the relationship between the forecast and the business plan. As a best practice, the demand forecast should never be forced to equal the business plan. Doing so not only has a negative impact on forecast accuracy, it destroys an important predictor of business performance. The forecast should, rather, serve as a predictor of performance relative to the business plan. Where discrepancies between the two exist, specific counter-actions should be planned and the forecast adjusted based on the expected impact of these actions (which may or may not completely resolve the discrepancy).

Typically, companies find it difficult, if not impossible, to reconcile different views of the forecast. One organization may plan by SKUs, while another uses revenue by product family. Meanwhile, sales may aggregate forecast by customer while operations aggregates by distribution centre or plant. It is these 'language barriers' that often present the most formidable hurdles to cross-functional forecasting. For cross-functional forecasting to be effective, the various groups which participate must be able to view the impact of everyone's input in terms that each group understands.

Top-down, bottom-up and adjustment capabilities

Fortunately, the ability to translate between different views of the forecast is available in several leading-edge demand-planning software applications. In a typical application, forecast data is stored at a very low level (such as SKU/customer group/distribution centre), which represents the least common denominator among required views. When combined with attribute data such as standard cost, price and product family, a variety of reports can be produced in different units and at different levels of aggregation. A good application will also take input in one unit of measure and level of aggregation and both propagate it down to more detailed levels (through some form of allocation) and roll it into other views and aggregations. Finally, a good forecasting system will distinguish between the initial or baseline forecast and subsequent adjustments to facilitate tracking of the amount of improvement or degradation in forecast accuracy produced by various sources of input.

Pull-based demand signals

Most companies forecast future demand based on historical customer order or shipment levels and patterns. However, actual consumer demand may be very different from the order stream. Each member of the supply chain observes the demand patterns of its customers and in turn produces a set of demands on its suppliers. But the decisions made in forecasting, setting inventory targets, lot sizing and purchasing act to transform (or distort) the demand picture. The further a company is 'upstream' in the supply chain (that is, the further it is from the consumer), the more distorted is the order stream relative to consumer demand. This phenomenon is a central finding in the 'beer game', as described in Peter Senge's *The Fifth Discipline*, and has become known as the 'bull whip effect' (Hau Lee, 1997).

Demand forecasts are inevitably more accurate when they are based on actual consumer demand, such as point-of-sale (POS) data, as opposed to, or in addition to, historical orders. A major toy maker was able to improve forecast accuracy by using POS data to validate customer orders. In the past, if the toy maker had received strong orders this would have prompted an increase in the forecast. Today strong orders are reviewed in light of consumer demand based on POS data and current and projected channel inventory levels. In cases where the data indicates that these strong orders are building high channel inventories (and are not the result of strong consumer demand), this review results in a decrease in the forecast in expectation that orders will drop when retailers become aware of their inventory position.

There is no one right approach to considering consumer or POS data in developing demand forecasts, as the availability and quality of this information vary widely across companies and industries. Common challenges in this area include the timely collection and processing of data and the need to extrapolate total demand from data collected from only a few key accounts (particularly when market share is fluctuating). Finally, regardless of the data used to generate them, forecasts should always be adjusted or 'consumed' based on actual orders received and, wherever practical, demand should be driven from actual orders, not forecasts.

Statistical techniques

While statistical forecasting techniques have been taught in engineering and business schools for decades, many companies continue to rely on primarily judgemental approaches to forecasting. To a certain extent, this is understandable given that software capable of handling forecasting problems on the scale of a typical large company or division has only recently become available. Nevertheless, statistical techniques continue to be under-utilized, largely because their proper application is not understood.

Statistical forecasting techniques provide a means of quantifying certain things about the past in order to predict the future. In doing so they are superior to judgemental forecasts in two ways. First, when implemented in software, statistical techniques can consider far more data than a human forecaster. This is true in terms of both the amount of time considered and the number of factors considered. Secondly, statistical techniques do not suffer from human biases, inattention to detail and imprecision. This does not mean, however, that statistical methods on their own will always perform better than a human forecaster.

Perhaps the greatest advantage of statistical techniques in forecasting is that they allow human forecasters to be much more effective by focusing their attention on only a subset of SKUs. In a typical consensus process, the forecasting group prepares a baseline forecast using statistical techniques. The group then addresses problem SKUs (those that fall outside some acceptable set of tolerances) on an exception basis. During the consensus process, the group provides input to help quantify specific actions being incorporated as adjustments to the forecast. For example, statistical analysis would be used to determine the increase in sales that should be expected when a certain type of promotion is run. By following this process, only a small fraction of SKUs would receive human attention in any given forecast cycle, but this approach focuses that attention on the items that need it most.

Performance monitoring or tracking

Demand forecast accuracy (or error) is the primary measure of performance for any demand-planning process. However, few companies actually track any measure of forecast performance and it is often difficult to identify a person or group accountable for forecast accuracy. Best-practice companies have clearly defined accountabilities and measurements, which often extend beyond the forecasting organization. Measuring all participants in the forecasting process on the accuracy of the result is critical to ensuring that demand planning gets adequate participation and attention and that inputs are free of organizational biases.

Process

One of the keys to excellence in demand forecasting is collaboration. The more information is incorporated into a forecast, the more accurate it is likely to be. Many of the best practices outlined above relate to the use of a cross-functional, consensus-based process. When different functions develop their own forecasts, they typically do so with different assumptions about the factors which will affect demand. A consensus process ensures a consistent set of assumptions based on a broader base of input.

When operations is involved in the consensus process of developing a demand forecast, the process is often known as sales and operations planning (S&OP). Sales and marketing will be the primary sources of information on actions being taken to stimulate demand. Meanwhile, operations provides critical information on product supply. In a well-functioning process the addition of operations has an impact that goes well beyond the accuracy of the demand forecast. For instance, based on feedback from operations, marketing may cancel a promotion scheduled for an item in short supply and redirect the associated spending to items with high inventory. Similarly, the salesforce may be redirected in terms of which products to push. Naturally, the inclusion of operations in the planning process increases in importance as a business becomes more constrained by supply.

A typical S&OP process has six main steps centred on a consensus meeting (see Figure 8.1). During the period between meetings, a forecast analyst solicits input from key members of the various functional groups participating in the process (such as sales, marketing and operations) These inputs are layered on top of a statistical forecast to create a forecast 'baseline'. The baseline is then translated to the 'language' of each group and distributed for review to identify issues in the forecast, such as conflicting assumptions, last-minute plan changes or problem forecasts. The review allows the consensus meeting to focus only on the contentious issues.

In order to come to agreement on a single forecast that will be used by all parties, the participants need to distinguish between the forecast, the business plan and any functional objectives. The forecast should reflect the most likely pattern and level of future demand given history, market intelligence and planned actions. Many companies fall into the trap of forcing the forecast to equal sales objectives or the business plan, or to reflect some other functional objective, such as sales targets. Where discrepancies exist, the other plans may be adjusted or specific actions may be planned to close the gap between the forecast and the particular plan. For instance, if the forecast shows revenue falling short of the business plan, the company may choose to provide additional salesforce incentives or promote the product in some way. Once a course of action

An effective forecasting process is highly cross-functional and usually more important than the forecasting technique or software

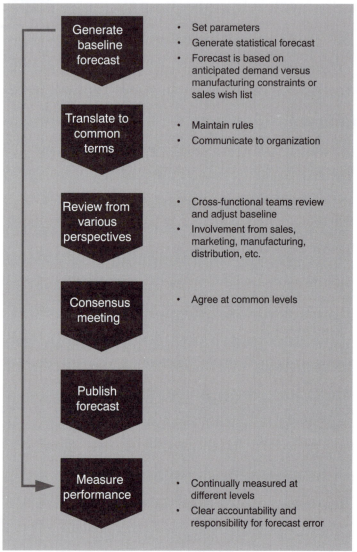

Figure 8.1   Forecasting process

is determined, it should be incorporated into the forecast based on the best available data as to its planned impact. This does not guarantee a forecast that will equal the desired number and several iterations may be required. The final forecast is published to each stakeholder group in the appropriate format for that group, either units, revenue, by plant or by market. Once a forecast has been agreed and published, it is the forecast analyst's responsibility to monitor performance and produce performance measurement reports (typically performance measurement would be an agenda item during the consensus meeting).

One of the key questions to be answered in the design of any demand-planning process is that of timing. Specifically, on what cycle will revised forecasts be developed? Quarterly? Monthly? Weekly? Frequent forecast revisions can consume a great deal of organizational resources, yet infrequent updates increase the damage done by a bad forecast by increasing the time required to correct it. The best solution to this problem is to operate two subprocesses on different frequencies. In this scenario, consensus meetings would be held between monthly and quarterly, while the forecast analyst would execute a forecast review and adjustment cycle weekly to monthly. This approach facilitates the identification and correction of large forecast errors (exceptions) on a short cycle, while reserving the bulk of the work to complete a forecast revision for a longer cycle. The weekly forecast cycle also allows for the incorporation of late-breaking information into the forecast between consensus meetings (although typically with the informal agreement of the consensus team members).

Integration

Best-practice companies are pursuing integration along three key dimensions: horizontally, vertically and geographically. Most companies begin by integrating horizontally, generally through a consensus forecasting process as described above. Vertical integration begins by expanding the consensus forecasting process to address supply-planning issues as well with complete vertical integration involving customers and suppliers in the planning process through forecast sharing or collaborative forecasting. Also, many companies are finding that it makes sense to integrate the planning process across geographical entities (such as regions or country units) to create a global planning process. The primary benefit of global planning is an improved ability to match supply and demand that comes from considering a broader set of supply options. Global integration is important in demand forecasting when product is sourced across geographical entities. Without this integration the benefits of consensus planning are limited to a portion of the total demand picture.

Global planning is not without its challenges. Language, time, distance and technology create obvious barriers. Companies often struggle to reconcile the drive to centralize planning that naturally follows from a global approach with the need to remain close to local sources of market intelligence in demand forecasting.

Performance measures

Demand forecast accuracy (or error) is the primary measure of performance for any demand-planning process. However, few companies actually track any measure of forecast performance, and it is often difficult to identify a person or group accountable for forecast accuracy. Best-practice companies have clearly defined accountabilities and measurements, which often extend beyond the forecasting organization. Measuring all participants in the forecasting process on the accuracy of the results is critical to ensuring that demand planning receives adequate participation and attention and that inputs are free of organizational biases.

Forecast accuracy, or conversely forecast error, is a key driver of product availability, customer service, cost and inventory levels. Focusing demand planning singularly on forecast accuracy eliminates the risk of driving the wrong behaviour that comes with a focus on a single dimension of business performance such as cost. Still, it is important for companies to balance the cost of the demand-planning process, organization and technology against the accuracy delivered.

Demand forecast accuracy is typically measured in the negative; that is, most measures are measures of forecast error. Various approaches to measuring forecast error exist in theory and practice, ranging from the simple to the complex in both computation and interpretation. The most commonly used and, we believe, effective measure is mean absolute percent error, or MAPE. MAPE has the advantages that it is relatively easily to understand and is correlated with business results. MAPE may be computed based on the following formula.

> ## Mean absolute percent error

$$MAPE = \frac{\sum |Forecast - Actual|}{\sum Actual}$$

Equation 8.1

This formula for MAPE is generally applicable across groups of items, for instance to evaluate forecast accuracy for the most recent period. It is important to note, however, that all errors are weighted equally. This means that a large error on a low-value item can skew the overall measure. For this reason, some companies prefer to use a weighted mean absolute percent error (WMAPE). WMAPE may be computed based on the following formula:

Weighted mean absolute percent error

$$WMAPE = \frac{\sum Weight \times |Forecast - Actual|}{\sum Weight \times Actual}$$

Equation 8.2

Typically item cost or revenue is used as the weighting factor. With this formula, those items driving the largest weighted volume have the greatest impact on the error measurement. WMAPE has the added benefit that it is highly correlated with safety stock inventory requirements, making it easy to relate performance on this measure to business performance.

In measuring forecast error it is also important to look for forecast bias. Bias is the tendency for a forecast always to be off in the same direction and when present indicates that there is a problem with one or more data inputs, or the process itself. Often bias is injected when an organization attempts to manipulate the forecast to match a functional goal such as a sales objective or manufacturing volume commitment. A high bias will drive increased inventories in proportion to lead times, while a low bias will hurt product availability and ultimately revenues.

Which formula is used in measuring forecast error should depend on where the forecast is being measured. Forecast error should be measured along several dimensions and at different levels of detail. Ultimately, the impact on the business is determined by forecast error at the SKU and location (warehouse/factory) level and thus the primary measure should be at this level. However, measures at higher levels of aggregation provide useful information both for managing the business and for ongoing efforts to improve performance. For instance, forecast error for total plant or distribution centre volume is useful in capacity-planning decisions and forecast error for total sales revenue is useful for financial planning. Similarly, measuring error by account or by product line may identify performance-improvement opportunities.

Forecast error measures should also be driven by who is being measured. Individual forecast analysts should be measured on the forecasts for which they have responsibility in a manner consistent with the division of labour. Where a consensus process is employed, all members of the team should be measured on overall forecast performance and on the quality of their individual input. Measurement of individual team members is critical to counteracting structural incentives to bias the forecast and to ensuring an appropriate level of attention from all team members.

Technology

Dozens, if not hundreds, of products are available when it comes to selecting software technology to support demand planning. These range from enterprise resource planning (ERP) systems to integrated supply chain planning tools to personal computer-based forecasting packages and even customized systems. The best solution for an individual company will depend on a variety of factors which largely relate to the six components of demand-planning strategy already discussed.

First and foremost, the choice of technology must be aligned with the needs and direction of the business. Business alignment has several different dimensions:

- Available statistical models must fit with the nature of demand. Most demand-planning software packages provide historical time series models. Other approaches, such as the use of causal factors, are supported by relatively few packages and sometimes require a customized solution.
- The software must support the process. If a consensus forecasting process is being used, then the ability to translate the forecast into the views required by different functional groups is critical, as is the ability to enter overrides at different levels of aggregation.
- The software must also support the way a company interacts with its customers in both demand planning and distribution. This would include support for collaborative planning, where applicable. If a company manages its customer's inventory, then the software must be able to forecast for customer sites (or store a forecast if provided by the customer).
- The investment in demand-planning technology needs to be compared to the expected benefit. In industries where demand is stable and free from the impacts of promotions, such as spare parts or medical products, the limited capabilities of an ERP system may be sufficient and investment in more sophisticated tools unjustified. However, in dynamic businesses, those with short product lifecycles or frequent promotions, significant investment in tools is easily justified based on the dramatic improvements in forecast accuracy they can deliver.

Another key consideration in software selection lies in the capabilities and skills of the intended users. The complexity of tools varies widely in terms of both internal processing and ease of use. Some vendors have chosen to take a 'toolkit' approach to demand planning which has the advantage of offering a great degree of flexibility, but at the expense of requiring a high degree of both user knowledge and user interaction. Other vendors have chosen to maximize ease of use, reducing both skill and time requirements, but at the loss of some flexibility. Which approach is best for any given company will depend on the value placed on flexibility and the existence of (or the commitment to obtain) appropriate resources. Companies that select software exceeding the capabilities of the demand-planning organization generally find themselves frustrated in their ability to deliver improved performance.

A final consideration should be the level of integration between the demand-planning system, ERP systems and other supply chain planning systems. To begin with, a timely, reliable source for required data must be identified, as demand forecasts will only be as good as the data used to generate them. If some data is not available it may be necessary to rethink the intended approach to forecasting. Another factor is the effort required to construct interfaces. Many software providers offer packaged integration to popular ERP solutions which dramatically reduces the time required to define data interchange requirements and construct interfaces. With increasing frequency, demand-planning software is becoming part of a larger, integrated supply chain planning solution. Often, this means that there are additional benefits to using demand- and supply-planning (distribution-planning, manufacturing-planning) solutions from the same vendor. Conversely, using a demand-planning solution from a different vendor may compromise some supply-planning functionality.

Conclusion

Companies today are faced with consumers who expect global access to high-quality and reliable products. Traditional channels for shopping have changed thanks to the Internet and home-shopping TV networks. Getting the right product, when and where it is needed, is becoming a competitive advantage for many organizations. That is why putting together the detailed components of demand planning is emerging as a critical factor in business success—and that is why the seven components of detailed demand planning working in concert can be so powerful.

References

Givens, Christopher P., *The Seven Principles of Demand Planning*, Andersen Consulting working paper.

Lapide, Lawrence and Smith, Todd S., *Demand Planning Strategy Framework*, Andersen Consulting working paper.

Lee, Hau L., Padmanabhan, V. and Whang, Seungjin (1997) 'The bullwhip effect in supply chains', *Sloan Management Review*, 38 (3), Spring.

Senge, Peter M. (1990) *The Fifth Discipline: The Art and Practice of the Learning Organization*, Doubleday/Currency, New York.

Effective demand management
Are you limiting the performance of your own supply chain?

Jamie Bolton

Many organizations may not realize this, but when it comes to managing the demand swings of their customers, they can often be their own worst enemy. Demand volatility is often increased through organizations' own policies and procedures. It is one of the chief causes of misalignment between the supply chain and customers. However, companies have the capacity to influence their customers to achieve smoother demand. When organizations implement demand management they gain significant benefits, including improved forecast accuracy, increased supply chain visibility, reduced supply chain costs and better customer service levels. Effective demand management is another tool to improve the potential for a company to align its supply chain operations with its customers.

Introduction

In an ideal world, customer demand would be smooth and growing. Demand would be perfectly predictable and therefore enable perfect planning of the supply chain for least total cost. Unfortunately, this is seldom the case. Customer demand can be, and often is, volatile, necessitating inventory and complex forecasting, planning and production processes to fulfil demand to the required level of customer satisfaction. Demand volatility places a significant burden on organizations in terms of both cost and complexity.

Closer inspection of the causes of demand volatility can, however, yield some surprising results. Given that demand volatility inevitably manifests itself through customers, it is easy to assume that this volatility wholly reflects the erratic, unpredictable consumption habits of customers. In fact, demand volatility is often driven primarily by organizations themselves through their own policies and procedures. Far from behaving erratically, customers are simply responding in a logical fashion to the signals sent to them by their suppliers. Organizations can understand and address these self-induced causes of demand volatility through improving their demand-management performance.

Demand management or demand planning?

The term demand management is not new to supply chain practitioners. It is often used interchangeably with demand planning to account for activities such as forecasting, production planning, inventory management and deployment. But important differences exist between demand planning and demand management.

Taken broadly, demand planning includes the processes that an organization takes to anticipate customer demand and ensure sufficient product is available—in the right place, at the right time, to the required level of service and at the lowest possible supply chain cost. Demand planning therefore includes such activities as demand forecasting, inventory management, capacity planning, production planning and scheduling and materials requirements planning.

Demand-planning processes have developed rapidly over the last ten years. For example, just-in-time (JIT) was developed to reduce lead times through smaller batch-size production to satisfy customer demand more effectively. Quick response (QR) takes JIT further and applies the principles to the retail industry. Efficient consumer response (ECR) was developed as an industry-wide demand-planning vision, linking all members of the supply chain to fulfil customer demand more effectively by integrating four key strategies: efficient store assortments, efficient replenishment, efficient promotions and efficient new product introductions.

All these approaches are useful in that they take time and cost out of supply chains. However, they all make one key assumption: that customer demand and the volatility of that demand is a given input into the demand-planning process.

Demand management, by contrast, actively seeks to ensure that the customer demand 'profile' that is the input into the demand-planning process is as smooth as possible as a means to simplify supply chain operations. It does so by reducing or eliminating the volatility of customer demand prior to input into the demand-planning process.

Demand management might be defined as 'the identification, reduction and elimination (where possible) of the causes of customer demand volatility with the objective of providing a smooth demand signal to increase supply chain visibility, planning accuracy and reduce total supply chain cost'. Consequently, where demand planning is reactive to customer demand, demand management is proactive to customer demand. Figure 9.1 illustrates this difference between demand planning and demand management.

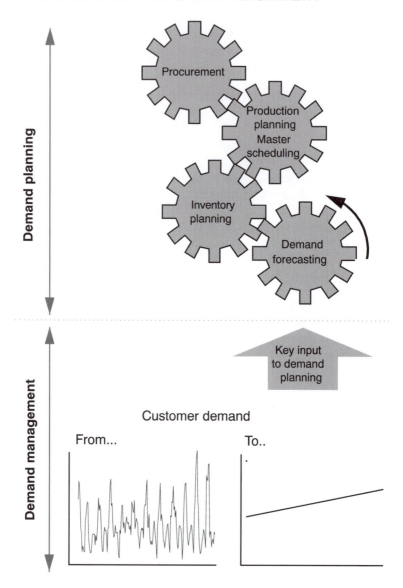

Figure 9.1   Demand planning vs demand management

Why effective demand management?

Ineffective demand-management practices manifest themselves as volatile customer demand and can have serious effects on business and supply chain performance. Servicing the excessive peaks and troughs of

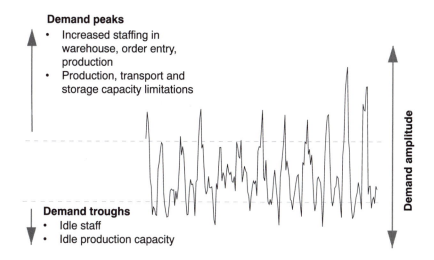

Demand peaks
- Increased staffing in warehouse, order entry, production
- Production, transport and storage capacity limitations

Demand troughs
- Idle staff
- Idle production capacity

Demand amplitude

Increased:
- Uncertainty
- Reliance on accurate and timely information
- Risk of stockouts
- Inventory to cover volatility risk
- Obsolescence
- Customer lead times

Decreased:
- Ability to accurately forecast
- Ability to accurately plan the business
- Quality

Figure 9.2   Volatility-induced cost and complexity

this volatile customer demand increases the cost and complexity of business operations, as shown in Figure 9.2.

Servicing a demand profile similar to that shown in Figure 9.2 will impose significant costs on an organization.

Demand volatility increases costs

A business that must continually service excessive demand peaks and troughs will suffer increased costs.

First, the *working capital cost* will increase as organizations seek to minimize the risks of running out of stock and maintain high customer service levels through increased inventory levels. And secondly, *variable costs* will also rise as a result of increased labour costs and the greater use of contract storage needed to hold the excess production during demand peaks. Labour becomes more expensive because of the casual or temporary staffing needed for order processing, production and warehouse operations. The overtime and adjusted shift patterns needed to cover demand peaks also increase labour expenses.

When the customer demand is low or in a 'trough', the same organization risks significant inefficiencies through idle labour and idle production and storage capacity. The greater this demand volatility, the more likely it is that these costs will occur and the greater they will be.

Demand volatility creates complexity

Demand volatility causes more than just additional costs. It also causes significant complexity which must be managed. The greater the demand volatility, the greater the complexity this demand creates for the organization.

This complexity may take many forms:

- *Increased supply chain uncertainty.* As demand volatility increases, uncertainty about future customer demand is likely to grow, increasing uncertainty about future pressures on the supply chain.
- *Increased reliance on accurate, timely information.* This heightened level of uncertainty greatly increases the organization's reliance on timely and accurate information as a means of gaining increased visibility of future customer demand.
- *Increased risk of stockouts.* As the magnitude of demand peaks can be unpredictable, the risk of running out of stock becomes greater if the organization operates in a make-to-stock environment. Furthermore, if it is operating on a long production cycle, the time taken to replenish inventory may be significantly greater than customer order periodicity. Back orders may result and become a chronic customer service problem.
- *Increased customer lead times (reduced service levels).* To guarantee the supply of product when demand is unpredictable and the risk of stockout is high, organizations may resort to increasing the lead time of customer orders to provide sufficient time to ensure that the product is available (increasing customer lead times is also a means of increasing the visibility of customer demand). For example, with 24-hour customer lead times, an organization has confirmed visibility of customer demand only 24 hours in advance. However a customer lead time of five days provides an organization with a confirmed visibility of customer demand of five days. Increasing customer lead times to increase demand visibility and mitigate against an organization's ineffective internal operations is, in effect, a reduction in customer service.

■ *Increased reliance on effective production-planning capability.* It is not uncommon for organizations to receive more than 70 per cent of total monthly customer demand in the first week of the month (in fact, many organizations use week-one sales to gain an early indication of total monthly sales). Consequently, organizations must ensure that a significant volume of monthly production is available in stock to fulfil customer orders prior to the beginning of the month. This misalignment between weekly production and weekly demand implies that organizations must effectively plan a mini stock build every month.

■ *Decreased ability to provide accurate information to manufacturing.* Generally sales and marketing divisions produce sales forecasts monthly and at a reasonably high level in the product hierarchy, that is, product-group level, not stock-keeping-unit (SKU) level. However, these forecasts are too aggregated and across too long a time frame to support accurate production plans for manufacturing. It is much easier to accurately forecast customer demand that follows a straight line than a demand profile. Volatile demand profiles make accurate sales forecasting extremely difficult. The smoother the customer demand placed on an organization the greater will be sales and marketing's ability to generate accurate forecasts and hence the greater the visibility the organization has of customer demand from which to plan manufacturing operations accurately.

■ *Increased risk of obsolescence.* Where inventory levels are inflated to cover increased demand risk for a given customer service level, there is the increased possibility of obsolescence if this demand fails to materialize, particularly for products with a short shelf life.

Causes of induced demand volatility

Given the resultant cost and complexity, organizations have a real interest in identifying and addressing the causes of demand volatility. While they may never achieve a perfectly smooth demand curve, organizations can certainly understand and address their self-induced drivers of demand swings. The primary causes of demand volatility are:

■ terms of trade (credit terms);
■ promotions and pricing;
■ specific company policies; and
■ distribution channel structure.

Terms of trade

Terms of trade or 'credit terms' refers to the conditions under which organizations require customers to pay for their purchases. Organizations are sometimes unaware that their credit terms drive particular customer behaviours which are reflected in demand volatility.

Organizations often require customers to pay for goods 30 days from the end of a given month (either they request payment 30 days from the end of the month in which the goods were purchased or 30 days from receipt of the invoice, which is often sent at the end of the month).

By fixing a regular date for payment, organizations are providing customers with an ideal regular date for purchase. In order to maximize credit terms, customers will order at the beginning of each month, effectively giving them 60 days' credit instead of 30 days'. Figure 9.3 shows the demand profile of an organization which posted invoices at the end of each month. The demand swings reflect customers taking the logical decision to order at the beginning of each month to maximize credit terms. By understanding the causes of these spikes in demand, companies can either eliminate them through effective demand management or, if this is not possible, manage their production and supply chain processes to accommodate them.

In order for this alignment of customer demand to supply chain operations to work, however, both organizations and customers need to be very clear about the payment guidelines. If an organization does not communicate its credit terms clearly to customers it can add further complexity to customer demands.

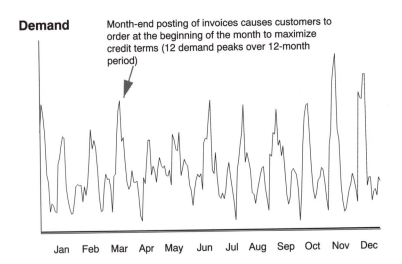

Figure 9.3   Impact of terms of trade

For example, some organizations choose to use an accounting month instead of a calendar month as a way of providing uniformity and consistency to business planning (a standard cycle may be four weeks, four weeks, four weeks, followed by five weeks). This enables routine meetings and processes to be performed on the same day of the same week each period.

One organization recognized and sought to account for the fact that customers placed orders at the beginning of the month as a way of maximizing credit terms. In acknowledging this customer ordering behaviour, the organization assumed that 35 per cent of total forecast monthly demand would be received in week one and 18 per cent of total monthly demand would be received in the last week of the month. This would have worked well, had the organization communicated to customers that its credit terms were based on an accounting month, rather than a calendar month. Customers continued to place their orders at the beginning of the calendar month, which mostly started at the end of the accounting month. So customers were placing their largest orders when the organization was planning for the smallest weekly demand, and were reducing their orders when the organization was planning for the largest customer demand. This created a complete misalignment between actual customer demand and supply chain planning, as shown in Figure 9.4.

Organizations need to be clear about their credit terms, communicate those terms effectively to customers, manage them to reduce volatility and plan their production and supply chain processes accordingly.

Promotions and pricing

Promotions and pricing are also a primary driver of induced demand volatility. Organizations have many reasons for offering price discounts or bulk purchase discounts for moving large quantities of product in a short period of time. Often, however, these discounts create demand disturbances that greatly distort the demand placed on organizations and do not represent the consumer's real end consumption or underlying demand.

For example, a convenience store offers a price discount on toothpaste. Instead of buying the usual one tube per week, consumers buy three tubes. As the end consumption of toothpaste is unchanged (consumers will not use more toothpaste when they clean their teeth), the effect of the price discount is to bring forward the customer's future purchase of toothpaste. This is illustrated in Figure 9.5.

Unless the organization is able to make a sustainable increase in market share following a price discount or promotion, the primary effect of the discount or promotion is greatly to distort consumer buying behaviour and generate significant demand volatility.

Demand

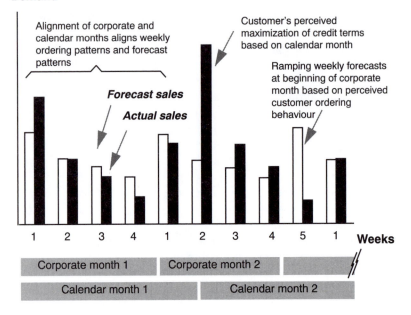

Figure 9.4   Ineffective communication of credit terms

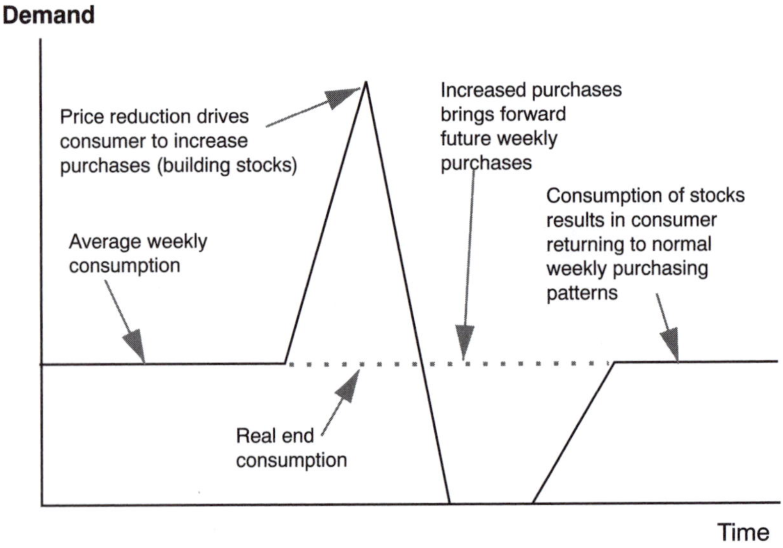

Demand

Figure 9.5   Impact of pricing and promotions

Demand

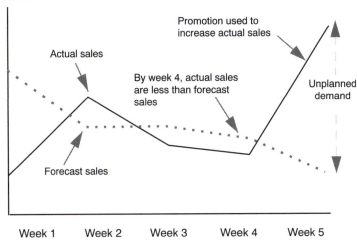

Figure 9.6   Unplanned sales promotions

A similar effect is created when organizations give customers (such as wholesalers) advanced warning of price increases. In this situation, customers will buy in bulk to lock in more purchases at a reduced cost, thus again bringing forward future consumption.

This problem can be further exacerbated when the sales promotions are unplanned, thereby giving the supply chain insufficient time to plan replenishment and increase production to meet the increase in demand. Figure 9.6 shows such an example where, in order to meet the monthly forecast budget, this organization aggressively promoted the product during the final week of the month to lift actual sales to meet forecast sales. However, with the weekly forecast being set by the beginning of the month and no prior warning of the sales promotion given to manufacturing, a significant amount of unplanned demand was placed on the organization.

Specific company policies

Organizations frequently put in place policies that result in customers adjusting their buying behaviour in an attempt to maximize the benefit of these policies. The resulting effect is that the policies distort customer behaviour, causing demand volatility.

For example, in an attempt to increase service to customers, an organization offered them two free deliveries per month. In taking advantage of this policy, customers created ordering patterns that resulted in two

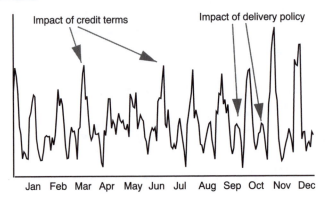

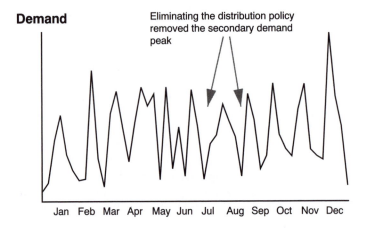

Figure 9.7   Impact of company policies

demand spikes each month. They would use one free delivery and order at the beginning of the month in an attempt to maximize credit terms. They would then use the second free delivery to 'top-up' their inventory and place an order in the middle of the month. This ordering pattern is clearly shown in Figure 9.7. By ceasing this policy the organization was able to eliminate one of the causes of induced demand volatility.

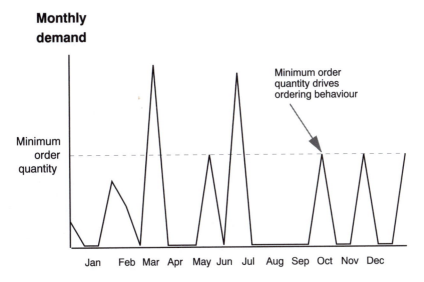

Figure 9.8   Impact of minimum order quantities

Minimum order quantities

Minimum order quantities (MOQs) are another example of policies that distort customer ordering behaviour and drive volatility. Although there are many good reasons for MOQs, care must be taken to include all the costs when calculating the MOQ, not just manufacturing costs. Figure 9.8 shows an example where setting a high MOQ relative to end consumption has resulted in significant demand volatility for the organization.

Distribution channel structure

The longer the distribution channel the greater the distance between suppliers and end customers. Figure 9.9 shows how each member of the distribution channel provides a possible source of demand volatility as each channel participant has the ability to distort the real customer demand. While it is economical (and often essential) for end customers to consume products on a daily basis, the rules of economic order quantities generally prohibit channel members from ordering on a daily basis. As a consequence, intermediaries stagger their ordering and generate demand volatility. The greater the number of channel members the greater the number of opportunities for demand to be distorted. Naturally there must be a trade-off between the value added by each additional member of the distribution channel and the resultant increase in demand volatility.

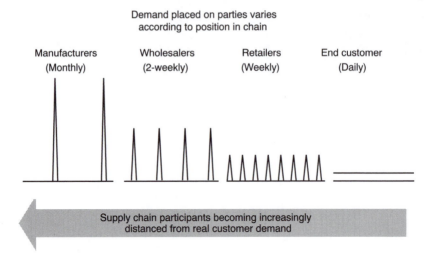

Figure 9.9   Impact of distribution channels

Spotting the symptoms of ineffective demand management

The key for organizations to determine whether their current demand management practices are ineffective is to investigate whether volatile customer demand represents the customer's real underlying demand or whether the organization is in fact the primary driver of demand volatility.

To do this, organizations must either gain access to end customer demand (which is often very difficult or impossible) or use analysis to approximate real customer demand.

Figure 9.10 shows the daily sales of a consumer product with very clear demand volatility. By aggregating demand on a monthly basis, the demand volatility disappears and the inherent demand volatility becomes visible, which better reflects the end consumption of this product (regular daily intake with some seasonality).

If end consumer demand is smooth then the organization must start to analyse whether volatile demand is caused by its own policies and procedures.

Making demand management effective

How does an organization know when a state of effective demand management has been reached? Effective demand management is realized

Demand

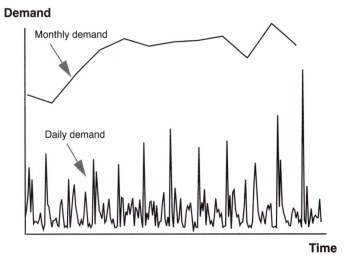

Figure 9.10   Inherent demand volatility

when an organization is no longer driving customer behaviour in a way that adversely affects organizational and/or supply chain performance. Realizing this state will result in significant benefits. These include:

- reduced risk/increased certainty of demand;
- reduced inventory levels;
- improved customer service;
- improved visibility of real/end customer demand;
- reduced reliance on forecasting;
- improved forecasting accuracy; and
- fewer staff required to cover demand peaks.

An approach to effective demand management

Before an organization invests significant amounts of money, time and effort in developing processes to enable effective fulfilment of volatile customer demand, careful consideration should be given, not only to whether the organization is adversely driving customer behaviour, but also the costs of this behaviour and the likely benefits of eliminating the volatility. By eliminating the induced demand volatility from customer ordering, the demand-planning approach adopted may be significantly different.

Figure 9.11 outlines an approach to effective demand management. This covers the basics of demand management discussed in this chapter.

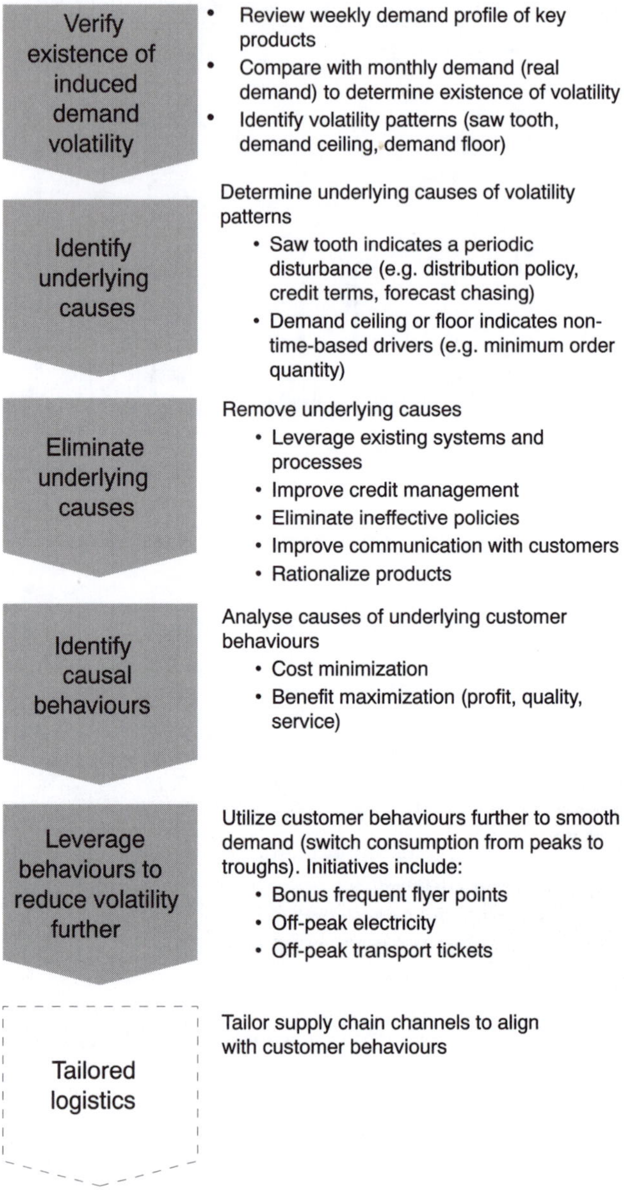

Verify existence of induced demand volatility	• Review weekly demand profile of key products • Compare with monthly demand (real demand) to determine existence of volatility • Identify volatility patterns (saw tooth, demand ceiling, demand floor)
Identify underlying causes	Determine underlying causes of volatility patterns • Saw tooth indicates a periodic disturbance (e.g. distribution policy, credit terms, forecast chasing) • Demand ceiling or floor indicates non-time-based drivers (e.g. minimum order quantity)
Eliminate underlying causes	Remove underlying causes • Leverage existing systems and processes • Improve credit management • Eliminate ineffective policies • Improve communication with customers • Rationalize products
Identify causal behaviours	Analyse causes of underlying customer behaviours • Cost minimization • Benefit maximization (profit, quality, service)
Leverage behaviours to reduce volatility further	Utilize customer behaviours further to smooth demand (switch consumption from peaks to troughs). Initiatives include: • Bonus frequent flyer points • Off-peak electricity • Off-peak transport tickets
Tailored logistics	Tailor supply chain channels to align with customer behaviours

Figure 9.11 Demand-management approach

However, it takes the principles further by showing that not only can customer demand be managed to eliminate induced demand volatility, customer behaviour may also be able to be managed as a way to reduce demand volatility. By identifying customers' underlying causal behaviours, organizations may be able to use these behaviours to smooth demand volatility even further.

This approach has been used successfully in service organizations, but is yet to be widely used in product organizations. For example, off-peak electricity and off-peak tickets for transportation represent an attempt to adjust customer behaviour to smooth demand. Furthermore, the rapid growth of frequent-flyer programmes has provided airlines with a mechanism for smoothing passenger loading by offering bonus points or discounts on low-volume routes, thus reducing the demand for the higher-volume routes.

After all possibilities of smoothing customer demand have been investigated, the organization may still be left with customer demand volatility and unique customer servicing requirements. Under these circumstances it must now look at tailoring or aligning logistics channels to the unique requirements of customer segments. For a complete description of this see Chapter 3.

Conclusion

Customers will never be completely predictable. But organizations can ensure that they themselves are not creating volatile customer demand patterns. Effective demand management represents a significant and often unexplored opportunity for organizations to simplify their supply chain operations. It has the potential to provide significant benefits to organizations in the form of improved forecast accuracy, increased supply chain visibility, reduced supply chain costs and complexity and improved customer service levels. The power of demand management lies in the fact that demand volatility is often induced by organizations through their own policies and procedures. Consequently it is within their capability to control and influence this demand volatility for their own benefit.

AlphaCo—Facilitating export order planning through effective demand management

The following case study illustrates a situation where an organization induced significant demand volatility. By eliminating the causes of this volatility the organization would realize significant reductions in supply chain complexity and improved service.

Supply situation

Twenty per cent of AlphaCo's sales were for export customers. These sales amounted to about $55 million per year.

To plan production for these export sales, AlphaCo's export department used a manual planning system. Production planning for domestic sales used a fully integrated enterprise system.

Planning for export orders was only performed every two months and export customers could only receive orders once a month.

All products for export customers were produced on a make-to-order basis, while all products for domestic customers were make-to-stock. However, 45 per cent of products sold in export markets were exactly the same as those products sold domestically. The remaining 55 per cent were specifically labelled products to accommodate country-specific labelling requirements, although the physical products were the same as those sold domestically.

When ordering export products, customers were required to provide firm orders four months in advance and were not allowed to change these orders within this confirmed order horizon. Nevertheless, order quantities, delivery dates and products were frequently changed during this horizon.

What was found

Analysis of export customer demand profiles indicated that the export demand placed on AlphaCo was volatile (see Figure 9.8 which shows the monthly export demand) and this volatility and unpredictability resulted in the adoption of the manual planning system and the make-to-order production strategy for export customers.

Analysis of export customer demand revealed that the demand placed on AlphaCo was not representative of the real underlying customer demand and was being driven by the company's own policies.

The key drivers of export demand volatility were found to be:

- *The use of minimum order quantities.* As the MOQs were set quite high and demand from many export countries was relatively small compared to the MOQs, export customers would only order once every two months.

■ *Viewing export customers as individual customers rather than as a whole*. This viewpoint eliminated any synergy gained from combining similar order types from individual countries to reach the required minimum order quantity.

Furthermore, it was found that the make-to-order production strategy for export products made AlphaCo reactive to export customer ordering requirements rather than proactive to meeting export customer needs.

What was recommended

By identifying and eliminating these causes of demand volatility there were many opportunities to improve the current process and increase its effectiveness. These opportunities include:

■ use make-to-stock production strategies for domestic and export products, where appropriate;
■ use the domestic planning system forecasting and production planning capability to generate the export forecast and develop production plans;
■ increase the formal export order planning frequency from two-monthly to monthly to enable AlphaCo to be formally notified of customer order changes on a monthly basis; and
■ amalgamate individual export orders where appropriate to determine if the total order quantity meets the MOQ criteria.

What were the benefits?

Reducing demand volatility and using the domestic planning process for export orders resulted in the following benefits to AlphaCo:

■ improved visibility of export demand;
■ increased capability to plan export sales;
■ improved customer service for export customers:
   — the majority of export customers were no longer required to order against a forecast;
   — export customers could order monthly for most export order products regardless of current minimum order quantity;
   — the need for export customers to confirm orders four months in advance was eliminated for 95 per cent of export sales;
■ It will be adopting a best-practice customer service strategy through:
   — forecasting customer order requirements (i.e. using the domestic planning system to forecast and plan export orders); and

— managing customer inventories (i.e. adopting a make-to-stock production strategy).

This case clearly shows that the right solution for improving export order planning was not to implement a completely new planning system or process to cater specifically for export orders. By recognizing that demand volatility was the key driver of ineffective export order planning and that this volatility was actually caused by internal procedures, AlphaCo was able to leverage the current domestic planning system and process and increase service levels to export customers without significant investment.

References

Plossl, George W. (1985) *Production and Inventory Control, Principles and Techniques*, 2nd edn, Prentice-Hall.

Silver, Edward A. (1985) *Decision Systems for Inventory Management and Production Planning*, 2nd edn, John Wiley.

Time compression in the supply chain
Compress your supply chain: expand your customers' satisfaction

Jon Bumstead

While supply chain reforms have traditionally been focused on cost cutting, leading organizations are increasingly analysing their supply chains for strategic opportunities to improve customer service and satisfaction. Time compression increases customer service and responsiveness, and also reduces costly imbalances in supply and demand and inventory holdings. Time compression is not easy. It requires a holistic view of the supply chain and often significant reengineering of processes right across the supply chain. But in an era of intense competition, no organization can afford to ignore the customer service opportunities offered by time compression of the supply chain.

Introduction

Customers in the 1990s will no longer tolerate unresponsive suppliers, and will ruthlessly switch brands in order to obtain what they want, where and when they want it. Intense global competition is rewarding those organizations able to provide their customers not only with quality, value and convenience, but also with products and services tailored to their exact needs and delivery requirements. The pressure is on all organizations to squeeze their supply chains in order to respond effectively to satisfy their customers.

Many organizations are struggling to adapt to these new pressures. An automotive company recently admitted that only 40 per cent of customers actually got the colour of car they wanted. A supermarket chain discovered to its dismay that it would normally be out of stock of 25 per cent of its promotional and key value items. In an attempt to address this, the company issued 'IOU' vouchers to allow the affected customers to benefit from the promotions—unfortunately it ran out of vouchers as well.

The model for excellence in the compression of the supply chain is not a conventional one, but it vividly illustrates the dramatic impact that time compression can have. Some years ago the Williams Renault

Formula 1 Grand Prix team tried a new approach. The team estimated that more short sprints in lighter cars with better tyres would be faster than running with a heavy fuel load from the start. It therefore introduced more pit stops for tyre changes and refuelling during the race. This approach would also accommodate unforeseen events such as a sudden rainstorm requiring a change of tyres or even a minor collision. The number of planned pit stops kept the team's options open.

With the time taken out for pit stops a critical competitive factor, this was a 'knife-edge' strategy. Williams used more than 16 highly trained mechanics with purpose-built equipment to perform the pit stops and invested a large amount of time in training them to attain the shortest possible time. The result was that four tyres could be changed and the car refuelled in less than eight seconds. By the late 1990s the Williams team had the highest win-to-start ratio in the history of the sport.

The strategic rationale for time compression

Supply chain reforms have until recently been driven largely by cost, with a narrow focus on tangible supply chain efficiencies. Like the Williams Formula 1 team, however, organizations looking for business success need to rethink their supply chain strategies. Innovative organizations are examining their supply chains, not for cost-reduction opportunities but for opportunities to serve their customers better. And those that have compressed their supply chain response times have found that the financial benefits have far outweighed the costs (see Table 10.1).

Customer service

A compressed supply chain provides a differentiated level of customer service by making the right products available to customers in the right place and at the right time. Many organizations with either substandard or non-differentiated service find themselves vulnerable to periodic 'margin bashing' from their customers. When customers embark on regional or global purchasing exercises, the only response from the non-differentiated suppliers is to lower prices if they wish to retain the business. Research undertaken by Andersen Consulting for a generic consumer products manufacturer shows that reducing the selling price by 1 per cent will require a 5 per cent cut in supply costs to avoid a profit shortfall, which usually has a further negative impact on customer service. Companies with differentiated service often avoid this ongoing price/service vicious circle.

Table 10.1
Financial value of time compression

Time compression feature	Benefit	Financial value
• Customer service	• Customer loyalty and retention	• Gross margin/ price protection
• Customer responsiveness	• Reduce lost sales • Conquest sales	• Sales growth with existing assets (higher return on assets)
• Balance between supply and demand	• Lower stock wastage or write-offs • Manufacturing effective	• Net margin improvement • Lower unit cost
• Inventory levels	• Less working capital employed in stock	• Improved cashflow

Customer responsiveness

Customer responsiveness enables organizations to adapt quickly to volatile and unplanned demand. Sales growth comes not only from capturing those previously neglected sales opportunities, but also in the longer term through taking market share from those less reliable suppliers. Increasing business through existing channels using existing fixed assets is a very efficient, low-risk and therefore profitable way to grow.

Balance between supply and demand

Achieving a much closer match between supply and demand leads to a reduction in the wastage caused by making or buying too much stock and having to write it off later. This is most obvious in the fashion apparel industry where stock writedowns are the main driver of year-end profits. When supply and demand are not in synchronization, spectacular order surges are often followed by significant order reductions. This common phenomenon encourages organizations to build more capacity than is required, only to see it poorly used.

Inventory levels

The reduction and even the possible elimination of the supply chain inventory, necessary in the traditional 'make-to-forecast' model, is not just a major business goal but also serves as a project enabler. Inventory ties up valuable working capital and chokes business cashflow. Time compression programmes can often release sufficient working capital to fund the overall initiative either partially or completely.

Making time compression work

The success of time compression is based on adopting new approaches:

- Take a holistic view.
- Take advantage of technologies.
- Cut out unnecessary steps.
- Source with service in mind as well as cost.
- Design your products with supply chain requirements in mind.
- Reduce forecast time and increase accuracy.
- Redesign production processes.
- Rethink distribution options.

Take a holistic view

Organizations trying to compress their supply chains need to look beyond their own boundaries. The complete supply chain is likely to consist of different organizations, and supply chain reform requires a holistic and integrated approach with all participants playing a role. Whatever service improvements may have occurred along parts of the chain, unless the whole supply chain is reformed the consumer does not experience those improvements as benefits. In fact, while many companies can quote their 'business-to-business' service levels, few can quote their true end-consumer service level. Often, therefore, it is the dominant player that must drive compression right along the supply chain from product design and manufacture through to delivery to the ultimate consumer.

Compaq Computer discovered this some years ago. By the mid-1990s, the rapid pace of innovation in the personal computer industry meant that product advantages were often short-lived as they were quickly emulated or overtaken by competitors. In addition, shortening product lifecycles meant that investments in inventory carried a large risk of obsolescence. As a result, Compaq Computer developed a strategy to improve response time not only to increase predictability but also to give its customers superior service.

Over three years, Compaq improved its delivery lead times from 21 to 6 days and its predictability from 50 to 85 per cent. Its sales channel satisfaction surveys reflected these improvements and Compaq reached the No. 1 position in customer satisfaction. End-consumer satisfaction surveys, however, did not show the same levels of improvement. The reasons lay in the behaviour that was taking place further down the sales channel.

Compaq's customers had taken advantage of its increased reliability and performance to cut down their own stocks. In addition, Compaq's sales reward system was based on monthly or quarterly quota and channel buyers were used to the month or quarter-end last-minute promotions. Channel buyers were holding back their orders waiting for these rebates and were willing to run out of stock to gain additional discounts.

Compaq could only attain the benefits of supply chain compression when it went beyond its company boundaries and pursued improvements across all the players and processes in the supply chain.

Take advantage of technologies

Many organizations taking a holistic perspective of their supply chains are discovering that new and converging technologies offer unheard-of opportunities to compress—and even eliminate some aspects of—their supply chain. By only using the Internet to sell book titles, Amazon.com has quickly generated quarterly sales of $28 million in less than two years of operation, but does not have a warehouse to call its own. A conventional bookstore is limited to around 150 000 titles with stock having to be deployed to all of its sales locations. Internet book sites do not restrict their customers' choice of titles, offer easy search tools to locate books quickly and allow a much smaller investment in centralized stock holding. It is not surprising that Internet book sales are growing at the rate of 50 per cent a year and major book retailers in both the US and the UK are having to respond with their own Web sites.

US software supplier Software.net not only allows all of its 22 000 lines to be ordered over the Internet but makes 2200 of them 'downloadable'. Customers can instantly obtain the products they have ordered without the need for a costly physical supply chain.

Cut out unnecessary steps

A revealing exercise is to measure the actual process time in supplying a product order as a proportion of the total order lead time—quite often the process time is a very small fraction of the overall time. Organizations reengineering their supply chains need to look aggressively at all opportunities to remove wastage and non-value-adding processes. Often progress is slowed by the number of pairs of hands that order information goes through before it gets to the people who will act on it. This can be exacerbated if those intermediate 'pairs of hands' do not work the same hours as the physical operations do. Optimum responsiveness requires the relentless pursuit of all delays in the end-to-end process. Many of the reasons for these extraneous processes reflect traditional divisions between functional areas, and the accompanying mistrust and lack of empowerment. Organizational realignment into 'cells' is a powerful way to get over these issues.

Source with service in mind as well as cost

Sourcing decisions were once primarily based on driving down input costs. But while concentrating all your sourcing in one organization located on the other side of world may give you access to very low prices, purchase order lead times might extend out to three to four months and supply intervals might be governed by intercontinental transport economics.

Sourcing decisions should, in fact, be viewed to achieve overall service improvement requirements. A leading UK clothing retailer achieved the efficiency/effective mix by sourcing the bulk of its textile requirements from Asia, but used top-up suppliers in the UK to respond quickly to specific sales requirements.

Some suppliers co-locate on their customers' premises, as in the case of a can supplier in the UK that supplies its products to its customer through a 'hole in the wall'.

A second important factor in effective sourcing is developing the right relationship with the supplier. Many Japanese companies invested heavily in first-tier suppliers in order to guarantee security of supply and to facilitate close collaboration on some of the early design stages. In other cases, the buyer and supplier have simply worked hard on developing relationships of trust and mutual reliance, with suppliers trusted to perform vital tasks such as quality assurance and self-invoicing. While risky at first, organizations soon realized that the comfort they got out of 'double checking' was far outweighed by the cost and the delay it caused. Working together across seamless boundaries is a prerequisite for time compression.

Design products with the supply chain in mind

Many of the current supply chain issues and complexities stem directly from product design. Products are not often designed with responsive supply chain management objectives in mind. In fact, products can often readily be designed in a modular fashion that can be quickly customized to the end product. This allows the modules to be made in bulk very efficiently but also ensures the flexibility to configure rapidly to a customer order requirement.

In addition, this enables the two operations to be decoupled and separated. The bulk items can be produced centrally for maximum efficiency and the customized items assembled just-in-time in a location close to the final customers to ensure maximum service effectiveness.

Process innovation can transform the traditional cost and service trade-offs. A consumer goods manufacturer developed the technology to produce colourless, flavourless products and inject the necessary flavour and colour just before they were packaged. This process breakthrough was the cornerstone of restructuring operations to meet challenging cost and service improvements simultaneously.

Reduce forecast time and increase accuracy

A key factor in effective time compression is both reducing forecast time and increasing forecast accuracy, preferably through use of actual rather than predicted demand. Traditionally organizations have suffered losses through operating on long and therefore increasingly inaccurate time horizons using the 'make-to-forecast' approach. Alternative approaches are outlined in Figure 10.1, where products are either partially or completely made when a customer order is received.

Businesses have stuck with the 'make-to-forecast' model despite its obvious flaws simply because alternative methods appeared to be too costly. In fact, many businesses have what they consider to be excessive stock holding in their supply chains but still experience significant service failures. It never seems to be the right stock. The forecast, more often than not, is singled out as the culprit leading to the double whammy of lost sales and possible expensive inventory write-downs and write-offs.

Despite its importance, forecast accuracy is only now starting to receive the attention it needed. Many organizations have found that by doing the simple things right they can dramatically improve the level of accuracy.

Experiences differ by industry, but best-in-class companies struggle to improve their overall forecast accuracy above 80 to 85 per cent over their planning horizons. At first glance this does not seem too bad, but grossly overstates the accuracy level for the slow-moving products. These products experience much larger volatility with actual demand either a fraction of the forecast or two to three times the size. This is often reflected in the high proportion of total inventory represented by slow-moving items. For example, 70 per cent of total inventory of a

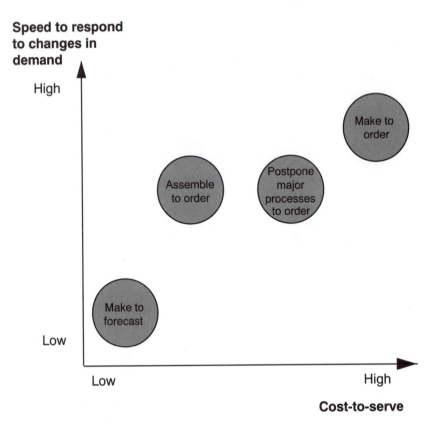

Figure 10.1 Alternative manufacturing approaches

supermarket chain was represented by lines that sold less than one case per store per day. It is the forecast accuracy of these lines that will determine supply chain performance and ultimately competitiveness.

Another factor often overlooked is the reduction of forecast accuracy over time. This varies from product to product and industry to industry, but can exhibit an alarming fall-off in accuracy within the planning horizon that cannot be accommodated by safety stock policies. It is not uncommon for organizations to undertake significant commitments to inventory, capacity and other resources in the supply chain based on forecasts beyond their legitimate planning horizons.

A real example is shown in Figure 10.2 of how the beer sales of a retailer varied over two months against an original forecast set in the first week. The first month showed sales 19 per cent above the original forecast, but in the second month the forecast accuracy had deteriorated threefold as sales raced to an alarming 57 per cent above forecast.

The beer manufacturer produces on a four-weekly cycle, setting their firm production plans one week before the start of the cycle. In this

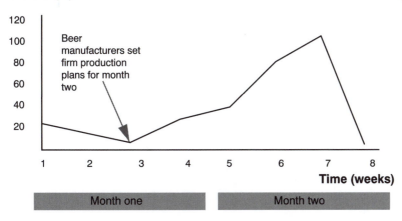

Sales above forecast (%)

Beer manufacturers set firm production plans for month two

Time (weeks)

Month one

Month two

Figure 10.2   Actual sales versus forecast sales

example it would have set the firm production plans for month two in week three. At that point it would have noticed its weekly dispatches to the retailer running about 15 per cent ahead of forecast and would have increased its production plans accordingly. It typically carries about three weeks' supply of safety stock in the supply chain to buffer against continuing strong sales.

However the stock levels, already reduced in month one, would not survive the battering they would take in month two, resulting in retailer stockouts in week seven and manufacturer stockouts in week eight. Both retailer and manufacturer would enter month three in a perilous position with further stockouts likely.

The irony is that the manufacturer could have produced more beer if it had known in time. Therefore it is likely that both retailer and manufacturer would increase safety stock levels.

In order to cut back the forecasting time horizons and dramatically increase accuracy, organizations can actually delay the requirement for some demand information until key stages of the process have been reached. This can provide a greater level of responsiveness even where further shortening of the overall process is not feasible.

Figure 10.3 demonstrates that many stages of the supply chain can proceed without the final end destination and quantity information being available until eight hours before the product goes on sale. Typically the total product requirement and requirement by the regional distribution centre are a great deal easier to forecast than the final store and product combination. Applying this approach can allow the less volatile decisions to be driven by forecast, based on older information. The latest information or even actual orders would

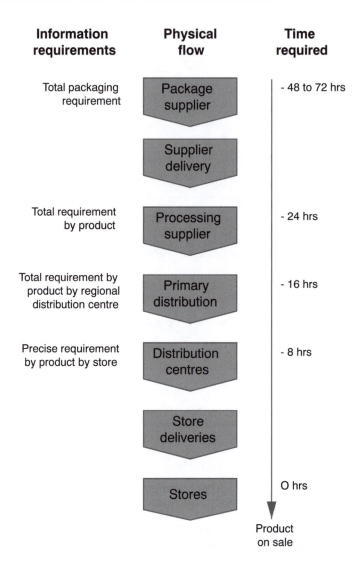

Information requirements	Physical flow	Time required
Total packaging requirement	Package supplier	- 48 to 72 hrs
	Supplier delivery	
Total requirement by product	Processing supplier	- 24 hrs
Total requirement by product by regional distribution centre	Primary distribution	- 16 hrs
Precise requirement by product by store	Distribution centres	- 8 hrs
	Store deliveries	
	Stores	O hrs
		Product on sale

Figure 10.3   Information deadlines in a consumer product supply chain

then drive the most volatile decisions.

To exploit these opportunities may require the current processes to be restructured but all of this will be in vain if the information systems cannot supply the necessary information at the right time. If, in the above example, the systems were only updated once a day, then the advantage gained would be lost. Therefore it is necessary to have responsive systems that can supply the latest information to the point of need in a timely fashion. This does not imply that systems have to work in real time but only in shorter update periods than the individual process steps.

The benefits of shorter and more accurate forecasting cycles are beginning to emerge. Recently a leading UK supermarket retailer announced that its capacity issues caused by its strong growth would not be solved by investing in another new £40 million warehouse. Instead it decided to invest in three new stores. With better forecasting, smaller production batches and more emphasis on customer service, the retailer was able to move away from costly, non-value-added warehousing and instead concentrate on continuing to improve its customer service.

Redesign production processes

Shortening response time often places onerous requirements on production. Long production runs were traditionally deemed necessary because changeover processes were complex, time consuming and wasteful.

However, production processes can also be reengineered, difficult subassemblies can be ordered and built to forecast information, and can be quickly assembled into one of many customized end configurations when the final order arrives. Therefore the actual response time is just the assembly and delivery time. This 'postponement' approach (see Chapter 5) is becoming the norm in the PC industry where unique computer configuration can be quickly assembled from a range of pre-assembled subassemblies, such as hard disk drives.

Where a process cannot be broken into intermediate stages and insufficient capacity occurs to make the total requirement inside the response time, an alternative approach can be taken. By using historical information on the level of order fluctuation by product, a confidence level can be established about what you can safely make in advance and leave making the 'top-up' amount to after the order has arrived.

It is important that the production processes and resources can make the top-up products in the sequence required. This may well be driven by distribution that requires all products for a specific customer to depart at a certain time. This may in fact require the manufacture of a same product with different end destinations to be made in many different batches during the course of the day.

This would normally challenge the conventional minimum run lengths driven by economic batch quantity (EBQ) calculations. But these calculations are based on current changeover time and cost, therefore the challenge is to reduce the changeover time so that the EBQ is 1.

Rethink distribution options

In the past, delivery frequencies were driven by transport economics. Product was shipped only when there was enough to fill the lorry or even the boat. Being responsive, however, requires that shipping corresponds, not with distribution economies but with customer needs. This can have large cost implications for smaller suppliers supplying slow-selling lines, unless significant rethinking takes place. The distribution cost per unit would soar if old methods were employed to meet new frequencies.

A simple answer is join together with a larger supplier of the same customer if the locations are convenient. Where this is not available, another option is to form a consortium with other smaller suppliers, use a nominated carrier and share the costs. Third-party service providers are increasingly able to provide a shared service with those inside and outside your industry and therefore provide the necessary economies of scale. Finally, many supermarket chains are developing flourishing primary distribution service offerings, collecting suppliers' product from the factory gate in return for being charged just the 'factory gate' price.

In this fashion, two competing supermarket chains have given their smallest suppliers the opportunity to deliver the daily requirements in a cost-effective manner. By recognizing that there was insufficient volume in either chain to make this possible, they appointed an agent to select and group common suppliers and share a delivery consolidation service to produce a competitive unit cost. This is an example of the market-level logistics concepts that are starting to appear. These alliances are born out of a common need and the mature recognition that cutting distribution costs would no longer be the basis of competition in the future.

Conclusion

None of these measures is easy. However, it is no exaggeration to say that customers will no longer tolerate failure and those organizations that fail to take up the challenge of time compression of the supply chain will lose their customers to those that do. With the continuing introduction of new technologies and an increasing willingness by organizations, not just along the supply chain but also competing for the same customers, to cooperate to simplify supply chain operations, organizations are confronted not just with a great opportunity—but with a compelling strategic imperative.

Safeway Stores: fresher food in the grocery supply chain

CASE STUDY

In the early 1990s an intense price war was waged in the grocery retailing industry in the UK, caused by recession and the entrance of low-cost discount operators. The market leaders' response to sliding margins was to improve the overall value proposition to the consumer in terms of service, quality and convenience. To achieve this, the market leaders needed to switch their focus from cost efficiency to supply chain effectiveness.

Safeway Stores plc, the third largest grocery retailer in the UK, recognized that the key to rebuilding lost profitability was to increase the yield in its existing store base, rather than relying on adding more stores to its portfolio. Safeway found that the majority of its customers did not do their main weekly shop at Safeway but preferred just to 'top-up' shop there instead. One of the key reasons was that the fresh food offered was weak in comparison with Safeway's main rivals. The food was not as fresh as it could be and the availability was not always reliable. With fresh food representing about one-third of sales and with some of the best margins, this was an issue Safeway could not ignore.

Safeway set a target of getting the fresh product from the farm or factory production line to the store shelf in under 24 hours, less than half the current response time. This would maximize the product freshness to the end consumer, but more importantly would enable crucial replenishment decisions to be taken with very recent sales information. Much can change in one day in a supermarket and late decisions would give a closer match between supply and demand, allowing improved availability without the penalty of higher wastage.

Safeway recognized that the success or failure of this initiative rested with its fresh food suppliers being able to respond quickly. However, the suppliers' ability to respond was limited by Safeway's internal practices that had enabled it to achieve the lowest logistics cost status in the industry. Therefore Safeway had to make the first move, reengineering its replenishment and warehousing methods together with completely changing the transportation schedules. The implication was that logistics costs would rise to secure the broader supply chain goals.

Despite Safeway's making these changes, the supplier requirements were still quite onerous:

- Any product could be ordered with 24 hours' notice.
- Specified product was to be made freshly on the day of delivery to Safeway.
- A daily delivery was made into each of Safeway's regional distribution centres.
- Products were to be delivered within a specified one-hour time slot.
- No on-cost was to be passed on.

Safeway realized that the suppliers would not succeed if they did not change their methods, particularly in transportation. Being one of the bigger fleet operators, Safeway was able to offer a range of transport options such as backhauling and consolidation to allow suppliers to meet the increased frequency of delivery cost effectively. In addition, Safeway buyers recognized that suppliers' locations and flexibility were now key influences on the sourcing decision, and not just price.

The new methods were not easy for any of the parties. Improving response time meant reducing the 'safety' time available to resolve the inherent day-to-day problems. As a result problems that could previously be lived with now needed to be solved. The emphasis on performance intensified and necessitated the introduction of standards not just between Safeway and suppliers but also within Safeway's internal functions. Line managers found that they needed to get much closer to their daily operations and try to anticipate problems.

The outcome was successful, providing the end consumers with fresher food and greater availability. In addition, methods were adapted to limit and even eliminate the rising cost pressures that this approach had initially implied.

The pay-off for all involved was expected to be long-term growth through strengthening Safeway's market offering. However, before the change programme finished, the initial stores were noticing a pick-up in sales, suppliers were noticing a reduction in day-to-day order volatility and Safeway had realized that it could put back planned capacity investments. Safeway now wish to apply this fresh food supply chain model to the remainder of its business.

The venture was successful because every party in the supply chain was prepared to make difficult changes (those they would not otherwise have made) to provide a more effective offer to the end customer.

Towards finding the perfect match

Matching supply with demand in supply chains

Ananth Raman

A firm's capacity to match supply and demand is a function of its reactive capacity (i.e. its ability to respond to market signals)—which is influenced by its labour and working capital costs and the incentives that drive it to stock more inventory. Firms have struggled to match supply with demand by focusing usually on improving forecasting, optimizing production and inventory plans and cutting lead times. But while these measures are useful, they don't offer a holistic solution. Firms need also to consider measures to address the costs of labour and working capital, and they need to find ways to align incentives both internally and across the supply chain.

Introduction

Retailers and manufacturers in many product categories have struggled to put together a match between supply and demand. Fashion house Liz Claiborne's 'unexpected earning decline is the consequence of "higher-than-anticipated excess inventories"', reported the *Wall Street Journal* on 15 July 1993. The same month, the Land's End Quarterly Report acknowledged 'a higher percentage of lost sales (orders received for merchandise not in stock and not back ordered)' for the second quarter of 1993. And consider department store markdowns, which climbed from a mere 8 per cent of sales in 1972 to 26 per cent of sales in 1990. This is the world of supply-demand mismatch—and it carries an enormous cost to firms.

A mismatch between supply and demand is not just a problem for clothing manufacturers and retailers. Toys 'R' Us, according to *Business Week* (7 April 1997), 'couldn't get enough stock of the popular [Nintendo] video games and turned away 100 000 disappointed customers "despite lobbying trips to Japan"'. Salomon Brothers Inc. noted in its *Investors Report* for 13 June 1996 that consumer electronics giant Best Buy's 'in-stock percentage has never been much above 75%, despite numerous efforts to improve it'. And the *Wall Street Journal* reported on

2 May 1994 that IBM 'continues to struggle with shortages in the ThinkPad line'.

Supply demand mismatch costs

The costs of a mismatch between supply and demand, measured as the combination of inventory carrying costs, markdown costs and stockout costs, are growing in many industries. Companies have tried to reduce these costs through better demand forecasting, improved production/inventory planning, increased production capacity and reduced set-up and transportation lead times. Companies have also tried to manage the demand process through pricing policies intended to smooth the arrival pattern of customers. These approaches, while useful, have failed to address a number of drivers of supply–demand mismatch.

A firm's ability to match supply with demand is a function of its capacity to react to market signals—its reactive capacity. Reactive capacity is affected by a firm's inventory and capacity levels—and these reflect its labour and working capital costs and the incentives that drive it to stock more inventory of its input materials. Supply-demand mismatch costs, therefore, are affected by the firm's labour costs, working capital costs and incentives for stocking inventory.

These factors—labour costs, capital costs and incentives to stock inventory—often differ from one firm to another, inducing firms within the supply chain to target different capacity and inventory levels. This goal incongruity with regard to inventory and capacity levels needs to be taken into account when trying to formulate solutions to the supply–demand mismatch problem in a supply chain. Even when each decision maker makes rational decisions that maximize his or her own profits, high factor costs and mismatched incentives can exacerbate supply–demand mismatch costs.

Impact of supply–demand mismatch

The benefits of reducing supply–demand mismatch are enormous. Earnings before interest and taxes (EBIT) at department stores in the USA average between 6 and 11 per cent of sales—meaning that even a slight reduction in markdowns (which average 26 per cent of sales) can significantly increase profits. Less mismatch between supply and demand can also lead to better customer service and therefore additional sales.

Supply- as well as demand-side changes can drive supply–demand mismatch costs. Increasing product variety has been cited by Fisher *et al.* (1994) and Pashigian (1988), among others, as one possible explanation for growing demand uncertainty which, in turn, could explain growth in inventory, markdowns and stockouts. Other authors, Hammond (1990) among them, have argued that recourse to cheaper production sources in countries such as China and India has lengthened some supply chains (that of apparel retailing in the USA, for example). The long lead times required to import from these countries dictates early production commitments based on poor forecasts, which leads to supply–demand mismatches.

Traditional approaches to mitigating supply–demand mismatches

Past attempts to address the supply–demand mismatch problem have focused on improving forecasting, optimizing production and inventory plans and reducing lead times.

Improving forecasting

Advances in information technology (e.g. point-of-sale, data warehousing, electronic data interchange) have increased the efficiency with which companies can capture and analyse historical sales data. Some companies are able to combine sales routinely captured by point-of-sale scanners with 'loyalty programmes' (such as airline frequent-flyer programmes) to understand demand by customer segment, or even by customer. Specialized software enables retailers to identify patterns in these data and make predictions based on them.

According to some managers, however, despite considerable progress in developing new demand-forecasting techniques, there is limited potential for these techniques to be implemented effectively. The short lifecycles of individual products in categories such as fashion apparel, toys and music limits the extent to which historical demand can be collected. To use historical data to predict demand for a new product in these categories, managers need to find products sold in previous years that are 'similar' to the new product, on the basis that demand for the 'similar' product would help predict demand for the new product. Given that identifying 'similarity' requires expert judgement, these companies need to combine such judgement with historical data analysis. Interestingly, few companies seem capable of blending analysis and institutional knowledge in this way.

Inaccurate recording of sales data also impedes the implementation of data-based forecasting at many companies. Through improper scanning at the checkout, sales data stored in the computer often does not reflect true demand at many retailers. In supermarkets, clerks frequently choose to scan a particular SKU more than once instead of single items of several SKUs with identical prices (for example, a sale consisting of a can of Coke and a can of Diet Coke might be scanned as a sale of two cans of Coke if the two products are priced the same). Clark *et al.* (1994) point out that even scanned items in a supermarket have only 95 per cent data accuracy and accuracy is much lower for items such as fresh produce that are not electronically scanned. This induces a mismatch between the demand data stored in the computer and real consumer demand, which makes it difficult to use historical data for demand forecasting.

Improving production and inventory planning

Companies can mitigate supply–demand mismatch costs by planning production and inventory commitments appropriately. Many companies have identified better ways to analyse the trade-offs involved in, and therefore to optimize, production and inventory plans. Early examples of such trade-off analysis include the economic order quantity (EOQ) model and the Newsboy model. The adoption of these and other more complicated procedures for identifying reorder points and quantities as a way to optimize inventory levels in the face of uncertain demand has been facilitated by the simultaneous development of large-scale computer systems. Large materials requirement planning (MRP) systems, for example, often have modules with the EOQ and Newsboy logic embedded in them. Savings realized from the application of improved production and inventory-planning techniques have been documented for example in case studies by Fisher and Raman (1996), who showed that stockout and markdown costs could be reduced by over 50 per cent through better production planning, thus leading to a 60 per cent increase in annual profits at a skiwear manufacturer.

A pitfall of most of these planning approaches, however, is that they are 'static', ignoring the possibility of future operational improvements. Consider, for example, the classic EOQ model that calculates optimal order quantity based on the trade-off between ordering (or set-up) cost and inventory carrying cost. In deriving the optimal order quantity, the model assumes that the ordering (set-up) costs are fixed exogenously and cannot be altered by management practices. This assumption is unrealistic over the long term. Companies such as Toyota have shown that set-up times can be reduced and conformance quality levels can be improved significantly over time. Cusamano (1989) noted that Toyota reduced the time needed to change stamping dies from two to three hours in 1955 to three minutes by 1971, even while major US automobile manufacturers reported two- to three-hour set-up times as recently as 1989. Moreover, in adopting techniques such as JIT, these companies have also shown that the pace of set-up time reduction is usually higher with lower factory inventory. The failure of these models to factor in the links between inventory levels and operational improvement reduces their relevance in many applications.

Reducing lead times

Companies looking to cut lead times can adopt a number of measures, including reducing set-up times, increasing conformance quality levels and reducing the frequency of machine breakdowns, thus reducing the inventory level required to achieve a target fill rate.

Many companies that face unpredictable demand have found that they can decrease lead times by reducing their dependence on forecasts that tend to be unpredictable and thereby improving their responsiveness to demand. The Quick Response movement in the US textile and apparel industry emphasized the importance of reducing manufacturing and transportation lead times and batch size, and using information technology (e.g. point-of-sale and electronic data interchange) to speed information transfer. Hammond (1990) estimated that annual stockout, markdown and inventory carrying costs in the US textile and apparel industry could be reduced by 5 per cent of sales (a reduction of approximately $12.5 billion) by reducing lead times in the supply chain. Similarly, in an independent study, Raff and Salmon (1997) estimated that lead time reduction could reduce financing costs and markdowns in US department stores by approximately 2 per cent of sales.

Towards a holistic approach

But while all the measures above offer firms some improved ability to reduce the mismatch between supply and demand, they don't address the problem in an integrated way. Firms can benefit from an integrative framework to understand the drivers of their reactive capacity and therefore explore the ways in which labour costs, capital costs and mismatched incentives affect a supply chain's target reactive capacity level. They can then target these areas to improve the match between supply and demand.

Fisher *et al.* (1997) have developed an integrative framework that identifies various mechanisms that can increase a firm's reactive capacity. To understand the framework developed in that paper, consider the model shown in Figure 11.1.

Take a situation where two production commitments are made to enable delivery of an order before the time of product delivery. The first production commitment, for speculative production, is made early based

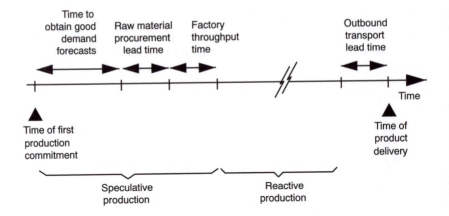

Figure 11.1   Identifying a firm's reactive production capacity

on the poor forecasts of demand available at the time. A second production commitment, reactive production, is then made once good demand forecasts are obtained. In many situations, forecasts exhibit dramatic improvement soon after additional demand information is obtained, for example through a trade show or after a meeting with important customers.

Figure 11.1 shows the lead time for procuring raw materials needed to start reactive production, the factory throughput time, and the lead time for outbound transport of finished goods. This information can be used to calculate a firm's 'reactive production capacity'—the maximum volume of production that can be committed after good demand forecasts have been obtained, as shown in the equation below.

Reactive production capacity

= Daily production capacity

   x (Time of product delivery

       – Time to obtain good forecasts

       – Raw material procurement lead time

       – Factory throughput time

       – Outbound transport lead time)

Equation 11.1

Knowing the reactive production capacity allows a firm to estimate the amount of speculative production to commit—the total demand forecast less the reactive production capacity. Clearly it is beneficial for

Figure 11.2 **Factors that exacerbate supply–demand mismatch costs**

a firm to increase its reactive production capacity so that a greater proportion of its total production is made after good forecasts are obtained, minimizing the amount of speculative production which is committed on poor demand information.

Understandably, this model is a simplification of what we observe in practice. However, it clearly demonstrates that a company may increase its ability to respond to market signals by reducing lead times in manufacturing, transportation, and materials procurement or by augmenting daily production capacity.

Figure 11.2 summarizes the drivers of supply–demand mismatch identified in this chapter. Consequently, to match supply and demand better, firms must consider not only production and inventory planning and operational improvements, but also differences in the cost of labour and in capital costs across firms, and incentives (for both firms and individuals) in a supply chain.

Labour costs

The ability to respond to market signals depends on production capacity. Higher production capacity enables a firm to delay a greater fraction of its total production commitment until more reliable demand forecasts can be obtained. Because demand forecasts in most industries become more accurate as the delivery date is approached, later production commitments are usually associated with lower stockout and obsolescence costs. Sport Obermeyer, for example, found that understocking and overstocking costs could be reduced from 10 to 2 per cent of sales, by increasing reactive production capacity from 0 to 100 per cent of projected season demand.

As we have seen, reactive production capacity can be augmented by increasing daily production capacity, K_r. Because increasing K_r usually involves hiring more workers, the cost of capacity expansion, especially in labour-intensive industries such as apparel, is determined partly by the cost of labour. The lower a firm's labour costs, the less the impediment to investing in capacity expansion to achieve higher reactive production capacity.

It follows that outsourcing production to low-wage suppliers can mitigate supply–demand mismatch costs. Labour costs can vary significantly across firms and countries. Wage rates in China and India, for example, tend to be much lower than those in developed countries such as the USA and labour costs for large firms with unionized workforces tend to be greater than those for smaller firms in the same region (by as much as three times in some instances). Firms need to recognize that low wage rates procured through outsourcing can not only reduce the cost of manufacturing, but also, by making it cheaper to invest in additional capacity, reduce supply–demand mismatch costs.

Working capital costs

Long lead times to procure raw materials can also impede a company's ability to respond to market signals. In Figure 11.1, longer material procurement lead time reduces the amount of time available for reactive production. Moreover, material procurement lead times can often be significant in many industries. At Sport Obermeyer, for example, lead times to source zips and fabric can account for as many as 90 of the 180 days that typically elapse between order placement and receipt of finished goods. Companies can reduce lead time (and thereby improve their response to market signals) by stocking raw material so they can commence production soon after market signals are observed. Sport Obermeyer, for example, could have another 90 days for reactive production if it did not have to wait for raw materials to arrive from its supplier.

Because demand for raw material can be forecast more accurately than demand for products, holding raw material is often less risky than holding finished goods. To forecast demand for raw material, a company needs only to estimate aggregate demand for all the products that share it to derive a demand forecast. Consider, for example, the difficulty of predicting demand for a specific size of a particular garment relative to that of predicting demand for all sizes of the garment put together.

That high working capital costs discourage firms from holding raw material inventory is manifest in the case below. Working capital financing costs are 3 per cent a month for Indian apparel exporters, which leads them to avoid carrying fabric inventory in anticipation of customer orders. Their decision to make fabric orders contingent on receipt of importers' orders accompanied by letters of credit occasions delays that drive importers to place orders earlier (when forecasts are poor) and, consequently, to incur higher supply–demand mismatch costs.

Apparel exports and the Indian economy

Many importers complain about the lead time to source apparel from India. Indian apparel exports account for $4 billion per year and the textile industry (which has similar problems) accounts for another $6 billion per year. The Indian apparel export supply chain is extremely fragmented (both apparel exporters and textile firms that supply apparel exporters tend to be small), partly because of diseconomies of scale in labour cost (larger firms tend to attract outside unions and also are governed by more stringent labour laws) and partly because of an explicit government-imposed barrier to consolidation that limits an apparel firm to fewer than 75 sewing machines. The motivation for this law lies partly in Gandhian notions of social equity and partly in the political power of small manufacturers.

Limiting the size of firms, however, makes banks and other financial institutions extremely averse to lending money to the supply chain, there being generally a higher risk and higher transaction cost associated with lending to smaller companies. High working capital costs lead to high raw material inventory holding costs, so Indian apparel exporters hold very little fabric inventory in anticipation of orders. Instead, procurement of raw materials begins only after a firm customer order and an accompanying letter of credit are obtained. This practice translates into extremely long lead times for this supply chain.

Misaligned incentives

Plans to increase reactive capacity have often not been implemented in many supply chains because of misaligned incentives along the supply chain. In many apparel supply chains, for example, retailers choose among different suppliers based on unit price with very little attention to lead time and responsiveness. Understandably, suppliers in this scenario have little incentive to make the necessary investments (such as in bigger factories or in more raw material) to improve reactive capacity. In recent years, some retailers have moved away from these practices by either rewarding more responsive suppliers or forcing suppliers to bear a portion of their markdown costs.

To understand the relationship between incentives, inventory levels and the fill rates in a channel, consider the following example. Willingness to carry inventory is a function of what is to be gained by doing so. Relevant gains are captured in operations research models through an opportunity cost such as stockout cost (the opportunity, or profit, lost from being out of stock of the particular item). Stockout costs, like labour and working capital costs, can vary significantly across the firms in a supply chain. For example, Wal-Mart stocks substitutable diapers (Pampers and Huggies) from different manufacturers (Procter & Gamble (P&G) and Kimberly-Clark, respectively). When a Wal-Mart store at a particular location is out of stock of Pampers and a fraction of the store's customers who prefer Pampers switch to Huggies, P&G has lost sales and incurred a stockout cost. However, because Wal-Mart has still made sales to the customer, it has a lower stockout cost, which leads it to target lower fill rates (carry fewer Pampers) than would P&G were it making the retail inventory decision. As a consequence, P&G stands to lose demand to the extent that customers who prefer Pampers experience more frequent stockouts. To understand and redress the problem, P&G must be aware of the differences between its stockout costs and Wal-Mart's stockout costs (see Figure 11.3).

Managers who fail to acknowledge the relationship between incentives and channel inventory levels can incur significant spoilage costs. Consider the case of a manufacturer of perishable foods that delivered products to supermarkets and convenience stores. Company drivers decided what to stock on shelves that were dedicated by the retailer to the manufacturer. In certain sales regions, the drivers received a commission equal to a certain fraction of sales from the stores on their route, but were not penalized for stale inventory. Consequently, the drivers in these regions were inclined to load the shelves fully, even when competing brands were being offered at sharp discounts, with the result that

Figure 11.3 Differing stockout costs

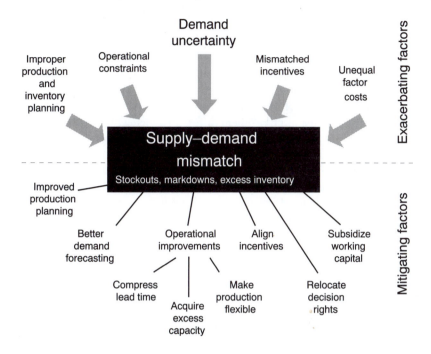

Figure 11.4   Exacerbating factors and mitigating actions

'stales' in these regions were substantially higher than those in other regions where incentives were structured differently.

Some supply chains have reduced supply–demand mismatch costs by identifying ways to reduce labour and working capital costs and align incentives. And intermediaries can play a useful role as mitigators of problems caused by high factor costs and mismatched incentives (see Figure 11.4).

Getting around the problem

Development of an effective solution to the supply–demand mismatch problem must begin with identification of its root cause. Sport Obermeyer, for example, having identified planning as the root cause of its supply–demand mismatch, explored new planning approaches (Fisher and Raman, 1996). Among the better-known operations-planning applications is American Airlines' yield-management system, which continually adjusts the number of seats available in each 'price bucket' to optimize the airline's profits; the airline realized savings of approximately $500 million a year from adopting the system.

An understanding of the impact of labour cost, inventory holding cost and mismatched incentives on supply–demand and mismatch costs is particularly important in the case of supply chains given the inherent variability of these costs across the firms in the supply chain. Because they often have very different stockout, labour and inventory holding costs, individual supply chain partners are likely to approach the supply–demand mismatch problem differently. Hence, firms need to identify ways to overcome their cost and incentive differences.

If mismatched objectives are the root cause of supply–demand mismatch, restructuring of incentives and contracts warrants consideration. The fresh foods company described in the previous section, for example, started penalizing its drivers for stales incurred on their route. This, understandably, altered drivers' stocking decisions and reduced the company's stale levels.

Altering commissions, strengthening brands and vendor-managed inventory (where the manufacturer takes over the decision of how much to stock at the retail store) are posited by Narayanan and Raman (1996) as possible solutions when mismatched incentives are responsible for supply–demand mismatch. Consider the circumstances of Wal-Mart and P&G described above. P&G could induce Wal-Mart to increase its Pampers inventory by offering the retailer higher commissions and thereby increasing its stockout cost. P&G could also increase Wal-Mart's stockout cost by making end customers more loyal to its products through, for example, investments in advertising. To the extent that customers who experienced a stockout of Pampers are less willing to switch to an alternative manufacturer's product at the same store, and perhaps even take their business to another retailer, Wal-Mart's stockout cost would be driven up, possibly even higher than P&G's if customers were willing to move all their purchases to another retail location. Finally, P&G could overcome the difficulty of mismatched objectives by making the stocking decision for Wal-Mart. Such vendor-managed inventory programmes have become popular in many industries.

If high inventory holding cost is at the root of supply–demand mismatch, ways might be found to make it cheaper to carry inventory. As noted earlier, larger firms frequently have lower working capital costs, which translate into lower inventory-holding costs. So it is common, and often advisable, for large companies to own the inventory at their small suppliers. In the US garment industry, for example, retailers often own all the fabric inventory held by the suppliers that cut and sew their garments. Similarly, General Motors owns most of the work-in-process inventory at some of its suppliers; and Bajaj Auto Ltd, a large Indian automotive manufacturer, purchases the raw materials needed for seat production and forwards them to the supplier as needed for production. In each of these cases, the supply–demand mismatch has been partially redressed by a large firm holding inventory on behalf of a small firm.

The likely alternative would be less supplier inventory and lower fill rates than the large firm would desire.

The role of intermediaries

Intermediaries can make it easier for a supply chain to match supply with demand. The classic analysis suggests that, because of scale economies in material and information flow, the distributor is better suited to matching supply with demand. This view emphasizes distributor functions such as breaking bulk, one-stop shopping and holding safety stock. But this view of intermediaries is limited and understates the capacity of intermediaries to facilitate the matching of supply with demand.

Electronics distributors are a particularly interesting example of supply-chain intermediaries, because they counter the notion that distributors are *passé* and do not have a future in the economy. In fact, electronics distributors' sales as a whole have grown by 20 per cent a year in the USA over the last few years and a few distributors' sales now exceed $5 billion per year. The immediate future, moreover, appears to promise greater growth as many high-tech firms revert to their core competencies of product development and manufacturing (Texas Instruments and Intel, for example, plan to leave many non-core functions to electronics distributors).

The case of two intermediaries in electronics distribution provides an illustration of the role of intermediaries. One intermediary, AESCO, an Akron, Ohio-based distributor headed by Bill Feth Jr, provides the classic distributor functions. But it also provides, as needed, cheap financing, cheap labour and trustworthy relationships, which help AESCO's customers better match supply with demand.

To understand AESCO's role as a supplier of cheap capital, consider a start-up OEM with an untested product idea and scarce working capital from the bank. Because most start-ups, owing to insufficient historical data, must deal with unpredictable demand, they require safety stock of various electronic components to be able to maintain high service levels to customers. The high cost of financing discourages them from carrying sufficient safety stock. AESCO will hold inventory on behalf of the OEMs, charging them a premium for the service. If the OEM is located near AESCO, AESCO's inventory can serve as the OEM's safety stock. A variation on this theme is the 'in-plant store', space at the customers' plants that is stocked with inventory owned by electronics distributors. The material in these in-plant stores is owned by the distributor (even though it is physically present at the customer's plant); the customer pays for the product only as it is withdrawn. The arrangement is efficient because AESCO's capital cost is lower than the OEM's.

Traditionally, the argument for a distributor carrying safety stock has been based on 'pooling' (that is, the distributor carries safety stock intended for more than one OEM and thereby diversifies its risk). This argument holds even if none of the distributor's other customers require a safety-stock component.

More interesting is AESCO's role as a supplier of cheap labour which may be understood in light of the wire requirements of OEMs, for example wire that must be cut to desired lengths or have its ends finished in a particular manner. Owing to the large number of ways in which wire can be cut and finished, demand for specific cuts and finishes is difficult to predict. Hence, OEMs are well advised to carry stock of uncut, unfinished wire and have reactive capacity to cut and finish it as surges in demand warrant.

The cutting and finishing of wire is a low-skilled, labour-intensive task for which OEMs' often inflexible, unionized labour is less than ideally suited. Their reluctance to hire labour at as much as $30 per hour, without assurance that it will be utilized, results in OEMs lacking 'slack labour' to chase sudden surges in demand. With AESCO supplying cheap, flexible labour, OEMs that experience such surges can accept the orders, rather than be forced to turn some away or to carry excess inventory of cut and finished wire to accommodate the demand.

Raymond Tse, Sport Obermeyer's buying agent in Hong Kong, plays the role of intermediary to perfection. Like many other supply chain intermediaries in Hong Kong, Tse arranges working capital financing in Hong Kong where transaction costs for such trades are much lower than in China. Without a Hong Kong-based intermediary, apparel manufacturing in China would have faced working capital shortages and probably incurred some of the problems related in the Apparel exports and the Indian economy case. Not surprisingly, the Hong Kong Chamber of Commerce, describing the growth in manufacturing activity in China, notes: 'The nimble fingers are on their side of the border, the brains are on our side.'

Intermediaries can often facilitate the matching of supply with demand in the face of markets (which are default coordination mechanisms) that perform poorly. Firms such as General Motors, Ann Taylor, Bajaj Auto and Benetton all have found ways to compensate for market failure. Italian garment manufacturer Benetton, for example, also acts as a supply chain intermediary since it arranges financing and manages inventory centrally (to take advantage of its cheaper capital), while leveraging smaller subcontractors' cheaper and more flexible labour. Thus, it effectively combines cheap labour and cheap working capital, which together facilitate the matching of supply with demand.

Intermediaries like Tse and AESCO enable supply chains to combine cheap labour with cheap capital; often a difficult task in their absence. For small firms, and firms in developing countries, cheap labour is often available at short notice, but the cost of working capital tends to be high. Most firms have either cheap labour or cheap capital, rarely both. In the Sport Obermeyer supply chain, for example, the Chinese factories have cheap labour but do not have cheap capital. By holding raw material inventory for these factories using cheap working capital in Hong Kong, Tse enables the supply chain to operate with cheap Chinese labour and cheap Hong Kong capital. Thus, by judiciously combining the complementary strengths of different firms, intermediaries can often secure both cheap labour and cheap working capital for a supply chain, both of which reduce supply–demand mismatch costs.

Fashion manufacturer-cum-retailer Benetton's role in the Italian apparel supply chain is similar to Raymond Tse's role in skiwear supply. Benetton was successful in reducing manufacturing costs and achieved higher inventory turns (that is, comparable to its competitors) even though it offered its customers very high product variety. Benetton's success could be traced partly to process innovations (the company developed a process to dye sweaters after they had been knitted) and partly to what has been termed 'external decentralization' (using a network of subcontractors). It utilized an extensive network of about 220 subcontractors for around 40 per cent of its knitting production capacity and around 60 per cent of its garment assembly capacity. These small units provided Benetton with cheap labour (wages and benefits at these units were much lower than in company-owned factories) and, because they could work extra hours and hire and fire workers more easily, absorbed much of the fluctuations in demand. Access to such cheap and flexible labour to perform these labour-intensive tasks was clearly a source of considerable advantage.

Even though the company relied on an extensive network of contractors, operations that had scale economies were managed centrally. Technical research, product design, production planning and raw material purchasing were all managed centrally. Also, some key production steps, such as cutting and finishing, that significantly affected the quality of the finished product, were largely conducted in company-owned factories. Thus, by acting as an intermediary, Benetton enabled the apparel supply chain to combine the benefits of scale economies in activities like purchasing and product development, with the benefits of inexpensive and flexible labour that result from fragmentation in manufacturing.

What does it take to be an intermediary? Effective intermediaries possess a portfolio of different capabilities. This is evident in each of the above examples. AESCO needs to be able to handle materials, but also to hire and fire low-cost labour easily and readily access credit. Tse needs to possess credibility with financial institutions and be able to manage skiwear manufacturing, to be able to generate working capital financing, communicate with various suppliers and, most importantly, be personally credible with Sport Obermeyer and local government officials in China. Indeed, personal credibility with other players in the supply chain is a critical attribute across all of the intermediaries we have studied.

Each of the skills in these intermediaries' repertoires is critical to their success. Tse's effectiveness, for example, would be seriously compromised if he were unable to enforce informal contracts in China or raise working capital or if he lacked trusting relationships with key people at Sport Obermeyer. There are many players in Hong Kong who possess some of Tse's capabilities, but probably only a few firms or individuals that encompass his entire skill portfolio. This is what makes him difficult to replace; it is the barrier to entry in his business and, hence, his sustainable competitive advantage.

Conclusion

Companies that have launched programmes simultaneously to decrease inventory and increase fill rates have often found their efforts stymied because they failed to account for differences in incentives and labour and capital costs, among the constituent firms in the supply chain. There may never be a 'perfect' match but, by focusing on these critical factors, firms can make significant progress towards achieving a match between supply and demand and thereby eliminating supply–demand mismatch costs.

References

A Tale of Two Electronic Component Distributors, Harvard Business School case study 9-697-064, Cambridge, MA.

Apparel Exports and Indian Economy, Harvard Business School case study 9-696-065, Cambridge, MA.

Benetton (A), Harvard Business School case study 9-685-014, Cambridge, MA.

Clark, T.H, Croson, D.C., McKenney, J.L. and Nolan, R. (1994) *H.E. Butt Grocery Company: A Leader in ECR Implementation*, Harvard Business School case study 9-195-125, Cambridge, MA.

Cohen, M., Agrawal, N., Agrawal, V. and Raman, A. (1995) 'Analysis of distribution strategies in the industrial paper and plastics industry', *Operations Research*, 43 (1), Jan/Feb, 6–18.

Cusamano, M.A. (1989) *The Japanese Automobile Industry: Technology and Management at Nissan and Toyota*, Council on East Asian Studies, Harvard University, Harvard University Press, Cambridge, MA/London.

Fisher, Marshall and Raman, Ananth (1996) 'Reducing the cost of demand uncertainty through accurate response to early sales', *Operations Research*, 44 (1), Jan–Feb, 87–99.

Fisher, M., Hammond, J.H., Obermeyer, W.R. and Raman, A. (1994) 'Making supply meet demand in an uncertain world', *Harvard Business Review*, May/June.

Fisher, M., Hammond, J.H., Obermeyer, W.R. and Raman, A. (1997) 'Configuring a supply chain to reduce the cost of demand uncertainty', *Journal for Production and Operations Management Society*, special issue on supply chain coordination and integration.

Hammond, J.H. (1990) *Quick Response in the Apparel Industry*, Harvard Business School note N9-690-038, Cambridge, MA.

Little, Ian, Mazumdar, Dipak and Page, John M. Jr (1987) *Small Manufacturing Enterprises: a Comparative Analysis of India and Other Economies*, a World Bank Research Publication, Oxford University Press.

Narayanan, V. G. and Raman, A. (1996) *Contacting for Inventory in a Distribution Channel with Stochastic Demand and Substitute Products*, Harvard Business School working paper, Cambridge, MA.

Pashigian, B.P. (1988) 'Demand uncertainty and sales: a study of fashion and markdown pricing', *American Economic Review*, 78, 936–53.

Raff, Daniel M.G. and Salmon, W.J. (1997) 'Economies of speed and retailing: the history, pathology and future of department stores', Harvard Business School working paper, Cambridge, MA.

Smith, Barry C., Leimkuhler, J.F. and Darrow, R.M. (1992) 'Yield management at American Airlines', *Interfaces*, 22 (1), Jan/Feb, 8–31.

Acknowledgement

Thank you to Professor Roy Shapiro for help in structuring the ideas presented in this chapter and also in developing specific figures. Thanks also to Professors Marshall Fisher, Janice Hammond, Robert Hayes, Ramachandran Jaikumar and Krishna Palepu for feedback on earlier drafts.

12

The personal computer supply chain
Unlocking hidden value
Terry Austin

The personal computer (PC) industry provides a unique and compelling case for creating value through supply chain integration. The industry's dramatic history of outstanding growth, its sheer pace and the magnitude of change and the increasingly complex and global supply chains have created large challenges for participants. Traditional channel structures and behaviours in industry supply chains have not kept pace with the changes. Three strategies are proposed to improve supply chain performance: compression of the supply chain, collaboration between supply chain partners, and designing products for market responsiveness.

Introduction

Unlike industries such as food service, consumer packaged goods, automobiles and apparel, the PC industry has not yet matured to high levels of integration in its supply chain. Inefficiencies have emerged that are now preventing potential growth. Supply chain inefficiencies have led to chronically delayed new products, demand distortions, scarcity and allocation problems, inventory obsolescence risks and unpredictable service levels.

With such a turbulent pace of change, participants in the industry are under increasing pressure to identify and exploit new value sources. Relationships among many supply chain participants, illustrated in Figure 12.1, are currently insufficient to provide solutions. Instead of seeking greater cooperation and interactivity, these four groups are displaying a degree of gamesmanship towards each other, serving to undermine rather than improve the supply chain's efficiency.

To assess ways to improve the integration of the industry's supply chain, Andersen Consulting initiated a study of the industry in conjunction with Stanford University and Northwestern University in the USA. The research team undertook a mail survey of more than 200 companies, site visits to leading companies and secondary research on supply chain performance and financial analysis—providing a comprehensive

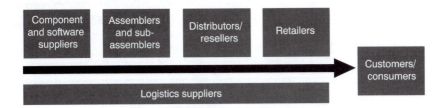

Figure 12.1   PC industry supply chain

picture of each segment of the industry. The goal was to understand how companies were integrating supply chains, to identify opportunities for improving performance and value creation, and to define critical factors for successful implementation.

The research provides a unique insight into how the supply chain can be approached on an industry-wide basis. Relationships between the participants were studied and initiatives developed for integrating the supply chain. Key features of the PC industry's supply chain, as revealed in the research and from Andersen Consulting's industry experience, are discussed in detail below.

Dynamic supply chain features of the PC industry

Changing product and profit dynamics

The pressures and tensions among PC supply chain participants stem from several sources, most of them by-products of rapid growth, which surged with the introduction of higher-density transistors in the early 1980s. The industry grew dramatically from $2.7 billion in 1981 to $150 billion in 1996, with compound annual growth levels of 13.7 per cent, which are expected to continue through to the year 2000 (Dataquest statistics).

The explosive growth has been fuelled by advances in technology; however, these same advances have wreaked havoc on product and profit dynamics. For example, technology breakthroughs have drastically shortened the lifecycles of microprocessors, components and desktop units from an average of seven years in the 1980s to a forecast four years by the year 2000, as shown in Figure 12.2.

Moreover, consumers are increasingly demanding products with unique configurations, which has resulted in proliferating product offerings. For instance, the number of models tripled from about 400 in 1990 to more than 1400 by 1995. And yet all this costly differentiation has

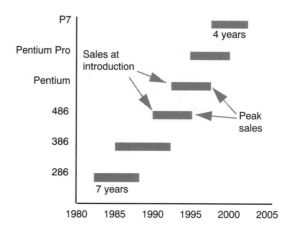

Figure 12.2   Microprocessor half-lives, 1982–2000

not stopped sweeping commoditization, as competitors have become increasingly able to emulate one another in ever shorter time frames. The result of these trends has been a rapid decline in average selling prices and margins, with the profit margins for the top assemblers such as Compaq, Apple, Acer and Dell falling by about a half between 1990 and 1995.

Supply and demand misalignment

With companies seeking to capture and maintain market share in a world of price cutting and falling margins, there is little room for error in getting products to market. If the product is not available to customers, particularly during the crucial days of introduction and ramp-up, when margins are at a premium, the impact on market share can be devastating. Figure 12.3 depicts the strong correlation between market share and product availability.

As shortages steadily increase, market share flattens as early as three months out, and then begins to decline precipitously only one month later. Despite this tremendous pressure on availability, adequate supply, particularly of the hottest new products, has typically been difficult to achieve in the PC industry. In fact, chronic shortages of hit products have plagued many industry participants. The graph in Figure 12.4 depicts the typical supply and demand misalignments that occur throughout a PC's product lifecycle.

As shown, demand is typically highest at, or shortly after, launch time when supplies are most precarious. During this period of scarcity, distributors and resellers often over-order as a way of hedging against con-

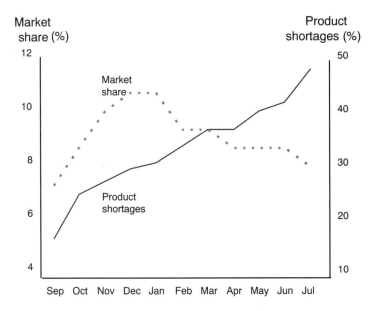

**Figure 12.3   Market share declines when product
shortages exist: Compaq**

tinuing shortages, creating 'phantom demand'. As planning systems typically use previous-period demand to forecast the future, the phantom
demand gets factored into forecasts, often triggering over-production. In
the meantime, true demand tends to taper off when competing products
come on the market.

Evolving supply chain structure

The PC industry's changing supply chain structure has itself created further challenges for supply chain value enrichment. Until the mid-1980s,
leading PC companies performed the majority of activities in the chain.
In the second half of the 1980s, however, the industry had evolved to a
networked structure, where many independent companies joined forces
to bring a product to market.

Today, many key supply chain activities in the PC industry have
evolved into myriad industries of their own. The industry's supply chain
was further altered as some components, such as microprocessors and
disk drives, became concentrated among fewer suppliers, both geographically and commercially. Conversely, sources for other types of
components began to proliferate rapidly at sites scattered all over the
world.

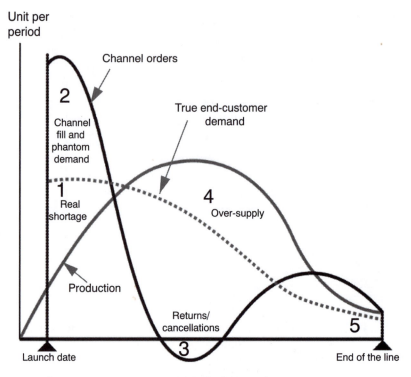

1   Production cannot meet initial projected demand, resulting in real shortages

2   Channel partners over-order in an attempt to meet demand and stock their shelves

3   As supply catches up with demand, orders are cancelled or returned

4   Financial and production planning are not aligned with real demand; therefore production continues

5   As demand declines, all parties attempt to drain inventory to prevent writedown

Figure 12.4   Supply–demand misalignment

Industry view of integration

Through the research work and the team's direct experience in the PC industry, it was apparent that the industry as a whole did not view itself as being highly integrated. The survey results reveal the level of integration with upstream suppliers and downstream customers, as shown in Figure 12.5. The highest score, 2.29, which represents significantly less

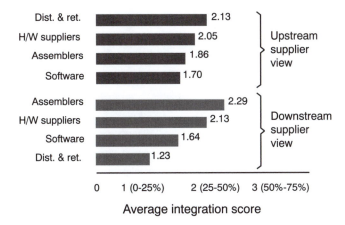

Figure 12.5   Segment integration level: all processes

than 50 per cent, is for integration between PC assemblers and downstream customers.

Ironically, these relatively low scores belie the extensive attention and activity related to improving supply chain integration, which is actually occurring in the industry. The flurry of current and planned activities appears to indicate considerable interest among industry participants. As depicted in Figure 12.6, substantial integration activity, both current and planned, has been reported among software developers, hardware suppliers, assemblers and distributors/retailers.

Despite all this movement, there appears to be considerable confusion among participants about the best ways to integrate. In many cases, significant value is being overlooked or simply not being captured. Many supply chain participants are still focused mainly on products and markets, neglecting aggressive management of the supply chain itself as a strategic source of value. Some are ignoring the chain's structure and dynamics as a source of added value. And others are limiting their integration efforts to quick, tactical solutions, rather than launching more far-reaching strategic initiatives. In some instances, implementation efforts have not been successful, mainly because relationships are not yet developed enough to support them.

Although the PC industry is experimenting with supply chain integration in many positive ways, some of it has backfired in terms of alienating the very participants whose cooperation was sought. The site visits revealed a wide spectrum of cooperation among supply chain partners. Some companies have done particularly well in achieving harmony. In other cases, however, there is discord among partners that have 'burned out' on trying various integration concepts that have been ill conceived and/or poorly executed.

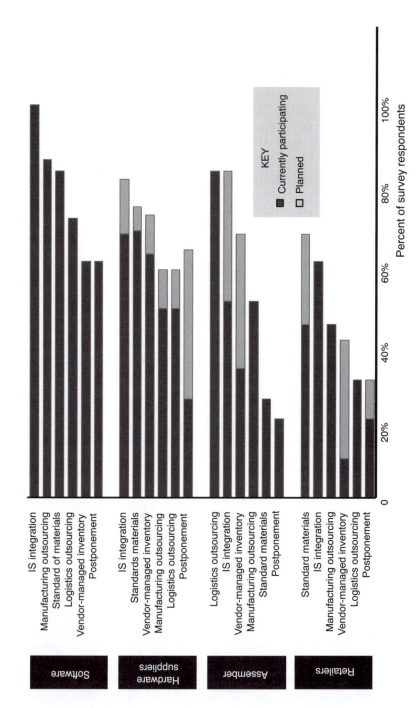

Figure 12.6 Integration initiative participation: industry segment

Strategies for integration

Analysis of the research reveals that there are substantial opportunities for supply chain integration in the PC industry; these vary in their suitability for different participants and the benefits they offer. Companies should vigorously pursue those integration opportunities that hold the greatest value potential for their own unique supply chain situations.

In order properly to assess the value of integration activities, the research team developed an economic model using performance indicators, such as inventory turns and gross margins, as well as economic value measurements. The value was driven by four levers: revenues, operating margins, the amount of capital employed and the cost of capital employed. Benchmarks were also established for improving inventory and margin performance, enabling the calculation of the difference between baseline performance and potential performance as a result of particular integration initiatives. The value-creation model and the benchmarks show that the three recommended initiatives, listed below, can create substantial value for supply chain participants, as summarized in Figure 12.7.

The three recommended strategies are for companies to:

■ pursue compression strategy;
■ implement collaborative planning with supply chain partners; and
■ design products for maximum market responsiveness.

These are outlined in detail below.

Pursue compression strategy

Supply chain compression is a strategy that focuses on the overall structure of a supply chain as a critical source of hidden value to the participants who form its various links. A great part of that dormant value is tied up in finished goods inventory. The more complex a chain's structure, the more likely it is that stock, at various stages of completion, is languishing on the shelves of several, if not all, participants. In addition, the more finished goods inventory there is dispersed throughout the chain, the more difficult and costly it is for the chain, as a unit, to switch gears when consumer demand shifts. Customer needs go unsatisfied, while obsolete goods accumulate.

For the PC industry, the problems caused by supply chain complexity are most evident in the commercial channel, where there can be as many as four or five different entities that hold various stages of finished goods inventories under their roofs: PC assemblers, retailers, distributors, resellers and value-added resellers.

		Software	Semicon	Storage	Assemblers	Distributors	Retailers
Compressed supply chain	Inventory	—	—	—	10-70%	10-100%	—
	Margin	—	—	—	0.7-4.7%	0.5-4.9%	—
	Value	—	—	—	$70-470m	$10-102m	—
Collaborative planning	Inventory	10-25%	10-25%	10-25%	10-25%	10-25%	10-25%
	Margin	0.6-1.5%	0.6-1.4%	0.3-0.7%	0.7-1.8%	0.5-1.2%	0.7-1.6%
	Value	$2-$4m	$9-23m	$4-9m	$70-181m	$10-26m	$26-64m
Design for responsiveness	Inventory	—	—	—	—	—	—
	Margin	7.5%	5.3%	2.0%	2.2%	—	—
	Value	$21m	$69m	$18m	$145m	—	—

Figure 12.7 Benefits summary

Inventory → Percentage reduction in inventory assets
Margin ←← Percent margin increase due to reduced obsolescence (1% margin for every 10 days in inventory)
Value ← Economic value increase from asset reduction and margin increase

The numbers achieved by supply chain compression are impressive. To calculate the impact on value, the research team measured inventory reduction and then factored in the margin improvement made possible through reduced obsolescence—1 per cent for every 10 days of inventory. The research indicates that compressed supply chain structures can deliver inventory reductions ranging from 10 to 65 per cent for assemblers and 10 to 100 per cent for distributors, depending on the level of compression achieved. Applying the value-creation model, this translates into value increases of from $72 million to $471 million for the baseline ($10 billion) assembler and $10 million to $102 million for the representative ($2.4 billion) distributor.

The research confirms that there are many more compression opportunities suitable for PC companies than those most prevalent today. Although there may be any number of variations, the research identified four basic options for supply chain compression that are available to commercial PC market participants. Each option can deliver progressively greater value, yet each is also progressively more challenging to undertake: intra-company postponement, inter-company postponement, the sales agent model and the direct model.

Intra-company postponement

This type of compression is probably the most manageable to achieve, since it occurs within a single company's operations. In this model, final product configuration is delayed, shifting those activities from manufacturing locations to distribution facilities. By doing this, a company can minimize its stock of finished goods and always have a ready supply of semi-configured product that can be customized just-in-time, according to shifts in demand. The research indicates that intra-company postponement can reduce the total inventory investment required by a PC assembler from 10 to 30 per cent.

Inter-company postponement

As with the intra-company model, this form of postponement has PC assemblers ship semi-configured product to distributors who add components, such as disk drives and memory, only when orders are received. The main difference is that final configuration is shifted from manufacturing to an outside distributor, such as a distributor, reseller or retailer. This one difference makes this strategy significantly more challenging, but it eliminates even more finished goods inventories. Under the value-creation model, both assemblers and distributors achieve 10 to 30 per cent inventory reductions.

Sales agent model

The PC industry has yet to embrace a true 'sales agent' model, although this strategy can enhance supply chain value even more than postponement. This supply chain design further compresses activities by drastically changing the roles of its partners. Instead of holding inventory or managing order fulfilment, distributors become sales agents, focusing on sales, service, training and network configuration. The chain's assemblers ship orders directly to customers. This eliminates virtually all inventory at distributor sites without increasing it at other locations. The sales agent model can deliver an increase in inventory turns of 10 to 60 per cent for assemblers and distributors, enhancing a representative chain's total economic value from $80 million to $500 million.

Direct model

The direct model creates the most compressed PC supply chain of all the models described here by eliminating all of the supply chain intermediaries between the assembler and the end customer. Within it, assemblers handle all sales and customer service functions in addition to final configuration and order fulfilment. Distributors and retailers disappear. This model eliminates all channel inventory and provides the clearest demand signal to the assembler.

Compared to a traditional supply chain structure, the direct model can reduce inventory investment by 50 to 70 per cent, increasing the value of a representative PC supply chain by $290 million to $470 million.

Implement collaborative planning

A critically under-utilized key to lean inventories and increased market agility is the degree to which supply chain partners collaborate in planning and executing the combination of tasks that bring a product from raw materials to market. The PC industry has barely scratched the surface in exploiting the available opportunities and technologies for this type of integration. Further, these opportunities and technologies are accessible to virtually any company and the risks are relatively low.

Rapid technological change, ever shorter product lifecycles and increased supply chain complexity in the PC industry have all compounded the challenge of matching supply to demand. Close collaboration among supply chain partners can better align them and thus enhance the value of the network's combined activities.

Value is increased through a number of levers. One of the most important, as it is with compression, is improved inventory performance. Study results suggest that collaborative planning can lead to chain-wide inventory reductions ranging from 10 to 50 per cent. As illustrated in Figure 12.8, a representative PC supply chain can translate these reductions into value increases of $135 million to $330 million. These rewards are shared by all participating partners, from manufacturers and assemblers to distributors and dealers.

Annual inventory turns

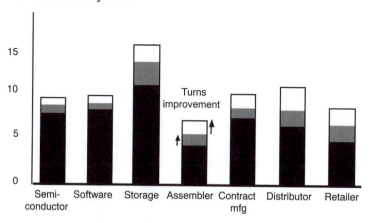

• Turns improve across the board by 12% to 33%

EVA™ as percent of revenues

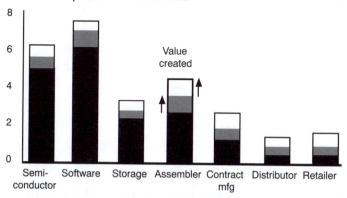

• EVA™ as percent of revenue improves across the board
• Total value grows by $135m to $330m
    — $35m to $90m from capital efficiencies
    — $100m to $240m from enhanced margins

Figure 12.8   Collaborative planning value-creation model

Collaborative planning and execution activities send a more accurate demand signal throughout the supply chain, serving to minimize waste and maximize responsiveness. The key activities are collaborative demand planning; synchronized order fulfilment; and joint capacity planning. Each activity requires progressively greater interactivity.

Collaborative demand planning

The goal of collaborative demand planning is to generate a truer demand signal for all the partners in the supply chain. This is accomplished by sharing customer and operational data among all partners and may also include joint decision making in forecasting demand. This continuous information loop eliminates, or substantially lessens, the type of incremental distortion that occurs when each participant puts their own spin on demand and supply information. The result is that everyone's understanding of demand remains unified, clear and more true to reality.

Synchronized order fulfilment

Synchronized order fulfilment goes further. It is characterized by negotiated or joint decisions, such as order size and frequency and by the transfer of management, and possibly ownership, of inventory from the supplier to the supplier's customer. So there is less incremental distortion of demand. The greater the synchronization, the greater the value added to the entire supply chain's performance. The most highly synchronized order fulfilment approaches let customer demand numbers directly drive orders, instead of basing orders on forecasts. While this form of total synchronization can do more to improve supply chain performance, it makes participants more dependent on one another and thus increases their risk.

Joint capacity planning

Currently there is little coordination among supply chain firms on jointly planning medium- to long-term materials and capacities. This lack of collaboration can lead to significant misalignment of capacity and demand over time. In addition to individual partners lacking vital information, supply chains that fail to do this will have difficulty gearing up or cutting back capacity when fluctuations in customer demand are large and long-lasting. Long-term, joint capacity planning is a critical source of further supply chain value and should thus be explored by all PC industry participants.

Use of collaboration-support technology

So much of collaborative planning and execution depends on timely exchange of quality information among supply chain partners. Hence, information technology plays a vital role in supporting such efforts. There are a variety of highly advanced tools available, which are specifically tailored to these applications. The challenge is for management teams to build their technology arsenals to support collaboration, not the other way around. Collaboration among partners is the real solution, while the technology is one important enabler among a number of others.

Some of the key technologies used are electronic data interchange (EDI), enterprise resource planning, decision-support systems and electronic commerce, or e-commerce. EDI, for instance, is used to transmit a range of data electronically between supply chain partners, including purchase orders, inventory, point of sale, demand forecasts and advanced shipment notices. But it is not a magic bullet when it comes to collaboration. EDI's power to enhance depends on how information is used, not just its availability. Without properly leveraging the information that EDI makes available, supply chain partners can only expect to benefit from reduced administrative costs through automation.

Design products for responsiveness

Designing for responsiveness seeks to maximize supply chain performance at the design stage of a product. It takes into account all the implications of a particular design, from raw material procurement to delivery at the end customer's site. The designer seeks to achieve the best possible balance between innovation and product performance on the one hand, and optimal supply chain efficiency and agility on the other. The result is building into every product release both maximum value for all supply chain participants and the best possible run for a new product.

PC assemblers who design for responsiveness can achieve impressive returns. As shown in Figure 12.9, design for responsiveness can reduce inventory and improve gross margins by 4 to 8 per cent, which together increase the value of a representative supply chain by $125 million to $255 million. Once again, the higher the level of integration and the greater the resulting supply chain efficiencies, the higher the rewards.

The highest-potential value-enhancement activities are supply chain structural analysis; design for postponement and product variety; and use of standard, off-the-shelf and inter-generational components.

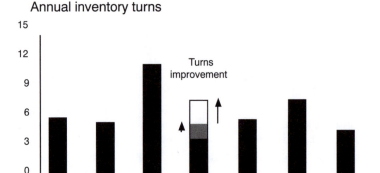

Annual inventory turns

- Margins improve 4% to 8.5%

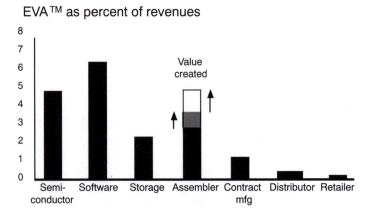

EVA™ as percent of revenues

- EVA™ as percent of revenue improves for suppliers and assemblers
- Total value grows by $125m to $255m
  - $125m to $255m from enhanced margins
  - No capital efficiencies assumed

Figure 12.9 Design for responsiveness value-creation model

Supply chain structural analysis

A fully realized design-for-responsiveness effort recognizes that product development is where the business case for a new product is made, and that it makes sense to evaluate fully, at that early stage, just how the supply chain will perform for the new product. As the development team makes decisions about suppliers, components and design details, it should be considering the optimal structure for the supply chain to support each new product design.

Design for postponement and product variety

In designing for postponement and product variety, the design team aims to minimize the negative impact of variety on time to availability and supply chain efficiency. This is accomplished by using modular designs and changing the order and timing of assembly. Postponement is a particularly important leg of a sound product-variety strategy. It calls for carrying modular, generic components to an optimal point in the supply chain, usually further downstream, where differentiating options will be added. By adding the desired variety features at that optimal point, demand can be pooled for the different product options, and final configured inventories kept to a minimum.

Use of standard, off-the-shelf and inter-generational parts

Another way to streamline the supply chain is by using interchangeable parts. The research found that many companies have programmes that encourage product designers to use standard and/or off-the-shelf parts whenever possible. Suppliers are also providing incentives to PC assemblers to standardize parts. However, programmes that encourage the use of inter-generational parts and the use of inter-generational suppliers are less common, and therefore appear to be an important source of untapped value potential for many companies. Every PC company should explore all three approaches.

Making it happen

As indicated earlier in this chapter, supply chain compression, collaborative planning and execution and design for responsiveness can present sizable implementation challenges to many companies. Which initiatives should be attempted? Which firms will make good partners? What are the risks? Since there is no one instant formula, the answers to these questions will vary for every company. To make an informed decision, supply chain integration can be considered from three key perspectives: rewards versus risks, reshaping relationships and execution as strategy.

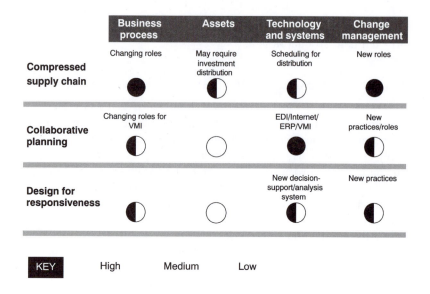

Figure 12.10   Summary of costs and risk

Rewards versus risks

In considering supply chain integration, a full and realistic assessment of potential value and the potential risks should be undertaken. The comparative risks and costs associated with the three initiatives discussed in this chapter are shown in Figure 12.10. As discussed earlier, integration can create value in several ways. All three initiatives can reduce inventory assets, which has a further positive net impact in that it also reduces inventory risk, obsolescence costs and time to availability, which increases margins. But the complete value picture also has to include the positive signal that bottom-line improvements send to stakeholders.

In addition to an assessment of value, management teams must also assess the risks of supply chain integration for their own companies and their supply chain partners. The flurry of implementation activity observed in the PC industry, which has not produced sufficient results, is due, in part, to insufficient risk assessments. Many companies, for example, have not considered the full cost and risk implications for their business processes, assets, technologies and systems, as well as change management.

Reshaping relationships

Most of the risks discussed above are relatively straightforward to assess. However, supply chain integration requires relationship building. In fact, all of the integration initiatives require some reshaping of supply chain relationships, ranging from transactional, to interactive, to interdependent. Transactional relationships do not require much shared information or decision making. Hence this should not be difficult to implement. A more interactive relationship, however, requires shared information, some joint planning and some shared decision making. This requires deeper cooperation, the willingness and capability to learn new skills and some degree of mutual trust. In the case of the interdependent relationship, the trust factor is most important, as the boundaries between companies become blurred information is shared extensively, as are decisions, investments and assets. The goodwill, candour and skill required in such relationships cannot be over-emphasized.

As the above range of variables indicates, whether a company chooses to integrate its supply chain, and how it chooses to do so, must take relationship building heavily into account. A large number of partnership experiences over time have shown that it takes a superlative fit to make even the best integration ideas deliver. Not every supply chain partner will be equally suited to the demands of integration. Companies must therefore select their integration partners carefully.

What are their capabilities? How flexible are they? Can they be trusted? Can they share your vision of the benefits and risks? These are the kinds of questions that must be answered before considering implementation of any but the most transactional relationships.

Execution as strategy

As the rate of change in the PC industry continues to accelerate and the availability of competitive information keeps expanding, the lead times for strategy formulation, design, absorption and implementation are shrinking, or disappearing. The firms that implement first will be the most likely to gain the advantage and realize the value they seek. Companies that want to integrate, or integrate further, their supply chains should consider the following guidelines:

- regularly implement strategies faster and more effectively than competition;
- define and utilize critical capabilities to their fullest, while not overreaching themselves;
- effectively launch and manage experiments; and
- learn, adapt and build from repeated successes.

As these guidelines indicate, learning through implementation has the potential to deliver incrementally higher value than deferring all implementation until a 'perfect' strategy can be forged. With due consideration of rewards, risks and relationships, the most important thing is to make the best possible choice for now and get started as soon as possible.

Conclusion

The traditional supply chain approach of the PC industry is failing to keep pace with the industry's dramatic rate of change. Products are being delayed, demand distorted and inventory obsolescence is a real risk. By adopting integration strategies, the PC industry has the potential to create substantial value in its supply chain. Companies need to consider compressing the supply chain's structure, they need to plan and execute activities with supply chain partners, and participants must also look at integrating supply chain considerations into product design.

Substantial value can be derived from each of the strategies, demonstrating the benefits of unravelling the complexities of the supply chain in a dynamic, new industry.

 # Value-creation model

The value-creation model was formed by integrating Stern, Stewart & Co.'s published value measure known as Economic Value Added™, or EVA™, into a larger model that was specifically designed to illustrate the impact of supply chain integration initiatives on value creation. The model, shown in Figure 12.11, works by identifying a specific supply chain integration initiative, quantifying the impact on profits and or capital and the impact this will have on value.

In addition, the research was used to develop a representative financial model for the PC industry (Figure 12.12). These baseline 'companies' are not actual entities, but model companies created using typical financial performance shown by true industry segment participants. The financial model constitutes the baseline supply chain employed in the study and yielded the value numbers outlined in more detail below.

Analysis indicated that the three recommended initiatives derived from the research, as outlined below, can create substantial value for supply chain participants. As shown earlier in Figure 12.7, financial analysis of the best integrators in the PC industry has yielded reasonable ranges of benchmarks for improving inventory and margin performance.

These benchmarks were used to calculate the difference between the value delivered to supply chain participants by baseline performance and the value that would be added over and above that by successfully executing the three main initiatives listed above. The value listed represents the gap, or value-creation opportunity possible, through implementing each of the initiatives. The results indicate that substantial value is not being realized.

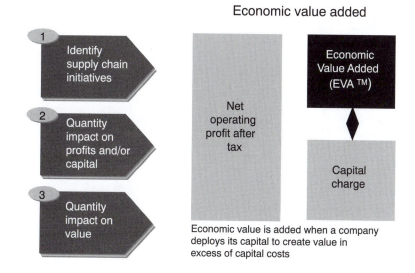

Figure 12.11   Value-creation model

Representative company financial results	Semicon	Software	Storage	Assembler	Contract manufacturing	Distributor	Retailer
Sales (billions)	$2.1	$.5	$1.5	$10.9	$1.5	$2.4	$5.1
Margins	64%	90%	23%	27%	13%	9%	14%
Capital (billions)	$2.3	$0.5	$0.7	$4.8	$0.4	$0.6	$0.7
EVA™ (millions)	$115	$30	$40	$290	$20	$10	$20

Figure 12.12 Representative financial results for typical PC supply chain

Part II
Strategic Response

Overview

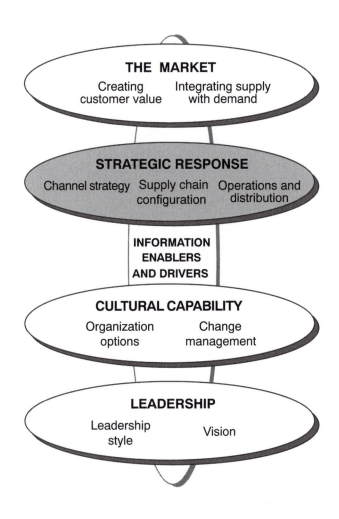

THE MARKET

Creating   Integrating supply
customer value   with demand

STRATEGIC RESPONSE

Channel strategy Supply chain Operations and
configuration   distribution

**INFORMATION
ENABLERS
AND DRIVERS**

CULTURAL CAPABILITY

Organization   Change
options   management

LEADERSHIP

Leadership   Vision
style

Traditional thinking about the optimum supply chain concentrated on consistency of performance and cost effectiveness. Supply chain management was inwardly focused, bound by company walls and an operational bias.

In this part, we argue that supply chain management is a strategic issue. It requires imagination, outward thinking and a capacity to build and sustain a web of relationships within the company and beyond it, indeed across an entire industry. Cost efficiencies remain important, but the real test of performance is effectiveness of value delivery to customers.

Supply chain management now requires a capacity to think through the relationships, resources and requirements to ensure the supply chain adapts itself to a customer-focused era. It requires a capacity to identify and plot the various possible physical pathways to get products and services to customers. And it requires a capacity for skilled and innovative planning and management, right down to the sorts of facilities which should be provided and who owns which part of the chain.

Chapters 13 to 16 challenge companies to rethink the very principles of their channel strategy—taking into account relationships and opportunities across the entire supply chain; the advent of direct channels to consumers via the Internet; and understanding the dimensions of alternative channels. Chapters 17 to 20 highlight the latest thinking and the leading tools to help companies configure the supply chain, in particular the need for a more relationship-driven approach. And Chapters 21 to 25 examine in detail the key operational components of the supply chain—manufacturing, facilities, transport and inventory management and new ways to resolve traditional challenges in these functions.

13 Strategic value networks
Redefining channel management
Randy Barba, Philip Roussel and Bruce Bendix

New and converging technologies, channel role redefinition and the
trend towards value-added services are reshaping the environment for
channel management. While some companies are adding new channels,
the more innovative players are entering into fresh arrangements with
channel participants, aiming to broaden their customer base, reduce
costs and deepen their customer relationships. But the challenges are
enormous. Top management leadership will be required to ensure that
the network is coherently designed, traditional channel roles are redefined, governance procedures are established, the information technology (IT) infrastructure is sound and appropriate measurement and
reward systems are put in place.

Introduction

E-commerce. Disintermediation. Coopetition. Many manufacturers
have heard about these concepts and recognize that all offer significant
opportunities to gain more value from sales and distribution channels.
What is less clear is the specific trends that underlie these opportunities
and, most important, their magnitude and the challenges to seizing
them. Some companies, however, are already trying to capture these
opportunities. Consider the following:

- Hewlett-Packard is testing a quasi-franchise channel concept called
  the HP Office Center; it requires retailers to pay a fee to join a third-
  party franchise called NetFire. Franchisees concentrate on delivering
  training, after-sales support and marketing, while HP focuses on manufacturing and logistics.
- Toyota is considering a direct electronic channel where customers
  would submit car specifications, as well as financing preferences, via
  the Internet, or a 1-800 telephone or facsimile number. The service
  would search the supply chain and dealers' inventories, and respond
  within 24 hours with the closest matches and estimated delivery time.

- Autodesk gives its resellers electronic access to its enterprise information systems. This enables dealers to place and track orders via the Internet, eliminating a call to a sales representative.
- Andersen Corporation's 'Window of Knowledge' point-of-sale kiosks allow selected dealers to design windows for consumers, get order quotes and place orders online. This system allows customers to visualize and configure their windows and links the Andersen retailers and distributors to an integrated supply chain.

All of these companies are transforming their once monolithic channel into a multichannel network. Although some are simply adding new channels, the more innovative companies are entering into different kinds of arrangements with channel participants. These arrangements have the channel participants—and the manufacturer—form a network in which members take responsibility for only those parts of the customer transaction that they do best and most cost efficiently, and rely on other network members' expertise to complete the transaction. By restructuring their channels in this way, these companies are attempting to capture several opportunities. The most important are an expanded customer base through the creation of new channels, additional opportunities to support the company's brand through multiple transaction points, and enhanced relationships with current customers by providing more responsive channels from which to buy products and services. Additional benefits include capturing cost efficiencies in the physical supply chain.

If these opportunities are substantial (as are new customers and deeper customer loyalty), why are companies slow to act on them? The answer lies in the difficulty of the process. Although the opportunities are significant, the challenges to capturing them are equally so. These include aligning current channel participants in a new structure based on cooperative relationships; identifying and using the demonstrated strengths of each channel participant; and investing the time and money to develop both the skills and the technology needed by the channel participants.

Top management must adopt a strategic approach and lead the migration to the channel network vision. The magnitude of the opportunities at stake, and their potential to affect a whole organization and to change industry structure, require top management understanding and leadership. Given that chief executive officers and boards of directors usually view 'channel management' as a functional or operational issue, this is no small challenge. Yet successful companies have treated the huge opportunities available and the difficulty of effective channel management as precisely the reasons that it must be raised to a strategic level.

This chapter explores why channel management should be a strategic issue for top management, identifies the opportunities and barriers to success that might be encountered, and proposes a framework to design and implement a network approach to channel management.

Underlying trends in channel management

Implicit in the opportunities are attempts to capitalize on several trends. Although they have been given labels such as 'e-commerce' and 'disintermediation', they are better and more easily described in terms of technology, channel role redefinition and expanded service offerings.

Technology advances such as virtual channels, Internet and intranet-based communication systems and 'data mining' all expand the potential range of value creation from channel networks. In the case of virtualization, it actually means creating a new, direct channel to reach the techno-savvy customer segment. Where this kind of electronic commerce is possible, much of the value previously delivered by physical channels migrates to the virtual alternatives. Internet and intranet applications and architectures create instant standardization across divergent platforms, allowing easier and faster communication between manufacturers, distributors and retail channel participants. This communication can vastly improve supply chain management to deliver products and information to the customer more quickly than ever before. Finally, data mining has significantly enhanced the ability to provide what the customer needs—sometimes before the customers know it themselves. In the appliance industry, Sears uses its database of equipment and appliance repair incidents and costs to predict customer needs and then sell its maintenance contracts through telemarketing.

Sometimes called 'disintermediation', the second trend relates to how channel partners' roles are being redefined or 'unbundled'. Rather than fulfilling many aspects of the customer transaction (from closing sales to delivery to after-sales service), specific partners take only those pieces of the transaction that they perform better than any other partner, such as in sales agent models. So logistics and distribution might be outsourced to an external carrier, and final assembly of a personal computer might take place at the dealer rather than in the factory, because both are cost efficient and more responsive to the customer's needs.

The final trend—providing value-added services—finds retailers acting more as information and service brokers and less like product salespeople. Instead, they concentrate on gathering information about the customer, or providing additional information on complementary products and services to the customer, or offering after-sales service. Supplying relevant information and services fills a definite customer need, while it also reflects a distinctive, valuable role that a dealer or distributor can play even after 'virtual channels' overtake the product sales function.

These three trends are opening up new opportunities in channel structure, opportunities which can contribute to an organization's bottom line and lay the groundwork for a strategic approach to channels for the long term (see Figure 13.1).

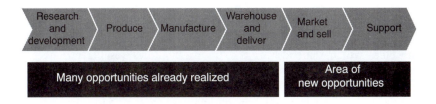

Figure 13.1 Integrated supply chain

New opportunities to capture

The new business opportunities that these trends present are enormous. They range from serving a whole new segment of customers with a virtual channel, to capturing cost efficiencies as a result of outsourcing a portion of the sales or supply chain transaction. The most important opportunity, however, is the potential deepening in customer relationships that result from obtaining and sharing data about customers' habits and needs, and responding to those needs with targeted information and services, e.g. customer relationship management.

Broader customer base

A good example of the potential of electronic commerce is seen in the automotive industry, where many of the functions performed by today's dealer can be handled through virtual channels. These functions include providing information on various models' features and available inventory, conveying terms and conditions of sales, negotiating price, preparing paperwork and arranging for and tracking delivery (from central inventory pools or factory direct). Consumers using the Internet can save time and money by electronic shopping. It is estimated that during 1996, 10 per cent of all new car sales bypassed the traditional dealer channel completely and were sold via the Internet.

Clearly, this is what Toyota has recognized and is responding to with its virtual channel concept. The new virtual channel would meet the needs of the techno-friendly buyer segment; at the same time it reduces new and used vehicle distribution costs, complements the traditional channel and leverages the strengths of the existing dealer retailing network.

Greater cost efficiencies

Both the technology advances and the unbundling of roles within channels enable organizations to improve their cost structure. The Autodesk interface, which depends on the Internet, allows resellers to access Autodesk's enterprise system to place an order and perform account-management activities, eliminating the need to call an Autodesk sales representative. This has saved the company more than $1 million annually from call volume reduction. Benefits to resellers include a 1 to 2 per cent improvement in margins as a result of a reduction in inventory support operations. Customers benefit by faster turnaround time at the reseller.

Leveraging technology has also dramatically reduced new vehicle sales costs. Whereas a sale costs traditional channels an average of $2050, it costs an electronic service such as Auto-by-Tel only $1015.

Persuading channels to assume non-traditional roles or outsourcing functions to a new channel participant can also improve the cost structure. Hewlett-Packard has implemented a form of postponed manufacturing that requires some dealers to perform final assembly operations. The company now can have a dealer conduct the final configuration on site, get the equipment to the customer faster and avoid the cost of carrying a lot of inventory and risk obsolescence. Autozone has outsourced its distribution to a national freight carrier, saving it the time and expense of developing its own transportation and tracking system.

Deeper customer relationships

Loyal customers are worth a lot. Andersen Consulting's research into OEMs in the automotive industry shows that loyal customers generate almost twice as much profit—59 per cent rather than 31 per cent—over their lifetime than do average customers for manufacturers. Channel networks will improve the customer relationship and provide better brand support by cutting down delivery time or by enabling the purchase of the vehicle in whatever way the customer desires.

But the third trend—providing information and services which add value beyond the product itself—may be the most important because service and information have become influential differentiators of products. John Deere and Caterpillar have found ways to deliver significantly higher value to their customers through innovative information and service initiatives.

Deere's approach to 'selling up-time'—after the sale of the piece of equipment—was to develop its John Deere Information Systems (JDIS). This satellite-linked system allows dealers to perform such functions as financial and inventory management. The system also enables customers to communicate with dealers and access an online parts catalogue through the Internet. Where previously John Deere received marketing information from its dealers monthly, it now receives real-time information. Sharing information with dealers and customers helps develop depth of knowledge and trust, which in turn results in long-term customer retention.

Caterpillar's approach is even more elaborate. A global, linked network of dealers enables Caterpillar to fulfil its service vision of delivering parts and service anywhere in the world within 24 hours of a reported problem. Dealers also provide a wide range of services before and after the sale of equipment. These include product selection and application advice, financing, insurance and operator training. Caterpillar continues to enhance its customer communication by developing monitoring devices for its equipment that would evaluate use and anticipate when a replacement part or service will be necessary. A dealer would then contact the customer and discuss arrangements for adjustments before they are needed.

Top management leadership—the imperative

While the benefits from new approaches to channel management are apparent, there are three significant challenges that can only be resolved with leadership from top management.

The first challenge is bringing about alignment—persuading channel participants to act in concert, share data and redefine their relationship *vis-à-vis* each other and the manufacturer. For channel participants who have viewed themselves as independent entities, all of whom seek to 'own' the customer, this may require a redefinition of their central role and how they do business. The second challenge is assessing and apportioning investment, risk and reward. The third challenge is managing complex decisions to design and implement a channel network that cross-multiple functions and business units within the manufacturer.

The first challenge in bringing about alignment of roles and skills cannot be over-emphasized, and is especially acute when a manufacturer seeks to integrate a 'virtual channel' into its traditional channel structure. Perceived or real channel conflicts mean that migration towards a network configuration must be optimized across all participants. If this integration and role redefinition are not done well you risk a mutiny and possibly retaliation. Consider the following: Compaq announced a direct channel targeted at 'microbusinesses' (less than 10 employees) in the UK. Fearing that they would be cut out altogether, distributors (which account for more than 70 per cent of Compaq sales) threatened to discontinue Compaq products and focus their resources on Hewlett-Packard or IBM personal computers. Compaq quickly responded to the threat by having its chief executive officer meet with distribution executives to discuss the company's strategy and quell their fears.

In addition to aligning roles, a manufacturer must ensure that all the skills necessary to serve all customer segments reside somewhere in the network. Undoubtedly, there will be overlaps and gaps in skills among channel partners. Assessing which participant is best suited to keep a certain segment of the customer transaction and who is best redeployed are difficult management issues.

If a company has enough influence it can impose a structure on dealers. To provide total solutions to the small-to-medium enterprise market, Hewlett-Packard required its channel participants to become franchisees of NetFire, so that it could better coordinate their efforts to provide training and support to users. Hewlett-Packard itself focuses on manufacturing and logistics. The customers win because they can expect a predictable level of quality from Hewlett-Packard and a predictable range of services from the franchisees.

The second challenge is making the *collective* decision to invest in the tools and time to develop the channel network itself. Depending on the current state of a company's technology, the investment in systems could be significant. Each of the kiosks used by Andersen dealers cost between $15 000 and $20 000. Andersen and its dealers are still negotiating how those costs should be allocated.

The third challenge is the difficulty of decision making within the manufacturer. Many marketing, sales and service managers have developed deep relationships, with existing channel participants making it hard to change. There are significant cross-functional and business unit issues that must be resolved. For example, it is difficult to gain agreement on channel-migration strategy in an environment where business units are managed decentrally but utilize the same channel, as in the automotive and heavy equipment industries. Often, changes in the network supply chain will affect the whole organization, including IT, sales and marketing, manufacturing and human resources.

These challenges underscore the need for top management leadership to guide channel migration. The framework described next provides senior management with an overview of the network design principles and the four key steps for developing the strategy for the value network of channel participants.

Developing a value network of channel participants

Given the complexity of redesigning channels, how should manufacturers begin to make value networks a reality? Pursuing an exhaustive but non-integrated set of activities does not make much sense when the goal is network 'optimization'. What manufacturers can do, however, is to concentrate their efforts on the following five areas: developing a coherent and workable design for the network, redefining the roles of traditional channel participants, establishing a governance process, developing measurement and reward systems and building the IT infrastructure. By following an integrated set of actions in each of these areas, a manufacturer will be able to move from the traditional channel architecture to the more profitable value network.

Network design principles

Persuading channel participants to work within a new framework requires demonstrating why the 'old' approaches will not work in the future and how the new approach would benefit channel participants and customers. Manufacturers should use four principles to design and describe their networks, all of which address the why and how issues. The principles require manufacturers to focus the network on creating maximum economic value for the customer, create a win–win situation for both the manufacturer and value-adding channel participants, create growth opportunities for each participant and, finally, develop trust-based relationships among all parties, channel participants as well as the manufacturer. While multiple channels will exist in the network, some marginal participants will probably be forced out.

Focusing on creating maximum value for the customer will be a new perspective for many network participants. Neither of the old models of channel relationships—the manufacturer-centred 'push' model or the more recent partnership model—focuses on customer needs or maximizes the total economic value that channels can deliver. The push model did not because it only sought to maximize the quantity delivered to a channel, with little thought as to how the products could best be sold.

The partnership model, where manufacturers team up with channels to improve the flow of products, was an improvement but still suffered from being focused on the needs of the partners rather than the customer. For example, a car dealer's paramount concern is obtaining an exclusive geography in which to work—on the assumption that a customer who wants the car the dealer sells will not have a convenient alternative from which to buy. As long as the dealer can sell the product, neither it nor the manufacturer needs to seek outside information or additional ways of delivering value. Consequently, both partners seek to maintain this stability, even though it may not fulfil customer needs in the purchase process.

Looking at channels this way, traditional structures seem less attractive. Channel participants compete among themselves in an attempt to control all aspects of a sale—even those they may not be best suited to deliver. The answer is to require channels to coordinate among themselves, with guidance from the manufacturer, to develop a network in which the aggregate expertise of the network participants combines to deliver all customer needs.

Ford recently took a step in this direction by announcing its plans to consolidate 18 metro-area dealerships into four or five superstores to meet the emerging competitive threat from national megachains such as CarMax and AutoNation. With fewer stores and tighter coordination, Ford believes it will be able to focus on beating the competition, rather than having its own dealerships competing against each other. With its margins getting thinner, Ford believes a new structure with closer relationships with dealers is required.

The second design principle is to create a win–win situation for all value-adding participants and move them from viewing channel management as part of a zero-sum game, where only one channel participant, or one kind of channel, can 'own' the customer. Instead, the network approach has several channels combine to satisfy all customer purchase process needs. Some customers' needs might be filled more quickly and cheaply by a direct channel to the manufacturer, while others are filled by an indirect dealer or distributor.

This approach sharply contrasts with the current discussion within the personal computer industry, where dealers and distributors are fixated on whether certain manufacturers use direct or indirect channels, and do not consider if there is room for both to exist and serve customers in different ways. In fact, in many if not most cases, there will be a need for both direct and indirect channels. For example, retailers give the customer wider selection, access to complementary products (software for a computer purchase) and after-sales service and support.

The third principle—creating growth opportunities for everyone involved—is closely related to the second. By aligning themselves with channel partners who have complementary expertise, a participant can concentrate on what it does best and generate a need for that specialty. For example, the strength of a retailer like Best Buy is in fulfilling an order for an appliance, yet the initial need for the equipment might have been generated by the manufacturer. Best Buy also adds value through its network of regional service centres and its extended warranty programmes.

Finally, developing trust-based working relationships must be both a principle by which the network operates and a goal of the participants.

Activities which promote trust include agreeing that all participants must invest in the network, sharing information about customer preferences and buying patterns and accurately evaluating their own and other channel participants' strengths and weaknesses. In particular, having everyone put some 'skin in the game' makes it more likely that participants will work for the common good, as well as underscore the collaborative nature of the undertaking.

Redefining roles of network participants

Once the design principles of the value network have been articulated and accepted, the next task is to define how the customers' needs will be met at each stage of the selling chain and who among the participants can best fulfil that need.

Participants must evaluate the value-creation opportunities for each segment of customers across the stages of the chain. Next, the manufacturer must identify the key players, in terms of demonstrated skills, developed tools and depth and breadth of relationships with customers. Finally, after roles and investments are determined, the group can design the channel network that maximizes economic value for each market segment. The product of this evaluation is a network grid that shows roles and responsibilities for each segment and stage in pre- and post-sale processes, as shown in Figure 13.2.

Defining roles requires a frank and open exchange of information between the manufacturer and channel participants to identify what value participants could add. Conversely, the definition process may result in the exclusion of some current players whose weaknesses cannot be overcome. Consequently, negotiating the specific roles and responsibilities can be a lengthy process and may require the use of external facilitation or legal services. When Ford sought to minimize its transportation costs by developing an alliance of vendors, it was its legal counsel who determined what information could be shared and whether it should be provided anonymously to avoid price-fixing and coercion concerns.

In addition to identifying optimal roles, the manufacturer will calculate the costs of participation for each member to play the role proposed. This calculation will indicate how much investment is required for the members to become truly 'networked' or knit together as a unit. Maximizing the value of the network not only requires increasing customer responsiveness, but also minimizing the costs associated with building and maintaining the network.

Roles in the network cannot be static, because as new customer segments are identified, or new channels developed to serve current customers, the network participants will need to bend to meet those needs.

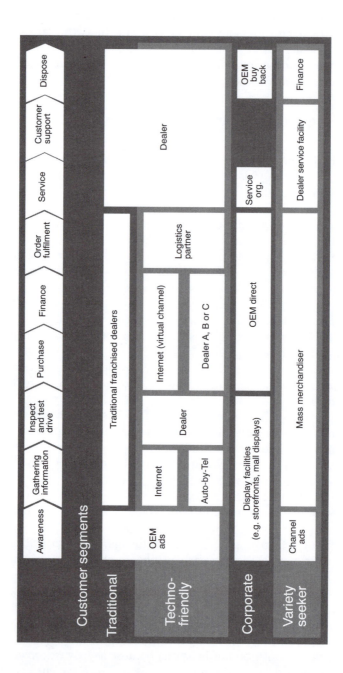

Figure 13.2 Optimal channels match market segments and selling stages to a member's skills

New participants with new skills, such as electronic capability or global reach, may be recruited. The network will be slightly reconfigured to incorporate those players and skills. Network participants should know that reconfiguration is a possibility and that adjusting to it will be an ongoing process.

These steps provide an agenda for companies who are attempting to form a network. Certain steps, such as tapping outside legal and facilitation support, can be done before network participants are brought together to agree on the specifics of roles, rewards and process.

Bringing the network members together

After roles are determined, the challenge of convincing the network members to work together begins. Although the specific governance processes of a network should take into account the members' preferences and experience, a few elements should be common to all networks.

The first critical element of making the network work is to establish leadership—both to reconfirm the commitment of the company and to ensure that some authority keeps the focus of the process and group on the strategic objectives. The emphasis has to be on doing business in a different way for the long term and finding how network members can best relate to and work with each other.

Second, the group should agree on higher-level goals, which should be to maximize value for customers and control costs. This requires the manufacturer to set aggressive targets for the group and demonstrate why achieving that target would benefit both it and the network participants.

The group then needs to determine what information should be shared and how the sharing will happen. It has to agree on what data—customer preferences, satisfaction ratings, buying trends—is most useful, how to gather it and when and whether it will be exchanged.

The most difficult aspect of convincing network participants to work together is identifying how equity and investments will be structured. There are several options available, from an alliance of independent companies rewarded based on their individual contributions, to forming a new company in which all the network members have an equity share and participate in all successes and shortfalls.

Ford has tried two approaches. To decrease distribution costs, it organized its transportation vendors to redesign how to transport cars from plants to dealerships. The members of the alliance remained independent, although they all shared information about capacity, turnaround times and connecting schedules to improve efficiency and cost. Participating vendors made varying degrees of investment, such as in facilities and equipment, and changes in service levels to build the network infrastructure. At the other extreme, Ford is facilitating an equity-based consolidation of its 18 dealerships around Indianapolis into four to five megastores. It has committed up to $155 million for this effort and the resultant business entity may be either a company wholly owned by Ford, or a distribution company with shared equity.

Regardless of the structure used to share equity and investment, the governance of the network is centred around an identified leader and agreed processes, as well as the shared goals of increasing customer value and improving cost effectiveness.

Measuring and rewarding network members

Just as governing the network requires new processes, rewarding participants in a value-based channel network requires a new approach. Using the traditional discounts off list price that had little correlation with actual customer value will not provide the right incentive to the network members. More often than not, these discounts were based on the relative power of the channel members. Indeed, many channel relationships today have deteriorated to the point where the value of the discounts is the primary motivation for each member.

In contrast, network participants are compensated only for the incremental value that they add to the customer, with an adjustment made for the investment that each channel member has contributed to developing infrastructure. Reward levels for serving separate segments should depend on the difficulty of fulfilling that particular segment's service needs and requirements. The compensation system must be flexible enough to accommodate additional participants and the changes in roles and value added provided by channel partners.

This approach is more complex than traditional discounting arrangements, but is more flexible and is based on proven performance. With the help of activity-based costing systems to calculate investments, and a balanced scorecard evaluation of participants' roles and contributions, value-based compensation can be done fairly and will strengthen trust among the channel members.

Building the supporting infrastructure

Delivering greater customer value is the focus of the network channel approach, but that delivery will be questionable at best without a well-thought-out technology strategy to support it. Companies such as Autodesk, AutoZone, Andersen Corporation and Ford have all built systems, or customized current systems, to allow a freer exchange of information among their partners.

Participants need to build an accessible and ubiquitous IT platform that will enable customer relationship management and electronic commerce. It should include a fully integrated database, a real-time update and verification process, qualified prospects as well as customers, comprehensive customer and prospect profiles (such as sales and service history, competitive products owned, lifestyle characteristics) and real-time transaction processing at all customer touch points. It will also be important to improve key sales and marketing and supply chain processes so that they work seamlessly together with the technology.

Convincing channel participants to make the required investments is often a challenge. System and training costs are frequently viewed as a profit and loss expense item with little recognition of their contributions to building customer loyalty and revenue. Rethinking processes as roles are unbundled is often unfamiliar to channel participants. Consequently, working with all participants—manufacturers and network members—to develop the business case is essential. John Deere spent a significant amount of time gaining input from dealers for their JD Vision programme. Accordingly, a direct TV, multimedia training programme was included.

Conclusion

New technologies are well recognized as offering great opportunities to a better supply chain. But creative supply chain managers have not only to capitalize on use the new channels created by technologies, but also consider the channel participants themselves. By building stronger, more effective relationships with channel participants, manufacturers can access a broader base of customers and offer them better products and services. Such an approach requires the vision and leadership of top management: they have to see the opportunities ahead, be prepared to create a new structure based on cooperation, and identify and capture the strengths of channel partners. This is a significant challenge for organizations and industries, but one that promises great rewards in adding value to the supply chain.

Formulating a channel strategy

How to master complex channel dynamics

John Miller

Faced with growing marketplace complexity in customer preferences, trading partner dynamics, product line expansions and fresh options for interfacing with consumers, manufacturers today are turning to innovative distribution channels as a tool for business success. Companies entering these uncharted waters should carefully analyse the risks and rewards of a new distribution channel by developing an effective channel strategy. This chapter outlines how to formulate and implement such a strategy, taking into account a range of key factors: consumer buying patterns, channel trends, product strength, competition, trading partner activities and business objectives. Woven through the discussion are examples of how several companies from different industries have decided whether to adopt a new channel strategy, and how such a strategy should best be developed and implemented.

Introduction

Changing consumer demographics, the emergence of new distribution channels, the consolidation of trading partners and the increasing use of computer and telecommunications technology are creating a changing environment for manufacturers. Each of these factors is producing new challenges, and new opportunities, in using different types of distribution channels to reach consumer segments.

'Channel strategy'—a company's decision about how it will distribute finished goods through possibly multiple supply/demand chains to end users—has emerged as both a theoretical concept and a practical tool for dealing with the growing complexity of the market. Channel strategy decisions by nature reflect the entire range and depth of a company's business objectives and operations. As they play such a significant role in a manufacturer's profits and market success, these decisions require the attention and understanding of all senior managers.

The key to formulating a successful channel strategy is to understand and minimize the risks of investing in too few, too many or the wrong types or combinations of channels for the consumers that a company serves or wants to serve. A company that approaches its channel strategy casually or without adequate knowledge faces great risks of lost opportunities or, even worse, business failure.

The complex distribution environment

Manufacturers must understand the changing market before embarking on a new channel strategy. These changes result from many factors including new consumer lifestyles, advances in information technology, new distribution capabilities, novel uses of traditional supply channels or changes occurring with trading partners. Today, the concept of an 'average' consumer is no longer meaningful. In the USA particularly, families in which both parents work place a premium on purchasing consumer goods in convenient, time-saving ways. Credit-card orders by telephone and, increasingly, by online communications such as the Internet have become common. Observers have estimated that by the end of 1997 more than 40 million US households had regular access to the Internet.

Advances in information technology have given market researchers a sometimes overwhelming wealth of detail about the preferences of individual consumers. It is possible for manufacturers—especially producers of mass-merchandised goods—to segment consumers not only by geographic region but also by gender, age, income, occupation, educational level, racial or ethnic type, type of dwelling, family size and composition, and even political orientation

Combined with technology, advances in physical distribution are also having an impact on distribution potential. Express shipping services enable consumers to receive products in exactly the individualized form they prefer, overnight or in a few days, at an affordable price. For instance, affluent and technically sophisticated end users, who represent the majority of purchasers for such products as home and small-business electronic equipment, routinely use toll-free telephone and online credit-card orders; products are typically shipped by overnight delivery. A company wishing to establish or increase its sales to such consumers must align its channel strategy with this demand for order-processing speed and convenience.

In addition, traditional supply channels are being used in new ways. It has become common for consumers to buy a family's entire weekly supply of grocery products from mass-merchant superstores which carry general merchandise. Purchases of everyday staple items such as bread and milk at convenience stores and drugstores have become routine. Thus, many manufacturers have been pressured to develop effective new strategies for simultaneously supporting multiple channels, and various formats of those channels, as shown in Figure 14.1.

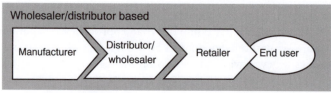

Wholesaler/distributor based

Manufacturer → Distributor/wholesaler → Retailer → End user

- Buying consortium
- One-step distribution
- Two-step distribution

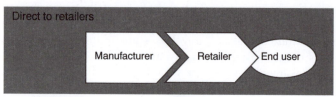

Direct to retailers

Manufacturer → Retailer → End user

- Mass merchants
- Clubs
- Convenience stores
- Chains
- Corner stores
- Speciality retailers

Direct to end user

Manufacturer → End user

- Mail order
- Internet/Web
- Phone orders
- Contract ('product of the month')
- TV shopping channel

Figure 14.1   Manufacturers need to support multiple channels

Finally, the increasing consolidation and growth of partnerships among distributors and retailers greatly affects manufacturers in many industries. The rising power of these middlemen has forced some manufacturers to meet more stringent information and logistics requirements. In the US, mass merchants such as Wal-Mart, Kmart and Home Depot set very specific and high service criteria for their suppliers, and some even dictate the type of distribution channel to be used. The manufacturer's channel strategy thus has a significant impact on its ability to achieve 'preferred supplier' status.

Understanding the consumer and channel partners

A solid understanding of consumer-driven logistics in the rapidly changing market environment is essential for formulating and implementing a successful channel strategy. This entails above all learning the value-added impact of meeting the consumer's wants and needs:

- providing products and services when, where and how the consumer expects them;
- assessing how these wants and needs are changing; and
- focusing on developing and implementing the 'best practices' required to meet these wants and needs.

Formulating a strong channel strategy also requires insight into the influence of trading partners (including distributors, wholesalers, jobbers and retailers) over how a product is purchased, promoted and sold. These partners may react in unexpected ways to the creation or elimination of channels.

For instance, a major US manufacturer of over-the-counter and generic prescription pharmaceuticals was considering dropping certain small accounts (often referred to as 'mom and pop stores') for its generic business because it felt that the cost of directly serving these trading partners was too high. Research showed, however, that these smaller accounts, rather than shifting their orders for the supplier's brands to wholesalers, were likely to drop these brands entirely and deal only with manufacturers who remained willing to do business with them directly.

These retailers recognized that their margins would suffer because of the change in source of supply and that, because the products being distributed were generic, alternative brands were available. Thus, what appeared initially to be a promising channel shift turned out to be a mistake that would cost the pharmaceutical manufacturer profits, goodwill and market share.

This example shows that a channel partner may have far more influence than a company's brand franchise on end users' purchasing decisions. This understanding is especially critical for commodity products and second- or third-tier brands. The more choices a consumer has among brands (or the more indifferent the consumer is towards any particular brand), the riskier it becomes for a supplier to replace an adequate but 'unprogressive' channel strategy with an untested one.

Finally, suppliers contemplating new channel strategies must also strive to understand what works, what does not and why. This calls for a knowledge of both the theory and practice of effective logistics management. It also demands a steady grasp of the risks and rewards of technology and insight into how competition—not only in the marketplace but also among factions or functions within a company—can

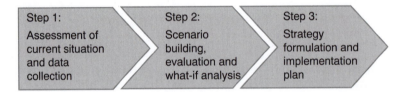

Figure 14.2   Developing and implementing an effective channel strategy

influence the success of channel strategy development and application.

Recent advances in information systems allow organizations to measure precisely the effect of various channel strategies on operating costs and ultimately to develop a complete profile of margins by customer type. This information about channel operating costs and customer profitability, combined with data about the likely actions to be taken by competitors and trading partners, allows an organization to develop a complete business case for or against a proposed channel strategy.

Formulating and implementing a channel strategy

Although channel strategy discussions often begin with sales and marketing, they eventually require input from every functional area and operating division of the company. Because of their understanding of supply economics, logistics executives are often tasked with the process of bringing clarity to channel issues. Through a process of open debate and rigorous, fact-based analysis, managers must strive to reach consensus on how a new strategy will affect consumers, trading partners and internal operations. Equally important is an understanding of how to develop and integrate a new strategy as efficiently and smoothly as possible in the marketplace and within the company itself.

The task of formulating and implementing a channel strategy, while not simple, presents a satisfying challenge to capable managers. A three-step process is recommended for developing and implementing an effective channel strategy, as shown in Figure 14.2.

Step 1: Assessment of current situation and data collection

An effective way to begin the channel strategy effort is by forming a steering committee which oversees all project activities, challenges the basis of recommendations and approves final recommendations and implementation plans. It is important that all stakeholders in the final strategy participate; this will require representation from marketing, sales, manufacturing, logistics, finance, IT and legal. Once the steering committee has been formed and the project team has been assembled and charged with their duties, the project can begin. Fundamental to the success of the project will be an assessment of the current situation.

The focus must be on facts rather than guesswork or emotions. Several categories of information need to be gathered and analysed: consumer and trading partner preferences, the strength of the brand or product line, the constraints on production and distribution systems, the economics of existing channels, competition and existing business objectives.

As anyone experienced in business logistics knows, many plans for improving operations fail because enough accurate, thorough, up-to-date, reliable—and, of particular importance, usable—information simply does not exist. This painful truth applies especially to the formulation and implementation of a new channel strategy. Minimizing not only the risks of choosing the wrong strategy but also its associated direct and indirect costs depends on possessing and using reliable data.

Consumer and trading partner preferences

A company must understand the current and projected behaviour of those who buy its products. This is normally achieved through interviews and other analysis, often conducted by outside consultants who specialize in such work. The knowledge gained from this study is invaluable in formulating the best channel strategy because the fit between a company's distribution actions and the preferences of those who purchase its products ultimately determines success.

A major producer of home entertainment software is one example of a company that analysed its end users' buying preferences well. Observing the sometimes ineffective in-store merchandising of its products by existing jobbers and distributors, the company reasoned that its strong brand identity could be leveraged much more powerfully if it asserted more direct control over this process. It discovered that in fact its brand was often the key factor in driving consumer buying behaviour. Furthermore, the product was frequently an impulse purchase motivated by strong merchandising programmes and advertising campaigns. Young families represented a large percentage of buyers, so the company saw an opportunity for developing in-store merchandising capabilities not only for entertainment software but also for selling tie-in goods such as clothing and toys. In short, the company wanted to develop its new channel strategy based on a sound understanding of individual consumers' preferences. By taking control of its product in the retail stores of large mass merchants, this organization was able to acquire dedicated shelf space for its brand, merchandise its products more effectively, improve product availability and inventory control and thereby improve sales and margins.

In the case of a supplier of industrial fasteners, what appeared to be a smart move into a catalogue sales channel turned out to offer fewer advantages than originally thought. After engaging a consultant to conduct a consumer segmentation analysis and trading partner service survey, the company realized that its existing network of middlemen would drop some of the company's products—which represented second- and third-tier brands in its market—if they became available through catalogue sales. In addition, catalogue sales would not yield profits at sufficient levels or soon enough to be worth pursuing. The company discovered that buyers of its products preferred to make purchases from speciality industrial suppliers who provided helpful purchasing and application advice. The company eventually decided to pursue other strategies to expand its presence in the marketplace.

Brand/product line strength

In the example of the supplier of industrial fasteners, the company's brands were not sufficiently strong to force existing trading partners (i.e. industrial suppliers) to continue to carry its products if it created a new catalogue channel. The situation was different for the manufacturer of home entertainment software. This organization was able to create a new channel and take activity away from existing trading partners (i.e. rack jobbers) because of the strength of its brand. The rack jobbers could not afford to stop carrying the manufacturer's products for its remaining customer base because of the lack of product substitutes.

Understanding the marketplace clout of a company's products is important for choosing and managing the best mix of channels. If substitutes for a product or product line are readily available, the company must approach a new channel strategy more carefully than if its brand is dominant. Retailers that might willingly purchase the products through, for instance, direct sales from a manufacturer may baulk at paying extra for the services of a middleman if substitutes are available from another manufacturer who does ship direct. As noted earlier, this is what happened in the case of the manufacturer of over-the-counter and generic prescription pharmaceuticals. It found that smaller accounts (which, like large mass merchants, have grown increasingly sophisticated in understanding the true sources of their profits and losses) would simply no longer carry its products if they could not obtain them through the direct-sales channel to which they had become accustomed.

Impact on production and logistics operations

A new channel strategy may require complex and costly changes in current manufacturing and logistics operations, information systems, staff and operations. A company may find, in fact, that the advantages to be gained by pursuing a new or revamped channel strategy will not in the long run justify the significant investments needed. Rigorous analysis of these trade-offs is essential for success.

To implement its new channel strategy, the supplier of home entertainment software went from shipping in case quantities to units of individual products. As a result, this supplier had to revamp its warehouse design, pick/pack equipment and systems to handle higher volumes throughout all operations, from order processing to customer service. It also had to implement a major contract with a third-party supplier to support in-store merchandising. Its total one-time investment reached tens of millions of dollars and it incurred a 20 to 50 per cent increase in some key operating costs. However, the decision resulted in significant increases in its sales and profits.

Economics of existing channels

Addressing channel economics may seem daunting but is unavoidable. Data must be gathered systematically over a sufficient time horizon so that managers can profile current operations accurately. Next, the data must be sorted, organized and analysed to convert it into a meaningful and comprehensive profile of existing channel economics.

All revenues and costs affected by a change in channel strategy must be collected and analysed. These include:

- sales revenue (for both products and services);
- production costs (costs of goods as affected by packaging changes);
- distribution costs (transportation, warehousing and pick/pack operations);
- sales costs (sales representatives, customer service, invoicing, deductions); and
- marketing costs (e.g. price discounts, rebates, market development, advertising co-op payments, payment terms and inventory-holding costs).

The goal is to gain a true understanding of profit levels and profit drivers in each channel. This exercise will require the profiling of customer activities and requirements that drive costs for each channel, including order size, ordering approach, packaging, payment practices and special services required. Although an ABC costing system is of great help, organizations lacking this system may use other analytical tools such as the sampling of costs associated with orders typical for each channel. Interviewing managers of functions affected by channel strategies is useful for reviewing and assigning costs to the orders processed by a channel.

Competition

Competitors may be leaders, followers or both. A watchful eye on their plans and performance is important to any company contemplating a new channel strategy. As stated earlier, the substitutability of its key products and product lines plays a key role in the success of any new strategy.

In the example of the manufacturer of industrial fastening products, the proposed strategy was to implement a new distribution capability through catalogue sales. Its two major competitors had stronger brand presence and were already marketing products through the catalogue channel. However, the project team discovered through research that the company's competitors were questioning the use of this channel—in fact, they were preparing to limit or drop catalogue distribution entirely because this strategy threatened to alienate existing trading partners and did not offer sufficient sales potential to offset the risk. For the company in question, which already had the weakest brand of the three suppliers, this information was particularly valuable.

Business objectives

Understanding the core values and goals of a company is not just the CEO's or chairman's job. All managers involved in developing and implementing a new or revamped channel strategy must understand and support them. Consensus among key decision makers is vital. As noted earlier in this chapter, for the supplier of home entertainment software, the decision to implement a new retail-direct distribution strategy involved all senior decision makers in the company.

At the end of Step 1, the project team should have a reasonably complete profile of its current distribution channels and business environment.

Step 2: Scenario building, evaluation and what-if analysis

In this step, the team engages in a visioning process to develop plausible what-if scenarios. The risks and rewards of new channels or new combinations of existing channels are evaluated on the basis of the facts gathered in Step 1. Decision trees and what-if modelling are used to assess the value of potential strategies based on the probability of various combinations of events occurring: changing sales volumes by channel, reaction of competition, changes in operating costs, reaction of trading partners. Although this process may begin with an assumption that new channels should be added, the examples presented in this chapter demonstrate that the team should also consider the value of reducing the number and complexity of channels, improving the management of existing channels, or both. Two categories of knowledge are important in building and testing scenarios: the impacts on supply chain partners and end users, and the calculation of risks and rewards.

Impacts on partners and end users

As already noted, for some companies the risk of alienating trading partners and thus losing business may outweigh the benefits of implementing new distribution channels. The wise approach calls for answering three key questions:

■ How will the new channel affect existing channels?
■ What will be the true net increase in sales (will the new channel take sales away from an existing channel)?
■ How much impact will the new channel have on trading partners' margins?

The supplier of automotive parts was using a complex mix of distribution channels, including sales to large OEM accounts, retail installers serving individual consumers, mass merchants providing both installation and do-it-yourself sales to consumers, regional distributors (both one and two step) serving small repair shops, auto dealers and independent mechanics. The company faced not only growing complexity in managing these channels but also resentment from some trading partners who felt that the company was competing directly with them as they created new channels.

Although the motivation to implement a new channel strategy should come mainly from perceived and actual incremental market demand that can be realized, some manufacturers put the cart before the horse by letting their strategy be driven by a perceived opportunity to reach additional end users. The need for understanding actual net increases in sales across all channels and not just by the individual new channel cannot be overstated.

A change in channel strategy can have a significant impact on trading partners' margins. This may result from either a change in sales volume or a change in the mix of customers served by these partners. When the home entertainment software supplier implemented its new strategy of serving key accounts directly, it took the larger, more profitable accounts away, leaving trading partners with customers whose smaller orders incurred higher distribution costs. Determining the exact impact of sales volumes and distribution costs on a trading partner's economics is difficult, but it is usually possible to estimate such results in ranges. This information will be essential in later discussions and negotiations with trading partners on the impact of the new channel strategy. It is also important to understand the strength of the company's product brand versus the strength of trading partners in the channel.

Calculating risks and rewards

The ultimate goal in evaluating a new channel strategy is to evaluate associated risks and rewards. This analysis may combine various management arts and sciences, including traditional decision trees and what-if modelling. The project team must eventually combine the economic models of existing channels developed in Step 1, with the estimated impacts on overall sales, impacts on trading partners and competitors and their potential reactions. The final output will be estimates of how the economics of existing channels will be affected by the new strategy, highlighting the specific revenues and costs and underlying reasons for these impacts. The team prepares a comprehensive economic profile across all channels to compare potential benefits of the new strategy over the old. Using this approach, the team develops, evaluates and compares various scenarios of how the market can be expected to react to the new channel.

The final activity in calculating risks and rewards is to estimate one-time costs associated with each scenario being evaluated. These costs, which can be significant, may include those for new information systems, changes in plant and equipment and investments in inventory. With this additional information, a business case can be prepared for each scenario; it should include a cashflow analysis, statement of impact on EVA™ (economic value added) and calculation of return on investment. This information might be organized in a table that quantifies the costs of the channel strategy, as shown in Table 14.1, with separate tables developed for each scenario.

Step 3: Strategy formulation and implementation plan

Selection of the new channel strategy must be supported by the entire leadership of the company. Channel strategy decisions ultimately affect and are affected by every major decision maker—not only the CEO but also executives in charge of manufacturing, logistics, finance, information systems, sales, marketing, research and development and legal affairs. Therefore, the review of the business case for each scenario, the probability of success, key assumptions made and necessary investments must be understood and supported by management.

With this knowledge, the final strategy should be selected with an understanding of priorities as well as implementation plans. Implementation plans must be developed in detail since the new strategy will probably require many new capabilities to be developed. These may include product packaging changes, changes in organization structure, new physical infrastructure, and new services provided by a third party. It is also important to plan the way these changes will be communicated

Table 14.1
Three channels with competitors' reactions

	Channel 1	Channel 2	Channel 3	Total
Ongoing costs				
Sales revenue				
Product costs				
Sales costs				
Marketing costs				
Distribution costs				
Inventory handling costs				
Competitor reaction				
One-time costs				
Physical infrastructure				
Other physical assets				
Systems				
Organization				

to trading partners, customers, employees and suppliers.

For the supplier of home entertainment software, discussions about developing new ways to go to market involved top-level managers from the very beginning. This company recognized that its new distribution plan would succeed only if the strategy supported overall goals for profitability, margins, market share and stock value. It began with the formation of steering committees involving senior-level decision makers. Marketing played a less important role than sales because the company's product brands were especially strong. However, since the company outsourced many of its production and distribution operations, the creation of a channel strategy also required the participation of its third-party service suppliers. In addition, because of the magnitude and scope of required changes, implementation of the strategy had to be planned carefully.

Implementation of the new strategy should occur in smoothly integrated phases. To reduce risks, some companies perform a pilot or test of the strategy at this step to assess results on a small scale. The supplier of home entertainment software, for instance, rolled out its new channel strategy only after testing it with selected retailers first.

As a strategy will have significant impacts on the company's logistics operations and systems, executives in charge of these functions should play a lead role in determining staff assignments, timing, testing and monitoring of results. Since several quarters may pass before the full impacts of the strategy are known, it is important to remain flexible and to fine-tune it as needed.

Conclusion

Complex channel dynamics are a fact of life today. The increasing sophistication of distributors, wholesalers, retailers and consumers has forced manufacturers to pay greater attention to how, when and where they take their products to market. Rapid changes in information technology and the growing importance of global logistics operations also present new challenges.

To the classic definition of logistics as 'utility of time and place' must be added 'value to the individual purchaser and end user'. Whether a given product or product line can be categorized as 'commodity' or 'one of a kind', an effective channel strategy must rest firmly on the principle of genuine value at a cost that is affordable to both supplier and purchaser. The strategy can and does play as big a role in a company's ultimate success as does the strength of its brands.

The winners in this contest will be those who best understand the economics of changing marketplace realities and who can master a disciplined, flexible, fact-based approach to formulating and implementing effective channel strategies. Both the risks and the rewards are great.

CHAPTER 15

The global retail supply chain

Conquering complexity through a new supply chain framework

Ken Bonning, Ed Rader and Rick Chavie

Today's global retailers are managing supply chains linking thousands of vendors to potentially millions of individual customers across the world. With diverse merchandise, varied selling formats and worldwide sourcing, supply chains are exponentially increasing in complexity. Retailers wishing to compete in this environment must find the supply chain solutions that will still enable them to deliver their products to the customer, at the right price and at the right time. This chapter outlines the main types of retail supply chains, and describes how merging the complexities of customer demand and supplier capabilities into a new supply chain framework, called logistically distinct businesses, provides a means to simplify retail supply chain management. At a time of increasing complexity, clever supply chain management will differentiate the winners from the losers in the retail industry.

Introduction

In any major retailer across the world, customers can commonly find within close proximity on the selling floor textiles from the USA, shoes from Italy, apparel from China and floor coverings from the Middle East. The consumer does not care how the merchandise made it to the shelves. Given the relatively high amount of retail selling space in many parts of the world and the rising use of direct-to-consumer services, retailers that cannot deliver the right merchandise quickly and cheaply will rapidly face a declining market.

There is not one 'retail supply chain' that is easy to picture or define. Rather, a retail supply chain is composed of thousands of supply chain paths stretching from the manufacturer to the end consumer. Left to follow their own routes, these paths would rarely become optimal without intervention. The retailer adds value in the supply chain by managing all of the diverse components of these thousands of supply chains in a common manner. By reducing the complexity from thousands to a few, the retailer can concentrate on operational excellence to help deliver a value equation to the end consumer.

Rarely do the same operating procedures and styles that served the retailer well in a one country environment transcend borders and work well in a global environment. The world's largest retailer, Wal-Mart, has learned this lesson as it has expanded from the relatively efficient confines of the USA to the rest of the Americas. Although the value proposition presented to the customer is similar to that in the USA, and customers are responding by choosing Wal-Mart over its competitors, the vendor community has lagged far behind the capabilities that the company expects. The net result is that it is forced to adjust its supply chain philosophy until the vendor community that it uses can support its traditional model.

Retail supply chain components

Although retail supply chains are made up of basically the same components as any other supply chain, it is the endless permutations of supply chain path possibilities that make them complex and difficult to manage. Imagine thousands of suppliers, each with their own ideas and supply chain operating strategies, all moving through a retailer's set of unique supply chains, all competing for resources. Typically, other industries strategically source certain products to reduce their vendor count and reduce supply chain complexity. Since many retailers base their offering on having a broad assortment to provide 'one-stop shopping', stock-keeping unit (SKU) counts are relatively high. Given high SKU and vendor counts, the retailer is forced to prescribe a given set of operating rules that all vendors must follow, in order to reduce supply chain complexity. The more vendors that can follow a set of operating conditions, the greater chance of combining those flows into manageable and distinct businesses.

Retail supply chains are composed of product sourcing and selection, inbound transportation, processing, storage, outbound transportation and store processing (see Figure 15.1). Some of the unique characteristics of how they operate and are different from other industries are outlined below.

Product selection and sourcing

Obviously, one of the core competencies of retailers is the value they provide by building a selection of merchandise for a consumer to buy. Product selection and acquisition mark the beginning of the retail supply chain, as the merchandising function within the retailer discerns consumer needs and wants and translates that into a category assortment. The sourcing of the products should be made to match an individual

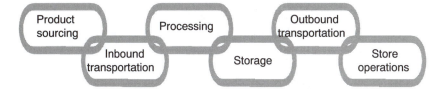

Figure 15.1   The retail supply chain

retailer's strategy as much as possible. For example, if a customer's number one value is low price then low cost should be the primary sourcing consideration, not lead time or breadth of assortment. Sourcing describes the method by which each retailer identifies, develops and maintains relationships with suppliers in order accurately to deliver the right products at the right price and at the right time.

Retailers distinguish themselves with two basic approaches to sourcing—branded product or private label. With branded product, the merchandising group builds the assortment based on close collaboration with a group of vendors that have built brand equity. These supply chains are typically already well defined and the retailer defines the set of operating procedures for the vendor to follow. With private-label merchandise the retailer must define the supply chain and manage all the processes from the manufacturing floor to the selling floor. This creates complexity in the supply chain that is especially difficult for global retailers to manage. Many apparel retailers support private-label merchandise and their supply chains have proved famously difficult to transport across global borders. Laura Ashley was successful within the confines of the UK but has had tremendous difficulties controlling costs on a global basis. On the other hand, Marks & Spencer succeeds by keeping the supply chain simple and easy to execute, but at a slight cost premium. Like many department stores on the continent, C&A Brenninkmeyer has focused on developing its own private labels and avoided reliance on manufacturer brands. At the same time, it has been able to achieve economies of scale by standardizing its product sourcing and offerings across operations in Europe.

Inbound transportation

By managing the 'rules' of how vendors interact in their supply chains, retailers determine both the mode (such as container, truckload, less than truckload or air) and the terms (such as prepaid or collect) of their inbound freight. Decreased emphasis on physical assets such as distribution centres has created the 'virtual network' of inbound transportation as retailers try to improve speed to market and channel flexibility.

Accomplishing these goals requires a global retailer to take control of the shipment as far back in the supply chain as possible, with complete visibility of progress, in order to coordinate shipments from the entire vendor base to their stores in the most economical and timely manner. Those manufacturers who are the most flexible in responding to the urgent needs of retailers recognize that transportation is a key component in minimizing the ever shorter cycle times on which retailers insist as they chase market trends.

Processing

All merchandise requires some kind of value added services to make it 'floor ready', available for the customer. This includes uniform product code (UPC) labelling, price labelling, building or creating assortments, removing or modifying packaging and customer presentation. Past retail supply chains were heavily focused on these services as the main role of the retailer, with corresponding warehouses and labour needed to perform the work, but gradually most of these requirements are being moved to the vendors. This enables cross-docking of merchandise directly to the selling floor from the vendor, which is currently a significant initiative among retailers. Global supply chains add the complexity of extensive coordination of country specific requirements for labelling and presentation which increases the need for vendor compliance programmes. These programmes define all the interactions and requirements of doing business with the retailer and are heavily focused on supply chain transactions.

Storage

Although a great deal of effort has been expended on quick response, efficient consumer response (ECR), vendor-managed inventory (VMI) and just-in-time supply and manufacturing (JIT), retailers must still carry inventory in order to buffer demand volatility and create acceptable service levels. Service levels are defined as the in-stock position of an SKU— whether it is available for sale when needed. Maintaining a high service level drives the need for inventory, whether at the vendor or the retailer. Previously, retailers held the majority of inventory available for sale in the most expensive real estate in their supply chain: the stores. However, retailers have moved to reduce backroom space faster than many manufacturers can respond. One of the main strategic considerations in the retail supply chain is the deployment of the inventory to enable rapid replenishment. However, retailers must critically analyse the reduction of inventories to ensure the availability of product, because the only place inventory can add value to the customer is when it is available for sale.

Outbound transportation

This portion of the supply chain moves the correct quantities of merchandise either to the store or direct to the customer and is commonly combined with inbound transportation to generate economies, flexibility, and control. The diversity of merchandise create several challenges for the retailer—how to build properly cubed and stable loads to the stores, how to separate by store zone without losing cubic efficiency and which mode to select given the variety of store volumes. As crossdocking increases, the ability to buffer spikes in demand is limited and outbound transportation assumes a greater role in balancing the tradeoff of expense versus delivery speed.

Store operations

As the final link in the traditional retail supply chain, this involves the effort required in the backrooms of the stores to prepare merchandise for sale, replenishing shelves and setting up displays. Retailers have aggressively pursued all means within the supply chain to minimize the amount of work required in this step because of the labour inefficiencies, high cost of space and renewed focus on customer service by selling staff. Speed to market means little if time is wasted preparing merchandise for sale or if the merchandise is not in stock. In the past, retailers would balance demand by transferring goods among stores to meet specific requests and respond to stockouts. Now, however, retailers have recognized that the handling costs and lack of asset productivity associated with transfers are too high to justify them and that the better approach is to resupply directly from the manufacturer. Not typically measured by the retailer is the time each consumer takes to shop the store, and consumers are increasingly trading some measure of cost for the convenience of avoiding the shopping experience through catalogue, mail-order or home-delivery services.

Retail channels

Although the above components combine into an infinite number of distinct possibilities, most retail supply chains can be generally described as falling into one of four main channels: direct to consumer, direct to store, single-level distribution and multiple-level distribution.

Direct to customer

Primarily defined by mail-order retailers in the past (telephone-order retailers), this channel is rapidly expanding with the growth of e-commerce. This is creating a fundamental change in the strategic design of retail supply chains, from store centric to customer centric. Typical retail supply chains are designed to funnel merchandise efficiently from many vendors to a finite number of store locations. A direct-to-customer supply theoretically allows for shipment from any place to any customer. The retailer must decide whether to own the inventory in centralized storage or deploy it further back in the supply chain at vendor warehouses. Achieving the cost and speed balance to match the needs of the target customers profitably is a key factor; this approach has particular value where a retailer faces high carrying costs and has exposure to obsolescence from on-hand inventory, such as personal computers. The success of this supply chain depends on seamless information transactions, coordinated shipments to customers' residences and minimized direct customer shipping charges.

Direct-to-store delivery

Typically this channel is dominated by high-cube, high-value or low-volume merchandise that can be economically delivered to each store location directly from the vendor, bypassing any retailer distribution network. This supply chain is common for food and beverage distributors and appliances. High-cube merchandise, such as insulation for homes, can go direct to home centres since the demand from individual stores can fill one or more trucks on a weekly basis; for jewellery, on the other hand, the high value of the items means that shipping costs are a very low percentage of their value—this means that even an overnight shipment can be justified by the reduction in inventory carrying cost.

Home Depot, a large do-it-yourself chain in the USA, built a core strength on its ability to offload supply chain responsibilities directly to manufacturers by forcing them to ship directly to stores in an industry that had traditionally relied heavily on distributors and wholesalers. By cutting out distributors and other intermediaries, by placing the burden for the supply chain on vendors and by offering substantial growth in volumes to suppliers who met their standards, Home Depot was able to connect manufacturers more directly with the end customers.

Single-level distribution

In this channel, merchandise moves to the consumer in one defined 'stop', usually to consolidate the goods from multiple vendors into the retailer's distribution centre. Store demands are pooled to create efficient and fast replenishment orders from each vendor that are then combined with others in the retailer's outbound shipping network. Inventory is held at the vendors' warehouses, the retailer's warehouse or in the stores, with the goal to reduce deployed inventory at the store level.

Multiple-level distribution

When merchandise cannot be ordered or manufactured in quantities to match demand because of long replenishment lead times, either the vendor or the retailer must warehouse the merchandise and replenish the stores based on demand. For example, many fashion apparel items have long lead times because of their distant manufacturing sources. Several leading global apparel retailers have reworked their supply chains to minimize the need for multiple-level distribution. The Limited, Inc. was one of the first to recognize the value associated with tailoring assortments to specific markets and to achieve this under a very short cycle time. By working very closely with manufacturers to redesign and segment processes to allow for later decision making, it was able to achieve both goals at once.

While retailers may have a dominant channel in which the majority of merchandise flows, typically they use several variations of the above channels according to the best flow for a particular type of merchandise. Common characteristics of supply and demand create these channels and make it easier for a retailer to manage the thousands of vendors and merchandise possibilities that occur. Retailers use the concept of logistically distinct businesses (LDBs) to simplify the channel and flow possibilities into manageable segments.

A strategic framework—logistically distinct businesses

The concept of logistically distinct businesses (LDBs), developed by Fuller, O'Connor and Rawlinson in 1993, focuses the supply chain design and development towards a family of products or businesses. A logistically distinct business is the collection of components of a supply chain that act similarly for a range of merchandise. Analysis of consumer purchase patterns, vendor manufacturing capability, product packaging, warehousing capability and replenishment lead times allows merchandise to be segmented into LDBs. Both supply and demand characteristics are analysed for each LDB, with vendor capabilities driving the supply side and consumer buying behaviour driving the demand side. Tables 15.1 and 15.2 demonstrate one set of supply and demand characteristics which can be used in the LDB framework.

As demonstrated by Table 15.1, products are grouped depending on the buying frequency and delivery frequency characteristics on the supply side. Based on this categorization, each product's economic order quantity (EOQ), based on time, can be calculated. The results demonstrate that for more functional, everyday products, the EOQ tends to be smaller, while specialized purchases are more economical in larger EOQs. The driver of these results is the predictability of demand for each. Merchandise with predictable and fairly stable demand, such as men's white shirts, lend themselves to be purchased automatically in smaller quantities with smaller buffer inventories. Hence, any cost minimization efforts should be focused on reducing production, transportation and inventory storage costs. On the other hand, fashion products have less predictive demand characteristics and shorter lifecycles, requiring larger up-front purchase quantities to ensure that adequate inventory is available.

In Table 15.2 products are grouped according to their demand characteristics. This categorization results in each product being ranked based on its demand volume, variability and predictability. Supply-side buying patterns can now be developed because the demand-side characteristics are known. This combination will enable the retailer to adjust their buying habits further in order to minimize either the physical costs or the market mediation costs associated with demand patterns. For example, seasonal fashion demand has characteristics of single purchase orders placed far in advance of the season—leading to the description of merchandising as an 'art'. Components of the supply chain receiving great focus in this retailer are inbound transportation and processing, in order to get an early read on demand to determine the need for an add-on order.

Results of the supply and demand analysis are combined in a matrix that allows the thousands of merchandise products to be summarized into the dominant logistically distinct businesses. Table 15.3 illustrates an example from a department store. Each box represents the percentage of volume that an LDB represents, and all of the merchandise categories can be summed to give the dominant businesses that require distinct supply chain support. In this example, the analysis demonstrated the need for the retailer to develop stronger capabilities in the replenishment channel to take advantage of new vendor capabilities for many categories of its merchandise. Previously this retailer had focused all of its logistics resources on a fashion-based channel, with characteristics of

Table 15.1
Logistically distinct business framework: supply analysis

Product purchase and flow characteristics	Buying frequency	Delivery frequency	Vendor- and volume-driven economic order quantity	Definition/example
Single order—small	Once	Once	Less than 2 weeks	Requires long-term purchase commitments or long manufacturing lead times—but can be produced and delivered in small quantities. Example: promotional breadmaker package.
Single order—large	Once	Once	More than 8 weeks	Long lead times, large order quantities and may only be available once in the selling cycle. Example: special-order logo items.
Multiple replenishment	Many	Many	More than 8 weeks	Can be ordered throughout the selling cycle but economically in large quantities. Example: imported rice cookers
Continuous replenishment	Many	Many	Less than 2 weeks	Can be ordered throughout selling cycle in small quantities. Example: microwave ovens.
High value	Many	Many	Once	Special orders or basics in quantities of one. Example: designer colour mixers.

Table 15.2
Logistically distinct business framework: demand analysis

Product demand and flow characteristics	Type	Volume	Variability	Predictability	Definition/example
Basics—regular	Year round	High	Low	High	High-volume merchandise with non-volatile demand—blowdryer
Basics—planned promotion	Year round	High	High	High	Regular item that is on a planned promotion—pan sets
Basics—unplanned demand	Year round	High	High	Low	Regular item subjected to non-planned demand peaks—water filters
Basics—sporadic	Year round	Low	High	Low	Sells year round but in low quantities—high-end microwave
Seasonal	Speciality	High	High	High	Speciality items with finite life—grills
Fashion	Speciality	High	High	Low	New item with short selling life and unknown demand—new model introduction

Table 15.3
Dominant customer buying traits and product-replenishment traits

Sample men's suits matrix (% of business)
Sample shoes matrix (% of business)
Sample electric housewares matrix (% of business)

Demand \ Supply	Single order—small	Single order—large	Multiple replenishment	Continuous replenishment	High value	Total sales %
Basics—regular	-	-	8%	43%	4%	55%
Basics—planned excessive	-	-	12%	18%	-	30%
Basics—unplanned excessive	-	-	-	-	-	0%
Basics—sporadic	-	-	-	4%	6%	10%
Seasonal	-	-	-	-	-	0%
Fashion	5%	-	-	-	-	5%
Total sales %	5%	0%	20%	65%	10%	100%

■ Dominant logistically distinct businesses

large, one-time orders and low inventory turn. Although some replenishment capability was in place, the volumes analysed were twice as high as expected and a new focus was developed to strengthen this channel.

Segmenting products based on either supply or demand will enable supply chain cost reduction, but segmenting products based on a matrix combining both supply and demand characteristics will enable supply chain cost optimization across each product family. Overall, carrying out the LDB framework allows the retailer to customize each of the main supply chains—direct to consumer, direct to store, single-level distribution or multiple-level distribution—with components that support all the supply and demand characteristics for each product family. For instance, for a given LDB, which of the dominant retail supply chains is correct and how must the individual components be modified to create the optimal supply chain? Does processing have to move to the vendor or can it be eliminated to speed merchandise to the selling floor?

The logistically distinct business framework provides advantages beyond the cost savings associated with rationalizing supply and demand patterns. Best practices can be compared easily across radically different types of business because the merchandise flow characteristics have been determined to be similar. This can be crucial if a retailer is considering a merger with or an acquisition of another retailer. Another advantage of the LDB framework is that it tailors supply chains to individual businesses, which results in focused communication to individual business managers. Finally, the framework enables each business to track their revenues and costs better, such that managers fully understand which products or families will yield the greatest returns from additional supply chain investments in order to allocate human resources and capital investments properly among growing, stable and declining product demand.

Strategic objectives driven by an LDB analysis

With the thousands of supply chains now effectively combined into just a few common supply chains, the retailer can focus on the correct financial, information and human resources to the strategically important LDBs. An LDB analysis typically generates several common strategic objectives to optimize supply chain performance: improved forecast accuracy, faster and more accurate replenishment, better in-stock position, flexible channel capability and strong informational linkages.

Improved forecast accuracy

Vendors and retailers have traditionally forecast demand for merchandise separately with multiple models and variations of data. Leading retailers are developing new integrated systems not only to share point-of-sale (POS) data but to develop jointly and share forecasts. Collaborative forecasting and replenishment (CFAR) is a means by which value chain collaboration is promoting the exchange of demand information throughout the supply chain. Its objective is to synchronize the supply side with the demand side of the supply chain, while lowering total supply chain inventories, improving asset utilization and decreasing non-value-added activities.

Three types of collaboration exist in the retail world: simple, formulated and modelled. Simple collaboration is the main type in the retail universe, as vendors and retailers commonly pass data unique to their businesses between each other via EDI or fax on a daily basis, where the demand stream is typically based on future orders, warehouse flow activity or sales forecasts. Fewer retailers participate in the next level up in sophistication, formulated collaboration, where one organization will provide a supplier with demand parameters and priorities, or a 'formula', to guide their replenishment activities. Typically it is the retailer driving the replenishment formula according to dictated protocols and priorities. Modelled collaboration involves the sharing of operational models between two firms so that each trading partner has real-time visibility into each other's capacities, factory loads, on-hand inventories and committed orders. However, this is extremely rare in retail because relationships have not been traditionally defined as mutually trusting. Modelled collaboration would nevertheless support an ideal vision of the 'virtual manufacturer,' as each partner can make unilateral (but informed) decisions that may affect another organization's resources.

Faster and more accurate replenishment

Originally driven by basic and everyday items, the principles of continuous replenishment are also being developed for seasonal and fashion-type merchandise. This includes smaller, more frequent orders, electronic transactions, shorter vendor lead times and smaller, assorted inner packs. Eliminating time in the supply chain allows more accurate forecasts since the purchase decision can be delayed until more demand data is known. Adopting these techniques also supports another goal of retailers, which is reducing investment in their main asset, inventory.

Better in-stock position

Retailers are continually working on the fine balance between reducing inventory levels and increasing sales demand. Increased pressure on the supply chain occurs as the inventory buffers are removed, first from the retailer and then from their vendors. Progressive retailers are closely monitoring sales velocity by item with their store layout, planogram (a precise description of the quantities and facings of the product assortment by shelf and area of the stores) and displays and fixtures to minimize out-of-stocks or over-stocks. Owing in part to the need to ensure product freshness while accommodating the velocity of their merchandise flow, large format grocery chains have worked hard with their manufacturers to increase the frequency of shipments needed to resupply store shelves on a just-in-time basis.

Flexible channel capability

An LDB analysis will generally point towards the need to support several dominant channel configurations. As volumes shift from one LDB to another, the retailer has the flexibility to support the sales demand without having to recreate channels or use existing suboptimal channels. Since retailers usually make tremendous investments in assets and systems for their present supply chain configuration, there is a tendency to layer change into the existing infrastructure, which can create a suboptimal solution. As long as the volume through a logistically distinct business remains low, this can be an acceptable strategy. Also, as volumes change through the various channels, global retailers entering a new market or category can gain an advantage by building and utilizing the ideal supply chain configurations from the beginning, frequently forcing manufacturers to advance rapidly to the end state or lose out entirely on supplying their business.

This is especially true of new retail entrants using e-commerce capability, such as Amazon.com. It does not have any retail store assets and does not even own the infrastructure to deliver books to individual customers. It did, however, design the correct supply chain to match the logistically distinct business of Internet book selling to individual customers. Amazon.com set itself up as an information intermediary, forwarding customer requests directly to the manufacturer to fulfil orders. Barnes and Noble was forced to match this supply chain advantage by building its own Internet presence and utilizing its existing distribution assets to match and even beat Amazon.com in the speed and ease of delivery to the customer.

Retailers may typically utilize several channels depending on the correct application of their LDB analysis. For example, in Home Depot's case, it eventually recognized that not all products could go direct to stores. One of the early configurations that departed from its standard model was lumber, where the company needed to take advantage of the lower cost of rail shipping and set up its own distribution centres with access to railroads. In contrast, for some of the smaller, assortment-intensive items such as bolts and screws, Home Depot has stepped away from managing the supply chain and instead relies on outside service representatives to manage ordering and shelf stocking.

Strong information links

Retailers who understand how to develop flexible, LDB-oriented supply chain structures in combination with advanced information networks will be increasingly able to extend their grip on the world market. Streamlined merchandise flow is difficult if the physical movement of goods is delayed waiting for correct information. Given compressed lead times and shorter selling cycles, the ability to maintain and share extremely accurate information is becoming a key competitive weapon. In the past retailers were able to avoid substantial investments in information technology (relative to other industries) by innovative merchandising strategies. In the future, successful retailers must do both. By putting in advanced systems and communications networks, those retailers who have a compelling merchandise assortment will raise new barriers to entry and hasten the consolidation of the retail industry. Toys 'R' Us is a good example of a global retailer that has used its information systems as a platform for common supply chain techniques around the world. Early on, it adopted a centralized platform for all of its international operations. In doing so, it was able to keep its administrative costs under control as it entered new countries, doing a better job than most international retailers in minimizing the losses typically encountered in opening in new countries.

Conclusion

The complexity of the retail business, driven by the diverse merchandise mix, worldwide sourcing and various selling formats, requires a strategic framework to create optimal supply chains that can deliver the right merchandise, at the right time and at the right price. Retailers that can deliver this value proposition to their customers will survive in a global marketplace that increasingly will have fewer but more dominant retailers as well as manufacturers attempting to sell direct to consumers. The logistically distinct business framework combines both the supply and demand characteristics to create the correct combination of supply chain components for each of the main retail supply chains possible within a company. The LDB framework also focuses effort on key strategic objectives that support optimal supply chains, such as new forms of collaborative forecasting, expansion of continuous replenishment, increasing in-stock position, creating flexible channel capabilities and making stronger informational links.

References

Fuller, Joseph B., O'Connor, James and Rawlinson, Richard (1993) 'Tailored logistics: the next advantage', *Harvard Business Review*, 71 (3) May/Jun, 91–3.

The consumer direct channel
How the virtual retailer is winning new customers

Steve Bartolotta

CHAPTER

16

Consumers today, with their changing lifestyles and expectations, are becoming increasingly willing to pay a premium for products and services for added convenience or other perceived value. 'Consumer direct' represents one such service that companies are offering to supply goods and services to these often cash-rich, time-poor consumers. The concept of consumer direct is to enable consumers to receive products and services without the need to shop for them physically. Some new businesses resulting from this new channel compete directly against traditional stores, while others are providing new capabilities made available through information technology and information management. This chapter investigates the impact of this 'virtual retailer' and how logistics professionals can capture the potential of the consumer direct supply channel. Consumer direct offers new options and new opportunities for winning consumers.

Introduction

The premise of consumer direct is for consumers to be able to place orders for groceries and other products and services and have them delivered to their homes or other convenient places. Consumers, particularly those in dual-income families who have increased incomes but little leisure time, have become increasingly discontent with traditional shopping models. Consumer direct is one of the solutions currently underway in several countries to satisfy these consumers, including the USA, Australia and the UK. While consumer direct is most developed in the USA, no one has yet demonstrated command of this new channel and proven its profitability.

Figure 16.1 depicts the essential elements of the consumer direct channel. This channel offers suppliers and manufacturers new options within which to distribute and market their products. It is not yet clear how the virtual retailer will evolve. What is certain is that it can play a role as a conduit between consumers and purveyors of goods and

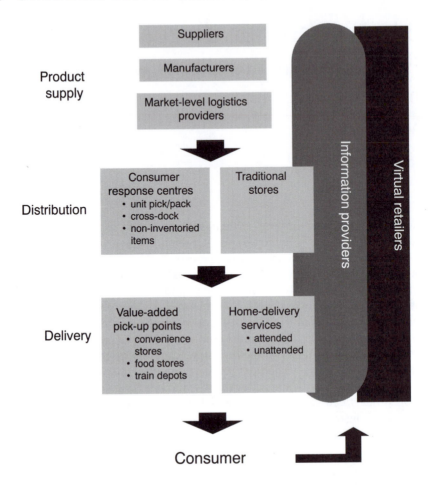

Figure 16.1 The consumer direct model

services. Additionally, the virtual retailer can be proprietary or act as intermediary for several companies.

The ability of this channel to deliver higher net profits rests on the fact that it is more efficient than the traditional models across several dimensions. A primary driver is the bundling of non-traditional services, which attracts extra customers and serves to increase average gross margins. Also important is the elimination of the need for a retail store: lease costs are lower when leasing warehouse rather than retail space, less inventory is required and labour costs are reduced. Electronic ordering provides critical data concerning demand, previously unattainable, to allow for increased forecast accuracy and one-to-one consumer marketing. And finally, requiring consumers to plan their ordering on a recurring basis results in larger average order sizes which can be processed more efficiently.

This chapter will provide a perspective on consumer direct for retailers wishing to enter the home delivery market and for manufacturers looking to exploit this new channel. First, it will outline the key drivers behind consumer direct, it will then examine the issues associated with start-up and achieving scale in the industry, describe the channel structures available for delivering products and services and discuss the technology required. Finally, the facilities and transportation aspects of consumer direct will be discussed, as well as the potential range of products and services that can be offered.

Overview of the consumer direct industry

Home delivery may represent perhaps the single largest trend in grocery retailing for the next decade. A major research study in 1996 (sponsored by Andersen Consulting and 14 major food and consumer packaged goods companies) found that home delivery has the potential to capture 8 to 12 per cent of the US grocery and related products market within seven to ten years. This equates to about $60 to $85 billion of the $720 billion market in the US. More interestingly, consumer direct has the potential to deliver net profits of between 4 and 6 per cent, far in excess of the traditional grocery channel.

The research study, called the Consumer Direct Cooperative, also found that:

■ consumer interest is high across all segments of the US population;
■ pricing and service provider account for nearly 50 per cent of the decision to use a consumer direct service;
■ consumers are more likely to use a service that has features with which they are readily familiar, but ultimately will evolve to a more efficient channel;
■ combined gross margins which include service fees and other revenue can equal 32 per cent;
■ to be successful, a company must operate across several markets to fully leverage the heavy investment required; and
■ supply-side activities will be the largest single operating expense and approach 13 per cent of sales.

Consumers have clearly demonstrated their appetite for this exciting new concept by virtue of the sheer number of companies scrambling to satisfy their demands. To date, more than 50 companies are involved in some fashion with home delivery within the USA alone. The industry has largely been entered by new providers, with the majority of existing food companies adopting a 'wait and see' approach.

Companies such as Peapod in Chicago, Streamline and Hannaford's 'Home Runs' in Boston and Gopher Groceries in Tampa Bay, Florida are springing up in most major markets throughout the US. The following are two examples of companies pursuing the home delivery market, each with a different strategy and supply channel configuration.

CASE STUDY Attended delivery model

Peapod, based in Evanston, Illinois, is the most successful home delivery company to date. It started in 1989 in a Chicago suburb. Peapod first established its online ordering software in 1990 and continues to refine its Web page which now includes over 40 000 products. The company markets and provides its services through current retailers and now operates in several cities, including Chicago, Boston, Columbus and San Francisco. Peapod is picking orders largely in the same fashion a consumer would, but also then delivers to the home at a pre-scheduled time. Customer membership has grown from 4600 in 1995 to over 71 000 in 1997. This customer base has provided revenues of around $59 million in 1997, a 104 per cent increase over the previous year, highlighting the rapid growth attainable through this new channel.

CASE STUDY Unattended delivery model

Streamline, based in Westwood, MA, offers a lifestyle solution that meets the needs of busy suburban families juggling time-intensive demands of family and dual careers. The company offers a broad array of essential and convenience services, including home shopping and delivery of groceries, dry cleaning and video rentals. Founded in 1993, Streamline currently serves Boston-area families weekly from its proprietary warehouse. A key feature is for delivery to take place at the consumer's home in their absence. To accommodate this, a receptacle has been placed in the customer's garage which houses a refrigerator and a shelving unit. The driver has access to the garage and delivers between 8 am and 6 pm. Customers leave items requiring dry cleaning or other service for the driver to pick up for processing and return the following week.

Consumer direct companies bring to the consumer a plethora of other value-added services. Much of these are exhibited on their Web pages in the form of meal solutions planning, standing orders to speed entry, announcement of specials and product information, to name a few. In all cases, changes are occurring rapidly as companies respond to new consumer demands once consumers have had an opportunity to try the service. Customer focus groups have also contributed to the knowledge capital of companies entering this market.

There are several primary drivers of the emerging consumer direct channel. Technological advancements in capabilities play a significant role in enabling companies to link processes in a efficient fashion to drive the business. This technology is increasingly becoming available at lower costs, helping to make the channel viable. Much of the more advanced technology is exhibited in the Web pages that consumers use in placing orders. Second, consumers are increasingly pressed for time and are discontent with the traditional shopping experience. This was clearly evident in 1996 when food service companies surpassed grocery retail as a percentage of total spend due to new retail formats catering to home meal replacement. In addition, this new channel offers a way to increase the profits normally found in grocery retail, by offering non-traditional products and services, such as dry cleaning, film development and prescriptions.

The success of this new channel has significant implications for companies within the food industry. Supermarket chains, with their high capital cost structure, have the most to lose. If consumer direct achieves its potential of 8 to 12 per cent market share, grocery retailers will lose about half of their earnings before interest, taxes, depreciation and amortization. To maintain existing levels of return on invested capital, retailers must eliminate fixed costs equal to 2 per cent of sales.

Consumer direct offers new marketing opportunities to 'lock in' brand loyalty, increase efficiency and create an exciting new shopping experience for consumers. Table 16.1 highlights several of those new opportunities and their related implications.

Significant investment in facilities, equipment, technology and transportation will be required to support this channel. Estimates range from between $11 and $13 million in capital to operate a single location. The total investment decreases to between $9 and $10 million when leveraging multiple facilities across several markets. Information systems assets are likely to be highly customized and expensive, yet are highly leverageable and a critical expense.

To achieve viability, a company entering the home delivery arena must obtain answers to a variety of critical business issues and tailor an appropriate market strategy. Questions surrounding stock-keeping units (SKUs) and service offerings, channel design, reverse logistics and pricing are abundant and not equally applied across all consumers. Selecting the right balance to attract adequate market share coupled with the right service level and cost structure, while fundamental, will challenge even dominant food industry players. In essence, a company must successfully become a market-level logistics provider to a customer of one.

One interesting note is that most of the capabilities to support home delivery already exist. Companies will be challenged to identify which capabilities are necessary to support their own strategy and integrate those processes efficiently. In some cases, companies may opt to

Table 16.1
Marketing process opportunities and implications

Opportunities	Implications
• Influence consumer consumption, 'lock in' brand loyalty, and increase switching costs on approximately one-third of household grocery needs through automatic replenishment programmes	• Importance of being first to the household • Need to help consumers forecast household consumption
• Targeted new product sampling can double repeat purchase rates, while simultaneously minimizing sampling costs	• Access to consumers and relevant household data required • Need to build competency in 'two-way' communications with consumers
• Replicate the excitement of in-store shopping in a 'virtual' channel through creative marketing/ merchandising programmes, such as sampling and bundling • Stimulate impulse sales	• Creative translation of traditional marketing processes required

outsource elements of the supply channel to focus instead on their core capabilities.

Entering the home delivery market

A prime barrier for a company considering entry into the home delivery market is the heavy investment of capital necessary to operate efficiently. Total capital requirements needed to achieve scale must be estimated and strategically deployed to mitigate risks to investors. Current estimates place total assets required for a single facility serving one market at between $11 and $13 million. As such, a consumer direct company will probably evolve through a series of stages in each market. Successful completion of each phase will be required by investors prior to the release of funds for subsequent phases. The evolution is likely to resemble Figure 16.2.

More than 50 companies across the USA today are actively engaged in Phase 1 and 2 activities. Few companies have yet progressed to Phase

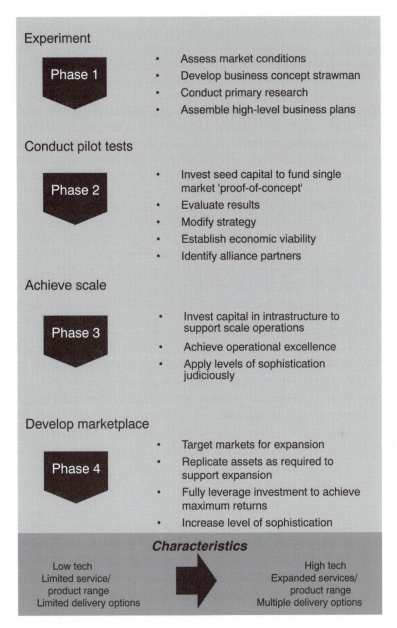

Figure 16.2 Phases in consumer direct evolution

3 or 4. No one has emerged as economically viable, but several exhibit promise in that they have been able to attract a substantial customer base.

A majority of companies involved in food retailing will participate to some degree in Phase 1 activities. Time will be spent developing an understanding of the business and service requirements. From this, decisions will be made regarding how consumer direct may fit into or require modification of their existing business strategy. Companies with no current intent of entering this business will keenly watch those engaged in Phase 2 and 3 activities as indicators of future success. It is within Phase 1 where companies such as supermarket chains with an already high capital investment will develop alternative strategies to secure their existing volume.

Phase 2 marks that point where hard assets are being secured to operate the business and prove the working model. Investments will be made as required, but with the caveat that they might be disposable in the event of failure to prove viability or seed capital runs out. Business process architecture will be defined for the short term and longer-term needs and capital requirements for operating at scale identified. Investors will scrutinize the data to assess whether the concept merits consideration for moving to Phase 3.

Reaching the third level establishes a firm commitment to the vision by all associated parties. The goal now becomes to create a replicatable asset. Heavy technological investments will be made to leverage across a network of markets. Infrastructure will be created to dominate markets currently serviced. Target markets will be identified along with a roll-out plan for expansion. Many companies will pursue public stock offerings to secure the capital necessary for funding expansion. Lastly, competition will begin to increase within markets where consumers have demonstrated an appetite for this service by both other home delivery companies and existing food retailers using alternative strategies.

Channel configuration

Home delivery companies must adopt a channel strategy to execute delivery of the products and services offered. Figure 16.3 highlights the existing food delivery channel and hypothesizes a number of potential 'consumer direct' options.

The options presented are not exhaustive in that other variations can and in fact do exist, such as mail-order groceries. The primary and most apparent difference is how the delivery is consummated. In both supermarket and restaurant options, the supply channel largely ends at the retail establishment that consumers must be attracted to patronize. Consumer direct channels in some fashion seek out the customer to extract their order with ultimate delivery a point of differentiation between consumer direct options. Consumer direct options also allow for the two-way exchange of product, opening the way to bundling other services such as film development.

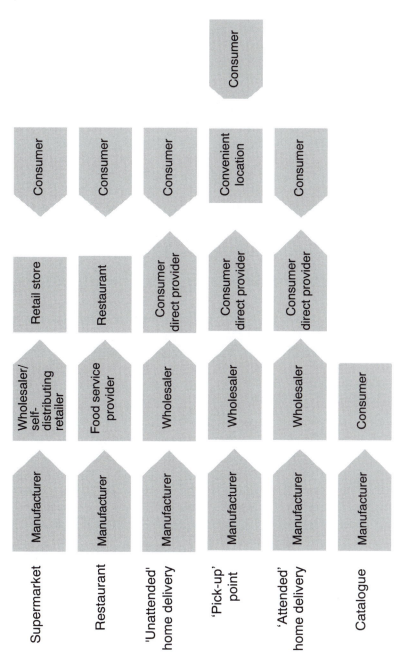

Figure 16.3 The consumer direct model

Each of the consumer direct channels offers a very different proposition to the consumer regarding delivery. Convenience to the consumer varies to some degree with each structure. Generally, as convenience increases, so does the representative cost to support the channel. However, cost should not be looked at in isolation as the consumer will ultimately dictate what their preference is and perform the necessary cost/benefit trade-off.

Besides consumer considerations, each channel has different and unique infrastructure needs. The current channels of supermarkets and restaurants require bricks and mortar in the form of retail establishments for consumers to patronize. These assets require a high capital investment and are inflexible to changes in demand. Consumer direct channels forgo a retail location and instead add a delivery component. This delivery element is further modified depending on the consumer direct channel being served. In the case of unattended home delivery, the provider maximizes its truck assets as it does not have to meet specific delivery windows, but must have some way to protect and secure the product at the home. Attended home delivery requires more sophistication in routing/scheduling packages to use the fleet best given specific day and time requirements from the consumer. Pick-up points, while efficient in that more than one order can be brought to a single stop, add an intermediary in the process and again must store and protect the product until it is received by the consumer.

Channel economics can be affected in other ways as well. Order response time, reverse logistics and peak demand variability, to name a few, will contribute to a channel's effectiveness. These and other factors must be considered in the overall selection process.

Technology

Technology will act as the glue that binds all activities of the channel together. Each function in the channel will rely on this glue to provide timely and specific information to meet customer requests and requirements. Some of the more important systems required are order entry, household data management, warehouse management and routing/scheduling systems, not to mention standard financial systems. Successfully linking all systems together in real time will be required to manage the overall operation effectively.

Establishment of a robust ordering device is probably the most critical system, as it sits at the beginning of all processes and sets the operation in motion. Consumers' increased access to technology such as the personal computer, Web television and facsimile machines is really the enabler for this channel to develop, as it provides retailers with a low-cost method to capture critical consumer information in the form of an order and allows for two-way exchange of information. Choices range from manual order entry via phone and fax orders, to development of an Internet site or even some form of in-home device where products to be ordered can be scanned.

Any system chosen must have the ability to capture exact customer requirements and convert that knowledge into an executable order which can be tracked through all processes. Information captured at this juncture can include not only customer name, SKUs and quantity, but one-off special instructions, comments regarding the ripeness of bananas desired or substitutions. Communicating this information in a timely fashion where required throughout the process will ensure that customer requirements and expectations are met. One caveat to any system chosen is that it must enhance the overall shopping experience for the consumer.

A second unique system requirement emerging from this channel is the previously unavailable ability to perform data mining. Not only can household purchases be tracked (much like scan-saver cards do) but original demand data can be captured that is missed today as consumers perform their own substitutions for items not on the shelf. This data will be highly valuable to not only manufacturers but purchasing agents performing replenishment by eliminating false demand. Providers will benefit by being able to maintain a tighter rein on inventory levels and offer greater in-stock positions.

While the order entry system serves as an important front end to all processes, the warehouse management system (WMS) serves as the heart of the operation. A unique feature of a WMS is its ability to handle effectively the sheer number of unit picks required in a consumer direct environment. Assuming a $50 million facility, a WMS will handle about 2.5 million cases on the receiving end, but 25 million units during order selection in a single year. In addition, a WMS for entities offering the broadest range of products and services must support time-sensitive cross-docking of products procured from outsourced vendors. Given the current offerings of home delivery companies in the market today, a WMS must also have the capacity to process all customer transactions within an 8- to 10-hour cycle.

Facility considerations

A critical element for entrants into the home delivery market is establishing a medium to facilitate the procurement of products and service. To date, there are few choices available from which to select. A company can choose either to leverage the existing supermarket channel or to establish their own proprietary warehouse. Regardless of the form chosen, it represents the linchpin where all processes culminate and must meet several objectives:

■ maintain product quality (through multiple temperate zones and product separation);
■ support a fleet operation and customer pick-up;
■ provide cross-dock and product consolidation; and
■ execute flawlessly against the expectations of customers.

While the first three objectives are fairly straightforward, the latter is where many entities will fail. Consider the following example:

Assume that a company with sales of $50 million has an average order size of $100. Also, assume that the order consists of 50 items. This would require 25 million picking transactions across 500 000 orders. If a company was able to achieve a picking accuracy of 99.5 per cent, one in four orders would contain an error. This is clearly an unacceptable rate from a consumer perspective, especially with 'time-starved' consumers looking for less stress. This can only be further compounded by errors occurring within other business processes.

Companies will need to pursue excellence relentlessly in all facets of their operation to prevent errors. Achieving excellence will be dependent on the establishment of a comprehensive set of processes against which to execute consistently, an extensive training programme to educate associates and integrating automation where feasible.

Evaluating the options available to home delivery providers against the requirements above yields significant differences between them. The dominant choice pursued by consumer direct companies to date is the existing supermarket channel. Supermarkets may offer the easiest and lowest initial capital cost entry into the market as much of the infrastructure is in place to procure products from vendors. The existing supermarket infrastructure was not designed to be an efficient order-processing format. It was designed with the consumer's overall shopping experience in mind. Inventory visibility, peak traffic demand and minimal dock space to support consolidation will all be significant challenges. Effective use of this model will require more emphasis on processes and training as it will be difficult to integrate automation into this format. Additionally, as volume increases, it will be necessary to leverage across multiple locations as inventory levels cannot be adequately increased beyond the levels that exist in a store today because of shelf-space constraints. Having to leverage across multiple locations will only increase the overall complexity.

Establishment of a proprietary warehouse would seem to be the only choice to sustain operations in the long term. Achieving the types of efficiencies required by this new channel will require the establishment of a piece-pick facility. There are several requirements for establishing a piece-pick warehouse capable of supporting a home delivery system. Multiple temperate zones consisting of ambient, perishable and frozen space are necessary to maintain product quality throughout the chill chain. Space within the facility, while limited, will still need to provide ample room for the separation of product that when placed together sacrifices quality. Racking to support a limited amount of on-hand inventory and store cross-docked products, as well as other storage mediums such as a skate rail for dry cleaning, will be necessary depending on the offering. Dock configuration and capacity will be the most critical component of the facility to enable the large number of deliveries that will occur.

Transportation

Transportation's mission is not only to deliver consumer orders but to maintain product quality and support reverse logistics while performing on-time in a profitable fashion. Maintaining product quality includes not only the provision of a proper temperate environment, but product segregation as well. Reverse logistics can be fairly broad and include product returns, bottle redemption, coupons and dry cleaning, to name but a few. Much of transportation's ability to operate profitably will be dictated by the offering to consumers around demand responsiveness, the delivery window and attended versus unattended delivery.

Delivery expense is perhaps the single largest variable expense that is not related directly to order value. As a result, a sufficient average order value is necessary to absorb the related delivery expense fully and maintain profitable operations. No other drivers of transportation expense impart the same level of variability.

On one end of the spectrum companies can strive to provide service at the lowest possible cost by limiting customers' ability to order on demand. Fixed delivery schedules, 24-hour lead time for order placement and seven-day-a-week delivery can all help to maintain an efficient operation. A few companies have even adopted unattended delivery into their offering, which enables delivery to be achieved in the absence of the consumer. Unattended delivery does, however, require additional capital to provide a medium at the home where the products can be left and continue to maintain quality. The other end of the spectrum is a bevy of services which offer the highest convenience to consumers. This essentially allows customers to place orders completely on demand without restriction. It could include delivery occurring within one hour of order placement or meeting specific delivery windows.

It is likely that a company will need to find some balance between the two extremes to provide a convenient solution at an affordable cost. One option for significantly controlling delivery costs would be to deliver multiple orders to a single location, also known as a pool point. In general, consumers have a number of locations that they frequent during the week such as church, work, schools or even gas stations that could be used.

Reverse logistics opens many opportunities, for example the ability to offer consumers a way to have someone else perform virtually any mundane errand such as dry cleaning, parcel shipment, film processing and others. The only real restriction is the value that consumers are willing to pay for the extra services and they must all be capable of using the existing equipment.

Product and service offering

The foundation for a consumer direct company is the value proposition it poses to consumers: how convenient are the products and services it offers? The right product and service offering must generate a sufficient average order value to cover the high variable costs generated with each order, which is largely a function of orders taken, not value. Figure 16.4 highlights the relationship between order value and transportation expense.

Clearly, the higher the average order value, the better a company will position itself for long-term sustainability. Consequently, simply offering a multitude of products and services across all categories is not enough, as increases in operational complexity cause greater variable costs and required infrastructure. Establishing the right mix given the resources and core capabilities available necessary to execute effectively will be the key to success.

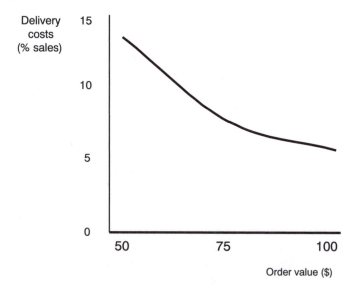

Figure 16.4 Order value

In theory, in a virtual world there are no constraints as to what products and services are offered as companies will no longer be limited by shelf space. Virtual companies will instead be constrained by their ability to execute flawlessly the demands of their customers. As such, a company may want first to limit its offering and add as it builds its capabilities.

Evaluating the current product offering by supermarket chains is a good start to developing a consumer direct offering. Reviewing products offered for sale by supermarkets today reveals an industry average level of SKUs in excess of 30 000. In many cases, this average is driven by marketing efforts to appeal to a broad spectrum of consumers through the proliferation of available brands and sizes and to obtain slotting allowances from manufacturers. SKU-level analysis would reveal that 55 per cent of SKUs account for 90 per cent of retail demand. Aggregating volume from similar product with different brand and size considerations should reveal even greater opportunity to a home delivery company in rationalizing their product assortment. To be effective, a company will, at a minimum, have to maintain category and commodity integrity so as not to cause a customer the inconvenience of having to go to the store anyway. Driving demand into a rationalized set of SKUs will enable a higher confidence level for predictability of demand, generating a high in-stock level. This high in-stock position will mitigate the complexity associated with substitutions and assist in maintaining customer satisfaction.

Services pose the greatest opportunity for a company to generate higher order sizes, attract more customers and supplement margins from the traditional grocery basket. Services also run the gamut from dry cleaning to premiums for expedited orders. This will ultimately be the largest point of differentiation between providers, as companies compete for share. Services can require very different supply channel needs than traditional products. Dry cleaning, for example, will require a company to develop not only reverse logistics capabilities but alliances with outsourcing vendors and to create a surety relationship for garments held. Video rentals must be tracked and noted when placed back in stock and available for rental, with late fee charging capability. Incremental costs for expedited services must be calculated and collected. A cost/benefit analysis for each proposed service can aid the selection process and ensure adequate returns.

Table 16.2 provides a perspective on potential services offered to consumers through this channel. This table is the synopsis of consumer research focused at understanding consumer preferences across a wide range of options. The primary drivers of the decision to use the channel are the price of the goods and services and who is the provider. These two factors account for more than 50 per cent of the decision to purchase. All other factors are equal in importance and individually are

Table 16.2 Summary of consumer preferences

Most preferred ← Relative preference → Least preferred

Group	Attribute							
Price	Monthly charges	$0	$25	$50				
	Cost of purchase	3% lower	Equal	5% higher				
Provider	Service provider	Current supermarket	New company	Group of manufacturers	Group of retailers	Delivery service	Other major supermarkets	Online services
Demand	Product availability	More than ave store	Same as average store	95%	85%	75%		
	Minimum order	$25	$50	$75	$100			
Supply	Delivery location and time	Home attended 1hr window	Home attended 4hr window	Attended pick-up point	Home unattended	Unattended pick-up point		
	Delivery lead time	Same day 4hrs	Same day 8hrs	Next day	Second day			
	Delivery day	Any day	Mon–Thurs	Fri	Sat or Sun			
Order	Order placement	Phone	Phone/voice recognition	PC	TV devide	New device	Fax	

Source: Consumer Direct Cooperative Market Research

relatively insignificant, allowing companies the latitude to tailor the offering. Largely, consumers want those services with which they are most familiar at the lowest cost.

Conclusion

As with any emerging industry, it is difficult to determine accurately how it may develop. Many of the concepts or views discussed here will surely require modification over time or even be proven wrong. Likewise, many new points of view will be developed in the quest to satisfy consumers' demand for this new channel. What will not change is the consumer's thirst for convenience and fresh ideas. Home delivery can certainly provide retailers with a tool to meet a broad range of demands. Finding the right mix of product and service offering that can be consistently and profitably provided will be key to success.

Relationships and alliances
Embracing the era of network competition
Martin Christopher

Perhaps one of the most significant breakthroughs in management thinking in the closing years of the twentieth century has been the realization that individual businesses no longer compete as stand-alone entities, but rather as supply chains. We are now entering the era of 'network competition' where the prizes will go to those organizations who can better structure, coordinate and manage the relationships with their partners in a network committed to better, faster and closer relationships with their final customers.

Introduction

In the past it was more often the case that organizations were structured and managed on the basis of optimizing their own operations with little regard for the way in which they interfaced with suppliers and, indeed, customers. The business model was essentially 'transactional', meaning that products and services were bought and sold on an arm's-length basis and that there was little enthusiasm for the concept of longer-term, mutually dependent relationships. The end result was often a high-cost, low-quality solution for the final customer in the chain.

The emerging competitive paradigm is in stark contrast to the conventional model. It suggests that in today's challenging global markets, the route to sustainable advantage lies in managing the complex web of relationships that link highly focused providers of specific elements of the final offer in a cost-effective value-added chain.

The key to success in this new competitive framework, it can be argued, is the way in which this network of alliances and suppliers are welded together in partnership to achieve mutually beneficial goals. Thus, Compaq and Dell compete not as independent businesses, but as two uniquely configured networks of alliances and partnerships.

In this chapter a distinction is made between alliances and suppliers—although some might see this as semantic since the aim is to achieve partnership with both. The definitions used are:

■ *Suppliers*: Suppliers or vendors are the providers of physical resources to the business. Sometimes these resources will be augmented by services but typically they will be characterized as the upstream source of raw materials, components, products or other tangible items that flow on a continuing basis into and through the customer business.
■ *Alliances*: In a sense, alliance partners are suppliers too. The difference is that typically they will be supplying competencies and capabilities which more often than not will be knowledge based rather than product based. They may well provide services and often these alliances will have been created in response to the perceived need to outsource an activity within the company's value chain.

Suppliers and alliance partners together form the web of relationships that we know as the 'supply chain'. The term 'supply chain management' is now widely used, although strictly speaking it is not a chain but a network and ideally it should be 'demand' not 'supply' that drives it. Whatever we call it, the crucial thing is that we manage it on an integrated basis. Indeed, the opportunities for achieving sustainable competitive advantage through the supply chain are considerable as the basis for competition switches from the single firm to the network.

The new rules of competition

The rules of competition are changing. It is no longer enough to rely on brand values or proprietary technology. Certainly, strong brands combined with product and process innovation can provide a firm foundation on which marketplace success can be built. But real competitive advantage comes from a combination of loyal consumers, committed customers and a superior supply chain. Figure 17.1 highlights the interplay of these three key competitive elements.

While no one element of this trinity is more important than the other, and they are highly inter-connected and inter-dependent, many companies are finding that the supply chain can provide them with an as yet untapped source of additional advantage.

The aims of supply chain management are aptly summarized by three words: better, faster, closer.

Better

It has now become an accepted fact of commercial life that customer service is a critical determinant in winning and keeping customers. Today's customer in virtually every market is demanding ever-higher levels of performance from suppliers, particularly with respect to delivery service.

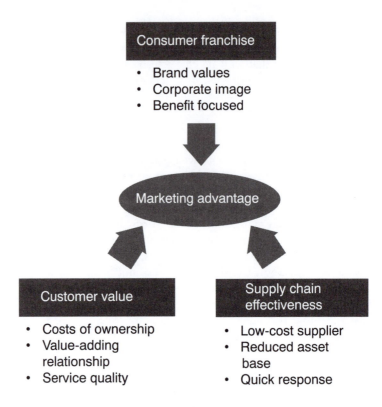

Figure 17.1   Marketing and logistics converge

The focus on inventory reduction has caused many organizations to look closely at the quality of the inbound delivery service they receive from suppliers. At the other end of the marketing channel, consumers have become equally demanding in their service requirements. In the era of fast food and convenience stores, there is less willingness to wait. As a result, on-the-shelf availability will often overcome brand preference.

The challenge to organizations aspiring to be leaders in service performance is to recognize the service requirements of the different segments that they service and to restructure their logistics processes around the achievement of those service requirements.

Organizations in virtually every market sector have come to recognize that differentiation through superior customer service offers an opportunity to avoid price competition. Whilst there will always be 'price buyers' in any market, there are also large numbers of service-sensitive customers.

Service quality is perhaps the most powerful element in the marketing mix. Organizations that have focused on managing the processes that lead to higher and more consistent levels of service tend also to be the most profitable, according to several recent studies. It is also recognized that increasing customer retention and hence customer lifetime provides higher-quality earnings and simultaneously makes competitive erosion of market share more difficult.

The key to improved customer retention, it can be argued, is in the provision of superior customer service. For that reason leading companies now measure their service performance in terms of 'perfect orders'. In other words, they are looking at service through the customers' eyes and are setting service standards based on the achievement of meeting customers' expectations 100 per cent of the time. In turn, these companies recognize that the only way these demanding goals can be met is through better management of logistics and an integrated supply chain.

Faster

In recent years, one of the most significant developments in the way that companies manage their operations and formulate their competitive strategies has been the focus on time. There are clearly many ways in which firms compete and through which they seek to gain advantage over their rivals. However, the ability to move quickly, whether it be in new product development or in replenishing customers' inventories, is increasingly recognized as a prerequisite for market-place success.

The late twentieth century has seen the emergence of the *time-sensitive* customer. These time-sensitive customers can be found in every type of market, be it in high-tech markets where short lifecycles demand short lead times, or in consumer durables manufacturing where just-in-time assembly requires just-in-time deliveries, or in everyday living where the pressures of managing a more complex, hectic lifestyle have led us to seek convenience—whether in banking, shopping or eating.

Whole industries have grown up around time compression, from overnight delivery to fast food. Technology has facilitated this process: cellular telephones, fax and satellite communications have all contributed to the continued search for the achievement of quicker response to the demands that customers place on us. Now, quality is measured not just in terms of product performance but delivery performance as well. Few industries have been immune from these pressures and managers must constantly seek ever more innovative ways of squeezing time out of every business process. Indeed, the main driver behind the business process reengineering (BPR) philosophy has been the search for more time-effective ways of doing things.

Time reduction does not only lead to faster response to customer needs but, just as importantly, can lead to cost reduction and greater flexibility. 'Time is money' may be a cliché, but in today's competitive marketplace it has never been more true.

Lack of responsiveness in logistics processes can heighten the risks both of stockouts, and therefore lost sales, and of over-stocked situations leading to markdowns or stock write-offs. Compaq Computer acknowledged that in 1994 its inability to respond to an upsurge in demand for its range of notebook computers led to estimated sales losses of up to $1 billion. At the same time, Apple Computer was reported to have been forced to scrap 30 000 brand new Newton personal organizers because of an over-estimate of demand. Similar examples can be found in industries as diverse as clothing and electrical components.

Closer

The emergence of the 'network organization' is a recent phenomenon that has given rise to much comment and analysis. These 'virtual' organizations are characterized by a confederation of specialist skills or capabilities provided by the network members. It is argued that such collaborative arrangements provide a more effective means of satisfying customer needs at a profit than does the single firm undertaking multiple value-creating activities. The implications of the network organization for marketing management are considerable and, in particular, the challenges to logistics management are profound.

To make networks more effective in satisfying end-user requirements requires a high level of cooperation between organizations in the network, along with the recognition of the need to make inter-firm relationships mutually beneficial. Underpinning the successful network organization is the value-added exchange of information between partners, meaning that information on downstream demand or usage is made visible to all the upstream members of the supply chain. Creating 'visibility' along the pipeline ensures that the manufacture and delivery of product can be driven by real demand rather than by a forecast and hence enables all parties in the chain to operate more effectively.

Supply chain management is concerned to achieve a more cost-effective satisfaction of end customer requirements through buyer-supplier process integration. This integration is typically achieved through a greater transparency of customer requirement via the sharing of information assisted by the establishment of 'seamless' processes that link the identification of a physical replenishment need with a 'just-in-time' response.

The important concept here is the idea of *process integration*. Processes are the fundamental ways through which value is created. Such processes include new product development, order fulfilment, supplier management and customer management. To achieve real integration in the supply chain requires ideally that these processes also be integrated—upstream with the supplier and downstream with customers. Take the new product development process. If suppliers as well as customers can become part of an integrated process team (as now happens increasingly in the car industry) then it is more likely that innovative products meeting the needs of customers and consumers will be developed—and at greater profit to the members of the integrated chain.

The same argument is true for all processes. The free flow of information up and down the chain, underpinning upstream and downstream integration, will enhance the recognition of mutual benefits and lead to a more responsive supply chain.

Supply chain management

As the critical role of suppliers and alliance partners comes to be increasingly recognized, the need for formal processes to manage the supply chain emerges. These processes are in effect an extension of the internal linkages that create the smooth flow of information and materials within a single organization into the other parties in the supply chain. Supply chain management has been defined as: 'the management of upstream and downstream relationships with suppliers, distributors and customer to achieve greater customer value at less cost' (Christopher, 1997).

The key to the achievement of this more responsive and cost-effective marketing process is buyer-supplier integration. What this means is that, rather than the totally separate decisions on critical issues such as production schedules, inventory levels and distribution plans that typify the uncoordinated chain, there is instead a single 'end-to-end' plan to manage the pipeline as a whole.

While many companies have begun the journey to supply chain integration, few have made it to the destination. It must be recognized that there are some significant hurdles to be overcome in the transition from a 'stand-alone' organization to supply chain partner. Stevens (1989) has identified four stages in this transformation process:

- ■ *The 'baseline organization'.* This organization operates the classical system of management, with the motivation of profit maximization and a high level of functional specialization. The company cannot adapt quickly to changes in the consumer market and has a low ability to exploit materials flow or market information.
- ■ *The functionally integrated company.* This organization has begun to erode the hierarchical structure and short-term financial focus by concentrating on customer service criteria and sales order processing. Its main competitive advantage is in the distribution efficiency of the system and the collaboration between the sales function and the distribution function.

- *The internally integrated company.* This organization has continued to restructure and align the activities of manufacturing and purchasing to create a systems approach to customer service. It has reduced the number of administrative functions required and operates effective interfaces between departments to optimize information exchange and hence the overall performance of the company. The planning horizon has also extended from the short term to the medium term and involves a limited interaction with suppliers. At this point the organizational structure may become product focused and involve a high level of cross-functional management.
- *The externally integrated company.* This organization's state involves externalization of the alignment process and integration of the supply base with the demands of the consumer in a transparent system of materials and information exchange. It seeks deliberately to manage the interfaces between companies to generate a flexible and responsive system of long-term collaboration. At this point the company has completed the restructuring of its internal supply chain and has recognized the importance of external supply chain management strategies and the need to synchronize the supply process. It operates internal cross-functional management structures, which may be product related, and typically develops supplier networking groups.

Figure 17.2 illustrates these four stages of supply chain integration.

If supply chain integration can be made a reality, then the potential impact on the final market can be significant. The point of supply chain management, it must be remembered, is not just to seek out efficiencies and cost-reduction opportunities, but rather to create a more responsive and flexible stance towards customers and consumers. In today's marketplace where time has become a critical success factor, the ability to move quickly in response to volatile demand is vital.

The achievement of a closely integrated supply chain will, however, ultimately depend on the recognition by all the parties involved of the need to work on the basis of collaboration and to seek out 'win–win' strategies.

Creating partnerships in the supply chain

The benefits of cooperation rather than conflict in buyer–supplier relationships have been set out in some detail by Axelrod (1990) among others. He demonstrates that cooperation can provide greater payoffs to both parties than can be achieved through the more traditional 'win–lose' scenario.

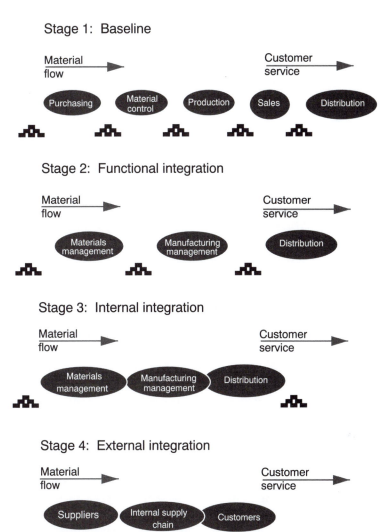

Source: Stevens (1989)

Figure 17.2   Achieving an integrated supply chain

In the same work, Axelrod describes the well-known example of the 'prisoners' dilemma' in which two outlaws are captured and can only escape a severe punishment by trusting each other not to confess. Because they are both offered lighter sentences if they convict the other (and knowing also that the other is inherently untrustworthy), the likelihood is that they will both confess and both be punished. While this may be an over-simplification of relationships in a supply chain, it graphically highlights the issues.

Lewis (1995) has studied in depth a number of companies which have strong partnerships with suppliers—companies such as Marks & Spencer, Chrysler and Motorola—and has identified that typical benefits include:

- *ongoing cost reductions* that can double those possible through market transactions;
- *quality improvements* that exceed what individual firms can possibly do alone;
- *design cycle times* 20 to 75 per cent shorter than those in traditional relationships;
- *increased operating flexibility*, which in some firms has yielded an economic lot size of one—the ultimate in flexible manufacturing;
- *more value for the customer's customers*, including faster and better responses to new needs and opportunities;
- *enhanced leverage with technology*, including earlier access to new concepts and more control over technological change; and
- *more powerful competitive strategies,* gained when a customer adds its supplier's expertise to its own.

One example of win–win thinking that is beginning to emerge in supply chains is the idea of vendor managed inventory (VMI) or—a subtle variation—co-managed inventory (CMI). The traditional approach to replenishment at each step in the chain has been for the customer to place an order on a supplier. Typically there would be no early warning of requirements from the customer and thus the supplier would have to carry inventory in the form of safety stock as a 'buffer' against this uncertainty. Similarly, the customer would also carry safety stock of the same items to guard against the possibility of non-supply. The result of this conventional 'arm's-length' approach was higher levels of inventory in the chain and paradoxically lower levels of service and responsiveness.

The idea behind VMI is that the customer no longer places orders on the supplier, but instead shares information on actual demand or usage on a continuing basis. As the supplier now has 'visibility' of the rate of offtake lower down the chain, it can plan and schedule production and transportation more efficiently, duplicated inventories are greatly reduced, service levels improve and the customer's cashflow is enhanced because it only pays for product as it uses it.

CMI is a further extension of the idea, where the customer jointly plans with the supplier appropriate inventory levels taking into account promotional activity, specific local conditions, competitive activities and so on. In either case, VMI or CMI, what is happening is what might be termed the 'value-added exchange of information'. Value is created through more responsive supply as a result of customers providing suppliers with information on offtake or product usage.

The key to supply chain integration is shared information. By working to the same data on demand, inventories and marketplace trends, a much more cost-effective logistics process can be developed. Under the conventional model—where no information is shared—both the supplier and the customer had to carry inventory on a 'just-in-case' basis. The supplier carried inventory because it had no forward notice of customer requirement. The customer carried inventory because it knew from experience that the supplier may not always be reliable. When information is shared then uncertainty is reduced and hence inventories can be dramatically cut.

The benefits of shared information go beyond cost reduction, however. There has been a clear tendency for companies to become increasingly mutually dependent as they start to link information systems together. The use of electronic data interchange (EDI) to create an environment where e-commerce can eliminate documentation such as purchase orders and invoices leads inevitably to the supplier's taking on more and more of the activities that previously were performed by the customer. For example, in retailing there has been a trend, particularly in North America, for suppliers to become very actively involved in 'category management'. This entails the supplier assisting the retailer in making decisions on shelf-space allocation, on layout and merchandising and by managing the flow of product from the factory to the shelf.

These patterns of collaboration in the supply chain are gradually starting to change the shape of the competitive environment. It was suggested earlier that companies no longer compete against other companies as single entities but rather as supply chains or networks. Under this model a key determinant of success or failure in the marketplace is the extent to which the supply chain can be managed as an integrated network with shared strategic goals and closely linked processes to support those goals. It follows from this argument that an increasingly important source of competitive advantage will be the strength and the quality of the relationships between members of the network—both 'vertical' supply chain partners and 'horizontal' alliance partners.

Integrating processes across organizations

True supply chain integration not only requires internal realignment in terms of managing processes on a cross-functional basis, it also requires that the company's processes align with those of its upstream and downstream partners.

Clearly it is not practical to contemplate inter-organizational process integration between the firm and multiple suppliers and customers.

Indeed, one of the main drivers of the current trend observable in many industries towards reducing the supplier base is the recognition that high-intensity relationships can only be managed with a limited supplier and customer base.

One interesting example of this type of thinking is provided by BhS, a UK high street retailer. At the beginning of the 1990s it had over 1000 suppliers of clothing products, by the end of the decade it was working closely with only 50 strategic suppliers. However, the nature of the relationships with those 50 suppliers is quite different from the past. There are now multilevel connections between BhS and its individual suppliers. Not only is EDI enabling quick-response replenishment to be achieved with significant financial benefits, but now there is a much higher level of supplier involvement in the development of long-term strategy at BhS.

It is perhaps the concept of joint strategy determination that distinguishes truly integrated supply chains from mere 'marriages of convenience'. While it should be recognized that the customer will always be preeminent in the determination of its strategic goals, the involvement of key suppliers in that process can only be to the benefit of both parties. However, making the transition from the conventional 'arm's-length' relationship to the new partnership model is not easy. The attitudes and habits of many years have to be discarded and replaced with mutual trust and commitment.

Structuring these types of relationships in a hard, competitive world is no easy task. The frequently quoted example of how Wal-Mart, North America's biggest retailer, and Procter & Gamble, one of the world's biggest manufacturers of branded goods, moved from a 'win–lose' to a 'win–win' model provides some clues. First, cooperation needs to start from the top with a recognition of the strategic opportunities that process integration can provide. For example, the founder of Wal-Mart, Sam Walton, was personally involved in structuring the terms of the relationship with senior vice-presidents from Procter & Gamble. He saw this type of arrangement as a way in which to improve both the efficiency and the effectiveness of the supply chain as a whole, in that close cooperation could lead to less inventory, faster response and lower costs, thus supporting the fundamental Wal-Mart strategy of 'every day low prices' (EDLP).

The second lesson is that it is not sufficient to have a single point of contact between buyers and suppliers. Instead there must be multiple contacts at all levels of the core processes of the business. So suppliers' logistics people must work with the customers' logistics people, sales and marketing on the supply side must form teams with sales and marketing on the demand side and so on. Furthermore, these buyer/supplier teams should be cross-functional and multidisciplinary. Figure 17.3 highlights the dramatic change from the traditional model—shown as two triangles that only connect at one point (the salesperson and the

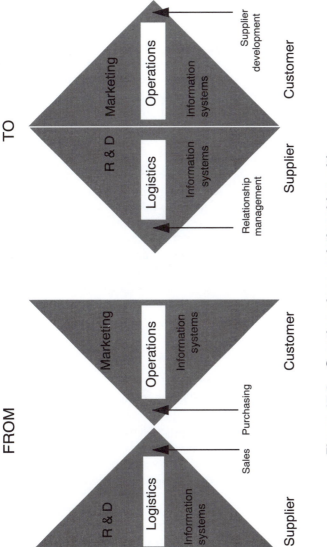

Figure 17.3 Creating closer relationships with supply chain partners

buyer), and the new model where there are multiple points of contact between corresponding people and processes within the two partners.

Conclusion

We are seemingly entering an era where the rules of competition will be significantly different from those that prevailed in the past. Brand loyalty can no longer be relied on to achieve competitive advantage. Equally, technology by itself cannot provide a defensible long-term advantage as clones and 'me-toos' inevitably appear. Instead the source of advantage in the future will increasingly come from the way in which superior brands and innovative technology are brought to market more rapidly and sustained and supported over their life through superior supply chain management.

In other words, a new paradigm of competition is emerging in which the supply chain network increasingly provides a source of sustainable advantage through enhanced customer value. If such an advantage is to be achieved, then it is critical for the organization to review the way in which it currently delivers value to its customers and to consider whether the time has come to reconfigure the chain to leverage the strengths of supply chain partners and alliances. One thing is for certain: companies which believe that they can continue to conduct 'business as usual' will find that their prospects for success in tomorrow's marketplace will rapidly decline.

References

Axelrod, R. (1990) *The Evolution of Co-operation*, Penguin Books, Harmondsworth.

Christopher, M. (1997) *Marketing Logistics*, Butterworth Heinemann, Oxford.

Lewis, J. (1995) *The Connected Corporation*, Free Press, New York.

Stevens, G. (1989) 'Integrating the supply chain', *International Journal of Physical Distribution and Materials Management*, 9 (8), 3–8.

Strategic sourcing

Aligning procurement needs with your business goals

Gregory Owens, Olivier Vidal, Rick Toole and Donovan Favre

Companies seeking to be competitive in today's global economy are reevaluating the role of procurement. Once a narrow, administrative function, procurement is now being moved to the centre of business decision-making and is creating a new source of value. This chapter uses a strategic sourcing model to identify the strategic importance and financial impact of procurement activities. The model provides a framework for determining how internal procurement skills and structures, external relationships with suppliers and enabling technologies can be aligned to the business goals of the organization. Adopting this strategic approach can result in lower total costs, greater revenue and improved competitiveness.

Introduction

The terms purchasing, procurement and now strategic sourcing are often used interchangeably in discussions about the buying activities of companies. However, they are not identical concepts; perhaps the best way to understand them is to place them in an evolutionary context. Purchasing applies to the transaction functions of buying products and services at the lowest possible price. Procurement is a broader activity: it involves the materials management of goods and services in addition to purchasing transactions. Strategic sourcing takes the process further, focusing on developing channels of supply at the lowest total cost to the company, not just the lowest purchase price. In strategic sourcing, all purchasing activities are assessed for their impact on the company and the company's goals. Businesses wishing to source strategically will identify the most appropriate purchasing relationship with their suppliers, according to the vital needs of their core business functions. Significant benefit can be gained from developing meaningful, often long-term relationships with suppliers that provide the most important goods and services.

Strategic sourcing realigns the organization with the aim of focusing the most time and energy on strategic purchases that can provide advantages in quality, speed or cost effectiveness. In many cases, strategic sourcing enables the total cost of goods and services procured to be reduced by more than 15 per cent, which adds tremendous impact to net income and market value. The transformation from a traditional purchasing function to a strategic sourcing focus often reduces the size of the supplier base, which creates economies of scale and long-standing relationships with suppliers. Advantages are achieved for the supplier and the purchaser: they can both leverage their core competencies to focus on increasing market share and improving market position.

The move from purchasing to strategic sourcing has developed as a result of the far-reaching changes that occurred in the marketplace during the 1980s. New production models based on just-in-time and total quality management, as well as outsourcing, commoditization and globalization, had a profound impact on the way goods should be sourced and on the relationship between suppliers and customers. Companies that wished to remain competitive had to shift their focus from a narrow transaction-based view of purchasing and take a wider, more strategic view of how the supply chain could be used to achieve broader corporate goals.

To achieve strategic sourcing, companies have to understand what are their most important goods and services and how vital they are to their day-to-day operation, as well as in achieving longer-term business goals. This chapter provides a framework for analysing procurement needs through a model, called the strategic sourcing model. This model puts sourcing in the context of how procurement will have an impact across an organization—in marketing, sales, research and development and finance. The chapter then discusses how to implement strategic sourcing, realigning the company's internal and external relationships using the model as a basis for analysis. The internal considerations are organizational structure, the skills needed by staff and management and the strategic sourcing processes, while the external factors are supplier management and partner relationships. Finally, the necessary technology is described as it underpins and enables the changes to take place.

The strategic sourcing model

Under traditional procurement methods, buying goods was carried out largely by the purchasing department using similar methods for buying widely varying products and services. The chief focus was on buying the items at the cheapest possible price. For example, when large capital items were purchased, the decision-making and purchasing process was often handed to managers with technical expertise, such as engineering or information technology. The negotiation and buying skills of the pur-

Figure 18.1   The strategic sourcing model

chasers were passed over in favour of so-called expertise in the function of the product.

In contrast, strategic sourcing recognizes the skill of purchasing professionals as necessary not only for purchasing itself but also for decisions in other areas—product design, direction of research and development and technology uptake. All these functions have purchasing implications and all have an impact on the overall profitability of the company. Rather than taking a blanket approach to securing products and services, strategic sourcing differentiates between items so that the most time and effort is spent on items that have the highest priority.

The strategic sourcing model, illustrated in Figure 18.1, provides a framework for adopting this strategic approach. The model identifies items along a scale of organizational priority and then places them along a financial impact axis. Combining these two axes creates four separate sourcing quadrants. The quadrants are critical in determining what approach should be taken in sourcing items that fall within these conceptual spaces.

Determining strategic importance

The strategic importance of a product or service is determined by whether it has an impact on the company's core business and future competitiveness. Needs of low strategic importance are not instrumental to the running of the company. They may be necessary, but they provide no competitive advantage in the marketplace and may have very little to do with a company's goals or mission. A good example is office supplies. Photocopying paper, pens and folders are daily business needs, yet their sourcing is unlikely to affect a company's competitive position.

On the other hand, needs of high strategic importance *are* likely to affect a company's position in the market. These sourcing requirements are often directly related to the company's core products or services and as such are an important part of the company's critical business functions. Silicon, for instance, is the nucleus of the product for a microchip manufacturer: it adds value and differentiates the product from its competition. The acquisition of the microchip is thus crucial to the overall product value and the future of the business. If a problem occurs with silicon supply, such as poor availability or a price increase, this creates a problem throughout the supply chain, from the microchip manufacturer through to the electronics manufacturer. Therefore, silicon is strategically important to a microchip manufacturer and should be purchased as such.

Assessing financial impact

In addition to understanding the strategic importance of a company's purchasing needs, it is also necessary to determine the financial impact of those needs. This will act as a guideline for the amount of time and effort that should be spent purchasing any particular item. Purchasing needs with low financial impact are often special or one-time purchases. Therefore, the time and effort spent on buying them should be minimal. Purchasing needs of high financial impact are most likely to be high-value items or recurring needs. As the dollars spent in the long term can be significant, it is worth some thought and effort to reduce total cost of these purchases.

The four sourcing quadrants

Figures 18.1 shows how the combination of strategic importance and financial impact defines the necessary type of sourcing arrangement that should be put in place. The benefit of analysing the organization's requirements in this way is that it identifies the most appropriate relationship and purchasing method to be used for a particular item.

Items of low strategic importance and low financial impact belong in the Automatic Pilot quadrant, where the aim is to spend as little time as possible on the purchasing process. The optimum solution is the automation of the processes, allowing time to be spent up-front to set up an automatic order and replenishment programme. Company-specific catalogues can be established to allow authorized employees to order certain items without going through formal requisition and approval processes. With replenishment programmes, once initial inventory needs are established and the programme is underway, orders will be automatically generated to replenish supplies or the inventory will be vendor-managed. This system frees the buyer or purchasing agent to spend more time on strategic purchasing needs.

The Price is Right is the concept used to describe needs that are of low strategic importance but have high financial impact. The best way to address these needs is by conducting a competitive bidding process to achieve the lowest-cost contract. As the monetary implications are substantial, the time and effort of a bidding process are justified by the cost savings that can be achieved. The lower strategic significance means that price can be the factor that drives the decision. Minor building works or portable computers are examples of Price is Right needs.

The Wheel of Fortune quadrant addresses needs of high strategic importance but that do not have a particularly high financial impact. The buying process needs to be more involved and supplier screening will be extremely important. This type of need is well suited to a blanket order contract, which establishes an arrangement for the supplier to furnish a specified number of goods or services over a set period. Blanket contracts allow for the necessary screening up-front to assure proper management, but then allow for flexibility and reduced involvement over the duration of the contract. Once the contract is negotiated, the orders are all filled using a 'release form' via a purchase order.

Finally, the Strategic Partnership corner of the grid addresses needs that are both strategically important and have significant financial implications. These needs should consume the majority of time. In order to address the importance of both sets of considerations, the best solution to this type of need is a formal partnership or alliance with the supplier. This type of arrangement provides the best opportunity to ensure that the proper emphasis is being placed on the strategic and financial considerations of the contract. If done properly, it joins both companies together working toward the same goals. An example of this kind of purchase would be aircraft for an airline.

The strategic sourcing model provides a framework for organizations to determine the needs of the highest priority according to overall corporate objectives. This can be used to determine which needs should be given the most time and resources within sourcing operations. Such an approach can reduce the total costs of procurement, increase sales, reduce lead times and improve competitive advantage overall.

How to achieve strategic sourcing

The perception and ability of the sourcing function within organizations must be changed if companies are successfully to implement strategic sourcing. This will involve redesigning and realigning the organization's internal and external relationships. Internally, companies have to consider the place of sourcing within the structure of the organization and the level of management abilities and professional skills available to support strategic activities. At an external level, the companies must develop appropriate partnerships with suppliers and learn how to manage those for the future. Finally, the strategic sourcing must be underpinned by enabling technology.

Internal relationships

Realigning organizational structure

Traditionally the debate about the role of the 'purchasing department' focused on whether purchasing was centralized or decentralized within the organization. But if strategic sourcing is to take place then 'purchasing' has to have a role that spans the organization's operations. This means that the purchasing activities should be linked with other departments, as seen in Figure 18.2. Purchasing interacts with many functional departments, such as manufacturing and marketing, and in a sense acts as the liaison between these departments and the company's suppliers. Without good internal relations between procurement and user departments, it will be impossible to build strong relationships with external suppliers.

The importance of strategic sourcing and the impact it has on different departments is detailed below:

- *R&D, engineering and design.* Strategic sourcing has a role to play in interacting with the R&D department. It must understand the products that are being developed and the subsequent purchasing requirements needed to achieve product success. Strategic sourcing can help ensure that the necessary components of a product design will be available, affordable and will meet necessary quality requirements.
- *Manufacturing and operations.* In order to source the most appropriate goods and materials, purchasing needs to understand such issues as quality, scheduling, production time and availability of supply. Strategic sourcing can add value and save money by working with operations to avoid emergency buys, production shutdowns and unscheduled changeovers.
- *Sales and marketing.* By understanding how products are sold to the consumer and at what cost, strategic sourcing can plan its buying

Figure 18.2   Purchasing needs to be linked with other departments

more effectively. It needs continually to communicate with sales and marketing to understand potential spikes in demand because of promotions or seasonality.

- *Accounting and finance.* Strategic sourcing is the intermediary between accounts payable and the supplier. Paying for items can have a large financial impact on a company. Therefore, it is important for the strategic sourcing and finance departments to have a good relationship and understand each other's goals and needs, as well as understanding the effects on cashflow and the costs of working capital.

Ensuring that departments interact across boundaries moves purchasing considerations beyond the traditional debate over centralization. In fact, successful strategic sourcing can deliver the advantages that are normally achieved by both the centralized and decentralized modes of operation. Strategic sourcing, for instance, is able to link key purchasing decisions to the long-term competitive goals of a company because it has a cross-organizational focus—an ability normally associated with centralization. Sourcing strategically can also enable a detailed, nuts-and-bolts knowledge of specific requirements and the costs involved, which is a characteristic of decentralization.

Many companies now realize that a hybrid organizational structure with elements of centralization and decentralization is the most efficient and effective structure. One popular hybrid, shown in Figure 18.3, involves forming procurement councils made up of personnel from multiple locations, including corporate headquarters as well as the operating

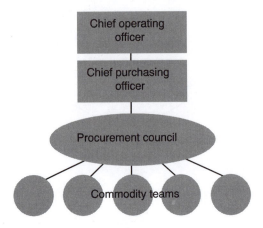

Chief purchasing officer
- Supports business strategy
- Develops strategic sourcing plan

Procurement council
- Identification and prioritization of initiatives
- Allocation of resources to commodity teams
- Advise and counsel commodity teams at key decision points

Commodity teams
- Implement total-cost-of-ownership reductions
- Negotiate with suppliers
- Develop rollout plan and timing for operating locations

Figure 18.3 Strategic vs tactical procurement organization

locations. These councils set direction and priorities in order to achieve the sourcing strategy outlined by the chief procurement officer. For material and service commodities that are common across multiple facilities, cross-functional commodity teams are formed by the procurement council on a priority basis.

These teams are lead by a representative of the operation with the most at stake for a particular commodity, which is generally the department with the largest spending in a commodity category. For materials or services outside the traditional procurement areas, such as electricity, travel or benefits, procurement personnel commonly take the role of key driver and/or team member, but usually do not lead the team. The leader of the commodity team becomes an expert on the commodity and the focal point for communications with the suppliers.

As supply relationships and contracts are set by the commodity team, the implementation and transactional functions, such as placing purchase orders, revert to the operating locations. The overall contracts are usually defined in broader terms, with individual locations defining their specific needs to the supplier. The leader of the commodity team stays in close contact with the operating locations during implementation to ensure that the supplier is complying with the requirements of the contract and that no recurring problems exist across multiple facilities.

Skills and training

The next important internal component for implementing a strategic sourcing approach lies in the knowledge and skills of the sourcing personnel. Whether they are on-line purchasers or managers of large operations, individual staff members must have the required level of skills appropriate to the type of sourcing they are carrying out. This will vary according to the quadrant in the sourcing model from which they are operating. For instance, if purchasers are buying items such as office supplies in the Automatic Pilot quadrant, then their skills will be far different to those needed for staff managing the supply chain relationships in the high-value, high-need Strategic Partnership zone. Potentially staff will need to operate in more than one quadrant, depending on the size of the company.

Undoubtedly, all staff will need to understand the strategic sourcing model if they are to prioritize their time and effort appropriately and they will need to be given the skill set required for each type of activity. Strategic sourcing means that procurement personnel are moving quickly from undertaking mainly clerical duties to much more of a decision-making role. They are also being involved in decisions across the organization. As a result, companies must invest heavily in retraining existing employees and if necessary recruit personnel with expanded skill sets that include a mixture of backgrounds in technical disciplines and advanced business degrees.

Some of the different types of skills required to carry out strategic sourcing are listed below:

- *Marketing and strategic analysis.* Identifying the best suppliers, including those who may be external to the current industry, requires strategic analysis skills. Buyers must be able to analyse and evaluate potential suppliers, perform constraint analysis, segment the supply market, pinpoint competition, analyse industry cost structures and understand pricing in accordance with a product's position in its lifecycle.
- *Information gathering and technical knowledge.* Buyers are also key players in the technical and commercial awareness of companies in that they develop both relational and technical skills. Besides buying, they must continually be seeking information, learning about new materials and products, checking for coherence and developing information networks outside the company.

- *Performance-evaluation skills.* Sales price was traditionally the only discriminating factor on which to evaluate suppliers. However, now with supplier-management techniques and cost-reduction practices, supplier evaluations are more detailed and include assessment of services, co-development capacity, innovation ability, quality and lead-time accuracy.
- *Product-development skills.* Acting at the forefront of the market, being responsible for costs, buyers are well placed to stimulate change within the company. They must initiate joint development programmes with suppliers, on products as well as services. Buyers must also be knowledgeable in value analysis and objective cost design and be able to identify opportunities to apply these techniques and propose product-enhancements pilot programmes to technical staff.
- *Negotiation skills and partnership development.* Adding on to day-to-day operation management skills, managing a partnership requires legal proficiency and negotiation skills. Once the partnership has been established, it is important to maintain and monitor the relationship.

External relationships

Managing suppliers and partnerships

A broad spectrum of potential relationships exists between suppliers and purchasers under the strategic sourcing model, ranging from low-value, transaction-based interactions to partnerships that are high in strategic and financial value to a company. As already discussed, companies wishing to adopt strategic sourcing should limit the purchasing resources devoted to the lowest-value quadrant; the most benefits can be derived from developing longer-term relationships with suppliers operating in the Strategic Partnership quadrant.

The strategic approach means that a radical shake-up is required of the traditional relationships pursued by buyers, suppliers and distributors. In particular, it requires the logic of the 'zero-sum game' to be abandoned, in order to escape its inherent opposition between players and competition between numerous suppliers. The win–lose thinking is replaced by the logic of the 'win–win game', where cooperation and common goals dominate, leading to the establishment of preferential relationships with a limited number of suppliers. This is naturally most applicable to the Strategic Partnership zone, where high-value relationships operate.

A partnership relationship can be advantageous to both suppliers and purchasers when a 'win–win' approach is adopted. Joint development of products and continuous improvement programmes can improve products while reducing their total cost, with both partners benefiting through a system of dividing the earnings. Where the competition is unable to match the relationship, the partners essentially benefit from a supplementary margin. It is important to shed any naïve thoughts regarding this type of partnership. Certainly it is based on mutual trust, but to maintain this, equilibrium must be maintained through joint tracking of the partnership's performance.

Allowing the partnership to fall into a disequilibrium of strengths between the players would swing the relationship towards a zero-sum game. Several means to maintain the equilibrium within a partnership are outlined below.

First, the partnership needs to be defined clearly from the start. Contractual relations must be established that guarantee an equitable division of effort and profit through the lifetime of the relationship. A rigorous definition of relations in the supplier/buyer contract is a key to achieving trade volume levels and stability. Precisely specifying both parties' involvement within the relationship will minimize opportunistic behaviour. If the duration of the partnership is well defined (for example the life of the product), then costs and service levels can be kept flexible and adjusted in order to take account of changes in consumer demand and internal process optimization, or indexed to raw material price levels. For example, a successful relationship contract will specify formulas for future price modifications, future distribution of productivity gains or supply chain cost enhancements.

Secondly, information must be transparent to both parties, providing full visibility on the economic performance of the relationship. At a high level, visibility on the mutual respect of the partnership requires rules, in particular the supplier performance assessment, the quality of the buyer's demand forecast and the stability of technical specifications. Monitoring of the total procurement costs is also essential to the smooth running of the relationship and often requires the reorganization of classical controlling processes. Costs need to be distributed by supply units, with details not only on direct raw material and manpower costs, but also on indirect costs (such as logistics costs, non-quality costs and overheads).

The next level of visibility necessary to a long-lasting partnership addresses not only the supplier's but also buyer's cost structures and profitability. Contractual agreements on price modifications and profit sharing require visibility on key performance indicators. The partnership remains competitive because its duration is fixed. To stay in business, suppliers must prove their competitiveness over their allowed time. Their cost structures are indicative of their internal performance and can help guide enhancement and innovation initiatives.

Thirdly, suppliers within a partnership should be evaluated on an enlarged performance basis, as discussed under Performance-evaluation skills above.

Fourthly, partners should have the ability to initiate cost reductions, either through product redesign or by contributing to an integrated logistics strategy. Product design is commonly seen to account for 40 per cent of an item's cost. Supply chain integration can also increase profits and reactivity. Change must be stimulated as discussed under Product-development skills above.

Finally, in addition to day-to-day management skills, managing a partnership requires legal proficiency and complex negotiation skills. Personal skills will become even more important with the greater participation of buyers in business strategic decisions.

Fact-based negotiation

Successfully implementing strategic sourcing relies largely on the ability to undertake fact-based negotiation. This method, outlined in Figure 18.4, takes a total-cost-of-ownership approach to selecting suppliers, rather than focusing on the purchasing price alone. It is a good example of a technique suitable for the high-need, high-value relationships belonging to the Strategic Partnership zone of the strategic sourcing model. It achieves a win–win outcome as opposed to the win–lose result of more traditional supplier–buyer relationships.

To carry out fact-based negotiation, a team is put together that has experience in a range of business functions, from procurement, engineering and finance, to maintenance and research and development. Specific industry and supplier analysis provides the team with strong factual knowledge about industry cost drivers and the unique capabilities of each potential supplier. Generally done as a first-stage screening, it provides a high-level understanding of which suppliers are aligned with the company's sourcing requirements. Issues to be considered are whether the potential supplier has the required capacity and the necessary breadth of product lines and whether it can perform R&D to support new product development.

Industry and supplier analysis may stretch the standard research techniques of the traditional procurement department to incorporate sources such as industry reports, trade publications, published work of industry associations and industry analysts, and Internet research. Site surveys of suppliers may be undertaken and raw material pricing trends will be critical to understanding changes in the commodity's price over time.

Analytical techniques have to be focused internally as well. Companies will not have credibility with their suppliers if they cannot demonstrate a detailed understanding of spending at the item level within a commodity group. Data on item purchase volumes, inventory levels, cost history and delivery and service requirements will help develop the quantitative portion of the request for quotation and begin to define the categories within the total-cost-of-ownership model.

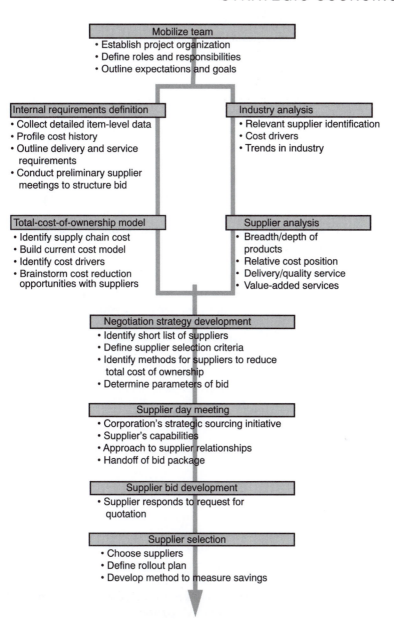

Figure 18.4   Fact-based negotiation process

The total-cost-of-ownership model must encompass the full cost of the commodity including price, use and administrative costs. Price is not only comprised of the actual price paid, but also includes volume rebates, gain-sharing benefits, payment terms and delivery terms. Usage reductions can drive lower total cost of ownership through standardization, elimination, functional equivalents, product redesign, specification changes and scrap reduction. Administrative and process costs are especially important for low-value, high-transaction commodities such as maintenance, repair and operating supplies. These costs can be driven down by automating purchase order processing, consolidated invoicing, stockless inventory and electronic data interchange.

Strategy development requires the team to consider issues such as: can we sole source, should we index to a base raw material price, how long should the contract run, can we source globally and should we qualify additional sources? In order to develop a quantitative supplier selection criteria with weightings and scoring guidelines based on pricing, delivery, service, value-added services and overall supplier capabilities, the team will identify, with respect to its company, the critical factors of each commodity. More time and effort spent up-front will drastically minimize issues when the bids are evaluated.

Communication between the sourcing team and the prospective suppliers is critical throughout the process, ensuring that the suppliers fully understand the requirements and can clarify questions. The team will have to decide the number of suppliers, the requirements for back-up capacity and percentage award to the suppliers if the bid is multi-sourced. Once the supplier is chosen, implementation planning with the supplier will ensure a smooth rollout. Communication throughout all levels of the organization is needed to resolve issues immediately. Follow-up meetings on a quarterly basis with the supplier will allow continuous total cost reduction and a successful longer-term relationship.

Technology enablers

The final key to the strategic sourcing model is information technology. By providing fast, direct links with supply chain partners, IT systems can enable organizations dramatically to increase the amount of information being processed and substantially to reduce the amount of routine administrative effort required internally and across the supply chain.

At almost every step of the purchasing process, technology has simplified repetitive tasks and provided greater capacity to gather and analyse critical information. At the planning stage, technology enables expenditure patterns to be forecast and once the transaction occurs, the data is captured and can be compared to the original forecast. As sourcing personnel start to analyse information regarding the use of products and services, IT can provide data about the internal consumption patterns of the organization, as well as information about longer-term consumption trends and the factors driving demand. These systems also extend to providing insight into the price, usage and process/administrative impacts of particular types of commercial deals.

At the stage of going to market and choosing suitable suppliers, requests for particular items can be gained much more efficiently with the use of online systems. Suppliers provide online catalogues comprising product information that can be drilled into for specifications or actually viewed using easy-to-use point and click techniques. For large customers, suppliers can even provide custom catalogues that include pricing and availability information.

In order for strategic sourcing personnel to gain competitive advantage from their IT systems, they require access to an integrated suite of software applications called a 'buyer's workstation'. Best leverage is gained from the workstation when the underlying applications are interfaced with the company's internal purchasing and budgeting systems and when access is available to the supply market through the Internet. Being linked with the Internet gives access to important data on industry trends and developments in the supply chain and can assist with supplier and product searches.

Establishing the approval to spend and choosing the correct account for the spend is made easier through the use of technology. Automatic routing for spending approval can be done on the system so that a request can be caught before the funds are committed. Being able to identify the spend early provides an opportunity for procurement cards to be used, or other one-off, transaction-based payment systems. Procurement cards fit the model for miscellaneous consumption at this point.

IT also allows the automatic consolidation of requests into orders using the company's own application to consolidate the product volumes ordered. However, the capability exists to over-ride this function, if necessary, to send approved orders without bundling. The technology can automatically release orders when the product, supplier, tax, logistics, approval and accounting requirements are all met.

Electronic communication such as electronic data interchange (EDI) minimizes the use of paper and reduces transaction costs, while ensuring that the transaction occurs instantaneously. EDI can also transmit consumption forecasts to suppliers, enabling them to calibrate production in order to get closer to just-in-time delivery and allow for key performance data on every transaction record to be obtained. At the same time electronic funds transfer is also possible, providing fully automated resupply.

For industrial companies, IT enables the integration of production and supply between the company and its suppliers. As new orders are received, the supply chain and production cycle of each partner are automatically put into action. This integration simplifies the management of supplier relations, establishes long-term partnerships and shortens supply lead times.

Similarly in the retail industry, electronic interface and computer-aided communication enable the automatic resupply of products, called continuous product replenishment (CPR). This system allows for the continuous update of sales/demand forecasts, the requirement for finished product and the issue of purchase orders or transfer requests with scheduled deliveries. The integration of accounting functions is also considerably simplified.

IT systems can release advance shipment notices (ASNs) which provide electronic information on the products in transit. This assists the receiving warehouse in planning the arrival of the shipment and in the subsequent updating of receipt records. The use of barcodes can simplify the receiving process and workstations are set up to capture the coded information. This information can be used externally for supplier communication and internally for invoice processing, quality assurance and inventory availability.

Finally, in terms of payment, IT systems allow for autodisbursement, which is a set-up based on evaluated receipt settlement. An exception base is built into the system to process mismatched transactions. The use of electronic funds transfer for payment and automatic reconciliation from banking and financial institutions means that in theory the buyer and supplier do not need to reconcile payments as this occurs automatically.

To ensure that technology is suited to strategic sourcing, one of the most important considerations is that the organization's business goals drive the information technology systems and not vice versa. This requires a separate information technology strategy to be developed, which should support the strategic sourcing model. Links with channel partners through EDI or other Internet-based systems should be periodically monitored to ensure that they are improving the performance of procurement.

Conclusion

Strategic sourcing is a new approach that promises substantial improvements to the competitiveness of an organization. Rather than adopting a singular, transaction-based method to procure all goods and services, strategic sourcing identifies the most appropriate method of sourcing according to the importance of the item to the overall business objectives of the organization. This means that most time and effort will be given to the items or contracts that carry the highest strategic and financial value to the business. Strategic sourcing will continue to evolve, but those companies that embrace the concept early will be positioned to meet or exceed customer service demands and providing more price-competitive products and services in the marketplace. Strategic sourcing will deliver a lower total cost for procurement, as well as improving product quality and service and ultimately providing competitive advantage.

Network-modelling tools

Enhancing supply chain decision making

Sue Jimenez, Tim Brown and Joe Jordan

Network-modelling tools are increasingly useful for firms trying to optimize their supply chain performance. Used properly, they offer a powerful resource for chief executive officers (CEOs) seeking to improve the basis of their supply chain decision making. They also have practical, tactical and operational applications. To make network optimization work, firms need to be fully aware of the available packages, able to capture all the required data and capable of managing the project through to success. Not only are network-modelling tools invaluable today—they are only going to improve in performance as firms and modellers find better ways to adapt them to supply chain challenges.

Introduction

Network-modelling tools are sophisticated computer modelling techniques for determining the impact of business scenarios on a company's operations and costs. Used effectively, they significantly contribute to enhancing supply chain decision making and optimizing supply chain outcomes.

Until recently, many supply chain decision makers hesitated to use these tools. They were costly and complex, requiring specialized database building and manipulation tools, expertise in computer programming systems and the skills to decipher the optimizer outputs and error codes. They typically used a large amount of computer processing time and required access to a mainframe computer. These factors made them prohibitively expensive for all but the largest businesses.

Now these tools are much more accessible. Computer technology has improved dramatically, so that network models can be run on relatively inexpensive personal computers or laptops under a windows environment, increasing their user-friendliness and vastly improving their reporting and analysis capabilities.

Network optimization defined

Network optimization involves modelling all the main supply chain network parameters and determining the optimal arrangement that will reduce cost or improve profit while satisfying given service requirements.

To model the supply chain, network-modelling tools require inputs on all main supply chain network parameters, including detailed cost and volume information. Key network components along or through which product flow must first be identified. The totality of the product flow pathways, the nodes through which they flow and links along which they travel define the supply chain's network structure, as shown in Figure 19.1. The network nodes are facilities in which the products are processed. Products travel along the transportation links that exist between these facilities. The product pathways are defined by the series of links and nodes along and through which products travel to pass from supplier to customer.

The supply chain network is complicated by the inter-dependence between the different network components of transportation, ware-housing, inventory, manufacturing, purchasing and customer service. For instance, warehouse and transportation are inter-dependent because decreasing the number of warehouse locations usually leads to a corresponding increase in the cost of outbound transportation and increasing customer service levels are associated with increased inventory holdings.

As the level of complexity of a supply chain network increases, it quickly becomes impossible simultaneously to take account of all these interactions manually or even to optimize the supply chain using simple analytical tools such as spreadsheets. In such cases sophisticated network models are a necessary condition for optimizing the supply chain.

Network-modelling tools represent supply chain parameters as a mathematical model of the network structure. Interactions and trade-offs that occur between the components in the network are represented using linear and mixed integer programming techniques. The supply chain network is optimized when the best possible balance is found between these parameters. This optimal configuration minimizes operating costs (or maximizes business profits) while simultaneously satisfying all supply chain constraints.

Once the supply chain model has been developed and optimized, it can also be used for scenario development. Scenario development is the process of evaluating potential business scenarios based on their impact on the supply chain infrastructure and costs. A *base case* model is first *validated* against known costs and is then used as a benchmark against which the costs and network structures of all future scenarios can be compared.

The base case model is also required to benchmark the optimized

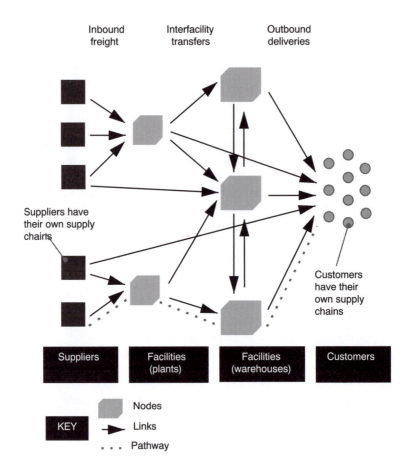

Figure 19.1   A typical manufacturer's supply chain

network. The key difference between scenario development and network optimization is that scenarios have predetermined conditions and situations to be tested, whereas a network optimization is relatively unconstrained, without a predetermined outcome.

Strategic applications

Network-modelling tools are a significant asset for supply chain decision makers. Specifically, they can be used to:

■ provide the CEO and his or her team with a 'whole of business' perspective;

■ identify opportunities for significant bottom-line savings;
■ aid the CEO in developing a long-term view of the business;
■ assist with business planning and business case development;
■ identify the inadequacies of existing management information.

Whole-of-business perspective

Network optimization involves the analysis of the supply chain from a holistic point of view. This enables CEOs to understand the cost drivers that affect their business and to have a better grasp of the interactions that occur along the supply chain. These tools may be used to derive meaningful key performance indicators (KPIs) for the business and to help overcome the functional 'silo' mentality that exists in many organizations. This has been especially useful for improving communication in retail operations between retail buyers and their internal logistics groups and in manufacturing organizations by improving coordination between the sales and marketing, manufacturing and logistics groups.

Bottom-line savings

A small change in operating costs can improve a firm's profitability by as much as 10 per cent or more. A study of 75 modelling projects has shown that sophisticated modelling tools, such as network-optimization techniques, have been able to identify cost reductions of 5 to 20 per cent of controllable supply chain costs (with an average of 11.63 per cent). As supply chain operations usually contribute about 10 per cent of business costs, and assuming an annual company profit of 15 per cent, this translates to an average 10 per cent improvement in annual profitability.

Experience in conducting network-optimization projects supports these findings. Significant annual savings have been identified in supply chains across a range of industries: from inbound transport to back-of-store receiving and reserves of a major department store, savings of 13.5 per cent; savings of 13.8 per cent for a discount chain (excluding inventory and store handling); and 10 per cent savings for a large industrial manufacturer, including manufacturing, raw materials, inventory and depots.

Long-term view

Network optimization and scenario development can be used to explore the impact of market, supplier and internal forces on the supply chain and to develop optimal long-term business plans that recognize these impacts. For example, future market projections can be loaded into the model (in terms of demand level, product mix and demography) to determine the effect of these changes on the current network and cost of operations.

Models are also useful in merger and acquisition analysis to understand the cost and structure of the organizations being merged or acquired and in decision making both before and after the merger or acquisition takes place for identifying synergies.

Business planning

Network models have several capabilities that make them useful for business-planning purposes. Scenarios can be developed with these models to understand the implications of changes in supply chain parameters over time. Although network-optimization techniques are usually 'single-period'—providing only a single 'snapshot' of a period of time (usually one financial year)—some modelling packages can be used to build multiperiod models, as illustrated in Figure 19.2. These models can be used to compare changes that occur between different time periods (e.g. between different years).

Optimization models also enable sensitivity testing of future scenarios to investigate the impact of best, worst and most likely trends. For example, the impact on the supply chain of a 20 per cent increase in transportation costs for all main routes can be determined and the network 'reoptimized' under the new conditions.

Network-modelling tools can support analysis of investment and divestment decisions and implementation timing. The model has the capability to select which facilities are optimal to 'open' or 'shut down' during the time periods of interest.

Network models can also be applied to the problem of developing supply chain contingency plans. These plans can minimize the impact of 'shocks' to the supply chain, such as those that occurred in 1990 when Source Perrier SA was forced to recall its entire worldwide stock of 160 million bottles of mineral water. If we were to apply network modelling to this situation, the 'base case' model would show the typical flow volumes and costs for several consecutive weeks or months, with the overflow capacities and costs built in. The expected recall and replacement volumes would be entered in the model to determine the optimal production and restocking routes for this contingency. The reverse channel flow could be modelled separately.

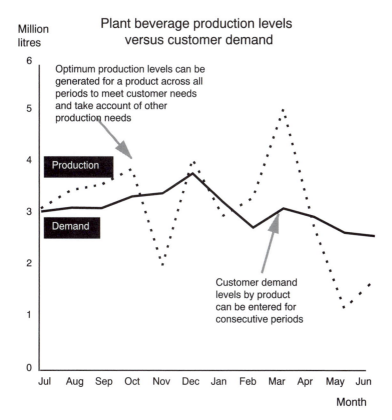

Million litres

Plant beverage production levels versus customer demand

Optimum production levels can be generated for a product across all periods to meet customer needs and take account of other production needs

Production

Demand

Customer demand levels by product can be entered for consecutive periods

Jul Aug Sep Oct Nov Dec Jan Feb Mar Apr May Jun

Month

* Discrepancies between production and demand levels are covered by inventory holdings.

Figure 19.2 Multiperiod modelling capability enables supply and demand to be tracked across consecutive periods

Executive decision-making information

The process of model building and scenario development can lead to a review of existing management reporting systems. In our experience the data-collection process needed to build a successful model often makes it apparent to those involved that critical data required for strategic decision making is not being collected by existing operational systems. This process may lead to the 'reverse engineering' of information-gathering systems.

For instance, it is quite common for companies to record goods purchased in terms of currency (COG) or quantity of items purchased, but for goods to be received into the warehouse in terms of number (and size) of cartons. This inconsistency in measurement makes it difficult to trace the flow of product through the supply chain. Such problems are often identified and rectified as a result of network-modelling exercises.

Tactical and operational applications

Network-optimization techniques are not only useful at the strategic level, they also make valuable contributions at the tactical and operational levels. This is particularly the case with manufacturing, logistics and marketing operations.

Manufacturing applications

Network-optimization techniques assist in the development and testing of the effectiveness of sourcing strategies and master production schedules. They can be used to determine the optimal plant to produce a given product for a given geographic market region.

For example, a beverage producer with five manufacturing locations (Sydney, Melbourne, Brisbane, Adelaide and Perth) that produces beverages in three formats (glass bottles, PET bottles and cans) uses the optimization model to determine the required changes to product-sourcing patterns from the current and proposed product flows shown in Figure 19.3.

The following differences in manufacturing are recommended by the model:

- Overall production levels in Sydney to remain static.
- The total number of production lines to be reduced.
- Melbourne PET and Adelaide glass bottle lines to be operated at capacity.
- Production to be scaled down at the Brisbane plant.
- New capacity limits to be set for the Melbourne plant.
- Perth plant to be operated at capacity.

The following recommended changes to beverage sourcing also result:

- Brisbane to supply some of Sydney's original production levels for glass bottles.
- Glass bottle production to shift from Perth to Adelaide for some markets.
- Glass bottle production in Melbourne to be maintained.
- PET bottle production to shift south (Melbourne production more efficient than Sydney or Brisbane).
- Adelaide and Perth PET bottle production increased.

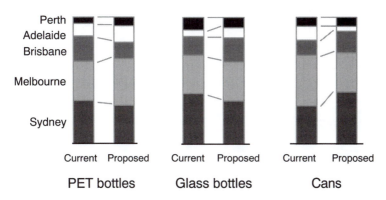

Figure 19.3 Optimization modelling used to optimize manufacturing

■ Can production in Sydney to remain static.
■ Can production in Melbourne and Perth to increase significantly.

A 15 per cent reduction in production and distribution costs could be achieved through implementing these recommendations that would involve relocating production capability between plants, changing sourcing pattern changes and developing optimal production plans for each location. In the longer term, further operating cost reductions could be gained through facility closures and the expansion of existing facilities.

Models with 'multiperiod' capabilities can also be used to manage seasonal stock builds required as a result of either supply-side or demand-side drivers and to optimize the location of inventory along the supply chain. Figure 19.4 shows customer demand fluctuations over a year for a given beverage that are provided as inputs to a multiperiod optimization model. The model has determined the optimum production and inventory levels to meet this demand. The pronounced variation in production levels is owing to the lack of available production capacity during the peak demand period (since peak demand also occurs at this time for a number of other products). The model compensates by building seasonal stocks prior to the peak period (August, September and October) and then depleting these stocks when production capacity is scarce (November, December and January) while keeping supply chain costs (including inventory-holding costs) at a minimum.

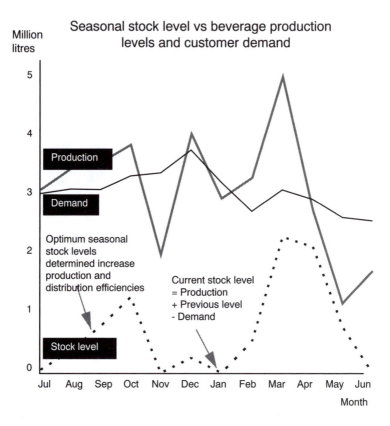

Figure 19.4   Modelling seasonal stock builds to allow optimal production while meeting demand

Logistics applications

Network-optimization techniques assist in warehouse location and selection decisions beyond the limitations of 'centre of gravity' models. Optimization models can determine the best warehouses or distribution centres for performing different processes and processing different products as well as the most appropriate pathway for a product from source of supply to end customer.

The development of a warehouse-location model requires the following five steps.

Determine structure of submodel

■ Determine the number of levels in the model.
■ Determine the number of product groups to model.
■ Determine how to model demand and supply from outer regions.

Split market into subregions
- Determine the number of subregions to be modelled.
- Select regional boundaries for subregions based on geography and size.
- Group postcodes into regions.
- Determine/verify demand by market region.

Determine potential warehouses
- Identify potential warehouse locations.
- Determine costs (fixed and variable) associated with potential warehouses.

Build transport rates
- Determine centre of gravity for subregions.
- Determine rates from each potential warehouse to each subregion.
- Determine rates from plant to potential warehouses.

Model runs
- Validate model.
- Carry out scenario testing and model optimization.
- Determine the preferred number and location of warehouses.

In the example shown in Figure 19.5, the model is given four alternative warehouse locations each with its own fixed and variable operating costs and transport rates. The model trades off the different warehouse and transportation costs and selects the best warehouse location or locations to service the key market segments. The use of a model becomes increasingly important as the number of warehouses increases.

Marketing applications

The development of new customer service strategies can also be assisted by network-optimization techniques. Customer segmentation provides key inputs regarding customer lead time and fill rate requirements. Network modelling tools utilize these inputs directly as service constraints that must be obeyed in the optimization process. By developing parameters at the customer class, product class and customer market area level, tailored supply chain channels are developed to meet (but not necessarily exceed) the needs of the varied constituencies, as illustrated in Figure 19.6.

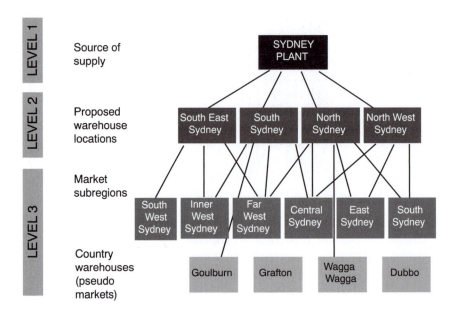

Figure 19.5 Sample network structure represented in warehouse selection models

Making network-optimization techniques work

Project sponsors must take a number of steps to make a network-optimization project successful. These steps include:

- selecting the appropriate modelling package for the specific application;
- following the correct development process;
- taking full ownership of the model;
- recognizing and managing the key success factors; and
- heeding lessons learned from the past.

Selecting a network-modelling tool

A large number of network-modelling tools are available, as shown in Table 19.1. Each has different areas of focus and strength and their suitability depends largely on the application.

In order to select the appropriate optimization tool for the job, the project manager needs to establish a set of selection criteria identifying

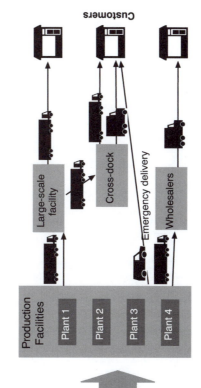

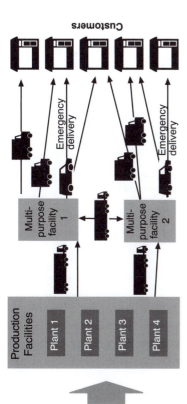

FROM...

- Customer receives multiple deliveries
- 2-4 day order lead time
- Stockouts in warehouse lead to delays in filling customer orders
- Infrequent deliveries to small customers

TO...

- Customer receives consolidated deliveries
- Order lead time reduced for bulk orders through cross-docking vs warehousing
- New wholesaler channel introduced to improve service to small customers
- Stockouts can be dealt with by emergency deliveries direct from plant to customer, reducing customer delays

Figure 19.6   Developing new customer service pathways

Table 19.1
Packages with network-optimization modelling capabilities

Package	Supplier/developer	Features
GSC	Insight Global Supply Chain Associates	Strong 'non-logistics' commerce functionality Multiperiod modelling
Linx	Numetrix	Multiperiod modelling Manufacturing focus Unlimited stages of production
Mimi	Chesapeake	Customizable toolkit Process industries focus
Navigator	Manugistics	Multiperiod modelling Manufacturing focus Unlimited stages of production Integrated to other Manugistics products
Network	Ron Ballou/Case Western University	Single-period modelling Centre of gravity functionality Regression analysis capabilities
Phydias	Synquest	Multiple stages of production Proprietary inventory calculation features
SAILS	Insight	Two stages of production Built in US freight rates Single-period modelling
SDPIM	Aspen Tech	Excel front and back end Mapping through data file exchange Multiperiod modelling
SLIM 2000	J. F. Shapiro Associates	Multiple stages of production Multiperiod modelling Windows version Profit maximization capability
Supply Chain Designer	CAPS Logistics	Multiple optimization and heuristics tools Batch run capabilities Strong graphical user interface and reports Customizable
Supply Chain Strategist	Intertrans	Multiple stages of production Proprietary inventory calculation features

the key model requirements. These criteria will vary between applications but will usually comprise most of those included in Table 19.2. It is also critical that these criteria are prioritized correctly.

The range, capabilities and functionality of these models are undergoing continual changes. Network-modelling tools are increasingly seen as 'bolt-ons' to 'enterprise systems'. In the short term, emphasis will be placed on automating the data flow between the optimization tools and the enterprise systems, as shown in Figure 19.7. Once the data-flow

Table 19.2
Application selection criteria and sample evaluation

Priority	Evaluation criteria	Application 1	Application 2
1	Modelling sophistication/features • Supply chain modelling capability • Level of modelling detail • Algorithm (linear/mixed integer) • Modelling (dis)economies of scale • Multiperiod capability • Manufacturing modelling capability • Profit maximization capability	Strong	Moderate
2	User-friendliness • Data uploading capability • Data manipulation capability • Menu system (easy to use/comprehend)	Strong	Moderate
3	Ease of debugging/problem resolution • Level of diagnostics • Availability of support • User base • Ongoing support	Moderate	Quite strong
4	Operating system/environment • Upgrade plan for platforms	Quite strong	Quite strong
5	Reporting capabilities	Strong	Poor
6	Efficiency/execution speed	Quite strong	Quite strong
7	Software cost	Poor	Quite strong

Key: ◖ Poor   ◑ Moderate   ◕ Quite strong   ● Strong

*Application 1 is the preferred package because of its enhanced functionality and user-friendliness.

issues are resolved, network-modelling tools will become a more standard component of the corporate planning process. Over time, new and creative uses of optimization tools will emerge such as utilizing the output of a network optimizer for the core data in an automated annual budgeting process. Additionally, as solver technology improves, multiperiod optimization will become more commonplace. This approach will lead to further refinement of network strategies that will be

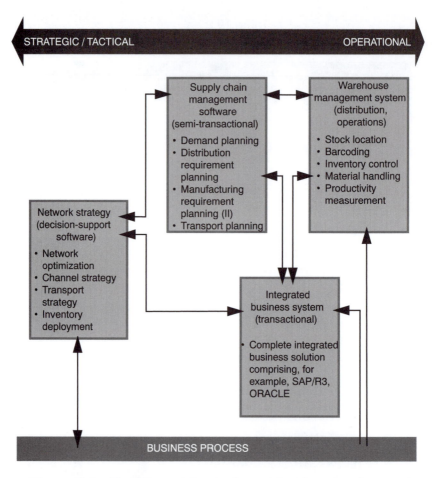

Figure 19.7   Enabling technologies to develop complete and accurate supply chain data

important to capital-intense process industries and industries with strong seasonal demand components.

Network-optimization process

There are four steps that should be followed to optimize the supply chain.

Base case development
The model developers must:

- select the appropriate modelling package;
- determine the modelling objectives and structure;
- specify data requirements and gather data;
- build the model structure and populate the model with data; and
- 'validate' the model against actual company financial data.

Recalibration
The base case model is rerun after the model developers:

- identify changes that have occurred in the business since the model validation period;
- identify new or proposed facilities or cost structures to be incorporated;
- determine demand forecasts for period to be modelled; and
- update model parameters.

Optimization
The model is run in optimization mode once the model developers have:

- determined economies and diseconomies of scale;
- determined the existing and future potential capacities of facilities;
- investigated new sourcing alternatives;
- removed validation constraints; and
- built capacities and economies into model.

Scenario testing and evaluation
The model developers need to:

- agree scenarios to test;
- specify scenarios in detail;
- specify data requirements for scenarios and gather data;
- document scenario assumptions; and
- analyse outputs and rerun until all 'realistic' scenarios have been developed.

Data gathering in the base case development phase and the scenario testing phase may involve the collection of data from external sources as well as internal sources. This is especially true where 'greenfield' sites are involved and cost estimates are required for labour, rent and other operating costs of the new facilities.

Key success factors

The success of network optimization depends on a number of key factors.

Stakeholder ownership

Key stakeholders who will be affected by the outcomes of the project or by the implementation need to be intimately involved in the process in order to develop ownership.

Quality data

The quality of the model and the value of its outputs will depend directly on the quality of the data used in its construction. All input data must be tested to ensure that definitions are consistent and that the data is accurate and complete. Data measurement must be consistent across the network. If the data is collected from different operating divisions, it is critical that it is standardized and derived consistently.

Enabling technologies such as those shown in Figure 19.7 can be used to avoid the need to approximate missing, incomplete or unknown data.

Sufficient data

Every effort must be made to elicit the necessary data. Clearly, where the data does not exist, then the approximations used in the model must be understood and validated wherever possible.

Sufficient resource allocation

The effort and commitment required to build the model should not be underestimated. The resources needed for the project must be defined and must be available for the full duration of the project.

Timely data acquisition

The allocation of the appropriate level of resources coupled with the correct level of detail in the model should allow for the data to be collected within the necessary time frame. Any slippage in this activity will cause a corresponding slippage in the duration of the project.

Customized model development

The range of modelling tools available should ensure that all potential applications can be satisfied. Significant deviations from these packages can add considerably to the time and cost of the project and can reduce the longer-term flexibility of the finished model.

Clarity of scope

The scope of the model must be clearly defined and agreed to by all stakeholders before beginning the modelling exercise. The investment of additional time up-front will ensure that costly, time-consuming modifications are avoided. This includes gaining consensus on the level and type of product aggregation, geographic region and parts of the business that will be covered in the model.

Managing complexity

A large number of variables may be used in the network-modelling tool, requiring a substantial amount of data. The size and complexity of the model are proportional to the product of the number of markets, the number of products and the number of time periods modelled. As the model size increases, the strategic value of the outputs becomes buried in the detail and the overall utility of the model decreases. This problem can be alleviated by reducing the amount of detail built into the model through judicious product and market aggregation, by reducing the number of levels represented in the supply chain and by reducing the number of time periods modelled. This aggregation is critical to the development of a useful and comprehensible model.

As the modelling focus shifts from strategic towards more tactical or operational decisions, it may be appropriate to construct models with added detail in one dimension (e.g. market subsegmentation or time-based segmentation) but with reduced detail in another dimension (e.g. fewer market regions or product groups), as illustrated under Logistics applications above.

Future applications

Network-optimization techniques have been applied to real-world business problems with great success. The challenge for the future will be to broaden the scope of this technology to embrace issues that have not currently been addressed.

We believe that network optimization has the potential to provide benefits in the following areas:

- inventory modelling;
- data integration;
- product profitability analysis;
- operational decision-support systems; and
- ownership of the supply chain.

Inventory modelling

Although effective transactional and predictive inventory models do exist, network-optimization techniques have not yet satisfactorily represented inventory. Inventory costs are typically non-linear owing to the economies of scale that arise when inventories are centralized or when volume flows through a facility increase. As a result, many inventory management considerations have fallen outside the capability of linear programming and hence many optimization models.

An approach exists, however, which model developers can use to model inventory factors effectively within the framework of an optimization model (using mixed integer programming). Consider the impact of production batch size on the level of cycle stock held as inventory. As batch size increases, so does cycle stock. While the increase in cycle stock cost is partly offset by a reduction in manufacturing costs (owing to the decrease in the number of changeovers or set-ups required), it may also lead to increased costs elsewhere in the supply chain. An increase in cycle stock can be treated in the model as an extra fixed cost that is incurred when the batch size is increased. Network-optimization models (using mixed integer rather than simple linear programming) can then choose the optimal balance between the fixed and variable costs.

While incorporating inventory into the network model can deliver richer solutions, it also adds significantly to the volume of data required. This added level of detail and modelling complexity needs to be balanced against the potential benefits to be gained. Typically, only major products that have a significant impact on inventory-holding costs would be modelled in this way.

Data-integration opportunities

Despite the usefulness of network-optimization techniques, further work is required to integrate them with existing data-capture systems. This is a great source of dissatisfaction for model developers because a significant amount of time may be spent translating data from operational systems into a form suitable for the optimization model.

Supply chain system developers are only now beginning to incorporate these tools into their offerings. Companies such as Manugistics and Numetrix are creating optimization packages that are integrated with their tactical and operational supply chain planning systems and are able to draw their data directly from those systems.

Ultimately, the development of a true electronic interface between the modelling package and the transactional databases of the business will vastly improve the modelling process. Optimization models will be developed in a shorter time frame, with improved data quality and will deliver better results with less effort.

Product and customer profitability

Sophisticated network-modelling tools capture not only the product price but true product costs across the total supply chain. In many cases,

Table 19.3
Sample logistics decision-support system for product distributor

Pathway	Logistics cost + Cost of goods sold			
	Product 1	Product 2	Product 3	Product 4
Channel 1 e.g. transfer order from another store	$16	$900*	$13	$875
Channel 2 e.g. direct delivery from a centralized distribution centre	$15	$975	$13	$800*
Channel 3 e.g. stocked item (service level=90%)	$15	$1200	$12	$850
Channel 4 e.g. stocked item (service level=80%)	$14*	$1000	$11*	$825
Volume	*Low*	*Low*	*High*	*High*
Sale price	*$20*	*$1500*	*$20*	*$1500*

*Optimum channel varies from product to product

the network model may provide an activity-based costing model of the network. This information can be harnessed to determine profitability by product and market region. Customer or market profitability can be analysed in a similar manner.

Operational decision-support systems

Although network optimization requires input of operational and transactional information, network-modelling tools can also be used to assist day-to-day decision making. These tools can provide cost information to operational staff and hence enhance the quality of their daily decisions.

Table 19.3 shows the alternative channels available for a typical distributor. Each alternative channel results in different cost and margin outcomes for each product type. Companies can develop decision-support systems using optimization model outputs, which provide this cost information to staff when purchasing products so that they can determine the best sourcing alternative. In this way, staff can be informed about both the cost and the service implications of their sourcing decisions at the time they are making the decision.

Table 19.4
Typical supply chain ownership arrangements

Supply chain components	Manage	Acquire	Operate
Inbound freight	○	○	○
Manufacturing	●	●	●
Inter-facility freight	●	○	○
Primary warehouses	●	●	●
Secondary warehouses	◑	○	○
Outbound freight	◑	○	○

KEY ○ Outsource   ● Inhouse   ◑ Both

Table 19.5
Supply chain costs incurred by different supply chain stakeholders

Model summary report ($m)	Company	Suppliers	Customer	Contractors	Total
Raw material cost		180			180
Inbound transport cost		20			20
Facility cost	40			30	70
Process cost	5				5
Resource cost	20				20
Inter-facility transport cost	15				15
Outbound transport cost	30		20		50
Total cost	110	200	20	30	360

Supply chain ownership

As more and more ownership options are made available to us, the question about the correct level and nature of supply chain ownership, as shown in Table 19.4, is becoming increasingly relevant and more difficult to answer.

Network-optimization techniques analyse who is incurring which costs along the supply chain. Model developers can depict various ownership arrangements within the network model by assigning cost ownership to the different supply chain components and identifying the costs incurred by each stakeholder in the supply chain, as illustrated in Table 19.5.

These costs may be transferred between these stakeholders. For example, the company may be paying a third-party contractor for running its warehouse and charging its customers delivery costs, while the third-party contractor is paying its own staff and paying rent for the warehouse. Once these costs have been identified and classified, some interesting options in supply chain optimization can be investigated, including viewing and optimizing the network from a number of perspectives:

- the company;
- the customers;
- the suppliers;
- the third-party contractors; and
- overall supply chain taking account of all trade-offs and interactions between all of the supply chain players.

This approach permits a focus on the areas of greatest cost in the supply chain and on promoting supply chain integration between key parties. It provides a better understanding of the forces driving the different supply chain players and gives a starting point for negotiations with these parties. The development of proper EDI channels between supply chain parties would further facilitate the development of these models.

Industry-wide supply chain perspective

A similar approach can be used to investigate industry-wide supply chain optimization by building a network model comprising both the company's and its competitors' supply chain networks in order to optimize the competitors' supply chains (to understand their operational capability and opportunities for joint ventures) and to optimize the entire industry supply chain.

Conclusion

Network-optimization techniques are powerful tools that use linear and mixed integer programming techniques to model and optimize the supply chain. They can help reduce the cost of supply chain operations by 5 to 20 per cent per annum. Network-optimization techniques can also be used by senior and middle managers to test and develop future business scenarios. They support business planning and also have strategic, tactical and operational business applications.

The usefulness and applicability of network-optimization technology will increase in the future as features are enhanced and as these models are progressively integrated with existing operational systems. Building an effective network model is not easy. Project sponsors need to manage the process carefully and ensure that sufficient resources and senior-level support are committed to the project to make the exercise successful.

References

Gattorna, J.L. and Walters, D.W. (1996) *Managing the Supply Chain*, Macmillan, London.

Goldberg, R. and Lorin, H. (1982), *Measuring the Value of Automated Decision Support Systems: The Economics of Information Processing*, Vol. I, John Wiley, New York.

Haverly, R.C., Coleman, M. and Whelan, J.F. (1995) *CLM (Council of Logistics Management) Logistics Software*, Andersen Consulting, Oakbrook, IL.

Robeson, J.F. and Copacino, W.C. (1994) *The Logistics Handbook*, Free Press, New York.

Schrage, L. (1991), *LINDO: An Optimization Modeling System*, 4th edn, Scientific Press, San Francisco, CA.

Shapiro, J.F., Singhal, V.M. and Wagner, S.N. (1993) 'Optimizing the value chain', *Interfaces* 23 (2), 102–7.

Wall Street Journal (1990) 'Perrier announces worldwide recall of its mineral water', 15 Feb.

Global supply management

Satisfying the global customer

Dave Anderson, Yamini Dhillon and Julian Remnant

The world economy is undergoing a rapid transformation. Globalization is changing the fabric of business from a patchwork of discrete national and regional markets to a boundaryless global market. The implications for business leaders are clear. The opportunities for growth and profit are growing exponentially; so too, however, are the potential risks. Companies wishing to compete in this environment must adopt a global supply chain management operating strategy. Success will require a new vision of supply chain management moving from a local and regional approach to a truly global operation. This chapter outlines three principles to guide supply chain leaders in their new challenge, focusing on how to satisfy the emerging global customer through supply chain integration and responsive operations.

Introduction

During the last decade the liberalization of trade, the growth and integration of global capital markets and advances in information and communications technologies have created an increasingly global marketplace. Companies that have relied on their seemingly unique competitive advantages can no longer expect that these will deliver continued success. The rules for competition have changed. The forces of globalization, combined with domestic pressures created by ubiquitous technology, shorter product lifecycles and lower-cost, seamless transport, are pushing companies to develop new capabilities to enter international markets.

Competing internationally creates a significant supply chain challenge. Consider the case of a global launch of a product—the worldwide release of the latest Michael Jackson compact disc (CD) within hours of its launch in Los Angeles. Underlying this event were a multitude of supply chain steps to ensure that the CDs arrived in retail outlets at the scheduled time. Contract manufacturers in key markets received electronically transmitted master copies of the songs from which hundreds of copies were locally manufactured. The printing of the CD cover and inserts was contracted and completed in advance. These were shipped to key markets where they were merged with the CDs. Contract manufacturers then produced the CD box and disk and combined the packaging items with the CD. On completion the CDs were loaded into containers and express delivered to local distributors. They were then delivered to retail outlets and stocked on the shelves in time to be purchased by consumers.

The supply chain task involved in the global retailing effort was enormous given that over 75 markets had to be supplied simultaneously, balancing supply and demand across the markets (for example, where should surplus production stock be shipped?) and determining appropriate sourcing, manufacturing and logistics options (for example, should the product be manufactured in Europe and shipped to Africa for the initial launch followed by local manufacturing?).

As this event highlights, competing globally requires several key supply chain challenges to be faced. First, companies need to adapt to significant increases in operational scale and supply chain complexity. This may also include adopting new operating models and building relationships with external organizations, for example outsourcing one or more supply chain functions such as manufacturing logistics and customer relations. Secondly, companies must accommodate and cater to diverse consumer needs. Reassertion of market-specific consumer preferences and the growth of the educated consumer will mean that homogenous products and services and a 'one-size-fits-all' approach to customer service will almost certainly guarantee a company's failure or demise. The concept of mass customization, which up to now has largely been theoretical in nature, will become a reality for more and more companies. This will require tremendous supply chain capabilities to allow the assembly and delivery of uniquely specified products to consumers in multiple markets. Finally, companies will need to adapt to variations in cultures, behaviours, languages and currencies over and above the constantly changing tax, regulatory and custom laws.

Moving towards global supply chain management

Becoming a true global competitor will involve nothing short of adopting a radically new vision of global supply chain management. Such an approach will indeed be radical, for the reason that management must adopt a holistic view of the company's supply chain operations and avoid producing a collection of fragmented local and regional sourcing, manufacturing and logistics operations. Often this will necessitate a change of mindset from operating on a traditional country or regional basis to a truly global basis. As Kenichi Ohmae described in *Managing in a Borderless Economy* (1989): 'building a value system that emphasizes seeing and thinking globally is the bottom line price of admission to today's borderless economy'.

Moreover, there is no single correct way of managing a global supply chain. Consider, for example, Vistakon, a contact lens manufacturer and subsidiary of Johnson & Johnson. The inherent nature of Vistakon's products requires little customization, allowing the company to begin implementing a global supply chain strategy. It has two manufacturing plants, one in the USA serving North America and the other in Ireland serving the rest of the world. Customer orders are manufactured on a just-in-time basis and express shipped to key distributors and retailers around the world. Single-plant global sourcing strategies continue to be evaluated to take further advantage of scale and cost efficiencies.

By contrast, Nike Apparel has adopted a mixed global supply chain strategy. Sourcing is global to ensure that the cheapest and highest-quality inputs are used in the manufacturing process. However, the company has adopted a localized distribution strategy. This partnering approach with local distributors and delivery companies has ensured that it has maximized its revenues in markets, especially in Europe, where access to retail chains is often tightly controlled by distributors.

The journey to successful global supply chain management must not only adopt a business integration perspective where strategies, processes, people and technologies are collectively considered to ensure that a robust approach is developed, but also adhere to three guiding principles. These are first, customers must drive the global supply chain; second, supply chain activities must be integrated across national borders; and third, supply chain operations must be responsive in order to respond to a diverse customer base. This charter for success of global supply chains appears deceptively simple, but in fact fulfilling all three guiding principles on a global basis can require an organization to make a radical change from the status quo.

Putting the customer in the driver's seat

Businesses seeking a competitive edge have tried recently to give all their activities a strong customer focus. However, this imperative takes on an even greater magnitude as a company expands its reach from national to global markets and the number of potential customers increases exponentially. While bigger markets present enormous opportunities for revenue and profit growth, they also raise a challenge of equal if not greater proportions—companies must maintain, as Ohmae put it, an 'equidistance of perspective'. Irrespective of which part of the world customers inhabit, a company must understand their needs and regard them to be of equal importance. Understanding the new global customer is the golden rule of competing effectively in a global marketplace.

Traditionally many companies have adopted an 'inside-out' perspective to serving consumers. Dimensions of cost and efficiency have tended to rate above that of customer service, causing companies to give precedence to managing their internal operations at the expense of addressing consumer needs. This mentality has resulted in many companies providing homogenous products and services to all classes of consumers and minimizing the cost-to-serve.

However, the new world view is distinctly different. Not only is an 'outside-in' perspective required in the future, positioning consumer service at the apex of company focus, but this customer approach will need to be adopted strategically. Companies cannot afford to apply a blanket approach to service for all market segments. The challenge will be to differentiate between consumer needs by providing tailored products and services, while simultaneously controlling cost and efficiency. This means that the cost-to-serve equation will cease to be uniform across consumers and instead will vary according to the level of consumer service required by different market segments and the efficiency of the organization to deliver the necessary services. As a result, the cost-to-serve will vary with consumer requirements; it will be higher for complex, sophisticated consumers and lower for simple, unsophisticated consumers. This will enable the 'ideal', rather than the lowest, cost-to-serve to be achieved.

Several companies have already succeeded in meeting this challenge. For example, US computer manufacturer Dell has made the following situation an operating reality:

> I, the consumer, sit in my living room, cruising the worldwide web. I see an interesting personal computer product on-line, proceed to customize features, functionality, and accessories. When completed, I order and pay via credit card, specify next day delivery via express courier and sit back and wait for arrival. Upon arrival, I receive a call from the company to help me set up, use and further customize the product. Answers to technical problems are handled on line through Dell's website or by service representatives via the telephone.

Providing this capability has resulted in first-mover advantage with many satisfied and repeat customers, a significant rise in shareholder value and major competitors seeking to emulate Dell's direct channel model.

But a direct channel model is not the only means of differentiating between consumers and providing customized products. In fact, before a specific course of action can be determined, global supply chain managers must have a solid understanding of current and emerging customer and consumer needs. Without such knowledge, companies will have little hope of anticipating and meeting the needs of a diverse, global customer base, nor will they be able to arrive at an ideal cost-to-serve equation. Unlocking the potential of the new customers will require two steps to be taken.

The first step is to collect consumer-level demand data. This requires the use of the right technology and for some manufacturers it may be appropriate to partner with wholesalers and retailers to obtain access to this information. For example, Fruit of the Loom, a US-based clothing manufacturer, has partnered with its distributors to collect consumer information from retailers via the Internet, rewarding participation in the programme by offering expedited delivery options at low cost.

The second step is to analyse consumer-level demand data. Analysis of historical consumer purchases provide very powerful insights into consumer preferences, for example the size, dollar value and frequency of orders, number of line items and delivery requirements can all be determined. For instance, Reader's Digest collects sales data by product by consumer. The company uses this information not only to increase sales to existing consumers by targeting new titles to individuals based on past purchasing behaviour, but also to identify new consumers by comparing current consumer data to US census data.

For both steps, new technologies are an essential tool in capturing and using consumer information at a global level. The Internet, as mentioned, is gaining popularity as a channel to communicate with consumers by retailers and manufacturers alike. For example, Amazon.com an Internet book retailer, uses past purchasing information to suggest additional titles to consumers; and Cisco, a global network computer manufacturer, has developed an interactive Web page to enable consumers to upgrade software and solve common service problems. Electronic commerce is also providing ways to get closer to the consumer. In 1994 Shell UK pioneered a smart card containing a microchip that collects data on consumer purchases. This information is used to develop store-specific assortments and customize product offerings in local markets and stores.

Integrating across national borders

The old paradigm for attaining efficiency of supply chain operations was premised on maximizing the efficiency within each functional and geographic area. For example, manufacturing efficiency could be attained by dedicating lines to specific products, increasing production run quantities and minimizing changeover time. However, functional and geographic excellence is clearly not the suggested way forward for global supply chain management as it would result in a horrendous number of fragmented local operations and gross supply chain inefficiencies.

The prerequisite for global supply chain management is to integrate supply chain activities. The three tenets of achieving integrated, cross-functional global operations encompass designing and implementing efficient sales channels and networks, collaborating between supply chain partners on planning and forecasting consumer needs, and using third parties to manage non-core activities and supply chain costs.

Efficient sales channels and networks

Companies must proactively look for ways to reduce channel costs to distribute their products and services. For example, following its initial success with the consumer direct channel, Dell is now working with traditional value-added resellers to tap into smaller business markets. This is a relatively less costly option compared to establishing the channel on its own and allows Dell to take advantage of the deep business relations developed by the value-added resellers with their customers.

Collaborative planning and forecasting

Past efforts in planning and forecasting frequently did not extend beyond sharing information on market trends. Forecasts of consumer level demand were not used to plan upstream supply chain activities, such as distribution and production scheduling. Instead, forecasts typically included 'just-in-case' estimates in the event that a channel partner may fail to meet actual demand in a local market.

Employing this approach in a global environment would spell disaster. Excessive levels of inventories would pile up in different locations around the world leading to inefficiencies, and the system would be in disequilibrium as supply and demand would be misaligned across markets.

Collaborative, cross-functional forecasting is an essential approach for managing inventory levels and supply and demand on a global scale. Collaborating with external organizations, for instance, such as retailers and wholesalers, is necessary for obtaining vital consumer-level demand data. Collaborating internally between the sales and marketing, distribution and production departments—in domestic and international locations—will enable one-number forecasts to be more accurately derived. This is critical given the complex mix of markets that multinational companies must serve. For inventory levels, a cross-functional approach allows inventory to be aggregated on a regional or cross-market basis, enabling regional inventory pools and improved balancing of supply and demand to occur. Better upstream planning across all supply chain activities can also take place, leading to improved production scheduling and more efficient raw material purchasing.

Key players in the consumer goods industry have gradually been implementing collaborative planning programmes with great success. Warner Lambert and Wal-Mart have implemented a revolutionary information-sharing programme via the Internet called CFAR (Collaborative Forecasting and Replenishment) which is expected to become the industry standard. It is a standardized way for manufacturers and merchants to work together on forecasts across the Internet. The system improves reliability of longer-term forecasts, which in turn eliminate excess inventory, rework, excess labour and waste.

Outsourcing non-core activities using third parties

Finally, third parties play an important role in managing costs (and service levels) in a complex environment by allowing companies to focus on core competencies. Ownership of the supply chain becomes an important issue for companies as they enter and exit markets because each country needs to be independently assessed in terms of its regulations, infrastructure and logistics market sophistication. For example, General Electric's appliance division has developed a tailored approach for Asia, of which the most important element is developing the right partnerships. In each region in Asia, GE located different third-party providers which had an appropriate fit with the GE culture. In China, the lack of transportation infrastructure made it impossible to find a manufacturing partner that could service the whole country, so GE teamed with a well-established distributor which was able to locate the appropriate factories scattered across the country. In Japan, the company was able to enter into a partnership with Kojima, a discount retailer, which enabled it to remove many layers from Japan's cumbersome distribution system. In India and the Philippines, GE found manufacturing partners which were able to service the whole nation. This strategy of using third parties has enabled it to avoid the high costs of investing in assets in Asia and at the same time take advantage of the knowledge its partners possess.

Achieving responsive operations

The fast-changing nature of the global market dictates the importance of the need for companies to maintain responsive operations. As customer needs change, supply chain operations must also change to retain customers and ensure continued customer satisfaction. The paradigm of the future is as follows: use consumer-level data to understand how consumers want to buy and use products; define supply chains that allow access to numerous global sourcing, manufacturing and logistics options, and develop the organization, people and operations based on these premises that allow a reasonable change in customer demand to be met.

Critical to establishing a responsive organization are the elements of structure and people. Companies need to design a flexible organization structure that can maximize internal expertise across countries and adapt to the requirements of customers with diverse needs. For example, Whirlpool used 'virtual teams' to access worldwide expertise to design new refrigerator technology. The company used insulation technology from its European business, compressor technology from the Brazilian affiliates and manufacturing and design expertise from the US operation. Similarly at Texas Instruments, engineers in the US and India work on new product development 24 hours a day, to speed products to market.

Preparing people to understand cultural differences and embrace diversity in the workplace is critical to the responsive organization. People must develop the mindset that change is part of their daily job function. Performance incentives and job descriptions must be aligned appropriately to facilitate this process. General Motors is developing a global manufacturing strategy which involves building plants in emerging markets in the hope of tapping into new markets. One key element of this strategy is that workers will be trained to do multiple tasks and they will be responsible for the entire process in the assembly operation, providing considerable flexibility for GM.

Once people begin to interact across countries, cultural differences are certain to emerge as different values, customs and ethics are brought into the workplace. Training staff to understand different cultures and to be flexible in their approach to ethnic diversity will be essential preparation for this environment.

Once the responsive organization and people are in place, companies must design responsive operational strategies. A variety of ways can be used to develop responsive operations. For example, in product development, Honda has designed a changeable platform to customize its Accord car to world markets. In other words, one platform will be used to make cars for all world markets, but the cars will be very different in each market. In the USA the Accord will be a mid-size car, but in Japan and Europe it will be a smaller, sportier model. This strategy greatly enhances worldwide supply chain flexibility and also reduces costs, making the supply chain more efficient.

In summary, responsive operational strategies are the key to supply chain success in a global environment. These strategies cannot be achieved without a responsive organization with people aligned to the needs of their global customers, prepared for differences in culture and business expectations.

Conclusion

The enormous size of the global economy offers business leaders a tremendous opportunity to boost their revenue and profits. However, satisfying customers across national borders involves a vastly different supply chain capability to that of business operations at home. The operational scale is larger and involves far greater complexity, with a greater number of supply channels and external parties to manage. The customers themselves are diverse and more difficult to understand. Before entering the global market, companies should first establish a set of clearly defined supply chain capabilities, through a global supply chain management operating strategy. Through customer responsiveness, integration and responsive operations, companies will increase their likelihood of becoming successful global competitors of the twenty-first century.

Globalizing the supply chain: SmithKline Beecham

SmithKline Beecham, one of the top ten pharmaceutical companies in the world, provides a good example of how the supply chain can be used as a lever for success.

In the pharmaceutical industry, escalating pressures are redefining the rules of competition. Pharmaceutical companies are evolving into global healthcare enterprises to keep apace with industry changes. As Figure 20.1 shows, the pressures on the supply chain are diverse and include the increasing globalization of the industry. As a result, companies are finding that their existing processes and infrastructure are lagging behind the growing scale and complexity of the businesses they must now support.

SmithKline Beecham has responded to this environment by focusing much of its management effort on building global supply chain capabilities through a clear strategy for global supply chain management.

The cornerstone of SmithKline Beecham's supply chain vision is a supply network configured and managed according to the principles of the value-creation model EVA™ to ensure optimal utilization of network assets and effective leverage of internal and external supply capabilities.

In support of its mission to become a fully integrated human healthcare company, delivering 'healthcare prevention, diagnosis, treatment and cure', SmithKline Beecham undertook a major realignment programme in 1994 that involved the purchase of Sterling Health, a prominent worldwide supplier of non-prescription products, the acquisition of a major US-based pharmaceutical benefits manager and the sale of its animal health business.

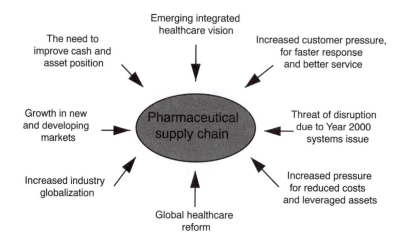

Figure 20.1   Forces affecting the pharmaceutical industry

The Sterling Health acquisition significantly expanded SmithKline's global network to 78 manufacturing sites and excessive distribution facilities. As a result, SmithKline Beecham established a new Worldwide Supply Operations (WSO) business unit to consolidate the group's worldwide manufacturing and distribution sites and manage the integrated network.

Challenges of competing globally

As mentioned earlier in this chapter, key challenges are encountered when competing in a global market. SmithKline Beecham, in pursuing its programme of integration and rationalization, faced its own supply chain challenges to:

- drive down network-operating costs by reducing over-capacity and duplication;
- reduce complexity in both the network and the supporting business processes;
- increase the company's ability to invest in the highest level of good manufacturing practice (GMP) and regulatory compliance by operating fewer sites; and
- supply larger geographic areas with greater product and process excellence from fewer sourcing points.

Building the path to supply chain supremacy

SmithKline Beecham has responded to these challenges by first identifying and implementing opportunities to consolidate the supply network, and secondly developing a common, integrated global supply chain management capability.

Supply network consolidation

SmithKline Beecham worked with Andersen Consulting to identify opportunities to focus investment, cut costs and ensure security and reliability of customer service in the supply network. The approach included extensive scenario modelling of manufacturing facilities and business case assessment to confirm the opportunities for network rationalization and reductions in product portfolio complexity, and implementation of the approved plans by local line management.

Each manufacturing facility was also analysed along cost and service parameters, with the aim of achieving the 'ideal' cost-to-serve level for SmithKline and its customers. The rationalization of the network was not only about avoiding over-investment in facilities, but achieving a greater degree of customer responsiveness through the efficient use of assets. For the pharmaceutical industry, the greatest service priority lies in timely delivery of the product the customer needs, so the careful planning of product supply through the new network of facilities was an important task and one that was well delivered.

SmithKline's manufacturing consolidation is already realizing benefits for the company and its customers. More than 2000 stock-keeping units (SKUs) have been transferred without any disruption of the supply of pharmaceuticals to customers. In addition, several manufacturing sites across the world have been sold or closed, while others have been refocused on selected manufacturing and product technologies, with some plants receiving substantial incremental volume. By 1999, the annual supply chain savings delivered by the programme will represent a payback period of some four years on the original global integration provision.

Integration in the supply chain organization

Historically, SmithKline Beecham's supply chain comprised a significant number of disparate processes, organization structures and information systems. The business was able to cope with this diversity as many of the day-to-day operations were carried out within geographic boundaries and tightly knit supply chain 'communities'.

However, growth in new markets combined with the restructuring of the supply network introduced a greater requirement for integration between internal customers and suppliers across the global supply chain. The need to reduce costs and eliminate non-value-added activities further accentuated the drive to integrate and standardize processes, information systems and organization structures.

SmithKline Beecham and Andersen Consulting developed an enterprise supply chain operating model (see Figure 20.2) underpinned by a set of principles designed to achieve uniformity of global supply chain operations.

This model comprises a common set of processes, standard configurations of application software and uniform roles and responsibilities across all

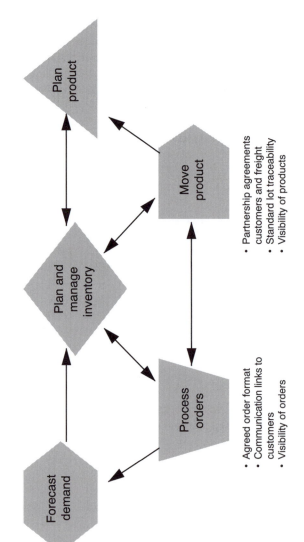

Figure 20.2   Enterprise supply chain

operational facilities. It is sufficiently robust to support local statutory and legal requirements, but other variations from the globally specified solution are subject to a rigorous process of justification and approval. SmithKline Beecham is adopting a deployment approach that devolves implementation responsibility to local commercial and manufacturing operations with support from global process owners and cross-functional deployment teams.

Benefits

As enterprise deployment gets underway, SmithKline Beecham should begin to realize the following benefits:

■ increased customer responsiveness and service levels;
■ improvements in operational and financial planning capability across the supply chain;
■ facilitation of millennium initiatives through establishment of a standard information architecture;
■ an increase in asset utilization by substituting management information for excess capacity; and
■ improvements in network efficiency (e.g. stock turns).

The SmithKline Beecham example illustrates the successful execution of a global supply chain strategy through a focus on network consolidation, integration across the supply chain and attention to the needs of customer segments. This strategy has improved SmithKline's competitive position in the rapidly changing and increasingly global pharmaceutical industry.

References

Ohmae, Kenichi (1992) 'Managing in a borderless world', in Bartlett, Christopher A. and Ghoshal, Sumantra, *Transnational Management: Text, Cases, and Readings in Cross-Border Management*, Richard D. Irwin, New York.

Lean synchronous manufacturing
'Hard-wiring' production to demand
David Kennedy, Barry Elliott and Frank Carbone

Traditional approaches to production planning and control systems, seeking to maximize efficiency and utilization, are no longer viable in a customer-centred world. Firms wanting to compete successfully need to look to new concepts, processes and technologies to help them adapt to this new era and to ensure that their production processes deliver customer satisfaction while retaining maximum efficiency.

Introduction

The guiding principle in modern manufacturing industries is, if you want to stay in business, get more competitive. Axioms about productivity and efficiency are still as valid as ever, but the focus has shifted towards reduced costs and improved customer service on a global scale. People now understand that both objectives can be achieved simultaneously. Success depends on doing what the customer wants better than the competition. It depends on reliably delivering products of better value with more benefits to customers more quickly, precisely when they want it.

As well as facing pressures from a more competitive marketplace, manufacturing has to cope with the many uncertainties inherent within its own processes, procedures and methods. These uncertainties include unpredictability in the day-to-day variation in demand, the capacity of suppliers to maintain a reliable service, the skills and cooperation of the workforce and the reliability and capability of plant, machinery and equipment. In the past, the response to uncertainty was to build inventories to serve as a buffer. The response now must be to eliminate the uncertainties. This achieves two benefits: reduced investment in inventory and increased responsiveness.

Manufacturing companies have long struggled to find production-control processes that helped them manage the inevitable disruptions. Generally they have contemplated one of two alternative strategies: either hold excess inventories to supply the customer in time of need; or maintain spare capacity that can be switched on to keep up or catch up.

But neither of these alternatives has proved acceptable to, or economically viable for, manufacturers. Holding excess inventories may cripple an operation, constricting valuable cashflows or reducing the plant's ability to respond. The stock held may not be the right mix, which opens the door to competition. Excess stocking increases the level of stagnation within the process. It extends lead times, causing earlier start-ups and compounding errors in long-term projections, which leads to increased inventories.

Maintaining excess capacity is not viable either. It flies in the face of principles of utilization and efficiency, in particular the goal of using the full capacity of the whole plant. Capital investments have traditionally been justified on the basis that any new piece of plant will be run at near 100 per cent, with little room for an increase in demand or any ability to recover from disruptions. Furthermore, the trend continues in expecting more and more from plant over the course of its useful life. This is made possible by more sophistication in process and product design and improvements to traditionally inadequate maintenance routines.

Having discounted excess inventory or excess capacity as viable methods to buffer the production process from inevitable disruptions, manufacturers turned to a solid but uninspired production paradigm. They were comfortable with monthly packets of information, customers and consumers were accustomed to long lead times. Utilization and efficiency were the key measures. This paradigm was reflected in the use of simple order points through the 1950s until materials requirements planning (MRP) emerged in the mid-1960s and became the basis for most production, planning and control systems. The additional sophistication of closed-loop MRP and, ultimately, manufacturing resources planning (MRP II) has contributed to improving the ability of production management to react to disruptions.

But the move to being even more responsive to the customer has largely invalidated the old production paradigm. The time has arrived to challenge the fundamental design of production-control systems, which are no longer acceptable to a demanding consumer population and globally competitive environment. Profound technological advances have made alternative production models a possibility and a reality.

This is where lean synchronous manufacturing comes in. The challenge of lean synchronous manufacturing is to move raw materials quickly and smoothly through the manufacturing process, producing finished goods in alignment with market demand while eliminating waste within the process itself. To achieve this, the process must achieve the following three objectives:

- maximize throughput (the rate at which the process generates money through sales);
- while minimizing both inventory (all the money tied up in the materials the process intends to sell); and
- minimizing operating expense (the money spent by the process in turning inventory into throughput).

The combination of initiatives that contribute to lean synchronous manufacturing focuses on the achievement of this goal.

Characteristics of lean synchronous manufacturing

First, 'synchronous'. The main objective is to have production triggered by—synchronized to—actual end-user demand. The reality is that most current manufacturing processes are anything but synchronous. A manufacturing process is a series of inter-linked and inter-dependent events. These events are consciously defined at the product design stage through the bill of material (BOM) and manufacturing routing. For example, it may be stipulated that an appliance shell must first be pressed before it is enamelled, or a precision rotor must be turned before it is heat treated.

Firms can alleviate the pressure caused by these trigger points through greater attention to design, such as through the concepts packaged as 'design for manufacture'. Indeed, this is an important element to enable lean synchronous manufacturing. But the reality is that discontinuities are inevitable in the manufacturing process. Even two identical and adjacent machines, which are rated at the same output, will often produce different output because they are being operated by different people, working on different materials, maintained by a different routine, are of different ages and so on.

It is therefore the understanding and management of the constraints within the process that will provide the key to successful implementation of synchronous manufacturing. The throughput of the entire process is totally dependent on the rate of its slowest resource, or bottleneck. Bottlenecks govern both throughput and inventories. Success in deriving a production schedule will be established by simultaneously considering all of the constraints (material, labour, equipment, cost) on the total process.

Figure 21.1 depicts the knock-on effect that happens as a change propagates backwards and forwards through a the process or, indeed, an entire supply chain: a small ripple in one part of the manufacturing process can ultimately cause a tidal wave in another. A small change in demand can have a tremendous impact on the smoothness of raw mate-

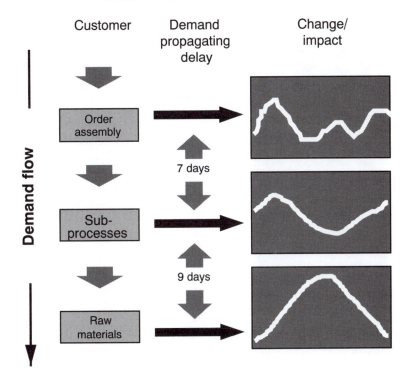

Figure 21.1   The knock-on effects of changes

rial requirements. A machine that is broken down for an hour can cause a failure to hit a due date by several days.

The traditional approach adopted to overcome this phenomenon is one of 'divide and be conquered'. Time horizons are broken up into immediate, medium term and long term and they are planned separately. The resources and materials are also planned separately. The sub-processes are further broken down into job functions and these are planned separately. Any exceptions found in any of these divisions will invalidate the plan, which is worked through again.

This approach has negative effects. Shop-floor personnel are expected to reconcile the informational inconsistencies, conflicts and surprises which inevitably result when the plan is conceived in parts, not as a whole. Higher inventories are sometimes used as a buffer to protect against the disruptions within the various parts of the process, but, as we have argued, represent economic inefficiencies. Figure 21.2 shows the disintegration between subprocesses. If changes occur in any part of the process, propagation of that change can only happen in one direction, slowly.

Secondly, 'lean'. Within the process of manufacturing many elements exist that would not exist today if process and control were redesigned

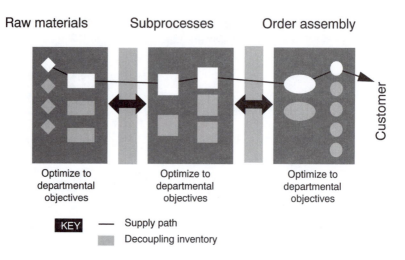

Figure 21.2   Disintegration between subprocesses

from scratch. In general terms, these elements have been defined as non-value-adding activities and account for around 96 per cent of time within modern manufacturing processes. Lean manufacturing concentrates on the identification and subsequent reduction of process 'wastes'.

The factors behind the main 'wastes' within the process today are summarized in Table 21.1.

In a practical sense, the main tool available to the lean synchronous manufacturing engineer is process mapping and focusing on activities which are wasteful. A review and subsequent mapping of documented and unwritten processes within an organization provides a powerful input to the development of change strategies for manufacturing. Exposing and mapping the processes of an organization in this way is a significant step toward the development of an understanding of value-adding versus non-value-adding activity. Focusing the design of new processes and performance-measurement criteria around value-adding activity is a key element for the development of manufacturing excellence capability.

In manufacturing operations it is important not only to map processes in detail but to represent the manufacturing environment in the form of an aerial view of the facility. This view should not only include details of the production flows into, through and out of manufacturing, but also highlight inactive links in processes, such as when product in the process is sitting idle. The actual lead times for the total process should also be analysed in detail, built up from the lead time for each individual step in the process and once again incorporating both idle and active steps. Analysing the manufacturing environment in this way very quickly and clearly highlights value-adding versus non-value-adding activity.

Table 21.1
Example and causal factors

Motion	If an operator has to wander about here and there in search of parts, materials or tools usually caused by poor layouts and ergonomics.
Waiting	An unbalanced line will be the situation where an operator is assigned to a job that has yet to be completed by a preceding operation.
Faster than necessary pace	If the operators of two adjacent operations work at different paces then the temporary storage area must cope with this dissociation.
Correction	The rework area, loop or department.
Over-processing	Extra work in a operation that is not necessary to meet customer requirements but, because of lack of work standards, operators add in to the process.
Over-producing	Long lead times and high inventories will have the effect of keeping running a specific job to maintain machine utilization with the result of building excess inventories.
Conveyance	Poor layouts and integration will necessitate the moving of parts between operations, departments and/or factories.
Inventory	The consequence of other wastes and inadequate practices.

This analysis often reveals that only a small percentage of time and resources is spent actually adding value to products in the manufacturing process. Details of how often the product was stored during the process, how many times it was handled and moved, the total number of steps in the process and the total and step-by-step lead times become very clear. The level of complexity of production flows is also clearly highlighted, affected by factors such as the number of storage locations in the facility, the capacity and location of those areas and the level of inventory holding in them.

Equally important to the operational analysis is a detailed review of the planning execution processes. Quite often, long-standing company habits or unwritten policy lead to inconsistent behaviours which, while not obviously wasteful in themselves, actually contribute to inefficient execution of the schedule. And sometimes a focus on optimum performance at the functional level can be at the expense of optimal outcomes for the total process or organization.

To achieve the objectives defined earlier, namely to be most responsive to the end user as well as most profitable, both the lean and the synchronous elements are required. Each enables the other. Leanness removes the 'fat' and enables the responsiveness to be synchronous. Sychronization allows the operation to run in such a lean manner. There is great synergy, which is how the result is maximized.

Initiatives to implement lean synchronous manufacturing

Performance measurements

Key performance indicators are a means of stimulating the correct behaviours within the production process—or indeed, in any other business process. The wrong measures will make people behave in the wrong way. If labour productivity and machine utilization are the only measures of how the shop floor defines success, then all behaviours on the shop floor will be to maximize these at the expense of other metrics.

A rounded, more balanced set of measures will ensure a rounded, more balanced set of behaviours, thereby ensuring that the 'correct' decisions are taken when the shop floor is faced with a trade-off. Linking this balanced set of measures to rewards is even more powerful. An amazing response can be achieved if, when a production line has achieved 100 per cent of its schedule, its members can go home without loss of pay.

Performance measurement and management will also be key to the continuous improvement and hence the ultimate success of the organization. Performance measurement is critical to operations excellence where daily decisions are pushed down to the lowest levels. Performance measures are indeed the vital signs of an organization: they quantify how well the activities within a process or the outputs of a process achieve a specified goal. On a regular basis they tell people what and how they are doing as part of the whole and communicate what is important throughout the organization. The messages communicated are confirmation of the strategy from top management down, process results from lower levels up and control and improvement within processes. With a consistent view everyone can work towards implementing strategy, achieving goals and improving the organization.

Continual and concurrent planning

Plans need to be made that integrate the short-, medium- and long-term horizons while considering the sequencing of task and taking into account resources and materials. Concurrent planning is the ability to simultaneously address capacity and material issues across all time-frames and processes, addressing issues in a holistic manner. Continual planning allows incremental planning, as opposed to 'throw everything up in the air', with less nervousness and rapid what-if capabilities. To describe this, Figure 21.3 shows the planning funnel with variable horizons allowing near-term detailed execution plans to mesh seamlessly with longer-term master plans. In the near term, the planning range is where the exact sequence is defined. In the medium term, there are small planning buckets of days or weeks, while, in the long term, there are larger planning buckets of months, quarters and years.

The combination of concurrent and continual planning will allow the reduction in the inventory needed to decouple the process of manufacturing. The plans produced from continual and concurrent planning will allow faster cycle and response times through ensuring a global optimum that is based on all the constraints simultaneously.

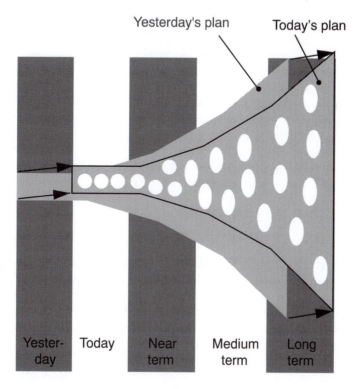

Figure 21.3   The planning funnel

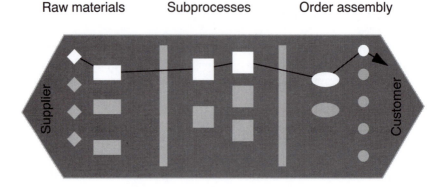

**Figure 21.4   Optimization based on overall manufacturing
process objectives**

Layout and facilities design

The design of a manufacturing facility has a major impact on its performance in terms of quality, timeliness, efficiency and cost. A facility designed around standard work flows and cells will achieve operational excellence in manufacturing by developing a flexible and responsive manufacturing environment. Designing a layout for the production floor that tightly integrates the flow of product through the facility will reduce cycle times and the need for buffers (see Figures 21.4 and 21.5). The move away from fixed batches progressing through functionally based departments will contribute towards this flexibility and have a dramatic effect on throughput, inventory and operating expense. In a practical sense, this is achieved by basing the throughput on a process-based, U-shaped manufacturing cell and splitting and overlapping batches. To demonstrate this, consider the following simple example of producing five items through four processes, each process taking one minute.

Set-up reduction

Changeovers have become an important opportunity for achieving lean synchronous manufacturing. A consequence of launching large batches on the shop floor is longer lead times, increasing inventories and poor customer response. On the other hand, however, reducing the batch sizes will appear uneconomical if the sometimes significant time taken to perform job changeovers is accepted without question. The time taken to perform the changeover can be reduced by understanding the elements that comprise it. The four-step process shown in Figure 21.6 can achieve significant results quickly and confidently.

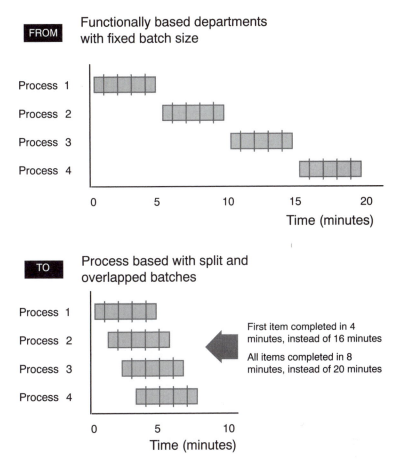

Figure 21.5 The shift from function-based to process-based design

The key to success is understanding what needs to happen in internal and external time. Internal time is defined as the actions that can only be done when the machine is idle. External time is the actions that can be performed while the machine is still producing throughput.

Effective plant-maintenance routines

Plant downtime and reliability are the two key areas of the productive capabilities of a manufacturing process that can be directly addressed by effective plant-maintenance routines. If not addressed effectively they can cause a reduction in throughput with increases in operating expense. These effects are aggravated when considered in the context of lean synchronous manufacturing. Formerly, inventory was a much-loved safety

Step 1   Analyse current time taken

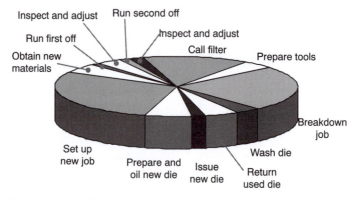

Step 2   Identify internal and external components

Step 3   Convert internal actions to external time

Step 4   Streamline both internal and external actions

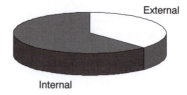

Figure 21.6   Four steps to reducing changeover times

blanket for fitters and maintenance engineers. If a critical piece of equipment went down, there was always plenty of stock around to keep the other plant going and retain output levels (even if the output consisted of the wrong stock). Nowadays, with lean synchronous manufacturing, even a short downtime period on a less critical piece of plant can result in stopping the whole manufacturing unit or factory. Another factor contributing to the need for a new generation in plant-maintenance strategy is the increase in the enabling technology available to production engineers. The growth in the mechanization and automation of machine tools, methods and procedures is placing more and more emphasis on improved plant reliability.

This must start with a clear understanding of what the piece of plant, equipment or system *does* (including measurable standards of performance) and not what it *is*. This statement of functionality helps ensure a clear understanding of how failures might occur, as well as suggesting the corresponding causal factors. Further analysis into the consequences of these functional failures brings an insight into the effects of equipment failure and what may be done to predict or prevent the failure. This is how one world-class methodology, reliability-centred maintenance, derives maintenance strategies, routines and services in a way that complements the vision of lean synchronous manufacturing.

Visual management

Visual management is key to the success of lean synchronous manufacturing. The impact of visual management can be summed up in one word: communication. Visual management can manifest itself in many guises within the manufacturing process: from posting a production schedule on a team noticeboard to the visibility of management on the shop floor. And there are also subtle, effective and more immediate ways to increase throughput and reduce both inventories and operating expense.

The first is kanban or, more precisely, the linking of the dependent events within the manufacturing process with a visual system of replenishment coupled with a powerful means to control over-production. Basically, kanban is shorthand for a mechanism that fixes the maximum inventory level held between two operations in the production process, allowing materials to be pulled from the upstream operation by the downstream operation. This has the effect of synchronizing the operations, joining them together with a logical 'rope' of inventory so that that maximum distance (or process time) between them is the length of the rope. Kanban can be implemented using cards (the literal meaning of the Japanese word *kanban*), containers, boxes or marked spaces on the floor.

A second and equally important aspect to the visual management of lean synchronous manufacturing is a clear understanding of the manufacturing plan and progress against it. To do this there needs to be an understanding of the issues, their causes and how they affect the daily throughput of the production line. One way of achieving this is through a multifunctional team review at the start of each production day or shift that focuses on the issues that will affect the team's ability to produce the required throughput on that day. For this meeting to be effective it should have a clear objective, be focused and be measured against stringent standards, such as timeliness, attendance, level of preparation, use of relevant questioning (methodology) and team working. Indeed, it is action based rather than discussion based in order to focus on today's issues and not yesterday's failures.

Additional benefits of using this approach are that it is a neat way to manage both the daily production and continuous improvement. It ensures daily communication. It keeps the emphasis on solving the problem and hence provides exposure to the use of problem-solving techniques. It is the link to the continuous improvement philosophy; and teamwork is improved as attendees contribute as team members first and functional specialists second.

The worksheet in Table 21.2 shows the format and structure of these daily meetings. This is posted within the production line, again for visibility and communications.

Firms which use this technique find that the meetings are highly valued, with everyone benefiting from a clear understanding of what is stopping throughput, what actions are required to solve the problem, who is responsible for these actions being completed and when this will occur. Once again, the checklist is a visual record of agreement and management.

Design for manufacture

Reviewing bills of materials (BOM) for opportunities to simplify their structure will also contribute to improved manufacturing performance. Aligning BOM structures with the manufacturing layout and looking for opportunities to increase commonality at lower levels will further simplify manufacturing requirements and improve flexibility within the plant. End product scheduling decisions can be varied late in the process if commonality exists at lower levels of bill structures, for like product groups. It is this point of differentiation within the BOM where a common part becomes sales order type specific, coupled with knowledge about lead times, that can make the difference between a make-to-order or make-to-stock environment. The need to decide what inventory to put into stock in a make-to-stock environment contributes a certain risk to the process and puts tremendous emphasis on integration with the sales and marketing functions in providing an adequate forecast. The other side of the coin is that in a make-to-order environment customers are required to wait for the production lead time to receive their goods, often an unacceptable response in today's competitive marketplace. Designing points of differentiation in the BOM allows stock to be held

Table 21.2
Daily meeting worksheet

Multifunction team	Issue (what)	Action (who)	Responsible (when)	Date
Production				
Packing				
Raw materials				
Planning				
Logistics				
Quality				
Maintenance				

with minimal risks of holding the wrong inventory and shorten the customer response time, resulting in an ability to finish or assemble to order.

As well as engineering BOM, component rationalization can have a dramatic effect on waste in manufacturing processes. Utilizing the same specification of raw materials or the same design of component parts will allow concentration of demand on less components. This concentration will contribute to the point of differentiation as above. But it will also reduce daily transactions within the process, decrease purchase orders raised and materials received or issued, cut inventories and safety stocks and reduce space requirements. Component rationalization will also support strategic purchasing initiatives by removing the dilution effects of spreading demand over several designs or specifications.

Enabling technologies

The premise of the fundamental design of many production-control systems has itself been constrained by the technology available. Technology has progressed over the years and is now at a point in its evolution that will allow the well-founded theory of constraints to become a reality. Client server-based systems have been developed that now meet the integration needs of organizations, along with leading-edge software solutions to provide powerful decision-support capability, enabling new ways to handle the challenges highlighted above.

Advanced planning and scheduling systems

The industrial software market segment that is currently generating the most interest is advanced planning and scheduling (APS) systems. This is well positioned to outstrip the 40 per cent growth enjoyed by enterprise resource planning (ERP) systems over the last three years.

As discussed earlier in this chapter, ERP systems are based on the fundamental design provided by the MRP philosophy. The sequential nature of these processes results in many iterations to understand the effect of making changes within the plan to reflect changes in demand or resource availability. The high-level nature of the details causes problems when considering the low-level details at execution. This is compounded when, as current trends indicate, multiplant planning is required. APS systems allow for all limitations to be considered when putting together a plan, resulting in plans that are not only feasible but flexible, removing the need to follow lengthy iterations. In using APS systems, the consequences both upstream towards the supplier and downstream to customers are totally visible. This translates into the business process of available-to-promise (ATP), which allows real-time order promising with levels of confidence never before achieved. At point of order the customer is provided with a promise date based on all the constraints within the production process, rather than referring to a master production schedule that is up to a week out of date.

The emergence of this technology has enabled immediate, medium-term and long-term planning horizons to be integrated while considering the sequencing of task and taking into account resources and materials. This will allow planning to be done concurrently and continually with a clear understanding of what is going on both upstream and downstream in the process, with fast, bidirectional propagation of changes.

Run strategy

A concept that pulls all of the concepts together is the run strategy. This is an approach to scheduling production that has all of the concepts presented in this chapter as prerequisites.

The concept is quite simple. Analysis is completed to determine the most streamlined sequence of products. This takes into account issues that minimize changeover times (for example, changing from product A to B takes less time than from B to A or from A to C), minimize run-in time and increase reliability. High-volume products may be planned to be run daily or weekly and low-volume products may be planned to be run only fortnightly or monthly.

Once this sequence is determined, it is considered set for the line and the variable then becomes the run length or batch size. This, of course, represents more of a paradigm shift for production people and, indeed, may require capital investment to enable variable batch sizes or run lengths.

Experience has been that this approach results in very predictable, maximized output. Production personnel become very adept at the specific changeovers that they perform on a more regular basis.

Electronic commerce

The Internet has emerged as the latest technology-enabling change tool. Web technologies continue to be developed which facilitate trade and simplify many business processes. Visibility between customers and suppliers has been significantly enhanced, opening up opportunities for reduced response times and significant savings for all players. Technologies have emerged which provide customers with real-time visibility of supplier inventory and manufacturing schedules and suppliers have visibility of customers' demand and inventory holdings. This seamless, speedy transfer of information enables better-targeted demand forecasts and manufacturing schedules to be developed between trading partners, leading to improved service performance with reduced inventory and resource consumption.

The number of links in supply chain relationships can be significantly reduced through the adoption of these new technologies. The ability to link customer outlets or distribution centres directly to supplier manufacturing facilities represents a radical reduction in process complexity. Response times and service performance which were once considered resource prohibitive because of the resource requirements are now possible. Internet commerce is likely to be the main trading arena of the future and the transition will be rapid as organizations seek to create sustainable competitive advantage.

Conclusion

The transition to a 'lean synchronous manufacturing' organization requires that a fundamental change in the way business is done in an organization. Change as deep rooted as this is difficult and requires significant commitment and focus. Organizations are challenged to explore concepts and process designs that previously would have been difficult to conceptualize.

True integration within the supply chain, providing linkages both at the customer and supplier ends, will call for the personnel in the manufacturing organization to be empowered and multiskilled, challenged, satisfied secure. Decisions will be made close to the customer and contribute to a simple and flexible process where every task adds value and information is captured at source. Product quality will meet, or exceed, the expectations of the customer with precise, on-time delivery. Throughput will be maximized and inventory and operating expenses will be the lowest ever.

Distribution operations
Managing distribution facilities for strategic advantage
Duane Marvick and John White

Excellence in distribution operations can have a profound effect on a company's performance, but to achieve this goal companies need to look beyond traditional approaches to the distribution facility. Innovative approaches and solutions are now available to ensure that distribution is a value-adding component of the total supply chain.

Introduction

Business leaders are continually focused on increasing shareholder value by reducing operating costs while increasing revenues. Firms that invest in superb distribution operations can strongly influence their performance—reducing costs, increasing revenues and raising customer satisfaction.

And the reality is that customers are increasingly demanding and will reward responsive and innovative distribution operations. They want products to be preconfigured and received, ready for immediate sale. To expedite the unloading process, they are asking for products to be properly sequenced in the trailer. They want products consolidated prior to delivery into store-ready display pallets. Some customers want to minimize the frequency of deliveries to their stores to increase store receiving efficiency and therefore seek larger, consolidated shipments less frequently.

Customers also want order accuracy and consistent quality which will expedite the receiving and check-in time at the store. In some cases, customers and distributors have developed partnerships whereby the customer will defer the check-in based on prior performance in delivering 'perfect orders'.

This highly demanding environment provides an opportunity for companies looking to create competitive advantage through their distribution operations and facilities management. The most successful companies are lifting supply chain performance by taking a holistic view of the supply chain, looking beyond the four walls of the distribution facility to see where it can add value along the chain. Once thought of simply as a warehouse in which to store inventory, today the distribution facility is fully linked into the supply chain. It serves a strategic role as a transfer point of both product and information as well as a vehicle to provide value-added services.

This transformation is being achieved through a combination of measures as suppliers, manufacturers and distributors are teaming with customers to 'pull' product through the supply chain to meet customer needs rather than 'pushing' product down the chain, which results in additional handling costs and excessive inventory levels. Companies are utilizing more advanced information technology and material-handling systems to streamline the flow of product pulled through the supply chain from source to customer. Flow-through distribution, cross-docking and continuous replenishment techniques are being utilized to reduce product handling and reduce inventory levels, thus lowering distribution expenses. So an electronics retailer, by cross-docking a large portion of its distribution volume, can decrease the costs of handling, labour and inventory levels. And a pharmaceutical company, by providing accurate order fulfilment quicker than its competitors, can achieve increased revenues via its supply chain distribution operations.

Aligning the components of distribution operations

In order for distribution facilities to fulfil their promise of satisfying customer demand, there must exist the correct match between the role of the operation to satisfy customer needs, the proprietor (owner or provider) of the products and services and the type of facility. A single facility can serve multiple roles and manage a variety of distribution operations.

The chart in Table 22.1 depicts the potential relationship between operational roles, proprietors and facility types.

Depending on consumer needs, distribution facilities are required to fulfil various roles in the supply chain. These include holding inventory, fulfilling demand, providing value-added services, assembling products, consolidating products, reworking and reclaiming and managing returns.

In the integrated supply chain, distribution facilities can be operated by different 'proprietors', including manufacturers, retail distributors, wholesale distributors and third-party distributors (see Figure 22.1).

Distribution facility types vary depending on the role that the facility is playing in terms of services and functions provided—including bulk storage, mixing, assembly, consolidation, break-bulk distribution, cross-docking and flow-through distribution facilities.

Table 22.1
Facility relationships

Operational role	Distribution centre proprietor	Facility type
Fulfil demand	Manufacturer Retail distributor Third-party distributor Wholesale distributor	Distribution centre Cross-dock facility Flow-through distribution centre
Consolidate products	Retail distributor Third-party distributor Wholesale distributor	Consolidation centre Mixing centre Cross-dock facility Flow-through distribution centre
Returns	Retail distributor Wholesale distributor Third-party distributor	Distribution centre Flow-through distribution centre
Hold inventory—raw materials	Manufacturer	Bulk storage warehouse
Hold inventory—finished goods	Manufacturer Retail distributor Third-party distributor Wholesale distributor	Bulk storage warehouse Assembly centre Distribution centre Cross-dock facility Flow-through distribution centre
Provide value-added services	Manufacturer Retail distributor Wholesale distributor Third-party distributor	Mixing centre Assembly centre Consolidation Distribution centre Cross-dock facility Flow-through distribution centre
Assemble products	Manufacturer Third-party distributor	Assembly centre Cross-dock facility Break-bulkcentre Flow-through distribution centre
Rework/reclamation	Manufacturer Wholesale distributor Retail distributor Third-party distributor	Distribution centre Cross-dock facility Flow-through distribution centre

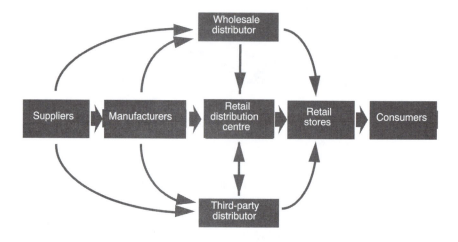

Figure 22.1 Distribution facility proprietors

Making the distribution operations work

In order to leverage distribution facility assets in the integrated supply chain, companies begin with the distribution operating strategy and then integrate enablers in the areas of people, process and technology to execute it. Effective utilization of people resources, including management, supervision, clerical and employee associates, combined with processes and technology will enable successful execution of the operating strategy.

Strategy

The first step in determining the operating strategy for the distribution facility is to develop a vision and conceptual design. A broad view of all the business environment factors is imperative to the success of the design process, including business direction, customer service requirements, customer order demand profile, product line characteristics, inventory policy, supply chain structure, supply chain partners and cultural, organizational and people components.

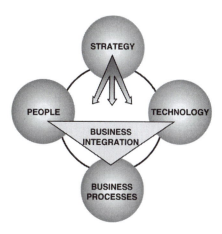

Figure 22.2   The business integration model

Process

Distribution processes align with policies and procedures and direct interactions among people, equipment and product flow. Process enablers of the operating strategy include receiving, put-away, storage and replenishment, wave planning, picking, value-added services (such as labelling, price marking and order consolidation), shipping, inventory management and control.

Technology

The flow of product into, within and out of the distribution facility is dependent on the integrated flow of information. Beginning with forecast and actual customer order demand information, the integrated supply chain will sense these demand signals and utilize data and information to fulfil customer demand. The key is for supply chain partners to share information freely with each other to enable the efficient flow of product through the distribution facility to the customer. Technology enablers of the operating strategy include warehouse-management system and material-handling equipment technology (see Figure 22.3).

Effective utilization of warehouse-management system (WMS) software will enable efficient management of the flow of product through the distribution facility, aid in the control of inventory, improve space utilization and reduce distribution operations labour expense.

Utilization of advanced material-handling system technology, including radio frequency terminals on forklifts, conveyors and sophisticated

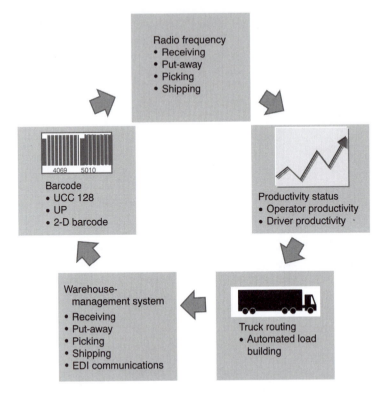

Figure 22.3   Technology enablers

sortation systems, barcode scanners, automated storage and retrieval systems, operatorless vehicles and robotics, enables the efficient movement of product through the distribution facility.

The distribution facility ultimately needs to be able to support an e-commerce capability for receipt and shipment of product. Advance shipment notices (ASNs) from vendors on inbound purchase orders will enable the receiving process. ASNs can be passed from the distribution facility to the customer. Routing, despatch, yard control and performance-measurement systems optimize operational efficiency.

The key is to determine what level of technology is required to enable the execution of the operating strategy.

People

Attitudes towards the distribution workforce are changing. Employees are not only the best resource in a distribution facility, they are typically the greatest single expense, so they should be understood and treated as assets. Progressive distribution facility managers are developing pro-grammes to make the most of this key resource, including training inside and outside the job, flexible and/or unique work schedules such as scheduled annual working hours. Additionally, employee empowerment and decision making at lower levels, self-managed work teams and new performance-measurement systems such as team incentives, pay for per-formance and profit sharing are being utilized to make maximum use of employee resources.

Distribution operations of the future

Applying a new supply chain perspective to current distribution opera-tions reveals that the product-delivery systems of 10 years ago are obso-lete today. Customers are demanding improved levels of service at the lowest possible cost as they struggle to control their own costs and fine tune their internal flow of products and information. The distribution facility of the future needs to represent the vital link in the supply chain that adds value to the overall chain—including maximizing customer service and minimizing costs.

Looking at the distribution facility of the future, the focus will still be on the four components of strategy, process, technology and people.

Strategy

The roles and responsibilities of the distribution facility are changing at a rapid pace. In order to meet the demands of customers for optimum service at low cost, distribution facilities will take on different roles within their respective distribution networks (see Figure 22.4).

Multiple facility operations

For example, in a network with multiple traditional distribution facili-ties, each servicing customers in their geographic territories, the move is towards development of a network consisting of a large regional full-line distribution facility which supports outlying downstream limited-line facilities, sometimes referred to as a 'hub and spoke' concept. Slow-moving items from each downstream distribution centre (DC) can be consolidated into the large regional facility. At the same time, the region-al facility takes on the role of a break-bulk facility whereby full truck-loads are purchased and received into the regional DC, the load is broken down and pallet quantities are cross-docked and 'shuttled' to the downstream facilities on a daily basis for replenishment of stock inven-tory. Customer orders continue to come in to the downstream distribu-tion facility for fulfilment in the local area. However, the slow-moving

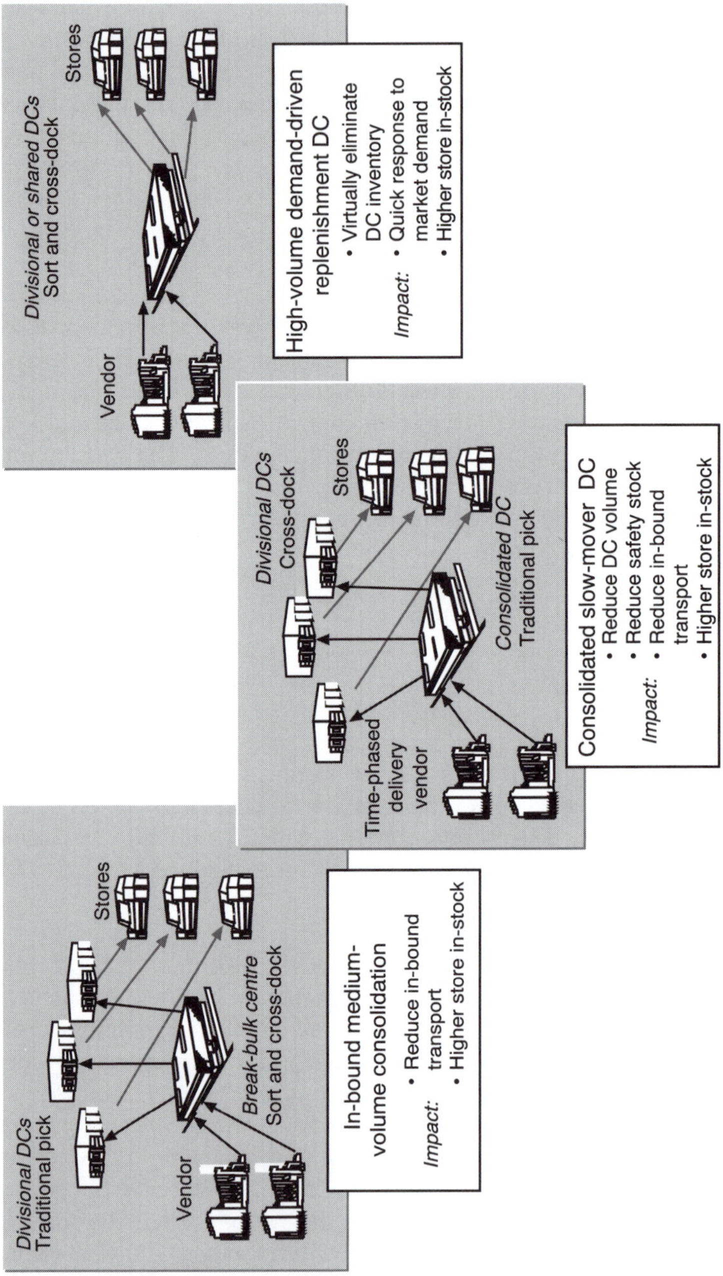

Figure 22.4   Distribution operations roles in network configuration

items on the customer order are fulfilled at the regional upstream distribution facility and shuttled daily to the downstream DC with break-bulk stock, where the slow-moving portion of the order is cross-docked and merged with downstream facility product for delivery to the local customer.

Rethinking the roles of the distribution facility brings significant benefits. Inventory at the downstream facilities for the slow-moving items is drastically reduced. Product is purchased at a discounted rate from the vendor and inbound freight costs are reduced if the centralized distribution facility procures full truckloads instead of each downstream facility individually purchasing less than truckload quantities. Efficiencies are gained at the centralized facility for handling the slow-moving items because of consolidation. Enhanced technology and material-handling systems can be justified to maximize efficiency through economies of scale.

Single facility operations

The strategy discussed above will work well for the multiple facility operator. However, single facilities can also take advantage of new concepts and technology to enhance their value in the integrated supply chain.

Distributed case movement cross-docking (DCM) combines continuous replenishment principles (CRP) with point-of-sale (POS) driven computer-aided ordering (CAO) to create a dynamic cross-dock environment. DCM consists of dynamically allocating inbound product to customer orders at the point of receipt into the distribution facility. Product does not move into traditional reserve storage and pick locations, but is cross-docked from the receiving truck to the shipping truck, typically the same day.

Product is received at the pallet level and barcode pick labels are printed based on allocation of the received product to customer orders in the order well. Pallets are depalletized on to a conveyor system while applying labels to individual cases. Cases are then scanned, sorted and diverted to palletizing lanes for loading on to outbound trailers shipping to customer locations.

The benefits of DCM can be significant. A grocery retailer projects that with DCM, inventories will be reduced by over 35 per cent and overall productivity will increase by at least 15 per cent. Additionally, service level is improved by expediting the receiving and shipping process, thus reducing order lead time. The customer's in-stock position is improved as POS orders drive the replenishment on a daily basis instead of projected orders with longer lead times based on forecast. With the replenishment activity closer to the point of consumption, the overall customer service level is improved. Utilization of DCM is a prime example of the distribution operation increasing shareholder value by increasing revenue through improved in-stock position and reducing costs by reducing handling labour and inventory.

Flow-through distribution

A second strategy worthy of consideration in future facilities is flow-through distribution. Essentially, distribution in a flow-through facility serves as a value-added service (VAS) function, performing customer-specific activities as product is continuously flowing through the facility.

Product is received on the receiving dock and placed on conveyors which move the product directly to the VAS area where pricing, labelling, ticketing, kitting, hanging, folding, repackaging and other value-added activities take place. The conveyor system continues to move the product from VAS through sortation and loading on to outbound trucks for customer delivery. The product does not go into traditional reserve storage and pick slot locations, but rather flows through the distribution facility, leaving with more value to the customer than when it arrived.

The benefits of flow-through distribution include reduced labour handling expense and reduced inventory costs, while providing customized store-ready product to the customer.

Process

The distribution facility of the future will continue to optimize various existing and new processes to enable execution of the overall operating strategy. For example, improved slot profiling and location assignment of items within the distribution facility will reduce travel time, improve productivity and increase space utilization. Continued use of batch order filling will reduce labour, formal and systematized daily staff planning will reduce labour expense by directing the workforce, and improved layout and material-handling systems will improve the flow of product while minimizing labour expense and maximizing space utilization. Specific utilization of alternative picking processes (batch, zone, wave, pick and pass etc.) together with enhanced wave planning, door per customer shipment (e.g. store) and fluid loading will improve overall distribution facility throughput and reduce operating expenses. Performance-measurement systems with engineered standards will track and report labour activities and will provide the basis for goal-based reward systems.

Technology

The distribution facility of the future will continue to utilize the ever-increasing availability of technology as an enabler of the operating strategy. Just a few sources of technology include those shown in Table 22.2.

The key to success will be to determine and utilize the appropriate

Table 22.2
Advanced technologies available for distribution centres

• Electronic data interface (EDI)	• Radio frequency
• Advanced shipping notice (ASN)	• Distributed case-movement system
• Computer-aided ordering (CAO)	• Cross-docking and flow-through systems
• POS interface to distribution systems	• Conveyor and sortation systems
• Enhanced barcode scanning	• Automated storage and retrieval systems
• Electronic routing system	• Carousels
• Inbound traffic system	• Pick-to-light
• Automatic truck loading/unloading	• Put-to-light
• Yard-management system	• Voice-recognition systems
• Operator-less vehicles	• Pick-to-belt mezzanine system

level of technology to enable execution of the distribution operations strategy.

People

With distribution operations becoming much more sophisticated and technology based, it will become increasingly difficult to hire and maintain qualified workers. Programmes need to be developed to utilize and retain this key resource.

One final thought about the distribution facility of the future. The future vision may well include shared distribution facilities servicing multiple suppliers and customers of different companies (see Figure 22.5). Why not maximize the use of the distribution facility infrastructure and share these assets among various companies? Today, these are the advantages that some third-party providers (3PLs) are already providing to the marketplace. The roles of the distribution facility are already changing to meet the needs of the customer—it is not too great a step to contemplate changing who utilizes these assets.

Picture the suppliers, the shared distribution facility and customers all connected via e-commerce, with the various partners in the integrated supply chain sharing a common physical distribution network. If distribution facilities are adding significant value today—tomorrow they will only have increased their significance in the total supply chain.

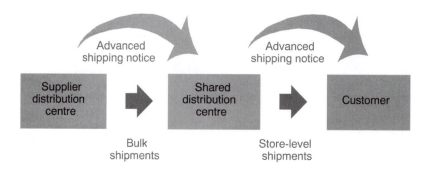

Figure 22.5 Shared distribution facility

Designing the facility

This chapter has discussed the strategic possibilities of distribution operations, and indeed the prospects for the facility of the future, the process of actually designing a distribution facility typically involves three phases.

Phase I, the conceptual design, defines the operating model for the facility and includes determination of short- and long-term business needs, review of current practices, comparison to industry best practices, alternative concept identification and evaluation, and selection of the best concepts which will fulfil short- and long-term business needs. Additionally, process, facility, equipment and systems requirements are determined to support and enable execution of the operating strategy.

The base case for the current operation is established. This step typically involves development of a database with a detailed analysis of the customer order, SKU and inventory profiles.

An analysis of the customer order profile provides volume and handling requirements for the design of the distribution facility, including order volume, order frequency, number of lines per order and quantity per line. Total product volumes in pallets, cases and units are captured together with an understanding of peak to average ratios and seasonal product volume fluctuations.

The SKU profile analysis provides a detailed understanding of each SKU's profile based on key characteristics including product style and class, space requirements, special characteristics (such as perishability, hazardous material, regulatory item, crushability), volume, velocity and seasonality.

The inventory profile analysis shows the relationship of the average and peak inventory levels by SKU and by category, with the corresponding movement rate of individual items and product groupings. Inventory turns and days-on-hand stock levels are determined and compared to the storage and picking space being occupied to support the inventory levels.

Table 22.3
Alternative picking and reserve storage concepts

Picking concepts	Reserve storage concepts
• 1 level selective	• Push-back rack
• 2 level selective	• Drive-through rack
• 3 level selective	• Drive-in rack
• Narrow aisle rack	• Pallet-flow rack
• Bin shelving	• Double-deep rack
• Case-flow rack	• Single-deep rack
• Case pick-to-belt	• Bulk storage
• Carousels	• Very narrow aisle (VNA) rack
• Push-back rack	• Decked shelving
• Drive-through rack	• Mobile rack
• Drive-in rack	
• Double-deep rack	
• Pallet-flow rack	
• Bulk picking	

After developing an understanding of the current operation, short- and long-term projections are developed for the operation, including order volumes, throughput volumes in pallets, cases and units by year, month, week and day, SKU count and inventory turns. This database model then becomes the basis for the targeted three- to five-year design horizon.

Current operating practices are documented, a comparison to industry best practices is completed and a gap analysis is performed that becomes the basis for generating alternative concepts for the new 'to be' operation. Input is received from operating associates and management and site visits are made to other operations as necessary to determine the concepts worthy of evaluation. A detailed operational and financial evaluation is completed before the preferred operating concepts are selected. Examples of alternative picking concepts and alternative reserve storage concepts are illustrated in Table 22.3.

As part of concept selection, an assessment is completed to determine the high-level facility and systems requirements to support the operating strategy. All aspects of process, technology and people are considered in the conceptual design. Phase I concludes with a financial business case of the costs/benefits of the conceptual design and the high-level implementation plan.

In *Phase II, detailed design*, detailed plans are formulated for the material-handling system, the warehouse-management system (WMS) and the physical facility. Material-handling systems are specified, bid out and vendors selected. The WMS software vendor is selected and a conference room pilot is executed. Equipment is ordered and the facility detailed architectural design is completed.

Phase III, implementation, begins with facility construction and involves the installation, testing and start-up of the material-handling and WMS systems. Employees are trained, systems are tested and construction is completed. The distribution facility design project concludes with transition and start-up of operations in the new facility.

Conclusion

Companies looking to make the most of their distribution operations are rethinking the traditional view of the distribution facility. No longer viewed as a dead point in the process, it is now an integral part of total supply chain excellence. The avenues for achieving greater performance through distribution operations are well mapped—it is up to companies to take advantage of these opportunities to achieve greater business success.

Transport management
Future directions: redefining the role of transport

Rich Bergmann and Craig Rawlings

Transport has traditionally been managed as a discrete functional activity, its prime role being to move inventory from one node in the supply chain to another. However, business leaders now recognize that in an increasingly competitive, global market, the supply chain must be seamless, providing the shortest possible lead times, reliable service and competitive pricing. This chapter describes how integrating transport into the supply chain is key to providing seamless service delivery. By developing multimodal capability and strong external alliances—supported by effective technology and low-cost infrastructure—companies can optimize the benefits of their transport operations. A synchronized supply chain will help companies compete successfully in a complex and changing market.

Introduction

Transport is a critical component of supply chain management. It creates value by providing time and place utility, that is, ensuring that product is available when and where it is requested by customers. Transport management has focused on moving product as quickly, cost effectively and consistently as possible from the point of origin to the point of consumption. The ability of transport to ensure time and place utility at a cost that does not disadvantage the organization is fundamental to competitive positioning in the marketplace.

The achievement of this objective has resulted in a highly complex operation requiring the coordination of multiple inbound and outbound shipments involving private fleets and/or third parties. Product must also be managed through multiple points of transshipment involving the transference of product ownership. The complexity of the system is illustrated in Figure 23.1.

Transport also represents one of the largest controllable costs within a product's supply chain. A 1996 study of US organizations has estimated that the cost of transport and associated activities represents just

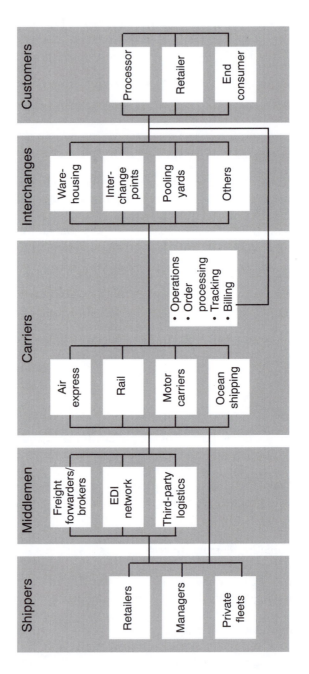

Figure 23.1 Structure of the freight transport industry

over 50 per cent of total logistics costs (*Logistics Management*, 1997). Organizationally, annual transport costs comprise about 3 to 5 per cent of total sales revenue for most retailers, wholesalers and manufacturers.

Given the strategic importance of providing time and place utility at a competitive cost, the complexity of transport-management activities and the significant expenditure involved, it is surprising that transport has perhaps the lowest level of process development and improvement of all activities within the supply chain.

The traditional functional approach to transport has resulted in organizations separating demand-generation activities, such as advertising, pricing and promotion, from the supply activities, such as manufacturing, warehousing and transport. This separation has allowed transport management to stay focused on functional efficiencies in isolation from benefits derived from integration with the rest of the supply chain.

However, successful operations recognize the need to integrate transport into the supply chain in order to optimize performance. The necessity to shift the management focus from a functional to supply chain perspective is driven by three forces of change: the rise in consumerism, the globalization of markets and the availability of technology-enabled solutions. The impact of these forces on the management of the supply chain is described in detail below.

The rise in consumerism

Customers and consumers are becoming increasingly aware of their power in competitive markets and are more discerning when assessing the supplier's value proposition. In response, suppliers are tailoring the service offering to specific customer requirements. This new operating environment requires a coordinated approach, ensuring a quick-response, high-velocity supply chain with the ability to react to market uncertainty and a rapidly changing competitive environment.

Historically, supply chains have operated on the basis of averaging, where product would flow through the supply chain at a rate to suit most but not all customers. So some customers received their product earlier than required and others later. In this situation, the supply chain was not able to adapt to the requirements of different customer segments without significant disruption to its processes.

In response to increasing market competitiveness and consumers' demands for higher service levels, suppliers are working together to reduce total supply chain costs and to offer value-added services in an effort to gain a competitive market advantage. Supply chains are now being realigned to meet the specific service requirements of the different customer segments. However, in this drive for increased effectiveness, significant complexity has been added to supply chain operations and, in particular, to the transport activity.

As an example, suppliers to the retail grocery industry are undertaking a number of initiatives designed to reduce supply chain inventories. The direct result is an increase in transport costs. These initiatives include:

- *continuous replenishment*—smaller, more frequent deliveries of product to replace units sold rather than to build inventory;
- *cross-docking*—sourcing products from multiple suppliers in small lots and consolidating in a cross-docking distribution centre for delivery to the final destination;
- *selective sourcing*—rationalizing the total number of distribution centres to reduce the total inventory, and selectively stocking products at different points in the channel based on sales volumes; and
- *postponement*—postponing the differentiation of goods, including geographic dispersion of inventories, until the latest point in the marketing flow to reduce both risk and inventory.

Although transport costs may have been increased as a direct result of initiatives such as these for the retail grocery industry, taking an integrated supply chain approach allows strategic and transactional decisions to be based on total supply chain costs rather than on incremental cost movements for individual functional areas.

Further, integrating transport into supply chain planning allows the transport suppliers to manage the requirements for faster order response times proactively.

Globalization of markets

As organizations focus on global strategies to improve market reach, establish off-shore production facilities and globally source production inputs, the complexity of the transport operations increases significantly. The ability to manage this complexity and ensure a responsive and efficient supply chain will be a significant determinant of how effectively organizations can service international markets. The challenge is not only to manage a supply chain spanning nations, but seamlessly to integrate the flow of both product and information with external partners.

The capacities and capabilities of transport infrastructure can determine the market boundaries of an organization for three key reasons:

- the more efficient the transport infrastructure, the more likely an organization is to compete on an equal footing in distant markets in terms of both price and product availability;

■ the broader the reach of the transport system, the more likely an organization is to develop new markets in locations remote from the production source; and

■ the deeper the penetration into new markets, the more likely the organization is able to take advantage of scale economies, because of
higher throughput volumes, and to increase competitive advantage in
both home and remote markets.

However, international trade poses interesting challenges for transport
operations. International transactions and shipments normally take
longer to complete, often involve the use of inter-modal transport operated and managed by parties external to the organization and are subject to government regulatory constraints such as tariffs and
environmental laws.

Once inside countries, shipments may also be subject to a different set
of transport regulations. For example, environmental requirements in
Europe differ significantly from country to country. Germany has strict
environmental regulations requiring suppliers to be responsible for
reverse as well as delivery logistics. It requires that all packaging is
returned to the source and disposed of appropriately. This has a significant impact on efficient vehicle management and scheduling.

The challenge

Successfully managing complex global transport operations requires
control of both product and paperwork through a number of modal
changes and compliance with a multitude of regulatory requirements. A
clear strategy must define issues such as ownership of product and payment terms for the modal partners. Importantly, compatibility of data
must be achieved across the inter-modal partners. As with shipments
within countries, it is equally important to be able to manage and track
shipments through each stage of delivery. One of the more important
types of communication involves the flow of operational data to coordinate product flow for decision making.

Given the number of product hand-offs and the complexity of the regulatory and cultural environment, compatibility of data throughout the
distribution chain becomes critical. If the data is not compatible at each
delivery point, it will need to be reprocessed at that phase, resulting in a
duplication of effort, greater chance of errors, mishandling and slowing
of both the product and the information.

Similarly, the greater the number of information sources, the greater
the chance that information will be misinterpreted, resulting again in
duplication of effort, potential conflict between inter-modal partners
and unnecessary delays.

Implications

With the challenges of managing the complex requirements for global transport operations and the necessity to coordinate information flows between a number of channel partners, organizations must either expand their own capability to manage the end-to-end process or develop close relationships with external service providers.

Increasingly, organizations are turning to third-party service providers for end-to-end solutions. The decision to outsource can be driven by the increasing complexity of the global logistics, principally owing to:

- the large volume and variety of logistics transactions affecting both physical and information tasks;
- divergence in the number and sequence of transactions which must be performed in various parts of the world; and
- inter-dependency of tasks within the supply chain process which places a premium on coordination and control.

These service providers have been quick to identify the opportunities and competitive advantage that can be gained from implementing fully integrated end-to-end logistics systems, with the result that the information they can provide to customers would be of a far higher quality and provide far more visibility of product than a customer's own internal systems.

Availability of technology-enabled solutions

Over the last five years, software vendors have integrated transport-management systems with other organizational planning systems to optimize supply chain performance. This has allowed transport management to be closely integrated with customers and suppliers and other internal supply activities such as order management, inbound materials management, available-to-promise functionality and service-level management (see Figure 23.2).

The advent of information technology-enabled distribution planning and scheduling tools has seen a radical increase in transport efficiencies. These tools coordinate transport shipments allowing for load consolidation, increase the utilization of transport assets and reduce variable costs through improved delivery routing and scheduling.

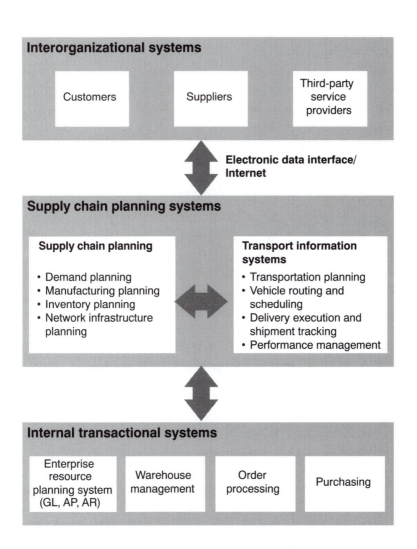

Interorganizational systems

Customers

Suppliers

Third-party service providers

Electronic data interface/ Internet

Supply chain planning systems

Supply chain planning

- Demand planning
- Manufacturing planning
- Inventory planning
- Network infrastructure planning

Transport information systems

- Transportation planning
- Vehicle routing and scheduling
- Delivery execution and shipment tracking
- Performance management

Internal transactional systems

Enterprise resource planning system (GL, AP, AR)

Warehouse management

Order processing

Purchasing

Figure 23.2   Supply chain technology infrastructure

Integrated supply chain solutions

To ensure a synchronized and efficient supply chain, transport management systems should integrate seamlessly with external enterprise systems, internal supply chain planning systems and internal transactional systems.

The interface with suppliers', customers' and carriers' systems allows for the efficient transfer of information via electronic data interchange (EDI) or the Internet. Electronic commerce is becoming increasingly important as more information is required to support business process changes across all supply chain stakeholders. As an example, some retailers request that advance shipping notices be sent via EDI from their suppliers, confirming shipment details and delivery times. Where the supplier has demonstrated accurate and consistent delivery performance, the customer may accept the advance shipping note as the confirmation of receipt, which can then form the basis of the payment transaction.

Transport-management systems must also be integrated with other internal supply chain planning systems to ensure that transportation constraints and costs are considered in overall optimization modelling. This is particularly important given that transport is estimated to represent more than 50 per cent of total supply chain costs.

Finally, transport systems must also integrate with internal systems to ensure that transactions are correctly reported to the general ledger and other financial modules such as accounts payable and receivable.

Transport-management solutions

The functionality of transport information systems can be grouped into four primary categories:

- *transport planning*—optimizing transportation resources within the constraints of the shipment plan;
- *vehicle routing and scheduling*—coordinating and optimizing of inbound and outbound shipments;
- *delivery execution and shipment tracking*—controlling shipments through the delivery process and managing post-execution activities such as freight payments; and
- *performance management*—providing management with a view of integrated transport and supply chain performance.

Transport planning
The need for and location of different distribution points are significant issues for national and multinational organizations. Opening, closing or

moving distribution depots can have a significant impact on distribution costs, particularly for high-volume operations.

Transport-planning systems allow organizations to model the cost impact of rationalizing or expanding the distribution infrastructure, primarily through a series of 'what-if' or scenario analyses. These tools are essentially used for strategic purposes by allowing managers to model scenarios quickly and easily, enabling the impact of various actions to be assessed and distribution costs minimized in relation to business cycles.

Vehicle routing and scheduling

Broadly, the objective of vehicle routing and scheduling packages is to develop a shipment plan focusing on the maximization of vehicle utilization and cost efficiency while meeting the specific delivery requirements of the customer. To optimize the fleet performance, it is necessary to drive efficiencies across both the inbound and outbound distribution network. Shipment plans cannot be developed in isolation. Planning must address customer orders, availability of transport resources and capacity constraints, the volume of goods to be handled, the geographic distribution of the depots, shipping and receiving requirements and the cost of direct delivery versus the cost of transshipment.

Specifically, vehicle routing and scheduling systems include:

■ driver productivity that recognizes the detailed handling requirements of orders and unique customer receiving conditions and methods;
■ ability to schedule routes within time windows to meet customer requirements;
■ ability to split loads for the same destination between vehicles or spread loads over several days;
■ ability to schedule both collections and deliveries on a single journey; and
■ complex, dynamic route assignment where suggested routes take into account detailed traffic and delivery patterns. Integration with motoring organization information systems, which detail roadworks and potential bottlenecks, allows the route assignments to be more responsive to actual conditions.

The areas listed below are still pioneering for most organizations:

■ in-cab computing to eliminate paper and reduce driver administration error; for example the use of pen-based terminals and printers mounted in the cabs of delivery vehicles to allow drivers to communicate with control systems and produce additional documentation, such as delivery notes and online proof of delivery confirmation;
■ multimodal or global transport optimization where specific rules manage performance, such as lead time or cost minimization;

■ load balancing, which is becoming increasingly sophisticated in order both to optimize the amount of product that can be loaded on to a truck and also support multidrop environments. Increasing regulatory pressures regarding the loading of trucks are making such software particularly critical.

Delivery execution and shipment tracking

Once the shipment plan has been finalized, the delivery documentation, including the delivery manifest and bills of lading, will be completed automatically and the load despatched. In transit, it is important to have the capability to monitor the status of the shipment proactively against the required delivery performance. Any deviation from this performance should require management intervention and/or notification to the customer.

To manage in-transit performance, organizations are adopting real-time communications and shipment-tracking technology using on-board communications, intelligent messaging capabilities, satellite technologies and shipment barcoding.

The advent of mobile communications is having a significant impact on transport operations. Using this technology in fleet management and vehicle tracking has several advantages: fewer delays, better management of truck movements on congested roads, and better allocation of slots for loading and unloading at warehouses. It therefore helps improve labour efficiency, fuel economy and control over fleet-management systems.

The combination of tracking and communication is regarded as progressive and has resulted in a number of key benefits, especially in the areas of customer service and increased efficiency:

■ a combined system can allow current positions to be relayed to base station for plotting on electronic maps;
■ overall delivery time is reduced due to the ability to reroute a vehicle to avoid blockages;
■ the vehicle's destination can be changed to a new collection or delivery point; and
■ automatic status reports can be provided periodically so that customers can be informed of delays, the cause of delays and the exact location of a shipment.

Post-execution activities, such as freight payments, also form part of the shipment activity. The form and structure of freight payments will often be determined by agreement between the shipper and the carrier. All systems need to establish how invoices are to be received from carriers, how they are to be validated and authorized for payment before being handled by the cash-disbursement activity.

Progressive shippers are managing payments on behalf of carriers. Based on the actual deliveries and the contracted terms and conditions, shippers are paying for freight services without receiving an invoice. Although this removes the need for a matching and reconciliation process, care needs to be taken to manage proof of delivery and claims.

Performance management
Whether private fleet, external fleet or both, it is important to define performance parameters and assess actual performance against this criteria. This is particularly so for monitoring the compliance of third-party service providers to agreed contract conditions.

Performance-management capability should allow the management of operations on an exception basis only and provide drill-down to levels of detail in the areas of cost, performance, customer service productivity and utilization.

Historical performance data can also be used as the basis for transport and supply chain planning decisions. Consequently, accurate and detailed performance information is necessary.

Conclusion

The traditional approach to transport has been to manage it as a discrete functional activity within a company's operations. Due to the rise in consumerism, the globalization of markets and the availability of technology-enabled solutions, organizations should be optimizing transport operations within the context of the supply chain.

The increased focus on integrated supply chain operations arises from both customer demand and the organization's need for seamless service delivery, within local and global markets, that focuses on short lead times, service reliability and competitive pricing. Seamless delivery means that organizations must have the ability to provide cost-effective, door-to-door service across multiple modes. To do this, transport operations must develop multimodal capability or strong alliances with specialist service providers.

The key to success lies in having the best service offerings supported by highly capable people, effective technology, a low-cost infrastructure and the best global support system.

References

Coyle, Bardi, and Langley (1992) *The Management of Business Logistics*, 5th edn, West, St Paul, MN.
Davis, Herbert W. (1995) 'Physical distribution cost and service 1995', *Annual*

Conference Proceedings, Council of Logistics Management, Oct. 8–11, 217–28.

Gill, Lynn E. and Allerheilgen, Robert P. (1996) 'Co-operation in the channels of distribution: physical distribution leads the way', *International Journal of Physical Distribution and Logistics Management*, 26 (5).

Logistics Management (1997) 'How big is the logistics market?', Sept., 55–9.

Inventory management
Keeping costs down while lifting customer satisfaction

Chris Norek

Today, firms can use innovative techniques to achieve higher customer satisfaction while lowering inventory investment, an achievement once thought impossible. Companies need to be aware of the new approaches available and apply them internally and, better still, across partners along the supply chain. In fact, where end-consumer inventory-management responsibility was once confined to retailers, now companies right along the supply chain can play an important role. Techniques such as materials requirements planning, distribution requirements planning, collaborative forecasting and replenishment and vendor-managed inventory are relevant for consideration by both retailers and manufacturers.

Introduction

Senior decision makers are becoming increasingly aware of the importance of the supply chain in improving the operations of their companies. Inventory management has always been an important aspect of total supply chain management. It represents a significant cost as firms can have millions or even billions of dollars invested in on-hand inventories. Freeing up even a small percentage of inventory can provide substantial capital to apply to other areas of the company. Not only is inventory itself an important cost, the carrying cost of the inventory has been estimated at anywhere from 25 to 40 per cent of the value of the inventory itself. This carrying cost or 'maintenance' cost of holding the inventory can be substantial.

Inventory is also an issue for shareholders. Capital tied up in inventory is not available. If it is freed up, it can be translated into applications that increase a firm's share value or dividends to shareholders (Cooke, 1997).

Today inventory management is made potentially more sophisticated, more effective and more efficient through the adoption of improved management techniques. But to move down the path of contemporary inventory management, companies need to internalize a new attitude to inventory. Superior inventory management once equalled lower inventory and therefore lower costs. This simple equation, while powerful at the individual functional level, failed to embrace opportunities for optimization of inventory performance across the entire company, and potentially across the entire supply chain.

In striving for lower inventories, companies can make the entire firm more cost and service effective rather than optimizing individual functions that can erode the efficiency of the total company. In certain situations it might actually make sense for a company to raise its inventory levels in order to have the lowest total delivered cost to the customer. A firm must be knowledgeable of and skilled in the logistics or supply chain tradeoffs, of which inventory is one.

Inventory defined

The American Heritage College Dictionary defines inventory as the quantity of goods and materials on hand or stock. Inventory's relationship to the overall supply chain is well summed up in a rudimentary definition of logistics, 'management of inventory at rest or in motion' (Coyle, Bardi and Langley, 1992).

Inventory can be classified in several ways, for example by stages of the production process. In this classification, there are three types of inventory: raw material, work-in-process or semi-finished goods and finished goods. These are self-explanatory on a continuum from materials used in a production process to the finished goods sold to customers.

A second categorization of inventory shows the types of inventory in the business process. In this scheme, there are seven types (Coyle, Bardi and Langley, 1992, 197–8):

- *cycle stock*—inventory necessary to meet normal daily demand and routinely replenished;
- *safety stock*—inventory that protects against uncertainty whether it be in demand, lead time or both;
- *in-process stock/in-transit stock*—inventory created in the steps to manufacture a finished product/inventory on route to a stocking or delivery point on some mode of transportation;
- *seasonal stock*—inventory held to meet increased sales volume during a particular time of year;
- *promotional stock*—inventory needed to meet the needs of marketing campaigns or advertising;
- *speculative stock*—inventory held to protect against price increases or limited availability; and
- *dead stock*—inventory that is no longer useable or saleable in the current market.

The role of inventory in the firm

Views on the role of inventory often depend on the perspective of the particular functional area of the firm. Inventory-management personnel strive to keep the levels of inventory as low as possible. Sales and marketing would rather have too much inventory so that fewer stockouts occur and customer satisfaction is as high as possible. Purchasing departments are often evaluated on the lowest purchase price per unit and therefore have an incentive to buy in larger quantities at a lower purchase price per unit. Manufacturing prefers longer production runs of like units to help spread the fixed costs of set-up and changeover, thereby producing increased levels of inventory. Transportation department personnel are often evaluated on the lowest cost per tonne-mile, resulting in large shipment volumes to realize truckload discounts and increasing the amount of inventory on each shipment.

This conflict of goals between the inventory manager and other departments must be reconciled for optimum inventory management. Many of the actions by various functional personnel are based on their current performance incentives within the firm. In each of these functional examples, people are only acting to meet their set performance goals; however, the end result is increased inventory investment for the entire company. Performance incentives should therefore be changed so that the efficiency of the whole firm is achieved, rather than the performance of a particular department. This requires a holistic point of view which does not play one logistics function off against another.

Innovative techniques are now available which will allow the seemingly conflicting goals of higher customer satisfaction and lower inventory investment to be achieved simultaneously. Traditionally this was a goal which was thought to be impossible; however today, it can be attained by evaluating and improving internal processes.

The role of inventory in the supply chain

If the perspectives of the firm with regard to inventory are broadened to include fellow members of the supply chain, the amounts of inventory in question increase substantially. However, companies traditionally have not done a good job of working internally to communicate and manage inventories, let alone across the whole supply chain.

Historical operating methods have resulted in increased channel inventory. For example, in the past, entities within the supply chain were not confident of the capabilities of their partners to deliver exactly as promised so they would carry extra inventory in case the partner did not deliver either on time or in the correct quantity. This extra inventory is often called 'buffer' inventory and reflects a lack of trust among supply chain partners. It has been estimated that almost one-third of total retail inventory is accounted for by buffer inventory. This supply chain perspective, coupled with the unnecessary build-up of inventories owing to traditional performance incentives within an organization, adds unneeded costs to individual firms as well as to the entire supply chain.

It is clear that because of the cost of holding inventory, minimizing the investment in it is a worthwhile goal. Getting inventories to zero—the goal of just-in-time—is obviously not possible. However, there are many ways to optimize the inventory investment in a firm and the supply chain while maintaining or improving required service levels.

One example of aligning the entire supply chain and thereby lowering total inventory requirements is shown by the actions of a major pharmaceutical producer. This firm wanted to streamline its supply chain and reduce overall inventories. It worked with supply chain partners through cross-functional teams to create pilot projects with inventory reduction goals of 10 per cent. These goals were met—and exceeded—showing how cooperation among supply chain partners can benefit the entire supply chain (*Inventory Reduction Report*, 1997). But supply chain inventory reductions are too often hindered because firms are often unwilling to share significant amounts of information with their partners to realize these reductions.

Inventory planning

Inventory planning was once thought to be confined to the downstream end of the supply chain. But responsibility for it is increasingly moving up the supply chain away from end consumers. Retailers have started to push inventory-planning responsibilities back to manufacturers of finished product. And even raw material suppliers are now being asked to perform certain logistics functions similar to those functions that the end players in the supply chain have asked of their suppliers. Understanding the principles and approaches of inventory planning is now valuable for partners all along the supply chain.

One of the most commonly recognized methods of inventory planning has been the concept of economic order quantity, or EOQ. EOQ optimizes the purchase quantity determination by balancing the costs of ordering against the costs of carrying inventory. The formula is as follows (Tersine, 1994, 93–4):

$$EOQ = \sqrt{\frac{2CR}{PF}}$$

Equation 24.1

Where:

    C = ordering cost per order
    R = annual demand in units
    P = purchase cost of an unit
    F = annual holding cost as a fraction of unit cost
    PF = holding cost per unit per year

While EOQ and its basic concepts have been taught for a long time, the concept has lost some usefulness in relation to inventory planning. One of the primary reasons that it is used less frequently today is that the assumptions used to calculate EOQ are too unrealistic to help plan inventory in dynamic environments. These assumptions are (Tersine, 1994, 95):

- the demand rate is known, constant and continuous;
- the lead time or replenishment time is known and constant;
- the entire lot size is added to inventory at the same time;
- no stockouts are permitted—since demand and lead time are known, stockouts can be avoided;
- the cost structure is fixed—order/set-up costs are the same regardless of lot size, holding cost is a linear function based on average inventory and unit purchase cost is constant (no quantity discounts);
- there is sufficient space, capacity and capital to procure the desired quantity; and
- the item is a single product—it does not interact with any other inventory items (there are no joint orders).

Obviously, these assumptions make a very complex situation overly simplistic. EOQ does not meet the needs of many companies which have become more sophisticated in their use of inventory-planning methodologies. Additionally, the recent transition to continuous replenishment-type initiatives (quicker replenishment of smaller quantities to reduce inventory and increase responsiveness) reduces order quantities in favour of lower inventories, thereby bypassing the logic of economic order quantity. EOQ is, however, often a good starting point for those companies just beginning to focus on inventory management.

Today several concepts illustrate the shift from traditional inventory management to a more responsive inventory planning system. Better-established concepts such as materials requirements planning (MRP) and distribution requirements planning (DRP) will be covered briefly in relation to manufacturers' inventory strategies. Two of the newer concepts that will be covered in relation to retailer inventory management are vendor-managed inventory (VMI) and collaborative forecasting and replenishment (CFAR).

Manufacturers' inventory strategies

Manufacturers must be prepared for relatively large orders in sometimes unpredictable time frames. Therefore, the level of safety or buffer stock for unpredictable orders can sometimes be substantial. However, the positive side of manufacturer inventory planning is that manufacturers' and wholesalers' demand patterns are often relatively stable and can be better predicted on average than the demand of end consumers. This idea is aided by the fact that the manufacturers' customers often know far in advance approximately how much and when they will be needing product. The key is to get customers to communicate their future requirements as far ahead as possible to allow suppliers to balance their own operations and inventory levels. This allows upstream partners to see changes to forecasts as they occur so that non-emergency production adjustments can be made. Communication of requirements to upstream partners avoids demand 'surprises' and the resulting shocks upstream. This means that customers should communicate requirements upstream as soon as they have the data.

Several tactics will allow manufacturers to plan and manage their inventories. Two well-known methods are materials requirements planning (MRP) and distribution requirements planning (DRP). MRP is a set of logically related procedures, decision rules and records (alternatively, records may be viewed as inputs to the system) designed to translate a master production schedule into time-phased net requirements, and the planned coverage of such requirements, for each component inventory item needed to implement this schedule (Orlicky, 1975). MRP essentially takes a total production schedule and converts it into the necessary raw material or parts requirements and synchronizes ordering timelines to ensure that the materials are on hand when needed.

Distribution requirements planning is the application of MRP to finished goods inventories. Where MRP starts with the master production schedule, DRP starts with the forecast at the lowest level in the distribution network and aggregates across facilities to give a total need by echelon in a network. With DRP, items are not replenished until there are future demand requirements that must be met (Tersine, 1994). Both MRP and DRP are designed to link end demand more logically to the process or product needed to meet that demand. In the case of MRP, raw materials needs and timing are determined by the master production schedule. In DRP, the end forecasts by location drive the flow of finished product from the production line to the location nearest customer demand.

Retailers' inventory strategies

One of the key shifts in business has been that of power from manufacturers to retailers. This is shown in the USA by the growth of Wal-Mart, which has annual sales in excess of $100 billion. Traditionally, logistics and supply chain management were not terms even used in most day-to-day retail operations. However, in the last five years retailers have begun to realize the leverage in logistics and have begun to pay this area much more attention.

Retailers have unique issues relating to inventory management. In fact, they have similar issues to manufacturers at a distribution centre stocking level and almost an entirely different set of requirements to control inventory at the store level. Retailers use several merchandising concepts in a store environment that can have a significant impact on inventory-management goals. Owing to some of these requirements, retailers often have to hold more inventory than is required to meet sales. Two merchandising strategies that have an impact on inventory management are presentation quantity or merchandising quantity and vertical striping. Presentation or merchandising quantity is the amount of store shelf inventory necessary so that the store looks like it is 'in business' or to show a full stock level. A store planner or manager wants the store to look full and appealing to shoppers. In many mass-merchandising stores, a large portion of SKUs sell fewer than one item per store per week. However, to hold enough to satisfy the presentation quantity, often a full case or an entire inner pack of product is on the shelf. The result is a much higher level of on-hand store inventory than is actually needed to satisfy customer demand.

Vertical striping is the concept of having multiple levels of shelves stocked with the same product to show a neat and complete merchandising appearance. The end result is the look of a 'stripe' of a product on a shelf. This merchandising technique requires a significant amount of inventory of a particular SKU. In this case, the appeal of a fully stocked series of shelves and the potential sales it might generate through increased customer attraction must be traded off against the cost of carrying inventory over what is needed to cover actual sales.

An idea that has arisen in the last five years to aid in retail inventory management is vendor-managed inventory (VMI). Vendor-managed inventory occurs when a manufacturer monitors inventory levels at its customer's warehouse(s) and assumes responsibility for replenishing that inventory to achieve predetermined inventory-turn targets and customer service levels (Copacino, 1993). The manufacturer now makes the replenishment decision, rather than waiting for the customer to reorder the product. In true VMI, the retailer does not review the supplier's suggested order at all. In VMI, the inventory is still owned by the customer, but it is often dramatically reduced with the aid of a continuous replenishment arrangement.

The previous description assumes that VMI is done at the distribution centre level. It has been talked about at the store level and can be done; however, distribution centre VMI is much more prevalent. There are only a handful of situations where VMI is used to replenish retail inventory at the store level. This is primarily because of complexity, since some retailers have thousands of stores and performing VMI for a few customers with several thousand stores is obviously difficult.

There are differing opinions as to the rationale for VMI. One retailer perspective has to do with the sheer number of SKUs. In a typical discount department store, there might be as many as 75 000 to 80 000 SKUs in each store. With this many, the retailer may have a difficult time monitoring the inventory levels and determining appropriate ordering quantities and times. Because of these large numbers, some retailers believe that their suppliers would do a better job of monitoring inventory levels because they might only have 100 SKUs to monitor for a single retailer. With fewer to monitor the supplier, in theory, could better manage stock levels of the smaller number of SKUs. Initially, VMI seems very appealing from the retail perspective; however, many retailers are sceptical because they are concerned that the suppliers might not perform and stockouts would occur at the stores.

VMI requires significant effort and expertise from a manufacturer. Therefore, in the first stages of implementation the manufacturer is learning the VMI process and often makes mistakes which can result in a retail stockout. If a manufacturer's VMI performance does result in a retail stockout, the supplier jeopardizes its future business with that customer.

Stockouts can be both a short-term and long-term expense for companies. In the short term it may simply result in a customer buying a substitute product; however, the long-term implication may be that the customer switches brands. The significant difference between manufacturer-level and retailer-level stockouts is that at the retail level there is often no contact between the buying consumer and the retailer. Therefore, the retailer might not know about buyer dissatisfaction, in contrast to the supplier/retailer stockout where there is communication (stockouts are discussed in further detail in Chapter 11). In addition, some retailers do not believe that a supplier can manage retailer inventories any better than the retailer can itself.

Conversely, a supplier perspective is that VMI is just a way for the retailer to push additional responsibilities on to their suppliers to reduce retailer costs. If a supplier is good at VMI, it can free up significant resources within a retail company. On the other hand, there are some suppliers which believe that if they perform VMI for a customer, they will have greater ties with that customer and possibly sell more product over the long run.

Manufacturers estimate that they should have 30 to 40 per cent of their sales volume on VMI to begin to gain some economies in distribution. If VMI is only done for one or two customers, the supplier must serve these two customers by exception, thereby not realizing economies of scale. Manufacturers also estimate that they would need 60 to 70 per cent of their volume on VMI to allow smoothing of production. With this large amount of sales on VMI, the manufacturer would have a good idea of future demand and therefore be able to plan production better to avoid production spikes in times of high demand. In addition, demand slowdowns would be noticed in advance, thereby allowing a reduction in excess or obsolete inventory.

VMI is most prevalent in discount mass-merchandising and grocery channels. However, the concept may add the most value in channels very different from those in which it was first conceived and implemented, especially those with high values per SKU. For example, many after-market parts companies do not have dealer networks with a high degree of inventory-management expertise. In these channels, VMI might have a significant impact by helping reduce stockouts and excess inventory. There are several software packages on the market which help manufacturers perform VMI for their customers.

Distribution strategies pursued by retailers also affect inventory. These include cross-docking and direct store delivery (DSD). Cross-docking is the concept of moving product through a retailer's distribution centre without putting the product into storage (see Figure 24.1). While this has more relevance to warehousing and finished goods distribution, it has a definite impact on the retailer's inventory-control plans. If a retailer can work with a supplier so that the latter provides shipments that can be cross-docked through a retail distribution centre, the centre will have to carry little inventory thus reducing the inventory investment. One example of cross-docking is where the supplier's product is received into a retailer's cross-dock and the product is diverted to waiting outbound trucks that go directly to stores. For cross-docking to work well, suppliers and customers have to have highly integrated distribution-planning systems. The retail distribution centre must know in advance what is arriving from the supplier so that the product can be quickly transferred to trucks bound for stores.

Another key distribution strategy decision is whether to deliver direct to store or use a company or third-party distribution centre to flow product through to stores. In the direct-to-store (DSD) scenario, either

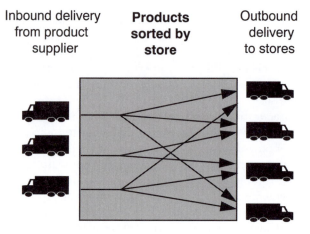

Figure 24.1   Cross-docking

transportation costs to the stores or inventory-carrying costs at the store level will be higher. If less-than-truckload (LTL) shipments are made directly to the store, the cost of the inbound freight will be high. The alternative is to ship full truckloads. This is prevalent in 'category killer' or niche retailing environments which are characterized by very large stores that often double as warehouses. These stores typically carry all of their inventory in the store rather than having a combination of regional distribution centres and stores. In DSD, with full truckload deliveries, the cost of carrying inventory is higher but transportation cost is lower than with smaller, LTL shipments. A difficulty that can be encountered with DSD shipments is that stores often do not have the receiving capacity for multiple shipments at the same time and many items do not sell enough to warrant large shipments.

Interaction between inventory management and technology

Several software applications are available to help plan inventory. Additionally, there are several pieces of technology which have aided inventory planners dramatically. Possibly the best known is the implementation and use of point-of-sale scanning. This allows a retailer to track exactly what is being sold, thereby also permitting a computerized perpetual inventory system. Unfortunately, many companies that have point-of-sale (POS) systems in place are not using them to plan their inventories. For these companies, POS is more a sophisticated price look-up feature than a valuable planning tool.

Electronic data interchange (EDI) is another technological development that can help inventory planners. It allows channel partners to communicate consistently, accurately and on a timely basis, thereby allowing lower stock levels across the firm. EDI standards have been developed to speed its implementation. As with POS scanning, many firms implement EDI only to meet customer requirements. In this case, they are missing the opportunity to leverage EDI in planning operations.

A key idea in this area of inventory is that software or technology should never be thought of as a panacea for a company's problems. Frequently, companies ask for the best inventory-management or forecasting packages rather than focusing on the more opportune issue—improving the processes that create inventory. Only if the necessary corrections are made to the process can the company choose the best software that will allow the inventory reductions to occur.

Having visibility of inventories either within a firm or across a supply chain can help alleviate some excess inventory. Often, within a company, one distribution centre cannot see the stock levels in other facilities. This can increase inventory levels across the company. This problem can be addressed by implementing the capability to see inventory across the company. This helps in two ways. The first is that a company does not have to carry as much safety stock to handle variations in sales and lead times for each individual facility. Secondly, it saves expediting costs in emergency stockout situations where product could be received from another company facility.

This concept of visibility can have as much or more impact if supply chain partners are linked together. However, there may be some push-back from some channel members. Firms might be concerned that if a customer sees they are out of stock, the customer may bypass the phone call and go to a competitor. In this case, a firm would lose the opportunity either to upgrade the customer to a higher-end product or to substitute with a product that can perform in the same way as the item initially desired. There are some examples of supply chains sharing this inventory-status information; however, they are only in the initial stages (Narus and Anderson, 1996).

A current example of information sharing to aid in the planning of inventory is the collaborative forecasting and replenishment (CFAR) project. CFAR is an initiative between Warner-Lambert (a consumer goods manufacturer), Wal-Mart and other software providers and logistics integrators, whereby forecast information regarding the sales of Warner-Lambert products in Wal-Mart stores is located on an Internet site and is updated regularly. By accessing this information, Warner-Lambert has a real-time idea of how its product is selling in Wal-Mart stores and is not surprised when Wal-Mart revises its order. CFAR has been expanded to CPFR—collaborative planning, forecasting and replenishment.

With the growth of the capability and popularity of the Internet, inventory planning can be done more proactively. The additional benefit of using the Internet versus EDI to share information is that the former does not have to follow stringent formatting standards to be successful. The biggest concern about using the Internet, however, is the security of the information. Safe 'firewalls' and other security features will have to be built in.

Future of inventory management

Inventory management is changing and will continue to change. The positive side will be that managers will have several additional tools to help in inventory planning. Some of these tools will be software products that will allow logical planning with little updating.

With the use of ideas like EDI, the Internet and other software tools, inventory management can be advanced to allow a 'sell one, make one' concept (the basis of continuous replenishment) become closer to reality. With better information links, data that will help in planning inventories will be moved more quickly across supply chains. With this speed, an accurate, long-term forecast becomes less important. By reducing the time between the forecast and the event it is intended to predict, forecast accuracy will go up substantially. In addition, the need for a forecast is reduced with a faster flow of information. For example, companies are beginning to transmit customer POS data further back up the chain so that even raw material suppliers will see what finished goods are being sold soon after the actual sale.

Owing to these changes, the next five to ten years will be exciting for inventory managers as the new ideas and tools will allow them to do their jobs more efficiently and more proactively than in the past. These concepts will be helped by an increasing focus from upper management, including CEOs, on the importance of inventory management.

References

Cooke, James Aaron (1997) 'The solid gold supply chain', *Logistics Management*, 36 (4), 57–8.

Copacino, William C. (1993) 'How to get with the program', *Traffic Management*, August, 23.

Coyle, John J., Bardi, Edward J. and Langley, C. John (1992) *The Management of Business Logistics*, 5th edn, West, St Paul, MN.

Inventory Reduction Report (1997) 97 (1), January, 15.

Narus, James A. and Anderson, James C. (1996) 'Rethinking distribution: adaptive channels', *Harvard Business Review*, 74 (4), July/August.

Orlicky, Joseph (1975) *Material Requirements Planning*, McGraw-Hill, New York.

Tersine, Richard J. (1994) *Principles of Inventory and Materials Management*, Prentice-Hall, Englewood Cliffs, NJ.

Warehouse-management systems technologies
Technology-enabled warehouse excellence

Bruce Richmond and Eric Peters

With the recognition that every aspect of the supply chain can contribute value to the process, the spotlight has fallen on the warehouse. Sophisticated warehouse-management systems (WMS) technologies can ensure that warehouses contribute strongly to supply chain excellence. But to implement WMS successfully, companies must drive forward from a strong business case and manage the project over all aspects, including people, processes, technology integration and linkages across the broader supply chain.

Introduction

Twenty years ago the warehouse was thought of as a non-value-added cost centre. Ten years ago we weren't sure if it added value or not, but it was still viewed as less important than sales or manufacturing. Today, not only is the warehouse viewed as a value-added process, but it is viewed as a critical part of a company's success equation. It is the critical link between the chain's supply and demand sides. From the supplier's viewpoint, the distribution centre focuses on efficient handling, inventory management, product flow, transportation and delivery. From the demand side, the distribution centre must meet all customer-specific requirements with maximum flexibility and responsiveness.

Warehouse-management systems technologies

This transformation in distribution philosophies is being supported by warehouse-management systems (WMS) technologies. A WMS is a software application that manages operations within the four walls of the warehouse. Several key components make up a WMS solution, including barcoding technology, radio frequency, computer systems and peripherals. A WMS therefore serves to support and enhance stock locating, barcoding, inventory control, material-handling and productivity measurement. Its applications comprise receiving, put-away, wave management, order allocation, replenishment, picking, shipment scheduling, shipping, inventory control and cycle counting.

Radio frequency technology coupled with the barcode serves to provide 100 per cent accurate information in real time, the foundation of a successful WMS installation. The barcode provides the most accurate method of entering information into the WMS, with radio frequency technology allowing that entry to occur in real time. Handheld or truck mounted scanners can be used to scan barcodes and, via radio waves, relay that information back to the WMS to ensure positive verification and to trigger the next task.

In addition to automatic identification technologies, the computer platform, paper printers and barcode printers are also required to support WMS technology. These peripherals can often be found on a company's LAN and in fact the WMS is often attached to a corporate LAN to maximize the accessibility to vital warehousing and distribution information.

Warehouse-management systems functions

The functions of a WMS fall into two categories: planning and execution. Planning includes order management, transportation planning, order wave management, labour planning and dock area management. Execution includes receiving, put-away, picking and shipping.

Planning

The role of the WMS in order release is to ensure the most efficient order-fulfilment methods inside the four walls of the warehouse. For example, the WMS provides a display of the pending orders to give managers the ability to review and sequence order release. It also provides order wave management routines that allow for the efficient release of order waves.

During the order-release cycle, WMS assists in rudimentary transportation-scheduling issues. It can provide basic cubing and weight information. It does not replace or perform the functions of a transportation-management system (TMS), but assists a manually based transportation operation in making intelligent loading and shipping decisions.

WMS technology also will provide labour-planning and management tools. A WMS provides warehouse managers with an understanding of the estimated labour to complete tasks in the work queue, allowing warehouse managers to plan activities and be proactive rather than reactive in their management decisions.

Finally, dock area management involves directing inbound and outbound truck traffic to dock doors to facilitate balanced receiving and shipping staging areas, minimal travel times from dock door receipt to physical put-away and managing trailers that are dropped in the shipping yard for later loading or unloading.

Execution

The WMS radio frequency performs the four basic functions of receiving, put-away and replenishment, picking and shipping. It is vital to design the receiving operation accurately. Unless it is built for 100 per cent accuracy, then receiving errors will be carried throughout the warehousing operations. With much of the information required for receiving is dependent on information sources outside the company, different interfaces and strategies must be developed for each information path into the WMS.

Real-time online WMS receiving can therefore replace manual processes. The WMS provides both receipt confirmation and validation of all inbound receipts. It can handle discrepancies such as count inaccuracies, order receipt inaccuracies and missing items. At the end of the process, the inbound receipt should have been accurately and quickly received into the staging area.

The second significant execution function of the WMS is put-away and replenishment. The WMS will direct the put-away of product from the staging area to the appropriate storage location. The key attribute of WMS put-away functionality is that it should always be system directed. Directed put-away results in system verification which in turn results in the highest levels of accuracy.

From the operator's perspective put-away is straightforward. The operator scans the pallet, the system tells the operator where to store the item, the operator goes to the storage location and puts the load away, scans the put-away location and waits for the next task. This simplicity masks the complex systems supporting the process in the background.

In the background, the WMS is managing forward pick location and reserve location inventory requirements. It may also be managing multiple logical warehouses under the same roof. It is trying to facilitate a good ABC storage philosophy, attempting to store the fastest-moving items closest to their points of use, as well as maximizing the capacity and density of the storage areas.

The third execution function is picking. Two types of picking can be facilitated with a WMS: paper based and radio frequency based. Paper-based picking is where the WMS generates pick requests and these requests are printed out for picking. High-volume, high-throughput, short-distance picking activities are generally best served with paper-based picking. All other picking activities are generally radio frequency based.

Radio frequency picking can be thought of as very similar to radio frequency put-away. The operator goes to a storage location, scans the location, picks the item and delivers it to its eventual staging location, scanning that location to close the transaction.

The final execution functionality is shipping. This is a straightforward functional activity. The WMS must ensure that the correct paperwork and order consolidation has occurred. It is the step that ties all of the information associated with the order into all of the documentation that is required to meet customer requirements.

Benefits of a WMS

WMS technology has traditionally been thought of as a tactical solution to either labour productivity or inventory inaccuracy problems.

Labour savings are tangible once the WMS has been installed. Four labour areas directly affected by a WMS include reduced deadheading, directed put-away and picking, reduced handling and the elimination of multiple reserve storage. There will also be administrative cost reductions as a result of less data entry and data-entry errors.

Inventory reduction is another key savings opportunity. Inaccurate inventory represents significant costs including lost sales, back orders, excess inventory, wrong inventory, reduced picking and put-away labour productivity and higher freight costs. A WMS will reduce the cost associated with inaccurate inventory by providing high levels of accuracy.

As the technology has grown and matured, strategic imperatives join the tactical reasons driving WMS implementation. The technology supports the transformation of the warehouse in the supply chain from a non-value-adding aspect of the process to a key player in an efficient, effective and customer-focused supply chain operation.

First, today's distribution centre must serve as an extension of the manufacturing process. Product must be prepared and shipped to the retailer so that the retailer has the ability to cross-dock the merchandise quickly and directly to the retail stores. More retailers are demanding this service, blurring the lines between manufacturing and distribution. Consequently, it is demanding a tighter linkage between trading partners.

Secondly, the distribution centre must assist in reducing inventory across the total distribution network. Hand-offs between trading partners are becoming tighter and tighter. This is required because of the demand to move product faster with high levels of accuracy. These tighter hand-offs are naturally reducing inventory. Supporting them are requirements that systems be more responsive and supportive of zero information errors.

Thirdly, today's distribution centre must be flexible in responding to an ever changing environment. Older warehouses are inherently inflexible because they are oriented to mechanisms, not systems. Storage and material-handling equipment (MHE) systems were often driving the distribution operations, instead of best operational practices. Because operations are ever changing to meet customer demands, distribution centres must be well-designed, not overly complex, functional and flexible. WMS technology helps serves as a foundation to this type of operation.

Fourthly, today's distribution centre manages inventory, product movement and transportation across corporate boundaries, with all chain members linked electronically. For a company to participate in this electronic information network, each member of the chain must have error-free information, an attribute of WMS technology.

And fifthly, information must be real time and provide instant feedback. This is necessary to provide a true picture of the business pulse points. Real-time information on orders, inventory and production status can all help better business decisions to be made. It can aid in reducing non-value-added steps in the business process.

Successful implementation

The reality is that purchasing a WMS is not of itself going to transform a business. A WMS is not off-the-shelf software that may simply be screwed into place. Companies need to drive its implementation and application from a compelling business case. WMS is a valuable tool, but the extent to which it transforms warehouse operations is entirely dependent on the quality of the business case and its execution. It cannot be seen as an information systems issue divorced from the business's overall strategy and operational requirements.

The development of the business case requires a strategic vision, an appreciation of the processes required to support that vision, including the design of storage and MHE solutions and operation processes, a commitment to the people who will make the transformation work and a solid understanding of the capacities of the WMS technologies which will underpin the transformation.

All these factors are interdependent and by attending to them everything comes together: process reengineering, software solutions, MHE solutions and also integration with existing software systems, such as order management and transportation planning. Effectively implemented, the WMS serves as a critical success component of the supply chain, dramatically strengthening the distribution link.

One of the most frequently asked questions is: 'How long is this going to take?' The question should really be twofold: 'How long will it take and what type of delays might I anticipate?' A recent survey of mass retailers showed that the time from start of the design process to funding is usually six to nine months. The time from funding to implementation is usually nine to twelve months. The cycle time can be reduced, but this requires exceptional planning, skilled team members and a vendor whose application is a strong fit for your solution. The more disturbing statistic is that more than 50 per cent of all WMS installations are late when compared to the original plan. These delays result from a combination of inadequate planning, improper team make-up or skills or a less than ideal vendor partner.

Implementation

To implement a WMS effectively, a business must understand the seven critical success factors for transformation.

Adopt a fully integrated approach

A fully integrated approach to change must be both developed and embraced. There must be a continuing balance among strategy, people, business processes and technology.

A competent project manager will have the primary role of integration. He or she will accomplish the implementation based on strategic insights into future directions for the business and industry, coupled with a deep appreciation of customer demands and how they can be satisfied.

Major transformation projects cannot be carried out in a vacuum. They must fit into the company's overall strategic plan, as it continues to evolve. Further justification should show that the project manager not only understands the corporate context but also makes sure the project is always synchronized with other company initiatives.

Solid coordination must occur between mapping out the desired outcomes and implementing the right technology solutions. Too often the wider effects of any technological change are underestimated. Some key interface challenges need to be addressed, especially as enterprise-level systems (order management, inventory management, transportation management and forecasting management) link to the WMS and the WMS links to material-handling solutions. With an integrated approach, smooth and predictable outcomes can be achieved. This integrated approach must also be extended beyond the warehouse walls, along the supply chain. Information should flow freely—all the way through to the product moving out of the door to the customer.

Worker acceptance of the solution is critical if long-term success is to be attained. The workforce must believe that this solution is *their* solution. An important part of this is developing an effective communications programme very early in the process.

Take a partnership approach with vendors

A partnership with the software vendor is important. The design and subsequent implementation of a WMS are complex tasks, because the systems integrate with so many functions in the organization. The challenge is that software vendors are generally not skilled at integration. Their core competency is building and installing the software, not interfacing with the host systems, not to mention relating to hardware vendors, human resource managers, architects, contractors and warehouse employees. By drawing them in as partners in the process, and showing them that they are participating in its success, the chances of problems are greatly reduced.

Use good methodology to leverage team members

Most companies demand that change occurs in a matter of months, not years. This reinforces the need to have a proven, well-defined and documented methodology. A proper methodology can minimize risk and assure on-time completion by clearly delineating roles and responsibilities and by maximizing the core competencies of all of the team members. A properly defined methodology can be a fail-safe road map for executing the project successfully.

Central to the methodology is an implementation approach involving three distinct phases.

Conceptual design

Phase 1 (see Figure 25.1) consists primarily of operations strategy and software selections. This is where you confirm the business strategy, develop logistics reengineering concepts, establish fundamental business requirements for MHE and select a WMS vendor. It concludes with an investment analysis that summarizes all of these steps, the definition of the budget and an estimated time frame. Skip Phase 1 and there is no blueprint and, potentially, you face long-term failure.

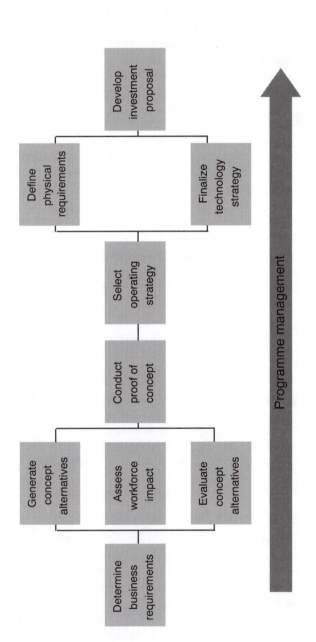

Figure 25.1   Phase 1—Operations strategy

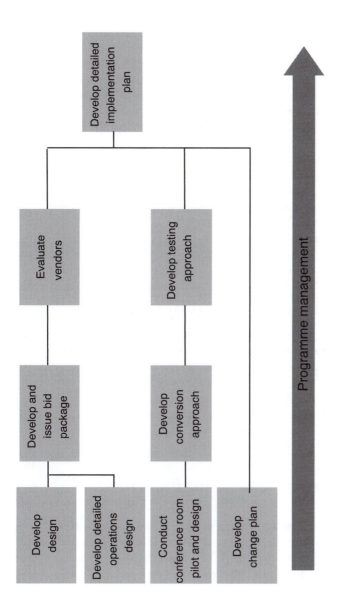

Figure 25.2 Phase 2—detailed design

Detailed design

Phase 2 (see Figure 25.2) is concerned with the detailed design and conference room pilot (the modelling of WMS software against reengineered processes) and the detailed design/specifications for the MHE solution. WMS modelling is essential because it exposes any gaps between what the software can provide and what the business case requires. In this way, a company can determine the costs involved in bridging the gaps and whether the business benefits justify those costs.

Along with the new process design, an understanding must be developed of the ability of the workforce to change. Often this calls for a change-readiness assessment to identify which groups or departments are most amenable to change and which will be most likely to resist.

Implementation

Phase 3 (see Figure 25.3) focuses on implementation and start-up. It addresses construction of the material-handling solution, organization structure, training, unit testing, systems testing, production simulations, conversion and ramp-up and support.

This three-phased approach calls for significant strategy involvement, particularly in the early stages. Major reengineering of business processes continues throughout the work. People issues are typically limited throughout the early stages but intensively addressed in the final steps.

Technology involvement is especially deep in the final stage to review and verify vendor-provided hardware, conduct network and database sizing, develop or review interface architecture, analyse system performance capabilities and execute a complete integration and customer-acceptance test.

For logistics/distribution management, a system methodology is essential in serving as a knowledge-transfer mechanism. As a result, the company is better equipped to operate the new distribution centre and to continue improving its performance.

Reskill, reorient, remotivate and retrain

Experience shows that the people equation is the toughest part to get right. It requires a strong, continuing effort to secure the organization's buy-in and commitment to change, empower employees to handle more responsibility and do what it takes to ensure that employees have a sense of ownership in the new processes.

Workers need to acquire new skills and gain a thorough understanding of how their jobs will be different. WMS affects the actual jobs that people will perform. Specialists who have prided themselves in doing one set of tasks for 20 years now must be multifunctional. The rules, pri-

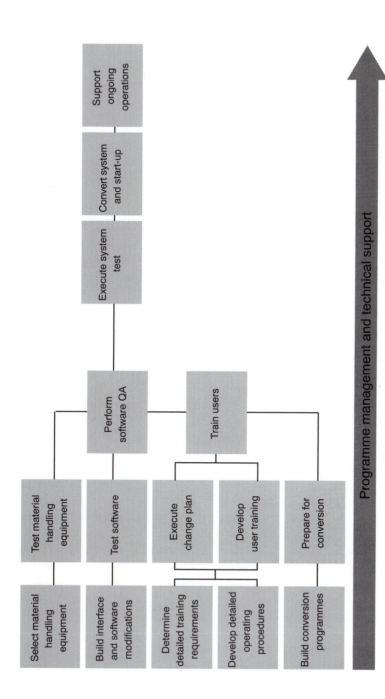

Figure 25.3   Phase 3—Implementation

orities, exceptions, standards and procedures that guide them are different, as is their sense of urgency, responsibility and decision-making powers.

Executives do not fully appreciate that reorienting their workforce requires employees to change mindsets, alter attitudes, demystify the changes and adapt to new tools. That is why executive communication is critical, in concert with focused non-classroom training. Managers are equally challenged, often underestimating how long it takes people to change long-standing work patterns. After doing the same task for 20 years, repetition and familiarity with a task are etched in the minds of the workforce.

People challenges are daunting. Workers must learn new skills, be reoriented, remotivated and retrained. If these issues are not addressed, the result is a functional system that delivers little or no business value.

Test and convert

Testing is a critical step in the successful implementation of a WMS. When a mechanic puts new brakes on a car, they are fully tested to make sure they work. When a new drug is being developed, it is tested, tested and then tested some more. If the brakes fail on your car or the drug has an unexpected side effect, the result could be catastrophic. If the WMS does not perform as anticipated, the effect on your distribution operations can be equally dangerous. The importance of testing and the development of a thorough conversion strategy cannot be understated. Many companies with a new solution underestimate how difficult it is to get all of the components to work together and to achieve an orderly conversion, while minimizing disruptions to the business.

Three levels of testing are critical: unit testing, system testing and stress testing. Unit testing makes sure that all stand-alone components function satisfactorily by themselves. This includes material-handling equipment, software packages and interfaces. Often a 'firewall' approach is the best answer. In effect, the project manager must draw a firewall to prevent any component from being system tested until all of the 'bugs' have been cleaned up. System testing makes sure that the parts are effectively integrated. This is where connectivity issues emerge and it usually reveals a few surprises. Stress testing makes sure that the new solution can handle the expected volumes. It may also test the performance of the interface between MHE and a WMS. These tests are critical as an improperly designed interface can result not only in poor response times, but in total system failure as it becomes too bogged down to operate.

Finally, there is the issue of conversion. It starts with the key questions: how do we ramp up the workforce? Have we done enough training? Do we want everything at once, by function, by best customer, or smallest customer? The answers to these questions then provide the information required to develop a methodical approach for turning on the new solution.

Various thresholds will be hit as the system ramps up: computer problems, MHE, people issues and so on. And in each case, guided by a good plan, the project manager can back away, down to the previous level, fix the problem and bring the system back up, with minimal or no impact. The beauty of this methodology is that it guides the conversion process.

Aggressively manage the project

Aggressiveness and schedule adherence must peacefully co-exist with testing and methodology. While it is important that a project manager is thorough in terms of testing and methodology, it is equally important for he or she to be aggressive in managing the overall programme. This includes integration of participants, partnering with vendors, monitoring and tracking progress and managing the executive's expectations.

Most important, the project manager must keep an eye on the 'big picture'. Warehouse management is generally focused on its own issues and does not maintain a perspective on what is happening to the overall business enterprise. For example, one retail chain went through a significant transformation of its logistics and distribution systems. Three weeks before the conversion to the new system the company acquired another retail chain, thus changing its product mix, delivery schedules, and so on. The result was that overnight the new system had to be changed, at a huge cost.

Make technology the enabler, not the driver

Technology should be the enabler of the integrated solution, not the driver. The evolution of a distribution centre as a supply chain focal point is a business issue. It is driven by strategic imperatives, not the selection of a database or hardware platform.

Technology is evolving from a centralized to a more distributed architecture. A few years ago, this trend troubled many people because the technologies were often unproven. But today, as vendors leverage the technologies, they can be counted on to support a new decentralized environment.

Once a company's strategic direction is set, a number of significant technology concerns need to be addressed. For example, because the typical information systems organization has old technology skills, it may be unable to partner effectively with, and leverage from, leading-edge vendors. A top priority, therefore, is to gain relevant skills and resources, via acquisition or training, to support the new technology infrastructures.

Conclusion

A distribution centre can be a potent competitive weapon, even a source of market differentiation. It can not only increase sales and reduce costs, but solidify business relationships by helping you consistently exceed customer expectations. The modern distribution centre is integral to the flow of products from the supplier to the manufacturer to the retail store.

WMS technology must be thought of as a key element in this transformation. And it must be understood that a 'quicker, cheaper, faster' approach to WMS technology and this transformation will only guarantee failure. Distribution is critically important in the supply and demand chain, so WMS must be done right, first time.

The warehouse was once thought of as a cost centre and a non-value-added process. Now it must be viewed as a critical part of company's success equation, with WMS a cornerstone in this success.

Part III
Cultural Capability

Overview

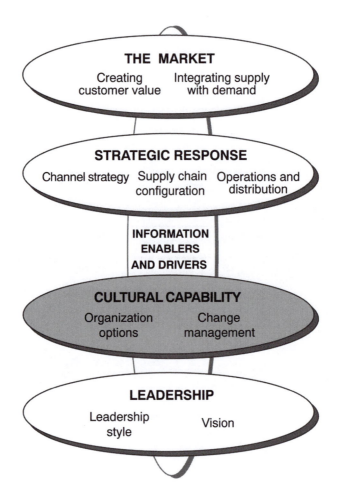

One of the great contemporary business axioms is that the goal of management is to create 'one culture' within any given firm. The argument runs that a dominant business culture lends strength and coherence to a firm and supports sustained performance improvements by its people. This belief should be challenged.

Customers are not homogenous, they are diverse. Their needs can vary widely. If a company's culture revolves around one set of systems, skills or working styles then it will find it very hard to align its operations to more than one customer segment.

Diverse cultures within one company will be far more powerful in this new era than will a monoculture. For example, a pathway delivering high-speed, innovative solutions to a small group of demanding customers requires a totally different management approach compared to a pathway delivering consistent cost-oriented services to high volumes of customers. The various pathways to each customer group should be entrusted to those with the skills best capable of meeting that particular group's requirements. The firm needs to look for, acquire and reward more specialized skills and approaches.

Once the principle of skill diversity has been internalized within the firm, then the process of achieving the appropriate mix will mirror the process by which the firm segments its customer groups. Chapters 26 and 27 suggest ways in which a company's corporate structure and internal organization might best be designed to identify, acquire and retain the right skill mix. Chapter 28 analyses how firms can manage change in the supply chain to capture the full benefits of proposed strategies.

Alternative organization options
Moving from lines of hierarchy to networks of alliances
Paula Giles and Anthony Hancy

Traditional forms of organizational structure are being buffeted by forces of emerging technologies, increasing consumer demands and changing markets. The old styles of hierarchical, command-and-control organizations are now having to adapt to these forces of change. The emergence of a myriad of structural forms, from integrated alliances and partnerships to outsourcing and 'spin-offs', has created a more complex set of internal and external environments for organizations. Today's supply chain managers must work in structures where boundaries are flexible and relationships with external parties have become paramount. In this world of networked organizations, information sharing, cooperation and control are the new keys to supply chain success.

Introduction

Organizations are operating in environments characterized by increasingly rapid rates of change. A range of forces are driving the change. Telecommunications, media and consumer companies are forming alliances and offering new products and services; the Internet is creating new channels of distribution; governments are reshaping the market through privatization and industry deregulation; and consumers are becoming increasingly more informed and sophisticated, more demanding and gaining more access to information. At the same time, employee expectations about work and careers are changing, with the increasing prevalence of career mobility across several companies and a working life consisting of a 'portfolio' of careers.

In response, we are now beginning to see the emergence of organizational forms that are designed for, or are in response to, the information age—where information is ubiquitous, cheap and in the hands of the user or consumer, where knowledge is meant to be shared across functional boundaries, and where the time and space between significant business changes is rapidly diminishing. This shift means the death knell for hierarchical, traditional forms of organizations and their attendant practices of 'command and control' and 'knowledge withholding'.

While executives in each new generation have felt that they are living in an era of unprecedented change—what is different today is that we are seeing more frequent experimentation and a greater diversity in the types of organizational forms being implemented. While this diversity is interesting for its own sake—there are more options out there to select—what is perhaps more significant is the range of structures within one organization. For example, a simple functional organization can also be one that participates in several interconnected alliances with suppliers, customers and, indeed, competitors. What this suggests is that the talent required of today's executives is to operate in an 'and' world. They must have the capacity simultaneously to employ skills of control and cooperation, rather than to use skills of one type or the other.

For executives in today's logistics and supply functions, internal and external alliances are rapidly becoming the norm. Where once logistics managers were the managers with the most resources—trucks, warehouses and distribution centres—now they have to work with many different internal and external structures. Logistics executives may have to share their resources with other companies in a supplier–customer arrangement; or operate internally as a service provider across several divisions in the organization, answering and accountable to many; or manage logistics contracts that have been outsourced to other organizations, so that the resources are now someone else's.

So what are the organizational forms which companies now face and, in particular, those that must be faced by executives in logistics functions? How can they help companies deliver the capabilities needed to be successful?

From hardware to software— organizational shapes to date

A vast array of organizational structures and shapes have emerged across industries. The earliest and most pervasive form is the functional structure (Figure 26.1) simply because it brings like functions, competencies and services together in one group. The logistics function is easily visible in most organizations—in downstream oil companies, for example, the logistics groups provide the product supply, trading, terminal storage and distribution functions and, in some cases, manufacturing as well.

The modern twist for the functional structure is to organize into strategic business units. This provides a notional profit-and-loss or return-on-capital-employed performance measure, even though this is through internal, transfer-pricing transactions with either upstream or downstream customers.

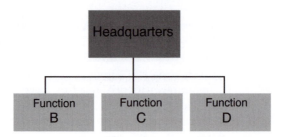

Figure 26.1   The traditional functional structure

This structural form has traditionally been regarded as successful when market conditions are stable and mature (where arrangements between competitors are relatively well defined and rules of competition well understood). This is the environment that has characterized the oil industry in particular over the last decade.

Traditional forms also include the product-oriented structure and the customer- or market-based structure (see Figure 26.2). Both of these are efforts to accommodate the level of differentiation residing under the one corporate roof. The product-oriented structure recognizes that the products (or services) offered are different, either by their features, the needs they serve, the type of good (e.g. wet versus dry), price (premium versus budget) or technology (batch versus continuous flow). This product structure is typically found in consumer goods organizations where separate divisions exist for snack foods, beverages etc.

The market structure is used to accommodate geographic spread and reach (such as domestic versus international, or regions such as Asia-Pacific, the Americas or Europe). At a time when British multinational companies were consolidating their offshore operations, the term 'Far East' was often used, betraying the companies' origins and mentality. Market structures are also used to differentiate customer segments and promote brands within those segments. Getting the right brand aligned with the right customer segment is a fundamental competency of consumer goods companies. Sometimes customer or market segments are differentiated by service standards and it is here where the impact on logistics activities is most often felt. Offering new service standards (such as overnight versus regular) can have an impact that reverberates back into the logistics chain. For example, to counteract competition from couriers, postal agencies introduced special express services and needed to introduce new processes, equipment and technology as a result.

However, any student of organizational design quickly needs to acquire a tolerance for contradictions. Scratch beneath the geographic layer of a multidomestic organization and you will find the functional structure in place in one of its regions. In recognition of the multiple structures that exist in organizations today, more and more of the debate

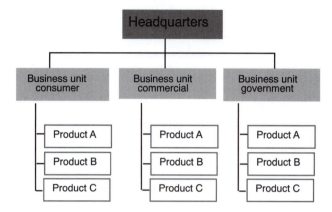

Figure 26.2   The product- or-market based structure

is centred around what goes in between the traditional boxes and lines on the organizational chart. Organizational design is not so much an architecture (of boxes, straight versus dotted lines, in functional or geographic structures) but an art (of processes, capabilities, mental models and paradigms).

Part of this move to look at what is between the boxes and bring the areas of apparent disconnection together is in response to business process reengineering activity. The process-oriented or horizontal structure has developed as the result (Figure 26.3). This is where end-to-end business processes are used to help align and focus effort. The term 'supply chain' is simply a reflection of this phenomenon.

Typically, discussions on the supply and demand chain are about how to organize horizontal, end-to-end processes that provide the glue to coordinate different functions. For example, one downstream oil company, which was organized into strategic business units (marketing, manufacturing and logistics), recognized that it was suboptimizing its supply and demand chain activities. In response, it developed cross-functional planning processes and teams to integrate demand planning more closely with the rest of its operational planning activities. In this case, the solution depended on both better functional practice, such as demand planning, and on developing more effective linkages and processes between the functions, such as creating cross-functional planning processes and teams.

These recent developments demonstrate the shortcomings in the traditional forms of organizing—specifically their capacity to handle more complex internal and external environments. In response, the organizational forms of the future will seek to accommodate and deliver greater flexibility and responsiveness.

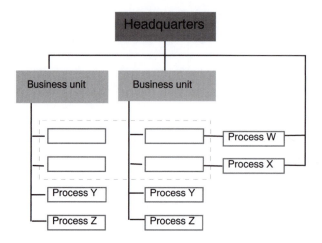

Figure 26.3　The process-based or horizontal structure

The organizational shape of the future

The organizational shapes now being adopted pick up the traditional forms and apply a new twist—that of the information age. Just as technology structures have shifted from centralized, mainframe technology to decentralized networks, so our organizations have begun to shift from head-office-dominated structures to networks of alliances, shared services or outsourced entities.

This shift is more profound than perhaps we realize. It is not just the new organizational forms which are interesting—it is that they also need to be accompanied by new behaviours (software) to be successful. Executives who have been brought up in a hard-wired, centralized mainframe, hierarchical environment are now struggling to confront the reality of decentralized, networked relationships that rely on trust, some loss of control, knowledge sharing, a 'common' culture and understanding of each other's processes and structures.

In the logistics organization this may mean moving from a relatively under-utilized and poorly regarded function (lower than manufacturing and marketing on the totem pole) to be a core, shared service for several divisions (internal network). It may mean entering into joint ventures with, or outsourcing to, third-party suppliers of specialized transport services (external network). In both internal and external networks, new skills are required of logistics personnel—a greater reliance on achieving a good chemistry fit between parties for example.

One petrochemical organization found that when outsourcing its warehousing and distribution activities and jointly investing in a greenfield facility with another firm, it required more than good project-management and financial expertise. One of the unforeseen benefits in jointly developing the business processes that would be used to manage their interactions and risks was gaining a better appreciation of each other's culture and decision-making style and, through this process, building the skills needed to make the alliance successful.

Internal network arrangement

Shared services

Shared services are where support functions and non-core processes are removed from the business units and performed by a separate internal group. Shared services typically provide transaction-processing and specialized activities. Hence key areas to focus on include:

- high-volume activities or routine transactions;
- specialized skills or expert services; and
- business process support requiring company-wide information.

What makes shared services different from the standard approach to centralization in the past is that they rely on information technology to provide many of the cost and service benefits to the businesses they are supporting and, through the use of service-level agreements, offer a method of assessing and controlling the quality of that internal service.

Logistics functions are now becoming candidates for shared service arrangements. This is a positive move, as while it puts the cost of logistics activity under the microscope it also elevates the function into a core capability, gaining more board-level attention as a result.

While the logic behind shared services is readily apparent, the reality of implementing it is often underestimated. Shared services is a visible example of the move towards greater corporate control. It requires largely independent business units to give away some of the levers of control that have enabled them to operate successfully. For managers who have prided themselves on their autonomy and being accountable only for results, 'giving up' some of these capabilities to corporate forces is often an anathema.

External network arrangements

More recently, organizations have been forced to look beyond their traditional boundaries and forge relationships and networks externally (see

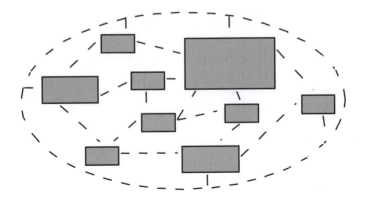

Figure 26.4   The virtual or network-based structure

Figure 26.4). This has created an 'alphabet soup' of options, including terms such as the virtual organization, outsourcing, netsourcing, co-sourcing, strategic alliances, joint ventures, spin-offs, third-party providers, fourth-party logistics. The following section provides an overview of a select few of these new organization options:

- *outsourcing*—where a company completely devolves itself of responsibility for non-core functions;
- *strategic alliance*—where an organization joins up with others to bring together the core competencies of each; and
- *spin-offs*—an innovative strategy whereby an organization manages an over-abundance of core competencies.

Several of these examples have been found in the downstream oil industry. To overcome the competitive pressures of over-supply in world and local markets, to reduce overall costs and to begin separating the respective capabilities required of refining by marketing, some of the oil majors are forming joint ventures of their manufacturing facilities to operate as a third-party supplier to their marketing arms. For an industry that has historically prided itself on having control over all aspects of its supply chain—from exploration, supply, transportation, refining, distribution and marketing—this is a significant and radical step and one that requires healthy amounts of pragmatism, superior negotiation and interpersonal skills to make it successful.

Outsourcing

While the concept of outsourcing is not new, it has been an important precursor to some of the new structures that have developed.

Outsourcing can be defined as: 'Contracting with an outside vendor to handle a function that formerly was handled internally.'

Companies have used external organizations to provide services traditionally part of the internal organization but deemed to add limited value to the company's bottom line or where the functions performed require greater levels of investment than can be provided. To mitigate risk for the outsourcer, sufficient numbers of alternative suppliers are needed. Typically, functions outsourced have been security, payroll processing, recruitment, warehousing, information processing and transportation. Supply chain activities such as warehousing and transportation have lent themselves well to outsourcing. These have long been considered as cost centres, draining both capital resources and operational cost and for which there are a range of alternative suppliers.

Traditionally the decision whether to outsource a function or functions has been based on risk versus strategic importance to the business. Companies have tended to outsource low to medium strategically important functions that are medium to low risk to the business. As the acceptance of outsourcing has grown, the services being outsourced have been developed and indeed functions have been bundled together to produce economies of scale. Instead of outsourcing security, cleaning and catering, organizations have grouped the services and had them carried out by contract facilities management, while joint warehousing and distribution activities provide logistics services. For example, organizations such as Drake and Skull Airport Services maintain many of the building and airport facilities for British Airways; Tibbet and Britton provide logistics services to Safeways, a UK retailer; and TDG provides logistics services for Lever Rexona in Australia. One of the early forms of outsourcing also occurred in the late 1980s in Australia when several downstream oil companies outsourced the property maintenance for their service station networks.

Radical variations of outsourcing have also included companies (especially in consumer goods, software and electronics) who are the overall 'deal maker'. Their model of organization is to be the organizer and integrator of a collection of specialist capabilities to deliver a product or service to a market. In this instance, it is not that the capability previously existed in-house and has now been outsourced, but that the firm never had the capability in the first place—the company is a 'virtual' corporation, a collection of third-party entities that come together for a particular purpose.

Some of the scenarios for a logistics manager are likely to include being a candidate for outsourcing (or insourcing through a shared service arrangement) or being a manager of outsourced suppliers of these services.

While many organizations have gained from the outsourcing experience by reducing cost, focusing on core competencies and providing access to additional skills and specific technologies, it has not necessarily delivered the expected cost reductions, perhaps not realizing that a new skill set is required. In addition, some organizations have found that substantial management time is required to manage the internal and external relationship effectively—or perhaps have not yet realized that managing the relationship is the job to be done!

Variations and extensions to this theme include alliances and joint ventures. These formal arrangements between two or more parties bring together knowledge, assets and capital to provide a service and revenue-gaining opportunities. An example of this is fourth-party logistics, discussed in more detail in the next chapter. Alliances and joint ventures are considered to be more flexible and to provide opportunities for revenue enhancement rather than simply cost reduction.

Strategic alliances: the attraction of opposites

Organizations use alliances to bring different core competencies together to achieve their strategic intent and mutual goals. Membership of an alliance therefore implies that one must already be excellent at something and have a value that is desirable to the alliance partner. Taking this idea further, a company is unlikely to form a successful alliance unless both parties' respective competence is of equal value, well known and acknowledged in the marketplace. The forces that drive alliances are shown in Figure 26.5.

Supply chain processes particularly lend themselves to alliance relationships. A company rarely has the capability to excel across the demand–supply continuum. Therefore alliances help acquire better relationships at the supply end of the chain and improve service to cus-

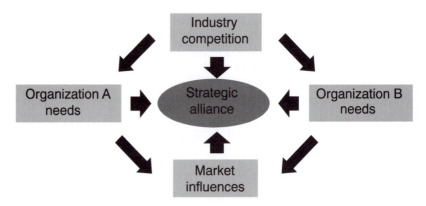

Figure 26.5   Drivers behind the formation of strategic alliances

tomers at the demand side. Typically, logistics service providers are used to improve supplier–customer relationships. Despite this intent, performance monitoring of the logistics service provider by both the supplier/customer is not widely practised and the alliance becomes more transactional/contractual in character.

There are several forms of strategic alliances. They include:

- *Networked alliances or 'promiscuous intent'*. Here several external organizations and internal business units have multiple partners. These structures are complex and difficult to manage. To be successful, they require intense levels of communication and are highly resource intensive. They are useful when wanting to 'up the ante' by shifting competition away from a company-to-company alliance towards group-to-group. These alliances are touching industries as diverse as industrial biotechnology and utilities.

- *Integrated alliances or 'serial marriages'*. This form is often used to integrate vertically or horizontally, either with suppliers and or competitors, without the capital or risk associated with mergers and acquisitions. For example, a large mass-merchandise retailer in the USA formed an alliance with a wholesaler. The two parties decided that advantages were available to them in several activities, including private-label and promotion buying, warehousing and transportation and information systems. The two organizations could then extend their supply network, reduce cost, build better relationships and work to manage the supply chain more efficiently even though they remain two separate organizations. This is achieved without the transfer of assets or employees. Horizontal alliances are visible in the airline industry where several airlines from different geographic regions have formed alliances to gain power and transfer passengers. For example, Qantas, British Airways and American Airlines have global reach through their alliance.

Companies enjoy several benefits from developing alliances. However, if they do not invest sufficient time in developing their 'compatibility' fit and really understand how the alliance is going to work in practice—for example which processes will be shared, how decisions will be made, what will be the response when business conditions or scenarios change and what culture differences between the alliance parties exist—then the process of operating the alliance can be unwieldy and time consuming and the benefits illusory.

Spin-offs and spin-outs—departures from the mother ship

Other organizations have taken more innovative approaches to the development of their business and core competencies. They have been prepared to tolerate and encourage diversity 'at the edge'. As people in the main corporation invent or develop a new market technology, service or product, an entirely new company is created in a strategy known as 'spin-out'. The name has been taken from a US-based organization called Thermo Electron.

This form is in many ways a revitalization of the early stages of divisional structures, with the role of the 'corporate office' being one of investor or portfolio manager. In Thermo Electron's case, the competitive features of its organization are derived from its leadership and culture, which is highly entrepreneurial in product and service development. To harness this and develop the business, it has sought to replicate these features and allow a large degree of individual management and control.

The spin-out strategy has also been used in reverse. Rather than wanting to replicate the leadership style and culture, spin-outs have been used to try to create something completely different from the 'mother ship'. For example, some downstream oil companies have recognized that their retail networks are competing in convenience store retail environments, which have completely different economic structures and cultures. They have sought to 'spin off' their retail business in an attempt to emulate the special skills focus and cost structures of convenience retailers, rather than those that accompany large, integrated oil companies.

Challenges arising from the new organizational shape

The network organization requires new capabilities, skills and competencies to those that have been acquired in working in traditional organizational structures (Figure 26.6). Just as the hierarchical hardware of organizational structures and shapes is being replaced with new network 'hardware', so must the accompanying 'software' of behaviour, values and assumptions about authority, work styles and practices be updated. This new 'software' consists of different approaches to human performance, cultures and knowledge sharing. In network organizations, 'getting the job done' means working with people over whom there is no direct authority, who are typically located elsewhere and work in differ-

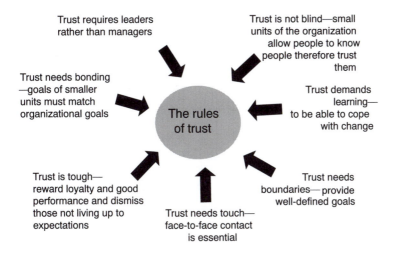

Trust requires leaders rather than managers

Trust is not blind—small units of the organization allow people to know people therefore trust them

Trust needs bonding —goals of smaller units must match organizational goals

The rules of trust

Trust demands learning— to be able to cope with change

Trust is tough— reward loyalty and good performance and dismiss those not living up to expectations

Trust needs touch— face-to-face contact is essential

Trust needs boundaries— provide well-defined goals

Source: Handy (1995)

Figure 26.6   Characteristics required to support networked organizations

ent time zones. The 'trust-based' way of working lies at the heart of making this successful.

The new organizational shape has important implications for supply chain professionals. Once they may have worked as a separate unit within a hierarchical organization where 'command and control' was the chief mode of operation. They now often need to work as part of a team with members from units across the organization, and potentially face myriad structures that have an impact on the supply chain, such as outsourcing of services, partnerships with other companies and integrated alliances. The challenge for the supply chain manager is to have a vision of how the supply can be maintained across a set of external structures and the capacity to manage the complicated set of relationships involved in a network of arrangements.

The capability and capacity of people to work (and be given sufficient discretion to work) with a high degree of autonomy and accountability is a key requirement of network organizations. This strikes at the heart of traditional 'command-and-control' management styles. Performance management systems containing stretch targets, specific performance contracts, individual- and group-based performance indicators and measures focused on outputs not inputs need to be used to act as incentives and reinforce the required behaviour to support the network form.

Figure 26.7 shows the development of organizational types, from vertical structures to deintegration through to the networked organization, and outlines the behavioural and cultural characteristics associated with each.

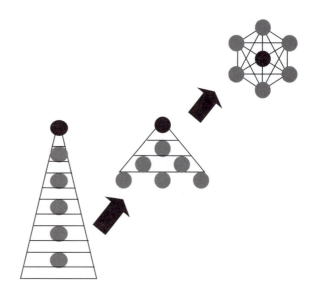

Organizational type	Centralized production	Decentralized process	Networked systems
Leadership style and control system	• Command and control hierarchy	• Efficiency and economic control	• Coordination and strategic control
Integration	• Vertically integrated	• Deintegrated	• Systems integration
Supply relationship	• Vendors	• Outsourcing	• Alliances
Size	• Large sized	• Downsized	• Logalized and globalized
Differentiation of specializations	• Functional organization	• Process organization	• Cross-function process organization
Focus for work group effectiveness	• Economies of scale	• Core competencies	• Synergetic capabilities

Source: Robert Porter-Lynch and Ian Somerville

Figure 26.7   The transition from vertical to deintegrated to network organizations

In addition, the capacity to share knowledge internally and among the parties in an alliance will be particularly important. The development of business-to-business e-commerce links makes knowledge-sharing behaviour and supporting knowledge-sharing systems a necessary component

Table 26.1
Shifts required to support knowledge sharing

From knowledge witholding	To knowledge sharing
From	To
• Power exercised by control over, and the withholding of, information	• Influence is gained by the knowledge one shares and connects people to
• Task independence	• Task interdependence
• Hierarchical and sequential pattern of formal communication	• Networked and simultaneous pattern of communication—blurring of formal and informal lines
• Concentration on knowing all there is to know	• Concentration on knowledge at point of need and use
• Skills in acquiring and holding information 'just in case'	• Skills in knowledge access, retrieval and reuse at point of need

of successful alliances and horizontal-style organizations.

However, knowledge sharing is not simply about information technology systems, electronic data interchange and data sharing—it is about managing and leveraging a strategic corporate asset. The most difficult issue is changing the organizational culture and employee behaviour from knowledge hoarding, 'knowledge is power', to knowledge sharing', 'my influence is based on who I can connect people to' across an organization. This requires significant shifts in the organization's culture, as shown in Table 26.1.

To support people in sharing and exchanging knowledge, knowledge-sharing behaviour must be part of the organization's recognition and reward system and actively monitored by its leaders. Incentives need to exist to encourage people to share, not hoard, knowledge and to contribute quality, not quantity, information, experiences and insights.

Conclusion

The 'best' organizational form is the one best able to distribute information, knowledge and capability to defend and enhance a strategic position. A variety of forms are available, all of which have their uses and advantages. Supply chain processes lend themselves to a variety of structures, including the functional, horizontal, and alliance forms. However, organizational structures are more than lines and boxes on charts, they are also the collective ability to organize and operate in a world of control and cooperation. Those working within such structures need to have significant range and flexibility of style to make them successful.

Reference

Handy, C. (1995) 'Trust and the virtual organization', *Harvard Business Review*, May/June, 40.

Porter Lynch, R. and Somerville, I. (1996) 'The shift from vertical integration to networked integration the emergence of extended healthcare enterprise', *Physician Executive Magazine*, May.

Fourth-party logistics
En route to breakthrough performance in the supply chain
John Gattorna

While outsourcing third-party logistics is now accepted business practice, fourth-party logistics is emerging as a breakthrough solution to
modern supply chain challenges. The fourth party logistics™ (4PL™)
organization incorporates the advantages of both insourcing and outsourcing to provide maximum benefit to the client organization, differing from a traditional third-party outsourcing arrangement in four main
respects:

■ the 4PL™ organization is often a separate entity established (typically) as a joint venture or long-term contract between a primary
   client and one or more partners;
■ it acts as a single interface between the client and multiple logistics
   service providers;
■ all aspects (ideally) of the client's supply chain are managed by the
   4PL™ organization; and
■ it is also possible for a major third-party logistics provider to form a
   4PL™ organzation within its existing structure.

The 4PL™ concept is not, however, a cure-all. It will only succeed if the
risks are managed appropriately and is applicable only to selected
industries.

The emergence of outsourced logistics

The outsourcing of logistics services is now accepted practice among
manufacturing companies. In the USA, logistics outsourcing has been
legitimate business practice since the 1980s. Between 1991 and 1995,
the proportion of Fortune 500 manufacturing companies making use of
third-party logistics services increased from 37 to 60 per cent (Leib,
1996; Figure 27.1).
    Services used by the large manufacturing companies have generally
been limited to six key areas: warehouse management, shipment consol-

Percentage of surveyed
Fortune 500 companies
using contract logistics

Percentage of surveyed
UK companies using
third-party warehousing

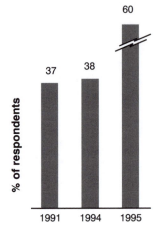

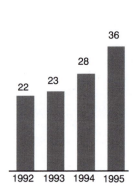

Source: Leib and Randall (1996); Harring (1996)

Figure 27.1   Use of third-party logistics providers

idation, information systems, fleet management, rate negotiation and carrier selection. Increasingly, however, key supply chain activities such as customer spare parts and inventory supply and replenishment are being outsourced to third-party providers.

With the use of contract logistics services widely accepted, the outsourced logistics market is potentially large in both developed and emerging economies. On a global basis, the market is estimated to be worth more than $900 billion per annum (Bain & Co. estimates, 1994).

Drivers of third-party logistics

The acceptance and growth of outsourced logistics services have been driven by strategic, financial and operational considerations:

Strategic factors
■ Allows senior management to focus on core competencies.
■ Improves customer service.

Financial factors
■ Reduces capital requirements.
■ Reduces supply chain costs.

Operational factors
■ Simplifies the industrial relations environment.

Allows senior management to focus on core competencies

The core competencies of an organization are the skills or knowledge bases that provide long-term, unique sources of leverage in its value chain (Quinn and Hilmer, 1994). Many companies recognize that logistics services, while ultimately critical to success, do not form the basis of competitive advantage. For example, one large Australian retail department store chain considers that its core competencies are centred on purchasing and merchandising (Andersen Consulting research). In the USA, Intel considers that its core competencies are centred around design skills and extensive test-feedback systems (Quinn and Hilmer, 1994). In these organizations, senior managers acknowledge that they can strengthen concentration on their core activities by outsourcing their logistics requirements to external parties:

> Companies are moving away from the 'lone ranger' approach to doing business. They're focusing on their core competencies and using people with expertise in non-core areas.
>
> Bill Zollars, senior vice-president, Ryder Systems (USA)

Improves customer service

Outsourcing delivery of production materials and finished goods can often increase consistent timeliness, delighting customers and enhancing a firm's reputation.

Reduces capital requirements

The assets required for an internal logistics capability are costly and can place a significant strain on the corporate balance sheet. If logistics services are outsourced, capital allocated to logistics assets can be diverted into areas in which a company can develop a sustainable competitive advantage:

> One of the main reasons we chose to outsource our transport function was to free up capital that would otherwise be tied up in a fleet of trucks.
>
> Head of logistics operations, major Australian beverage manufacturer

Reduces supply chain costs

Cost reduction is one of the most frequently cited reasons used to justify the outsourcing of logistics operations (Leib, 1996). Savings are primarily made by reducing the effective labour cost of logistics staff and by economies of scale and scope that can be realized by dedicated logistics service providers. In a US automotive firm, union-mandated warehouse labour rates were about $35 to $40 per hour. Third-party logistics (3PL) providers were able to offer the same services using free-market warehouse labour costing $10 to $14 per hour, a 60 to 70 per cent reduction in direct labour cost.

Simplifies industrial relations environment

With warehousing and transport staff typically belonging to some of the more demanding and militant unions, in-house logistics services have been a source of industrial relations turmoil, particularly in the UK and Australia. Outsourcing these services to a third-party provider potentially eliminates most of the industrial relations problems faced by a manufacturing firm in its day-to-day operations.

Drawbacks of third-party logistics

Despite the apparent attractiveness of the 3PL solution, the expected benefits have not always been fully realized. In fact, a 1994 Andersen Consulting survey of 250 organizations in the UK found that, on average, only one-third of respondents actually felt that their initial expectations of 3PL providers were being met, as shown in Figure 27.2.

At a *strategic* level, much senior management time is still required to manage the 3PL providers. Typically, no single third party is able to satisfy a firm's total corporate logistics requirements. While many third-party providers can deliver warehousing, transportation and fleet-management services, few are able to cover the full range of supply chain requirements that include services such as logistics information technology development and management, provision of pre- and post-sales customer service and order processing. This shortfall in service capabilities means that the client organization—the organization that has outsourced its logistics operations—needs to assemble a combination of in-house and outsourced service components to manage its supply chain requirements effectively. Senior management, therefore, is required to spend a disproportionate amount of time managing the web of relationships and resources required to make 3PL work.

A lack of shared goals between 3PL providers and client organiza-

Percentage of customers surveyed who felt
that their expectations were met
(by industry type)

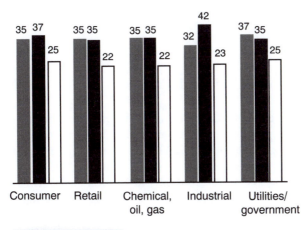

Source: 1994 Andersen Consulting Survey of 250 UK
organizations

Figure 27.2 Delivery of customers' 3PL expectations

tions usually means that *financial* gains are obtained once only, at the
time when the 3PL arrangement is established. After this initial 'honey-
moon' period, the benefits from many 3PL relationships begin to
decrease. In the worst cases clients feel that the 3PL providers are not
passing on reductions in costs, and the 3PL providers feel that the clients
are trying to cut margins 'to the bone'.

In fact, a capacity to identify and eliminate inefficiencies in all aspects
of the client supply chain through process reengineering has not been
adequately delivered by traditional third-party logistics providers.
Without this capacity, despite initial productivity and cost savings
obtained by outsourcing logistics functions, the performance of the
overall supply chain inevitably fails to keep pace with global best practice levels:

> In Australia, transport prices have been falling but we have not been able to
> reap any of the benefits.
>
> Head of logistics and operations, major beverage manufacturer

In the *operational* sphere, the client's desire to 'outsource' the associated industrial relations problems has not always been achieved. While management of the problems may have moved from the client organization to the third-party provider, nevertheless the disruption to service levels and potential cost increases continue to be experienced by the client organization and its customers.

The fourth party logistics™ solution

Given the problems inherent in traditional third-party logistics arrangements, a new organizational form has evolved which, to a great extent, overcomes these problems and enables clients to achieve significant, sustainable improvements across their supply chain.

The 4PL™ organization represents a solution that incorporates the advantages of both outsourcing and insourcing to provide maximum overall benefit.

The advantages of logistics outsourcing have already been discussed: reduced senior management time required on non-core activities, improved customer service, financial benefits and simplifying of the industrial relations environment.

Logistics insourcing also has its advantages. If the client performs all logistics operations internally, it is able to maintain and grow its logistics skills within the organization, retain control over customer service levels and logistics costs and maintain the vital interface with its customers.

The 4PL™ organization is one of the intermediate stages along the logistics sourcing spectrum (Figure 27.3) that combines the benefits of outsourcing and insourcing. It differs from traditional 3PL arrangements in four main respects:

■ the 4PL™ organization is often a separate entity established (typically) as a joint venture or long-term contract between a primary client and one or more partners;
■ it acts as a single interface between the client and multiple logistics service providers;
■ all aspects (ideally) of the client's supply chain are managed by the 4PL™ organization; and
■ it is also possible for a major third-party logistics provider to form a 4PL™ organization within its existing structure.

4PL™ organization: set-up

The 4PL™ organization is most often a separate management company whose role is to provide logistics services to a few primary client(s) and,

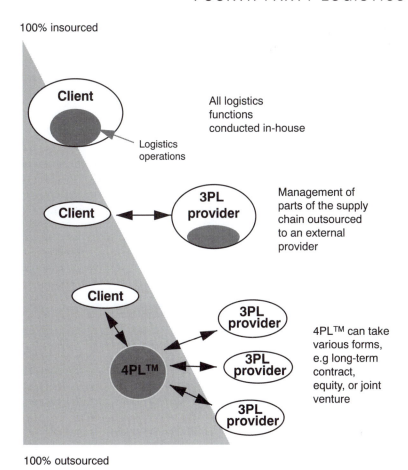

100% insourced

Client

Logistics
operations

All logistics
functions
conducted in-house

Client ↔ 3PL provider

Management of
parts of the supply
chain outsourced
to an external
provider

Client

4PL™ ↔ 3PL provider

4PL™ ↔ 3PL provider

4PL™ ↔ 3PL provider

4PL™ can take
various forms,
e.g long-term
contract,
equity, or joint
venture

100% outsourced

Figure 27.3   Logistics sourcing spectrum

at a later stage, to a few other clients in the same or related industries. It is usually established as a joint venture or long-term contract between at least two parties, consisting of the primary client(s) and at least one other partner, which contribute the start-up capital for the venture and also provide assets and expertise for ongoing operations (see Figure 27.4).

The 'primary client' is so named to reflect its two roles—it is simultaneously a 4PL™ organization partner and a client to the 4PL™ organization. Besides contributing capital, typically the primary client also sells its entire logistics and procurement operations, consisting of assets and logistics management and operational staff, to the 4PL™ organization. The 4PL™ organization, in return for a fee, is charged with the responsibility for managing and operating logistics and procurement functions across the client's entire supply chain.

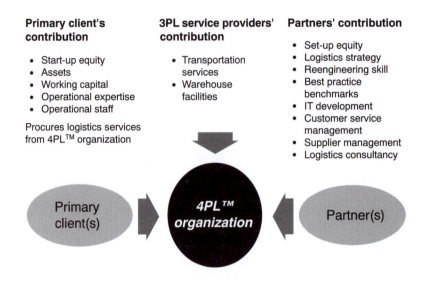

Primary client's contribution

- Start-up equity
- Assets
- Working capital
- Operational expertise
- Operational staff

Procures logistics services from 4PL™ organization

3PL service providers' contribution

- Transportation services
- Warehouse facilities

Partners' contribution

- Set-up equity
- Logistics strategy
- Reengineering skill
- Best practice benchmarks
- IT development
- Customer service management
- Supplier management
- Logistics consultancy

Primary client(s) → 4PL™ organization ← Partner(s)

Key characteristics

- Hybrid organization—formed from a number of different entities
- Typically established as a JV or long-term contract
- Alignment of goals of partners and clients through profit sharing.
- Responsible for management and operation of entire supply chain
- Continual flow of information between partners and 4PL™ organization
- Potential for revenue generation

Figure 27.4   4PL™: Set-up

For two principal reasons, a 4PL™ operation is likely to achieve a greater level of success and acceptance if it is established with at least two primary clients. First, scale and scope benefits are established from the outset. Secondly, the venture is immediately perceived as being an independent entity. Non-alignment with a particular client organization makes the 4PL™ organization a more attractive proposition to potential non-equity-holding clients and increases the prospect of its quickly establishing a significant external client base.

Evidence from existing 4PL™ ventures suggests that an independent image is essential to attract non-equity clients to use their services. Having at least two primary equity partners establishes this independent image in the minds of potential non-equity clients. For example, a 4PL™ organization was established by a major utility company in the UK to provide procurement and logistics services to itself as the primary client, then to other non-equity clients in the industry. Limited success has been achieved to date selling services to non-equity clients. With competition in the marketplace being extremely strong, potential non-equity clients are reluctant to purchase services from the 4PL™ organization as they doubt its independence and fear that using its services will overly assist the primary client, who is also their main competitor.

4PL™ organization: operations

The 4PL™ organization is a supply chain integrator. To its clients, it differentiates itself from other 3PL service providers by acting as the single interface between clients and the full scope of supply chain services. The 4PL™ organization delivers supply chain management services from its own internal staff and contracts the services of external logistics service providers as required (Figure 27.5).

It is staffed with the best skills from the founding partners. With logistics excellence as its core competence, all 4PL™ operations are best practice and are regularly assessed against global benchmarks, developing a strong culture of continuous improvement.

4PL™ organization: model variations

The 4PL™ concept is a flexible model that can be adapted to include different partner organizations according to its charter and objectives, which in turn are shaped by industry structure and conduct.

Industry solution model

As an example (Figure 27.6), the UK pharmaceutical industry consists of a large number of relatively small manufacturers, each with independent distribution operations, resulting in a high degree of duplication of distribution operations within the industry. There is an opportunity for consolidating the distribution operations of a number of manufacturers within the industry, with the view to realizing substantial cost savings.

The 'industry solution' model comprises a 4PL™ organization whose role is to coordinate and manage the distribution operations of its primary clients initially, and then those of other pharmaceutical companies within the industry. The proposed structure of the arrangement is a joint venture between three major UK pharmaceutical companies in the role

Clients (limited in number)

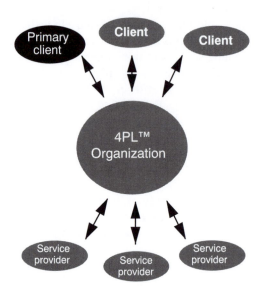

External service providers

Key characteristics

- Single interface between client and service providers
- Manages performance of 3PL service providers to achieve continuous improvement
- Actively benchmarks against world's best practice
- Maintains leading-edge logistics technology and processes

Figure 27.5 4PL™: Operations

of primary clients; a major 3PL provider to perform the logistics operations; and a supply chain management consulting firm to manage operations.

Total savings from this 4PL™ arrangement are estimated at 39 per cent per annum, resulting from consolidating the shipment activities of the three primary clients, greater efficiencies from the increased scale of operations and implementation of best-practice processes.

Pharmaceutical
products
manufacturers

Service
providers

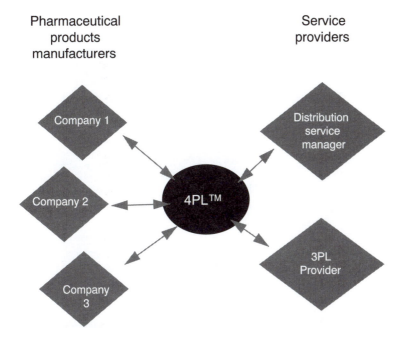

Figure 27.6   Industry solution: pharmaceutical industry

Supply chain partners

The 'supply chain partners' model comprises a 4PL™ organization in the beverage-manufacturing industry, established with the objective of managing an integrated industry supply chain (Figure 27.7). The proposed parties to the venture consist of two beverage manufacturers, two key packaging materials suppliers, a 3PL provider and a supply chain management consulting firm to manage the 4PL™ operations.

The 4PL™ organization provides supply chain management, inbound and outbound transport, warehousing and materials-management services initially to its primary clients, and later to other beverage manufacturing companies. Benefits consist of savings from improved rates for goods and services enabled by the increased scale of combined purchasing, and improved efficiencies brought about by greater integration of operations across the supply chain.

A 4PL™ arrangement will address most of the problems experienced by users of 3PL services and provide some important additional benefits.

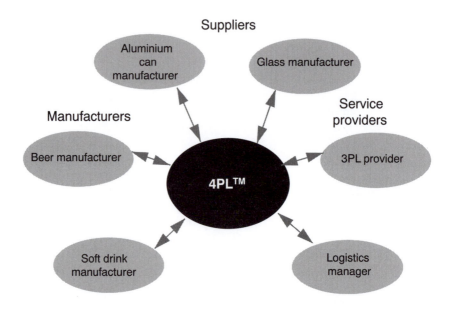

Figure 27.7 Supply chain partners: beverage manufacturing industry

Addresses strategic failures

Time and effort spent by senior management within the client organization(s) to manage supply chain activities are kept to a minimum. The 4PL™ organization is a single point of contact with which the client chief logistics officer can deal to manage all aspects of the client supply chain. Management of multiple logistics service providers is handled by the 4PL™ organization.

A 4PL™ arrangement addresses the shortcoming of typical 3PL providers that deliver competent transportation and warehousing services, but do not have the skills required to provide broader supply chain services, such as information technology development and management or supply chain integration strategies. By sourcing specialists from a number of organizations to provide 'best of breed' capabilities across the entire supply chain, the 4PL™ organization provides an entire suite of world-class supply chain management services through a single point of contact.

Addresses financial failures

Capital within the client organization can be freed for more productive uses by selling the clients logistics assets, either to the 4PL™ organization or on the free market. By ensuring that common goals are established between all parties in the 4PL™ organization, actions taken by individual parties are aimed at reducing the overall cost of managing the supply chain and improving the service delivered to internal and external customers.

Processes and performance of the 4PL™ organization are continuously monitored and improved to minimize supply chain costs. Individual processes are benchmarked against global industry and process peers and process reengineering is undertaken as required to ensure that best-practice levels are maintained. Service-level agreements between the parties are modified periodically to ensure that appropriate levels of service are delivered to customers and all parties receive appropriate benefits.

The 4PL™ organization can draw as required on deep cross-border and cross-industry functional expertise possessed by the partner organizations in the venture. This expertise includes, but is not limited to, supply chain design and reengineering skills, IT systems design, value chain planning systems and implementation experience. This 'intelligence' at the core of the 4PL™ organization is one of the main benefits inherent in this solution.

Addresses operational failures

Establishing a new entity creates new opportunities for the client organization to address old industrial relations issues. The client organization is able to transfer personnel selectively into the 4PL™ organization and reduce labour requirements, without having to encounter typical union disruptions. In establishing the new workforce, the client organization has an opportunity to negotiate flexible and more relevant wage structures and escape antiquated union agreements. In fact, in some cases the 4PL™ organization may operate with non-unionized labour. A new entity allows the creation of a totally new culture, 'cutting loose' the anti-competitive practices that may previously have existed.

Additional benefits of the 4PL™ organization

In addition to addressing the failures of 3PL organizations, the 4PL™ solution can deliver unique benefits resulting from the nature of the new organization.

Revenue opportunities can be realized by selling the supply chain

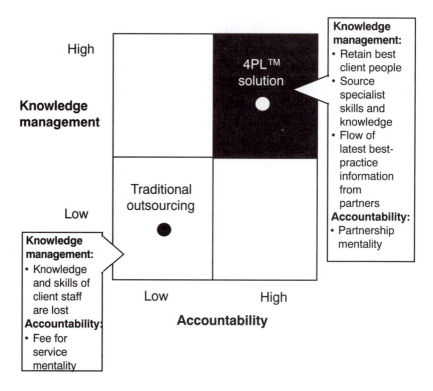

Figure 27.8   Knowledge management and accountability

services provided by the 4PL™ organization to external clients. The revenues from providing these services would be shared between participants in the venture in proportion to their stakeholding. Selling services to external clients also increase the economies of scale that can be realized by the venture, further reducing overall net supply chain costs.

The 4PL™ organization enables the primary client organization to retain corporate supply chain knowledge and accountability for results (Figure 27.8).

Knowledge management is defined as bringing together and effectively sharing knowledge capital among identified stakeholders. Accountability is defined as taking responsibility for achieving desired performance or outcomes. A 4PL™ arrangement enables a high degree of knowledge management and accountability when compared with traditional outsourcing.

Supply chain management knowledge is maintained within the founding partners by retaining the best internal people to staff the 4PL™ organization. This knowledge pool is constantly updated by ensuring an active flow of information between these partners and the 4PL™ organization.

Accountability is high in the 4PL™ arrangement as the organization requires a partnership mindset and is guided by clear performance targets. This is contrasted with a traditional 3PL arrangement where client organizations will transfer accountability for maintaining supply chain performance to the 3PL provider.

Risk management and careful industry selection

Successful implementation of a 4PL™ organization requires a clear understanding of establishment and operations risks and of the industries within which a 4PL™ arrangement will deliver the maximum benefit.

Establishment phase risks

As stated earlier, it is preferable to establish the 4PL™ organization with at least two primary clients. However, there is a risk that it may be difficult to convince a potential primary client to cooperate with one of its competitors (the originating primary client) to form the 4PL™ venture. The approach to managing this risk is to communicate clearly the independent stance of the venture to the potential partner. It will be necessary to establish procedures that serve as a 'firewall', effectively separating information between competing client organizations so that no confidential information can be accessed by any clients of the 4PL™ organization.

Another factor which may prevent a potential primary client from taking part in the venture is the existence of long-term contracts with 3PL providers. The cost of switching to another logistics service arrangement may be perceived as prohibitively high by the potential primary client, as it would not only include penalty costs in breaking the long-term contract but also an initial drop in efficiency of logistics operations as the new service provider grew accustomed to its operations and invested time to establish a good working relationship with the relevant personnel within the 4PL™ organization. This risk can be managed by determining 3PL commitments at the earliest possible stage of potential partner assessment, so that they are a key consideration in identifying the most suitable partners. It may even be advantageous to include the 3PL provider as a partner in the 4PL™, as it may also be able to fill any gaps in the operational expertise or assets of the 4PL™ venture.

Industries are constantly undergoing change. As such, there is a risk that changing industry dynamics may make obsolete all or some of the services that the 4PL™ organization originally provides. To address this risk, an assessment must be made of the long-term viability of the 4PL™ organization through scenario planning for the clients and industries in question. It should then be structured so that it retains the ability to change the nature and mix of service providers to the venture as the nature of the industry or supply chain also changes.

Once the contractual arrangements for the 4PL™ organization have been established, and operations are on the verge of being transferred to it, there is a risk of excessive disruption to the client's existing business which may have a negative impact on performance. To mitigate this risk, a detailed transition plan must be developed up-front which will include initiatives to communicate the change being undertaken and appropriate procedures to move client personnel into their new roles in the 4PL™ organization.

Risks during the operational phase

The 4PL™ organization may not be able to attract external clients to the venture on a revenue-paying basis. This can arise due to a reluctance by competitors of the primary client to engage in transactions that may be perceived to be beneficial to a competitor. To prevent this situation, the organization must be perceived to be an independent entity. This can be achieved by ensuring that there are at least two primary founding clients in the 4PL™ organization.

Industry applicability

Several attributes have been identified which characterize industries and companies suited to a 4PL™ venture: low industry concentration, small margins, companies that consider logistics as a non-core competency and companies with multiple business units.

Wherever there is low industry concentration, there are a large number of small, independent players. They are likely to have minimal scale benefits in their supply chain operations. Significant opportunities exist to consolidate the operations of a number of players to exploit scale economies. Consumer electronics and pharmaceuticals are two examples of this type of industry.

Where companies are currently experiencing small margins, they are likely actively to be seeking profit-enhancing opportunities. Most 'obvious' cost-reduction opportunities, such as reducing the size of administration areas, will probably already have been exploited. Further cost reduction by focusing on the corporate supply chain through a 4PL™ arrangement may therefore be readily accepted by the executive group.

These companies are also more likely to be committed to following through with the large-scale changes required to bring about the 4PL™ organization, increasing the likelihood of success. Examples of these low-margin industries include downstream oil processing and large-scale consumer retail.

Companies for which logistics is not a core competency will welcome the opportunity to outsource logistics to a high-performing operator. Public (or newly privatized) utility companies have been identified where the logistics associated with spare parts and maintenance would not be classified as a core competency.

Companies with multiple business units are able to benefit from the economies of scope that shared 4PL™ services deliver across the entire organization. Examples of these types of organizations have been identified in food-processing companies where multiple business units often have similar supply chain requirements.

Conclusion

A 4PL™ concept addresses the shortfalls of traditional 3PL arrangements and offers the opportunity to achieve substantial incremental benefits. In addition, the concept can be extended to an existing 3PL, converting it into a 4PL™.

A major Australian downstream oil company

CASE STUDY

Company A was a major Australian downstream oil company which, along with its industry competitors, had been experiencing declining profitability for the previous few years as a result of industry deregulation. As the threat of increased competition loomed larger, and forecasts of future profits remained low, Company A sought a new business model for its supply and distribution business that would enable it to achieve a sustainable breakthrough in performance.

The 4PL™ solution

Company A selected a 4PL™ arrangement that involved forming an equity joint venture in which the main equity holders consisted of itself, another major downstream oil company and two third-party transport providers to offer logistics services, first to the two oil companies and then to other companies within the same or related industries (Figure 27.9).

The 4PL™ venture was to be responsible for managing and performing deliveries to most customer segments, including customers for bulk fuels and lubricants, solvents, C-store products, bitumen, LPG and aviation fuel.

The arrangement was structured with the two major oil companies contributing equal majority equity capital and the two major third-party service providers contributing equal but minority capital. The rest of the equity was to be owned by minor service providers and the employees of the company.

At set up, there was to be a total of about 600 staff within the 4PL™ organization consisting of about 30 managerial staff, mostly from the two major oil companies, and around 570 operational staff, consisting of drivers from the two major oil companies and the two third-party transport providers.

The assets of the 4PL™ organization consisted primarily of the trucks that were purchased from the two major oil companies and the two third-party transport providers.

The organization was responsible for managing deliveries to all customers. This involved managing its own staff who would perform deliveries for some customer types based on demand and location requirements, and managing third-party providers who would carry out deliveries for other customer types. The original supply chain costs of the company are illustrated in Figure 27.10.

Owing to existing initiatives that had commenced prior to the start of the 4PL™ exercise, only 70 per cent of total supply chain costs were within its scope.

By establishing the 4PL™ venture, the oil company identified that it could reduce its annual supply chain spend by 26 per cent (Figure 27.11). The main source of benefits arising from the arrangement came from synergies created by combining the operations of the two major oil companies and savings from centralizing distribution of C-store products. Synergies from combined distribution operations resulted from greater purchasing power when negotiating rates with third-party transport providers and the ability to optimize routing across the combined network. Savings from centralized distribution of C-store products arose from moving away from direct-to-store supplier deliveries to having suppliers deliver to a central warehouse and outsourcing deliveries to stores from the central warehouse.

Further benefits were identified through offering logistics services to other clients. This was estimated as an equivalent of 3 per cent of operating costs which would be accrued to Company A, in the form of dividends from the 4PL™ organization.

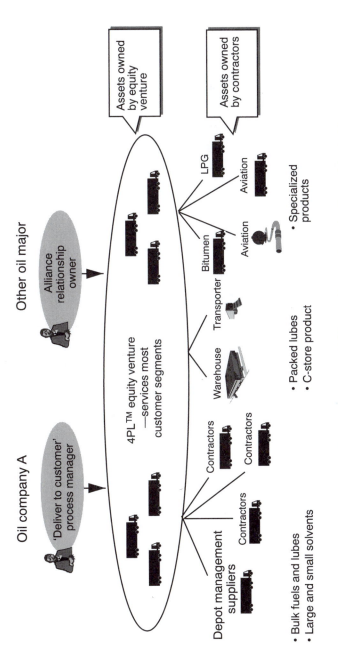

Figure 27.9 Example of a 4PL™ equity venture in the oil industry

Percentage of total supply chain expenditure

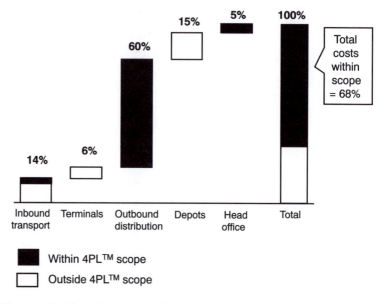

Figure 27.10   Company A's current supply chain costs

Percentage of 'within scope' supply chain costs

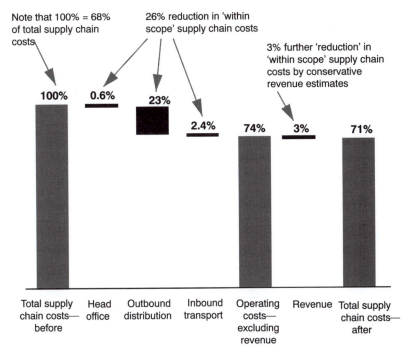

Figure 27.11   Supply chain savings

References

4PL™ is a registered trademark of Andersen Consulting.

Harring (1996) 'Special report on contract logistics: unlock profits', *Transport and Distribution*, 1 Sept.

Leib, R.C. and Randall, H.L. (1996) 'A comparison of the use of third party logistics services by large American manufacturers, 1991, 1994 and 1995', *Journal of Business Logistics*, 17 (1), 305–20.

Quinn, J.B. and Hilmer, F.G. (1994) 'Strategic outsourcing', *Sloan Management Review*, 35 (4), Summer, 43–55.

The dynamics of change in the supply chain

Translating supply chain strategies into action

Robert Easton, Robyn Brown and Duncan Armitage

In the search for supply chain excellence beyond the year 2000, managers are developing new strategies to improve supply chain performance. While these strategies may have voluminous detail about the supply chain operations, they often neglect to focus on a key factor for success: managing change itself. Successful change requires careful planning to ensure that the behaviour of people 'fits' with the behaviour of the market, products, systems and the supply chain itself; that is, to align culture with strategy. Four factors are keys to managing change: recognizing the pressure for change, enunciating and sharing a clear vision, having the capacity for change and, finally, taking a series of first steps to embed the change. No supply chain strategy can succeed without managing people and their response.

Introduction

Managing change has been compared with attempting to change a Boeing 727 into a Boeing 747 in mid-flight. On the one hand, the change seems worth the trouble, because the 747 will be a more effective transport vehicle. On the other hand, there will be a point where the craft is neither a 727 nor a 747 and the whole thing could crash. For supply chain professionals change is inevitable as current paradigms are tested and retested to attempt to attain excellence. Yet few will argue that translating supply chain strategies into action is often more difficult and less successful than was initially anticipated. Indeed, many initiatives to implement a new supply chain strategy either fail or fall short of expectations. A key reason for this is that supply chain professionals neglect the behavioural element: they pay insufficient attention to managing resistance and to reskilling and developing people to operate in the new environment. In significant change, they do not ensure that the culture of the group of people concerned matches the new strategy.

While these problems are inherent in change management in general, they are exacerbated in managing supply chain change. Clearly, for most

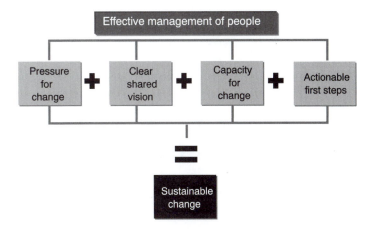

**Figure 28.1   A framework for fast and effective
management of change**

organizations, implementing a new supply chain strategy spanning
material and product flow from vendors to final consumption, across an
array of different organizations or functional groups, is a complex and
awesome task. Somehow over the months and years following the definition of a supply chain strategy a range of changes are required.
Employees must do different things, make different decisions and perform in different ways. New networks of suppliers, manufacturers, distributors and customers will have to be forged. Customers will need to
understand the benefits of the new services and pricing; suppliers will
have to react with their own change process; alliance partners will need
to share the same vision. New infrastructure across these networks must
be built or reconfigured including computer systems, distribution centres, factories and support organizations. To make matters more challenging, this must all be achieved in a framework of continuous
operations—systems cannot be shut down while we remodel!

For many supply chain professionals who are used to dealing with
concrete things like facilities and systems, dealing with the complex
behavioural aspects of change—that is, how to manage change through
people—does not come easy. This chapter sets out to respond to this
need by providing a framework which outlines the critical path to fast
and effective change management. While no single path holds in all situations, our research and years of case experience indicates that there
are four prerequisites to fast and effective change management (see
Figure 28.1). Although each of the prerequisites can be examined individually they are mutually supporting so, as Hewlett-Packard clearly
found during its change initiatives to outsource logistics in Asia Pacific
(see Figure 28.2), if any one element is missing, change is likely to fail.

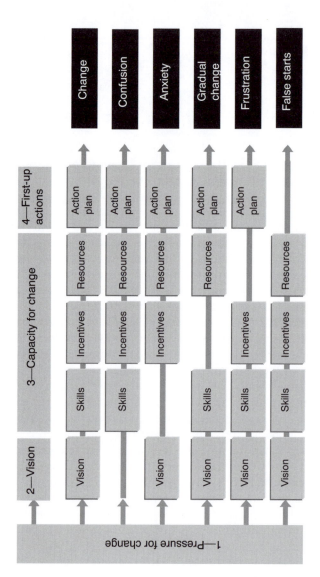

Source: HP way, Barry Newland, May 1997

Figure 28.2 The four prerequisites for change in the context of the HP 'outsourcing' way: change attributes

A governing thought underpinning this chapter and one encapsulated in Figures 28.1 and 28.2 is that change management is about building business success through managing people and it is people who in the end provide the critical path to effective and sustainable strategic change. This chapter points out that for successful change, pragmatic logisticians will have to move beyond proficiency in the hard areas of cost, time, benefits and quality to become proficient at managing stakeholders and their emotions, team building, communicating, commitment building, risk management and people development.

Prerequisite one—pressure for change

Pressure for change is the first prerequisite for successful change. The most successful change programmes begin when there is a compelling need or pressure that provides the incentive and motivation for change. To be effective the pressure must be well documented and researched and must convince virtually everyone in the organization. In successful change programmes the pressure for change comes from a rigorous analysis of customer needs, the company's competitive situation, its market position, financial performance, identification of the barriers to be overcome and the potential payoffs. This analysis is then communicated dramatically, often in terms of organizational survival or continued effectiveness, to convince managers and employees alike that change is imperative and desirable, and not a management ploy to downsize or restructure. The importance of pressure for change has even led some companies to generate the pressure for change by manufacturing a crisis.

The pressure for change, therefore, is an essential precondition to successful change because it provides the basis for inspiring cooperation and motivation and for pushing people out of their comfort zones, without which the programme will go nowhere. Since supply chain change spans inter- and intra-organizational boundaries, inspiring and motivating the various stakeholders is difficult and demands that the voice of the customer be injected into the pressure for change from the outset. The voice of the customer proves a powerful force in encouraging discrete elements of the supply chain, regardless of their different priorities and goals, to cooperate fully in bringing about change.

Prerequisite two—clear vision for change

The second prerequisite for change is a clear vision. Many change programmes that fail are characterized by plenty of plans and directives (in some cases, pages and pages of detail) but no clear compelling statement that communicates the goal sought and the mandate for change. Where a vision does exist it is often blurred, complicated or not market focused. Under these conditions a great deal of unfocused activity occurs with little movement towards the change objectives, both of which result in increased costs and little impact. If different managers or stakeholders have varying perceptions of the required result then the expected benefits will not be achieved. For example, in one major consumer products company, senior management set the goal of achieving competitive advantage from a finished goods logistics strategy. A newly recruited senior logistics manager, however, focused initial project activities on cost reduction within his function. This, combined with a lack of appreciation among sales managers of the role that logistics has in creating profitable customer relationships, stalled the change process. At the time of writing, this company was projecting greater cost reductions than those planned in the strategy, but will not achieve the initial goal of competitive advantage without revisiting the entire strategic-development process. In this example the incomplete vision statement resulted in managers having an inconsistent understanding of the change goal.

A clear and concise statement of the goal of the change programme, stated in customer-focused terms, which amplifies the voice of the customer, provides the essential means to harness and focus the energy of the organization in pursuit of that goal. From our experience a good vision for change should be expressed both in terms of the things the organization needs to do and in terms of the things individuals need to do to meet the customers' needs.

Prerequisite three—capacity for change

Capacity for change is the third prerequisite. As Figure 28.3 shows, the link between a clear, shared vision with commitment to change and the organizational and individual capacity for change is compelling. Despite having a great commitment, many change programmes fail because the organization lacked the necessary capacity to change. This capacity is derived from redesigning the organizational structure, jobs and performance measures to enable new performance and changed behaviours to occur; systematically and methodically training and developing staff to attain the required skills and behaviours in the new environment; and creating organizational slack or some temporary reduction in performance standards while the organization moves through the transition. Successful change necessitates generating and harnessing increased energy to keep the organization performing while its capacity for the new environment is being developed. This creates the need for building and fostering high-performing change teams, a need which receives particular emphasis during supply chain change owing to the necessity to span many boundaries.

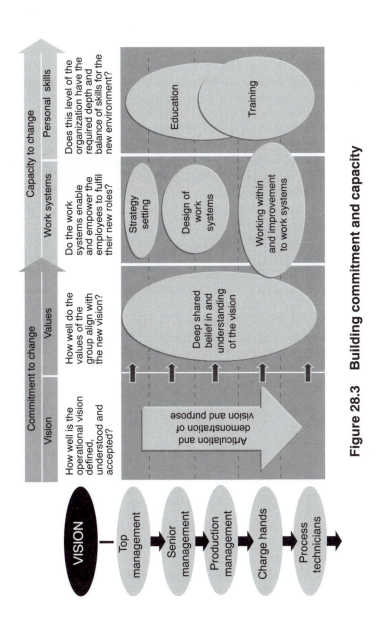

Figure 28.3   Building commitment and capacity

Of course, even though the pressure for change may be evident and a clear vision for change communicated, high levels of frustration and anxiety will occur if the capacity to undertake the change does not exist. People who know what is required and why will begin focusing their energy on making the changes asked of them, but will be frustrated by the lack of capacity to change, be it a lack of skill—both change management (group facilitation, communication and leadership) and technical job skills—or appropriately defined accountabilities and responsibilities, or simply a lack of respite in existing business demands.

Within the context of supply chain change, recognizing the company's capacity for change is essential as numerous project initiatives will compete for limited resources and different stakeholders will have different opinions about the priority of each initiative. Pareto's law is an immutable truth when applied to supply chain change; that is, in general, 80 per cent of the major gains or changes sought will result from 20 per cent of the initiatives. Failure to establish and clearly communicate priorities, which are within the organization's capacity to achieve, early in the change process is a recipe for disaster. For success, the change journey must be broken down into manageable phases, each planned in detail and each asking only what is within the capacity of the company to deliver. Following this formula will ensure that change initiatives can be realized step by step, as the capacity for change is increased through organizational redesign, training and development, reskilling and creation of organizational slack.

Throughout the change programme, finding the right balance between what we set out to do and what the organization is capable of is not easy and will require refinement. If too much is asked, the plan may fail and attract cynicism towards future projects. Yet if the scope is too limited, success may not matter because little is accomplished. Remember, success breeds success. Where resistance to change is high, early small successes will enable the company incrementally to expand the content and pace of change to match capacity until the end goal is achieved.

Prerequisite four—first-up actions

The final reason that change programmes fail is because they do not carry out the essential actions required to direct the efforts of people. Unless the workforce is skilled, motivated and organized for the new environment and there is focus on integrating change in the human, technology and process areas, it is unlikely that intended business results will be delivered. The essential first-up actions are listed below:

■ Align culture with strategic response.
■ Appoint a process owner.
■ Reshape performance measures.
■ Develop and train the workforce.
■ Communicate and demonstrate top management commitment.
■ Involve stakeholders and gain commitment to change.
■ Implement a system to track benefits.
■ Communicate with all stakeholders.
■ Create an integration map.

Action 1—Align culture with strategic response

Supply chain organizations should be designed to meet the requirements of the market they face. That is, organizational design should start from the customer and move back towards the chief executive officer (CEO). The supply chain should be organized around a few key processes, such as order fulfilment, to ensure that the goals and plans of all related functions are aligned with customer service requirements. The notion of strategic alignment and the creation of market-based organizations has been discussed in previous chapters, but the importance of culture in the context of managing change demands detailed examination. Many managers complain that their change programme failed because 'culture' got in the way. But what is 'culture' and how can it influence success in change programmes?

In simple terms organizational culture means the shared values, beliefs and norms in an organization which tend to evolve and persist over time and influence individual and group behaviour patterns. In other words, culture guides the way things are done within an organization in the same manner in which a person's cultural background guides the way they behave and act. Culture provides the internal fabric to deliver the business strategy. When mapped and understood, it can be a predictor of the likely success of implementing a strategy. Both research and case evidence are conclusive on one thing: regardless of the strength of the logic for a strategic response, change is unlikely to be achieved unless there is alignment with the corporate culture. Indeed, logic will count for little if aspects of the existing culture are misaligned with and work directly against the change.

Achieving alignment, however, is a complex process. All the time the alignment is being sought, customers in the market are changing their behaviour, the corporation is trying to change its strategy, the different subcultures are resisting the change and managers and leaders in the firm are trying to respond. For the supply chain professional attempting change across a number of cross-functional and cross-organizational or network interfaces, the complexities that arise in achieving cultural alignment are magnified many times. Of course, perfect alignment is an ideal state which is continually sought but rarely achieved. The key task for the change manager is to understand and manage the inter-dependencies that exist between the situation, strategy, culture and leadership style in implementing change. Achieving closer alignment between them will always result in more effective performance than if no actions are taken.

The strength of culture also plays a significant part in this relationship. If we accept that culture drives behaviour and decisions, then inevitably it is the key driver of organizational performance. In a 'weak' organization, there is a distinct lack of awareness of, and identification with, the mission. There is a lack of clarity and commitment about what the organization is about. Rather than empowering employees through a sense of shared values, strategic initiatives are imposed through rules, methods, policies and procedures. In large companies with 'weak' cultures the structures and systems necessary to implement and monitor strategy through imposed rules and controls invariably creates a conservative and unresponsive bureaucracy. On the other hand, evidence suggests that strong cultures, such as Procter & Gamble, Coca-Cola, IBM, Honda and Toyota, excel at implementing strategic plans. Nevertheless, a US study of cultures in 207 companies by Kotter and Heskett (1991) found that 'strong cultures with practices that do not fit the company's context can actually lead intelligent people to behave in ways that are destructive—that systematically undermine an organization's ability to survive and prosper'. Scholz (1987) argued that the stronger corporate culture is, 'the more it limits the feasible space for strategy decisions'. A strong culture with good fit will propel the company to higher levels of performance, but a strong culture with poor fit will often lead it well away from where it wants to be.

Culture has profound implications for achieving a new supply chain response, but in many ways it is like an iceberg. Above the surface lies only the tip of the iceberg: the rules, structures, behaviour patterns, rituals and style are relatively easily changed. But nothing could be further from the truth, because just as the bulk of an iceberg lies beneath the surface so too the real essence or core of the company's culture lies hidden.

Attitudes, values, beliefs and assumptions about the company underlie the observable behaviours and structures. The invisibility of these underlying variables means that their decisive impact on how the organization thinks and behaves is often not even considered in the process of undertaking a strategic initiative, yet they act as an invisible barrier to change. For example, a beverage company was attempting to introduce new processes and tools for the route managers to capture vital information quickly on competitors. New personal computers were bought, software developed and the managers were all trained—but many of the managers failed to use the tool. Why? Because there was a strong 'local ownership' culture in each region that rejected head office involvement in activities.

This was reinforced by clear regional management performance objectives which management failed to adjust to reflect the way this additional data would be used for corporate decision making. A strategic competitive weapon—vital competitor information—was never deployed as the existing culture was stronger than the change project. Clearly, as this example shows, culture at all levels must change.

The larger and more diverse or complex an organization, the more difficult changing the culture will be. The complexity of supply chain change requires an array of intra- and inter-organizational subcultures to be considered and brought into alignment along the supply chain. Each of the subcultures will have differing goals, priorities, beliefs, standards and values driving behaviour. Areas of clashes or inconsistency will have to be negotiated, although working through fundamental differences takes time and energy. In the context of supply chain change, an intermediary, such as another channel member, may be used to bring differing cultures into alignment, just like a transformer or adapter is used in electrical engineering to change the voltage of alternating currents.

In one simple example, a wines and spirits wholesaler was used as the mechanism to align the diverse cultures of a large Australian beverage manufacturer with that of a major customer group of restaurants. The manufacturer was dominated by an administrative culture characterized by systems, quality and consistency, and the restaurant group's driving culture gave primacy to productivity and action tempered by systems and stability. The restaurants wanted frequent deliveries of small, mixed cases and 30-day terms; the manufacturer was geared to weekly deliveries of pallet-size loads and seven-day terms. Rather than asking either party to undergo a significant cultural shift, a wines and spirits merchant/wholesaler was engaged to act as an 'adapter' or switching mechanism in the system, to interface at one end with the manufacturer's systems, but then to reshape the offering to match the restaurant's lesser systems capabilities.

The solution in this example portrays a particular paradigm and contradicts the belief held by some that strategic fit or alignment means creating one culture across the supply chain. Advocates of this approach believe that where necessary parties across the supply chain should make significant cultural shifts in pursuit of one unifying and homogenous culture. Research, however, shows that companies with strong cultures with homogeneity across departments are low performers in the long run. Joanne Martin of Stanford University (1992) has warned that shaping culture into unity can leave the organization stuck in the status quo, unable to make needed changes. According to Hilmer and Donaldson (1996):

> Effective organizations foster distinct subcultures so that differences are
> respected and can flourish. They foster communication and collaboration

Table 28.1
The four logics

Logic		Means	Outputs	Associated phenomena
Production	(P)	Action	Results	Objectives, goals, energy
Administration	(A)	Control	Order	Systems, measurement, stability
Development	(D)	Create	Change	Innovation, creativity, discontinuity
Integration	(I)	Integrate	Cohesion	Synergy, teamwork, cooperation

among subcultures so that differences between them remain intact ... successful corporations—especially if innovative, large, and diverse—have anything but a unified corporate culture ... attempts to impose a unifying culture other than at the most general level would be counterproductive.

These findings are consistent with years of research and experience by John Gattorna and associates (1990, 1991, 1992) who found that each of the four forces (competitive situation, strategy, culture and leadership style) has its own behavioural 'logics'. In Gattorna's model, the 'logics' are characterized by a behavioural orientation to one of four main activities: production, administration, development or integration (Table 28.1). Change effectiveness is likely to be optimal when all four logics in the four forces are aligned (complement or bear a close similarity to each other), as illustrated in Figure 28.4. For example, change effectiveness would be optimized when an organization responds to a predominantly competitive (P) environment with an operational (P) strategy, rational (P) culture and a growth management (P) leadership style. Through use of cultural surveys and experience Gattorna and his associates observed that differing customer segments represent differing customer behaviour logics, each demanding different logistics service requirements. Their observation has important implications for supply chain change.

In developing supply chain strategy world-class companies segment their logistics according to specific customer requirements and competitive advantage is derived from offering different service propositions to each of these segments. For example, some customers of a particular company may require a flexible response in very small sizes, supported by high-technology tracking, such as express or time-sensitive freight. The requirements of other customers of the same firm might be scheduled (and hence predictable) deliveries in large quantities, such as regular replenishment of product in full truck and pallet-load quantities from a supplier to a manufacturer. Rather than trying to build one culture or

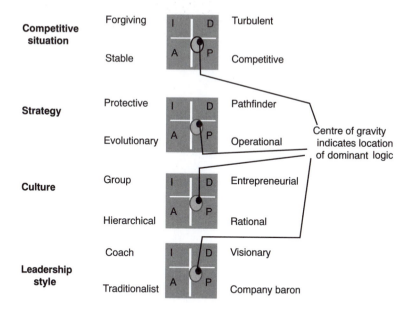

Figure 28.4   Achieving strategic fit

one pathway, the key to success, according to alignment theory, is to have different and distinctive service pathways through a supply chain to match the different customer-service requirements. Since each of these pathways represents market-facing alignment of each of or combinations of the subcultures required to meet specific customer needs, the secret to successful change then lies in ensuring that the logics of all of the pathways are in alignment. Clearly, Gattorna offers a prescriptive typology for cultural change that is anchored in the principle that alignment of different service pathways to meet the needs of each customer segment is the key to achieving supply chain change outcomes.

The failure to recognize the importance of, let alone achieve, strategic alignment is one main reason that change outcomes are not achieved. As we have already stated above, strategic logic counts for little if alignment between culture and the new strategic market response is poor. Moreover, there are two prerequisites to alignment that many organizations fail to address (see Figure 28.5). First, the mandate for change must be based on alignment with the market and customer base; that is, we must have studied our market and know where we are heading. Secondly, companies must know what they are or what their culture is; this is normally achieved through mapping our culture. Having attained this knowledge, a fact-based coherent strategy to bring the organization's cultural capability into alignment with its strategic response to the market can be developed. If neither is known then companies have no

Figure 28.5   The goal

hope for achieving alignment. In essence, organizations of this type do not know what their actual capability is, nor where they are going but they will have a lot of fun on the way. This is change management in search of coherence, a strategy doomed for failure.

The important point being made here is that the change journey should commence with an assessment of the gap between the current state of alignment and the target state. Culture mapping or profiling the capability of the organization to implement specific change strategies is the essential first step. The mapping exercise identifies to management the changes and refinements on critical dimensions that need to be made to optimize the implementation of the desired strategic response. Once the gap has been recognized the organization must be redesigned to support the culture or values and behaviours of the new organizational state. This will require redesign of organizational structures and jobs. Identifying the gap between current and target states also provides the basis for altering performance measures, training and skilling people or retrenching and recruiting others.

Lever Brothers provides a useful example of the importance of conducting an audit of current cultural capability at the outset of a change programme. In 1993, at the outset of radical business transformation, a culture audit provided Lever Brothers' leaders with insights into the realities of the company's culture and the role its employees could play in the change process. The audit uncovered cultural barriers such as strong bureaucracy, deep functional silos, risk aversion and control orientation that meant Lever lacked the structure, willingness and ability to read and react rapidly to major changes in its market. John Gillespie, senior vice-president of human resources, reported: 'We had to integrate all our organizational components, from business strategy to processes, to structure, to culture and all the HR support systems.' For Lever, the cultural and attitudinal transformation was pivotal to improved profitability, regaining market leadership and revitalizing innovation.

Action 2—Appoint a process owner

Supply chain change is invariably about moving from a functional or subprocess orientation to one where the process covers all functions and subprocesses across the entire supply chain network. Subprocess owners will have neither the perspective nor influence to deal with the new environment. The change process involves managers defining who does what in the new environment. If these managers report to different functional heads, then the process of reaching consensus can be long and painful. Moreover, the complexity of achieving change across supply chain networks will lead to a higher occurrence of boundary issues, resource prioritization conflicts and questions over the perceived need for change. Indeed, without a single process owner coordinating the supply chain in total, change initiatives will result in optimized performance along functional lines without regard to the impact on the total system. One study across five industry groups reported that outstanding performers in all industry groups 'focus responsibility for total inventory in one organization/leader'. This best practice was agreed on by all industry groups. Table 28.2 shows three possible supply chain process owner options for management to adopt in implementing a change project.

Table 28.2
Supply chain process owner options

	Pros	Cons
Supply chain director	Direct control of operations and change programmes Tensions between functions can be resolved quickly	Introduces another management layer Decreases regional/customer focus through becoming centralized
Supply chain change programme manager	Focus on developing future supply chain capabilities Defines processes to ensure integration between functions	No coordination of day-to-day activities Difficulties in building consensus for different regions/functions
Supply chain planner	Creates consistent plan across supply chain and forum for resolving issues Maintains regional/functional autonomy	No real responsibility for operations and lacks authority No focus for supply chain strategy and change programme

In many parts of the world, companies are already getting this message. For example, out of a sample of ten of Australia's largest consumer products manufacturers, seven had created one of the roles listed in Table 28.2. Five of these have been appointed in the last two years.

Action 3—Reshape performance measures

Performance measures provide the means by which the vision is translated into a specific set of performance objectives. Changing performance measures is one of the few ways for change leaders directly to affect and change people's behaviours quickly. People will focus their own activities to maximize their performance to achieve individual and workgroup goals that are measured. In the absence of new performance measures, there is no incentive for managers and employees to adopt the change as it is not considered important enough. The saying 'people behave as they are measured' is true. Without a change in measures, there will be no sustainable behavioural or performance change.

If existing performance measures are driving current behaviour, then to change behaviour we must reshape measures; paradoxically, to build we must tear down. Indeed, as soon as new business targets are set, these should be cascaded to organizational unit and workgroup level, then down to individual worker performance goals. New performance measures signal to managers and workers alike what the new behaviours are and how they will be rewarded.

Tearing down old performance measures will not be easy. New approaches to performance appraisal, rewards and incentives, which encourage behaviour that supports the change, will play a critical role in replacing old measures with new. In one example a supplier and distributor involved in implementing a continuous replenishment programme experienced initial distrust until they undertook a joint process-mapping exercise. Each then realized that their unhelpful behaviour was driven by the financial incentives (embedded in the old performance measures) that encouraged the old and not the new behaviour. As a result incentives were changed and the programme progressed smoothly. The complex array of interactions across supply chain processes, such as bringing a new product to market or fulfilment of customer orders, makes deriving an incentive system a difficult and time-consuming process. A simple formula will inevitably leave some important measures out; conversely, a complex formula may be confusing and encourage individuals to play games with the numbers.

Our experience has shown that reward or incentive systems will be most meaningful, and hence successful in embedding change, when they result from informed consensus between key stakeholders, managers and staff, on both qualitative and quantitative measures. Experience has also shown that, for supply chain change, there are four prerequisites for successful incentive systems:

- At the strategic planning and resource allocation stages, appropriate funds should be set aside to reward employees for supply chain improvements based on key performance measures. Strong positive cultures result when rewards are strictly linked to performance against objective criteria.
- Team incentives should be paid for improved team performance, with the entire team sharing in those rewards.
- Strong disincentives need to be established to reinforce the unacceptability of inappropriate behaviours.
- Significant shifts in rewards are necessary to underpin behavioural change. Disproportionately small rewards are a waste of money and actively work against the serious realignment needed in supply chain work.

Supply chain change is an organic process, a continuous programme of improvement that is evolving and never complete. The desired strategic vision can never be a static end state and continual renewal is required. Given the power of performance measurement and management, the supply chain change master would be prudent continually to ask the following question: is my performance measurement system (measures, incentives, rewards and appraisal systems) driving different parts of the supply chain organization towards the change goal? If the answer is no, then rather than reinforcing change success, the measurement regime may well unknowingly be undermining the goals of the change programme. In this case it needs to be reshaped quickly until alignment is achieved.

Action 4—Develop and train the workforce

A comprehensive development and training programme has been shown to be a key vehicle for helping organizations change through conveying alterations in values and beliefs and developing the knowledge, abilities and skills needed to perform in the new workplace. In the initial stages of a change programme, the focus of development should be on those key individuals who, by virtue of their personal and/or positional power, have the ability to change the organization by applying leverage at the key pressure points. These change leaders have the positional power to make or break the transmission of key aspects of the programme. In supply chain change many of them will be logistics or supply chain professionals who will be called on to make more rapid and complex decisions, coordinate action across multiple product, geographic, functional and organizational interfaces and interact with and manage several rapidly forming teams. According to one estimate cited in a study by Michigan State University (1995), only 20 per cent of a logistical change initiative involves the direct work of logistics; the remaining 80 per cent involves the responsibilities of other managers affected by the logistics process. Michigan also reported that few logisticians are either trained or experienced to manage true business integration and concluded that the tasks of formulating a change strategy and managing the change are outside the comfort zone and experience of many supply chain professionals.

This research, together with our experience, suggests that as a minimum individuals at key leverage points across the supply chain should be developed in the following four areas:

■ *Group and workshop facilitation skills.* Specific training in facilitating workshops and leading discussions in the areas requiring change will enable managers to elicit ideas and responses from staff, confidently involve their people in the change process and make presentations to senior management.
■ *Organizational behaviour and change skills.* Since the key individuals will act as change agents they would benefit greatly from knowledge of the techniques and theories of organizational behaviour and change. Understanding the psychology of change and even a little about organizational behaviour will help prepare them for the specific interventions that may be used to shift the company towards its desired state.
■ *Cross-cultural communication skills.* Where change spans international boundaries or workforces with differing cultural composition, key individuals would benefit from insight into the behaviours and perceptions between the cultures in question that might lead to misunderstanding or which could be leveraged to help reach the change goals.
■ *Leadership and performance-management skills.* Key supply chain change agents require skills that enable them to influence, motivate and manage personnel around them and from functions and organizations different to their norm. These skills are necessary to move people from existing positions towards the change goal, to generate confidence that the changes are in the organization's and their best interests, and to monitor and manage the extent of movement of people towards the change goals. Just as the key managers will need to be rewarded for their commitment to, and participation in, the change programme, so they need to learn how to reward those reporting to them.

Of course, all affected employees will require some form of training and development to enable them to achieve new performance targets. Supply chain change often results in process redesign requiring workers to carry out new tasks and interact with different people. For example, a person who previously just took customer orders may now be required to check inventory, check credit, confirm the order and handle many product types. Carefully crafted training programmes are required which allow the worker to understand the new job, its performance objectives, new systems, tools and techniques.

In complex change where the cost of employee failure to perform is high, it may be necessary to develop employees' higher-order cognitive and analytical capabilities using simulations of business activities—just as simulators are used to train cockpit crews. Technology (e.g. multimedia) is now a powerful learning tool when combined with deep understanding of employees' learning needs, within the context of specific business and individual performance objectives.

Action 5—Communicate and demonstrate top management commitment

When an organization strives to implement large-scale change, it is crucial that top management communicate to organizational members the why, what, when and how of the change programme. Communications must be honest and relentless. Actions and words of the CEO and other top managers will do more than anyone else to reshape attributes of the culture and propel the organization towards its change goals. These leaders must demonstrate commitment by giving full support to the change, setting a detailed course of action for its implementation, allocating the necessary resources and removing barriers to progress. Most importantly, managers at all levels must act and behave in accordance with the new models. For example, a manager who encourages her direct reports to accept changes in responsibilities must not ignore them herself. Doing so would confuse the change message and destroy momentum. Equally, senior managers will undermine an enterprise-wide cost-cutting initiative if they try to preserve their own departments and luxuries. Where the leadership team demonstrates commitment to the change goal by personally adopting the change and communicating by word and action, the change has a better than average chance of success.

Action 6—Involve stakeholders and gain commitment to change

Change is a competition between the need to change and the barriers that resist it. Michigan's research suggests that supply chain change will often be widely resisted because:

- change often involves changing or improving something that is not broken and the imperative for change is not obvious;
- change challenges long-standing paradigms, which are the accepted way; and
- quality and performance are elusive and difficult to measure across the array of relationships in a true supply chain.

Research also tells us that resistance to change is a natural human response. It will occur. We also know that people resist change more when it is imposed on them. The question therefore is how best to address it. The answer: stakeholder involvement in a meaningful way.

While gaining involvement can appear complex and is very time consuming, particularly at the outset, doing so is one of the best ways we know to alleviate the unnecessary fear and uncertainty that lead to resistance and to assist in building commitment towards, and ownership of, the change goals. If people are involved it sends a powerful message that things will be different and employees are playing an important role in making the difference. If they are not involved from the outset they feel left out and unfairly treated and the chances of success will be significantly reduced. Our experience is replete with examples of change programmes that have failed through not giving adequate attention and time to involving stakeholders in defining the change content. In one important supply chain project in a major consumer goods company, for example, the change effort stopped after a successful first phase but before any benefits could be realized. In retrospect, it was clear that failure occurred because:

- local managers were not committed to the change;
- a policy of secrecy suppressed, rather than overcame, resistance;
- a short-term focus resulted in lack of involvement; and
- current high levels of profitability meant that there was no clear imperative for change.

Such problems were overcome in the initial stages by a strong sponsor. However, when he left the company these contextual factors overwhelmed the programme.

Identifying all stakeholders is also a critical precondition for change success. Many programmes have been headed for the finishing line only to have the ribbon moved at the last minute by a stakeholder whose interest had not been identified and involvement not attended to. Supply chain change projects must identify all stakeholder groups so that their fears, expectations and needs can be addressed.

Action 7—Implement a system to track benefits

Implementing a system to monitor continuously the success of the supply chain change programme and track the capture of benefits is important in order to:

- ensure that the progress to date and planned actions will still achieve the business benefits;
- provide early feedback to stakeholders that will reassure those funding the project, motivate those engaged in the programme and quieten the sceptics and cynics who may otherwise undermine the change; and finally to
- provide feedback to senior management so that further refinements can be made to programme plans.

In implementing a benefits-tracking system it is important to create a link to the budgeting process so that the business benefits are reflected in the targets of operational managers. Links also need to be created to the product-pricing and customer-profitability monitoring systems. Strategic change will deliver improved margins by affecting both revenue and costs. Actively managing the pricing decision as it relates to new services and key customer segments is essential to achieving the expected benefits.

This is particularly important in supply chain change because, despite all the focus on partnerships and win–win relationships, the benefits of change (or its value) are rarely distributed evenly across the companies participating in the change process. In fact, if the process of value capture is left to chance some very odd things can happen. Imagine a consumer products manufacturer that has worked closely at the logistics level with a retailer to implement best-practice supply chain integration resulting in significant logistics cost reductions for both companies. Its competitor is a logistics laggard but has shrewd sales managers negotiating deals for promotions and shelf space. It would be folly for the company that has made all the logistics changes to leave to chance the possibility that it will gain a fair proportion of the benefits from its effort. Even assuming that there is goodwill all round, the reality is that costing information is incomplete and communications between logistics and sales in manufacturers, and logistics and merchandising in retailers, are imperfect. It is inevitable that without proactive management the benefits of change will be dissipated across the product category—in the worst case even resulting in some of the benefit reaching the logistics laggard.

Action 8—Communicate with all stakeholders

Rumour and distrust can undermine any change programme. Communication, particularly from top management, must be a continuous process, conducted in an honest, effective and open manner, so that people understand in advance what is required of them. Successful change programmes are characterized by constant, frank and timely communication to all stakeholders.

In supply chain change, communication also is required across company boundaries—to suppliers, customers and other organizations in the chain. And the investment community in publicly traded organizations must also not be ignored. These other parties are affected differently to internal employees and require radically different messages using different means. For example, one company involved several full-time people from its public relations group to manage these external communications throughout the change.

Action 9—Create an integration map

It is essential to create a map of organizational or supply chain-wide initiatives and compare these with goals, performance measures and resources. Just as a picture is revealed to a child when the dots in a puzzle book are connected, a picture is revealed when change initiatives are mapped. By its very nature, supply chain change will lead to a multiplicity of programmes springing up across the supply chain. This, together with the array of other change programmes that might exist in the organization, provides a recipe for confusion and potentially failure. The integration map is the mechanism for identifying the array of change initiatives and programmes going on in the organization and reveal conflicting time and resource priorities and change goals that have not been addressed. The map proves useful in helping to decide which projects to launch first and which may need to be jettisoned. Since concurrent initiatives often lead to confusion, action taken to integrate initiatives is essential if the change programme is not to degenerate into a hodgepodge of well-intentioned individual and otherwise conflicting initiatives.

Conclusion

The challenge of supply chain change is pervasive and significant. Current best practices are merely steps along the path to supply chain excellence beyond the year 2000, as existing paradigms are tested and retested in the search for excellence. For supply chain managers, technology and functional expertise are not enough to effect sustainable change. People provide the route to fast and effective management of change. To achieve change through people, they need to know what to do, why and how; they need the resources to do it; and they need to be motivated and guided. The supply chain change master of the future will be able to reconcile the paradoxical demands of managing costs, time, benefits and quality with managing stakeholders and their emotions, team building, communicating, commitment building, risk management and people development.

In this chapter we have outlined a prescriptive framework for managing change through people. As we noted at the outset from the Hewlett-Packard experience (Figure 28.2), if any one of the prerequisites shown in the framework is missing success is unlikely and failure probable. Without pressure for change, initiatives go to the bottom of the 'in-tray', they just are not important enough; without a clear vision shared by all, a fast start is likely to fizzle out; without the capacity for change, anxiety and frustration will arise; and without the right actions at the outset, there are likely to be many false starts and a great deal of haphazard activity. For supply chain managers the message is simple yet compelling—address all of the prerequisites and you have a sound base for success; ignore one of them and you have a recipe for failure.

References

Alexander. J.W. (1989) 'Sharing the vision', *Business Horizons*, 33 (3), 6–9.

Bowersox, D.J., Daugherty, P.J., Droge, C.L., Rogers, D.S. and Wardlow, D.L. (1989) *Leading Edge Logistics Competitive Positioning for the 1990's*, Council of Logistics Management, Oakbrook, IL. Comprehensive research conducted by Michigan State University Materials and Logistics Management Program.

Davis, S.M. (1985) *Managing Corporate Culture*, Ballinger, Cambridge, MA.

Denison, D. (1984) 'Bringing corporate culture to the bottom line', *Organizational Dynamics*, Autumn, 5–22.

Dichter, S., Gagon, C. and Alexander., A. (1993) 'Leading organizational transformations', *McKinsey Quarterly*, 1, Spring, 89–105.

Economist Intelligence Unit (1993) *Building Process Excellence Lessons from the Leaders*, Economist Intelligence Unit in cooperation with Andersen Consulting.

Forbrum, C. (1983) 'Corporate culture, environment and strategy', *Human Resource Management*, 22, 139–52.

Gattorna, J.L. (ed.) (1990), *The Gower Handbook of Logistics and Distribution Management*, 4th edn, Gower, Aldershot.

Gattorna Chorn Business Strategies Pty Ltd (1991) 'Pathways to customers: reducing complexity in the logistics pipeline', *Strategy Spotlight*, 1 (2), October, 24.

Gattorna Chorn Business Strategies Pty Ltd (1992) 'The challenge of change', *Strategy Spotlight*, 2, November, 20–25.

Global Research Team Michigan State University (1995) *World Class Logistics: The Challenge of Managing Continuous Change*, Council of Logistics Management, Oakbrook, IL.

Gordon C. and DiTomaso, N. (1992) 'Predicting corporate performance from organizational culture', *Journal of Management Studies*, 29 (6), 783–98.

Government Accounting Office (1994) *Organizational Culture Use of Training to Help Change DOD Inventory Management Culture*, GAO/NSIAD-94-193, 4.

Hassad, J. and Sharif, S. (1989) 'Corporate culture and strategic change', *Journal of General Management*, 15 (2), 4–19.

Hilmer, F.G. and Donaldson, L. (1996) *Management Redeemed: Debunking the Fads that Undermine Corporate Performance*, Free Press, New York.

Kotter, J.P. (1995), 'Leading change: why transformation efforts fail', *Harvard Business Review*, Mar/Apr, 59–67.

Kotter, J.P. and Heskett, J.L. (1991) *Corporate Culture and Performance*, Free Press, New York.

Leibfried, H.J. and McNair, C.J. (1992) *Benchmarking: a Tool For Continuous Improvement*, Vision Publishing.

Martin, Joanne (1992) *Cultures in Organizations: Three Perspectives*, Oxford University Press, Oxford.

Novak, R.A., Langley, C.J., and Rinehart, L.M. (1996) *Creating Logistics Value Themes for the Future*, Council of Logistics Management, Oak Brook, IL.

Schneider, B., Gunnarson, S. and Niles-Jolly, Kathryn (1994) 'Creating the climate and culture of success', *Organizational Dynamics*, 23 (1), 17–30.

Scholz, C. (1987) 'Corporate culture and strategy: the problem of strategic fit', *Long Range Planning*, 4 (4), 78–87.

Stace, D. and Dunphy, D. (1994) *Beyond The Boundaries: Leading and Re-creating the Successful Enterprise*, McGraw-Hill, Sydney.

Stewart, G. (1995) 'Supply chain performance benchmarking study reveals keys to supply chain excellence', *Logistics Information Management*, 8 (2), 38–44.

Tompkins, J.A. and Harmelink, D. (1994) *The Distribution Management Handbook*, McGraw-Hill, New York.

Part IV
Leadership

Overview

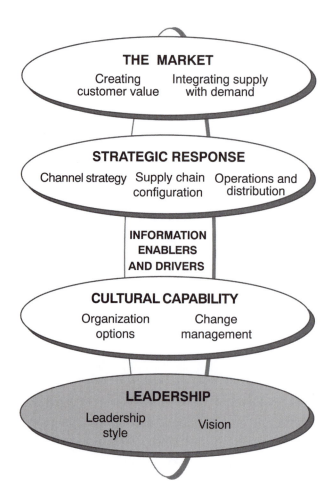

THE MARKET
Creating customer value   Integrating supply with demand

STRATEGIC RESPONSE
Channel strategy   Supply chain configuration   Operations and distribution

INFORMATION ENABLERS AND DRIVERS

CULTURAL CAPABILITY
Organization options   Change management

LEADERSHIP
Leadership style   Vision

Throughout this book we have argued that high-performance supply chain management requires the sophisticated application of leading-edge techniques to understand customers and align the whole of the business in order to meet their various needs. This is not a functional issue, but for too long management of the supply chain has been approached as if it were. As firms begin to recognize the pivotal role that the supply chain performs in achieving competitive success, that limiting view of the world is starting to change.

The reality is that supply chain management calls for supply chain leadership. And leadership is not about managing the resources, it is all about leading and directing the people who manage the resources. It is about formulating and articulating a vision and then developing the internal capabilities to realize it fully.

A supply chain leader today must be comfortable with diversity and complexity. This leader needs to be able to cope with the seismic shifts in customer values or behaviours which occur infrequently, but which can profoundly reshape the operating environment. He or she has to be able to recognize and reward the diverse skills required to identify and sustain various relationships and channels to target customer groups.

Chapter 29 looks at the leadership skills required to thrive in this new era, and particularly focuses on the need for leaders to build and sustain relationships across the entire supply chain network from suppliers to consumers

New dimensions of leadership in the supply chain

Aligning leadership style to the supply chain challenge

Cathy Walt and John Gattorna

Leadership is a widely discussed concept in business theory, yet too often 'leadership' itself is poorly understood. Very little is known of the underlying mechanisms at work and, consequently, the errors of former generations of management are being repeated. This chapter seeks to provide a framework for assessing and using leadership as a tool for business success. Leadership style is not prescribed, but defined according to combinations of four behavioural 'logics'. These logics are also common to the company strategy, its culture and, most importantly, to the market. To optimize company performance, the style of the leader should be aligned with, or 'fit', the market. An exceptional leader will use the power of the supply chain to introduce change and ensure an ongoing strategic fit with the market. This is the key to winning a stronger competitive position in a rapidly changing competitive environment.

Introduction

The outcomes of successful—and unsuccessful—leadership are well chronicled. Historical accounts describe at length the performance of political and military leaders. The libraries of the world's business schools bulge with accounts of corporate leadership. Unfortunately, the lessons of success and failure in leadership are usually descriptive at best and lack careful analysis. Descriptions of leaders as 'strong', 'weak', 'charismatic' or 'wise' are simply not adequate for developing a body of leadership knowledge.

The early students of human behaviour, the likes of C.G. Jung, Ichak Adizes and others, clearly understood that the study of why people behave the way they do was fertile field for research. Previous thinking tended to favour the view that behaviour was random, but Jung found that visible behaviour was largely driven and shaped by the individual's 'values'. Unfortunately, most of the work of Jung, Adizes and later Katherine Briggs and Isabel Myers (of Myers-Briggs Type Indicator™ fame) focused on individual rather than group behaviour. No attempt was made to extend their thinking to groups of individuals in a corporate context (such as top management teams) or to the world of the consumer, where large groups of people exhibit similar 'buying behaviours' for particular categories of products or services based on values. The potential to use these patterns of buying behaviour as a means of segmenting the market and aligning corporate strategy and culture remain largely untapped.

Leadership and the concept of 'strategic fit' or alignment

The breakthrough understanding of the connection between the market, strategic response of the organization, cultural capability and leadership style was achieved relatively recently (Chorn, Myres and Gattorna, 1990). All four elements are essential to achieve optimal organizational performance.

The common factor in three of the four is human behaviour and the fourth (strategy) can have a dominant 'personality' designed into it. Each of the four elements can be broken down into two sets of opposing logics, each exhibiting particular behavioural characteristics. An organization's orientation on each can be mapped, providing an accurate indication of the extent of its strategic alignment.

Our work in numerous organizations over the last decade has led us to the firm belief that organizations exhibiting superior performance, ultimately measured in terms of ROI and the share price, generally have a CEO (or top management team) who has a deep understanding of the competitive operating environment and of the dominant behavioural segments present in that marketplace. In our view, an understanding of the market and a leadership style that 'fits' the market are the two fundamentals for corporate success. The remaining two elements, strategy and cultural capability, will be derived almost as a matter of course if the market and leadership style are aligned.

Leadership style

The mechanics of the alignment model rely on the underlying logic frameworks for classifying market conditions, corporate strategy, organizational culture and leadership style respectively. The starting point is Carl Jung's theory of psychological types, which states that all conscious mental activity occurs in two perception processes—sensing and intuition – and two judgement processes—thinking and feeling.

By extending Jung's theory, four behavioural logics have been

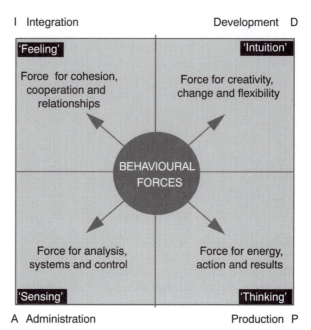

Figure 29.1 General characteristics of the four dominant logics

developed to help determine the 'dominant' tendency and to apply type theory to group situations. These four logics, referred to collectively as the PADI framework, are:

■ development—D
■ production—P
■ administration—A
■ integration—I

The four dominant logics have common themes that are reflected throughout the alignment structure. The general characteristics of the logics are shown in Figure 29.1, which also indicates the relationship with Jung's classifications of sensing, intuition, thinking and feeling.

The frameworks for competitive situation, corporate strategy, organizational culture and leadership style are shown in Figure 29.2, each indicating the specific characteristics exhibited by the four dominant logics.

The competitive situation is the fundamental driver of the alignment model. The market is characterized by its levels of uncertainty and competitive intensity.

Strategy provides the bridge linking an organization's internal capabilities with the external market requirements. Unlike the competitive situation, the strategy component of the model is derived, formulated by

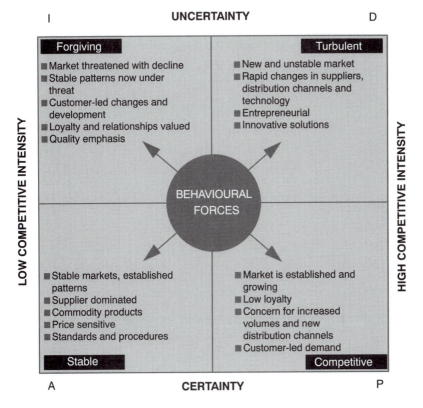

I UNCERTAINTY D

LOW COMPETITIVE INTENSITY

HIGH COMPETITIVE INTENSITY

Forgiving
- Market threatened with decline
- Stable patterns now under threat
- Customer-led changes and development
- Loyalty and relationships valued
- Quality emphasis

Turbulent
- New and unstable market
- Rapid changes in suppliers, distribution channels and technology
- Entrepreneurial
- Innovative solutions

BEHAVIOURAL FORCES

Stable
- Stable markets, established patterns
- Supplier dominated
- Commodity products
- Price sensitive
- Standards and procedures

Competitive
- Market is established and growing
- Low loyalty
- Concern for increased volumes and new distribution channels
- Customer-led demand

A CERTAINTY P

Figure 29.2 'Competitive situation' logic framework

the company leadership in response to environmental conditions. Strategy is characterized by its level of risk and by its proactive or reactive posture, as shown in Figure 29.3.

Successful implementation of a strategy requires that the organizational culture supports the necessary capabilities (Figure 29.4). Like strategy, this is a derived component of the model, shaped by leadership where possible to align with market demands. It is characterized by orientation towards direct or indirect control and internal or external focus.

Along with competitive situation, leadership style is a fundamental component in achieving strategic alignment. The intermediate or derived elements of strategy and culture will follow from an appropriate alignment between competitive situation and leadership style. The 'orientation' dimension in the framework measures the extent to which a manager is sensitive to teams or individuals (Figure 29.5). The 'preference' dimension measures the extent to which a manager tends towards thought or action.

In performing their role as organizational leaders, managers must perform four discrete functions as interpreted from the work of Jung:

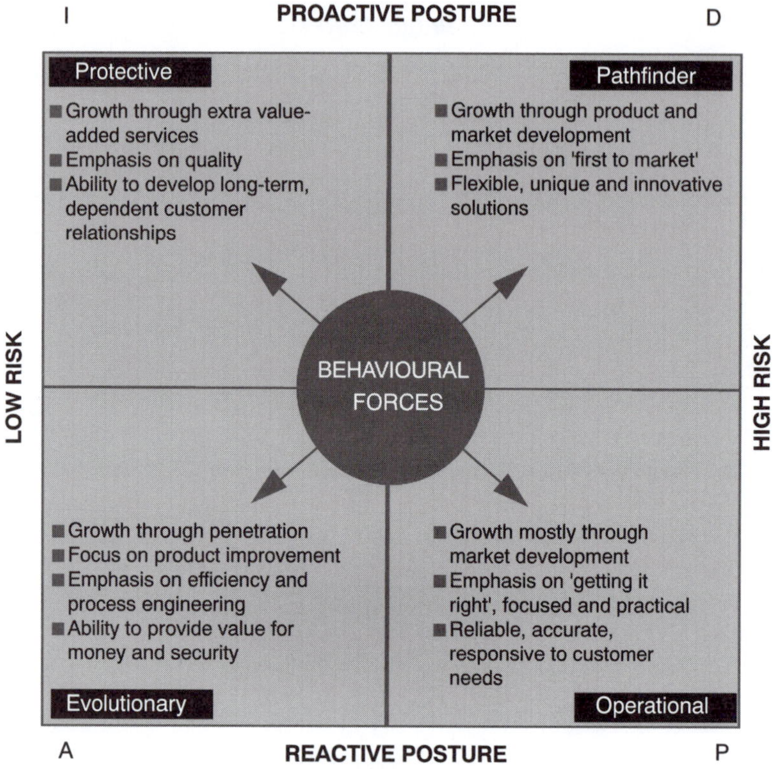

Figure 29.3 'Strategy' logic framework

■ *Production (P)*: the action-oriented contribution that he or she makes to achieving corporate objectives.
■ *Administration (A)*: the planning, maintenance and control of systems and resources.
■ *Development (D)*: the anticipation of alternative futures and determining the creative responses to them.
■ *Integration (I)*: the coordination of resources and energy to achieve cohesion and synergy.

The extent to which each of these roles or functions predominates will largely determine an individual's leadership style—although not necessarily the extent to which a particular manager is effective. To be a good fit with the prevailing organizational style is sometimes of great advantage. At other times (generally when a sea change is required or necessary), managers who are completely different in style are most successful.

This is often the case when a leader, sensing a change in the operating environment, adopts a style appropriate to the new competitive conditions. He or she formulates a strategy appropriate to the new environ-

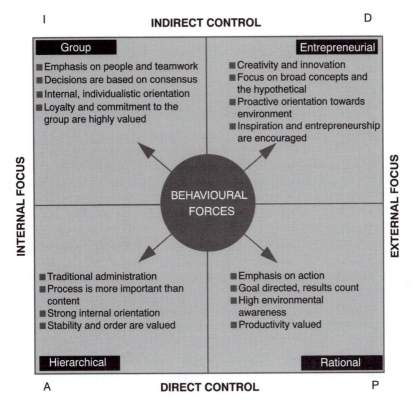

Figure 29.4 'Culture' logic framework

ment and begins to transform the old organizational culture towards a new alignment with the market. These circumstances frequently call for a change in leadership, as the entrenched style of the old leadership becomes inappropriate to the changed market demands.

While an individual may demonstrate aspects of all of the above competencies, mapping of his or her leadership style is likely to reveal a 'dominant logic'. The four dominant styles can be broadly classified according to the following:

- *Coach*: a thoughtful realist whose strengths include a concern for others and perseverance.
- *Visionary*: a thoughtful innovator, whose strengths include flexibility and enthusiasm.
- *Company baron*: an action-oriented innovator whose strengths include practicality and the ability to find compromises.
- *Traditionalist*: an action-oriented realist whose strengths include reliability and thoroughness.

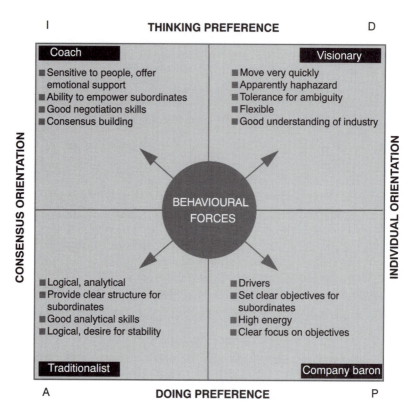

I   THINKING PREFERENCE   D

Coach
- Sensitive to people, offer emotional support
- Ability to empower subordinates
- Good negotiation skills
- Consensus building

Visionary
- Move very quickly
- Apparently haphazard
- Tolerance for ambiguity
- Flexible
- Good understanding of industry

CONSENSUS ORIENTATION

INDIVIDUAL ORIENTATION

BEHAVIOURAL FORCES

- Logical, analytical
- Provide clear structure for subordinates
- Good analytical skills
- Logical, desire for stability

- Drivers
- Set clear objectives for subordinates
- High energy
- Clear focus on objectives

Traditionalist

Company baron

A   DOING PREFERENCE   P

Figure 29.5 'Leadership' logic framework

The PADI frameworks correspond very strongly to the widely known Myers-Briggs Type Indicator™ (MBTI™) framework, both being based on the work of Jung. The MBTI™ provides an indication of personality by considering eight personality preferences that all people use at different times. These eight are organized into four bipolar scales as in Table 29.1.

An individual's personality 'type' is then expressed as one of the 16 possible combinations of these preferences.

The similarity between the MBTI™ and PADI frameworks allows an individual to use the Myers-Briggs type indicator™ to map his or her leadership style accurately on the PADI framework illustrated above. The complementary relationship between the Myers-Briggs framework and the strategic alignment model allow the two to be used in combination to great effect (Figure 29.6). The PADI classifications allow an easy assessment of the extent of management's fit with the other three key variables in the alignment equation. Analysis of the dominant logic in each of the four variables reveals the extent of strategic alignment.

The most significant role that senior managers can undertake is to shape the organization's cultural capability such that it is able to drive

Table 29.1
The four bipolar scales used in the Myers-Briggs type
indicator™ framework

Scale	Refers to
Extraversion (E) — Introversion (I)	How a person is energized
Sensing (S) — Intuition (N)	What a person pays attention to
Thinking (T) — Feeling (F)	How a person decides
Judging (J) — Perceiving (P)	Lifestyle a person adopts

the appropriate strategies into the market, and to manage the inter-dependencies between competitive situation, strategy, culture and leadership style towards improved strategic fit.

Change and leadership style

The relationships between the four elements in the strategic alignment model are largely reciprocal. Management can both react to change and create change in order to maintain alignment. Strategic fit can therefore be achieved in several ways, including:

- management 'reacting' to change in the competitive environment by altering strategy and culture;
- management 'preempting' competitive change by proactively changing the organization strategy and culture ahead of the market;
- management 'creating' a shift in the competitive environment by altering strategy and culture and so influencing customers and competitors; and
- a new leader 'changing' the culture of the organization through his or her leadership style.

The model reinforces the idea that management is neither 'reactive' nor 'proactive'. Rather, management is necessarily 'interactive', simultaneously creating and responding to situations. It is nonetheless true that in a perfectly stable and predictable environment, the need for effective leadership is minimal. It is in the face of change and turbulence that the capacity of a leader to manage effectively comes to the fore.

In 1995 the New Zealand dairy industry moved towards deregulation. Prior to that time, New Zealand Dairy Group (NZDG) had sold 95 per cent of its produce to a single customer, the NZ Dairy Board. With deregulation, the market changed fundamentally, from a stable,

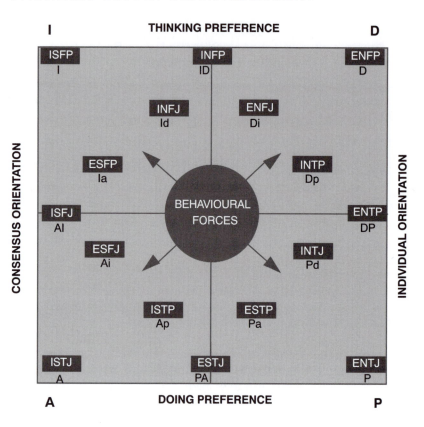

Figure 29.6 MBTI™ overlay with PADI framework

supplier-dominated environment, to one that was highly competitive, diverse and customer driven. The transition required significant strategic change, necessitating a correspondingly radical shift in organizational culture, from one preferring stability and emphasizing internal processes, to one emphasizing responsiveness and productivity, with an external focus and driven by results. To implement the change, new leadership was required, with a vision and style that aligned with the new market conditions and with the ability appropriately to reposition the organization's strategic and cultural orientation. Implementation of these changes under new leadership has seen the organization adapt to its new environment with considerable success.

The paradox is that, in the face of change, leadership requires vision, risk taking and a preparedness to respond quickly in line with the operating environment. Indeed, our work indicates that the more quickly change initiatives are implemented, the better the odds that the full benefits predicted in the business case will be delivered. Go slow and too cautiously, and the benefits evaporate quickly. At the same time, however, strong forces act to enforce the status quo. Pressure to reduce risk and to maintain stability often induces leaders to delay organizational change, leading ultimately to loss of alignment with market conditions. The key, once again, is that the leadership style be appropriate to market conditions. A market that is turbulent and rapidly changing needs leadership which is visionary, responsive and flexible. In a market that is stable, with established patterns, leadership that emphasizes productivity and structure is more likely to be effective.

At a time when change is accelerating throughout markets, the incidence of 'misalignment' between market, strategy, cultural capability and leadership style is increasing. The leader's role is becoming more and more that of a change agent or change leader as the organization struggles to remain aligned with its market segments, which themselves are constantly being reconfigured in size and mix. For exceptional corporate leaders, this situation offers the opportunity to introduce genuine and sustained change into the organization using logistics as the vehicle.

David Hearn at Goodman Fielder in Australasia recognized that significant potential existed to take advantage of the overlapping customer bases of several independently run divisions of the organization. Rather than focusing on any single division, he undertook a logistics review at the corporate level. Analysis revealed the potential synergies of integrating the separate divisional logistics functions and acted as a catalyst for implementing substantial organizational change. An integrated logistics strategy was developed, allowing extensive process reengineering in all divisions and the formation of a shared services-style logistics entity.

Principles of leadership

No prescriptive set of guidelines exists that characterizes good leadership. Rather, the effectiveness of a leader's style is a function of its appropriateness to the dictates of the market. Many recent corporate failures have occurred under the control of individuals who previously, and in different circumstances, had earned reputations as being among the world's most capable business leaders. Different market characteristics, a shift in consumer behaviour or new stages in product lifecycle all demand different leadership styles if strategic alignment is to be maintained. Where distinct patterns of consumer demand are identified by one organization, several distinct parallel strategies might be pursued. Here too, each might require different cultural capabilities and consequently a different leadership style to align with each particular market segment.

Ichak Adizes (1983) observes that no one individual can have all the qualities that are needed for effective management under all circumstances. The perfect manager, he claims, simply does not exist, 'because too many personality traits are required to perform all the managerial roles equally well, and because some of the traits required are incompatible'. Peter Drucker (1980) expresses a similar idea in his observation that 'the four temperaments are almost never found in the same person' and that therefore, 'the top management tasks require at least four different types of human beings'.

A person cannot excel in performing all of the roles identified in the four quadrants of the leadership logic framework, since the roles require internally conflicting personality traits. While the roles are not mutually exclusive, they are mutually inhibitive, in the sense that the capacity to excel in one of the four styles is likely to inhibit performance in another. A person ideally suited to managing under certain conditions is likely to be quite ineffective elsewhere.

Adizes suggests that what is needed is a managerial team, comprising a number of individuals each of whom can perform all the roles, albeit with different degrees of excellence. Since no one person can assume all the roles, a 'managerial mix' is the only way of implementing all necessary elements of effective leadership. The role of each person in the team is determined by his or her particular leadership style and by the particular tasks to be managed.

However, given the nature of personal interactions between individuals with different leadership orientations, it is likely that even within a diverse management team, a 'dominant logic', a definitive style, will emerge. Furthermore, if an organization is to succeed in its particular market, it is necessary that this does occur and that the dominant logic aligns with market conditions.

We recently applied the Strategic Alignment Model during work in a large financial services company. A detailed PADI analysis revealed a significant lack of alignment between the competitive situation and the other elements of the model. Results of the study are shown in Figure 29.7.

All but one of the alignment elements exhibit a single dominant logic as measured by the position of the centre of gravity data points in Figure 29.7. However, the company's leadership, comprising different individuals with diverse leadership styles, has no single dominant logic. A shift to the right in leadership style will therefore be necessary in order to align the organization more closely with the market. The dominant characteristics of this organization are outlined in Figure 29.8.

Irrespective of a leader's dominant style, certain capabilities are vital to effective leadership.

If the leader's primary responsibility is to achieve and maintain strategic alignment, then a prerequisite skill must be that of assessing and understanding the marketplace. A leader who not only thoroughly understands the dynamics of his or her current market, but who is able to predict future trends in consumer behaviour, gives an organization a

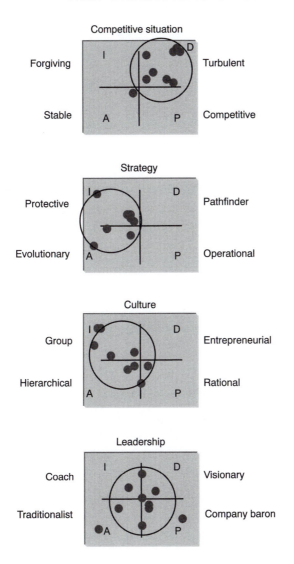

Figure 29.7 The organization's strategic fit

competitive advantage by aligning strategy and culture in anticipation of market changes rather than as a reaction to them.

Having understood market conditions, a leader must have the ability to formulate an appropriate strategic vision, one which aligns with market trends and which exacts optimal organizational performance.

Implementation of a strategy then requires appropriate cultural capabilities to be cultivated in the organization. This might at times require significant change in focus or orientation. An effective leader has the

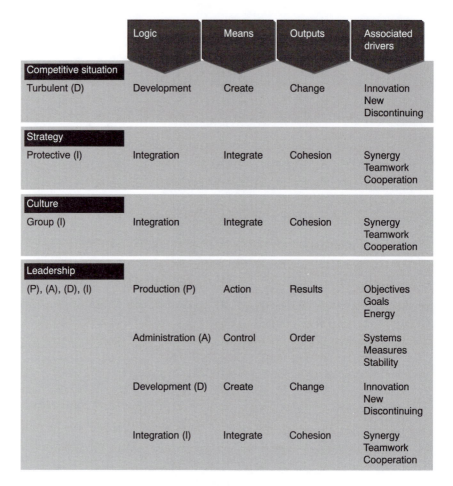

	Logic	Means	Outputs	Associated drivers
Competitive situation				
Turbulent (D)	Development	Create	Change	Innovation New Discontinuing
Strategy				
Protective (I)	Integration	Integrate	Cohesion	Synergy Teamwork Cooperation
Culture				
Group (I)	Integration	Integrate	Cohesion	Synergy Teamwork Cooperation
Leadership				
(P), (A), (D), (I)	Production (P)	Action	Results	Objectives Goals Energy
	Administration (A)	Control	Order	Systems Measures Stability
	Development (D)	Create	Change	Innovation New Discontinuing
	Integration (I)	Integrate	Cohesion	Synergy Teamwork Cooperation

Figure 29.8   The organization's dominant characteristics

ability to motivate subordinates and to manifestly influence the culture of an organization.

Leadership comes to the fore during times of change. During these periods, an effective leader demonstrates a deep conviction in his or her own ability, an over-riding individualism which through initiative, determination and persistence empowers the organization to shift away from the status quo and to direct efforts towards achieving newly defined goals.

A leader sets the agenda and has the skills to gain the necessary organizational support in pursuit of the desired vision.

Leadership style in a logistics context

Achieving successful change through inspired leadership in the corporate logistics function draws on all the general principles of leadership outlined above. Indeed, acceptance of logistics strategy as an integral part of an organization's business plan has in turn had an impact on the role of key logistics personnel. These days, senior logistics executives operate more as internal consultants and culture managers than as subject-matter experts. The paradigm shifts that need to be addressed and managed in modern-day logistics include moving from:

- functions to processes;
- profit to physical performance;
- inventory to information;
- fragmentation to integration;
- functional to market focused;
- transactions to partnership relationships;
- fully controlled to 'arm's length' via third parties and extended enterprises; and
- insourcing to management of alliances (at both supplier and customer ends).

In relation to the study of corporate performance in general, one important insight (Gattorna, 1991) has led to an entirely new perspective on the logistics function. This involved the recognition that merchandise moves through a logistics network (or pipeline) in a manner that largely reflects the buying behaviour of customers (and end consumers) and the behaviour of company personnel. The two influences are interdependent. For example, if a retailer decides to display a low-price 'special' and runs a promotional campaign to alert potential consumers, it will be necessary to place a bulk-buy order on the supplier and cope with the subsequent surge in demand from consumers—a case of influencing buyer behaviour.

In effect, what was previously a scrambled mess of merchandise moving through the logistics pipeline can now, with the aid of the same behavioural principles outlined above, be resolved into a limited number of conduits or discrete 'pathways' with different operating characteristics. These pathways are designed to align with the dominant segments evident in the market. In this way the logistics function is able to achieve 'multiple alignment', perceived by the untrained eye as flexibility.

We have named the three fundamental types of pathways base, wave and surge. Their respective characteristics are as follows:

- *Base*—large systems; high capital investments; low management involvement; permanent staffing; focus on fine tuning.

- *Wave*—some systems; hire rather than purchase equipment; periods of high management involvement; mostly casual staff; focus on responding quickly.
- *Surge*—low system requirements; low capital; high management involvement; permanent (multiskilled) staff; focus on unique solutions.

All three types of flow can be present in a single facility at any one time; or a particular facility may be dedicated to only one type of flow if the volume is sufficient. In any event, by recognizing the presence of these three types of flow and managing them accordingly, customer satisfaction levels can be increased significantly and costs can be simultaneously reduced.

Coca-Cola Japan provides an example of a single organization which deliberately and effectively pursues three distinct channel strategies, corresponding to three distinct customer segments. The three segments are supermarkets, vending machines and 'mom and pop' stores respectively, and the logistic responses demanded by each are significantly different. The supermarkets require consistently reliable and regular deliveries. Vendor-refill machines rely on short lead times and flexible and responsive service. 'Mom and pop' stores require high levels of support and stable long-term relationships. The company serves each of these channels quite separately, with dedicated, segment-focused activities, supported by a shared infrastructure. Despite the uniformity of the product, this multiple-response approach to the market is vital if the organization is to remain aligned with the buyer behaviour characterizing each of its distinct market segments.

The capacity demonstrated by Coca-Cola to implement multiple responses is often mistakenly referred to as 'flexibility'. This would imply a single logistical response which could be adjusted in some way as the demands of the channel vary. In contrast, the company's channel strategy is deliberately to pursue three distinct logistics responses, each appropriate to a particular market segment. Each of these will have a degree of flexibility, dictated by the demands of the target market.

Shaping the three core roles of logistics

Ultimately, the logistics leader has the responsibility for setting the logistics vision (or desired competitive positioning in the market) in support of the marketing and sales functions, and operating in such a way as to deliver the 'contracted' range of service levels for the agreed price(s).

An actual vision statement is included below in full. It has simultaneously an internal and external focus. It clearly articulates the company's strategic direction and objectives relative to its external stakeholders, while at the same time serving as a positioning (or boundary) statement, providing a guide to employees about what their internal obligations and focus should be. This draft was prepared in conjunction with the logistics personnel of a general merchandise discount store group which we will call D-Store.

D-Store Logistics vision statement

CASE STUDY

D-Store Logistics is the custodian of the supply chain (or pipeline) which links D-Store customers with suppliers. Logistics is charged with the professional management of those considerable resources which are involved in the complex task of moving merchandise through the pipeline, i.e. facilities, systems, personnel and capital. The actual inventory in the pipeline remains the 'property' of Merchandise, but we are the facilitators. In effect D-Store Logistics is an *internal contractor* which has the potential to significantly influence D-Store profitability by optimizing the *service–cost equation* and contribute to the growth of D-Store's business.

D-Store Logistics has several 'stakeholders', and in meeting their respective needs we effectively define our role:

Suppliers: D-Store Logistics has to fulfill elements of the strategic partnership arrangements entered into by the Buying Group for the purposes of achieving mutual profitability. We provide them with access to facilities to convey their merchandise to the point of sale.

Merchandise: is an internal customer which requires D-Store Logistics to minimize the lead times that inventory is in the pipeline between Suppliers and Stores. Management of this lead time has leverage on merchandise profitability. We aim to provide a delivery system which is at least as efficient and reliable as suppliers, and at a lower cost. We also assist Merchandise by providing space for bulk buys and liaise with Merchandise in regard to promotional campaigns, packing, and other special conditions which influence the flow of merchandise.

Stores: is another internal customer which requires D-Store Logistics to deliver merchandise to every store in the network according to an agreed service level, i.e. manageable quantities and pack sizes, reliable schedules etc. We also liaise with Stores on a range of matters which affect the management of merchandise, such as packing allotments, storage, facilities, design and handling practices to improve store receiving. It is our ultimate intent to contribute to customer satisfaction by collaborating with internal functions as well as suppliers.

Logistics owns the *methodologies* and procedures which facilitate the cost-effective flow of merchandise from suppliers to stores and on to customers. These methodologies include leading-edge physical and information systems, supported by a logistics orientation among all our personnel. Our size gives us a significant edge in buying power, for both local transport and overseas freight, and also affords us more *flexibility* in operations.

For the future, D-Store Logistics intends to reconfigure its infrastructure and systems involving implementation of a blueprint for quantum change which will take D-Store to the forefront of logistics practice in discount stores worldwide. To achieve this, we must institute and manage major changes in the way we currently do things. Our task is to ensure that no competitor out-performs D-Store in a logistics sense, that stock in the pipeline is managed expeditiously, and that the entire supply chain, including the supplier component, comes under our influence—all of which adds up to a competitive advantage for D-Store at point of sale. We are determined to realize most, if not all of the potential savings available through improved logistics practice. For this reason micro measurement systems and corresponding standards will be instituted along the supply chain. Technology will be applied as appropriate. We are mindful that D-Store Logistics manages major elements of the company's assets and as such we will seek to ensure acceptable rates of return on these investments.

In implementing a vision, the logistics leader must understand how to manipulate the levers of change to achieve the desired alignments. These include organization design, movement of key people into key roles, training, appropriate communications at different levels, selective recruitment and monitoring of the relevant key performance indicators. The appropriate combination of these variables will achieve the required alignment at a given point in time.

As well as driving the necessary change through the logistics organization, the logistics leader must also develop several core competencies in his or her organization. These include:

- *core technology*—getting the job done in a timely and consistent manner;
- *building infrastructure*—developing people, integrating all the systems, building the physical network; and
- *interface management*—managing the interfaces between the logistics function and internal customers, external customers, suppliers and third-party providers.

From logistics to supply chain management

The logistics manager limits his or her efforts to functions internal to the organization. The supply chain manager moves beyond the boundaries of a single firm, focusing on the entire value chain and on the interdependencies between contributing companies. He or she aims at achieving a high degree of integration with suppliers at one end, and customers at the other, and seeks to lead, manage or, at the very least, influence the string of interdependent organizations comprising the entire chain.

The two primary mechanisms for achieving this are:

- alliances with major suppliers and customers for mutual benefit; and
- complete integration of enterprise and application systems into a seamless decision-support system providing visibility at every point along the supply chain and to every key channel party involved.

Under this scenario, leadership of the entire supply chain is the prize. While the rewards are considerable, the change challenges become correspondingly more complex. These include:

- joint reduction of inventories along the channel—facilities are rationalized and shared;
- movement away from cost minimization at the individual level and seeking instead channel-wide or even industry-wide economies;
- rationalizing the supplier base; and
- focusing primarily on inventory velocity across the entire supply chain.

In all, the emphasis is on achieving radical improvements in performance rather than embracing the 'creeping incrementalism' of yesteryear.

Conclusion

In a world where the rate of change in many markets is accelerating, the need to align leadership style with market conditions is all important. New, rapidly developing markets will require leadership that is visionary, responsive and flexible. Stable, more mature markets will benefit most from leadership that emphasizes productivity and structure. In this environment all leaders must have the capacity to embrace and manage change. The challenge for leaders will be to assess the competitive environment and strategically steer the cultural capacity and business strategy of their organizations into alignment with the market. Management of the supply chain can play a pivotal role in this scenario of sustained success.

References

Adizes, Ichak (1983) *How to Solve the Mismanagement Crisis*, Adizes Institute, Santa Monica, CA.

Briggs Myers, Isabel (1993) *Introduction to Type®: A Guide to Understanding Your Results on the Myers-Briggs Type Indicator®*, 5th edn, revised by Linda A. Kirby and Katherine D. Myers, Oxford University Press, Oxford.

Chorn, N.L., Myres, K.L. and Gattorna, J.L. (1990) 'Bridging strategy formulation and implementation', unpublished paper presented to the 10th Annual International Conference of the Strategic Management Society, Stockholm.

Drucker, Peter F. (1980) *Managing in Turbulent Times*, Pan, London.

Gattorna, John L. (1991) 'Pathways to customers: reducing complexity in the logistics pipeline', *Strategy Spotlight*, 1 (2), October, 21–30.

Part V
Information Enablers and Drivers

Overview

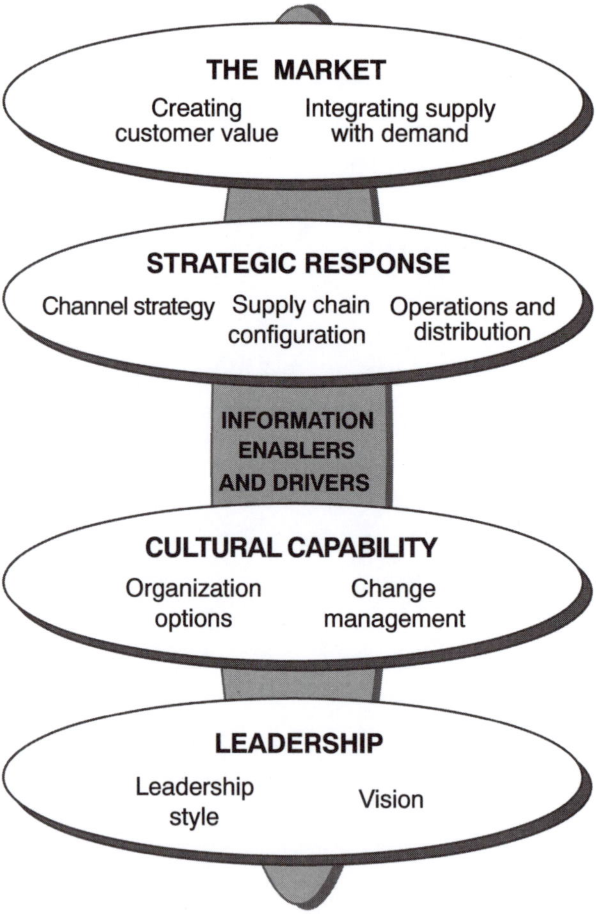

THE MARKET

Creating customer value   Integrating supply with demand

STRATEGIC RESPONSE

Channel strategy   Supply chain configuration   Operations and distribution

INFORMATION ENABLERS AND DRIVERS

CULTURAL CAPABILITY

Organization options   Change management

LEADERSHIP

Leadership style   Vision

With the proliferation of sophisticated information technology solutions, the IT investment decision for businesses has become a complex choice between custom or standard systems, and point or enterprise solutions. Even more challenging is the realization that most IT solutions are no longer likely to provide strategic advantage, but simply the business basics. The competitive advantage for companies will originate from developing creative information technology strategies and implementing them superbly.

Information systems enable existing strategies to be realized; more importantly, they drive the creation and realization of new strategies. Information flows provide the linkages which enable the supply chain to operate effectively. Indeed, information is the life blood of supply chain management. The Internet and electronic data interchange provide the linkages to the market and neighbouring companies. Enterprise resource-planning systems enable the execution of strategy at an operational level. Communications systems such as common databases, e-mail and various reporting and decision-support systems ensure that knowledge is shared across the firm. Managing these tools and using them to achieve business advantage is a tremendous challenge for companies.

Chapters 30 to 32 assess the new business paradigms created by information technology and explore how firms can adapt to the changing environment which demands increased integration to drive breakthrough performance.

Strategy, information technology and the supply chain

Managing information technology for success, not just survival

Tom Nickles, James Mueller and Timothy Takacs

Aligning information technology (IT) to existing business strategies was once sufficient to deliver competitive advantage. But tomorrow's achievers will reverse this process, using IT to drive strategy development. With the proliferation of cheaper, enterprise-wise IT solutions, tailored closely to the recognized needs of firms and industries, supply chain managers need to ensure that they make the most of proven solutions for their business simply to stay competitive. But with shrinking opportunities for innovation, significant advantage can only be achieved by exploiting information skilfully to draw benefits from existing IT investments; shifting discretionary investment from bottom-line cost cutting to top-line growth; and developing skills in nimble IT 'arbitrage'.

Introduction

IT has dramatically transformed the way companies use their supply chain operations to achieve competitive differentiation. Successful firms have used IT to support their business strategies and priorities (Figure 30.1). In so doing they have generated tactical efficiencies, created operational excellence and enhanced decision-making capabilities across their supply chains. One of the most discussed examples of this IT alignment is Wal-Mart, which reinvented the industry through its quick-response capability and was able substantially to improve its operating performance over competitors. Companies like Levi Strauss, USAA and Federal Express have also demonstrated the power of using IT to create advantage and business value.

But a new challenge confronts firms seeking to leverage the extraordinary power of IT. Where business strategies once drove the adoption and use of IT, companies in the future will need to think through their capabilities and redesign their supply chain strategies on the basis of optimum management of IT investments and the superior use of the information stream generated by IT.

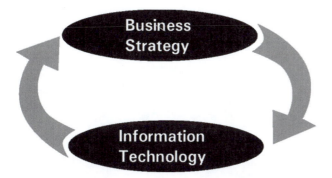

Figure 30.1 **Business strategies have traditionally driven IT development, but IT can now be used to enable new business strategies**

In this chapter, therefore, we argue that the key to creating successful supply chain strategies relies on the management of IT investments and exploitation of information. These skills will be vital for any company thinking about investing in supply chain systems which are to be amortized over several years, or looking to make the most of the information systems and capabilities already in place.

Putting IT into the supply chain context

Early corporate leaders in IT recognized that bottom-line savings could be achieved by automating the more clerical and labour-intensive aspects of their businesses. General Electric broke ground as the first firm in the world to install a computer in a corporate environment in 1952. It hired an Arthur Andersen group, which would later become Andersen Consulting, to install a system to automate a complex accounting department with a general ledger. The system filled up a small warehouse and packed computing power dwarfed by today's laptops. This installation sparked the change in the way business strategists thought about using computers to deliver specific results.

In the 1960s and 1970s the corporate computing revolution built momentum. Business strategists found logistics functions an early target for automation. Mainframes and minicomputers were employed to automate processes within clerical departments such as the transportation and warehousing functions. These systems were typically built from the ground up within a corporation's electronic data-processing group. They were highly customized, unique solutions tied to investments in computer hardware.

Historic IT solutions

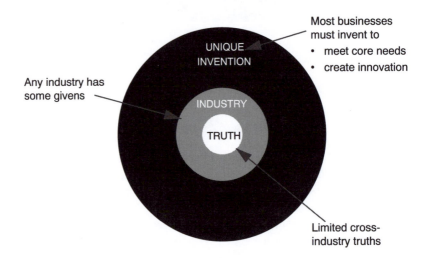

Figure 30.2   Historically IT solutions were created by unique invention

As companies were developing these IT systems, they were concurrently developing cross-industry 'truths' which applied to any type of business and industry-specific 'givens' which applied to firms within a particular industry. These truths and givens reflected the commonly understood business requirements of firms across and within industries. For example, products firms in general recognized the 'truth' that the flow of inventory must be tracked. The perishable goods industry, in particular, recognized the 'given' that tracking the dating of inventory was important. But at this stage, areas of recognized common need (and the common IT solutions to address these areas of need) were small relative to the recognition of, and capacity for, unique, customized solutions (Figure 30.2).

These unique IT solutions helped divisional and functional leaders capture and automate the flow of information in their company. They helped deliver significant competitive advantages. But the systems created were expensive to maintain, very user unfriendly and typically did not communicate with other systems in the company. The competitive advantage these companies achieved was not going to be sustainable in the coming years.

Software and hardware vendors began to understand and address the applications and features (truths and givens) that firms wanted for these departmental and divisional systems. In the 1980s multitudes of firms sprang up to offer solutions based around the commonly accepted requirements of firms across and within industries. Although the systems developed still required a great deal of specific company customization, these 'packaged' systems worked on common platforms and brought computing power to the masses of companies unable to develop applications internally. For example, IBM's AS/400 platform, coupled with software solutions, gave smaller companies the capacity to add standard systems gradually, which supported key supply chain strategies. Companies dealing in highly cost-competitive industries installed tactical logistics systems to reduce administrative logistics costs and burdensome paperwork.

While these systems were easier to install and learn, they often led to complexity because they were not common across an entire company. An example might include a geographically dispersed company leaving systems selection in the hands of local division heads, resulting in competing systems for the same purposes. Another example might include a distribution requirement planning system used in a company's operations, not tied to the forecasts generated by its finance or marketing groups.

This was not the only problem. Not only did many companies find it difficult to ensure that their IT investments fully supported the achievement of their strategic goals, for many their strategic goals were not properly aligned with the end objective of creating maximum value, resulting in further under-performance of IT assets.

To take some examples: different business units operating with different performance metrics; individual markets within a multinational firm having little visibility into the rest of the company; warehouses in a distribution network using different systems and working off different data; systems generating inappropriate aggregated generic solutions; systems inflexibly designed to deal with a specific task the same way all the time. Circumstances like these led business strategists and software developers alike to realize that different systems working independently from each other, and separated from key data sources, were producing less than optimal results.

Moving to enterprise-wide solutions

Today, common enterprise solutions are beginning to link processes across companies and provide for enterprise-wide flow of information. The supply chain management process is a significant beneficiary of shared company information, especially when these systems are linked to relevant customer and vendor systems. Enterprise resource planning supports all of an industry's core needs or truths and incorporates specific company options or givens. As industry truths and givens have become more apparent to IT developers and business strategists, it has become easier to leverage existing knowledge. These solutions are

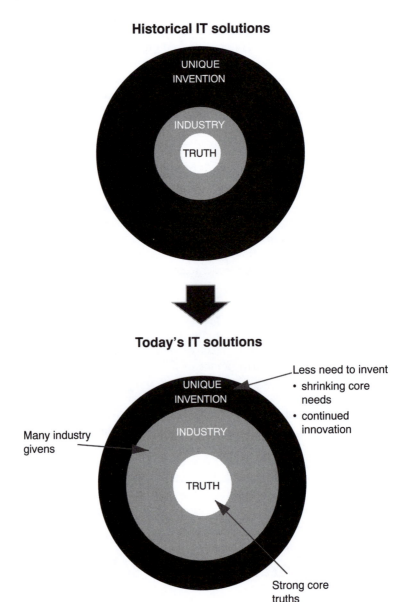

Figure 30.3   The emphasis of IT investments is changing from unique innovation to leveraging 'truths' and 'givens'

ensuring a much closer fit between IT systems, business strategies and the creation and management of information. Figure 30.3 illustrates the extent to which the degree of unique invention required has diminished as common issues and requirements have been recognized and addressed.

These packaged solutions and components have effectively eliminated the need for heavy in-house expertise and programming skill. For example, supply chain managers can simply import whole IT solutions rather than spend excessive time inventing or working out the details of transactional systems. Executive information systems (EIS) help manage outsourced components of the supply chain (including transactional systems), tools are available to help optimize the supply chain alternatives and software can be obtained that analyses the promotional forecasting implications.

Equally, the growing agreement on industry and firm truths and givens also helps supply chain managers reduce areas of complex decision making. For example, a supply chain manager in the pharmaceutical industry typically knows that customers need to have inventory almost instantly available in case of a shortage. The manager may know that demand is fairly predictable for maintenance drugs which a patient refills every few weeks or months. The manager may also know that cost becomes the driving factor of drugs which are coming off patent and can be produced generically. IT solutions that automatically address these truths and givens can then ensure that these issues are constantly and consistently being managed. To take another example, the trucking industry will always need applications to price or rate shipments. Again, third-party warehouses will almost always find benefits with load-planning and optimization software.

Therefore, companies which have waited to make investments in supply chain IT have the opportunity to consider their own industry supply chain truths and givens and invest in readily available solutions to address those needs. An important parallel opportunity is to avoid being locked into old and inflexible technologies when so many flexible alternatives are now available to provide the necessary information.

Supply chain software vendors, for example, create enterprise solutions which make connecting with customers and vendors increasingly easy. IT service providers or third parties provide basic capabilities by providing standard solutions. As the marketplace changes, these firms can adapt the core software across an industry. This creates great advantages for industry followers, and significant disadvantages for industry leaders which have made heavy entry-level IT investments.

Investments need to be driven by a clear sense of the value that will be created, with custom solutions only adopted when it is clearly demonstrated that standard solutions won't suffice. Companies must consider whether a less robust IT solution would work and whether outsourcing of components of the supply chain to third parties could negate the need for the complex, enterprise solutions. Third-party IT and logistics service providers offer the flexibility to manage ever changing and logistically distinct supply chains.

The reality is, however, that no matter how they are acquired and sustained, most IT investments of themselves will no longer serve to deliver

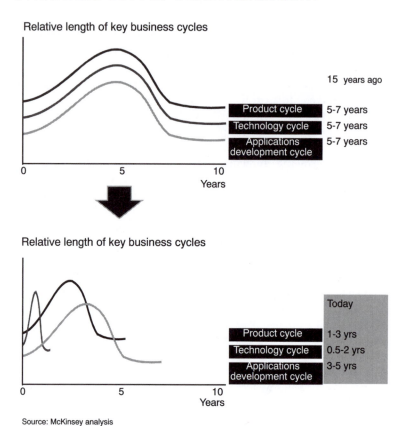

Figure 30.4 Contracting development cycles are reducing IT's role in sustaining competitive advantage and requiring faster payback on investments

competitive advantage. They are too easy to replicate. Most IT investments will simply be a condition for continuing survival in the marketplace, in the same way that phones or faxes are a given in the office. Figure 30.4 represents the historical product, technology and applications development curves and how these have contracted today.

In this context, then, the role of the supply chain manager is changing. The supply chain manager obviously needs to ensure that the truths and givens of the firm are being fully addressed by the standard, readily available IT solutions. But those looking to go beyond survival and build competitive advantage will recognize the need for unique innovation in the firm and accept that this will be point specific rather than enterprise wide. The supply chain will, therefore, need to be managed by exception, with the real focus on seeking out new opportunities to create value. In so doing, the supply chain manager will be spending more time dealing with strategies and information rather than tactics and goods.

And to make the most of these shrinking opportunities for innovation, firms need to work on three related tasks: exploit information skilfully to draw benefits from their IT investments; shift their discretionary investment focus from bottom-line cuts to top-line growth; and as part of this strategy, develop skills in nimble IT arbitrage.

Exploiting information skilfully to draw significant benefits from IT investments

As Figure 30.5 suggests, leading companies don't just import proven IT solutions and apply them uncritically to their business strategies, they actively leverage the opportunities provided by IT and the information flow it delivers.

Supply chain managers need to apply proven IT solutions to their own unique company circumstances—their truths and givens. Successfully putting these ingredients together will lead to nine key

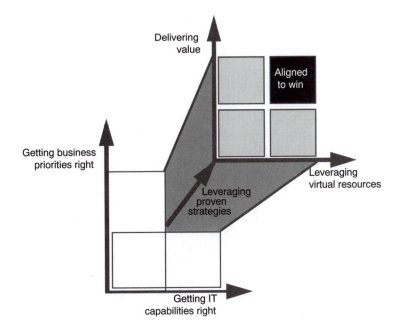

Figure 30.5 Historically companies focused on simply aligning business priorities and IT capabilities, but today's successful IT investors will leverage proven strategies

outcomes for leading firms which will enhance their competitive edge:

- new customer/vendor relationships;
- new insights about customers and markets;
- market efficiencies and channels fully exploited;
- transformed products and services;
- restructured multienterprise/cross-industry value chains;
- the capacity for real-time decisions and simulated outcomes;
- the ability to manage global complexity and mass customization;
- a radical acceleration or elimination of traditional processes; and
- continuous learning and innovation.

New customer/vendor relationships

IT enables supply chain managers to set up new forms and types of customer relationships, with customers and suppliers mutually establishing communities which improve the flow of information and knowledge. These communities are establishing new forms of relationships. General Electric, for example, has given its vendors improved access by establishing an online network where GE can request bids for materials it plans to purchase. GE is assured of access to the best available prices for goods and approved vendors will never be left out of a GE purchasing decision.

GE's Trading Process Network (TPN) aggregates internal demand across all of the company's divisions and posts a consolidated order for suppliers to bid on in an electronic marketplace. In 1996, this marketplace cleared approximately $350 million in goods. In 1997 it is expected to clear some three billion dollars. Benefits include reducing material cost, streamlining procurement functions and providing internal buyers with access to a global market. Suppliers also like it because they have electronic access to GE's needs at any given time.

Geffen, a major recording company, is in the process of piloting the use of the Internet to support order management through transportation and shipping electronically. Customers will be able to shop electronically and hear selected cuts of music. When they find the music they like, they can order it and have it distributed electronically to their PC. Beyond these market-facing opportunities, the company eliminates processes/intermediaries and allows for continuous learning about what the marketplace likes, based on order flow. Vendors are enabling new business capabilities through the use of IT by directly dealing with end consumers worldwide.

New insights about customers and markets

Using the Internet to exchange information about customers is providing new insights into market activities. For example, some supply chain managers are linking their demand-planning systems to information clearing houses which provide a secure means for sharing sales and forecasting information. The process of benchmarking partners has aligned leading consumer products manufacturers, distributors and retailers in one such clearinghouse of supply and demand information. Large companies such as Ford are finding that they have to become much more knowledgeable about their end customers around the world. IT is being used to extend their reach on a global basis.

Market efficiencies and channels fully exploited

IT has enabled new market efficiencies and channels. Heineken established a new model for dealing with its distributor channel, avoiding the large expensive proprietary systems employed by some of its US competitors, such as Anheuser-Busch. Several years ago, Anheuser-Busch gave its distributors ordering and inventory systems which allowed instant access to information about product availability and sales patterns. While this system gave the distributors a competitive advantage over smaller competitors such as Heineken, it was a stand-alone system which left integration with distributor systems up to the distributor. Heineken recently launched a system that achieves the same objectives using the Internet as the platform for communicating this information and thereby greatly improving the efficiency of doing business with this channel.

Land's End deals with over-stocks electronically at its Web site by continually dropping the price until the item is cleared out of inventory. With this type of capability, it is possible to program rather sophisticated pricing algorithms into systems to try to optimize the trade-off between inventory cost and price and deal with items on an exception basis. In this world, all pricing is dynamic and IT can be used continuously to seek the best price points *vis-à-vis* supply and demand for all products.

Transformed products and services

The virtualization of products and services is transforming the way products are being delivered and used. New software releases have for many years been distributed on floppy disks or CDs. This required a significant picking and packing operation. Most of these products are now electronically distributed.

Restructured multienterprise/cross-industry value chains

Information is beginning to restructure multienterprise value chains by leveraging core competencies of experts and industry-common solutions. As manufacturers and distributors begin to use logistics and IT outsourcing capabilities, firms are finding it increasingly challenging to manage and monitor aspects of their supply chains that they do not own. The airline industry, for example, has been using industry-wide ticket-accounting services for years instead of creating unique solutions internally. We expect other industry-specific solutions to emerge for manufacturers and distributors.

The capacity for real-time decisions and simulated outcomes

The plethora of information now available to supply chain managers is enabling them to make and simulate changes. These changes affect the supply chain and allow supply chain managers to manage on an exception basis. A manager may want to understand what the impact would be of moving a warehousing facility or changing a manufacturing location. Armed with detailed cost and service information, many companies are making optimal decisions based on hypotheses about a changing marketplace. For example, one large consumer products manufacturer wanted to rationalize excess manufacturing capacity worldwide. Using sophisticated modelling techniques, the firm was able to model the cost and service impacts of these supply chain changes, resulting in millions of dollars of operating savings.

In today's fast-changing environment for highly engineered products, many of these decisions need to be made frequently as product lifecycles shorten. The variables associated with these decisions, while available within a company, have traditionally been difficult to model owing to both the complexity and inter-relationships of data sets. Ongoing supply chain modelling tools give the supply chain manager the ability to determine the least-cost way of delivering what the customer wants when he or she needs it.

The ability to manage global complexity and mass customization

Companies are increasingly required to work in global markets but still deal with the uniqueness of local requirements, needs and tastes. Many companies have developed IT solutions which allow for this capability. For example, there are 1.5 million ways that Deere can schedule production of 90 models. Deere leveraged proven scheduling techniques to develop the best production schedule through 'natural selection'. It used to take a day to produce the schedule for the coming week; now it is an instantaneous process. In this technique, the algorithms themselves (rules or criteria) are lines of code that act like living organisms. Through chance matings, different sections of code come together to produce unique combinations. Through deliberate mutations, in which some parts are randomly altered, the algorithms are continually modified. Eventually, only code approaching the desired solution remains. This technique often comes up with solutions that humans wouldn't normally see.

Dell Computer's Web site enables customers from anywhere to produce highly customized machines available for overnight delivery. This electronic commerce strategy has allowed Dell to strengthen ties to its end consumers, while companies such as Compaq and IBM leave much of the end configuration of machines in the hands of resellers. Dell has the ability to manage the customer relationship directly, more effectively market to its best customers and minimize expensive supply chain costs associated with distributed inventory and the administration of resellers.

The radical acceleration or elimination of traditional processes

IT is accelerating and eliminating traditional supply chain processes and blurring the relationship between products and services. For example, 3Com's US Robotics division has historically sold modems either directly or through a large network of resellers. Because modems are continually improving and changing, new product releases are frequent, making demand difficult to plan for. The challenge of coordinating manufacturing and distribution for these highly engineered products is expensive both in terms of logistics and administration costs. Advancements in IT completely transformed product delivery for US Robotics' x2 modem technology. Once a consumer purchases the basic modem, upgrades can be purchased electronically over the Internet, completely overturning the modem supply chain. Modem upgrades have practically become a service provided by 3Com which has virtually no material constraints. Even if millions of customers simultaneously place orders for modem upgrades, the company is no longer bound by its planning, production and distribution capabilities.

Continuous learning and innovation

Supply chain managers will need to continue to improve their supply chain processes and share usable information within the enterprise. It is important to capture information that leads to process improvements and new capabilities. Knowledge-management systems are being put in place to codify this usable knowledge and make it accessible across the company.

Shifting IT supply chain investments to top-line growth

IT has been enormously successful in streamlining costs and reengineering supply chain processes. But the strategic investments will now be based on using IT supply chain investments to enable top-line growth while still keeping an eye out for opportunities for cost savings. Figure 30.6 illustrates that IT spending is already heading in this direction.

Chrysler recognized that car-purchasing decisions were perceived by consumers as being tedious and unpleasant. In 1996 it started an online method for customer purchases which achieved $900 million in sales. By the year 2000, Chrysler estimates that this IT investment will generate $15 billion in revenue (source: *The Economist Survey of Electronic Commerce*). Granted, some of these revenues will come at the expense

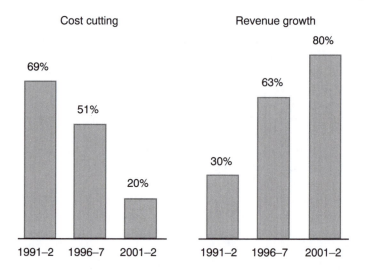

Figure 30.6 Main goal for IT investment: use IT to create revenue growth

of existing sales channels, but if having this capability makes it easier for customers to do business, they will shift more business in your direction.

Barnes & Noble, a retail bookseller, is also directing IT investment towards growth by creating a global, virtual bookstore in response to early leaders such as Amazon.com. The Web-based marketplace will be available anywhere, at any time, to anyone (with a PC and Internet access). People in remote locations will have the same easy access to literature that only customers in large cities have today.

Competing on IT arbitrage opportunities

One of the first steps in shifting IT investments to revenue growth is to understand what information is truly valued by customers, in what form, and whether there are changes in paradigms of how they get information that might be changed.

Typically 'windows of opportunity' emerge driven by marketplace or competitor changes which have created a situation for quick response and need for information. Figure 30.7 shows how more companies are investing their discretionary IT dollars in these arbitrage opportunities consistent with the collapsed time for catch-up.

Consider the last ten supply chain innovations in your industry (such as load-optimization software or EDI links) and the pace at which you adopted these capabilities compared to your competitors. What processes do you have in place to identify and adapt arbitrage opportunities? Does your company have the resources in place to be first to market with innovative approaches or is it generally risk averse? How often does the first player with a new technology in your industry develop the industry standard?

In an environment of rapid marketplace and technology change, the reality is that quick, potentially less robust responses to business

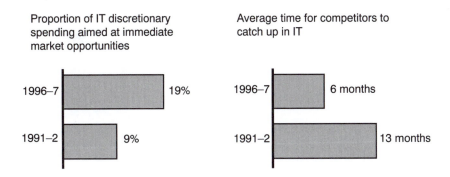

Figure 30.7   Create budgets for discretionary IT spending

challenges are emerging as preferred solutions and can deliver the edge over competitors. However, your business must be able to react quickly to market or 'arbitrage' opportunities to create top-line growth.

Conclusion

Putting together strategy, information technology and the supply chain to achieve success is not easy. The more packaged solutions have become available, the harder it is to find that unique advantage over the competition. But firms can do it, through wise investment in proven strategies and through creative, nimble and growth-oriented approaches to future opportunities. The future of IT in the supply chain is all about value creation. The steps outlined in this chapter establish the groundrules for achieving that goal.

Supply chain management tools
Minimizing the risks: maximizing the benefits

Bruce Richmond, Ann Burns, Jay Mabe, Linda Nuthall and Rick Toole

In an environment of rapid business and technological change, the challenge for each individual company is to determine which is the right individual or set of management tools to solve its specific supply chain requirements. This chapter outlines some of the key functionality of the various software components, reviews their inter-relationships and boundaries, then discusses the key decisions to be made in choosing the appropriate technology and ensuring that the benefits of such an investment are realized.

Introduction

A multitude of supply chain management tools are now available to provide intelligent decision support and execution management. However, no single tool provides the complete suite of desired capabilities to manage today's complex supply chain processes. Most tools have a functional focus on a single link, or a small set of links, in the chain. Changing market conditions and increasing acknowledgement within companies of the importance of supply chain concepts and process orientation have created the demand for a totally integrated supply chain solution.

In the absence of a total packaged solution, companies are looking to link their supply chain support systems, particularly enterprise resource planning (ERP) with 'best of breed' supply chain planning and real-time decision-support tools to achieve a totally integrated supply chain solution, which may even extend past the enterprise wall directly to the disparate applications of their suppliers, distributors and end customers.

Supply chain management tools

Supply chain management tools support the operation of and flow of information in the supply chain. They can be transactional systems—focused on day-to-day operations; planning systems—used for weekly or

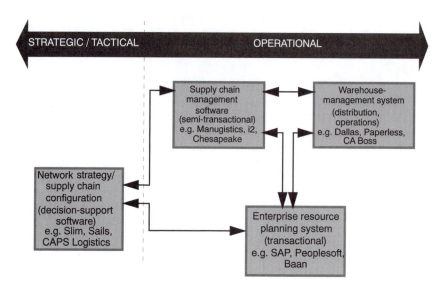

Figure 31.1   The inter-relationship between supply chain planning tools

monthly operational planning; or strategic tools—used to redesign the supply chain infrastructure. Many manufacturers feel that their current systems do not provide adequate support for their supply chain initiatives and, as a result, there is an ever increasing need for fully integrated information technology supply chain management solutions. Supply chain management solutions are those that incorporate all the functionality of network strategy/supply chain configuration, demand planning, manufacturing and distribution planning (supply planning), transportation management and warehouse management.

While there is no single supply chain management solution, there are hundreds of supply chain management products to choose from, ranging from ERP systems to sophisticated supply chain planning tools and PC-based forecasting packages.

In order for companies to take the best decisions they must understand the capability of the tools available, their inter-relationships and most importantly the degree of integration between these different software components (Figure 31.1). A useful starting point is to define what is meant by each of these components of supply chain management and what the leading functionality is for each.

Supply chain configuration tools

Supply chain configuration tools deliver quantified information to assist management in determining, at a high level, the infrastructure and other physical characteristics of an organization's operations required optimally to fulfil demand and/or achieve service-level objectives. These tools support strategic decision making by determining the number, capacity requirements and preferred location of distribution centres, warehouses, terminals and plants; supplier and transportation mode preferences; optimal material-sourcing locations and product group manufacturing sites. The information requirements of supply chain configuration tools include time-phased demands by customer or region; resource constraints and costs; transportation, warehousing and manufacturing costs; customer-service objectives; and profitability targets.

Demand-planning tools

Demand planning is the process of predicting the future demand for product. Demand-planning tools assist management in understanding the key drivers of demand and use historical data to forecast future demand patterns statistically. Sophisticated forecasting tools use multiple forecasting algorithms and simulation, multiple time horizons and aggregations, and can incorporate promotional demand, price elasticity/ sensitivity and even external forecasts (such as customers, suppliers, industry) in their calculations. Other value offerings of demand-planning tools include product lifecycle modelling; graphical representation of demand data; exception-based performance indicator tracking, reporting and management; and tracking and reconciliation of multiple internal forecasts (marketing, financial, annual etc.)

Supply-planning tools

Supply-planning tools are designed to help match supply to the expected demand. This requires planning at the strategic, tactical and operational levels. Supply-planning tools assist management with decisions such as which products to make, how to make them, what order to make them in and where to source materials from. They require input information such as product profitability, alternative production routings, methods and run rates, multiple stocking and sourcing locations and costs including changeover, work in progress (WIP) and inventory carrying. Typical capabilities of supply planning tools include the ability to determine seasonal prebuild needs; available to promise (ATP) and capable to promise (CTP) logic; and ability to locate capacity bottlenecks and potential stockout problems.

The more sophisticated supply-planning tools use interactive production planning Gantt charts and simulations, and also incorporate advanced constraints such as capacity utilization, customer priority and due dates.

Transport-planning and management tools

Transport-planning and management tools are designed to determine the most efficient inbound, outbound and intra-company transportation solution to meet all service needs at the lowest possible cost. Typical capabilities of transportation tools include preferred carrier, consolidation and backhaul opportunity identification; load creation and sequencing; vehicle-utilization optimization; shipment tracking; and dynamic routing and route scheduling. Advanced transportation tools also incorporate special service-level requirements such as specified delivery windows.

Warehouse-management tools

Warehouse-management systems (WMS) are primarily transactional tools which manage operations within the four walls of the warehouse. The functionality of these applications includes receiving; radio frequency/handheld scanning; quality assurance validation; put-away; wave management; order allocation; replenishment of product to pick locations; inventory control (cycle counting, aging, lot control, expiry date tracking); and load/shipment scheduling and confirmation.

Enterprise resource planning tools (ERP)

Traditionally, ERP tools were not considered under the umbrella heading of supply chain management tools. However, many manufacturers now view ERP systems as the core of their information technology strategies on which to build their supply chain management solutions.

ERP tools have grown out of a variety of products such as single-plant materials requirements planning (MRP) systems and financial systems. By adding applications to cover other functional areas, such as order entry and plant maintenance, ERP products have become enterprise-wide transactional tools which capture data and reduce the manual activities and tasks associated with processing financial, inventory and customer-order information.

One of the fundamental keys to improving core business processes for most organizations is fast and accurate integration, capture and retrieval of information. ERP systems achieve a high level of integration by utilizing a single data model, developing a common understanding of what the shared data represents and establishing a set of rules for accessing data. ERP systems within a single company utilize a common database as the basis of communication within the organization, with individual information systems accessing data via any number of standard networking protocols.

Although the concept of a single data model across a supply chain is an elegant solution to the problem of sharing data, it has proved difficult to implement, even inside large enterprises. Unlike today's ERP systems, supply chain solutions must be able to cope with the complexity of integrating information across any number of disparate information systems spanning the entire length of the supply chain. This issue has been partially addressed—previously by EDI and more recently, by universal acceptance of the Internet and associated protocols as a standard communications mechanism between businesses. However, communications have been limited to standard transactional information, not proactive decision-support data.

While integration of key business transactions across the supply chain is crucial to success, it is only part of the equation when the desired outcome is a fully integrated supply chain management solution. The need for integration of business processes across the supply chain is being driven by demanding market conditions including:

- shorter product lifecycles;
- product proliferation and mass customization;
- increased pressure on profit margins;
- predatory competition, globalization and larger-scale companies; and
- core competency focus, to survive in the age of the virtual enterprise.

This new process-oriented focus within the supply chain is forcing ERP vendors to address their capability gaps, specifically in the areas of decision support, demand and deployment planning, capacity and resource planning, warehouse management, network optimization and electronic commerce. Despite the efforts of many ERP systems vendors to link with other supply chain decision-support software vendors, in order to bridge their capability gaps, integration of these 'best of breed' systems carries its own set of complications and shortfalls in terms of information sharing and communications. ERP vendors are now feeling the pressure to supplement their internal functional orientation with process-oriented intra- and inter-company supply chain solutions.

The functionality boundaries are blurred

Selection of the right supply chain support is now a very complex task. One of the drivers of this complexity is the ever changing functionality offered by each system. The traditional core capabilities of some software packages are fast becoming just another module in a suite of offerings. As a result, the functional boundaries between tools have become somewhat blurred and it can often be very difficult to determine the extent of coverage possessed by a particular system.

For example, originally the core functionality of ERP applications was to link back-office operations such as manufacturing, finance and human resources into a single system. Today leading ERP software is being extended beyond this core functionality to include supply chain management functionality previously provided by niche players in specific supply chain solutions (Figure 31.2).

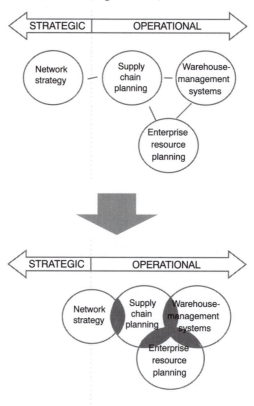

Figure 31.2   The changing inter-relationships between supply chain management applications

The challenge is figuring out what is the right software solution set for the specific supply chain being addressed.

Success factors for supply chain applications

Companies invest heavily in supply chain management applications, particularly ERP. However, it is often not clear how to maximize the benefits. The value of implementing a complex piece of software can be uncertain as management priorities and the business environment itself change. A number of critical decisions and questions must be addressed to ensure that the benefits are correctly identified and realized.

Develop/define business strategy and requirements

Above all, the choice of any technology must be aligned with the needs and direction of the industry and the individual business. It is critical to understand how technology can enable future corporate strategy and shape the dynamics of a supply chain. An expensive technology solution based on meeting today's requirements will rapidly be leapfrogged by the next generation of software and outdated by industry trends.

Identify the potential benefits

Another important step is the identification of opportunities for achieving significant business benefits through the implementation of supply chain management tools. The highest value-creating opportunities should be the starting point of any supply chain implementation. The focus should be on value drivers which enhance competitiveness and stakeholder value. Identifying the company's supply chain leverage point for creating value will focus the company on doing the 'right things' and consequently on selecting the right supply chain tool. For example, an opportunity to reduce working capital may lead the company to consider supply chain components which include sophisticated demand-planning and inventory-planning functionality.

Deciding which tools are required

In making a selection, identifying the required capabilities and functionality is a priority. Owing to the demand for visibility of information throughout the supply chain, it is critical to choose software that supports the way in which a company interacts and communicates with its suppliers and customers, particularly in demand planning, supply planning and distribution. In selecting an appropriate tool, consideration should be given to the level of integration with their trading partners' existing legacy systems.

With no one vendor currently offering a fully integrated supply chain management solution, companies are still faced with a great many tools and software vendors. Deciding which tools are really required is a difficult task. Is the functionality of ERP sufficient? Is a suite of tools required which fill the gaps to provide the full range of capabilities? The current versions of ERP successfully automate internal processes and provide a solid foundation on which to build, but they do not provide the dynamic, more strategic planning and forecasting tools and, more significantly, they lack the capability to integrate across enterprises. Although most software vendors have some degree of alliance and integration, such as SAP and Manugistics, selecting a combination of tools still has its difficulties, particularly win the design of interfaces between new and existing legacy systems.

A useful first step in deciding what systems are required is to understand the fundamental differences in their implementation:

- *Value*—ERP provides a transactional backbone and ties all facilities into a worldwide financial system but does not provide the necessary information to decide what should be made, when, where and by whom. These questions are better addressed by supply chain planning applications which function more as decision-support tools.
- *Time frame*—Depending on the functional and geographic scope, ERP implementations typically take 12–36 months, whereas a standard supply chain planning application typically takes 6–9 months to implement.
- *Payback period*—ERP systems have payback periods of at least two to five years. The average supply chain planning system has a payback within 6–12 months.
- *Disruption*—Typically the scale of disruption to an organisation implementing ERP is significant owing to the high numbers of end-users who need to be equipped, trained and supported. By comparison, supply chain planning tools are used by a select group of end users and consequently cause relatively less disruption.

The question is: how do I evaluate all these tools to decide what I need now and in the future? The two critical factors are the extent to which the systems will support the business by increasing customer value and the time it takes for the project to produce net value (see Figure 31.3).

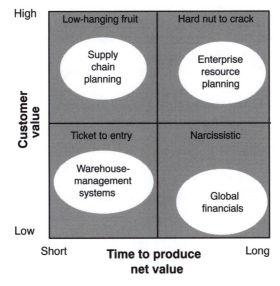

Figure 31.3   Evaluation model

Choosing a vendor

Faced with a choice between many software providers, often with few differentiating characteristics, it is difficult to decide on a vendor. This choice can be simplified by considering three key questions:

What is the vendor's specialization?
■ Manufacturing centric—Concentrates on supply side, i.e. sourcing expertise/focus.
■ Market centric—Concentrates on demand side, i.e. delivery expertise/focus.
■ Industry expertise—e.g. fast-moving consumer goods, utilities, healthcare etc.

What systems do your supply chain partners have?
Ideally you want to integrate with the suppliers/manufacturers in your supply chain. Even if the architecture is not the same, software and processes should be collaborative to enable information sharing etc. Different software providers are at varying stages of development in enabling their applications to function across enterprises.

Does one vendor offer all the required supply chain capabilities?
Although at this point no one vendor offers a one-stop solution, a number of key players are rapidly developing their supply chain capabilities. With future strategies in mind it would be advisable to consider a vendor who continues to develop its products and could offer future upgrades to your systems as they are developed.

Driving implementation from a rigorous business case

Technology alone is unlikely to deliver the full range of business benefits. Regardless of the specific type, all supply chain tools will require a significant degree of change to be successful. It is unlikely that technology alone will provide the 'quantum leap' improvement sought by the organization as the new technology will need to be supported by new or improved business processes and by a workforce with the right skills and motivation to perform the new job responsibilities. Consideration must therefore be given to how operational activities and processes must be changed to support the new IT solutions and how the organization and workforce must change to best utilize the new capabilities offered by the supply chain applications.

Traditional approaches for measuring the success of IT-related implementations rely heavily on whether particular project budgets and 'go live' dates have been met. While time and cost measures are important, these are not consistent with maximizing business benefits and attainment of these two metrics does not guarantee that the implementation will deliver value to the organization. To maximize the benefits of a supply chain implementation it is critical to develop a rigorous business case which is used to drive and direct the implementation effort to specific business outcomes. The business case needs to be developed to do more than just provide justification to senior management to move ahead with the project; it must be used to refocus the implementation continually and track the progress of the benefits capture.

The starting point is a rigorous business case which should ideally:

- cast the benefits net wide not only to focus on short-term requirements but also to target longer-term opportunities to maximize total possible benefits;
- understand the context for change by not only considering the environmental and competitive conditions in depth but also identifying the key implementation decisions to be made;
- be realistic with the nature of benefits achievable, the type and scale of the organizational impact and the rate of implementation. The key is to balance goals and objectives with what it is possible to achieve;

■ consider sustainability from the outset by taking into account the change required to make the benefits sustainable across all organizational dimensions. Sustainability is achieved by not only thinking through the process changes but also verifying the link to the organization strategy, establishing an appropriate technology foundation and proactively managing the overall change; and

■ have sufficient rigour to define the measurement process clearly, allocate ownership and responsibility for specific benefit areas, agree baseline and stretch goals to allow a degree of flexibility and identify reporting requirements to monitor progress.

Following a summary checklist to guide the development of the business case will ensure that it is sufficiently rigorous:

■ Look at all benefit opportunities.
■ Balance what you must achieve with what you should achieve.
■ Understand what your limitations are and set a realistic ambition level.
■ Take a holistic approach to business change sustainability.
■ Translate into quantifiable and measurable benefit targets.

It is critical to use the business case to drive and direct all activities throughout the implementation process. Ensuring this occurs requires that the following be considered:

■ Structure work around benefit delivery. Benefits need to be broken down in a quantifiable way, level by level, until each task has clearly defined responsibilities, deadlines and budgets.
■ Use the business case to monitor and report progress. Translate the benefits in the business case into operational metrics and associated measurement methods that can be used to track the progress of benefits capture continuously both during and post implementation.
■ Analyse the progress of benefits capture and refocus project activities, resources and priorities accordingly.
■ Allocate appropriate resources and provide the team with incentives which are directly tied to achieving targeted benefits.
■ Differentiate between project delivery and benefit delivery. Time and the right resources should be made available for benefits management while also focusing on the traditional project-management tasks.

Conclusion

Manufacturers are increasingly focusing on and undertaking significant initiatives to become more effective participants in their supply chains.

Information technology, not surprisingly, is the key enabler of these initiatives and, as such, investment in the right supply chain management IT support is critical for success. But the sheer number of tools available, and their evolving functionality, have made the task of software selection a complex, time-consuming and potentially expensive exercise. A structured approach helps companies ensure that they extract the best from the selection process. And the key to successful benefit realization in any implementation of a supply chain management application is to build a rigorous business case and be obsessive about using it as the driving force for implementation.

Internet logistics

Creating new customers and matching new competition

Grieg Coppe and Stephen Duffy

In the space of less than four years, the Internet, World Wide Web and electronic commerce have become household words. Much attention has focused on topics such as Web-based advertising, Web site proliferation, site security and business-to-consumer sales. Proportionately little coverage has addressed the use of these technologies for the improvement of supply-chain-related business processes. This chapter explores how the Internet can support supply chain management efforts, from both external and internal perspectives. It also identifies some of the risks and challenges that companies are likely to face along the way.

Introduction

While it is true that there has been much hype surrounding the Internet and its capabilities, it is hard to ignore the rapid penetration of this technology or the numerous predictions of continued explosive growth. By way of comparison, the Internet has reached the same number of users in three years that television took 15 years to reach. Although those users are largely exploring the Web for its information content and entertainment value, market research firms such as IDC, the Yankee Group and Forrester Research predict that between $115 billion and $196 billion of electronic commerce will take place over the Internet by the year 2000, compared with between $0.85 billion and less than $10 billion in 1996. Furthermore, a recent survey of e-information systems managers indicates that a high proportion of companies are already using the Internet to support key supply chain business processes with suppliers and end customers.

Much of the Internet's success can be attributed to its open standards, rapid adoption, relatively low cost and standard graphical user interface. These characteristics have enabled new classes of competitors to enter seemingly mature markets quickly and are driving existing players to change the way they do business. Take the automotive industry as an example. Today, new online purchasing services, such as USA-based

Auto-By-Tel and Microsoft Corporation's CarPoint are educating consumers, reducing shopping time and allowing customers to guide the shopping process according to their needs. New hybrid channel models involving new classes of intermediaries, such as online brokers, are helping consumers find the right vehicle at the right price, without haggling. Individual dealers and dealer collectives are providing consumers with a window to vehicle inventory, helping the consumer to reduce the number of dealers they need to visit before finding the car they want. And some dealers have gone so far as to enable online vehicle purchase, coupled with home vehicle delivery. Collectively, these market movements are increasing consumer power and changing the competitive landscape. This new breed of competition and increasingly informed and demanding customers are forcing traditional players to adapt. Certainly, the time has come to take note of the impact the Internet may have on all kinds of industries.

Benefits of the Internet supply chain

Companies have realized several supply-chain-related benefits through the use of the Internet. These are:

- more collaborative, timely product development through enhanced communication between functional departments, suppliers, customers and even regulatory agencies;
- reduction of channel inventory and product obsolescence owing to closer linkage across the supply chain and better insights into demand signals to drive product schedules and ultimately achieve build-to-order capability;
- reduction in communication costs and customer support costs with more interactive, tailored support capability inherent with Internet technologies;
- new channel capabilities to reach different customer segments and further exploit current markets; and
- ability to enhance traditional products and customer relationships through customization driven by Internet connectivity and interactivity.

Interacting with customers, suppliers and channel partners

Conventional supply chain management approaches have difficulty matching the cost-effective, dynamic and customer-driven nature of Internet-enabled approaches. Recognizing this, companies such as

Federal Express, Auto-By-Tel, Dell, Williams-Sonoma, Amazon.com, Jaguar, Toyota, Compaq and Cisco have leveraged the Internet to streamline their supply chains and to benefit channel partners and customers. For companies to exploit the Internet successfully, they must have a long-term vision, strong planning skills and technical insight.

A useful tool is the Internet presence framework, as illustrated in Figure 32.1. This provides a comprehensive guide to companies in developing their Internet-based supply chain strategies. This framework shows that use of the Internet ranges along a continuum, from Stage 1 for simple information dissemination to Stage 2 involving dynamic retrieval of more complex information, to Stage 3 where full-scale transactional services take place. At each stage the type of information, the nature of the interaction with the customer and the primary business objective differ. These stages are described in more detail below.

Information dissemination

For many technology companies, product complexity and configuration and integration requirements require that product specifications and technical information be made readily available to the channel and end customer. Because of short product lifecycles and the sheer number of people to inform, this is a challenging task. All too often, the end result is high paper-based publishing expenditures, burdensome inventory-carrying costs, high shipping expenses, high risk of collateral material inventory obsolescence and inconsistent or out-of-date information dissemination. Efforts to address the challenges of paper-based methods, with such approaches as proprietary-based electronic tools, have also failed owing to the high cost of establishing and maintaining a customized, proprietary installation and the subsequently limited number of audiences that can be reached via this medium. The Internet, by contrast, both extends the audience reach and increases the degree and richness of the interaction, as shown in Figure 32.2.

Companies such as Cisco and Compaq have turned to the Internet to take advantage of these characteristics and improve access to information at the same time. Channel partners and technical personnel at the end-customer location now turn to the Web for key product and technical information. Content is tailored by audience and secured from the eyes of unintended parties by password-protection features. Information is always up to date, published once and consistent. Furthermore, previously harder-to-reach small resellers and small to medium businesses now have access to the same mission-critical content as larger players. From an economic standpoint, these benefits justify the investment required to support the initial and ongoing Web site costs. Other examples include the following:

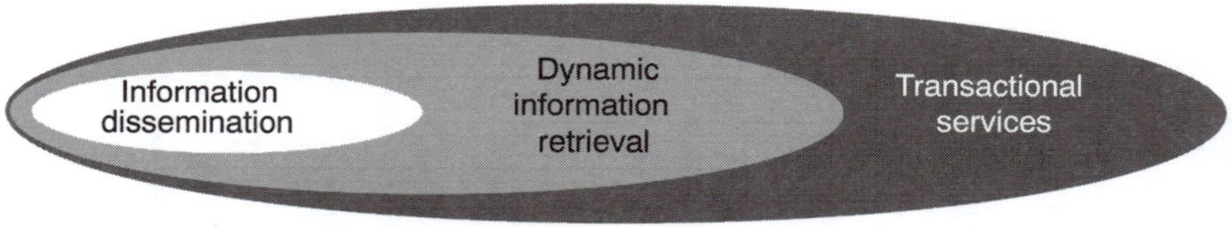

	Information dissemination	Dynamic information retrieval	Transactional services
Information exchanged	Stable information: documents created with few anticipated changes and relatively long shelf life	Dynamic information: information with ongoing changes and significant levels of depth/complexity	Real-time data: Transaction event specific data. Typically created in real time and not stored
Nature of interaction	Read only	Read and prescribe the format and depth of the content	Read, modify and create content
Primary business objective	Marketing and public relations	Customer service	Day-to-day operations
Key functions	Advertising, marketing communications, product and channel information	Order tracking, customer inquiry responses, technical support and service	Order entry, financial processing, order processing, transaction confirmation

Figure 32.1   Internet presence framework

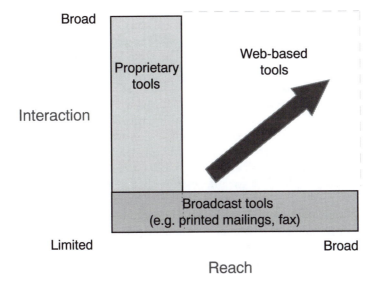

Figure 32.2 Matrix of reach and interaction

An electronics component manufacturer used the Internet to publish and disseminate technical documentation on its products. Previously this was accomplished by publishing specification books that, owing to the thousands of products offered, were expensive, published infrequently and became quickly outdated once in print. The new Internet-based approach saved millions a year in publishing costs and, equally important, greatly increased the utility of the product information for the customer. The Internet-based product specifications now include real-time updates, links to substitute component comparisons and interactive circuit design assistance.

A major computer manufacturer uses the Internet to communicate with its reseller channel partners, replacing a conglomeration of paper-based, fax-based and proprietary electronic-based communications channels. The benefit of this approach is a much greater audience reach, reduced communication and publishing costs and more accurate and timely reporting of sales data. The impact of this latter capability has been a significant reduction in working capital because of better forecasting and reduction in inventory and obsolescence costs.

Dynamic information retrieval

Beyond information publishing, the Internet's interactive capabilities can be leveraged dramatically to enhance the experience of doing business with a company. By placing information at the customer's fingertips, relying on a standard graphical interface, the browser, and rendering content to customers based on their specific requests, companies can customize the customer interaction. Furthermore, companies can add value-added services to assist the customer during purchase and before ultimate product delivery. One such success story is Federal Express. Customers can easily determine the exact package location and expected (or actual) time of package delivery by entering a simple tracking number. Imagine doing this for your customers—allowing them access to up-to-date order status. Not only does this provide a service, but it also diminishes costly calls to customer-service centres.

Cisco's use of the Web for information dissemination has been taken one step further to provide a complete online service and support around the clock. Customers logging into the appropriate area on the site will find tailored responses to frequently asked questions and supporting information. This has lifted a burden off the shoulders of call centre staff, and improved overall responsiveness to customer needs. Cisco has seen a significant reduction in information requests to its call centre and a reduction in overall 'publishing' costs.

In the consumer market, Jaguar and Lexus, along with many individual car dealerships, have used the Internet to provide customers with visibility to pre-owned vehicle inventory. Customers can search the online database to find cars that meet their needs. During this discovery process, the customer is free from potentially unwanted salesperson interruption or sales pitches, and the dealer eliminates investment of salesperson time in the prospective customer. Once such customers enter the dealership doors, it typically takes much less salesperson time to get the customer into the car that they want, thereby improving the dealer's bottom line. In Jaguar's case, the customer can actually reserve a pre-owned automobile even before its existing lease is up. In this way, Jaguar significantly improves its pre-owned vehicle inventory turns and the overall economics of the pre-owned vehicle programme. Customers get the added benefit of finding the exact car they want and reserving it so they know they will get what they want.

New product development

Another successful supply chain implementation of dynamic retrieval via the Internet is new product development. Cross-functional product development has been hailed as the most reliable way to bring creative, market-driven, manufacturable and profitable products to market on a consistent basis. A cross-functional team avoids over-reliance on one key individual, and incorporates outside resources that are too specialized or costly to employ on a continuous basis. A cross-functional approach synchronizes the perspectives of marketing, finance, manufacturing and engineering, as well as those of suppliers and customers, so that time and effort in the design process are not wasted. The key aspect required to make this team work well is frequent and focused communication.

Using the dynamic information-retrieval capability of the Internet offers a solution to many of the communication hurdles common in any product-development effort. All members of a design team can be given access to a shared design Web site through which much of the knowledge and information sharing that is necessary for the completion of the design can be conducted. By tailoring the information accessed to suit their needs, users can also avoid unnecessary sifting through unwanted data and further speed the design process.

The process of translating designs into workable, manufacturable solutions could also be enabled through the Internet. Design for manufacture could be facilitated through the creation of a knowledge database that could reduce the review cycle. Design guidelines, part specifications, vendor lead times, part availability, component costs and preferred suppliers could be accessed by both engineers and manufacturers to ensure that the creative design process was also leading towards a practical, cost-effective, manufacturable solution. By creating tailored reports from the back-end knowledge database, users can speed up their inclusion of critical information. Suppliers could be linked into the design process early via the Internet to avoid conflicts or surprises in later stages of design, where changes are more costly and require more rework.

This use of the Internet offers many benefits, including improved coordination, increased process efficiencies, reduced manufacturing and materials cost, greater creativity and a tighter market focus. Customers will be offered the products that they want sooner and cheaper. More importantly, these factors taken together will lead to increased speed to market, which can dictate the eventual success of the product launch. Studies indicate that effective use of the Internet in the product-development process may reduce product-introduction delays by between 12 and 37 per cent.

Transactional services

The use of electronic data interchange (EDI), bulletin boards and commercial online services to conduct inter-entity exchange of information is relatively common among today's business community. Fortune 500 companies use EDI to exchange business information with their larger vendors and customers. Other organizations have used commercial online service providers (such as AOL and Prodigy) to support their customer-service operations. Numerous benefits have been associated with these forms of electronic communication, particularly improved process efficiency and better customer service.

Unfortunately, several issues with these technologies have limited their ability to serve the broad market for electronic transactional services. Traditional EDI is expensive to implement, ongoing communication via value-added networks is costly, conforming to EDI standards is difficult and only the largest enterprises have the economies of scale to benefit from an EDI installation. Bulletin boards are often a patchwork approach requiring manual maintenance because of the lack of interfaces with back-end enterprise systems. Commercial online services limit control over the channel of communication.

The use of Internet-based transactional services promises to overcome the drawbacks associated with traditional means of online communication and radically increase the effectiveness and efficiency of electronically mediated communication. Transactional services, the real-time, event-specific exchange of information between an organization and its customers or partners, offer the largest potential economic benefits of the Internet and demand the highest degree of technical sophistication. A transactional service may take the form of either a monetary exchange for a product or service or information exchanged between two entities for decision-making or planning purposes.

Internet-enabled supply chains are a significant use of Internet technologies for interaction with both vendors and customers of an organization. Traditional batch EDI transaction sets can be transported via the Internet, with the advantage of far more trading partners being able to afford connectivity. Beyond the limited scope of EDI applications, a wide array of new applications will be developed that will allow real-time use of the Internet. Using a Web-based front end, authorized partners will connect directly to enterprise systems and data warehouses. Partners then find their own secured or password-protected areas in which to gain access to key business information and transaction applications.

Internet-based transactional services are significantly improving production and logistics efficiencies. Vendors can access demand-projection pages to obtain their rolling forecast update for the period and integrate that information into their own master production schedule. Vendors can obtain purchase orders via the Internet to initiate their own production process and also confirm receipt and acceptance of the purchase order. Advance shipping notices can be submitted via the Internet on completion of an order for immediate integration into the receiving entity's warehouse-management system. Online freight rate tables and global shipment 'track and trace' capabilities are also being developed to automate the shipping process.

In the area of order management and distribution, transactional services also promise to improve customer satisfaction and efficiency. An order-entry module provides a porthole into a variety of customer queries. From here the possibilities include direct routing to an available-to-promise module to calculate lead times and shipment dates. Order confirmation (including commitment dates) can be sent to the partner via e-mail or EDI over the Internet. Business partners can per-form real-time inquiries about order status through Web pages linked to materials management, manufacturing and sales and distribution mod-ules. Finally, payment via secure bank transfers can be authorized.

In comparison to traditional approaches, Internet-based transactional services offer significant advantages to businesses implementing elec-tronic communications. Duplicate paper-based systems are minimized or eliminated as all vendors and customers can be brought online. The implementation cost per connected supplier/customer is reduced as the number of connected partners increases. Total supply chain visibility is improved as more pieces of the supply chain, including subcontractors and small vendors, achieve connectivity and provide current informa-tion. Small vendors are offered a level playing field with larger vendors, potentially improving the creativity and speed-to-market of new con-cepts. Small customers are offered the same access to critical informa-tion as large customers, eliminating potential restraint-of-trade issues. All customers will be more satisfied with the breadth and immediate availability of information regarding their orders.

Dell Computer, like many catalogue-based companies, uses the Internet to provide a natural extension of its already prosperous cata-logue business. The combination of an online catalogue, product con-figurator and online order-placement capability permits customers to configure product bundles to their liking and then place an order directly to the build plan. Dell is then able to fulfil these orders in days, incurring very little variable selling costs in the process. Like the Federal Express example, Dell customers are in the driver's seat during the whole process, creating a customized shopping and purchasing experi-ence. The success of this model is underscored by the more than $1 mil-lion in Internet-based business that Dell closes every day and a much higher than industry average number of inventory turns.

Customer relationship management

Another use of Internet-based transactional services is in interactive mar-keting and selling. For years marketing experts have advocated the idea that companies need to know their customers better. To manage market-ing and selling cycles effectively, managers need a knowledge of customer values, needs and preferences. Such information will allow for targeted, specific marketing and correspondingly higher sales conversion rates.

Unfortunately, gathering information about customers is expensive and time consuming—and the information quickly becomes outdated. At best, the quest to target customers has yielded a limited set of cus-tomer segments representing a broad range of underlying values. Modern segmentation techniques represent an improvement over the past, but ironically not the intimate level of understanding obtained by the corner grocer of years past.

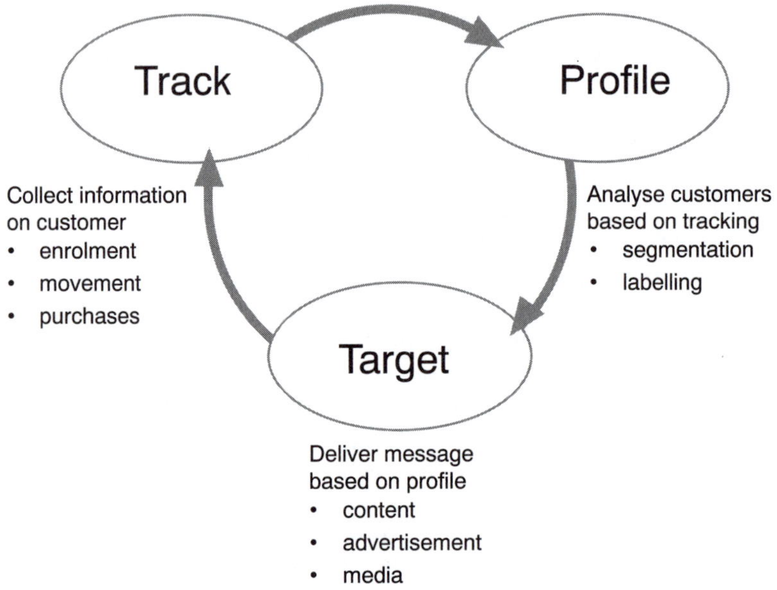

Figure 32.3   The marketing and selling cycle

The Internet offers companies the opportunity to overcome some of the shortcomings of past marketing efforts through the use of an integrated Internet marketing and selling channel. Instead of the broad segments of the past, technology enabled 'markets-of-one' can be developed based on individually observed behaviours, buying patterns and preferences. Using real-time tracking, profiling and targeting engines, these relationship-marketing Internet sites will allow companies to execute the marketing and selling cycle on a person-by-person basis.

Figure 32.3 shows how such an application would work. Users might visit an organization's site and on entering be prompted to log in—the company might offer a coupon if they register. After filling in relevant marketing data—demographic, personal and financial—the users would be presented with personalized pages. These tailored pages would include specific content, product offerings, advertisements and editorial commentary, all based on the customer's registration profile. A user may choose to purchase a product, which they may preview on screen. Product records for items within the site will be tied to the enterprise inventory system, ensuring ability to commit. After selecting shipping options and payment preferences, secure payment information will be transmitted to the bank and fulfilment systems notified via an enterprise system interface. In some cases, the entire order-fulfilment cycle will be completed with little or no manual intervention.

Throughout this process, as users negotiate their way around the site, movements will be tracked in real time by back-end activity logs. Registry information, viewing activity (movement), purchase intention and actual purchases can all be tracked and analysed to update users' profiles. As more information is gathered, the site experience is further tailored to their preferences. After the users log off the site, the history of their activity will be stored and analysed by back-end tools for future marketing.

For the marketing professional managing this channel, real-time feedback on the elements of the marketing mix and the ability to tie the channel directly to legacy systems make the Internet 'market-of-one' concept a powerful medium. The effectiveness of all promotions and advertisements on the site can be measured and reviewed during the promotion, allowing for immediate course corrections. A variety of potential product locations and pricing options can be tested in real time to understand which yields the best results.

Internet-enabled interactive marketing and selling will revolutionize how companies do business with customers. As online purchasing becomes more common, Internet technologies will allow companies to deliver increasingly attractive (relevant and personalized) marketing offers with little or no expensive human intervention. Such applications position a company to establish themselves in a rapidly emerging channel—one in which the average user has markedly higher disposable income than the population at large. And while costly, these implementations will produce new high-margin revenue streams.

Companies such as Cisco, Williams-Sonoma and Amazon.com have all established ongoing dialogues with their customers over the Internet.

Williams-Sonoma provides recipes and cooking-related information to customers at its site, letting customers keep recipes and items of interest in a personal storage location. In that way, customers are motivated to maintain an ongoing relationship with Williams-Sonoma after purchase. In the process, the company retains top-of-mind brand recognition with customers and can stay in touch with their needs and interests over time. When the next occasion to purchase cooking-related items occurs, customers who are still in touch with this relationship-building service, are likely to return.

Amazon.com, an Internet-born success story, captures book-purchase information about a customer. When new book titles are released on a topic in which the customer has previously shown interest, Amazon notifies the customer. The company is smart enough, however, not to bombard customers, but rather passes on only the best matches it can find. In this way, it stays in contact with the customer, enticing them to return for more purchases when they are ready. It can provide this customized relationship and a virtually unlimited selection with a fraction of the logistics cost, inventory and capital investment of a traditional bookseller.

At Toyota.com, Toyota owners can register to join an online owners' club where topics of a general automotive nature and specific care and maintenance tips are offered. Around this site, Toyota has built a sense of community which tends to foster loyalty. And, even if they do not return, a positive experience is likely to be shared with potential brand new customers, thereby generating sales lift.

Future challenges for the Internet

By providing customers with direct access to up-to-date information and a window to supply chain data, online interactions provide high value at little variable cost. Since the experience can be highly tailored to the needs of the customer, the customer feels well taken care of. However, these benefits should be understood in balance with some risks and challenges imposed by Internet-enabled supply chain management approaches.

While providing channel partners and customers with ready access to internal data, including inventory availability and order status, companies remove a buffer layer of risk protection. In conventional dealings with customers, internal mishaps or complexities can often be dealt with by quick employee decision making, trade-offs and stop-gap solutions. However, once you provide a window into the enterprise, much of this buffer goes away. Customers can see at first hand how smoothly things run inside the organization. And, given that the Internet-enabled consumers are also more informed and in control, companies will have to be prepared to respond to their demands and concerns.

If things were bumpy before adding Internet services, it is possible for them to get a great deal worse unless appropriate planning for process and system integration has taken place. Internet-enabled solutions ultimately have touch points with conventional business processes. These touch points need to be addressed in advance to ensure integration. Similarly, Internet-based applications ultimately need to interface with back-end or legacy systems. This interface can be complex. If it is not appropriately addressed, companies can be making promises they cannot keep to their online customers. Take the example of the online inventory-reservation application. The customers search an online database, find products to their liking, reserve them and place orders against that inventory. However, the online application is a stand-alone application with nightly batch-based replication to legacy systems. If a conventional, offline customer reserved the same piece of inventory earlier in the day, there may be duplication.

Integration is only part of the puzzle. Online solutions may require completely new processes, not just integration with existing ones. While it is often relatively easy to design these new processes from the ground up, care must be taken to adopt a holistic approach. For instance, though Web sites will reduce aggregate call centre volume, they will result in some new types of calls. If appropriate steps have not been taken to educate some or all of the call centre staff about your online offerings, they may not be appropriately equipped to respond to customer enquiries.

Similarly challenging, if not more so, are the cultural and organizational shifts inherent in migrating to or supporting supply chain processes on the Internet. Internet-based solutions inevitably change the rules of the game and extend the roles and responsibilities of various departments. Since for most companies a complete shift to an Internet platform is inconceivable, there is a need to operate simultaneously under conventional and virtual business models. Unless appropriately trained and prepared, staff may find this confusing. In the automotive industry, some dealers have implemented Web-based shopping services but kept the same in-dealer sales processes. Consequently, Internet-informed customers who walk in the door ready to purchase an exact car for the price they have researched to be appropriate are likely to be subjected to the same lengthy and high-pressure sales process served up to a customer who walks through the door with no information or pre-determined expectations. Thus, it is imperative for organizations to support their Internet-enabled solutions.

Lastly, the co-existence of different channel structures gives rise to potential channel conflict. Care must be taken to define guidelines for salespersons and channel partners to ensure that potential conflict is addressed. In many cases this can be accomplished by serving different products in different channels. If this is not feasible, the total product bundle needs to be differentiated in some way, so that additional services are or are not available to the online customer. This ensures that no two competing channels offer exactly the same value proposition. Although this approach makes sense for legal reasons, it also makes sense from a customer-segmentation perspective. It is likely that the Internet customer has different buyer values than the traditional buyer, and thus is better served by a different value proposition. Given this hypothesis, you would be well served to investigate these potential differentiating factors before defining your online value proposition.

Conclusion

The rapid penetration of the Internet into the market is dramatically changing the competitive landscape. New competitors are fast entering mature markets, while consumers with direct access to information and transaction services are driving changes in the way companies do business. Conventional supply chain approaches cannot match the cost-effective and dynamic nature of the Internet. Companies wishing to exploit the Internet must understand its capacity to distribute both basic and complex information and enable transactions to be conducted in real time. The Internet can streamline the supply chain in ways that have not previously been possible without this dynamic technology. Clear vision, strong planning and technical insight into the Internet's capabilities will ensure that companies maximize its potential for better supply chain management and, ultimately, improved competitiveness.

Part VI
Special Interest

Overview

A closer inspection of specific industries and geographic markets raises specialized supply chain challenges. This collection of chapters presents perspectives and insights on the critical supply chain challenges facing a range of industries, including the automotive, consumer goods, telecommunications and healthcare industries. And businesses contemplating the challenge of the world's biggest market of the future will benefit from insights into China's unique supply chain issues.

To round off, the emerging field of reverse logistics points to the continuing evolution of supply chain thinking and the necessity for managers to get ready for the next generation of supply chain challenges.

Australia's fast-moving consumer goods industry

Challenging manufacturers to join the integration revolution

33

Peter Moore

Australia's manufacturing firms have limited time to prepare for the revolution in supply chain integration. While retailers have forged ahead, manufacturers have so far taken only limited steps towards supply chain integration. To move forward they need to take immediate action to respond to retailers' efficient consumer response (ECR) programmes. They must also look to the longer term by appointing senior managers with cross-functional responsibility for the supply chain. And they must develop an explicit supply chain strategy that sets out how each firm will derive business advantage (whether through efficiency, customer service or competitive advantage); position the company to gain advantage from the shifting industry structure; capture the value of change within the business; and provide for a focused implementation around a small number of high-priority supply chain capabilities.

Introduction

A recognition of inter-dependence among functions and companies in the supply chain is emerging as a driving force in the Australian consumer products industry. Even before the current ECR initiatives, other programmes, such as quick response and lean manufacturing, championed supply chain integration. Driven primarily by retailers, a turning point has been reached in the development of the fast-moving consumer products supply chain in Australia.

The retailers, as well as making further progress with their own initiatives, now need the manufacturers to respond—the retailers' initiatives cannot realize their full potential without action from manufacturers. The latter must formulate strategies based on supply chain integration principles and strive to implement them effectively. It is only when retailers and manufacturers align their objectives and activities that increased value can be delivered to the end consumer.

It is estimated that the fast-moving consumer goods industry in Australia could reduce its collective operating costs by over 5 per cent

Table 33.1
Examples of supply chain improvements

Company	Supply chain features	Benefits
Food company, Australia	• Integrated finished goods logistics across several business units	• $15m cost reduction • $10m estimated service benefits

Beverage company, Australia	• Optimized supply chain performance
	  • finished goods logistics
	  • production
	  • procurement
		• $30m cost reduction
		• Targeted service levels to each customer group

Automotive company, Australia	• Consistent supply chain strategy • Global supply pipeline precisely synchronized with Australian production schedules • Flexibility in sourcing—local and overseas	• Low inventories • High level of responsiveness to customer demand • High-quality components
Food company, US	• Reengineered supply chain processes • Rapid response manufacturing capabilities • Greater integration between R&D, procurement, manufacturing, distribution and sales and marketing	• Increased sales • Rationalized sourcing and stronger relationships with fewer suppliers

($1 billion) combined with a 25 per cent reduction in inventory through the pursuit of ECR. For individual companies, the scale of benefits and diversity of achievements involved can be conveyed by looking at a few examples taken from the USA and Australia, as seen in Table 33.1.

Australia's food manufacturers are behind

An in-depth study has shown that, overall, Australian food manufacturers are relatively unsophisticated in the development of their supply chain integration capabilities. As part of its continuing research on supply chain integration, Andersen Consulting partnered with Professors Norma Harrison and Peter Gilmour of Macquarie University to conduct a study into the supply chain practices of leading food manufacturers in Australia. The study involved six of Australia's leading consumer prod-

Table 33.2
Profiles of the six companies in the study

Product	Food/beverage	5
	Packaged goods	1
Market	Australasia	6
Ownership	Australian	3
	International	3
Size (Total sales)	A$100–500 million	3
	>A$500 million	3
Total sales	All study companies	$A 4.4 bn

ucts manufacturers, five food and beverages companies and one consumer packaged goods company. Together they represent total sales of about AUS$4.4 billion (Table 33.2). The study examined their supply chain capabilities across all functions from procurement, through manufacturing and distribution to planning and performance reporting. Senior management from each participating company made a self-assessment of their supply chain capabilities. Additional information and performance levels were collected using a questionnaire.

The key findings of the study were:

- The study companies remained unsophisticated in their supply chain capabilities, falling well short of best practice.
- The study companies all had ambitious targets to increase supply chain sophistication within two years.
- Few of the companies had coordinated change programmes that would deliver against the targets.
- None of the study companies (at the time of the research) had a clearly articulated supply chain strategy covering both market impact and internal effectiveness.

If the study companies are any gauge of the broader consumer products industry, then the rhetoric of supply chain integration is far ahead of actual implementation. As Figure 33.1 shows, the average sophistication shown by the study companies in implementing integrated supply chain practices varied between 2.0 and 2.7 on a four-point scale. As this diagram indicates, Level 4 represents best practice commonly recognized in

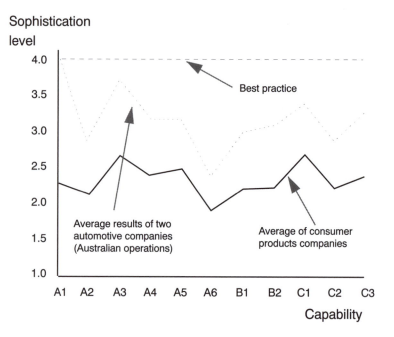

Figure 33.1 Average current capability sophistication: consumer products vs automotive products

supply chain literature. The top line, showing the performance of two Australian automotive companies, demonstrates that high levels of performance are achievable in practice. The automotive companies are expecting to increase their supply chain sophistication still further over the coming two years, particularly in integrated supply chain management capability.

Signs of the supply chain integration revolution

Companies that have been the early movers towards supply chain integration will have a significant business advantage, at the same time being able to deliver superior customer service levels. Retailers, and also logistics providers and some manufacturers, are making rapid progress towards integrated supply chain operations. Australian food manufacturers, therefore, have only a short window of opportunity to influence the development of the supply chain. The evidence for rapid progress towards supply chain integration is clear:

■ Australian retailers are advancing their ECR programmes to the point that action is now required from manufacturers.
■ Significant investment is being made in logistics infrastructure by retailers, manufacturers and logistics service providers.
■ The available information technology solutions have significantly improved logistics functionality.
■ Several Australian success stories in supply chain integration have proved that there are real benefits to be achieved.

Well-advanced retailer ECR initiatives

Of all the key players in the grocery supply chain in Australia, the major retailers and wholesalers are most influential in delivering progress towards an integrated supply chain. Their relative size compared to the manufacturers that supply them, as well as the key position they hold in the supply chain directly interfacing with the end consumer, ensures that they will take a leading role in shaping the fast-moving consumer goods supply chain.

Intense activity is now underway in supply chain development among Australia's leading grocery retailers and wholesalers, in part resulting from the ECR initiative championed by the Grocery Manufacturers of Australia. One of the frustrations for food manufacturers is that each of the major retailers is pursuing a different approach to supply chain integration. Indeed, there are sometimes differences in the approaches within a retailer with significant variations by state and product category. Nevertheless, there are three aspects of supply chain development that are common to all the retailers: the development of supply chain capabilities through pilots; restructuring to manage the supply chain more effectively; and greater utilization of electronic commerce (e-commerce).

Supply chain pilots

All the major retailers have a number of pilots (both internally and with manufacturers) underway to develop their capabilities in supply chain integration. Woolworths is trialling its 'quick response' programme built around forecasts and three-hourly response with Uncle Tobys and others. Coles has an initiative with Smiths Snack Foods on POS-driven direct-store delivery. Franklins is working to develop its capabilities with staff from suppliers seconded full time to Franklins' project teams. Davids has a number of initiatives including developing its cross-docking capability in key warehouses.

Restructuring

Significant consolidation is taking place in retailers' and wholesalers' logistics operations as they seek to gain critical mass in their operations and achieve synergies within business units. Grocery Holdings is an example of the latter and was established to consolidate the purchasing functions of Coles Supermarkets and Bi-Lo. Woolworths is moving to a more consistent national model for its logistics operations and has recently acquired Australian Independent Wholesalers (AIW) as a significant push into wholesaling. Davids has moved, primarily through acquisition, to consolidate the independent wholesalers. Among a long list of purchases, John Lewis is now being used in Victoria as Davids' primary food service operation with a parallel supermarket chain distribution channel for its Jewel supermarkets and the franchise chains.

E-commerce

Electronic commerce is also an important area where consumer products retailers and wholesalers appear to have made significant inroads. Most progress has been made in the electronic communication of purchase orders and it is estimated that some retailers have already established EDI links with 30 per cent to 35 per cent of their supplier base. Electronic commerce is also being extended to include purchase-order confirmations, ASNs/SBNs and invoices. Woolworths is well advanced, with plans to drive store replenishment from point-of-sale (POS) scan data. Internal pilots have been operating successfully since 1996. Distribution centre replenishment-planning capabilities have reached the stage where Woolworths can extend the availability of electronic information to include forecast data by stock keeping unit (SKU) and location up to 90 days ahead for selected suppliers. Using an example outside of food retailing, one of Australia's major non-food consumer products retailers has for several years provided forecast data to its key suppliers by SKU and by store, each week, on a 90-day rolling basis.

The wild card still to be played in the electronic commerce arena is home shopping. It is no longer a question of whether home shopping will be a major event but of when and how it will become a mainstream channel. In the USA, organizations such as Peabody have been operating city-based programmes for many years. In the UK, Tesco is already trialling Internet home shopping, with Sainsbury planning to launch its 'Internet supermarket' early this year. In Australia, many grocery retailers have home shopping sites on the Internet, with the rest currently investigating the viability of implementation in the near future. For instance, Woolworths has been trialling computer home shopping in the Queensland town of Gunpowder (near Mt Isa) and now has plans to roll out the scheme nationwide.

All this activity clearly points to Australia's retailers and wholesalers having made significant progress in implementing the basic capabilities required for supply chain integration. With many of the pilots now reaching completion, the retailers will be expecting the manufacturers to respond quickly. They will also be expecting to achieve the supply chain cost savings that were put forward to justify their multimillion-dollar investments.

Significant investment in logistics infrastructure

A number of highly sophisticated distribution centres (DCs) are now being developed around the country to move goods more efficiently. The key attributes of these DCs include advanced conveyer and sortation systems, radio frequency technology used to enable automatic identification and time slotting of products, more advanced warehouse-management systems and layouts that support cross-docking.

Progress towards supply chain integration is unaffected by who owns and operates these DCs. The retailers, manufacturers and logistics service providers are all trying to stake a presence in finished goods logistics infrastructure as they seek to capture the value from the supply chain within their businesses.

The retailers, through their major DCs, are leading the way in developing logistics infrastructure. Woolworths' DC in Warwick, Queensland, and Franklins' DC in Brisbane are examples of the sophisticated operations needed for supply chain integration. The logistics service providers are considering ways of operating industry-wide logistics operations, either leveraging off their contract work with manufacturers or alternatively investing in new facilities as Linfox has done in Homebush and Clayton.

In the road freight sector, loading, unloading and transporting goods throughout the supply chain is becoming a more sophisticated process. The emphasis on just-in-time inventory management means that road freight deliveries are becoming smaller and more frequent. More sophisticated route-planning processes are allowing consolidation of loads in the main transport corridors allowing use of efficient vehicles such as B-doubles. Other techniques such as slip-sheeting, more effective load compilation and roll-on roll-off are increasing the efficiency of pick-ups and drop-offs. Real-time communication and tracking capabilities are also becoming available. For example K&S Freighters (part of Scott Corporation) has been trialling a satellite-based global positioning and data-processing technology known as 'Rockwell' for its fleet of trucks.

In the USA it is now common practice for retailers to coordinate and manage third-party transport provider relationships so that goods are picked up from suppliers FOB and delivered to the retailer's DC, rather than delivered by suppliers FIS. Sears, Eaton's, Kmart and Wal-Mart are just a few of the retailers that have achieved greater control over inbound freight and scheduling and the associated costs.

In parallel to the physical infrastructure, an information infrastructure is being developed. Gemmnet is perhaps the best established of these, derived from its support by Woolworths. EAN Australia is working to standardize the underlying data protocols for information capture and e-commerce. Many other organizations are also resolving to create the components of the information infrastructure, although many trading partners continue to exchange proprietary EDI messages.

Internet commerce and EDI will exist side by side, each serving a different purpose. EDI will be used for high-volume business-to-business communication, while the Internet will be used for customers and suppliers in lower-volume transactions.

Improved logistics functionality of information technology solutions

As with many business revolutions, technology is a key driver of the supply chain revolution. The increasing functionality and variety of packaged software, communications developments including the Internet and the decreasing cost of hardware are dramatically improving the capability of information technology systems available to manufacturers and retailers.

The options are now so numerous that one of the main barriers to making progress in deploying the technology is the time taken to understand, prioritize and implement the newly available systems. Examples of recent technology advancements are shown in Table 33.3.

In parallel with the new technologies, the functionality of business systems is also improving significantly. Driven by the success of SAP R/3,

Table 33.3
Logistics information technology

Capability	Supporting technology	Examples
Customer connectivity/ supplier partnering	• ED • Internet commerce • Product catalogues	Gemmnet, EAN net Oracle Web browser
Efficient distribution	• Warehouse-management systems • Specialist packaged systems (slotting, route planning, etc) • Conveyancing, sorption and other handling systems	Paperless, Dallas, Slot-it, Trucks, Transit, Roadshow
Demand-driven sales planning	• Supply chain planning	Manugistics, IRI Logistics, IZ
Lean manufacturing	• Manufacturing/ warehouse simulators • Finite capacity/constraint-based scheduling • Manufacturing execution systems	Cinema, Taylor II Scheduler, i2 MES
Integrated supply chain planning	• Supply chain planning tools • Supply chin network models	Numetrix Linx

the business system market is now measured in billions of dollars and we are now seeing market success and new offerings from a number of companies such as Oracle, Baan, J.D. Edwards and others.

Australian success stories

Already several companies are proving in trials—both internally and with trading partners—that supply chain integration delivers business success. These pioneers are developing the skills and experience that will filter through the industry and, by raising the bar on their competitors, will force others to follow. Examples of Australian success stories are shown in Table 33.4.

A change agenda for food manufacturers

Few Australian food manufacturers are well positioned for this new world. Those that do not have major change programmes underway

Table 33.4
Australian success stories

Company	Logistics actions	Market impact
Coca-Cola	Direct-store delivery to some CBD supermarkets	Maintaining control of distribution channel
Smiths Snack Foods	Trailing use of POS data to drive direct store replenishment	Reduced stockouts and back-of-store inventory
Goodman Fielder	Consolidating finished goods distribution across business units	Improving customer service and gaining significant efficiency
Hilton Hosiery	POS scan data linked directly to pantyhose production machinery	Reduced inventory and improved customer service

must take urgent action at both the operational and strategic level. The winners will be those that have made the investment in resources and management time to adapt their supply chain operations to meet the challenges and opportunities ahead.

Growing number of logistics director appointments

One trend providing evidence that manufacturers are preparing to respond is the growing prevalence of cross-functional supply chain or logistics roles at the senior management level. The appointments demonstrate commitment to the principles of supply chain integration and show a willingness to support the rhetoric with leadership and senior management sponsorship.

Of the top ten leading food and beverage manufacturers in Australia (ranked by revenue), seven have cross-functional logistics roles in place, with five of these positions being created in the last two years. Table 33.5 shows the sample companies that have made senior logistics appointments with cross-functional responsibility and gives a more detailed breakdown of their roles and responsibilities.

For the organizations with cross-functional logistics directors, responsibility was analysed in terms of three categories: authority, scope and focus. In terms of authority, the majority have line responsibility for the supply chain and show that there is a commitment to manage supply operations as an integrated set of activities. Scope demonstrates that the appointments are truly cross-functional, with all logistics managers

Table 33.5
Logistics appointments

Year role created	Goodman Fielder	1996
	Coca-Cola Amatil	1995
	Fosters Brewing	1996
	Lion Nathan	1996
	ConAgra Holdings Barrett Burston	1992
	Nestlé	1996
	Unilever	1993
Authority	Line	5
	Advisory	2
Scope (Function areas)	Two or more	3
	Full supply chain	4
Focus	Business unit	4
	Cross-business unit	3
Nature of appointments	Cross-functional logistics appointments	3
	No cross-functional logistics appointments	3

responsible for at least two supply chain functions and most logistics directors overseeing the entire supply chain.

On the other hand, the majority of the appointments have a business unit focus, suggesting that cross-business unit synergies in the logistics arena are yet to be widely pursued.

While a sample of ten food manufacturers does not tell the whole story, it does point to a positive trend: some of Australia's largest manufacturers are structuring their organizations to provide a cross-functional perspective of the supply chain.

An agenda for action

But while recognizing the importance of the supply chain function through appropriate appointments is a positive move, it is only the beginning. For manufacturers to play their role in the supply chain integration revolutions the following actions must be taken:

■ Companies must move quickly to adapt their customer-facing processes to meet the ECR needs of their customers.
■ To bring about substantial change in the supply chain, companies must organize to provide a cross-functional perspective of the supply chain.
■ Companies must develop and implement an explicit supply chain strategy that:
  —focuses on one of the three possible benefit areas (efficiency, customer service or competitive advantage);
  —deals with shifting relationships between industry players;
  —captures the new value created within the organization; and
  —defines a small number of practical change initiatives for urgent action.

Meet the ECR needs of customers

Retailers are now making rapid progress in the development of ECR initiatives, which will put significant new demands on the supply chain capabilities of their suppliers. The large fast-food chains and industrial customers with their smaller number of inbound SKUs and suppliers are also increasingly expecting manufacturers to be more sophisticated in their supply chain capabilities.

All manufacturers need to take urgent action to change their customer-facing processes to meet the ECR demands of their customers. Broadly, the ECR demands of customers fall into two categories: electronic commerce and aligned distribution operations.

E-commerce requires manufacturers to conduct business transactions with customers through an electronic interface. At the simplest level this involves documents that were once posted or delivered with the goods to be transmitted via EDI. Electronic commerce also enables new ways of doing business such as the elimination of invoices or changes to the ordering cycle that place greater emphasis on medium-term forecasts, with electronic orders being sent for replenishment confirmation.

Aligned distribution operations require that manufacturers deliver goods in a way that optimizes the customer's inbound logistics operation. At the simplest level this requires the product to be identified with the appropriate barcodes at the pallet, case and item level. A further requirement is that the delivery is performed at the time specified by the customer (sometimes down to a 15-minute delivery window) so that the operations of large distribution centres can be organized for maximum efficiency. At a more complex level, customers can require specific pallet make-ups (small size, multiproduct etc.) that allow the customer to cross-dock the stock for onward delivery to the store without the need for storage or breakdown.

For manufacturers which still have to make substantial progress in these areas, there is an urgent need to make the required changes:

- Create a dialogue with customers at the logistics operations level—do not leave it to sales or senior management.
- Embark on electronic commerce by building a front end to existing systems to meet the immediate needs of customers.
- Change warehousing and distribution processes to meet customers' labelling, pallet presentation and delivery requirements.

Focusing on efficiency, customer service or competitive advantage

A strategy should not try to be all things to all people. It must provide guidance to managers for their day-to-day decision making, enabling the organization to focus on priority actions. Phrases such as 'to be the best' or 'strive for excellence' may serve as motivational catchphrases, but do not help managers who face the real world of choices, trade-offs and competing demands for investment. Table 33.6 shows the three areas of focus for a supply chain strategy: efficiency, customer-service improvement or competitive advantage. The position a company takes with its strategy depends on its assessment of the industry; its position in the market; and a realistic assessment of how its logistics function can contribute to the business strategy in the medium and long term.

Focusing on efficiency results in a reduced cost of supply chain operations of a company directly improving profitability or gaining a cost advantage in the market. Focusing on customer service provides a differentiated service to a customer where the value of the service is worth more than the cost of providing that service. When the customer comes to evaluating its choice of suppliers, factors other than just price are considered. Focusing on competitive advantage is about exploiting the unique position of a company in the industry to offer a service that cannot easily be replicated. For example, a multidivision company can use synergies between business units to package together products and services that other companies cannot achieve without developing complex partnerships with third-party organizations. Alternatively, the company could exploit the scale of its distribution operations to provide a reliable and frequent service that cannot be effectively matched by smaller organizations.

Table 33.6
The three benefit areas

Strategic focus	Rationale	Examples
Efficiency	• Business strategy based on cost or non-logistics-based attributes • Differentiation on service impractical	Medium-sized company outsources its distribution to a logistics provider to benefit from scale efficiencies
Customer service	• Specific service attributes valued by customers • Can deliver service more effectively than competitors	Manufacturer creates specialist logistics service to win sole supplier status at food service organization
Competitive advantage	• Market position allows shaping of industry structure and balance of power	Consolidation of wholesalers to gain control of specific channel

Reorganize to achieve cross-functional management of the supply chain

Changing the front end of the supply chain may satisfy the immediate needs of customers, but it is no more than a short-term remedy. Without significant reengineering of internal logistics processes, the new requirements will add complexity to existing operations and result in increased costs. If the new customer-facing processes are not aligned with internal processes there will be an internal tug of war with conflicts arising periodically, resulting in customer service failures.

An extreme example comes from an Australian automotive assembler which extended its just-in-time programme by requesting that suppliers increase the frequency of delivery from daily to three times a day, delivering small batches of the required parts direct to the assembly plant. After a few weeks the new operation seemed to be going smoothly until the assembler found out what was actually happening. A major supplier had been unable to adapt its internal processes to the new level of service and so dispatched the traditional-sized truck with a full day's supply to the assembler. Instead of dropping off the full amount, the driver dropped off a third, waited four hours, dropped off another third and finally returned again in the evening to complete the delivery. The only organization that seemed to be benefiting from this arrangement was McDonald's where the driver spent his waiting hours!

Table 33.7
Supply chain organizational options

Role	Pros	Cons
Supply chain / logistics director	• Direct control of operations and change programmes • Tensions between functions can be resolved quickly	• Introduces another management layer • Decreases regional / customer focus through becoming centralized
Supply chain / logistics change programme manager	• Focus on developing future supply chain capabilities • Defines processes to ensure integration between functions	• No coordination of day-to-day activities • Difficulties in building consensus for different regions/functions
Supply chain planner	• Creates consistent plan across supply chain and forum for resolving issues • Maintains regional / functional autonomy	• No real responsibility for operations and lacks authority • No focus for supply chain strategy and change programme

Companies seeking to implement supply chain integration must develop an organization that provides a cross-functional perspective of the supply chain. The extent of this necessary reorganization varies from company to company, but the successful ones are bold in their organizational change, bypassing compromise solutions based on functional perspectives.

Table 33.7 shows the three possible organizational options.

In an ideal world the logistics function should be given responsibility over the full supply chain, but the real priority is to focus on areas that require most attention and not allow the span of control to become so great that management attention is dissipated across too many initiatives. For example, one Australian company created a logistics function across the full supply chain from inbound to outbound, but carved out production as a separate department because of the complex and unique production processes. Another Australian company created a logistics function focused solely on finished goods, but gave the new function the challenge to integrate distribution across all business units.

As noted earlier, some of Australia's largest manufacturers are making good progress in focusing senior management attention on supply chain integration, with seven out of the ten sampled having one of the roles listed in Table 33.7. Five of these have been appointed in the last two years. It is vital that senior management continues to endorse and develop these appointments in the context of a total supply chain strategy.

Develop and implement a supply chain strategy

Few manufacturers can articulate a supply chain strategy that passes the four-question test:

- Does the strategy go beyond the generic to focus on one of the three benefit areas (efficiency, customer service or competitive advantage)?
- Does the strategy position the company to deal with the shifting relationships between consumers, retailers, wholesalers, manufacturers and third-party logistics providers?
- Does the strategy explicitly state how the added value is going to be captured within the organization rather than dissipated across other players in the industry?
- Does the strategy define a small number of practical supply chain capabilities that give direction to the implementation project?

Define a role in the new industry structure

With the focus on the current day's issues, it is easy to forget how fast the consumer products industry is changing. The combination of changing consumer demands and technology has resulted in significant shifts in supply chain relationships. The continued rise of the supermarket chains; the increasing trend to food service and convenience; the changing role of transport providers; and consolidation among manufacturers and suppliers have all changed the way the different organizations interrelate within the grocery supply chain.

Australian manufacturers need to be proactive in defining their role in the industry. The key to doing this is to develop a supply chain strategy that defines the organization's position with respect to other players and aligns the company's internal supply chain activities with the broader industry supply chain.

The starting point is to understand the changing needs and make-up of customers and define the logistics needs of each customer group. This definition should focus on the role of all players in the industry in delivering the goods or service to the end consumer. The second step is to create a vision for the new supply chain that provides a value-added service proposition to customer groups in the most efficient way.

The third step is to consider which activities are best conducted internally, or by supplier and customers, or by third parties. At one stage the trend was towards outsourcing as many logistics activities as possible. There are now a greater variety of outsourcing models, including one where planning and management activities are retained, with third-party transport and warehouse operations used where they can offer specific advantages over internal operations.

Finally, it is critical to consider the options for delivering to, and communicating with, the end consumer. Significant direct-delivery channels already exist through catalogues, vending machines, home-shopping services and home delivery for fast food. This will dramatically increase as organizations leverage off Internet technology.

In summary, a supply chain strategy must deal with changing industry relationships by defining:

- priorities and approaches for different channels (chains, independents, industrial, food service etc.);
- differentiated logistics service propositions for each of the different customer groups;
- roles and relationships with wholesalers, transport companies, third-party logistics providers, suppliers' and customers' logistics activities; and
- direct delivery/communication with consumers.

Capturing the added value in the organization

Despite all the focus on partnerships and win–win relationships, the benefits of change (or the value of change) are rarely distributed evenly across the companies participating in the change process. A company has a duty to its shareholders to capture a fair proportion of the value of change within the company and, arguably, the industry as a whole has an obligation to pass on a proportion to the end consumer.

In fact, if the process of value capture is left to chance some very odd things can happen. Imagine a manufacturer that has worked closely at the logistics level with a retailer to implement best-practice supply chain integration resulting in significant logistics cost reductions by both companies. Its competitor is a logistics laggard but has shrewd sales managers negotiating deals for promotions and shelf space. It would be folly for the company that has made all the logistics changes to leave to chance the result that it will gain a fair proportion of the benefits of its effort. Even assuming that there is goodwill all round, the reality is that costing information is incomplete and communications between logistics and sales in manufacturers, and logistics and merchandising in retailers, are imperfect. It is inevitable that without proactive management the benefits of change will get dissipated across the product category—in the worst case even resulting in some of the benefit reaching the logistics laggard.

The retailers are acting as good business people, maximizing the profits of their own company. In response, manufacturers must put in place

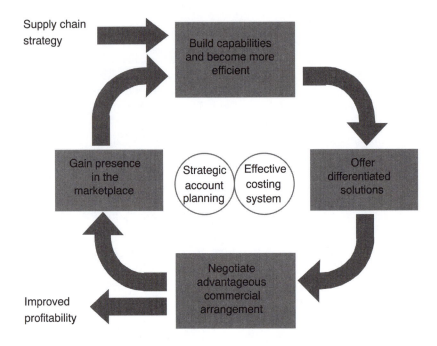

Figure 33.2   Supply chain profitability: the virtuous circle

an approach and processes that ensure that they reap benefit from supply chain integration. Figure 33.2 shows a strategic account planning process that ideally becomes a virtuous circle in improving supply chain capability. New supply chain capabilities provide a differentiated service to a customer, which allows an advantageous commercial arrangement to be negotiated, resulting in improving market presence. The improved business results allow further investment in supply chain capabilities, starting the cycle again.

To begin this virtuous circle requires effective coordination between sales and logistics, good costing and modelling systems, but most of all an explicit account plan as part of the supply chain strategy. The strategy sets out how the logistics changes will result in capturing the value of change in the company given the likely behaviour of other players in the industry. This process will not yield immediate results, but when consistently applied over time it can make a significant difference to product margins.

Table 33.8
Focused change projects

Company	Change initiative	Focus of change initiative	
Consumer products company	Customer service	A1	Customer connectivity
		A3	Demand-driven sales planning
Pharmaceutical company	Logistics network configuration	A2	Efficient distribution
		A4	Lean manufacturing
Consumer products company	Customer service/ material flow effectiveness	A1	Customer connectivity
		A2	Efficient distribution
Beverage company	Logistics reengineering	A6	Integrated supply chain management
		A2	Efficient distribution
Clothing company	Quick response	A3	Effective distribution
		A3	Demand-driven sales planning

Deliver results by focusing on a small number of practical capabilities

A strategy is only a success if it is effectively implemented. It is critical therefore that as an outcome of the strategy process there is clear direction for what operational capabilities are to be developed. These need to be expressed in practical terms that allow an effective change programme to be formulated.

The trick in structuring the implementation project is to define a change initiative that primarily focuses on one or two of the process capabilities, but also recognizes the inter-relationships with other capabilities. Table 33.8 shows how several companies have structured their change projects.

Conclusion

A turning point has been reached in the development of the fast-moving consumer products supply chain in Australia. Within a few years, a supply chain revolution will require manufacturers and retailers to have developed new capabilities in order to survive.

As with any revolution there will be winners and losers from the changes. The results of the supply chain revolution are still to be determined, but experience elsewhere in the world suggests that the early adopters of change will have a greater chance of influencing developments to their advantage.

The supply chain in the telecommunications industry

34

The secret weapon for future competitiveness

Michael Mikurak, Rick Tullio and Scott Wiskoski

Fundamental changes are occurring in the communications industry around the world, driven by deregulation, new competition and rapid technological innovation. For communications companies wishing to leverage that change, rather than be swamped by it, the supply chain offers an as yet untapped weapon for improving competitiveness. By improving supply chain alignment, operating costs can be cut, customer retention increased and the value of new products and services maximized. This chapter discusses four perspectives for creating value in the supply chain; these perspectives are strategically important to communications businesses wishing to survive and grow in the global marketplace of the future.

Introduction

Evidence is all around of the far-reaching developments in the telecommunications industry. In the USA, the Telecommunications Act of 1996 opened the market for new entrants by enabling local telephone companies, long-distance carriers and cable television operators, among others, to enter and compete in each other's markets. The Act has also had the effect of accelerating consolidation in the industry, with the Bell Atlantic–NYNEX and Southwestern Bell–Pacific Telesis mergers being just two examples. In short, the competitive landscape is dramatically changing in the US telecommunications industry.

Significant change is also underway outside the USA. In Japan, the government is dismantling NTT, the local giant, into smaller national companies. In Europe, the European Union (EU) has agreed to create a single market for telecommunications services and to allow full competition. At the time of writing, 70 per cent of EU nations had adopted the open market approach, with the remaining countries delaying liberalization until the year 2003. In the developing countries, the 'big telephone company' still exists, largely as a public-sector monopoly, but this is also expected to change. In February 1997, 69 countries within the

World Trade Organization adopted an agreement to open their markets and dismantle state-run monopolies. This agreement is significant because the participating countries represent more than 90 per cent of worldwide telecommunications revenues.

Technology is also fuelling the rapid change. The introduction of fibreoptics, video conferencing, wireless, cellular, satellite, the Internet and soon single-number portability are all bringing new meaning to the global communications marketplace and extending the mobility of its customers. Consumers across the world can now more than ever access people and data on a global basis at costs lower than ever before. Technology is expected to continue to bring new and innovative services along with added complexity in managing the lifecycles of these innovations. Companies will no longer be able to be passive players and provide only long-distance or local land-line services. They will need to expand their service offerings and compete on a global rather than a local market basis. New bundled services (such as long distance, local, cellular, voicemail, caller ID, Internet access and single billing) as well as lower overall prices are currently being required to keep customers from switching to other service providers, hence with each new technology breakthrough current services have to be reviewed, replaced or bundled to provide continued value.

Many of the changes will require different types of expertise, which will demand the application of quick and decisive management techniques to stay ahead of the competition. In most cases the current and previously protected giants of the industry have not had to compete in this type of business environment. They have been to some extent internally focused, highly layered and budget driven rather than profit driven. To keep their competitive advantage in the future they will need to be more agile and ready to make changes quickly to bring new innovation to the marketplace or meet market demands. Accomplishing this feat will require immediate actions to protect their current and future revenue streams and market bases by:

- reducing operating expenses;
- managing new product and service introductions to maximize value realization; and
- retaining customers.

The supply chain can contribute substantially to each of these areas. Telecommunications companies can use it to reduce operating expenses by better aligning sourcing strategies, supplier capabilities and inventory strategies with their overall business strategy. Maximum value realization of new product and service introductions can occur when inventory development is synchronized with sales performance over product lifecycles and the right amount of inventory is available when needed; no more, no less. Finally, customer retention can be enhanced when customers are supported promptly and accurately.

Telecommunications companies' current supply chain

Although there has been rapid change in the telecommunications industry, telecommunications companies have yet to change significantly the way they deploy their supply chains. The typical communications company competes in the traditional wire-line business and/or in the newer wireless markets (such as satellite and cellular communications). In the wire-line business, the supply chain functions support building, expanding and maintaining the network as well as installing, servicing and maintaining wire-line telephone service to customers, both residential and commercial. As this business has been both regulated and stable for many years, the supply chain organizations and operating processes required to support it evolved into 'smoke stack' organizations focused on supporting several very distinct 'customer' groups: network build and construction, network maintenance and end-customer servicing. The business strategy for supporting each group meant separate people, processes and information systems. Sourcing is also accomplished separately, first by technical engineering on new equipment and technology and then by the purchasing department for replenishment or repair. This partitioned process does not readily take into consideration the total supply chain impact that each purchasing decision will have on the company's bottom line, nor does it focus on using the company's full leverage with a vendor or for building meaningful, long-term alliances with vendors.

The supply chain functions are required to support the emerging wireless markets in the same three areas. Although wireless businesses do not have a history of regulation or strong bureaucracies, their supply chain organizations have followed the same pattern as their wire-line counterparts. They have also split their supply chain organization around the traditional areas, which have not been designed to respond to a nimble, product-driven market.

As can be seen, the extent to which the supply chain is being used to both create and realize value is currently under-appreciated in the telecommunications industry. It is unclear as to whether or not all within the industry consider supply chain costs to be significant elements of their operating costs. Before continuing, it is useful to compare the significance of supply chain costs to operating costs in the telecommunications industry with those of high-technology electronics. Table 34.1 displays the 1996 revenue, operating expense, capital expenditure and

Table 34.1
Logistic metrics comparisons

Logistics metric	Long-distance carrier	US RBOC	International long-distance carrier	Fortune 20 electronics manufacturer
Net sales	$18 500	13 100	$52 200	$38 400
Operating expenses US$m *(%Rev)	16 200 (88%)	10 200 (87%)	43 400 (83%)	34 700 (90%)
Capital expenditures	3 300	2 500	6 800	2 200
Total assets	23 000	24 900	55 600	27 700

Source: 1996 year end US Securities and Exchange Commission filings. All numbers rounded to nearest $100 million.

*Operating expenses include cost of goods/services sold, R&D, SG&A and debt and amortization expenses.

total asset values for three telecommunications companies beside those of a Fortune 20 electronics manufacturer. In absolute terms the numbers are relatively similar. On a percentage basis, operating expenses are between 80 and 90 per cent of net revenues. Although telephone companies and manufacturing concerns report operating expenses differently, research indicates that payments to suppliers for both operating and capital expenses comprise about 65 per cent of net revenues for both telecommunications and manufacturing companies. The remaining percentage represents labour and other costs not directly affected by supply chain improvement. This high-level comparison shows that supply chain costs are a significant segment of operating expenses, hence improvements in supply chain performance can have a significant effect on bottom-line performance.

End-to-end supply chain perspective

The traditional communications company has faced logistics-oriented problems, which were largely considered to be related to network support, in a fragmented manner. The solutions developed for network logistics support were usually point solutions, only minimally integrated across the business. For example, inventory management is distinctly different in warehouse and field inventory operations and is in most cases managed by two different business organizations. Although such segmented approaches were effective in a stable, regulated environment,

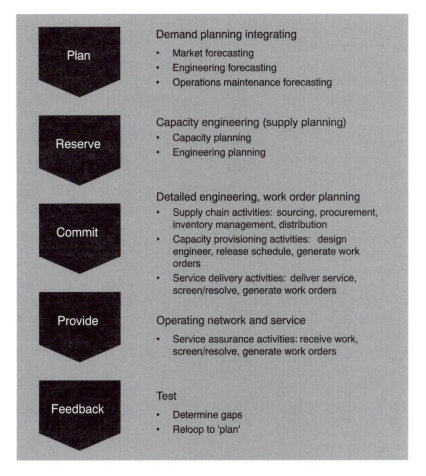

Figure 34.1   Telecommunications industry supply process

they are less and less valid in the increasingly competitive, cost- and service-sensitive environments of today, as illustrated previously. Communications companies must start to build and manage their supply chains on an integrated basis, from customer to supplier, 'end to end'. This will require a restructuring of their supply chain organizations, but the benefits from this restructuring will outweigh the cost through reductions in inventory, product delivery and improved customer service. The new supply chain organization will have visibility across the entire business.

Figure 34.1 illustrates the new supply chain process flow and how the supply chain will be managed end to end, beginning with demand planning through to end-customer feedback and integrated into a communications company's core process flow. The supply chain links suppliers to customers and supports the integration of functional entities across a company. The differences between the current situation and an end-to-end perspective include creating visibility of both logical and physical inventory across the supply chain. This enhances the ability to provide end-customer requirements on a just-in-time basis. Companies that have adopted this concept have reduced their overall supply chain costs by more than 5 per cent (for example one such company with a supply chain cost of $1 billion has achieved more than $50 million in end-to-end supply chain savings). In addition to the obvious customer-service improvements, this would have significant benefits in the opportunity to remove costly redundant physical inventories from the supply chain. It would also provide protection against inventory write-offs and write-downs, an especially important factor given the increasing likelihood of obsolescence due to short product lifecycles.

By integrating across the supply chain, a more cohesive framework for value maximization would be developed. The typical planning, capacity-engineering and capacity-provisioning activities focus on providing a financial benefit through minimizing economic value lost or overall costs. On the other hand, the customer-acquisition and maintenance activities of service delivery and service assurance typically focus on maximizing economic value added (EVA™) without identifying the impact on the cost of ongoing operations. Since both sets of activities operate simultaneously, there is the opportunity to maximize value when they are managed together.

Global logistics perspective

Globalization is currently underway in the communications industry. This evolving landscape presents an opportunity to employ the supply chain to assist communications companies in preparing for competition and liberalization. The lines between what is an international communications company and what is a local communications company are blurring. Many companies will operate without respect to international borders, provide an array of products and services and deliver a consistent level of service, both domestically and internationally. Many telecommunication companies are investing overseas and, as more overseas markets are deregulated, greater opportunity for investment will exist. SBC Communications' investment in South Africa Telkom, GTE's investment in the telephone company of Venezuela (CANTV) and World Com's bid for MCI Communications are but a few recent examples of cross-border investments. In addition there are global alliances, such as Global One, the alliance among Deutsche Telekom, France Telecom and Sprint International.

The supply chain contribution in global situations will vary, in part with the mission and objectives of the individual company, investor or

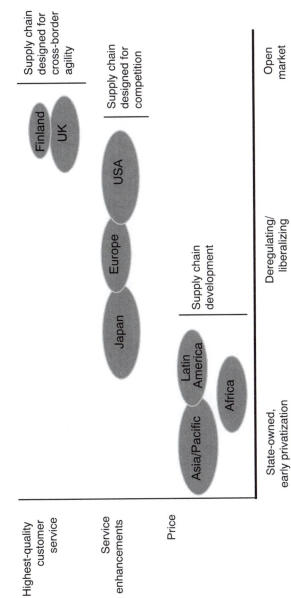

Figure 34.2 Telecommunications industry market development

alliance, but also with other factors. One way of looking at the potential contribution from supply chain improvement is to consider the conditions in each communications market. This can be displayed in a simple matrix (see Figure 34.2), which compares the stage of market development with the degree of market competitiveness. 'Stage of market development' can be defined to mean the key competitive factor at each stage of market development. For example, in the basic stage, the competitive factor is the availability of a basic telephone service. As the market develops and a basic telephone service is widely available, then the basis for competition becomes price. In the subsequent stages, competition is on the basis of enhancements to the basic service and finally on outstanding customer service. The second dimension is 'degree of competition' and is intended to describe the level of competition within a geographic market, broadly defined.

Consider the state-owned, early privatization and service-availability scenario. Typically, the organization or system undergoing privatization is already non-competitive in the global marketplace. Its key business processes are likely to be well below international standards. Sometimes, in exchange for private investment, the national government commits to an aggressive expansion of capacity and service availability, such as a telephone in every home or village. For example, when the Chilean government privatized its main telephone carriers, it set up a fund offering a subsidy to any company willing to provide telephone services in areas where there was a significant telephone service shortage. Today, Chile has one of the developing world's most open telecommunications market. While this is a good example of a successful privatization, there are circumstances where the pace of change is not met and it risks damaging goodwill and brand image, both for the government and the company. When expansion fails to occur as expected, it is often because the existing supply chain was not redesigned to respond to the new aggressive expansion or to increased standards of customer service. Setting up new networks, maintaining and upgrading networks and servicing customers all require efficient supply chain management. Thus, an integrated supply chain is a key to effectively capturing (building networks) and growing (servicing customers) in new markets.

With global investments in communication companies around the world, it is extremely important to assess legacy supply chain systems carefully. The degree of 'brokenness', or distance from international performance expectations, must be determined. Consider the example of a privatizing telephone company system. An assessment showed that its supply chain was unable to meet its most basic requirement—delivering the right materials at the right time to the right place. The logistics pipeline was empty, warehouses were filled with non-conforming, obsolete inventories, virtually all equipment and materials to support the aggressive expansion programme were internationally sourced and international sourcing partners were unable to be paid for six months or longer due to failures in the supporting processes. The solutions to this company's dilemma were first to keep the network expansion programme on schedule. Once this problem was addressed, the next step was to develop a supply chain infrastructure that would support international standards of performance. This included developing requirements forecasting, inventory strategies, inventory management, warehousing management, procurement and strategic sourcing strategies and supplier alliances as well as change management and information systems development.

In a deregulating, liberalization or service-enhancement scenario, the situation may not be as severe as that described above. However, even where a communications company is operating in an industrialized 'rich country', the supply and demand chains are typically not designed to operate in highly competitive environments, but rather in a highly bureaucratic and stable one. The opportunity for logistics improvements in these organizations is often extremely high, but less obvious because of the entrenched, well-developed, well-documented—and often wrong—logistics approaches. Finally, in the open market or highest-quality customer-service scenario, the supply and demand chains will increasingly need to be designed for cross-border and agile operations.

Global telecommunications company

A Third World, state-owned telecommunications company realized that it needed to change to compete in the increasingly global telecommunications marketplace. Combined with decades of isolation from competitive forces and technological advances, the company had to act quickly to improve its operations prior to the projected deregulation of the domestic telephone industry in 2003. Additionally, under pressure from the government to provide universal access for all people, the company initiated an ambitious plan to add three million new telephone lines and upgrade an additional one million lines in the five years between 1996 and 2000. Traditionally, the line-penetration rate in the country varied widely by socioeconomic group, with 60 lines per 100 people for one area and one line per 100 for a poorer area. Given that the company's existing network in 1996 consisted of 3.75 million lines, the task of doubling the network in five years certainly seemed daunting.

Approach

To meet the aggressive growth targets, improve its competitiveness prior to deregulated competition and make itself more attractive to potential equity partners, the company began reengineering in 1995. This effort included supply management process design for the preferred method of operating in the future. Six process areas were identified and reengineered:

- understanding customer needs and managing performance;
- planning material requirements;
- procurement;
- managing inventory and materials;
- warehousing and distribution; and
- product returns and repairs.

To ensure improved performance for the future, design team members were encouraged to think creatively and to envision how they would design supply management's operations if it were a new company entering the country's market for the first time. This served to represent the impending competitive environment which the company would be facing in the future. Expected customer needs were derived from direct customer surveys and detailed information gathered from other companies within the industry who had already begun to make the transition. The supply chain reengineering team used best practices from across industries. They were then adapted to this company's operations and geographic location to create new forecasting and inventory-management process. A high-level distribution network model was developed to assess how many distribution warehouses would be required and where they would be strategically placed for maximum efficiency. And finally, fact-based procurement strategies were developed to leverage the unique position of this company with its vendors and to establish cost-effective returns and repairs processes. Throughout the project, the process designs were reviewed and validated with appropriate stakeholders, specifically the consumer, commercial and network-build business units within the company.

Benefits

Currently the company is developing detailed plans for implementation of this newly designed supply chain. Preliminary benefit targets include a 10 per cent reduction in annual purchasing spend, which could reap $100 million in annual savings, with a corresponding 75 per cent reduction in requisition to delivery cycle times. Additionally, inventory management has shifted from a regional focus to a country-wide approach and is projected to result in a 30 per cent reduction in inventory levels. Additionally, the forecasting process has become more iterative, resulting in smaller, more frequent orders. This is expected to increase forecast accuracy and minimize obsolescence.

Based on this new supply chain strategy this company has been able to attract new investment from an international consortium as well as additional support to implement this future design.

Consumer logistics perspective

In the communications industry of the future, 'relationships will more closely resemble those of the retail industry than today's communications industry. If they [communications companies] are to survive, they must ... move from technology organizations to merchandising organizations prepared to meet individual customer needs' (Burgess, 1995).

It is common today for communications devices, products and services to be sold much like consumer products. When mass merchandisers learned logistics creativity, it enabled them to meet the highest customer service levels and maintain the strictest cost controls. Learning logistics creativity will be equally critical for communications companies seeking a competitive advantage.

With an increasing consumer focus, communications companies must seek out creative ways to assure that the right product is at the right place at the right time at the least cost. First and foremost, this will mean adopting an integrated view of their supply chain activities, beginning with identifying customers' requirements for products and services and developing a supply chain strategy that effectively supports their needs. Again, this integrated view will need to encompass the key supply chain functions of demand planning, vendor sourcing, supplier alliances, inventory management, transportation and distribution. Moreover, a consumer logistics focus requires a recognition that customer segments exist and these need to be serviced differently, not only from a marketing point of view but from a supply chain perspective.

Logistics tools used in the consumer environment include demand-based planning and forecasting, point-of-sales data management for continuous replenishment, vendor-managed inventory initiatives, cost-service trade-off analyses and selection of push versus pull distribution strategies. Competitively astute players will recognize that the consumer focus indicates the presence of logistically distinct businesses within their markets and will seek the right supply chain balance within different customer segments.

When the supply chain is inadequately considered, the impact on customer satisfaction and financial strength can be profound. A history of insufficient inventory of the right product to meet customers' needs can damage a company's brand image and compromise customer retention. On the other hand, too much inventory is a drain on working capital and with today's frequent technological changes, too much 'old product' often needs to be written off or sold for cents on the dollar. When logistics strategy is integrated properly with overall business strategy, then the right logistics response, including inventory levels, inventory positioning, channel partners and service strategies, can be determined.

Another important challenge in a consumer environment is how to manage the product lifecycle (see Figure 34.3). With the rapid

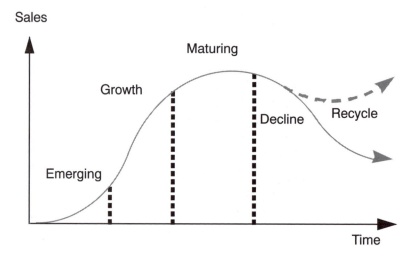

Figure 34.3   Product lifecycle

deployment of advanced communications, information and computing technologies, the industry is characterized by shortening product life-cycles and increased likelihood of building inventory. Shorter lifecycles require a different approach to demand planning relative to long life-cycle products. Moreover, the product lifecycle itself must be planned and managed with well-defined launch, migration and exit strategies. Without supply chain savvy, inventories will build quickly and to a far greater level than in the past. Obsolete inventories could become prolif-ic—and disastrous from a financial perspective (when it is considered that network equipment could cost millions of dollars and plug-ins could cost tens of thousands of dollars). When a supply chain strategy is specifically linked and tailored to the stages of new product introduc-tion, growth, maturity and decline, the best supply chain mix will be achieved to deliver different business objectives at each stage of the cycle.

The supply chain mix can be determined by asking certain key ques-tions. What are the customers' service and distribution channel service requirements and what supply chain strategy should be pursued to meet these requirements? Which strategies are feasible for a given company? Companies should consider applying multilayered, demand-based plan-ning and point-of-sale data to improve forecasting and reduce inventory risk. The cost-service trade-offs would vary by product lifecycle stage. The right supply chain mix would be designed to achieve the right bal-ance within the lifecycle and for the company's multiple performance objectives.

Logistics enterprises

As emphasized, the communications industry is rapidly transforming. Until recently only a few regional holding companies, such as regional Bell operating companies (RBOCs) and GTE, controlled telephone communications in the USA. The regional holding companies were given incentives through government regulation and marketplace dominance to build network asset inventories to support and maintain their networks. Because inventories were managed regionally at the distribution centre level, rather than on an overall basis, inventories became suboptimized throughout the system.

When the US government intervened to break open this marketplace and allowed companies from other industries to enter the communications business with new services and features, its actions not only increased the number of competitors but also the importance of factors that drive the need for a supply chain strategy: cost reduction and customer service improvement.

As with the service providers, it will become increasingly important for the manufacturers of equipment for the communications industry to extend their supply chain strategies to include more of a demand chain perspective. Technology will force the current non-compatible equipment manufacturing strategy to change and require development of more standards and inter-changeability. As this happens, manufacturers will need to look for more innovative way to achieve competitive advantage. Based on these market-driven requirements, there will be an opportunity for a 'logistics enterprise' to emerge.

The hypothesis is this: if one or more of the leading communications providers were to align with a third-party logistics provider, potentially a financial institution and one or more manufacturers of equipment, a new enterprise could offer a unique set of value-added services to both current participants and future entrants into this marketplace (see Figure 34.4). The participants in this programme would set up a new business entity owned by one or more of them. The involved parties would set up new supply chain operations (including demand planning, inventory management, warehousing and transportation) to support the service providers' supply chain needs, using cross-industry, best-in-class supply chain practices. Selected personnel from all parties' current supply chain organizations with deep supply chain skills would become part of the new company. It would be structured to provide cost-effective services centred on global management of the network assets, from initial build through repair, upgrade and replacement cycles, including all traditional operations and field-maintenance services. This new enterprise would allow the service providers involved with the new company to have the necessary supply chain support and to focus on their position within the marketplace and on their current and future required core competencies

Figure 34.4   Integrated network management

as competitive weapons. It would also drive network asset management, on a total company if not industry basis, to the least-cost, most-efficient posture. Communications companies could achieve significant financial benefits from outsourcing their supply chain management functions as an alternative strategy while reducing current operational cost.

To prove the point, data was collected from both internal and external sources across industries as shown in Table 34.2. Similar operations were sought for the types of savings they have received from supply chain integration and outsourcing. The research shows that, for example, companies with $20 billion in annual revenue could achieve bottom-line benefits from improvements in supply chain functional operations through this type of outsourcing.

Annual savings of $410 million would increase earnings per share of a typical RBOC by $0.20, which would equate to an 8 per cent increase in their 1996 bottom-line revenues.

Additional benefit could also be realized through service improvements which would include improvements in on-time delivery, component quality and reduced cycle times. From an organizational perspective, achievable benefits could come from a leaner, more efficient organizational structure, improved decision-making capabilities and cross-functional integration without directly reducing headcount

Table 34.2
Financial benefits through outsourcing

Supply chain focus area for improvement	Baseline costs (US$m)	Potential improvement range	One-time benefits (US$m)	Ongoing savings (US$m)
Materials planning	1000	2–5%		20–50
Network procurement postponement	4500	5–10%	225–450	
Field inventory reduction	9000	1.5–3%	135–270	20–40
Distribution network efficiency	2000	5–10%		100–200
Transportation leverage	1000	8–12%		80–120
Total savings and bottom-line impact			360–720	220–410

through direct downsizing. And from an overall supply chain view, companies could achieve closer linkages to core suppliers, additional value-added vendor services and most importantly increased end-to-end process efficiencies.

This type of approach could significantly change industry dynamics. Establishing a new business venture of this kind would require a business integration methodology that embraced a strategic vision. Managers and facilitators with deep supply chain skills would also be needed to understand how to execute the vision using the capabilities of each of the participants. This group (the business integrator) would need to bring proven software-development tools and business process-management capabilities to the table. A new company as described could truly provide a competitive edge for those involved and could set the stage for the future direction of the telecommunications industry, using the supply chain as a competitive weapon (Figure 34.5).

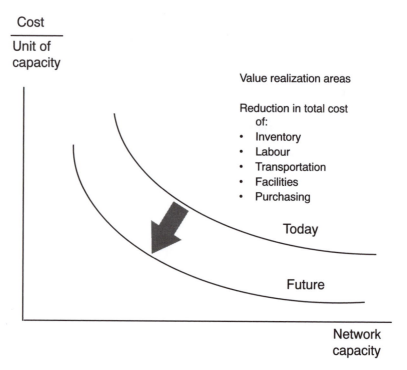

Figure 34.5   Telecommunications industry cost curve

Conclusion

Value can be created in the communications industry through the enhanced application of supply chain technologies and methodologies. The far-reaching changes occurring in the industry are expected to continue, rather than abate, as new innovations and technologies emerge; these will have an impact on the industry's supply chain operations. Companies that effectively address the supply chain areas identified will be positioned to gain competitive advantage within the marketplace and to stake a claim as leaders in the communications industry of the future.

The healthcare supply chain
Applying best-practice remedies to the healthcare sector

Kim Wigglesworth and John Zelcer

Healthcare supply chains around the developed world are under pressure to reform. A number of push and pull factors are driving this process, including rising costs, new technological and business solutions and the introduction of new healthcare approaches. The future for the healthcare industry is very different to today—more customer focused, IT based and efficient. To get to that future will require the application of global best practices in supply chain management, greater outsourcing and stronger alliance partnerships.

Introduction

Health systems around the world are experiencing intense pressures from rising costs, fewer resources, growing consumer dissatisfaction with the quality of care and value received and fragmented funding arrangements. In response to these pressures, leaders and policy makers in health systems are looking beyond their borders and beyond the healthcare industry itself to identify best practices, tools and concepts that can be applied to yield improvements. One of the key opportunity areas is total supply chain management.

The health system within a particular country is defined by several factors, including its evolving social system, its political environment and its level of economic prosperity. Community attitudes towards the role of government and the application of concepts of access, equity and universality are also profoundly influential. These factors, shown in Figure 35.1, significantly affect the design of a health system; they also influence the degree, type and pace of change possible.

Most western democracies established health-insurance programmes as a form of social welfare. Their motivation was, among others, to provide all citizens with a basic level of healthcare—to provide equity. Governments created a system to provide universal coverage; hospitals and physicians provided care within the constraints of the system.

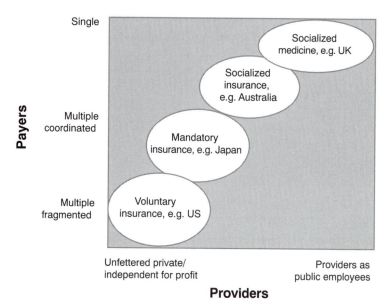

Source: Andersen Consulting global health futures forum, 1997

Figure 35.1   Healthcare provider system archetypes

The US system, for example, was established as 'employment insurance' and has been dominated by providers who created private insurance in response to the increasing cost of surgery. Hospitals and physicians created a system to protect their livelihoods. Consistent with the US tradition of limiting the intervention of government in citizens' lives, government took on a regulatory role. Employers played a fundamental part in determining who received healthcare insurance coverage, while pricing of that coverage was largely driven by competitive market forces.

The elements unique to individual countries complicate efforts to forge supply chain links across healthcare boundaries. Within individual markets, unlike a majority of other industries, the manufacturers that supply the healthcare environment are, in most cases, restricted in their capacity to influence the final consumer (the patient or health professional) to consume their products (Figure 35.2). In some countries several players intervene between the manufacturer of a product (for example pharmaceuticals) and the end consumer. These factors have created a diverse, complex and fragmented environment across the global healthcare industry.

The business of healthcare is provided by a wide variety of enterprises. Products and services provided include medical consumables, pharmaceuticals, catering and food, laundry cleaning, waste manage-

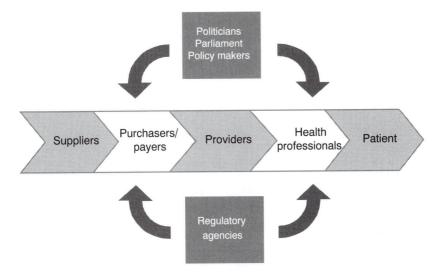

Figure 35.2 Healthcare supply chain

ment and disposal, home-care products, information technology, vehicle fleet management and general research supplies. In a majority of countries the management of products, inventory and processes for both clinical and non-clinical services is largely independent and non-integrated, resulting in great inefficiencies.

A number of participants play clearly defined roles in the healthcare supply chain. These are the suppliers and/or manufacturers, who develop, create and/or supply the product; the distributor, who manages distribution and transportation; the provider, who makes the product/ service available to the end consumer; and the end consumer, who may be a health professional or patient in the healthcare system.

In a majority of countries there is relatively limited communication between most of the key members of the supply chain, beyond simple ordering and billing. The supply chain is characterized by high inventory levels, discontinuous product flow, paper-based information management and inconsistent technologies (see Figure 35.3). Each of these characteristics is further complicated by a lack of trust and unwillingness to consider partnering.

Pressures for change

Healthcare supply chains are under pressure to change. The increasing cost and complexity of healthcare management under present arrangements, coupled with the rise of new business and technological solutions

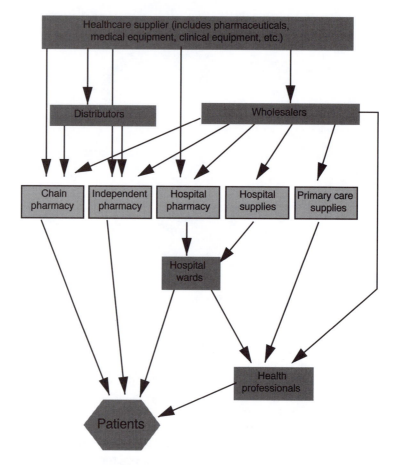

Figure 35.3   High-level view of a healthcare supply chain

to facilitate reform, combine to create strong push and pull factors for change. The high cost of healthcare is making the current system unsustainable. Changes to healthcare practices are improving service, opening up new opportunities for reform but adding complexity to the present situation. A number of players within the current healthcare supply chain are profiting from adopting new approaches. Information technology (IT) solutions are well advanced in other industries and could be readily applied to healthcare. Finally, inefficient business processes such as the rebate and contract system which operates in the USA, present an ideal opportunity for significant reform.

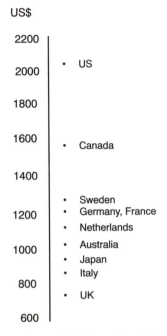

US$

2200

2000 • US

1800

1600 • Canada

1400

1200 • Sweden
• Germany, France
• Netherlands
1000 • Australia
• Japan
• Italy
800
• UK

600

Source: Harris, Harvard, and IFTF Special Survey 1990

Figure 35.4   Per capita spending on healthcare

Cost pressures

Delivering healthcare consumes a significant portion of a country's gross domestic product (GDP). This varies from country to country depending on how healthcare costs are managed and accounted for related to other social costs. Per capita spending ranges from around $700 in the UK up to around $2100 in the USA (see Figure 35.4).

For example, total healthcare expenditure in the USA is $1.2 trillion per year (1995 figures), second only to defence spending as a portion of total GDP. It is growing faster than inflation (recent annual growth is approximately 4 per cent).

Of this, $23 billion is directly traceable to supply chain costs (see Table 35.1). Transportation and distribution represent 38 per cent of the spending; order and inventory management the rest. These figures represent an enormous opportunity for improvement. The Efficient Healthcare Consumer Response study by CSC Consulting Inc. (EHCR) identified $11 billion of improvement, calculated by assuming fairly conservative changes to the current system (such as electronic data interchange (EDI) and partnering), falling well short of the radical adjustments that are likely to occur in the future. Even greater industry savings may be possible.

Table 35.1
Estimated supply chain costs in US healthcare

TOTAL healthcare spending	$1200 billion
Deduct: dental, vision, admin., R&D, government, veterinary	($392 billion)
TOTAL personal healthcare	$808 billion
Deduct: retail pharmaceutical, capital equipment, professional fees, services other providers (example: chiropractors, insurance administration, facilities etc.	($725 billion)
TOTAL non-retail ethical pharmaceutical products/service	$ 83 billion
Deduct: products and service costs	($ 60 billion)
TOTAL healthcare supply chain costs	$ 23 billion

Source: CSC Consulting, Inc., 1996

New models of service delivery

Traditionally the healthcare delivery process was focused on either a general practitioner (primary care) in the local community or within a hospital-based environment (secondary or tertiary care). This simple model limited the channels that needed to be served.

However non-hospital (ambulatory) and home care are increasingly taking the place of traditional inpatient and institution-based outpatient services. The associated reduction in demand for hospital beds has led to the consolidation of large hospitals, the growth of small local health-care centres and the emergence of new clinical and allied health services which directly support the ambulatory and home-care needs of health-care consumers.

Healthcare providers are finding that their role in the supply chain requires redefinition as a result of this shift. There has been a strong standardization of business practices within countries (such as purchasing, facilities management etc.) for healthcare providers as they close inefficient hospitals and create economies of scale. However, offsetting the economic benefits of these closures is the growth in alternate care sites such as doctor's offices, outpatient care units and minor emergency care clinics. These sites are being grouped into networks, which in the

USA are being referred to as integrated delivery networks (IDNs), controlled by the provider (see Figure 35.5).

These healthcare networks give the patients closer, more convenient access to healthcare services and illustrate a significant shift for healthcare providers as they attempt to provide more service away from the traditional hospital environment. However, they give rise to significant additional complexity in the overall healthcare products supply chain.

These shifts in the structure and scale of healthcare provision provide an opportunity for injecting new business practices and solutions to lower costs and reduce complexity.

Changing role of product distributors

Some participants in the chain are moving closer to integration than others, signalling that change across the healthcare supply chain is both possible and inevitable. For example, many global pharmaceutical or medical products manufacturers are embracing current best practices for supply chain management within their own segment of the chain. EDI and electronic commerce are widely used for interactions between the manufacturers and their suppliers (in many cases commodity or specialist chemical producers) or manufacturers and their distributors.

More significant, however, is the emergence of the distributor/wholesaler as a potential key player in a new supply chain model. In some countries distributor/wholesaler consolidation has led to the formation of very large companies which have the ability to serve their customers in several new ways. For example, Baxter Healthcare Corporation of Deerfield, Illinois, is a $9 billion sales and distribution company that has the capability to supply 70 per cent of a typical hospital's day-to-day needs. Its product line includes over 200 000 items. It is predicted that companies like Baxter will expand their supply chain role from simple provider to supply chain integrator.

As the proximity to the end consumer increases for these distributors, they will become important sources of usage trends and patterns. They will have access to data that pharmaceutical and medical products companies will need. With this knowledge they will be required, and able, to provide services that have previously been performed by the providers, including kitting (the creation of pre-packaged items that are required for specific procedures, such as packs containing needles, swabs, saline and forceps for specific sterile procedures); inventory management at the user site (vendor-management inventory); and recycling/disposal.

Partnering with medical and testing laboratories and with general hospital supplies companies will allow the distributor to become a 'one-stop shopping' point for providers. As this develops, the function of a pharmaceuticals-only distributor may disappear as this requirement is

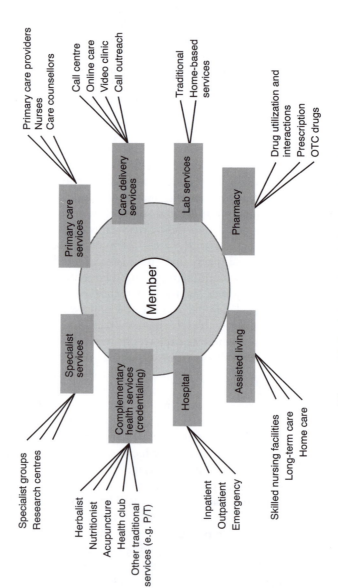

Figure 35.5   Integrated delivery network

progressively eliminated by closer electronic interaction between the provider and the manufacturer.

For a majority of segments of the supply chain, however, there is still reliance on manual, non-integrated, laborious and error-prone methods for managing products and inventory.

Information technology

Of the many current inefficiencies in the total healthcare supply chain, the varying use and sophistication of information technology at each level stand out most strongly. An increase in the use of technology aligned with a wider adoption of EDI transactions would significantly ameliorate some of these inefficiencies. However, this change will require a significant investment in technology along with new methods of doing business.

Technology used for business solutions has not been accepted widely across the healthcare supply chain. While there has been some adoption of EDI for transactions between members, there are few examples of the integrated use of electronic transactions continuously across the entire chain from supplier to end user. Even within organizations (such as hospitals) different technologies survive, which reduces both internal communication effectiveness as well as external communication opportunities.

Even inter-company integration represents just one link in the supply chain. Only by pushing this integration both up and down the supply chain will healthcare organizations be able to realize efficiency gains.

Rebates and contracts

Another problem, encountered most specifically in the USA and one which adds significant cost to the overall supply chain, is that of rebates and contracts. These practices developed before strict price controls were in place in the US healthcare industry and have become ingrained in the process. They involve selling to the distributors at a higher price than directly to the end consumer/healthcare provider, allowing a rebate to be claimed by the wholesaler, depending to whom the product was sold. The elimination of rebates and related contracts among manufacturers, distributors and providers will require a change in business structure. For some manufacturers, this contract/rebate practice involves more than 90 per cent of all transactions. The distributor is obliged to document each end-user sale and calculate the rebate due in order to arrive at an adjusted cost. Theoretically, the product price could be different for each customer.

The processing and management cost involved in these practices is significant and is an additional burden placed on the healthcare system. No value is added by these repricing steps, yet they involve the majority of transactions. Even when these transactions occur electronically they are still inefficient. Standardized pricing and supply chain margins based on the value added at each step must be the ultimate goal when redesigning this process.

Vision of the future for the healthcare supply chain

It is likely that the healthcare supply chain of today will disappear within the next 10 years. Government and public concerns about spiralling healthcare costs have already illuminated high physician salaries and drug costs as issues. The 'baby boomer' generation has begun to turn 50 and will be demanding more and better healthcare in the future. It is only a matter of time before the current process of distributing healthcare products and services is targeted for significant change.

Healthcare providers linked to suppliers, manufacturers and distributors will have to enter the 'information age'. They will be forced to be responsive to issues, such as cost-effective service and quality outcomes, that have been addressed and ingrained in most other industries.

The new supply chain will be characterized by electronically linked participants with overlapping roles. For example, hospitals will own no inventory—items used in the treatment of patients will be stored at nurses' stations, but will be owned by the distributor or even manufacturer. As an item is used for a patient, its barcode will be scanned, electronically sending usage information to the distributor or manufacturer and transmitting the required information to the healthcare payer, whether that is a government agency or insurance company. The distributor or manufacturer will then restock the items. Healthcare product inventory will exist not only at hospitals but also at all types of alternate care points (such as doctor's offices, outpatient care units, minor emergency care clinics). The distributor will electronically receive payment from the relevant authority (such as government or insurance company) directly as usage information is matched (see Figure 35.6).

In the local community, pharmacies may no longer exist in their current form for fulfilment of physician-created drug scripts. They may maintain some role for the provision of self-medication products (over-the-counter, herbal and naturopathic remedies, vitamins and so on). However, it also is possible that this role will be embedded within that of a general consumer goods or food retailer.

A primary care physician, or other health professional, will enter a

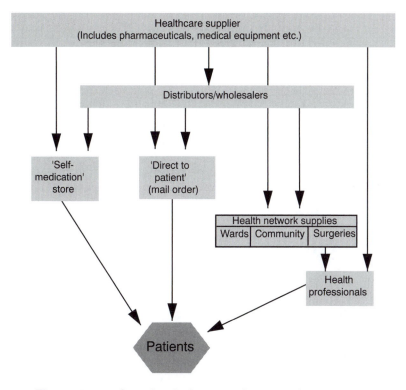

Figure 35.6   Supply chain gets closer to the customer

prescription into a computer, where it will be validated against a defined patient-care plan and protocol. These care plans will depend on the patient needs and/or the related health authority's requirements and will be based on industry best practices. On an exception basis this prescription information may be transmitted to the patient's insurer or healthcare organization to authorize the prescription (should the product be either not on the 'preferred list', not recommended for the identified disease state or a high-cost item). Whichever route the prescription takes, it will be automatically forwarded to either a pharmaceutical manufacturer's or distributor's 'direct-to-patient' (or mail-order) organization. The medication would then be delivered to the patient via overnight delivery at the latest. Refills would be delivered to the patient automatically when required, according to a defined care protocol. These direct-to-patient organizations may also be involved in medication-compliance management and associated services.

Distributors will have the important value-added role of making healthcare items 'consumer ready'. For example, 'kitting' of surgical supplies will involve sorting and aggregating all of the supplies needed for a surgical procedure, boxing them and barcoding the kit so that it can be tracked within the supply chain. Responsibility for 'accelerating' the product along the supply chain (that is, breaking the manufacturer's shipments of pharmaceuticals/supplies into patient-ready quantities) will then be the distributor's value-adding responsibility.

With the improved information available regarding individual patient usage of products and supplies, the distributors will be positioned to take a key role in determining separate hospital demand profiles. This information could be aggregated into regional profiles and even into entire market-level profiles. Since the transactions are tracked electronically, distributor information can be passed on to the manufacturer's system at an almost real-time level, which would improve forecasting and planning.

Getting to the future

This future will happen through the application of world's best supply chain practices, sensible use of outsourcing and greater use of alliance partnerships.

Application of world's best practice

The application of supply chain strategy to healthcare, using supply chain principles drawn from many industries, can help transform healthcare businesses into lead enterprises. Traditionally, product-based industries have received most attention, but as competitive intensity and cost pressures escalate, supply chain thinking is being systematically applied in utilities, government, telecommunications, financial services and increasingly to health.

Shown in Table 35.2 are some of the leading-edge best practices in managing supply chain processes. Key elements of these practices must be considered and applied to the healthcare supply chain to realize efficiencies.

Outsourcing opportunities

The supply chain requirements of the healthcare industry could be well served by outsourced supply chain management enterprises. Such enterprises essentially seek to synchronize the process (from demand planning to manufacturing, procurement, inbound and outbound supply chain) all the way to the point of patient healthcare delivery.

Three powerful motivations exist for the industry to accept such a solution:

Table 35.2

Leading-edge best practices in managing supply chain processes

Determine strategy and policy	• Integration of planning and transaction systems with suppliers and customers • Cross-functional teams focused on customers • Well-defined and documented methodology or supply chain network strategy assessment • Total cost and service perspective for supply chain network analysis • Use of comprehensive modelling tool for analysis of supply chain infrastructure
Manage sourcing	• Supplier selection criteria reflects relative bargaining positions of organization and vendor in supply market • Strategic purchasing perspective—align purchasing with overall strategic goals • Where appropriate establishing long-term strategic supplier relationships • Investing in the supplier's company and single sourcing
Procure goods and services	• EDI for purchase orders, manifest, invoice, shipping notice 'paperless transactions' • Usage information integrated with supplier for JIT sourcing • Supplier access to forecast purchases • Supplier-managed purchase inventories • Consolidated purchasing power within organization, fragmentation eliminated • Eliminate approval process
Manage inventory	• Regular cross-functional meetings to agree organization's supply requirements • Differentiated approach to inventory planning based on product demand characteristics • Regular review of functional performance against targets • Regular, system-driven review of inventory parameters • System-driven cycle count • Daily stock count only for items that have moved
Manage distribution	• Carrier scheduling and tracking using computer tools • Joint buying and transportation team to identify inbound opportunities • Automated despatch systems integrated into other operating and financial systems • Minimal freight auditing due to electronic exchange of POs, tenders, acceptances and delivery notices • EDI invoicing and EFT freight bill payments

- it allows provider networks and hospitals to outsource non-core but critical activities to a competent, process-oriented organization;
- it shifts the burden of information technology (IT) infrastructure investment for managing the supply chain to specialist organizations

whose core business capabilities can be leveraged to achieve the business objectives of the enterprise; and
■ it allows for critical mass to build up and achieve economies of scale exceeding those existing today.

Key change must also take place in the distributor role in the supply chain. Although traditionally viewed in some supply chains as the non-value-adding 'middleman', the distributor must become the focal point of integration for the healthcare supply chain. For example with EDI enhancements, if the distributor is not leading the advancement of EDI and a provider or manufacturer adopts EDI, the distributor becomes the bottleneck. It would be unable to meet the demands of its EDI equipped partners and the partner's information technology advancement would be wasted. However, a distributor which adopts EDI is in a position to 'drive' the supply chain forward by offering advancement and savings to both the provider and the manufacturer. Even if only the provider or the manufacturer adopts EDI, at least a partial improvement would be realized.

Alliance opportunities

Alliance formation is a relatively common business strategy in the healthcare industry. The pharmaceutical sector has been pursuing alliances in product research and development for at least a decade. These alliances seek to leverage operational diversity between alliance partners who share both strategic objectives and cultural style.

The emergence of integrated care and virtual care delivery systems will be associated with new arrangements for shared services across current enterprise boundaries. The skills required to plan, implement and manage integrated supply chain operations across the healthcare supply chain are non-core capabilities for most business operators in that chain. This provides an opportunity for comprehensive, end-to-end supply chain infrastructure and service providers to offer efficient, cost-effective services as third-party operators.

Conclusion

There are several inefficiencies in the healthcare supply chain that could be significantly improved through the application of best practices from other industries. However, change in the industry will mean that supply chain decision makers will have to work far more collaboratively, rather than pursuing individual actions that secure their own position to the detriment of the whole chain.

The healthcare industry is probably the last major industry to enter the information age. Consequently, the degree of infrastructure investment and the extent of business process change required to adopt and realize the benefits of integrated supply chain management are extremely large. But these steps must be taken if the healthcare environment is to make the savings needed in order to maintain costs at an affordable level for governments, employers and patients worldwide.

Once the shift occurs the improved efficiencies and quality of both product and service delivery will generate enormous benefits for the entire industry. The business operators who embrace these best practices first will be optimally positioned to capture those benefits in both regional and global healthcare markets.

References

Almon, Ted (1996) 'Price discrimination plagues a medical product Turkish bazaar', *Health Industry Today*, July.

Colletti, John J. (1995) 'Healthcare reform and the hospital supply chain', *Hospital Materiel Management Quarterly*, February.

CSC Consulting, Inc. (1996) *Efficient Healthcare Consumer Response: Improving the Efficiency of the Healthcare Supply Chain*, November.

Harrington, Lisa H. (1997) 'Supply chain integration from the inside', *Transportation & Distribution*, March.

Moynihan, James J. (1997) 'Improving the healthcare supply chain using EDI', *Healthcare Financial Management*, March.

Nathan, Jay, and Trinkaus, John (1996) 'Improving healthcare means spending more time with patients and less time with inventory', *Hospital Materiel Management Quarterly*, November.

North, Lee H. (1995) 'Beyond just-in-time: the UCLA Medical Center experience', *Hospital Materiel Management Quarterly*, February.

Speer, Tibbet L. (1996) 'Just say grow: Cardinal Health looks beyond drug distribution and sees a healthy future', *Hospitals and Health Networks*, August 5.

Strong, John W. (1995) 'Effective alliance—hospital partnering: beyond price', *Hospital Materiel Management Quarterly*, February.

Werner, Curt (1996) 'Distributors find big opportunity in alternate site sales', *Health Industry Today*, December.

China's supply chain challenge

Creativity in a giant marketplace

Denis Simon and David Ashton

China is making rapid progress, but a modern, comprehensive, national supply chain is still far from completion. Until that time, whether foreign firms choose to import or produce in China, they need to consider carefully their supply chain strategies. For the most part they must be willing to invest in unique supply chain solutions, combining existing methods with innovative, often unorthodox means to reach China's consumer and industrial markets. Key aspects of this will include selecting the right transportation options; creating the best distribution centres and warehousing arrangements; overcoming distribution headaches through creative solutions; and managing information technology to succeed.

Introduction

From 1949 until the onset of its economic reforms in 1978, China's supply chain was based, not on the principles of supply and demand, but on a government-planned system of allocation, production and distribution. For national security reasons the Chinese government discouraged development of a nationally integrated transportation and communication system that might make it possible for an invading force to move easily from either north to south or west to east. Today, profound shifts in the global geopolitical environment and 20 years of economic and technological modernization have spurred increased attention to, and an expanded need for, a well-orchestrated, well-equipped transport and communication infrastructure. But China has a long way to go before a truly modern, national supply chain infrastructure is developed. Ironically, according to some commentators, Coca-Cola may possess the most extensive network in all of China, reaching nearly 70 per cent of the population.

China's supply chain situation today

While many observers like to think of the Chinese market as the 'market of one billion plus', the reality is that China is a vast economy made up of a series of regional and subregional markets, all at different stages of economic and, therefore, infrastructure development.

The challenge of distribution throughout the regions of China is made even more problematic by various types of local protectionism. It is not uncommon for products manufactured in one section of the country to be denied entry to local markets in another region because of the existence of a local competitor. The 15th Chinese Communist Party Congress held in 1997 may have sanctioned further advance of a market economy in China, but many foreign firms still find it difficult to succeed without access to political middlemen capable of 'horse trading' with officials in the targeted markets.

In fact, many of China's interior rural regions remain economically very challenging indeed for foreign companies. They are characterized by low incomes, undeveloped infrastructure and a lack of reliable wholesalers. The government has tried to upgrade the overall interior infrastructure and continues to encourage foreign companies to move west, but the task is enormous. Until the still appreciable shortcomings present in central and western China are to remedied to some degree, distribution to these areas will lag far behind that in the urban areas of the east and south.

So despite the fact that two-thirds of China's population resides elsewhere, an overwhelming majority of its foreign-invested consumer and industrial products companies distribute and sell only in its faster-developing urban areas in the south and along the east coast. Realistically, China's currently addressable consumer market size is somewhere between 80 and 120 million people. The area along the eastern seaboard forms the main hub(s) for sales and distribution of many of the upscale products being offered to the Chinese populace.

Over the last 10 years, the government and foreign companies have invested billions of dollars in developing China's transportation and communications infrastructure, focusing specifically on the coastal areas stretching from Shenyang in the north to Shenzhen in the south. Fourteen coastal cities along China's eastern seaboard have been designated commercial centres for attracting foreign investment and facilitating economic contacts with the outside world. Recently built or improved highway segments between Tianjin–Beijing, Shenyang–Dalian, Shanghai–Nanjing, and Guangzhou–Shenzhen (see Figure 36.1), among others, have made product and component transport between these urban areas faster and easier.

With Chinese facilities generally under-equipped and ill prepared to handle the demands of modern logistics and distribution, several

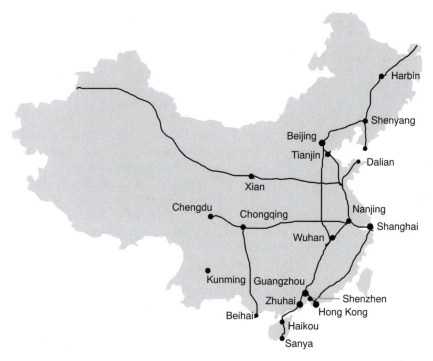

Figure 36.1   PRC highway projects: recently finished and in development

logistics service providers from Asia, Europe and the USA are building modern, world-class facilities, combining them with reliable intermodal transportation and communication options. TNT Logistics, Inchcape, APL, Trammel Crow and Sea-Land Logistics are just a few of the well-known providers now operating and expanding in China. There is still much to be done, however. According to the *China Trade Report* (September 1997), 'nowhere in Asia is the need for warehouse and distribution centres as great as it is in China'.

With few domestic suppliers and growing pressures from their global customers, some foreign logistics firms now offer services along the entire supply chain. For example, in mid-1997, a business unit of APL named American Consolidation Services announced a joint-venture plan to develop and operate one million square feet of consolidation, container storage and repair and distribution space (including 500 000 square feet of world-class warehouse space) in Shenzhen. The purpose of the facilities is to provide consolidation space for cargo distribution to northern and central China.

Even more innovative, through a 1996 bilateral agreement between the US and Chinese governments, Sea-Land Logistics became the first foreign logistics provider licensed to operate a wholly owned subsidiary in China. Several other foreign providers have since received the same licence and are aggressively moving inland and/or constructing modern facilities throughout China. The unique feature of these ventures is that they have been authorized to offer logistical services without local middlemen or joint-venture partners. In late 1996, APL announced the opening of a daily, rail-based inter-modal service from the port city of Dalian to Harbin, a northern industrial city about 1200 km inland.

Options for distribution strategies

Under China's planned economy, most consumer goods were distributed using the 'factory–wholesaler–retailer' method. Over the last 15 years, however, several new methods of distribution have gained favour. Specifically, many foreign investors feel that the 'factory (or import agent)–distribution centre–retailer' and 'factory–consumer' (direct marketing) methods represent the best ways not only to save time and money, but also to retain closer control over distribution.

To take charge of their destinies in China, foreign firms need to make several key decisions. They need to weigh up the costs and benefits of importing versus production within China; and they need to decide whether to invest significant amounts of human and financial resources to manage their own supply chains or wait for further developments in China's distribution network. Below we set out the options in more detail and highlight some proven strategies for success.

Making importing work

To make importing work, companies require a high degree of patience and ingenuity. Chinese trade law prohibits foreign companies from selling imported products directly to customers, as part of the government's effort to encourage actual investment over importing (see Economist Intelligence Unit (1996): Nestlé and Ferrero Rocher case studies). Even foreign companies that manufacture products in China do not have the right to import additional products directly and independently to fill out their product lines.

Once their products have entered China, multinational corporations have two distribution options: send their own people into China to follow products throughout the distribution chain, or spend less money and allow goods to be distributed by wholesalers.

The vast majority of imported consumer goods (some say as high as 90 per cent) cross the border into China at Guangdong (in Shenzhen, Guangzhou and Zhuhai) after going through a Hong Kong trade agent or 'converter'.

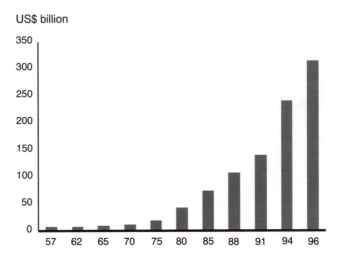

US$ billion

Figure 36.2   China's total value of imports and exports, 1957–96

Hong Kong-based converters have always been in high demand for their ability to move imports quickly and cheaply into China through south China's relatively lax customs areas. Like any hired import agent, converters will handle the paperwork and cargo transfer for a set fee. Their real job, however, is to avoid the tariffs and value-added taxes (VAT) that can add as much as 250 per cent to the cost of an item. This is accomplished through the use of 'grey channels', which can involve anything from slight infractions of tax and duty regulations to outright smuggling. If a company wants to avoid illegal activity it must keep a close watch on its converters, as turning a blind eye is accepted practice.

Quite a few Hong Kong converters provide distribution services as well, using companies with existing ventures and distribution networks in China. After reaching the port of Hong Kong, the company's goods are turned over to the Hong Kong partner, who ensures their safe transport into south China. There is some evidence that these same channels may be used to violate export controls on the sale of sensitive technologies to China. American officials from the US Departments of Commerce and Defense have expressed their concerns to Hong Kong officials about the need to monitor more closely the movement of so-called dual-use technologies and equipment into China via the Hong Kong window.

The problem is particularly acute with the import of personal computers and related peripherals, frequently referred to as 'water goods'. Many foreign firms actually producing the same or related products find their China-based factories competing with goods imported through these grey channels. The aggressive nature of Hong Kong distributors, combined with the unique access that these distributors seem to have in terms of penetrating the Chinese market, has forced many foreign firms to look the other way as they have few other viable options within the current environment. Estimates are that the Chinese government loses many millions of dollars every year in uncollected import duties and VAT.

Notwithstanding its return to Chinese rule, the role of Hong Kong as a door into the Chinese market has only been reinforced by the rapid development of infrastructures connecting Hong Kong with southern China. The relative wealth of south China's citizens, and a well-established distribution infrastructure, ensure not only a strong market demand for foreign goods but an effective medium through which to transport those goods. As long as import tariffs and customs duties remain high, there will always be demand for those individuals or groups providing ways around them. And 'the mountains are high and the emperor is far away', as the ancient saying goes. The former colony's status as a Special Administrative Region brings with it stated assurances by Beijing that certain economic privileges will be protected through to the year 2047.

While reliance on Hong Kong-based distributors does have significant short-term cost advantages, it can result in a multitude of long-term problems, many of which stem from a loss of control over intra-China distribution. One multinational essentially stopped doing business with several state-owned distributors after finding its products, supplied by a Hong Kong distributor, being improperly displayed among products comparable in neither quality nor cost (thereby creating an inaccurate and unhealthy product reputation) and displayed in undesirable retail outlets.

In an effort to discourage the use of grey channels and encourage investment at certain port areas, the government has established several free trade zones (FTZs) over the last decade. Many, such as Waigaoqiao near Shanghai, offer tax incentives and access to more direct trade with Chinese companies operating outside the zone. Often located in close proximity to some of China's most modern ports, roads, railroad links, warehouses and container facilities (not to mention the country's wealthiest consumers), these free trade zones may represent the most reasonable alternative to grey-channel importing.

Recently, the government has allowed some foreign companies, AT&T and Matsushita being two prominent examples, to establish their own 'maintenance centres' within free trade zones to help expedite the importing process. Despite the initial expense, those who can afford to do this usually become convinced that having such a presence at the port significantly reduces customs headaches. GE Medical Systems previously needed a full day to clear one shipment of spare parts through customs. With its own maintenance centre in the Waigaoqiao FTZ, the company can now clear a month's worth of goods in several hours (Yatsko, 1996).

Regardless of the methods used, multinational corporations that import products into China should follow several guidelines in order to succeed:

■ Work with converters and port authorities to negotiate the lowest possible duties on imports. Aside from China's free trade zones, other low- or zero-duty channels can be utilized for significant savings on many customs duties.
■ Know the import laws. Loopholes exist that allow companies to find preferable alternatives inside of China's import regulations. Knowing the law will save money and effort in the long run.
■ Designate one company as responsible for import operations. Having multiple, dissociated importers at several ports encourages parallel trading and causes a loss of control over product pricing.
■ Closely monitor the operations of all hired converters, importers and distributors.

Do-it-yourself supply chains

For an increasing number of companies, however, the most effective solution to the challenges of doing business with China is to set up full-scale production and distribution networks within China. Prior to 1986, foreign companies manufacturing in China were not permitted to sell direct from their factories to end users. Since then, however, literally thousands of companies have undertaken this challenge. Those which have chosen to build and manage each stage of the supply chain have generally been the most successful.

Perhaps the best example is McDonald's. Faced with the monumental task of moving bread, meat and related food products to its various stores in China, the famous fast-food chain had no alternative but create its own trucking company to ensure sustainable delivery schedules. Moreover, the lack of domestically available cold storage via rail and highway meant that the challenges were even more vexing. Of course, McDonald's venture into the trucking business went beyond its traditional core competencies, but the company had no alternative if it was to approximate a supply chain resembling what it was able to build in more developed markets.

This experience shows that implementing an effective distribution system in China is indeed possible. Successful foreign firms understand that constructing such a system of optimal warehousing and transporting methods across a developmentally diverse country can be a significant short-term investment. Yet short-term perseverance, ingenuity and a long-term investment strategy largely determine the degree to which a foreign firm succeeds in China.

For companies choosing to establish full-scale distribution networks within China, key areas of attention should be:

■ selecting the right transport options;
■ creating the best distribution centres and warehousing arrangements;
■ overcoming distribution headaches through creative solutions; and
■ managing information technology.

Selecting the right transport options

Constraints on the distribution of both raw materials and finished products remain the single greatest hindrance to effective supply chain management in China. In a 1995 survey conducted by the Economist Intelligence Unit, respondents 'ranked distribution as both the most essential task to achieving success in China and the most difficult' (*EIU Business China*, 1996b). Similarly, in an Andersen Consulting-sponsored study of joint-venture success in China, the same distribution issue was highlighted as a significant obstacle to business profitability in China (Andersen Consulting/EIU, 1996).

Distribution mainly relies on pivot cities and transportation hubs supported by key ports, commodity distribution centres and a combined use of rail, road and waterways. Price ceilings, capacity constraints and unpredictable delivery times make rail and water transport challenging, forcing most foreign companies to use road transport. Air transport is too cost prohibitive to be commonly used, except for emergencies. Over the last 10 years the Chinese government has made concerted efforts to upgrade services, particularly in railways, but improvements have lagged far behind demand growth (see Figure 36.3). So establishing an effective distribution strategy can be an unexpected cost and potential problem for foreign companies. As one US corporate executive recently confided, 'We take things like reliable transport facilities for granted when we operate in the US and Europe. Foolishly, we made some similar assumptions when we came to China and this error almost killed any chance of profitability for our business.'

Water

The use of water transport as a means of distributing products throughout China is, for the most part, impractical. Water routes flow mainly east to west in China and, once at port, products must somehow be moved to warehouses or retail outlets. A bigger difficulty may be timely and safe delivery of product. Goods transported by water have been known to be delayed due to storms, lost in transit or badly damaged. Rail and road transport are better methods.

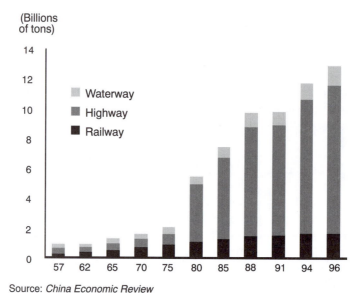

Source: *China Economic Review*

Figure 36.3   China's freight traffic by water, road and rail, 1957–96

Rail

Despite recent modernization and expansion plans carried out through the Eighth and Ninth Five-Year Plans by the Ministry of Railroads, it is estimated that 25 to 30 per cent of demand for cargo space on railroads cannot be met. Even after successfully booking rail space several months in advance, many companies find that their cargo is often taken off the trains mid-route by local officials to make room for items deemed higher priority. Tracking freight sent by train is also difficult and freight often disappears due to pilfering, going to the wrong destination and/or simply sitting interminably at some unknown rail yard. One foreign multinational in Shanghai has a full-time railway supervisor, responsible for tracking the company's cargo as it comes and goes through Shanghai only (*EIU Business China*, 1994).

Nevertheless, an appreciable number of corporations use rail as their main distribution method. Existing subsidies to the rail sector make cost savings significant. With close monitoring of cargo in transit, firms can reduce damage and loss. This option is not always advisable for a wholly foreign-operated venture, however, as a lack of *guanxi* (relationships) can mean a total inability to resolve potential scheduling, pilfering and product damage issues as they arise. At the very least, hiring a reputable, local rail supervisor is a must. One of the attractions of having a local joint-venture partner in China is the ability of that partner to gain access to transport facilities when needed.

Road

Most foreign companies rely on road transport. Despite its higher costs, road offers foreign players the greatest degree of control over their own products, both in terms of time taken to arrive at the assigned destination and product condition on arrival. Although China's road milage per square kilometre is less than one-fifth that of the USA and construction growth cannot keep up with increasing freight traffic, overall length and quality have improved tremendously during the last decade. As any recent visitor to China can attest, however, traffic in most urban areas is highly congested. The government is working to ameliorate the problems. Some large cities, such as Shanghai and Beijing, have imposed strict limits on where and when trucks can deliver, even going so far as to restrict on what days vehicles can be driven based on the last number of their licence plates. Also, over the last few years several foreign and domestic logistics providers have introduced long-haul trucks capable of carrying large loads of paletted and even containerized goods, making intermodal transport much more efficient. Trans-provincial logistics, however, can be a nightmare if appropriate permits and fees are not paid in advance.

There are other negatives with road transport as well. Cargo theft, for instance, is a frequent occurrence. A former driver of long-haul trucks for a domestic logistics provider recently admitted that when he carried large goods, such as industrial items or raw materials for factory use, he could bribe the highway bandits to leave him alone. But when carrying appliances or other consumer durables, he expected to be robbed of at least some of his cargo before arriving at the assigned destination. Even those trucks crossing from Hong Kong into southern China carrying so-called grey goods have often found security to be a significant issue. Local law enforcement does attempt to control such behaviour, but doing so is difficult because of the length of common distribution routes, such as Hong Kong to Beijing, Guangzhou to Shanghai and Shenzhen to Chongqing.

Owing to the need for more and better highways and roads, efforts are being made to build 'two vertical and two horizontal lines' and three road sections totalling 17 000 km. The two vertical lines refer to the Tongjiang (in Heilongjiang Province)–Sanya (in Hainan Province) highway and the Beijing–Zhuhai highway. The two horizontal lines are the Lianyungang (in Jiangsu province)–Torrogort (the juncture of the borders of Xinjiang and Kazakhstan) highway and the Shanghai–Chengdu highway. The three key sections include the Beijing–Shenyang, the Beijing–Shanghai and the Chongqing–Beihai (in Guangxi Zhuang Autonomous Region) highways. Thereafter, China's main economic zones will be connected with the four leading state trunk roads along the coast, the Yangtze river, the

Lanzhou–Lianyungang and Beijing–Guangzhou highways, as shown earlier in Figure 36.1.

Creating the best distribution centres and warehousing arrangements

Except for those few companies shipping directly from Hong Kong to customers (and/or retailers), access to a modern, reliable warehouse in China is an absolute necessity. Until recently, however, locating suitable warehouses and finding available space in them was a seemingly impossible task. An expatriate manager who had previously worked in China for an ice-cream producer and retailer once advised his close friends in Beijing against buying his former company's products because 'at night the electricity in the warehouse frequently goes off and the ice cream melts all over the floor'. Fortunately, this sad, almost comical experience is more representative of the past than the future of China warehousing, for the outlook is very positive.

Better roads and highways are opening large areas of lower-cost land for development. A larger range of available building materials is contributing to improved structural quality for China's warehouses. Buildings are getting larger (both in height and total area) and have increasingly sophisticated systems to enhance operational services and meet customer requirements. Such developments are bringing with them the ability of distribution centres and warehouses, such as APL's new 500 000 square foot facility in Shenzhen, to handle a greater variety of stock-keeping units to be shipped to more places more often and in better condition than was previously possible. As more logistics providers and individual companies build their own warehouses in China, and as the government begins to loosen regulatory control over warehousing and storage, access to effectively managed, modern facilities will increase and rental/usage costs may even fall. To some extent, this is already happening in larger cities.

Several aggressive and forward-looking companies have also managed to take advantage of the Chinese government's loosening of certain regulations to build their own distribution centres in China. The government still tries to discourage foreign participation in distribution and warehousing, while seeking the transfer of foreign technology and experience. Recognizing this, Japanese companies such as Mitsubishi were recently able to open integrated distribution centres in Shanghai and Guangdong. Prior to its demise, Yaohan's Shanghai distribution centre doubled as a retail outlet for local consumers, while storing products for transport to more than 100 of its other supermarkets in major cities around the country. In another twist, Mitsubishi hopes to lease extra space in its new Guangdong distribution centre for use by other home-appliance manufacturers. With close proximity to Hong Kong, major rail lines and several new expressways, the location is optimal for storage of imported products slated for inter-regional distribution. Although these companies are fairly high profile, lesser-known companies are also establishing their own distribution centres, some of which have space available for lease by interested parties.

Overcoming distribution headaches through creative solutions

Companies operating in China must remember that it is one of the world's largest nations in terms of geographic spread. With the exception of a few major players such as Coca-Cola and Unilever, multinational corporations have been unable successfully to distribute nationwide. Those with the furthest-reaching supply chains generally operate several regional factory and/or distribution hubs around which distribution to outlying areas is centred. Raw materials and imports of components are sourced from a specific location, such as a port area close to a large market (e.g. Shanghai), and from there are sent to either the regional factories for value-added production or the distribution centres for transport.

Distributing to such remote areas as Urumqi (about as far from Beijing as Seattle, Washington is from New York City) and Lhasa (the equivalent of Phoenix, Arizona from New York), however, is currently not much different to shipping from New York to California in the 1860s. Long stretches of arduous, undeveloped terrain make distribution very difficult. About 70 per cent of China's roads are Class III and IV (Class IV is inaccessible to most vehicles). The vast majority of these roads mark the only way to get to China's northern- and western-most areas. This helps to explain why infrastructure development has become such a high priority in terms of the country's economic development plans.

The most effective supply chains use creative methods to work effectively within the existing infrastructure. Finding its trucks unable to deliver to many stores in Beijing because of traffic congestion (and concerned with the cost of buying and maintaining an army of large refrigerated trucks), in 1994 Wall's began delivering its ice cream to various stores and kiosks throughout the city on the back of bicycles equipped with small freezers. Distributors on bicycles and motorbikes pick up ice cream at Wall's main Beijing distribution centre and transport it to assigned stores, many of which are equipped with freezers given to them by Wall's on condition that they are only used to store and sell Wall's products. This method proved so successful that it was adopted in Shanghai in 1995 (with some modifications) and has since been used in other cities as well and by other companies (EIU *Business China*, 1996a). Wall's is now one of the most widely recognized brand names in China.

As one of the most successful foreign companies in China, and one of the few that can say it truly has a nationwide presence, Coca-Cola has chosen to expend the necessary resources to develop an independent distribution operation. During more than 15 years in China, the company has found independent distribution to be the only way to get product exactly where it should be, while at the same time offering optimal customer service. Before opening its Beijing plant in 1981, Coca-Cola imported product from its plant in Hong Kong and used various outside distributors within each targeted urban market.

After gaining more of a foothold in China, the company hired its own distributors to service an area within a 50 km radius of each bottling plant and outsourced distribution to retail outlets in more remote areas. This trend has continued throughout years of expansion (Coca-Cola now has nearly 20 bottling plants in China) and by the year 2000 the company expects to be personally distributing half of all product sold.

Some of the ways in which Coca-Cola has achieved this degree of independence are truly unique. In Shanghai, the company hired hundreds of elderly 'street committee' members, who enjoy special privileges, to do its distribution in hard-to-reach areas. Able to go where they like and do whatever they want, these contracted distributors sell only Coca-Cola products out of refrigerated push carts and tricycles stocked straight from the bottling plants. Most of these distributors seem to be doing a brisk business and the company is considering implementing its new-found distribution method nationwide, if circumstances permit (EIU *Business China*, 1997).

As with Wall's and a few other foreign players, this shift from outsourcing to in-house capability requires ingenuity and investment. Coca-Cola's success in China, however, is attested to by its ubiquitous product and strong nationwide sales. Simply put, the companies that invest most heavily in distribution find that they usually develop the most reliable networks. This point is highlighted by the fact that many multinationals in recent years have been taking measures to gain better control over where and how their products are marketed to the Chinese consumer.

Information technology

While much of the world began running supply chains electronically in the late 1980s, most organizations operating in China were not afforded this luxury. It is only over the last three to four years that the country's enterprises and government organizations engaged in commerce have begun to join the information technology revolution. Even today, the vast majority of state-owned and other indigenous enterprises are still run manually and China's IT infrastructure, despite impressive modernization efforts over the last decade, remains in its infancy. Programmes such as the nationally oriented 'Goldens Projects' are aimed at allowing China to make rapid progress in terms of integrating the entire domestic market. In fact, some observers suggest that the Goldens Projects will contribute to China's national integration in the same way that railroads contributed to the integration of the US economy in the mid-nineteenth century.

Currently, however, it is precisely the lack of adequate information technology that makes data on customer needs and preferences hard to gather, cargo tracking almost impossible, communication with suppliers, distributors, wholesalers and retailers spotty and payment collection difficult and labour intensive. Also, since nearly all domestically owned warehouse systems in China are run manually, it is hard to control costs and ensure high levels of operational efficiency. Although the financial cost is significant, many corporations, especially those expanding outside one municipality and/or customer segment, are finding that the benefits of IT expansion outweigh the costs and have chosen to build their own systems or outsource the same. In part for this reason, many consulting firms have well-established, thriving practices in China.

Other companies, whether because of size, depth of commitment to China and/or other financial concerns, find it more attractive to pay for the use of another IT network. Aware of this burgeoning demand, many logistics providers are moving into or expanding existing operations, while placing an emphasis on their IT capabilities. The majority of these organizations take the form of Sino-foreign joint ventures, combining western IT standards and management techniques with local knowledge of suppliers, customers and distribution networks. Given the greater emphasis placed on IT capability over the last few years, many foreign logistics providers operating in China have upgraded to business software applications such as SAP R/3 or other comparable enterprise resource planning systems (*Business Wire*, 1997). For a price, any multinational corporation's China operations can enjoy the same IT infrastructure found in the most developed countries. Of course, the challenge of training the staff to utilize these capabilities on a consistent basis remains a fundamental problem—even if the commitment to invest in the hardware and software is made.

Conclusion

Foreign firms doing business in China will find that effective twenty-first-century supply chain management is challenging, but possible. By combining a regional approach with a commitment to continual investment in improved performance, and meticulous management of products at every stage of the supply chain, foreign players can succeed.

References

Anderson Consulting/EIU (1996) *Moving China Ventures Out of the Red and Into the Black: Insights from Best and Worst Performers*, Economist Group (Asia/Pacific), Hong Kong.

Business Wire (1997) 'Contract logistics helps businesses open new opportunities throughout Asia', 7 July.

China Trade Report (1997) 35, Sept., 16–17.

Economist Intelligence Unit (1996) *Difficulties in Distribution*, EIU Business Reports, Economist Group (Asia/Pacific), Hong Kong.

EIU Business China (1994) 'Moving goods in Shanghai: transport travails in China', XX (13), 27 June.

EIU Business China (1996a) 'China: why conquering Shanghai is not like Beijing: no wall's too high', XXII (3), 5 February.

EIU Business China (1996b) 'Distribution remains the key problem for market makers in China', XXII (10), 13 May, 6.

EIU Business China (1997) 'Those ever resourceful Coke boys: distribution is it', XXIII (9), 28 April, 12.

Yatsko, Pamela (1996) 'Another way in: "grey channels" are a boon—and a trap', *Far Eastern Economic Review*, 160 (49), 5 December, 63–6.

Reconfiguring the automotive industry supply chain

Driving a new focus on customer value

Mark Reynolds and Scot Eisenfelder

The automotive industry has been a leader in managing complexities in technologies, product development, global supply, production, distribution and sales and marketing.

However, the industry has largely failed to deliver at the customer end of the supply chain: in the critical areas of sales, service and support. Customers today are expecting high levels of service, ample information and open, honest pricing. Their rising dissatisfaction with the traditional car-purchasing experience is forcing change. This chapter describes how the industry can make the break from its production-driven push-based sales, marketing and distribution traditions and redesign its customer service and supply chain activities around a pull-based system. By putting the customer firmly in the driver's seat in the supply chain, manufacturers will be able to respond more quickly and cost effectively to customers' needs.

Introduction

Customers the world over frequently loathe car dealers and their practices. The treatment of customers in many car showrooms has hardly changed from the days of horse trading when sharp practices abounded. Customers respond by avoiding car showrooms and salespeople. Meanwhile, almost every other retail business from groceries and clothing to fast food and furniture has learned to put the customer in charge and make it easy for them to buy.

In automotive sales, however, this concept has developed slowly, with a few automotive exceptions such as Saturn in the USA, which aims to be the industry 'good guy' by providing a simple, friendly and honest purchasing environment for its limited range of small cars. The sort of 'customer-first' approach achieved by Saturn and taken for granted by most retailers seems to have escaped the majority of automotive retailers. Instead, car dealers persist in treating customers with less respect than they deserve and are often accused of offering unrealistic prices,

Table 37.1
Primary automotive sales process dissatisfiers

• High-pressure sales tactics	• Dishonest pricing
• Poor needs assessment	• Turnover gaming between finance and sales
• Difficulty of comparison shopping	• 'One size fits all' approach
• Poor vehicle selection	• Excessive time required
• Haggling	• Poor problem resolution

Source: Andersen Consulting project work, 1997

wasting time and forcing them to haggle over every detail. The primary sources of customer dissatisfaction listed in Table 37.1 indicate the depth of the problem.

These dissatisfiers lead to customer avoidance of car sales locations, creating a huge loss of buying opportunities for the industry. Paradoxically, in countries like the USA where car dealers traditionally close on Sundays, their yards are often busiest with visitors checking out the vehicles free from any risk of interference by salespeople but dependent on other sources such as newspapers, magazines and consumer reports for information.

A new factor became significant in the mid-1990s: the Internet. A remarkable range of product and pricing information has been published on the Internet, particularly in the USA, and has created a new class of well-informed purchaser. The buyer armed with detailed printouts of vehicle specifications and dealer pricing has seriously shifted the balance of power against the dealer salesperson. Some people have obtained good deals, although most still feel cheated by the buying process and disinclined to show the dealer any loyalty for subsequent service needs, even where its service department may be doing an exceptional job.

It gets worse. Outdated supply chain planning and information systems are the norm among car manufacturers who consequently have great difficulty giving their dealers reliable delivery dates. When nobody will give them a firm commitment, customers who have chosen to order a car may begin to believe that the entire industry is incompetent. Stories abound of customers cancelling orders after the third or fourth change in delivery promises, only to have the missing vehicle arrive unexpectedly the next day. Unfortunately, the few car companies that can provide accurate delivery information are rarely distinguished in the public mind from the many who cannot.

Creating better alternatives through the supply chain

Mastery of the supply chain has become a critical success factor for prosperity in retailing. The key objectives for supply chain performance vary from lowest possible cost in grocery retailing to fastest possible response in high-end fashion goods. Successful supply chain configurations follow many patterns according to product and positioning needs. The common characteristic is greatest possible use of end-customer demand to drive supply chain planning and execution. Such a model is often described as pull based and requires a powerful set of supply chain capabilities to deliver exactly the product the customer wants, when the customer wants it.

Several highly visible industries from clothing to personal computers have shaped the expectations of today's customers. Using lean, flexible supply chains with customer-focused sales processes they can deliver exactly what the customer wants without a significant price premium or even at a discount. Automotive customers are rightly asking, if manufacturers can deliver such tailored products and experiences for a $60 pair of jeans or a $2000 computer, why not for a $20 000 vehicle?

It can be argued that retail shopping experiences are not relevant to car sales because customers think differently about major capital purchases. Evidence against this argument includes the extraordinary success of direct selling in the personal computer business, where unit price is much higher than most consumer purchases. Direct seller Dell Computer, for instance, has progressively developed one of the most fully integrated customer-direct supply chain models in any industry. The cost, responsiveness and customer-service advantages provided by Dell's pull-driven model could well be applied to the automotive industry.

The most significant characteristic of the Dell model is that almost every activity is directly driven from the 'buy' signal sent by the customer. The PC is assembled or configured to order from very small inventories of parts. Dell's logistics supplier coordinates delivery to the customer of the PC and all other items ordered such as printer, monitor, software or accessories. And every detail of the customer's purchase and the path towards the purchase decision is instantly available to Dell's own marketing staff and to their supply chain partners to help them plan their future product and service offerings.

The pull-based supply chain

The pull-based supply chain is the right answer for the automotive industry because it is essential to deliver better customer value and has finally become technically feasible for complex manufacturing and distribution environments.

For decades the automobile industry has operated under a push distribution system. Under such a system, manufacturers produce to long lead-time forecasts and rely on their dealers and periodic incentives to move inventory. Push distribution is characterized by high levels of inventory held in a distributed manner, thereby simultaneously driving high costs and low fill rates.

Perhaps more critically, push distribution has created and sustained sales processes which are the antithesis of developing lifelong relationships with customers. The focus on 'selling what you have' rather than 'making what sells' results in sales processes driven from the manufacturer's need to push often unwanted vehicles, not in identifying and responding to customer needs. In such an environment, the constant pressure to move volume through short-term incentives undermines pricing and brand strategies. The result is a constant boom-and-bust cycle as new products drive higher sales at the expense of satisfaction, followed by lean years of staggering incentives to buy customers back into the franchise.

The alternative pull-based model is built around integrated information systems which enable effective processes and encourage customer input. Dell has shown how this can be done for computers and the race for automotive supply chain leadership is now on.

Benefits of pull-based distribution

Creating the capabilities to deliver the exact product to the customer in a timely manner will have tremendous benefits throughout the value chain. Most analyses have focused on the impact on inventory carrying as the primary or sole source of benefits associated with a pull-based distribution system. In fact, our findings suggest that the reduction in inventory costs is only the 'tip of the iceberg' (Andersen Consulting analysis and project work in North American markets during 1996 and 1997).

We have identified four main benefit sources from implementing pull distribution, which together yield $635 in increased profits per new vehicle sold for car manufacturers and their dealers: reduced fulfilment costs; higher revenue realization; lower selling costs; and improved retention throughout the ownership cycle.

Benefit 1—Reduced fulfilment costs

Much of today's fulfilment cost—shipping, storing inventory on dealer lots and physically trading inventory between dealers—does not add

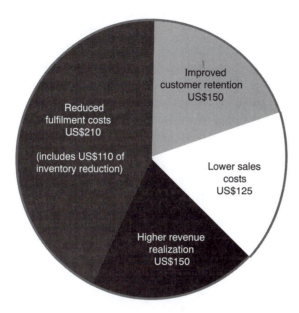

Total profit increase per new vehicle sold = US$635

Figure 37.1   Benefits of pull distribution, US$ profit increase per new vehicle

value for the customer. Even in the USA where buying from the show-room floor has been common, recent data indicates that 70 per cent of customers are willing to wait two weeks or more for the vehicle of their choice. Therefore, most customers do not value inventory beyond the minimum required to 'show the line' and provide test drives.

Reducing the inventory in the system can eliminate about 50 per cent of today's physical inventory. Shifting it to manufacturers' regional pools will reduce carrying costs through lower interest and insurance rates. Furthermore, a pull distribution system will greatly reduce costly physical trades between dealers. Over the long haul, dealers can reconfigure their real estate and take additional costs out of their infrastructure and overhead. The total fulfilment saving of $210 per vehicle comprises $110 from less inventory in the system, $75 from lower interest rates and $25 from less physical inventory trading.

Benefit 2—Higher revenue realization

Even with today's high inventory levels and dealer trades, fill rates are relatively low. The average customer shops at three same-brand dealers for selection. As a result, 15 per cent of customers bypass their nearest dealership for selection reasons. Furthermore, poor selection at the local dealer results in 3 per cent of all customers defecting from the brand, equivalent to $50 lost profit per vehicle sold.

Other customers who do not find the vehicle they want at their local dealership compromise on vehicle content. Some customers buy more content than they truly want, while others drive away with less content than they actually desire. With the average customer willing to buy an extra $700 of content, the sale of vehicles with too little content to 20 per cent of buyers suggests that $140 is lost in revenue per new vehicle on typically high margin add-ons, resulting in perhaps $70 per vehicle in lower profit. Those who purchase a vehicle with too much content presumably do so at deeply discounted margins, leading to an assumed profit loss of around $25 to $50 per vehicle.

Benefit 3—Lower sales costs

Buffer stocks slow the feedback between sales and production, leading to excessive inventory in pockets of slow-moving vehicles, frequently those in unpopular colours. The high inventory levels and long lead times between ordering and production make car companies particularly vulnerable to forecasting errors and changes in customer tastes. While 'stale' vehicles—those more than 90 days old—are a small percentage of total inventory, they represent almost half of the inventory-carrying cost, as shown in Figure 37.2. Surprisingly, the bulk of 'stale' inventory is not

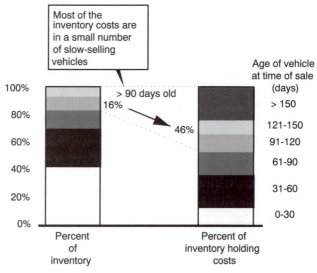

Figure 37.2   Drivers of inventory costs

slow-moving models, but rather slow-moving variants of otherwise healthy models.

To clear the inventory pockets, car manufacturers must offer substantial discounts. However, industry practices raise the cost of doing so. Current incentives do not distinguish between slow-moving and fast-moving variants within a model, so a substantial proportion of incentives are spent on vehicles that were selling in any case. The negotiated sales process also disguises the significant cross-subsidization employed by dealers to shift slow-moving inventory both within and across models. Without an understanding of both 'velocity' and price realization, the manufacturers cannot model the true demand for their products. Therefore, not only does the current system fail to respond quickly with changes in product mix to meet market changes, it muffles the market signals. Providing a more responsive order-to-delivery system would enable manufacturers significantly to reduce the number of slow-moving vehicles and virtually eliminate 'wasted' incentives on less popular variants of high-volume models, potentially yielding savings of $100 per vehicle.

In addition to requiring increased incentives to move stale inventory, the push-based approach affects sales productivity. The current system forces the customer to shop at multiple dealers not just to find the lowest prices, but also to find the vehicle they want. This activity has an impact on the shopping costs and satisfaction for the customer, but it also lowers salesperson productivity by 10 per cent, which translates into an extra cost of $25 per vehicle.

Benefit 4—Improved retention throughout the ownership cycle

Unlocking the $20 000 lifetime profit potential from each customer requires meeting his or her needs at each point of the ownership experience, which is made up of a chain of experiences as illustrated in Figure 37.3. The sales experience establishes the context for the potential service relationship and, in turn, the dealer service experience has significant impact on the likelihood of repeat vehicle purchase. For instance, a customer satisfied with the sales process is more likely to return to the dealer for servicing. Satisfaction with servicing will inspire service loyalty and ultimately service loyalty will lead to repurchasing.

As the first link in the chain, obtaining the exact vehicle desired has a substantial impact on the future revenue stream from a given customer. Purchasers of vehicles with too much or too little content have between 4 and 18 percentage points lower satisfaction than purchasers receiving the exact desired content. Such lower sales satisfaction translates into a 2.5 per cent lower service intent and ultimately 2.8 per cent lower

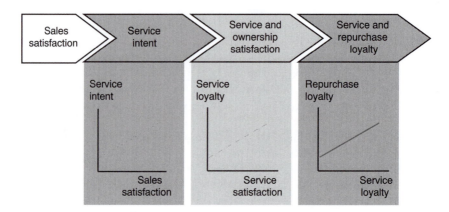

Figure 37.3   Drivers of loyalty

repurchase loyalty, shaving $75 from the service and repurchase value of each customer per purchase cycle.

The current push system affects lifetime customer value even among those customers who found the exact vehicle of their choice but had to travel outside their market area. While customers are willing to travel 100 km to purchase a vehicle, most prefer to service their vehicle within 10 km of their home or business. Therefore, when customers leave their market area to find the vehicle of their choice, their propensity to service at the dealer drops significantly, particularly after the warranty period. The associated loss in service retention reduces the value capture by $50 per ownership cycle.

The challenges of change

Changing the automotive industry's established ways of producing, distributing and selling vehicles is exceptionally difficult because it requires aligned action from three groups with very different histories, capabilities and interests, namely:

■ the manufacturer's production organization, especially the production planners and schedulers;
■ the manufacturer's sales, marketing and distribution organization; and
■ the dealers.

Where other industries have redesigned their supply chains from the customer backwards, car manufacturers have a problem. Car dealers are an independent-minded group, well aware of their legal rights in many countries and disinclined to do anything that may not show them a quick return. Gaining agreement from dealers is difficult. Large and small, metro and country, truck and car, import and domestic, dealers are united only in making relatively little money from new vehicle sales. Observers monitoring dealer profitability in the major car markets of the world consistently report that dealers lose money on new car sales, barely break even on used cars and make all their money on parts, service, accessories, finance and insurance. The dealers' objectives are therefore only partly focused on new vehicle sales and can be hard to reconcile with the manufacturers' interests, let alone with an overall supply chain view.

A few individual dealers have made remarkable changes through their own initiative. Some have introduced no-haggle pricing following the Saturn model. Others have gained scale economies by creating mega-dealerships. Others have reached a wider market by embracing the Internet. In various ways such dealers have cleaned up their sales and customer relationship processes and have often found, as has AutoNation (the innovator in national used-car retailing in the USA), that the cultural and behavioural changes required at the point of sale are so great that 'non-car' people from outside the industry are more likely to succeed than the classic car salesperson.

Manufacturers have recently introduced some variations on the dealer model, especially where they are latecomers to a market, like Hyundai and Daewoo, or making a fresh start as Jaguar and Land Rover had to do in the US during the 1990s. Daewoo in the UK has bypassed traditional dealership approaches by establishing its own retail network. Its showrooms have a small inventory of demonstration vehicles and enable customers to obtain product information from multimedia kiosks. And unlike the traditional model, servicing was initially outsourced to another company.

The bigger challenges are faced by the long-established players such as Ford and GM, which already have extensive dealer networks that tend to foster margin-sapping inter-dealer competition. Dealer numbers have been steadily falling since the 1950s and in the USA both Ford and GM are now trying to accelerate rationalization in selected locations. By merging dealerships the car companies aim to bring down costs through inventory pooling and reduced dealer-against-dealer advertising and to introduce customer-friendly practices such as no-haggle pricing. Some of the barriers to change in the industry are highlighted by the difficulties that Ford in particular has faced. Its first two attempts were torpedoed by unyielding dealers in Indianapolis and Salt Lake City.

In taking the lead on dealer mergers Ford has had to overcome internal barriers between its sales and marketing and its manufacturing arms. Historically these groups have operated at arm's length in almost every car company, with sales complaining that they never get what they order while manufacturing keep their eyes tightly focused on product quality and production efficiencies. The gulf between the groups has become particularly embarrassing because of the extraordinary success of lean production. By any measure today's cars deliver remarkable product quality, equipment levels and performance through a production system that has cut out every possible waste and extra cost during design and manufacture. Yet nothing much has happened to take out cost and waste from marketing, selling and distribution.

From production's point of view it has the factories running like clockwork with sequenced deliveries of major subassemblies and systems united with the correct body in perfect time. The processes that make this happen begin from a forecast provided by sales and marketing and from dealer orders, but it is common to find that manufacturing believes it knows best and makes extensive changes to forecasts and orders, for all the best reasons. Requirements such as corporate average fuel economy, component availability and assembly time all influence the final production schedule. Some companies report that as few as 25 per cent of dealer orders are actually built as ordered. Clearly something is seriously wrong when a dealer cannot get what was ordered two months previously.

Getting started—priorities for action

For the majority of car manufacturers the challenge is to reform an existing supply chain of great complexity and depth of capabilities, interlaced with many vested interests and conflicting objectives. The scale of the challenge suggests an evolutionary approach—start small, build capabilities, prove concepts and demonstrate value before making significant investments in radical solutions. While the ultimate goal is a true pull system, where a significant percentage of vehicles are not produced until there is a firm order, manufacturers can build toward this system incrementally. Four distinct building blocks make up a pull system, which can be implemented sequentially:

■ improving allocation and trading procedures;
■ compressing order-to-delivery processes;
■ creating regional inventory pools; and
■ increasing production-scheduling flexibility.

Priority 1—Improving allocation and trading procedures

Unlocking the tremendous value in the supply chain starts with allowing any dealer to sell any vehicle that has not already been sold to a customer. This vehicle may be on the dealer's lot, on another dealer's lot, in transit, in production or planned for production. To facilitate this transaction, the manufacturer must provide participating dealers with complete supply pipeline visibility and the means to acquire any vehicle in that pipeline for the customer.

Providing the required visibility is relatively straightforward. Most manufacturers have a vehicle locator that enables them to know where any vehicle is in the pipeline. In some cases, manufacturers may have to link the 'physical' pipeline with the 'virtual' pre-production pipeline. Some companies may need to improve their search capability to locate vehicles based on more precise product attributes. Adding an algorithm that translates the vehicle's current schedule position into days to delivery would add further value to the dealer, allowing the customer to choose delivery date along with other product features and price in the vehicle-specification process. Whether existing or not, deploying the technology is not difficult.

The implementation challenge centres on creating policies and processes acceptable to all stakeholders. The manufacturers need to design incentives to ensure that dealers share all inventory, not just slow-moving models. The incentives need to incorporate a fair dealer-to-dealer transfer-pricing model. Mechanisms have to be created to ensure that dealers do not use the system to accumulate 'hot products', rather than meet customer needs. While the system works best when all dealers participate, participation must be contingent on strict adherence to policies. This becomes less of an issue as order-to-delivery time is shortened and inventory pools are implemented, dramatically reducing the percentage of inventory held at the dealership.

In addition, dealer sales processes must be changed. To realize the improvements in profit and satisfaction, customers must be encouraged to trade off features, price and delivery dates. Most manufacturers are developing information kiosks and sales-support tools to provide customers with information on vehicle specifications and capture 'true demand' data. But under prevailing practices pricing is a major hurdle. A customer needs to know the 'real price' on each option when configuring his or her ideal vehicle. The current negotiated sales process denies the customer the required information and hence limits the effectiveness of allocation changes or technology investments.

Similar culture change is required at the manufacturers. In an environment of periodic swings of excess supply followed by shortages, manufacturers have widely used allocation of scarce product to 'reward' dealers who helped move slower-selling units or met other objectives. Allowing dealers open access to inventory throughout the pipeline will undermine both the traditional lever exercised by the manufacturer's field staff to control the dealer body and the tendency of the franchise's largest dealers to acquire inventory for competitive reasons.

One compelling new lever that could be used to break down resistance to change, and change dealer behaviour, is customer information. As manufacturers reduce their dependence on mass advertising by building better customer relationship-management capabilities—capturing and using information to sell to individual customers—access to the manufacturer's customer information will become a more effective lever. Using information as a lever will have an impact on the dealer's lead stream directly, without adversely affecting the customer. In the new environment, manufacturer's field staff roles will change to supporting new dealer processes and technology. Again, this will require substantial reskilling.

Priority 2—Compressing order-to-delivery processes

Once customers can be offered the opportunity to purchase any vehicle in the pipeline, the next priority is to speed up the order-to-delivery cycle. The speed of this cycle determines the amount of buffer stock required to meet the demands of customers unwilling to wait more than the two weeks usually regarded as acceptable. Since the scope of order-to-delivery goes from the dealers through sales and marketing to production, then back through distribution to the dealers again, managing all the resource constraints on the way, it is a fearsomely complex process. Redesigning this process along pull-based lines requires a complete rethink of all the existing roles, relationships, behaviours, responsibilities, incentives and systems support at every point. Ultimately the rethinking must extend right back to product design and development where significant contributions can be made to manufacturing flexibility and new possibilities can be created for customizing vehicles as close as possible to the point of sale.

Fortunately there are incremental steps that can be taken to redesign the order-to-delivery process. Taking advantage of its relatively small-scale home market with only one factory and one locally manufactured vehicle line (the Falcon), Ford Australia has developed highly refined order-to-delivery processes based on collaborative forecasting and planning between dealers, sales and production schedulers. The system encourages realistic ordering by dealers and allows for vehicle specification changes to be made online right down to the last few minutes before the body enters the paint shop. Ford in the USA has managed the introduction of some of the Australian concepts by starting with its specialist car lines such as the Mustang. Introducing new order-to-delivery processes on a low-volume vehicle line has allowed Ford to iron out issues with a North American implementation at low risk while demonstrating the value of a pull-based approach across most of the dealer network.

Ford US provided an overview of its progress up to late 1997 in a conference paper (Patton, Preston and Wujciak, 1997) where it described its key change objectives as: 15 day order-to-delivery cycle time (reduced from as high as 60 days); more choice; production schedule stability; customer delivery schedule stability; and halving of inventory from 86 to 43 days.

The pervasive nature of the order-to-delivery process is shown by the eight key elements of Ford's changes, which go a long way towards addressing product allocation, regional inventory pooling and production-scheduling flexibility as well as specific order-to-delivery issues. Ford's eight key elements are:

- production and dealer business planning using agreed time horizons and rules;
- dealer-suggested order creation (Ford provides a sophisticated forecasting model which incorporates a wide range of demand drivers and helps dealers develop orders which are 'buildable', contributing strongly to volume stability);
- joint team order management by sales and production scheduling using a single set of constraints;
- sequenced assembly production;
- vehicle-destination management that allows dealers to trade 'virtual' vehicles;
- dealer order amendment allowing dealers to change some aspects of vehicle specification as late as eight days prior to production;
- regional material logistics; and
- vehicle transport mixing centres.

Among other issues, the Mustang pilot highlighted changes to organizational roles and responsibilities. Implementation of the eight key elements required changes from director level downwards to sales, marketing, planning, distribution, manufacturing, purchasing and finance. Interestingly, the IT system changes for the pilot were kept to a minimum with only three added functions—a suggested order algorithm, a dealer business-planning toolset and an order-allocation levelling package.

Initial results from the Mustang pilot have been most visible in ordering simplification and schedule stability. Production schedule stability has improved remarkably from 40 to 60 per cent of promised orders built over a week to 95 per cent of promised orders built to the day. Major reductions in inventory and cycle time are expected to follow once the final process refinements are in place. Nevertheless, the measurable performance improvements achieved to date have convinced Ford to proceed with rollout to higher-volume vehicle lines like Taurus during 1998.

Priority 3—Creating regional inventory pools

Distribution changes such as regional inventory pooling are highly attractive. The concept is relatively simple. Dealer inventory is reduced to a level sufficient to 'show the line' and provide test drives, while sales inventory is held in pools. The customer can then choose from a much wider selection of vehicles but must wait a day or two for delivery. According to Ford, regional pools can take more than $1000 per vehicle out of current distribution costs in some parts of the USA. This is an area which cries out for leadership from the manufacturer and there are plenty of good examples of optimum inventory deployment around the world. In the UK, most manufacturers now centralize their vehicle stocks at one or two locations which has largely eliminated costly shuffling of vehicles from dealer to dealer. Step one is to introduce physical

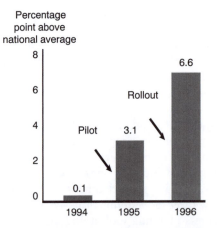

Percent of customers rating
availability excellent in Florida

Source: General Motors, Andersen Consulting analysis

Figure 37.4   Cadillac regional pool results

inventory pooling. Step two is to extend the concept to pooling of the virtual inventory of yet-to-be-built cars.

A well-documented example of the sort of improvements that can be achieved is provided by Cadillac's trial of pooling in Florida. Cadillac benefited from customer satisfaction gains, as shown in Figure 37.4, as well as overall inventory reductions.

Barriers to implementing regional pools range from risk management, particularly with slow-moving vehicles, to concerns that customers associate more visible inventory with better deals. Ultimately the car manufacturers cannot afford the negative customer-service impacts of current practices and will have to find ways to resolve dealers' concerns.

Priority 4—Increasing production-scheduling flexibility

Production scheduling is of critical importance to both assembly plants and their networks of suppliers. The situation is made even more complex where key systems and components are supplied from overseas on long lead times, as is happening more often with increased globalization.

The challenge is to develop sufficient supply chain integration to allow different order lead times to be provided accurately for various vehicle options depending on resources and parts availability without introducing unmanageable complexity. The first requirement is to achieve production schedule stability through improved order-to-delivery processes. The next requirement is to synchronize resource planning including labour requirements and material release with the production schedule. In the past it has been common for assembly plants to reschedule activities and material requirements every night. Paradoxically, more responsive order-to-delivery and production-scheduling processes may require less nightly rescheduling by improving overall schedule stability at the weekly level, which will create savings in expediting effort for both assembly plants and their suppliers.

Conclusion

The challenge for all automotive manufacturers is to agree their priority actions, establish focused pilots such as the Ford US work and steadily extend the scope of the pilots until the pull-based model becomes the norm instead of the exception. Very soon there will be significant pain among the dealer sales staff and their car company sales and marketing counterparts who find that the new attitudes, skills and behaviours required to deliver customer value and satisfaction are far outside their level of comfort. Manufacturers and dealers who fail to focus their energies around competition based on customer satisfaction will soon find that customers are deserting them in favour of those who offer alternative supply chain approaches.

Reference

Patton, S., Preston, A. and Wujciak, M. (1997) 'Implementing change in the automotive supply chain: redesigning Ford's order-to-delivery process', Council of Logistics Management annual conference.

Reverse logistics
Bringing the product back: taking it into the future
Theresa Jones

Creating and sustaining best practice in the forward logistics flow is a hard enough challenge for most companies. It's no surprise, then, that so few are inclined to embrace wholeheartedly the reverse logistics challenge. But the proliferation of used products, aggressive new environmental legislation and a drive for maximum utilization and efficiency are forcing companies to tackle this relatively new supply chain area. Companies can move ahead of their competitors by thinking through the opportunities and implications of this new era, including the prospect of managing a life-long product responsibility.

Introduction

Having ensured delivery of the product to the customer, the last thing the average supply chain manager wants to think about is the product's eventual return. The reality is, however, that all or part of the product is likely to become the responsibility of the manufacturer, distributor or retailer once again, at some stage during the product's life. Most companies still regard reverse logistics as a problem and react to it passively: however, smart companies such as BMW, Sears, Tesco and Xerox are actively implementing reverse logistics strategies to obtain competitive advantage.

Reverse logistics is here to stay. Most firms in industrialized markets will be forced to deal with this concept whether they want to or not—to stay in line with environmental legislation in industrialized countries or to keep up with their competitors who are using and reusing their resources to maximum efficiency.

Reverse logistics defined

Reverse logistics is very simply defined as: 'An organization's management of material resources obtained from customers' (Giuntini and

Andel, 1995). It encompasses any materials, packaging or products received from the customer. At its most simplistic, reverse logistics tends to be thought of as the collection of used, out-of-date or damaged products and packaging from customers to a point of ultimate disposal. But increasingly it is understood as the coordination of processes to ensure complete, efficient and effective utilization of products and material throughout their entire lifecycle.

Figure 38.1 illustrates a typical reverse supply chain and reverse information flow.

Reverse logistics and information

Contemporary definitions don't highlight a key attribute of reverse logistics: the critical dependence of the process on the management of returned information. If the producer retains a stewardship role over the product until its final disposal, then it needs to be able to track the historical course of the product, including its ownership, for its entire life.

This information will help the producer understand the attributes of the product—whether the design is good, whether the product is durable, what attributes the component parts possess. Product and parts usage profiles can be utilized at an operational level to improve the inventory management of products and spare parts in the forward flow and to generate return profiles in a manner similar to the demand data used in the forward flow. These patterns will be helpful in planning and managing the operations of the reverse supply chain. At a strategic level the information will be used to develop and understand customer consumption patterns more thoroughly and to manage new product ownership models and their financial impacts on the business. By understanding the product intimately, its producers can contemplate design and durability improvements.

Drivers of reverse logistics

For those companies for which reverse logistics is already a fact of life, senior managers have all too often pushed its management down to operations. This approach will no longer work. Powerful drivers are forcing companies to move reverse logistics on to the strategic agenda of senior management. The main drivers of this change of attitude are:

- government legislation;
- new channels of distribution;
- shifting power in the supply chain; and
- shortening product lifecycles.

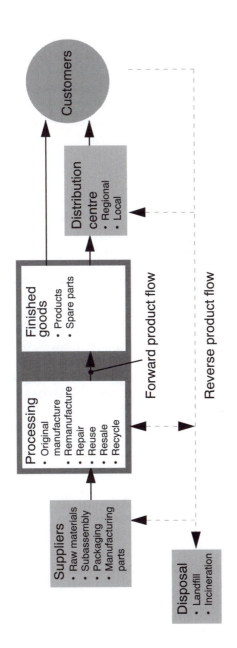

Figure 38.1 Reverse logistics product and information flows

Government legislation

Government environmental legislation throughout the industrialized world is effectively forcing companies to take life-long responsibility for the products they create. Consumer concerns over issues such as global warming, the greenhouse effect and increased pollution will advance this trend. In the USA, over 2000 Bills on solid waste disposal have been introduced into Congress over the past few years and in 1997 the Japanese parliament legislated for compulsory recycling of certain materials.

In Europe the message is even stronger. To reduce the waste being disposed of at landfill, the European Union (EU) has produced a Directive on Packaging and Packaging Waste, which has been translated into statutory law by each of the member states. This Directive stipulates the reduction, reuse and recycling of packaging material, requiring specific tonnages of packaging waste to be recovered and recycled by each individual member of the supply chain, based on its role in the supply chain and its annual turnover. The aim of this regulation is to develop shared producer responsibility.

All firms handling more than 50 tonnes of packaging a year that have an annual turnover of more than £5 million are obliged to register and prove that they have undertaken material recovery and recycling by 1998. The packaging materials to be recovered are aluminium, glass, paper, board, plastic and steel. Raw material producers have a 6 per cent share of the responsibility; packaging manufacturers 11 per cent; packer fillers such as food canners and spare-part makers 36 per cent; and anyone who sells the product to the end user, 47 per cent. Recovery targets are substantial at 38 per cent for 1998, rising to 52 per cent in 2001. The UK government has also implemented a landfill tax to force firms to change the way they deal with the waste they produce, in effect to 'make the polluter pay'.

These aggressive legislative moves are just the beginning, as governments force companies to change the way they develop and manage their products through to their ultimate disposal as waste.

Smart firms are not waiting around passively to be forced into legislative compliance. They are preparing for the next generation of environmental legislation and actively rethinking the producer's role, responsibilities and opportunities in relation to the products they make. Indeed, they are preparing for the inevitable day when the producer will be made fully responsible for the disposal of the product at the end of its useful life. When this legislation is in place, the traditional notion of transfer of ownership and liability will disappear and the relationship between buyer and seller will change forever.

Shortening product lifecycles

Product lifecycles are shortening. This phenomenon is evident everywhere in industry and most visible in the computer industry. New and upgraded designs are brought on to the market at an ever faster pace to persuade consumers to buy more often. While consumers benefit from greater choice and performance, inevitably this trend results in more usable but unwanted products, more packaging, more returns and more waste. Shortened product lifecycles have increased the volumes of waste entering reverse logistics systems and the cost of managing them.

New channels of distribution

New channels are also being developed to provide consumers with easier and quicker ways to buy. Consumer-direct channels TV shopping networks and the Internet facilitate the delivery of goods directly to consumers. Direct channels increase the likelihood of returned products, as items are damaged in transit or simply don't appeal to the customer in a real rather than virtual state. These direct channels will add pressure on the reverse logistics systems. Where the average retailer can expect that between 5 and 10 per cent of its product will be returned, those selling to catalogue and shopping-network customers can expect that a massive 35 per cent of products purchased will be sent back (Eisenhuth, 1997). As direct channels find customers around the world, not simply locally, nationally or even regionally, managing returns will become increasingly complicated and expensive.

Shifting power through the supply chain

Increased competition and a larger supply base have meant that buyers have more power in the supply chain. Retailers can, and do, refuse responsibility for the burden of disposing of unsold products and unnecessary packaging. Most product returns to the top retailers in the USA (either direct from the consumer or through non-sales) will be taken back by the original suppliers for rework or disposal. This trend is occurring in all industries, even in the airline industry, where airlines as buyers are specifying that their suppliers take back and dispose of unwanted packaging.

Reverse logistics in action

The size, cost and complexity of reverse logistics are therefore beginning to change the attitude of management towards the discipline. While it is not yet considered to be a boardroom activity, companies are beginning to consider management approaches to tackle the problem. Best-practice firms are finding that the right reverse logistics methods will result not only in a reduced cost for reverse logistics, but in improved revenue streams as well.

Reverse logistics in practice consists of a number of processes designed to gain maximum value from the returned products and materials at minimum cost. In order to achieve this objective firms must develop appropriate systems to manage the incoming products, including rapidly identifying the most cost-effective reverse process for the products to undergo.

Firms must therefore address two different issues. First, they must develop a system by which products can undergo one of six different reverse processes; and secondly, they must configure a physical network to facilitate these processes. Two main systems are available to firms to manage their reverse logistics: closed loop and open loop. Many firms will use both to maximize the life and value of their assets.

Tesco (a leading supermarket chain in the UK) uses both a closed- and open-loop system to manage the requirements of the EU Directive on Packaging and Packaging Waste. The system has been designed to manage the elimination and recycling of all the packaging waste returned from their supermarkets. The waste is recycled and either processed into a Tesco's own-label product such as bin liners (closed loop) or sold into secondary markets (open loop). Nine purpose-built recycling and service units (RSUs) are being used by Tesco to manage the recycling process.

Closed loop

A closed-loop system is where used materials are returned and processed by the producer, which makes use of the returned product, any of its elements or any reusable parts of the product. Tesco uses a closed system to eliminate as much as possible of the transit packaging (cardboard outers) used by suppliers for the delivery of product to its stores. To achieve this, product is delivered to the stores in returnable transit packaging (RTP) or plastic trays. Suppliers pack product directly into the trays, which are delivered to Tesco's central distribution centre and sent on to the individual stores. Once the product has been unpacked, the trays are collected and returned to a recycling and service unit, where they are washed and reissued to suppliers. The use of the RTP has removed the equivalent of 50 000 tonnes of card from the waste stream. The trays are owned by Tesco but rented to its suppliers, which also pay a deposit for the tray. This is refunded on receipt of the tray at the RSU. Tesco uses an information system to manage these payment reconciliations.

A more traditional use of a closed-loop system would be the management of the refurbishment of spare parts for vending machines or other capital items such as trains or heavy moving equipment.

Open loop

An open-loop system means that materials and products are collected by the originator, but processed by other parties. The resulting products or materials are not reused by the originator. Tesco has an open-loop system for the remaining card and soft-wrap secondary packaging used by its suppliers. This represents about 120 000 tonnes of card and 6000 tonnes of polythene each year.

This packaging is collected at the supermarket and returned with the RTPs to the RSUs. The packaging is sorted and baled into appropriate material and is sold to recyclers, who will reprocess it and put back into the market.

Benefits
According to Tesco the system is more than paying for itself by providing the company with an estimated £12 million worth of business benefits. The benefits come from the reduction in the amount of packaging bought and the reduction in landfill charges.

Reverse processes

On receipt of the returned product, firms select one of six possible reverse processes for it to undergo—the product is either to be refurbished, repaired, reused, resold or recycled (broken down into constituent elements for resale). If the product is unsuitable for any of these processes, it is ready for the final reverse process, scrapped to either landfill or incineration.

Refurbishment or remanufacture
Product refurbishment or remanufacture is not a new concept, but it is increasingly attractive. Equipment that has been recovered in a usable condition but lacks current functionality can be remanufactured and replaced in inventory for reuse. Recovered assets can often be remanufactured for a fraction of the cost of manufacturing new equipment. The most effective refurbishment programmes will minimize the cost of refurbishment but get the parts back into stock quickly.

This approach has traditionally been used in capital-intensive industries such as airlines and railways, where the cost of remanufacturing is manifestly lower than that of building anew. Increasingly, however, it is being used by firms with large inventories of mechanical equipment with heavy usage patterns, such as vending machines, automatic ticket machines and photocopiers. Xerox, for example, remanufactures 'recovered equipment' to strict performance specifications. The company estimates that remanufacturing results in annual savings of $200 million, which are passed on to its customers. It see this as a significant advantage over its competitors (Witt, 1997).

Repair

A product is returned for repair because it is not fit to perform the task for which it was designed. Returned goods fall into two categories, warranty and non-warranty. Non-warranty products are repaired at the customer's expense, so the real problem area for firms is warranty returns. The objectives of the repair process are to minimize the cost of the repair process, minimize the turnaround time and increase the life of the product.

Firms need to consider and balance the cost of repair carefully against the cost of a new product. At Black and Decker, a power tools manufacturer, action on warranty returns is decided on this basis. Anything with a manufacturing cost under $12.50 is sent straight for scrap or recycling. All other warranty products are sent to storage for repair (Giuntini and Andel, 1995).

Repair of warranty products is a large problem for computer hardware and software distributors and resellers. The products they sell tend to have high failure rates and become obsolete quickly. But many of these companies lack the rigorous systems required to process warranty claims accurately, and therefore returned products wind up sitting around distribution centres. This results in a number of problems. Lack of tracking means that management gathers no information to assist in rectifying and preventing future problems and more importantly it has no idea how much the warranty returns are costing the business. Without tracking control, future design and process improvements will be impossible.

Reuse

The reuse of product mainly applies to spare parts. Equipment that has reached the end of its life can be broken down into its subassemblies and original parts, some of which will be in a suitable condition to be reused without remanufacture or repair. These will be put into inventory as spare parts and used in the repair process.

Resale

Some products will be returned in a state that allows them to be resold. These are likely to be products that don't sell at all, that customers buy but return (such as catalogue returns) or that customers lease and return. Some high-technology organizations advanced in the reverse logistics field are aggressively reusing their products. Original buyers in the USA take a two-year operating lease for equipment that has already been pre-sold to developing countries such as China and South America, giving the equipment a much higher residual value. These firms are exploiting technology lags and servicing the same products progressively to different customers, matched to each customer group's readiness along the technology curve (Andel, 1997).

Recycling

Products which are unsuitable for refurbishment, repair or resale can be broken down into their component parts and recycled. Until recently, recycling was considered to be time consuming, expensive and unrewarding. However, as firms face increasingly large waste-management bills, they are reexamining alternative means of disposal. Some companies are reaping rewards for their recycling efforts as they develop revenue streams. Black and Decker, for example, avoided $500 000 in landfill costs and collected $463 000 for commodities it sold, directly as a result of its recycling initiatives. The company has stated that its ultimate goal is to have nothing going to landfill and all products being recycled (Giuntini and Andel, 1995).

The reverse logistics system needs to be well managed to gain the maximum benefit from recycling initiatives. This includes minimizing transportation, processing and handling costs and maximizing scrap value.

Scrap

When no alternative course of action is appropriate, products need to be disposed of either by scrapping at landfill or through incineration. Even this is no longer a simple matter. In most industrialized countries, products deemed hazardous must be separated from other waste and disposed of responsibly. Failure to do this can result in a high cost, as the disposer will remain liable for the waste even after disposal.

Proactive companies are developing schemes to ensure that their products are disposed of responsibly. For example, BASF's carpeting division has a programme whereby it voluntarily takes responsibility for the disposal of used carpeting. Any chemically treated carpet is accepted back for free so that BASF knows it will be correctly disposed of and therefore avoids any risk of liability (Giuntini and Andel, 1995). With the question of ultimate liability for the product increasingly under legislative scrutiny, companies like BASF are voluntarily assuming responsibility for the disposal process in an effort to dissuade legislators from further action.

Reverse logistics challenges

Reverse logistics is hard work. Managers of reverse logistics don't have the level of control over their inventory they exert in forward logistics flows. While products move out to customer through efficient, established channels, their return or collection is unpredictable and often in uneconomic quantities as small as single items.

The supply of returned product is not yet subject to sophisticated forecasting techniques. The uncertainty is twofold. Companies don't know how much product they will receive back nor what condition it will be in. A personal computer manufacturer, for example, was offering an aggressive warranty programme to customers to match the offerings of its competition. But it found that it was shipping warranty replacement spare parts to customers who were not returning the impaired product back promptly. Those customers who bothered to return the impaired product were taking six weeks to do so. The programme was creating uncertainty about the number and type of spare parts required to support all the customer warranty claims, resulting in an increase in spare-part inventory.

It resolved this problem by hiring a third-party organization to deliver the replacement spare part and collect the impaired original, while charging customers for non-returns.

The proactive management of the returned spare parts meant that the manufacturer reduced the inventory investment needed to support its warranty claims and its product-repair cycle was reduced from 14 to 6 weeks, resulting in savings of $2.5 million over a period of a year (Giuntini and Andel, 1995).

Delays in processing are costly. Those companies which manage their supply forecasting are in a better position to manage processing. High-technology products, for example, risk becoming obsolete if they are not processed expeditiously. It has been estimated that electronics inventory in the reverse pipeline loses about 10 per cent of its value per month (Knapp, 1995). Products to be sold into secondary or salvage markets need to be processed rapidly to reduce inventory management costs and maximize the return on sale.

Trends in reverse logistics

Firms are moving towards the next millennium knowing that developing faster, more efficient and cost-effective reverse logistics systems will be an imperative. And some firms are already investing in the search for opportunities to strengthen their reverse logistics capabilities.

Design for disassembly

An array of firms from white goods to car manufacturers are investigating ways to design their product with disassembly in mind. The investigation has three strands of enquiry: to understand how new products can be designed in order to be dismantled; to understand how current products can be dismantled; and to improve opportunities for recycling the product and its component parts.

Manufacturing systems have traditionally been based on the most efficient assembly methods, but now the time has come to ensure that products are designed and manufactured in a way that makes them easier to pull apart, for disposal or recycling. For example, this may mean the redesign of an assembly that can be put together with fewer bolts (of course the functionality must stay the same), which facilitates faster dismantling. While most products can be dismantled, the objective must be to dismantle a product at a lower cost than the revenues obtained from the component parts. Consequently, different discarded parts offer different profitability opportunities.

BMW has a stated strategic goal to offer a car designed for disassembly by the twenty-first century. At the end of the useful life of the car the BMW dealers take it back from the consumer when it will be disassembled, with the parts being put back into the new car-manufacturing stream (Giuntini, 1995).

Recycle more material

Many industries are investing in systems that allow them to use more recycled material. The car industry is particularly advanced. For example, the US Council for Automobile Research (USCAR) was formed in 1992 by General Motors, Ford and Chrysler to conduct 'precompetitive' research into new technologies. One of its research groups, the Vehicle Recycling Partnership, consists not only of the major car firms but also relies on input from suppliers, raw material producers, universities and related industry associations.

The Partnership is compiling a database of parts and materials taken from used cars to identify how they can be reused and recycled. Scrap dealers already extract about 95 per cent of the aluminium and steel and the majority of copper and brass from 10 million used cars annually and sell those materials into secondary recycling markets. While the residue of car materials, such as rubber weather-stripping, foam seat cushions, composed glass and plastics, is currently regarded as worthless, the Vehicle Recycling Partnership is actively considering how these materials might be reclaimed and reused (Couretas, 1997).

Increase product lifecycles

To increase product life, many firms are establishing modular design techniques and using standardized product interfaces. Products built of a variety of standardised components can easily be upgraded instead of discarded, simply by changing an out-of-date component for a new one.

Maintaining standard components and/or modules from previous versions in new products presents an opportunity to reuse older components. When disassembling one of the old models, there is a higher chance that these 'old' components can be reused in one of the new models.

Materials

Firms have made significant steps in the last few years to use recycled and recyclable materials in their products. These materials provide immediate efficiencies and reduce long-term disposal costs. The fuel tank of Saab's new 9-5, for example, is made from polyethylene, consisting of 35 per cent recycled plastic (Woodward, 1997).

The future: reverse networks

The development of first-class reverse logistics will continue, with many best practices emerging from, and converging with, trends that are evident in the forward-flow supply chain.

Physical structure

Organizations must ensure that their reverse systems are as efficient as their forward flows. While this will take some time to develop, it is important that companies have a physical logistics structure that allows them to get the products back quickly, but at the lowest possible cost. This may well mean that third-party operators manage the reverse system or that dedicated facilities in distribution centres are provided to manage the reverse flow.

The reverse logistics system will become a complex network rather than a single chain. It will contain first- and second-tier customers, as some customers will purchase new products while others will buy component parts or resold products. In some instances, customers will become suppliers. The network will be further complicated with the additional suppliers in the network providing specialized services for waste disposal and product returns.

Financial impact

A key driver moving reverse logistics from an operational system to a strategic part of the business will be the financial impact that it has on the operation of the business. The trend towards allocating ongoing liability for a product is challenging the nature of the transfer of ownership and liability and transforming the dynamics of the traditional buyer–seller relationship.

In the future it is probable that many more products, such as mobile telephones, will be leased rather than sold to customers. Customers won't be encumbered with obsolete or out-of-date products but, more importantly, producers will be able to track, receive and dispose of the product at the end of its life.

Information technology

One of the most important areas for development in the reverse logistics flow will be information systems. New and sophisticated technology will allow firms to collect data on their returned products. The movement of this information will be as important as the movement of the product itself. In the future data is expected to be collected from two-dimensional barcodes which will contain a multitude of information about the ownership and use of the individual product and even a part within a product. Miniature coding will be used for small items, meaning that even individual computer chip will be traceable. For the reverse logistics system this will make life significantly easier. All products will be traceable at all times and a real-time picture of product and part failures will allow logistics managers to understand the requirements of their reverse system.

This data management will ensure that companies track the movement of products between customers, but it will also allow companies to identify how often the product has been returned for recycling purposes. This information will be used to improve the reliability of products and identify particular problems in the reverse supply chain.

The information will also be used to improve forecasting of the supply of goods.

Conclusion

Reverse logistics is having an impact across many industries as firms seek opportunities both to reduce the costs of their waste programmes and to increase revenue throughout the life of their products. This is being largely driven by government legislation in the industrialized world forcing organizations to take responsibility for the liability of their products, even if ownership would appear to have been transferred.

Reverse logistics is still in its early days. But the signs are that those companies prepared to invest now will be far better placed to manage this developing trend than will the laggards. This is an area ripe for strategic attention and operational innovation. The rewards are worthwhile today; in the future superb reverse logistics may be a condition for company survival.

References

Andel, T. (1997) 'Reverse logistics: a second chance to profit', *Transport & Distribution*, 38 (7), July, 61–6.

Couretas, J. (1997) 'Back to the future—big 3 research project is developing ways to recycle vehicle parts', *Automotive News*, 24 Feb., 161.

Dawe, R. (1997) 'Tackle 21st century technology today', *Transport and Distribution*, 1997 Buyers Guide Issue supplement, July, BG21–2.

Eisenhuth, D. (1997) *Asset Recovery: Adding Value to Assets Report.*

Giuntini, R. and Andel, T. (1995) 'Advance with reverse logistics: Part 1', *Transport and Distribution*, 36 (2), Feb., 73–7.

Giuntini, R. and Andel, T. (1995) 'Reverse logistics role models: Part 3', *Transport & Distribution*, 36 (4), 97–8.

Knapp, J. (1995) 'And now, back to you', *Warehousing Management*, www.chiltonco.com/warehouse/reverse.htm (online exclusive).

Materials Management and Distribution (1996) 'Take it back! Reverse logistics, returning packaging and products to the original supplier, is becoming common practice', 41(11), 25–6.

Melbin, J. (1995) 'The never ending cycle', *Distribution*, 94 (11), 36–8.

Miskelly, B. (1997) 'UK: Recycling pilot for old mobile phones', *Electronics*,6 Feb., 2.

Penev, K.D. and deRon, A. (1994) 'Development of dissembly line for refrigerators', *Industrial Engineering*, 26 (11) 50–53.

Prendergast, G. (1995) 'The EC directive on packaging and packaging waste: current status and logistical implications', *Logistics Information Management*, 8 (3) 10–17.

Witt, C.E. (1997) 'Distribution: let someone else do it', *Material Handling Engineering*, 52 (2), Feb., 38–45.

Woodward, B. (1997) 'Sweden: Saab takes itself apart for recycling purposes', *Canberra Times*, 4 July, 21.

A final word

In 1980, Peter Drucker wrote in *Managing in Turbulent Times*:

> The one certainty about the times ahead is that they will be turbulent times, and in turbulent times the first task of management is to make sure of the institution's capacity for survival, to make sure of its capacity to survive a blow, to adapt to sudden change, and to avail itself of new opportunities.

How right he was. Indeed, in the intervening decades we have witnessed an ever increasing rate of change, perhaps even beyond Drucker's original expectations.

Over the past two decades, progress in business thinking has moved us from the limited perspective of 'distribution management' to 'logistics management' and, more latterly, 'supply chain management'. But the words and concepts have all too often outpaced the reality on the ground. Corporate leaders and managers have generally been reluctant to go beyond their 'comfort zones' and push the implementation of the various disciplines involved in supply chain management at anything beyond what might be described as a timid rate.

Because supply chain management is by its very nature cross-functional, inter-company and borderless in terms of geography, it will always pose conceptual, operational and systems difficulties for those who would prefer to contend with singular parameters, stable equilibrium, predictable futures and apparent simplicity. Unfortunately the world is not like that any more, if indeed it ever was.

Visionary leaders and managers recognize that a certain level of instability can be used to improve organizational effectiveness—eliminating executive comfort zones, producing positive tension, facilitating creativity and, ideally, generating a net improvement in financial performance and therefore shareholder value. So the old paradigm of stability, harmony, predictability, discipline and consensus is now only relevant where operating conditions are stable and the playing field is tilted favourably—a rare condition these days.

What works for firms today is a type of 'bounded (or constrained) instability' where the firm reacts and interacts with its environment, not unlike the fly-by-wire control mechanisms now in use in the latest military and civil aircraft. In essence, the firm is forced to cope with and manage the ambiguity of an ever more turbulent operating environment and seek to be in dynamic equilibrium with it.

In a dynamic environment, the 'strategic alignment' framework that shapes this book is very relevant, as it allows for the four levels (market, strategy, culture and leadership) to seek a moving or dynamic equilibrium, rather than struggle unrealistically to achieve a static or stable equilibrium. And the reality is that the supply chain will become one of the pivotal vehicles of corporate change, with untold opportunities for value creation if companies are prepared to embrace the opportunities.

The major sources of improved performance in the supply chain over the next five to ten years will be as follows:

- Whole industries will rethink their sales and marketing channels and these new channels to customers will require newly reengineered processes and technologies, in turn demanding significant changes at all levels.
- Leading companies will recognize the close relationship between customer relationship management and the supply chain; taken together these two will open up new avenues for shaping trading terms, from both supplier and reseller/customer perspectives.
- A much more aggressive search for additional organization design options for supply chains in particular industries will eliminate polarized thinking in terms of 'insourcing' or 'outsourcing', opening the way to new solutions and combinations along this continuum.
- The best supply chains will have fully integrated enterprise systems and indeed will go beyond transactional information and decision-support systems to 'knowledge management'. In turn this will affect organization design and lead to improved coordination (rather than 'control').
- Companies looking to embrace supply chain regimes at the global level will require a much better understanding of country cultures as a necessary ingredient for success.
- Strategic sourcing approaches at the supply end, and mass customization approaches at the consumption end, are likely to be fertile areas for relatively quick large-scale benefits.
- 'Reverse logistics' will loom large on the agenda, with issues such as extending product usage lifecycles, product-recovery processes and bidirectional logistics channels coming to the fore in the search for new competitive dimensions.
- Organizations other than product companies will begin to recognize the huge untapped potential that the application of logistics and supply chain principles to their businesses will release, such as telecommunications, utilities, healthcare, education, entertainment and financial services.

Finally, as with all movements, there is always a leader industry and in the case of logistics and the supply chain that is fast-moving consumer goods. By observing developments in the FMCG industry we are able to observe the 'markers' and anticipate some of the changes that are sure to confront many follower industries

In this context, Glen Terbeek and John Hollis (1996) predicted, among other things, that the FMCG industry had reached the plateau of the industry's 'logistics productivity' S-curve, and that the 'future of the industry will be played out on a new "marketing productivity" based S-curve'.

What Terbeek and Hollis were in effect saying was that the cross-bar of consumer satisfaction (what they termed as meeting the consumer at their 'moment of value') was being raised to such heights that those companies that do not reach a certain minimum performance capability will simply not have a ticket to play in the next game. That will be about issues such as one-to-one marketing, branding, product innovation and creating the best shopping experience for consumers.

For those companies that have not reached the minimum entry level referred to by Terbeek and Hollis, there is much to do.

We hope that many of the insights included in this book will act as the catalyst to bridge the gaps and, indeed, strike out ahead with demand chain solutions that consistently deliver for consumers at their 'moment of value'. In the words of Terbeek, this means 'bringing products and services closer to consumers, how, when, and where they value them most'.

References

Drucker, Peter F. (1980) *Managing in Turbulent Times*, Pan, London.

Terbeek, G. and Hollis, J. (1996) *The Supermarket of the 21st Century*, presentation at the Food Marketing Institute (FMI) annual convention, May 6, Chicago.

Contributors

Dr David Anderson (Chapter 20) is the managing partner of Andersen Consulting's European supply chain management practice, based in London. He specializes in supply chain management, logistics strategy, customer service, logistics information systems and operations outsourcing strategy. Before joining Andersen Consulting, Dave was vice president of logistics consulting at Temple, Barker & Sloane and vice president of Data Resources, where he founded the firm's transportation and logistics consulting practice. He has published numerous articles on supply chain compression, global logistics trends, outsourcing and operations management. David holds a BA in economics from the University of Connecticut and a PhD in econometrics from Boston College.

Duncan Armitage (Chapter 28) is an associate partner in Andersen Consulting's Australia and New Zealand change management practice, based in Sydney. He has experience working in manufacturing, food and packaged goods industries as well as financial and entertainment industries. His particular focus is on helping clients build and sustain the necessary levels of leadership to launch and sustain major change programmes and to realize the anticipated benefits. Prior to joining Andersen Consulting, he managed the post-merger organization change issues in a large UK financial services company. He holds a Bachelor of Science in applied psychology and a postgraduate diploma in human resource management.

David Ashton (Chapter 36) is an analyst with Andersen Consulting's China strategy practice, based in San Francisco and Beijing. He specializes in logistics and distribution issues in China and has extensively researched and written papers on China's infrastructure development. He has experience working with clients in the transportation, telecommunications and high-tech industries. David holds a BS (international relations and Chinese) from Brigham Young University and has lived and worked in both the PRC and Hong Kong.

Terry Austin (Chapter 12) is an associate partner in Andersen Consulting's Americas supply chain practice, based in San Francisco. His primary consulting expertise is in the areas of supply chain management and logistics, business strategy, organizational development and productivity improvement. Terry has spent eight years in the US focusing on supply chain management issues in the high-technology industry and previously spent four years in Melbourne, Australia, serving clients in the Asia Pacific region. Terry holds a Bachelor's degree in operations research and industrial engineering from Cornell University.

Randolph Barba (Chapter 13) is a partner in Andersen Consulting's Americas strategy practice, based in Chicago. He co-leads the industrial products and automotive strategy practice in the USA, focusing on distribution channel strategy and channel migration issues. He specializes in developing business and market strategy and designing large-scale enterprise change programmes. Prior to joining Andersen Consulting, he was a vice-president of marketing and sales for a computer company and a consultant with another major strategy consulting firm. Randy has a BA in geology from Princeton University, a MS in oceanography from University of Rhode Island and an MBA from the Wharton School, University of Pennsylvania.

Stephen Bartolotta (Chapter 16) is a senior manager in Andersen Consulting's Americas supply chain management practice, based in New York. He has experience working with food and consumer packaged goods and retail companies in the areas of distribution operations, third-party outsourcing, conceptual and detailed facility design and performance management. He participated in Andersen Consulting's consumer direct cooperative and was responsible for the conceptual development of all supply-side activities. Prior to joining Andersen Consulting he was a vice-president with the Coast Distribution System and a CPA in Connecticut. He holds a BBA in accounting from the University of Texas, Austin.

Jeff Beech (Chapter 6) is a partner in Andersen Consulting's Americas supply chain management practice, based in Atlanta. He leads the food and consumer packaged goods group of the supply chain strategy practice. His areas of expertise include supply chain strategy, distribution operations strategy, inventory management, network configuration, materials handling and system design. He presents at national forums on supply chain strategy, regularly writes articles for several industry publications and was president of the Warehouse Education Research Council. Jeff holds a BS in management from the Georgia Institute of Technology.

Bruce Bendix (Chapter 13) is a senior manager in Andersen Consulting's Americas strategy practice, based in Chicago. His expertise is in strategic marketing and channel management and he serves clients in the technology industries. Prior to joining Andersen Consulting, Bruce was vice-president of marketing for a manufacturer of architectural and engineering imaging equipment and a product manager for a large computer manufacturer. He holds an MBA from Harvard University and a BS from Stanford University.

Richard Bergmann (Chapter 23) is a partner in Andersen Consulting's Americas supply chain management practice and head of the transportation area, based in San Francisco. Rich has extensive experience in warehouse operations, company fleet operations, common carrier modal management and alternate delivery programmes such as direct-store delivery and promotional direct delivery in the food industry. Prior to joining Andersen Consulting, Rich managed the logistics function at Frito Lay, part of PepsiCo. He has also worked in the common carrier trucking industry in operations, sales and planning.

Jamie Bolton (Chapter 9) is a manager in Andersen Consulting's Australia and New Zealand supply chain management practice, based in Sydney. He has experience working with consumer and industrial products companies in the areas of supply chain integration, demand management, strategic sourcing, distribution, inventory management and supply chain modelling. Prior to joining Andersen Consulting Jamie worked as an engineer with Pacific Power in Australia. He holds a Bachelor of Mechanical Engineering from the University of Technology, Sydney, and an MBA from the University of New England, Australia.

Ken Bonning (Chapter 15) is an associate partner in Andersen Consulting's Americas supply chain management practice, based in New York. His experience has focused on working with retailers in the areas of distribution network strategy, global supply chain strategy, conceptual and detailed facility design and distribution operations. Prior to joining Andersen Consulting he was vice-president of international logistics and franchise operations for Toys 'R' Us and also worked previously as a retail consultant for one of the large international accounting firms. He holds a BIE from Georgia Institute of Technology.

Robyn Brown (Chapter 28) is a partner in Andersen Consulting's Australia and New Zealand change management practice, based in Sydney. She specializes in the management of change, working with executives in formulating and implementing the organizational change components of significant business change initiatives. She has experience working with energy (oil and gas), industrial equipment and consumer goods companies with a particular focus on organization redesign, culture change and workforce performance development critical to the success of business reengineering. She holds a Bachelor of Commerce degree in accounting and economics from the University of Queensland.

Tim Brown (Chapter 19) leads Andersen Consulting's supply chain configuration solutions group, based in Atlanta. His areas of expertise include logistics network strategy, supply chain optimization, transportation management, site selection and decision-support systems. Prior to joining Andersen Consulting, Tim held positions in logistics at a major consulting firm, Frito-Lay, Tropicana Products and Georgia Pacific. He is certified in production and inventory management and holds a BS in management science/industrial engineering from Georgia Institute of Technology and an MBA from Georgia State University.

Jon Bumstead (Chapter 10) is a senior manager in Andersen Consulting's UK supply chain management practice, based in Manchester. Jon specializes in the grocery consumer products area and has worked extensively with suppliers, manufacturers, carriers and retailers throughout the European grocery supply chain in his six years with the firm. Prior to this, Jon worked in industry for Mars confectionery in a variety of manufacturing and distribution roles. He holds a Bachelor of Mechanical Engineering from the City of London University.

Ann Burns (Chapter 31) is a consultant in Andersen Consulting's Australia and New Zealand strategy practice, based in Sydney. Ann's areas of expertise are in communications, sales and marketing, supply chain strategy and logistics management relating to FMCG clients. Prior to joining Andersen Consulting, She worked in the construction industry with a UK-based multinational in various roles, including project finance for large infrastructure projects, international business development in emerging markets and regional sales management. Ann holds an MBA from Warwick Business School, a postgraduate diploma in marketing and a BA in architecture.

Frank Carbone (Chapter 21) is a manager in Andersen Consulting's Australia and New Zealand supply chain management practice, based in Sydney. Prior to joining Andersen Consulting, Frank spent 15 years in materials and logistics management roles in several industries in Australia, including consumer goods, automotive parts, retail, paper products, chemicals, food, textiles and consumer electronics. Frank holds a BA majoring in economics from the University of New South Wales and a graduate diploma in logistics management from the Macquarie Graduate School of Management, Sydney.

Douglas Castek (Chapter 4) is a partner in Andersen Consulting's Americas supply chain management practice, based in Atlanta. He currently leads the supply chain management practice in the utilities industry. During his consulting career, Doug has focused on the development and implementation of supply chain strategies across a number of industries, including consumer products, pharmaceuticals and healthcare, industrial products, retail energy and utilities. Prior to joining Andersen Consulting, Doug was a managing associate at another major consulting firm. He has also held positions with Avco Lycoming (AlliedSignal) and Goodyear Tire & Rubber.

Rick Chavie (Chapter 15) is an associate partner in Andersen Consulting's Americas supply chain management practice, based in Atlanta. His areas of expertise include market and segmentation analysis, strategic sourcing, operations reengineering, retail concept development and merger/acquisition strategy. Prior to joining Andersen Consulting, Rick occupied a number of senior positions as a director of strategic planning for The Home Depot, executive vice-president for the American Retail Group and a partner at Deloitte & Touche. Rick holds an MBA from Harvard Business School, a BA in German and accounting from the University of St Thomas and studied international trade at the University of Cologne, Germany.

Prof. Martin Christopher (Chapter 17) is a professor and deputy director of the Cranfield School of Management, UK. He is head of the Marketing and Logistics Faculty and chairman of the Cranfield Centre for Logistics and Transportation. In 1987 he was awarded the Sir Robert Lawrence medal of the Institute of Distribution Management for his contribution to the development of logistics education in the UK. He has written numerous books and articles and is on the editorial advisory boards of a number of professional journals in the marketing and logistics area. Martin has also consulted with major international companies in North America, Europe, Asia and Australia and is a director of a number of companies. He is a fellow and council member of both the Chartered Institute of Marketing and Institute of Logistics Management.

Grieg Coppe (Chapter 32) is a partner with Andersen Consulting and is responsible for the firm's electronics and high-technology strategy practice, based in San Francisco. He has experience developing corporate and business unit strategies, market assessments and channel strategies for a wide range of high-technology companies. His recent engagements have focused on working with high-tech clients to exploit Internet market opportunities as well as developing Internet operating strategies to leverage clients' business. Grieg has an MBA from the Harvard Business School and a BS from the University of California, Berkeley.

Alister Danks (assistant editor and Chapter 2) is a senior consultant in Andersen Consulting's Australia and New Zealand supply chain management practice, based in Sydney. He specializes in supply chain management, strategy formulation and new business development. He has extensive experience in the construction industry and has worked in retail banking, telecommunications and manufacturing. Prior to joining Andersen Consulting, Alister worked for a major engineering consultant in Melbourne and Hong Kong and a global chemical manufacturer in London. He holds a Bachelor of Civil Engineering from the Melbourne University and an MBA from the London Business School.

Yamini Dhillon (assistant editor and Chapter 20) is a consultant in Andersen Consulting's Australia and New Zealand supply chain management practice, based in Melbourne. Yamini specializes in the development of customer strategies and segmentation, and sourcing strategies. Her consulting experience includes projects with leading consumer product and utility companies in Australia and Hong Kong. Yamini holds a Bachelor of Economics, majoring in accounting and econometrics, from Monash University, Melbourne.

Stephen Duffy (Chapter 32) is a senior manager with Andersen Consulting and a member of the firm's electronics and high-technology strategy practice. He has experience developing corporate and business unit strategies, assessing and enhancing sales and marketing capabilities, and defining channel strategies for high-technology companies. Over the past three years, he has helped clients assess the relevance of the Internet and electronic commerce for their industry and business model, as well as identify specific product, service and operations-enhancement opportunities. He holds a BS in industrial management from Carnegie Mellon and an MBA from the Haas School of Business, UC Berkeley.

Robert Easton (Chapter 28) is a senior manager in Andersen Consulting's Australia and New Zealand supply chain management practice, based in Sydney. He has logistics experience in both military and commercial organizations in Australia and Asia, focusing on supply chain strategy, outsourcing, warehousing and distribution centre operations, inventory-management systems, performance measurement and achieving supply chain performance improvement. Robert has a BCom from Victoria University, a graduate diploma in psychology from Massey University, a Master's in defence studies from Deakin University and an MBA from Macquarie University. He has also completed the US Army's logistics executive development course and graduated from the Singapore Command and General Staff College.

Scot Eisenfelder (Chapter 37) is an associate partner in Andersen Consulting's Americas strategy practice, based in Los Angeles. He has specialized in helping clients more effectively utilize distribution channels, pricing and incentive policies and service offerings to raise customer satisfaction. Prior to joining Andersen Consulting, Scot worked for a major consulting firm and JD Power & Associates in the automotive, telecommunications and aerospace industries. Scot has an MBA from the Wharton School and a BA in economics from Princeton University and studied international economics at the University of Mannheim, Germany.

Barry Elliott (Chapter 21) is an associate partner with Andersen Consulting in Sydney and is part of the leadership team of the supply chain management practice for Australia and New Zealand. He has been consulting for 12 years in North America, Asia and Australasia and specializes in manufacturing and logistics operations. In recent years, he has focused on issues of streamlining the supply chain, both physical supply and information flow, in a variety of industries, including grocery, pharmaceutical, wholesale and retail. Barry holds a degree in engineering from the University of Waterloo, Canada, and is a Certified Fellow in production and inventory management from APICS.

Robert Evans (Chapters 2 and 4) is the managing partner of Andersen Consulting's Americas supply chain management practice and is based in Chicago. He is also responsible for Andersen Consulting's customer support practice area. Prior to joining Andersen Consulting, Bob was vice-president of customer support/parts and service for Mazda Motor of America. He was also the founder and president of Caterpillar Logistics Services and held other executive positions at Caterpillar. Bob is a frequent speaker at both Council of Logistics Management and the American Production and Inventory Control

Society events, as well as at other international logistics and customer service conferences. He has a BA in economics from MacMurray College and a MA in economics from Western Illinois University.

Donovan Favre (Chapter 18) is a senior manager in Andersen Consulting's Americas supply chain management practice, based in Cleveland. He has experience working with food and consumer packaged goods, industrial products and energy clients in the areas of strategic sourcing and supply chain management. He is leading the Consumer Driven Demand Network project, a joint Andersen Consulting, Stanford and INSEAD effort researching innovation in the food and consumer packaged goods industry. Prior to joining Andersen Consulting, he worked in several line management positions for Westinghouse and Asea Brown Boveri. He holds a BS in industrial and systems engineering and a MA in operations management from the Ohio State University.

Peter Fuchs (Chapter 1) is the managing partner-in-charge of Andersen Consulting's worldwide strategic services practice and is based in London. He has been a partner since 1975 and has led the strategic services practice since 1987. Peter has been involved in numerous projects during his career in the areas of business planning and strategy development, business process reengineering, information technology planning and industry and market studies. He has worked with a wide range of clients in the consumer products, retailing, pharmaceuticals and high-technology industries. Peter holds a BS in accounting from Lehigh University and an MA in economics and finance from the Wharton School of Management.

Dr John Gattorna (editor, Introduction, Final Word and Chapters 27 and 29) leads Andersen Consulting's supply chain management practice in Australia and New Zealand/Asia and is based in Sydney. John has an international reputation in the fields of logistics strategy, distribution channels strategy, supply chain strategy and business planning. He is widely renowned as a lecturer, author and task force leader. John has written a number of articles and books and has pioneered the application of 'strategic alignment' thinking to logistics and the supply chain. Prior to joining Andersen Consulting in 1995, he ran a successful Sydney-based specialist consulting firm serving a select group of domestic and global clients in both product and service industries. He has a Bachelor of Engineering from Melbourne University, an MBA from Monash University and a PhD in marketing and logistics from Cranfield University.

Paula Giles (Chapter 26) is an associate partner with Andersen Consulting, based in Melbourne. She is responsible for the organization design and development practice in Australia and New Zealand. Paula has extensive experience in the oil, industrial and consumer products industries. She has specialized in working with executives to help their companies accomplish successful mergers, create new businesses and achieve benefits from their change programmes. Prior to consulting she held line management positions with Shell in Australia and lectured in organization and human behaviour. Paula holds a BA and MA in organization sociology.

Anthony Hancy (Chapter 26) is the managing partner of Andersen Consulting's products and resources portfolio in Australia and New Zealand and is based in Melbourne. His main areas of expertise are in strategic and business planning, organization strategy, supply chain management and merger and acquisition strategy and implementation. He has extensive experience advising global consumer products companies on corporate and organization strategy. Prior to joining Andersen Consulting in 1984, Tony was a director of a US-based multinational consumer foods company responsible for strategic business planning, finance, information technology, regional sourcing and production. He has a Bachelor of Commerce, a Bachelor of Education and an MBA from Melbourne University.

Richard Hill (Chapter 7) is a partner in Andersen Consulting's UK practice and works exclusively within the food and consumer packaged goods industry, specializing in the area of food retailing. In his consulting career, over more than 17 years, Richard's experience has spanned the areas of strategy development, business process reengineering as well as the planning, design and development of administrative information systems for clients in the US, Sweden and the UK. Richard has a BS in mathematics, electrical engineering and computer science from the Rose-Hulman Institute of Technology in Indiana, US.

Susan Jimenez (Chapter 19) is a senior consultant at Andersen Consulting's Australia and New Zealand supply chain management practice, based in Sydney. She has extensive experience in developing network models for strategic decision making. She has worked with major discount chains, department store groups, FMCG manufacturers and spare-parts distributors in Asia Pacific developing network models for their supply chains and testing alternative supply chain scenarios. Prior to joining Andersen Consulting, she worked at Gattorna Business Strategists in the area of logistics strategy. Susan holds a BE and BSc from the University of New South Wales and an MBA from the University of Sydney.

Theresa Jones (assistant editor and Chapter 38) is a senior consultant in Andersen Consulting's Australia and New Zealand supply chain management practice, based in Sydney. She has extensive experience in supply chain strategy, particularly in the service sectors, and her key areas of expertise are logistics strategy, procurement and strategic sourcing and reverse logistics. Prior to joining Andersen Consulting, Theresa was responsible for recycling programmes at British Airways. She holds an honours degree in business from the University of Northumbria, a MSc in logistics and distribution from Cranfield University and has professional buying qualifications (CIPS) from the UK.

Joe Jordan (Chapter 19) is a manager in Andersen Consulting's Australia and New Zealand supply chain management practice, based in Sydney. He has extensive experience in developing network models for both strategic and tactical decision making, having worked with a range of manufacturers and distributors in the Asia Pacific region. These models were used by the clients to develop and test alternative operating scenarios. Prior to working as a management consultant, Joe held a range of operational roles within the Australian fast-moving consumer goods industry. He holds a BSc in engineering from the University of New South Wales and a graduate diploma in business administration from the New South Wales Institute of Technology.

David Kennedy (Chapter 21) is a project manager with i2 Technologies, a major vendor of advanced planning and scheduling systems, based in Sydney. He is responsible for the delivery of value to clients through the effective implementation of the family of Rhythm Products. He has experience in world-class automotive manufacturing organizations, where he has secured grounding in the theory of constraints, bottleneck management and supporting IT systems. More recently he has successfully applied lean manufacturing techniques throughout several industries, including textiles, appliance, personal care, food and agribusiness. He holds a BSc in mechanical engineering from the University of Glasgow and an MSc in manufacturing systems engineering from Warwick University.

Prof. Hau Lee (Chapter 5) is the Kleiner Perkins, Mayfield, Sequoia Capital Professor and Deputy Chairman of the Department of Industrial Engineering and Engineering Management and Professor of Operations Management (by courtesy) at the Graduate School of Business at Stanford University. He has lectured, written and consulted widely on supply chain management, global logistics system design, inventory planning and manufacturing strategy. He is the founding and current director of the Stanford Global Supply Chain Management Forum, an industry–academic consortium to advance the theory and practice of global supply chain management. Dr Lee is the current editor-in-chief of *Management Science*. He holds a BS from the University of Hong Kong, a MSc from the London School of Economics, a MIS from the Institute of Statisticians and a MS and PhD from the University of Pennsylvania.

Lucinda Holdforth (assistant editor) is the business communications manager for Andersen Consulting's Australia and New Zealand strategy practice, based in Sydney. She has a background in government, politics and communications. Lucinda spent ten years in the Australian diplomatic service, which included serving in the former Yugoslavia and advising on Australia's relations with North Asia. She was speechwriter and adviser to the former Australian Deputy Prime Minister and Finance Minister. She holds an honours degree in Australian and English literature from Sydney University.

Jay Mabe (Chapters 8 and 31) is an associate partner in Andersen Consulting's Americas supply chain management practice, based in Atlanta. He has experience working with food and consumer packaged goods and chemical companies in the areas of supply chain strategy, supply chain planning, manufacturing operations, supply chain planning technology and performance management. Previously he was a partner with Kurt Salmon Associates and has held positions in information systems and manufacturing operations with DuPont, Johnson & Johnson and Avery International. He holds an MBA from Drexel University and a BS in finance and MIS from the University of Virginia.

Duane Marvick (Chapter 22) is a senior manager in Andersen Consulting's Americas supply chain management practice, based in Dallas. His areas of logistics expertise include supply chain and distribution operations strategy, distribution network and facility design, material-handling system design, warehouse inventory-management systems and performance measurement. Duane has held previous senior management positions in industry with McLane Company (Wal-Mart), Supervalu, Ben Franklin and Gillette. He is an active participant in Food Distributors International and the Food Marketing Institute and has spoken at numerous industry conferences. Duane has a BS in industrial engineering from the University of North Dakota.

Michael Mikurak (Chapter 34) is an associate partner in Andersen Consulting's Americas supply chain management practice, based in Florham Park, New York. He leads the supply chain activities in the communications industry. He specializes in supply chain strategy, procurement, materials management, distribution operations, logistics information and systems planning and implementation. Before joining Andersen Consulting, Mike was a partner at KPMG Peat Marwick LLP and held logistics managerial positions with a major consulting firm, Textron Lycoming and GTE. Mike holds a BSBA Degree from Rider University and a certificate from the product development and manufacturing strategy program at Stanford University Graduate School of Engineering.

John Miller (Chapters 3 and 14) is a partner at Andersen Consulting's Americas supply chain management practice, based in Atlanta. He has helped numerous clients in the US and Europe maximize supply chain cost/service performance by developing and implementing new customer service and channel strategies, improved manufacturing/distribution networks as well as improved processes for inventory and demand management. His engagements cover a wide range of industries including manufacturers of pharmaceuticals, electronics, consumer durables and industrial equipment. Prior to joining Andersen Consulting, John was a director at Cleveland Consulting Associates. He has an MBA, a BA in economics and has completed additional studies in systems science engineering, all from Michigan State University.

Peter Moore (Chapter 33) is an associate partner in Andersen Consulting's Australia and New Zealand supply chain management practice, based in Melbourne. He specializes in supply chain strategy covering both strategy development and implementation. His consulting work has included projects for many successful companies in Australia, UK, Europe and Asia across consumer products, transportation and process industries. Peter has a MA in engineering from Cambridge University and a postgraduate diploma in accounting and finance.

James Mueller (Chapter 30) is a partner in Andersen Consulting's Americas supply chain management practice, based in New York. With over 17 years of management and consulting experience, he has worked extensively in over 60 countries around the globe leading and developing international and domestic supply chain strategies, process outsourcing strategies, long-range facility planning strategies and domestic and international transportation strategies. Jim received his BA from the University of Texas at Austin.

Tom Nickles (Chapter 30) is a partner in Andersen Consulting's information and technology strategy practice, and is based in Boston. He leads the group in the manufacturing/industrial sector. Tom has over 20 years of experience working with major corporations in the transformation of their businesses to achieve significant business value through the use of information and advanced technologies. Prior to joining Andersen Consulting, Tom held positions as vice-president at CSC Index, marketing representative at IBM, consultant at Deloitte & Touche and IS director at Underwood Company. He holds a BS in finance and an MBA from Northwestern University.

Dr Christopher Norek (Chapter 24) is an assistant professor of logistics and transportation at Auburn University. Prior to this, he was a manager in Andersen Consulting's supply chain practice in Atlanta. He was responsible for research and thought leadership at Andersen Consulting's Logistics 2020, a centre focusing on the future of logistics. Chris has a PhD and MABA in logistics and transportation from Ohio State, an MBA (logistics and transportation) from Tennessee and a BS (business logistics) from Pennsylvania State University. He also has gained logistics experience with Office Depot, Cleveland Consulting Associates, Apple Computer and Kimberly-Clark.

Linda Nuthall (Chapter 31) is a consultant in Andersen Consulting's Australia and New Zealand strategy practice, based in Sydney. Linda has experience working with consumer and industrial products companies in the areas of demand management, distribution, inventory management, supply chain modelling and optimization, customer segmentation and supply chain strategy alignment. Linda holds a Bachelor of Applied Science in industrial mathematics and computing from the Charles Sturt University, Bathurst, NSW.

Gregory Owens (Chapter 18) is the managing partner of Andersen Consulting's global supply chain management practice, based in Atlanta. His primary areas of focus are strategic sourcing, integrated supply/demand chain management, distribution network strategy, facility planning, inventory management and demand planning. Greg was previously executive vice-president of The Garr Consulting Group. He is a member of the Warehousing Education and Research Council, Materials Handling Management Society, Council of Logistics Management and National Retailers Federation. Greg has a BS in industrial management from Georgia Institute of Technology.

Eric Peters (Chapter 25) is an associate partner in Andersen Consulting's Americas supply chain management practice, based in San Francisco. He has presented over 100 talks on the subject of logistics and warehouse-management systems technology and has written over 50 articles and contributed to several books. Eric has been involved in over 25 warehouse-management systems designs and/or implementations. He holds a BS in industrial engineering from the Pennsylvania State University.

Ed Rader (Chapter 15) is an associate partner in Andersen Consulting's Americas supply chain management practice, based in Atlanta. He has over 20 years of experience working with many consumer products and retail companies in the areas of logistics strategy, distribution operations, facility design, manufacturing strategy, global supply chain management and strategic sourcing. Prior to joining Andersen Consulting, he was vice-president of operations for an integrated consumer products manufacturer and retailer and the director of operations services for an international consumer products and retailing consulting firm. Ed graduated from Georgia Institute of Technology.

Dr Ananth Raman (Chapter 11) is an assistant professor at Harvard Business School, in the technology and operations management area. He has taught technology and operations management, quantitative methods and supply chain management to MBA students and in various executive education courses. His research focuses on supply chain management for short lifecycle products with unpredictable demand and emphasizes production and inventory planning and the role of incentives. He has recently received a multiyear grant from the Sloan Foundation to research retail merchandising approaches. Ananth has consulted with a number of leading US companies and recently advised the Indian government on strategies for increasing apparel exports. He holds a Bachelor of Technology from the Indian Institute of Technology, an MBA from the Indian School of Management and a PhD from the Wharton School, University of Pennsylvania.

Craig Rawlings (Chapter 23) is a manager in Andersen Consulting's Australia and New Zealand supply chain management practice, based in Melbourne. Craig has worked with clients in industrial and fast-moving consumer goods industries in the areas of distribution operations improvement, supply chain strategy development and strategic sourcing. Prior to joining Andersen Consulting, Craig worked in operational roles with Caltex Oil and Air Liquide. Craig holds a Bachelor of Business in transport economics from the Royal Melbourne Institute of Technology and an MBA from the Macquarie Graduate School of Management, Sydney.

Julian Remnant (Chapter 20) is a manager within Andersen Consulting's pharmaceutical and medical products practice in London. His primary focus has been on global supply chain integration programmes within the pharmaceutical industry. Julian's experience includes working within the programme management function of a global supply chain integration initiative to design, develop and deploy standard supply chain processes and systems and in developing business case proposals to integrate, consolidate and optimize the manufacturing network following acquisition of additional capacity.

Mark Reynolds (Chapter 37) is a senior manager with Andersen Consulting's Australia and New Zealand supply chain management practice, based in Sydney. He has expertise in manufacturing, distribution and supply chain planning in a wide variety of industries including automotive, aerospace, food, beverages and consumer products. He has worked in the UK, Australia, New Zealand and Asia. The focus of his recent work has been on the application of advanced demand and supply chain planning tools. Mark has a Bachelor of Mechanical Engineering and a Master of Engineering in industrial electronics from the University of Auckland.

Bruce Richmond (Chapters 25 and 31) is a partner in Andersen Consulting's Americas supply chain practice, based in Atlanta, with global responsibilities for the distribution practice. He specializes in all areas of physical distribution including facility design and operations, performance management, distribution strategy and warehouse-management systems. His clients include retailers, consumer packaged goods manufacturers and service providers. Prior to joining Andersen Consulting he was vice-president of distribution for Haggar Apparel Company. He holds a Bachelor of Industrial Engineering from Georgia Institute of Technology in Atlanta.

Philip Roussel (Chapter 13) is an associate partner with Andersen Consulting, based in Chicago. He has over 20 years of international business experience, identifying market and strategic opportunities for top management and boards of directors with geopolitical insight and cultural sensitivity. He specializes in helping automotive and industrial clients analyse their markets and competition to grow their businesses and penetrate new markets; evaluate their operations to improve processes and costs; and restructure their organizations to bring about significant change. He holds a BA and an MA from Cambridge University.

David Sharpe (Chapter 7) is an associate partner in Andersen Consulting's European retail practice, based in Manchester. He also leads work in ECR and has worked widely within the retail industry in grocery, textiles and general merchandise in convenience, supermarket and department store formats in Europe, Australia and Asia. He specializes in complete supply chain integration, working with consumer products companies and retailers to improve and leverage their trading partner relationships. Prior to joining Andersen Consulting, David worked for another major consulting firm and for Bass in logistics operations. He holds a BA in geography from Cambridge University.

Dr Denis Simon (Chapter 36) is the managing partner of Andersen Consulting's China practice. He has spent substantial time over the last 15 years working with multinational companies doing business in China and assisting them with both their entry and operating strategies. Prior to joining Andersen Consulting, he was a full-time faculty member specializing in international business strategy and global technology management at the Sloan School, MIT, and the Fletcher School of Law and Diplomacy. Denis, who is fluent in Mandarin, has edited and written numerous books and articles on business and technology in East Asia. He holds an MA and PhD from University of California, Berkeley.

Todd Smith (Chapter 8) is a director in the global business services organization of Bristol-Myers Squibb in Princeton, New Jersey. He has ten years of consulting and industry experience, specializing in forecasting and inventory management. Prior to joining Bristol-Myers, Todd was a senior manager in Andersen Consulting's supply chain management practice focusing on forecasting and inventory-management programmes. He began his career with the operations research department of AT&T Bell Laboratories where he focused on inventory management issues for what is now Lucent Technologies. Todd holds a MS in operations research and a BS in industrial engineering from Stanford University.

Timothy Takacs (Chapter 30) is currently an MBA student at Cornell University's Johnson Graduate School of Management. Previously, he was a senior analyst in Andersen Consulting's supply chain management practice, based in Boston. Timothy has helped clients in high-tech, consumer products, publishing, distribution and retail industries develop and implement creative supply chain solutions to improve profitability and market position. Timothy has also held operations and marketing positions with Framework Technologies, Black & Decker and Motorola Asia Pacific. He holds a BA in economics and psychology from Syracuse University.

Richard Toole (Chapters 18 and 31) is an associate partner in Andersen Consulting's Americas supply chain practice, based in Atlanta. His areas of expertise include procurement, global sourcing strategy and execution, logistics strategy, channel management strategy, performance measurement, total cost management and materials management. He has previously worked at another major consulting firm and in manufacturing and logistics management with Kimberly-Clark Corporation. Rick is a certified CPIM by the American Production and Inventory Control Society.

Liane Torres (Chapter 3) is a manager in Andersen Consulting's Australia and New Zealand supply chain management practice, based in Melbourne. Over the past five years, Liane has worked extensively with consumer and industrial products organizations and has specialized in customer service analysis, customer segmentation and supply chain strategy alignment and development. Liane holds a BS in industrial management engineering, minoring in chemical engineering, from De La Salle University, Philippines.

Rick Tullio (Chapter 34) is a senior manager in Andersen Consulting's Americas supply chain management practice, based in Philadelphia. His areas of expertise include supply chain management, logistics outsourcing and distribution network strategy. Prior to joining Andersen Consulting, Rick was a consultant in the transportation practice of another major consulting firm. He has previously held line and staff positions within Mobil Oil's operations and supply divisions and the corporate planning department of Sea-Land Service. Rick has an MBA from the Wharton School of Business and a BS in business logistics from Pennsylvania State University.

Dr Olivier Vidal (Chapter 18) is an associate partner in Andersen Consulting's European supply chain management practice, based in Paris. He specializes in operations and logistics and has experience designing supply chain strategies, facilities reengineering programmes and global distribution channels and systems for a wide range of consumer products and industrial products companies across Europe. He is a member of the ASLOG and has written several papers presented at professional societies and magazines. He graduated as an engineer and holds a PhD in systems analysis from Lille University, France.

Dr Cathy Walt (Chapter 29) is a managing partner in Andersen Consulting's change management practice, based in New York. The majority of her recent work has been in the electronics and high-tech, utilities and financial services industries. In her 15 years of consulting and teaching experience she has developed a strategic practice area for Andersen Consulting. She has deep skills in executive leadership coaching specifically in partnering, new business ventures and alliances. She is a regular speaker at conferences on large-scale change initiatives involving supply chain issues. Cathy has a PhD in behavioural science.

John White III (Chapter 22) is a manager in Andersen Consulting's Americas supply chain management practice, based in Atlanta. His areas of expertise include supply chain strategy, distribution operations strategy, operations reengineering, facility and material-handling system design, warehouse-management systems and distribution operations implementation. He has held previous positions at Mitsubishi Consumer Electronics America and another major consulting firm. He is vice-president of Warehousing Education and Research Council and holds a Bachelor of Industrial Engineering from Georgia Institute of Technology.

Dr Kim Wigglesworth (Chapter 35) is a senior manager in the pharmaceutical and medical products practice of Andersen Consulting's Australia and New Zealand practice, based in Melbourne. She has worked in a broad range of areas including disease management, clinical and medical applications and regulatory systems. Kim has had experience with a number of the major pharmaceutical companies, as well as government agencies. She has been a regular speaker at conferences on subjects such as patient information technology, disease management and health data networks. Kim holds a BSc and a PhD in biochemistry, Liverpool University, and an MBA from the Open Business School, UK.

Scott Wilfreda Wiskoski (Chapter 34) is a senior manager in Andersen Consulting's Americas strategy practice, based in Washington, DC. Her expertise is in strategic sourcing and supply chain strategy across diversified industries, including process, communications, products and services. Prior to joining Andersen Consulting, she worked at two other major consulting firms and in the US Navy as a supply corps officer. She completed a Bachelor in Economics at Yale University, School of Management, earning a Master's in Public and Private Management.

Dr Andrew Young (Chapter 1) is a consultant in Andersen Consulting's Australia and New Zealand strategy practice, based in Sydney. He has worked with clients in telecommunications and healthcare and has gained experience with scenario planning and vision-development techniques in particular. Andrew has worked on large research efforts in engineering and management, including two major initiatives which aim to determine what company strategies and activities will contribute most to company success in the future. He holds a BE and PhD in mechanical engineering.

Dr John Zelcer (Chapter 35) is a practising anaesthetist who is a senior healthcare adviser to Andersen Consulting's Australia and New Zealand strategy practice, based in Melbourne. He has extensive consulting, academic and clinical backgrounds. His consulting experience spans strategic planning, process reengineering, change management, information technology implementation and medical technology development. His has researched and published articles in clinical and basic sciences and held postgraduate teaching roles in both Australia and the USA. John has worked in private practice as an anaesthetist since 1979. He holds a MB, a BS and a BMedSc from Monash University, Victoria.

Alida Zweidler-McKay (Chapter 1) is a senior consultant in Andersen Consulting's Americas strategy practice, based in Boston. She has worked with clients in consumer packaged goods in the areas of salesforce effectiveness, customer strategy and procurement strategy. She participated in the firm's Redefining Strategy research initiative, studying the components of strategic positioning and execution capabilities to understand better how each contributes to success in the marketplace and how companies maintain alignment between them.

Index